A HISTORY OF

ENGLAND

BEFORE THE

NORMAN CONQUEST

William Derington

A HISTORY OF

ENGLAND

BEFORE THE

NORMAN CONQUEST

SIR CHARLES OMAN

BRACKEN BOOKS
LONDON

A History of England Before the Norman Conquest

This sixth edition first published in 1924 by
Methuen & Co, London

This edition published in 1994 by
Bracken Books, an imprint of Studio Editions Ltd,
Princess House, 50 Eastcastle Street,
London W1N 7AP, England

ISBN 1 85891 336 5
Printed and bound in Guernsey by
The Guernsey Press Co Ltd

INTRODUCTORY NOTE

BY THE GENERAL EDITOR

IN England, as in France and Germany, the main characteristic of the last twenty years, from the point of view of the student of history, has been that new material has been accumulating much faster than it can be assimilated or absorbed. The standard histories of the last generation need to be revised, or even to be put aside as obsolete, in the light of the new information that is coming in so rapidly and in such vast bulk. But the students and researchers of to-day have shown little enthusiasm as yet for the task of re-writing history on a large scale. We see issuing from the press hundreds of monographs, biographies, editions of old texts, selections from correspondence, or collections of statistics, mediaeval and modern. But the writers who (like the late Bishop Stubbs or Professor Samuel Gardiner) undertake to tell over again the history of a long period, with the aid of all the newly discovered material, are few indeed. It is comparatively easy to write a monograph on the life of an individual or a short episode of history. But the modern student, knowing well the mass of material that he has to collate, and dreading lest he may make a slip through over-

looking some obscure or newly discovered source, dislikes
stirring beyond the boundary of the subject, or the short
period, on which he has made himself a specialist.

Meanwhile the general reading public continues to
ask for standard histories, and discovers, only too often,
that it can find nothing between school manuals at one
end of the scale and minute monographs at the other.
The series of which this volume forms a part is intended
to do something towards meeting this demand.   Historians will not sit down, as once they were wont, to
write twenty-volume works in the style of Hume or
Lingard, embracing a dozen centuries of annals.   It is
not to be desired that they should—the writer who is
most satisfactory in dealing with Anglo-Saxon antiquities
is not likely to be the one who will best discuss the
antecedents of the Reformation, or the constitutional
history of the Stuart period.   But something can be
done by judicious co-operation : it is not necessary that
a genuine student should refuse to touch any subject
that embraces an epoch longer than a score of years,
nor need history be written as if it were an encyclopædia,
and cut up into small fragments dealt with by different
hands.

It is hoped that the present series may strike the
happy mean, by dividing up English history into periods
that are neither too long to be dealt with by a single
competent specialist, nor so short as to tempt the writer
to indulge in that over-abundance of unimportant detail
which repels the general reader.   They are intended to
give something more than a mere outline of our national
annals, but they have no space for controversy or the
discussion of sources.   There is, however, a bibliography
annexed to each volume, which will show the inquirer

where information of the more special kind is to be sought. Moreover, a number of maps are to be found at the end of each volume which, as it is hoped, will make it unnecessary for the reader to be continually referring to large historical atlases—tomes which (as we must confess with regret) are not to be discovered in every private library.

C. OMAN.

Oxford, 1st September, 1904.

PREFACE

THE main purpose of this short preface is to express my deep obligation to many friends who have given me their assistance in revising and correcting various parts of this volume. Three must be specially named. Mr. T. Rice Holmes, the author of *Cæsar's Conquest of Gaul*, and of *Ancient Britain and Cæsar's Invasions*, was good enough to look through the first four chapters, forming the prehistoric and early Celtic section, to make most valuable criticisms thereon, and to give me many fruitful suggestions. This part of my volume, indeed, may be said to be founded in a large measure on his researches, for his two books abovementioned were invaluable to me.

For the Roman section, Chapters V. to IX., I am no less deeply indebted to the help of the present holder of the Camden Chair of Ancient History, Professor Haverfield. I was indeed fortunate to obtain the assistance of such an unrivalled specialist in all that concerns Roman Britain. He placed at my disposal a number of pamphlets and papers which would otherwise have been practically inaccessible to me—for many of them were scattered broadcast among the proceedings of learned societies, English and foreign, where they are hard to

find without a guide.   He put me under a still greater
obligation by looking through the text of my chapters,
and furnishing me with much comment, and a considerable number of corrections.   The extent to which I
have been aided by his published treatises may best be
gauged by a glance at the footnotes to Chapters V.,
VI., and VII.   Practically all the conclusions as to the
Walls of Hadrian and Severus are drawn from his
reports to the archæological societies of Cumberland
and Northumberland.   I may add that I carefully
walked over the whole central section of the wall with
these treatises in my hand, to verify his observations on
the spot.

The third friend to whom I must express my thanks
is Mr. H. C. Davis of All Souls and Balliol Colleges,
who was good enough to read Chapters XI., XII.,
XVII., XVIII., XXIII., XXIV., those which deal
with the more difficult problems concerning the early
settlements of the Anglo-Saxons, and their social and
political institutions.   I rewrote or retouched many a
paragraph after considering the weighty comments
which he sent to me.

In addition I must express my acknowledgment for
help given from other quarters.   My old friend Mr.
C. H. Turner of Magdalen College looked over the
chapter on Early Christianity in Britain, and revised the
paragraphs on the Paschal Controversy in Chapter XIV.
Mr. David Macritchie of Edinburgh took me round
several interesting sites in Lothian, including the Roman remains at Inveresk, and the Pictish *weems* by
Crichtoun mentioned on page 127.   The Rev. C. S.
Taylor of Banwell gave me some valuable notes as to
early Mercian history.   I owe to Mr. Craster of All

Souls College not only a closer acquaintance with the
excavations at Corbridge, but other recent information
as to discoveries along the Northumbrian wall.

A few words of explanation on the plan which I
adopted as regards the spelling of Anglo-Saxon names
may be necessary in self-justification. I have not the
courage of Professor Freeman, who logically and consistently wrote of Aelfred and Eadward and Eadmund.
Nor, on the other hand, could I consent to use time-
honoured but mutilated forms for names, such as Edwy,
Elgiva, or Edith. Steering a middle course, I have
kept the modern and familiar shapes only for a very few
famous names—such as the three mentioned above with
Professor Freeman's spelling, Edwin, Charles, and one
or two more. For the rest I have used contemporary
spelling—even at the risk of being a little pedantic—
following coins, charters and chronicles as best I might.
There are, of course, many difficulties—some kings spelt
their names in three or four different ways. Other
personages are mentioned only by Bede or other Latin-
using authors, and the actual way in which their names
would have been spelt by a contemporary, writing in
his native tongue, is not to be recovered with certainty.
I have done my best to use common-sense methods
when problems of this kind cropped up.

In a volume in which the criticism of sources has
to be carried out in the text—for a discussion of the
authority of Cæsar and Tacitus, of Gildas and " Nennius " (not to speak of the Anglo-Saxon Chronicle),
forms no small part of my task—I have thought it
unnecessary to write a separate appendix on sources.
This would, indeed, have been equivalent to repeating
in a second place almost the whole of Chapters XI. and

XII., and many long notes and paragraphs out of other sections. But copious references to authorities will be found in the Index.

My last and not least pleasant duty is to give one more testimonial to the indefatigable compiler of the Indices of this and many another volume of mine, whose ardour has made this weary task a labour of love.

C. OMAN

Oxford
March, 1910

NOTE TO SECOND EDITION

I MUST give my best thanks to Mr. R. B. Rackham and several other scholars who have enabled me to correct slips and misprints in the first edition of this book.

NOTE TO THIRD EDITION

I HAVE to thank Mr. Leonard Wooley and some four or five other kind correspondents for useful corrections of errors that still lingered in the second edition.

NOTE TO FIFTH EDITION

POST-WAR excavations seem to have settled the long disputed point about the building of the great Northumbrian Wall. It is now certain that Hadrian built the stone wall no less than the turf wall, and that the attribution of the former to Severus must be given up. The admirable monographs of Dr. George Macdonald, proving that the Scottish Lowlands were not abandoned by the Romans after Agricola's departure, have led me to rewrite great part of Chapter VII.

CONTENTS

BOOK I

BRITAIN BEFORE THE ROMAN CONQUEST

CHAPTER I

CONTENTS

BOOK II

ROMAN BRITAIN, A.D. 43-410

CHAPTER V

CHAPTER VI

CHAPTER VII

CHAPTER VIII

CHAPTER IX

CONTENTS

XV

PAGE

sions by the Picts and Scots—Their Origin—Campaigns against them by
Theodosius the Elder—Usurpation of Magnus Maximus—Stilicho pro-
tects Britain—Britain in the *Notitia Dignitatum*—Problems in the
Notitia—Renewed rebellion in Britain—Usurpation of Constantine III.—
He removes most of the garrison—End of the Roman power in Britain.

CHAPTER X

CHRISTIANITY IN BRITAIN DURING THE ROMAN PERIOD . . 177
Early mentions of Christianity in Britain—St. Alban and St. Augulus—
Bishops from Britain present at the fourth-century councils—Character
of early British Christianity—Pelagius and his followers—Survivals of
heathenism.

BOOK III
THE ANGLO-SAXONS IN BRITAIN (A.D. 410-796)

CHAPTER XI

THE ANGLO-SAXON INVASION (A.D. 410-516) 186
Authorities for the fifth-century history of Britain—Coroticus and the
defence of the North—Legend of Cunedda and his conquests—General
condition of the British lands after A.D. 410—The visit of St. Germanus
and the " Hallelujah Victory "—Gildas's account of the coming of the
Anglo-Saxons—Ambrosius Aurelianus—The *Historia Brittonum* and its
narrative—Legend of Vortigern and Hengist—The narrative of the
Anglo-Saxon Chronicle—Extent of the early Anglo-Saxon conquests—
The legend of King Arthur and his battles.

CHAPTER XII

THE SETTLEMENT OF THE CONQUERORS—THE EARLY
KINGDOMS (A.D. 516-570) 213
Character of the Invaders—Origin of the Saxons, of the Jutes, of the
Angles—The old kingly houses—The early history of Kent and Sussex—
Of the East Saxons—Of the West Saxons—Its doubtfully authentic char-
acter—Legend of Cerdic—Settlements of the Angles in Mid-Britain—
The Celtic kingdoms of the sixth century as described by Gildas—In-
vasion of Gaul by the Britons—The Celtic states of North Britain,
their struggle with the Angles of Northumbria—Wars of Urien and the
sons of Ida.

CHAPTER XIII

THE SECOND ADVANCE OF THE INVADERS—CEAWLIN AND
AETHELFRITH (A.D. 577-617) 245
Ceawlin and the West Saxons—Battle of Deorham—Fall of Ceawlin—
Aethelbert of Kent—Aethelfrith of Northumbria, his victory over the
Northern Celts at Dawston—His victory of Chester.

CONTENTS

CHAPTER XXII

CHAPTER XXIII

BOOK V

THE KINGS OF ALL ENGLAND (A.D. 900-1066)

CHAPTER XXIV

CHAPTER XXV

APPENDICES

MAPS

CONTRACTIONS

THE FOLLOWING OFTEN-USED CONTRACTIONS SHOULD BE NOTED:—

Ag. . . . . . . = Tacitus, *Agricola.*

A. S. C. or A. S. Chronicle = Anglo-Saxon Chronicle (Plummer's Edition).

B. C. S. or Birch C. S. . = Birch's *Cartularium Saxonicum.*

B. G. or Bell. Gall. . . = Caesar *De Bello Gallico.*

C. I. L. . . . . = *Corpus Inscriptionum Latinarum* (vol. vii. *ed.* Hübner).

E. H. or Eccl. Hist. . . = Bede's Ecclesiastical History of the English Nation (Plummer's Edition).

Eng. Hist. Rev. . . = *English Historical Review.*

H. B. or Hist. Brit. . . = The *Historia Brittonum* (" Nennius ").

H. Y. . . . . . = Historians of the Church of York (Rolls Series).

K. C. D. or Kemble C. D. = Kemble's *Codex Diplomaticus Aevi Saxonici.*

Liebermann . . . = Felix Liebermann's *Gesetze der Angelsachsen.*

M. H. B. . . . . = *Monumenta Historica Britannica* (Petrie, 1848).

Num. Chron. . . . = *Numismatic Chronicle.*

Thorpe Dipl. . . . = Thorpe's *Diplomatarium Aevi Saxonici.*

W. M. . . . . . = William of Malmesbury (Rolls Series).

W. P. . . . . . = William of Poitiers (M. H. B.).

Freeman N. C. . . . = Freeman's Norman Conquest.

Hist. Eccl. Dunelm. . . = *Historia Dunelmensis Ecclesiae* in Simeon of Durham (Rolls Series).

Crawford Charters . . = Stevenson's Edition of the Crawford Charters in *Anecdota Oxoniensia.*

BOOK I
BRITAIN BEFORE THE ROMAN CONQUEST

CHAPTER I

PREHISTORIC BRITAIN

GEOLOGY is not history in any proper sense of the word, nor is prehistoric anthropology, though both of these sciences may prove useful handmaids to their greater sister. It is therefore unnecessary to follow the successive changes in the contour of North-Western Europe, or the character of its climate, and its fauna and flora, in the days when there was as yet nothing that could be called Britain. So long as the land of which some remnant now forms the British Isles was a part of a great European continent, not yet cut up by the existence of the North Sea or the Channel, we have no concern with it, or with its successive rises and fallings in level, or its alternations between a glacial and a tropical climate. They may be very interesting to the student of geology at large, but they are not British history.

Nor need much more attention be paid to these regions, which had not yet settled down into their final geographical shape, when the first faint traces of man begin to be found in them. For there seems to be in Britain a break between the days of the " palæolithic period " as it is called, when the first human beings, provided with uothing but the simplest stone implements, are found existing in this remote corner of North-Western Europe, and the more definitely known period of " neolithic man " that was to follow.[1] There were still no Straits of Dover when these earliest aborigines appeared, presumably drifting (like all their successors) in a westerly

[1] So Boyd Dawkins and Sir John Evans. For doubts on this point see Rice Holmes's *Ancient Britain*, pp. 59-61, 385-90.

direction. The greater part of the North Sea seems to have been a marshy plain, over which the Thames meandered to join the lower course of a greater Rhine, which discharged itself into the distant Arctic Ocean. The worst of the ice age—or rather of the ice ages—which had made North-Western Europe a desert, had passed away, and animals suited to a more temperate climate, the woolly rhinoceros, the hippopotamus, the mammoth, the grizzly and brown bear, the lion, and the hyena, were roaming over the land, when man first appeared as a hunting and fishing savage. His rude weapons, of flint or other stone, have been found in river drift, or in the caves which were his habitual dwelling-places. He was certainly contemporary with all the formidable beasts mentioned above: apparently he even dared to contend with them, trusting to the cunning of his human brain—little developed though it may have been—and to the advantage which the hand that can wield a weapon has over the paw or the tusk of the animal. Probably he acquired the art of making fire from the flints that were his favourite weapons, or from the friction of sticks, such as is still practised by savage tribes : he may have used it not only for cooking his food, but as a formidable weapon of offence or defence against the beasts with which he contended. He was not destitute, strange as it may appear, of artistic instincts; numerous carvings on bone found on the Continent, and a single solitary instance from Britain, show that it sometimes pleased him to make reproductions of the animals that surrounded him, from the mammoth that may have been the supreme terror of his life—though he perhaps plotted against it by pitfalls and suchlike devices—to the horse, which was still nothing more than an eligible source of food.

But between palæolithic man and his more advanced successors there seems to be, in Britain at least,[1] a distinct break, corresponding to a contemporary change in the geological conditions of North-Western Europe. The Channel had broken in between England and France, the North Sea had overflowed the plain of the lower Thames and the lower Rhine, seventeen of the forty-eight various species of mammals which were contemporary with palæolithic man had disappeared, when the later race came upon the scene : there is often a thick deposit, implying a gap of many centuries, between the strata in which the remains of the earliest aborigines are found

---

[1] Not, however, in France and other continental regions. See Rice Holmes, as quoted on the previous page.

and those in which the better-finished neolithic tools and weapons occur. Did the older race die out from some change of climatic conditions, or retire before them to more southern regions—or was there some cataclysmic disaster to account for their disappearance? Or did some of them survive to be conquered or exterminated by their successors? None can say ; but whatever may have been the case farther south and east, there seem to be few or no remains that link palæolithic and neolithic man in Britain.

The land had become an island, the greater part of the terrible beasts of old had disappeared, and conditions of climate and geography had apparently come to be not very different from what they are at present, when neolithic man begins to be discernible. Whether the gap that divided him from those who went before is to be numbered by thousands of years, or was comparatively short, in would be dangerous to say. The evidence is as yet insufficient to enable us to speak with certainty. But since his first arrival there has been no cataclysmic break in the occupation of Britain, even though race after race may have pressed forward into its borders. His occupation of the island must have lasted for many ages, since the first relics show tools not very much advanced beyond those of the palæolithic people, and imply a life of hunting and fishing under squalid conditions, while the later ones show something that might almost be called without exaggeration an early civilisation. Enough of bones and skeletons of this age have been found to prove that the neolithic people were a race of moderate stature and slender proportions, with skulls that were markedly long in shape, whence they have often been called simply the Early Dolichocephalous people, in order to avoid the use of misleading national names. The archæologists who have called them " Iberians " seem to imply that they had some special connection with the well-known people of later Spain who bore that name. But all that it is safe to say is that they were kin to the similar races that occupied in the same age all the territory in the basin of the Mediterranean, of which Iberia is but a small part. Another name for this race that is often used is the " people of the Long Barrows," for, in contradistinction to their successors of the next age, their characteristic form of tomb was an oval mound, which sometimes did and sometimes did not include an elaborate central core of stones.[1] The most

[1] The Long Barrow, it must be remembered, is not the sole type. The neolithic people, at least in their latest period, sometimes used a round barrow.

typical form of their sepulchre was a "dolmen" or chamber of large
stones set on their ends or their sides, and roofed in on top by other
large stones placed horizontally, after which the whole was covered
in by an immense heap of earth.   There were, however, districts
where large stones were not easily to be found, and where burial,
for want of them, merely consisted in the placing of the body of the
defunct under a long mound of earth.   Where the stone sepulchre
had been prepared in the normal fashion described above, it was
sometimes single-chambered, but often consisted of a more or less
complicated system of recesses or compartments, each containing its
one or more corpses according to the needs of the family.   In the
earlier days of the neolithic age simple inhumation seems to have
been universally prevalent, but before it was over cremation had
begun to be practised, though it would still seem to have been
comparatively unusual.   Whether or no the change in the method
of sepulture had any relation to the changing conceptions entertained by man as to the fate of the soul after death, it would be
profitless to inquire.   Burning and burying were practised simultaneously and in the same districts, so that any generalisation is dangerous.   There seems to be clear proof, from the bones found in certain
barrows, that in some cases the slaves or concubines of a dead chief
were slaughtered at his graveside, in order that their spirits might
follow him and minister to him in another world.   The same belief is
indicated when we find animals buried at their master's side, or tools,
weapons and drinking cups, broken or intact, left within his reach.

The neolithic man was still a hunter and a fisher like his palæolithic predecessor, but he was also a herdsman. He had domesticated
the dog, the ox, the sheep, and the hog, and lived largely on the
produce of his folds and stalls, so that he was not dependent on the
chances of the chase. He had an ample provision of pottery,
though it was still extremely rude. His tools and weapons, however,
were often elaborate, and sometimes shaped with an evident regard
to ornament, though the material was only flint or other hard stone.
But the practice of ages gave men marvellous skill in the trimming
of the flint, or the cutting and polishing of the lump of rock, so
that a wonderful symmetry was attained from very unpromising
material. Spear and arrow heads, scrapers, knives, and even saws
were made, but the most typical instrument of the age was the
celt or stone hatchet, which could be used equally as a tool of
carpentry or as a weapon of war. Bone, as in older days, supplied

the rest of the instruments of mankind, and especially the needles which served to sew, with threads of fine sinew, the garments of skin which were the universal wear. Apparently weaving and the cultivation of cereals by agriculture were unknown ; for vegetable food the neolithic man evidently depended on the fruits, berries, and roots supplied to him by nature : in winter he must have fallen back almost entirely on to an animal diet.

At the very end of the neolithic age a new race of invaders came upon the scene, intruding among the older people whose graves and tools are found everywhere, from Syria and North Africa to Scandinavia and the remotest British Islands, for even in the Shetlands neolithic remains are found in profusion. The new-comers were two races of a new physical type, the Brachycephalous or round-headed peoples, who were about to introduce the bronze age, though the first few traces found of them in North-Western Europe show them armed with stone implements only. They were equally well distinguished from the tribes whose lands they invaded by the fact that they generally buried their dead in round, and not in long, barrows. Very soon after their first appearance they are found in possession of bronze tools and weapons, so that by the discovery of the use of metal the whole face of human life was changed. The majority of the Brachycephalous invaders of Britain belonged to a race far larger and more powerful than the neolithic men ; their average height, as deduced from their skeletons, must have been as much as five feet eight inches. But in a few districts the first round-skulled immigrants seem to have been of a shorter type, not exceeding in stature the Dolichocephalous people whom they superseded. Whether by superior vigour or by reason of their know-ledge of the use of metal, the Brachycephalous races evidently got the better of the older inhabitants : but that they did not wholly exterminate them, but retained many of them as serfs or tributaries, is shown by the fact that skulls of mixed type, evidently those of people in whom the blood of the long-headed and the short-headed races was mingled, are frequently to be found in interments of the bronze age. In a few regions the elder people seem to have re-tained their independence for a considerable time. There is no reason to doubt that a strain derived from the neolithic man not only diversified the race of the metal-users, but persisted on from these again to the later coming Celts, and from the Celts to the

inhabitants of Britain in our own day. On the whole, however, it
would be true to say that the brachycephalous invaders absorbed
the race that went before them.

The age of metal, in Britain at least, starts at once with the
use of bronze, there being little or no trace that unmixed copper
was used, before the method of hardening and alloying it with tin
became known. This is not the case in certain other countries, and
even in Ireland there is some trace of a copper age : but the copper
of Britain was found where tin, its invaluable corrective, was also
easily to be won. Copper from the outcrops or boulders, found on
the surface in many parts of Wales, could be mixed with the tin
that came easily enough from very light working in Cornwall,
so there was no need for any further importation from the Continent, from which (no doubt) the first bronze tools had been
brought over.[1] The general shape of these implements does not
seem traceable to direct copying from the old flint implements
which they superseded, but rather to have been thought out on
new principles, which could only be used in melted metal, and would
not have been possible with stone. These tools are very varied in
size and design, and, in their later stages at least, very ornamental.
It is curious to find that two classes of implements alone continued
to be made from stone, when all the rest were now designed in
metal. These were hammers, which very seldom occur in bronze,
and arrow-heads, which (whether for war or for hunting) still continued to be made of flint, even by tribes whose other tools, even
the smallest, were now of metal. Early bronze arrow-heads seem
hardly to be known at all in Britain.

The brachycephalic people used other metals besides bronze,
though this formed the main staple of their manufactures. They
had gold, sometimes in considerable quantities, which was made into
torques, bracelets, pins, breast ornaments, and other jewellery in
great profusion. They had also lead, to be used for metal work
that required neither a cutting edge nor a strong resisting power.

From the enormous number of camps of the Bronze Age found
in Britain, it is clear that the tribes of that time were very small in
numbers, and always were liable to plunge into internecine war with
each other. Otherwise there would be no need for the tribal

[1] But certain types of bronze implements continued to be imported nevertheless.
See Rice Holmes, pp. 126, 144.

strongholds to be so numerous, and (for the most part) so small. Most of them are found enclosed by one or more concentric lines of ditch and palisade on isolated hills; but a few are constructed on the edge of the sea, or with their backs to a sheer precipice, so that only their front side required the artificial protection of a stone or earthen wall. But, despite their wars, it is clear that the bronze-age folk were not so continually engaged in strife as to render commerce impossible. Many of their luxuries must have been brought from very far afield, such for example as the amber with which they decorated their persons; much of their pottery and metal utensils seems to have been introduced from Gaul and the Rhineland, and there is every reason to think that they may have communicated with Scandinavia also.

They were dispersed over the whole of the British Isles from Shetland to Cornwall, but the distribution of population was very different from that which obtained in later ages, since they seem to have sought not the most fertile ground but that which was most open and easy to clear. Hence they were found very thickly on poor soils, like the chalk downs of Wiltshire and the wolds of Eastern Yorkshire, while in some of the richest river valleys there is little trace of them, since such tracts were originally covered by woods and morasses, into which they had no wish to break so long as more easily cleared ground was available. But swamps were not always considered impracticable, as is shown by the interesting lake village on piles, belonging to the later Bronze Age, which was discovered half a generation ago in Holderness. This was a settlement very similar to the larger establishments which have often been found on the Swiss lakes, but by no means so rich as its continental prototypes. The larger and more interesting lake village near Glastonbury belonged to the iron age, and probably to the Celts.

The men of the Bronze Age not only possessed flocks and herds like their neolithic predecessors, but cultivated the soil for several sorts of grain. Wheat was grown as far north as Yorkshire; other cereals were known all over Scotland. Weaving was also generally practised; spindle-whorls are among the commonest finds in sites of this age. Man was not, therefore, any longer dependent on skins alone for his clothing. Pottery was elaborate, highly decorated, and differentiated into many shapes, according to the purpose for which it was required. There seems even to have been a special manufacture for funeral purposes—many of the typical vessels which occur in graves being hardly found in any other conjunction. The typical decoration was in stripes, chevrons, and angular geometrical figures, the curves which were to be the special mark of the iron age and the incoming Celt being not at all usual. Dwellings were usually round huts, which stood together in villages, but pit-dwellings were well known, and even caves seem occasionally still to have been inhabited.[1] In the extreme north the curious subterranean chambered burrowings called " weems," which persisted into historic days, seem already to have been in existence, though they were still being used long after the Christian era began.

Cremation had already, as we have seen, begun to be practised in neolithic times, and it grew steadily more usual as the Bronze Age wore on. In many districts it was universal. The custom was of course not calculated to preserve for the archæologist of the future nearly so many relics as were left by the earlier practice of inhumation ; it also rendered the calculations of anthropometry impossible, since burnt bodies cannot be measured. Thus in some ways less is known of the physical type of the later Bronze Age men than of their neolithic predecessors.

The most notable monuments of the period are its great circles of standing stones, of which Stonehenge is the best known, but not the largest, example. They are very widely spread, from the islands of the extreme north down to Cornwall. They are of various designs and sizes, some more and some less complicated, but they all seem to have been associated with burials. Some of them are the centres of such immense numbers of " round-barrow" tumuli—there are three hundred close around Stonehenge—that it has been suggested that bodies or burnt bones were brought even from distant places, in order to be deposited in the neighbourhood of some spot considered sacred. The theory of the seventeenth and eighteenth century antiquarians that stone-circles were " Druidical Temples " has long been discredited ; but some measure of truth may lie beneath it. It is even possible that the enormous wrought-stone temple to Apollo in " the Hyperborean Island " mentioned by Hecatæus of Abdera, the Greek geographer, from

---

[1] The most fruitful excavation of bronze age objects in Britain was in a cave, that of Heathery Burn in the county of Durham.

whom we get one of our earliest notices of the extreme north, may refer to Stonehenge, or to the still larger, though not so elaborate, stone-circles of Avebury, not far from the better-known monument. The endeavour to work out Stonehenge and certain of the other circles as astronomical monuments, intended to point out the rising of the midsummer sun by their Orientation, need not, however, be taken seriously.[1] Nor need any attention be attached to the various dates, 1680 B.C. or 1460 B.C., deduced by very hypothetical and dangerous astronomical calculations for the erection of these strange works. It is safer to hold with Dr. Arthur Evans that "Stonehenge was built comparatively late, that its connection with sun-worship, if any existed, was at most a secondary object in its structure," and "that it is one of the large series of primitive religious monuments that grew out of purely sepulchral architecture". Its late date is proved by the facts that two ordinary barrows of the round type, such as are typical of the Bronze Age, are encroached upon and partly cut through by its containing rampart, and that chippings from the two sorts of stone employed for the structure, "sarsens" and "blue-stone," were found in one of the closely-neighbouring barrows along with bronze objects, a dagger and a pin; the débris of the stones therefore was being shovelled about by Bronze Age grave-diggers. But the most conclusive discovery was that of clear stains of bronze or copper on one of the great sarsen-stones, seven feet below the surface.

With the end of the Bronze Age we are at last approaching the commencement of true British History, which for us begins with the arrival of the Celts, the people who were found there by Pytheas of Massilia, the first visitor from the civilised, record-keeping, peoples of the Mediterranean who wrote a full account of his travels in the extreme North-West. He was a contemporary of Alexander the Great, a man of the end of the fourth century before Christ. There is no reason whatever to doubt that, when he landed on the shores of what he called the "Pretanic Isle," the same people were in possession of it of whom Poseidonius, five generations later, and Caesar, six generations later, have left us more elaborate accounts.

But it is a more difficult thing to settle how long before Pytheas

[1] See Rice Holmes's *Ancient Britain*, pp. 479-82.

the Celts had crossed the Channel and subdued the Bronze Age
people, with whom they afterwards intermingled, much in the same
way as the Bronze-Age men had mixed their blood with that of
the earlier neolithic races.   The Celts seem to represent for us the
triumph of iron over bronze, and for North-Western and North-
Central Europe that triumph seems to have taken place between
600 and 450 B.C., if deductions may be generalised from the great
excavation at Hallstatt in the Tyrol, the only place in barbarian
Europe where the transition from bronze to iron can be followed
in detail.   It is not impossible that the first Celts may have come
hither before the Bronze Age was over, but it is clear that the
greater part of their invasions must have taken place after iron was
thoroughly well known.   Roughly speaking, therefore, we should
be inclined to place their appearance in Britain somewhere about
600, and to allow another couple of centuries, if that is not too
much, for their establishment of a complete domination in the
land.   The invasion period may perhaps have fallen a little later,
but at any rate it was well over before Pytheas landed on the coast
of Cornwall, and circumnavigated the whole island, in the end of
the fourth century.   The mere fact that he gives a purely Celtic
name to the land is conclusive, not to speak of other evidence to
be deduced from the fragments of his work that survive.

CHAPTER II

THE CELTS IN BRITAIN, DOWN TO THE INVASIONS OF JULIUS CAESAR
(B.C. 600-55)

THE entire history of Europe, from days long before written history begins, is occupied with the southward and westward movements of a series of races who start from the unknown darkness of the North and East—from Scandinavia or Central Asia or regions yet more remote. These movements did not entirely come to an end till the tenth century of the Christian era, when the Magyars, the last to arrive of the nations of modern Europe, conquered their position on the Middle Danube. It would be wrong however, to count the still later establishment of the Ottoman Turks in the Balkan Peninsula as part of the same story of the "Folk Wanderings": it belongs to a different category of invasions.

The Celts in successive waves were moving westward when first we get a glimpse of them. Already in Herodotus' day (440-30 B.C.), they had got so far, that the "father of history" reckons them, with the Cynetes, as the farthest of mankind in the direction of the Atlantic. But the head of the column had reached the Western Sea, thrusting aside Ligurian and Iberian and many a primitive tribe more, long before the bulk of the army had reached its ultimate home. The main body of the Celts were not only in the Black Forest or the Alps, but far back by the Danube, or even farther off, when their forerunners were occupying Gaul and Spain and Britain. Of the movements of their southern wing we have a fair, if intermittent, knowledge, because it came into collision with the literary peoples of the Mediterranean. It is clear that the main movement was *north* of the main chain of the Alps, because it was not from Dalmatia or Pannonia but from Gaul, and by way of

the Western Alps, that the Celts, somewhere about the end of the
sixth century[1] swarmed down into the plain of the Po, and all
Northern Italy, driving out the Etruscans who had previously
occupied in force the modern Lombardy, and confining them to
Etruria alone.[2] At the same time, or a little earlier, they had
pushed the Ligurians, who had shared with the Etruscans the control
of the lands between the Rhone and the Mincio, into the Maritime
Alps and the Provençal and Genoese Rivieras. The high-water
mark of this southern line of Celtic invasion is, for us, the sack of
Rome by the Gauls, in 387 according to the accepted chronology :
but it must not be forgotten that their armies were seen in Central
Italy for many generations later, indeed it was not till after the
battle of Telamon (225 B.C.) in the period between the two Punic
wars, that the Gaulish danger may be counted to have wholly come
to an end.   Nor was it till Hannibal had been finally crushed, twenty
years later, that the Romans made an end of the Celts of Italy as
an independent Power.

It was more than two centuries after the time when the
South-Western wing of the Gauls entered Italy, and cut short the
Etruscan power, that their South-Eastern wing, descending from
the middle Danube, the land afterwards called Pannonia, overran
Thrace and Macedonia in the days of the Diadochi, and pushed as
far as Delphi and Thermopylæ. A section of this same Gaulish
swarm even crossed the Bosphorus into Asia Minor, set the whole
of that peninsula aflame, and finally settled down as permanent
inhabitants in the old Phrygian region around Ancyra, whose name
was consequently changed to Galatia. Pannonia was still half Celtic
in the days of Julius Caesar and Augustus, and Celtic elements
were to be traced among the peoples of the northern part of the
Balkan peninsula down to the moment of its conquest by the
Romans. The great tribe of the Boii, one section of which had
occupied the lands between Po and Metaurus in the fourth century
before Christ, had a greater establishment in the quadrangular plain

[1] Roman tradition, as given by Livy, places the Gallic passing of the Alps in the
time of the Tarquins, or a generation before the ending of the Roman Kingship in
510 B.C.—or whatever the real date may be.

[2] This statement would not be altogether admitted by all French scholars. See
Rice Holmes's *Caesar in Gaul*, pp. 549-50, and Camille Jullian's, *Hist. de la Gaule*, i.
pp. 281-96.

of the Upper Elbe and Moldau, where the name of Bohemia still preserves their memory, though the German Marcomanni crushed them in the days of Augustus. Meanwhile the forefront of the southern Celtic column of advance had entered Spain, subdued much of it, and finally coalesced with some of the earlier inhabitants into the tribes that were known as Celtiberians.

All this is clear enough : the movement took place between the sixth and the third centuries before Christ, in lands that were within the ken of the Greek and the Italian ; sometimes it actually penetrated into Greece and Italy. But at the same time a similar advance was taking place along a northern line of progress, in lands absolutely hidden by the mist of a past without records, such as Northern Germany, the Netherlands, and the British Isles. All that we can know of this advance is that it was in successive waves of tribe behind tribe, each impelling the other westward, while at the back of the whole Celtic flood there was another oncoming tide of nations, that of the Germans, who only reached the Rhine and the Alps at the end of the first century before Christ, when they forced themselves on the notice of the civilised world by their irruption into Celtic Gaul and the northern frontiers of the Roman Republic. But the Teutons and their kinsmen were still far out of sight when the Celts came to the Rhine and the British Channel.

There seems no reason to doubt that the three Celtic swarms which successively crossed into the islands of the remote North-West all came originally by the obvious route across the Netherlands and the narrow seas, between the mouths of the Rhine and the Seine on one side and Southampton Water and the Humber on the other. Legends that bring some of them from Spain to Ireland or South-West Britain, or which land others directly upon the north-east coast of Scotland are late and literary, not genuine survivals of the prehistoric memory of the tribe. Such long navigations seem incredible, when the passage from the Rhine mouth to the Thames, or from Picardy to Kent, is so easy and obvious.

Be this as it may, the three Celtic waves of population in the British Isles seem clearly marked by geographical position, by linguistic differences, and (in the end) by definite historical statements. The first wave must have been that of the various tribes whom historians have called the Goidels, the ancestors of the races

which in the British Isles afterwards spoke the kindred dialects of
Erse in Ireland, Gaelic in the Scottish Highlands, and Manx.   On
the Continent the descendants of the similar tribes were to be found
among the Pictones and certain other septs of Western Gaul,
whose tongue (from the small traces of it that survive) is held to
have been very similar to that of the Goidels of the British Isles.
The second wave was that composed of the vast majority of the
tribes of Central and Eastern Gaul, those whom Caesar calls the
Celts proper; in Britain it was represented by the peoples who
overran the central and western parts of the island, as far as the
Firths of Forth and Clyde and the Irish Sea, from whose language
descended the Welsh that is still spoken to-day, the Breton that
still survives in the extreme west of France, and the now extinct
tongue of the Cornish people.   Lastly the third wave, which had
only reached Britain in the second century before Christ, and probably about the middle of that century, was that of the Belgae, the
race whom Caesar found in occupation of Northern Gaul and
Belgium on the hither side of the Channel, and of South-Eastern
Britain from Somersetshire to Kent, and as far north as the farther
edge of the Valley of the Thames.   We incline to place the commencement of the Celtic invasion of Britain about 600 B.C. or a little
later, because the parallel irruption into the slightly more remote
Italy is recorded to have begun about 540 B.C.

The language-division between the early coming Goidels and the
later-coming Britons and Belgae has many marks, but the clearest
of them is that which has caused the former to be known as the Q
Celts and the latter as the P Celts.   That is to say that whenever
in Irish, Gaelic or Manx a Q sound is to be found, the corresponding
word in Welsh, Breton or Cornish would be spelt with a P.   Celtic
philology is a mysterious science, because the written records from
which it has to be deduced are extremely late.   Putting aside a
few coins and inscriptions, they all belong to centuries long after
the Christian era had begun.   These coins and inscriptions, supplemented by a modicum of Celtic names and words preserved in
classical authors, are all that we possess to enable us to deduce the
early history of the language.   Their evidence is so scanty, and so
liable to diverse interpretations, that even to the present day the
wildest divergencies of opinion prevail among linguistic specialists
as to the early history of its various dialects.   All will agree that

Celtic is one of the great family of Aryan tongues, and that of all its sisters the one to which it has the greatest affinity is the Primitive Italian—from the Hellenic, German, or Slavonic groups it differs in a much greater degree. But whether we are to consider that the Goidelic dialect of the Western Celts is nearer the original language of the whole race than is the " Brythonic " dialect of the later comers, or whether both are parallel developments of equal antiquity, who shall say, when the few skilled philologists who are entitled to an opinion differ hopelessly among themselves? The greatest continental Celtic scholar will have it that when the first invaders reached Britain the difference between Goidelic and Brythonic was not yet developed, so that it is an anachronism to call the early comers Goidels—though their descendants might correctly bear the name. The majority of authorities, on the other hand, see no reason to doubt that the tongues were thoroughly disassociated before we can get the earliest glimpse of the tribes that used them.

The all-important point for the chronology of the successive Celtic invasions is that if we take the dialectic differences between the families who preferred the Q and those who preferred the P to have been in existence in the fourth century before Christ, then the Goidels had long been in Britain and the Brythons had already followed them to its southern parts, when Pytheas made his great voyage somewhere about the year 325.   For the Massiliot explorer calls the land " the Pretanic Isle," a form which shows that he got its name from P-using Brythons and not from Q-using Goidels, unless indeed he learned the name in Gaul, and not in Britain itself.

This all-important name, which has stuck to us to the present day, and has spread to so many Britains beyond the seas, simply means the land of the painted or tattoed men. In Irish, which preserves the Goidelic form of the word, these folks, the " Picts " of the Roman, the Pechts of the Anglo-Saxon, are called Cruithni or Cruthni. The archaic form, if writing had existed among the Celts six centuries before Christ, would have been Qurtani. The corresponding form used by the Brythonic " P Celts " would be Priten, or in later shape Pridein, Prydyn, or Pryden. Since therefore Pytheas called the land that he visited the Pretanic and not the Kuertanic Isle,[1] he must have heard its name, when he visited its

---

[1] Greek having no Q, he would have called it so, I suppose.

southern shores, from Brythonic and not from Goidelic inhabitants.
The various spellings of the name which prevailed in later days,
when B was substituted for P as the initial letter, has been attributed to a bad Latin pronunciation of the forms Pretanic, and Pre-
tani, and Pretannia, which the Romans first heard from their allies
the Greeks of Massilia a century after the time of Pytheas.[1] This
seems preferable to the other view which has been put forward by
some Celtic scholars, to the effect that, entirely independent of the
word Priten, the painted, there was another Celtic word Brittŏnes
(from an archaic form of the Welsh word Breithyn, cloth) meaning
"the clothed people," which was applied to themselves by the inhabitants of the southern parts of the island to distinguish them
from the more scantily garbed aborigines whom they had been
driving out. This seems unlikely, considering that archæological
evidence seems to show that the brachycephalous men of the round
barrows, whom the Celts conquered, wore just as much clothing of
both woven woollen material and of dressed skins as did their successors—so that the name would be entirely inappropriate.

The story therefore of the invasion of Britain by the Celts would
seem to be that somewhere about the year 600 B.C. Goidelic tribes,
the forerunners of the whole race, began to cross into the island,
and to subdue or intermingle with the men of the short skulls and
round barrows who had been dominant in the Bronze Age. The
earlier people were mainly thrust North and West into the Scottish
Highlands and Ireland, where they were ultimately followed by
their conquerors. But enough of them always remained, mingled
among the Goidels, to influence the physical form and perhaps also
the customs or even the language and religion of the victors. Then,
some considerable time after 600, but also some considerable time
before 325 B.C., the second Celtic waves of Brythons crossed the
Channel, and treated the Goidels just as the latter had treated the
brachycephalous races. This second invasion, which forced the
Goidels into the North and West, completely swamped the last
remains of the pre-Celtic population, who were absorbed by the
tribes driven in upon, and over, them. The Brythons occupied the
whole land from the Channel, as far as Forth and Clyde, absorbing,
in their turn, so many of the Goidels as were not content to flee to
Ireland, the Highlands, or the remoter isles of North and West.

[1] Though the change of a Greek Π into a Latin B is to say the least unusual.

Thus in the Goidelic lands the governing classes would be Celtic, the servile classes largely non-Celtic, while in the Brythonic lands the dominant aristocracy would be Brythonic, the serfs Goidelic, with a surviving dash of blood from the earlier people whom the Goidels had subdued a couple of centuries before. Both Britain and Ireland, in short, would be Celtic lands, but in both there would be a percentage of the blood of the older non-Aryan aborigines. But this percentage would be much smaller in the South than in the North and West. There is no clear proof that in any part of either island a non-Celtic speech survived a century or two after the Brythonic invasion, *e.g.*, in the time of Julius Caesar. The whole population of both islands may be treated as Celtic, though the proportion of non-Celtic blood in the remoter Goidelic districts may have been considerable.

The survival of this blood is marked by the existence of a dark-haired race of shorter stature among the conquering Celts who, as all authorities, both Roman and Greek, assure us, were a tall race with red or fair hair. That this was the characteristic appearance of the Celtic chiefs and their warriors cannot be doubted, but even before arriving in Britain both Goidels and Brythons may have already mixed their race somewhat on the continent, by conquering and absorbing other shorter and darker peoples, of race similar to that of their later victims in the island. In their progress by Danube and Rhine they must surely have picked up some serfs and dependants, or ever they crossed the Channel. Be this as it may, the comparatively few remains of bodies of the Celtic period in Britain, the relics of the Iron Age men, are by no means all of the large stature that we should have expected, though they define themselves clearly enough from the skeletons of the Bronze Age, through the fact that their skulls are more or less dolichocephalous. It must be remembered, however, that the Celts were addicted to cremation, and that their kings and chiefs and warriors were very often burnt, so that there is small chance of systematically inspecting or measuring the bones of the ruling class. Still, the bodies discovered are often those of men of moderate stature, even those of persons who had been buried along with their chariots, and who must therefore have been of some importance. Yet the whole number discovered is so small, owing to the preference for cremation, that all inductions are dangerous.

The third Celtic wave of invasion in Britain was that of the
Belgae, whose settlements, as Caesar informs us, took place only a
comparatively short time before his own visits to Britain, perhaps
as late as 180 or even 150 B.C.   They were apparently akin to the
Brython rather than the Goidel,[1] but had evidently no mercy on
their relatives, whom they conquered or drove northward or westward in the usual style.   Caesar remarks that the Belgae beyond
the Channel still showed their ancestry in his day by the fact that
they preserved in Britain the tribal names which they had borne
on the continent.   From this we may deduce that the Atrebates of
Berkshire and Surrey, whose name is identical with that of the
Atrebates of Artois, the Catuvellauni of Hertfordshire, Bedfordshire and Oxfordshire, whose fathers were the Catuvellauni or
Catalauni of Chalons, as well as the confederacy of small communities in Hampshire, Wiltshire, and Somersetshire, who called
themselves by the racial rather than tribal name of Belgae, were
in Caesar's mind.   But to the same Belgic race must also have
belonged the tribes of Kent, who simply bore the local name of
Cantii, taken from the word Caint, and also the men of Sussex
(Regni) and Essex (Trinovantes), for it is inconceivable that Belgae
should have occupied the basin of the middle Thames and the
whole of the downs of Hants and Wilts, unless they were already
in possession of the estuary of the great river and the Kentish
promontory, through which lay the easiest entry from their original
continental seats.

These, to the best of our knowledge, were the Belgic tribes:
beyond them to the North and West were their Brythonic kinsmen
—the Eceni (or Iceni) in the eastern counties,[2] the Durotriges and
Dumnonii in the South-West (Dorset, Devon, and Cornwall), the
Dobuni of the lower Severn Valley, the widely spread but apparently thinly scattered Coritani and Cornavii of the woodland
district of the North Midlands, the Silurians, Demetae, and Ordovices of the modern Wales.   Then, from sea to sea, came the
Brigantes, most numerous of all the Brythonic tribes, who held the
six northern counties entire, save the district round the Humber-
mouth belonging to the Parisii, and the part of Northumberland

[1] But see objections to this statement in E. B. Nicholson's *Celtic Studies*.
[2] But some will have it that the Iceni were Belgic.

beyond the line of the later Roman Wall, where the Otadini dwelt.
Lastly, in the Lowlands along the Solway and the Irish Sea were
the Novantae and Selgovae. The second section of the Dumnonii,
a name identical with the distant Cornish tribe of the South, lying
northernmost of all the Brythons, on the spot where the island is
narrowest, and the two firths of Clyde and Forth almost meet, ends
the roll. Beyond them the Goidelic races began.

It has been sometimes alleged that several of this list of tribes
were Goidelic, or had a preponderant Goidelic element in them,
such as the Dumnonii of the extreme South-West, the Demetae and
Silurians of South Wales, and the Novantae and Selgovae of the
Lowlands. The evidence alleged for this statement seems insufficient, as it is all drawn from facts of too late a date, mainly
inscriptions of Roman or post-Roman date found in the territories of some of these tribes.[1] Since it is acknowledged that there
was in the fourth century after Christ, and later, a Goidelic immigration from Ireland into South Wales, and possibly into Devonshire also, any dialectic traces of that race in fifth or sixth century
inscriptions may be ascribed to late-coming visitors, without it
being necessary to suppose that the whole region was originally
Goidelic. The place-names of these districts which are to be found
in Ptolemy and other classical authors seem mainly Brythonic: the
Celtic tongues which survived in them into post-Roman days was
most certainly Brythonic, not Goidelic, viz., Welsh and Cornish.
So was the other dialect which was borne into Gaul in the fifth
century by exiles from Britain, who carried with them not only the
racial denomination of Bretons, but local names like Cornouailles
and Domnonie, showing the exact district from which they had come.
The same seems the case in the western Lowlands of Scotland,
where the tribes of historic days, with the exception of the intruding Picts of Galloway, were reckoned "Welsh," and not "Picts,"
by their Anglian neighbours, and were, according to their own
legends, connected with kinsfolk to the south, in Wales proper,
while they held the Goidels north of them, whether Picts or Scots,
to be alien. Indeed, all that can be said in favour of the theory
that the Dumnonians or the Silurians and other tribes along the

---

[1] Especially an Ogham inscription at Silchester, and three or four South Welsh
tombstones of post-Roman date which show names of a Goidelic cast.

western shore of Britain were Goidels, is that there probably was
a larger proportion of men with Goidelic (and we must add pre-
Goidelic) blood in their veins among the servile classes of this
region, than there was among the other Brythonic peoples of
Britain, and specially more than among the south-eastern tribes,
which were not only Brythonic but Belgic, and had the least percentage of non-Celts in their ranks. The survival of the pre-Celtic
and pre-Aryan blood is marked by low stature and dark complexion,
of which one or both may be found clearly prevalent in some parts
of Brythonic South Wales and Damnonia, no less than in many
districts of the Goidelic Scottish Highlands, where the typical
conquering Celt, the tall red-haired man described by the classical
authors, is less numerous than the small black-haired man. But
there is no reason to suppose that anywhere in Britain did the
pre-Celtic population maintain itself independent, or succeed in
swamping and denationalising its conquerors. The Goidel-Picts,
Caledonians, or whatever we choose to call them, are to be reckoned
predominantly Celtic like their southern neighbours, though the
predominance of the Celtic element in their blood was less marked
than among the Brythons and Belgae.

Pytheas, whom we already have had occasion to mention
so often, gives us the first definite literary picture of Britain,
though he does not help us, except indirectly, with its ethnology: probably one sort of Celt seemed to him much the same
as another. He was a younger contemporary of Aristotle, and
his journals are said to have been published after the death of that
philosopher, so that no information from them got into the encyclo-
pædic works of the greater man. He was a professional explorer,
mathematician and astronomer, who was employed by the government of Massilia, or perhaps by a syndicate of Massiliot merchants,
to head an expedition into the Atlantic waters, in order to see
whether anything could be done in the way of developing trade
in that direction, where only the Phœnicians of Carthage had yet
ventured to advance. But being a scientist by nature, and a commercial explorer only by force of circumstances, he evidently put
more of geography than of trade information into his works. Perhaps his employers directed him to keep the practical information
for traders dark, that they might have the monopoly of it, while
permitting him to say as much as he pleased about tides, climate,

solar equinoxes, longitude and latitude and such like things. It is sad that Pytheas's work (or two works) has perished, and is only known to us by copious extracts in Polybius, Strabo, Diodorus Siculus, Pliny, and other later writers, of whom Strabo and Polybius were bitterly hostile to the earlier geographer, and mentioned him in a carping way, disputing many of his statements which there is no real need to reject.

Pytheas sailed through the Straits of Gibraltar and up the coast of Spain, being fortunate enough to escape the notice of the Carthaginians, who would have stopped his voyage if they had been able. He then felt his way all along the Bay of Biscay to Corbilo, a great port at the mouth of the Loire, where in this age the British tin was wont to come ashore, in order to be taken overland all over Gaul and as far as Marseilles. He next rounded Cape Ushant, where he reports the existence of the Osismii, the same tribe who were there three hundred years later, in Caesar's day. From Uxisama, as he calls this cape, he struck across the mouth of the Channel, and in one day's sail reached Belerium, the Cornish Land's End, where he found the people comparatively civilised and ready to trade for their tin. He then pushed right along the south coast of Britain to Cantium, or Kent, for a distance which he calculated at 833 miles, the voyage not being very much more than half that number of miles in reality. But calculations made (like those of Herodotus in an earlier day) by the day's journey of a ship, are notoriously untrustworthy. In Kent and the neighbouring regions he noticed that corn was produced in abundance, but that owing to the damp and gloomy climate it could not be thrashed on open floors, as in the Mediterranean lands, but had to be dealt with in covered barns. Wheat was common in the South, but the more northern tribes had to be content with oats, which suited better their still more inclement climate. The national drink was a sort of beer, or rather mead, prepared from grain fermented with honey : this remained the favourite beverage of the Celts right down into the post-Christian Middle Ages. He reports that the tides were portentous, as indeed they must have appeared to a navigator from the tideless Mediterranean, but states their maximum at eighty cubits, which exceeds by the proportion of two to one even the bore of the Bristol Channel, the greatest tidal wave of the British Isles.

After visiting Kent, Pytheas went into the North Sea, in search
of the sources of the amber trade : for amber was much esteemed by
the Greeks, who had, however, been compelled to depend for it on
overland trade from the Baltic through Central Europe.   How far
in this region the explorer made his way is difficult to determine,
it is pretty certain, however, that he did not round Denmark, or
get to the real amber-coast of Pomerania and Prussia, though
he reached the district east of the Helder, where tide-washed
amber is thrown ashore, then inhabited by the " Ostiones " and
Cimbri.   Apparently he returned round the north of Britain, where
he gives curious notes about Thule, which he calls a great island
under the Arctic Circle and near the Frozen Ocean, six days' voyage
from the northernmost of the British Isles.   In the last point that
he visited himself, the Shetlands probably, the shortest midsummer
night was only four or five hours long, but farther off, in Thule,
there was no night at midsummer, and no day at midwinter.   This
would seem to show that Thule must be Norway, wrongly conceived
of as an island, where the midnight sun is a reality which could not
fail to strike any observer.   There seems no reason to think that
Pytheas visited Thule himself ; he had to rely on reports from Britons
who had been in more or less direct touch with the inhabitants of
Scandinavia, where (as we have already mentioned) there was a
well-developed Bronze Age, and considerable trade, long before the
Celts came to Britain.

Finally Pytheas came back to the Channel, apparently without
having seen Ireland.   For this the carping Strabo calls his veracity
into account, saying that, if he had really rounded the extremity of
Britain, he must have been close to Ireland, which Strabo wrongly
conceived to be north of Cape Wrath, instead of west of Galloway
and Wales.   He finally concluded his voyage by going overland
from Gaul to Marseilles, probably from Corbilo.   Presumably his
report must have been that the sea-voyage to the extreme North-
West was so long that it had no preference for practical purposes
over the land route across Gaul, which the Massiliots were already
wont to use for their tin trade.

Poseidonius, more than 200 years after Pytheas, gives us much
more information about that trade : we have from him a long
account of the region of " Belerium," of the working of the tin in
superficial veins near the surface and from streams, how it was cast

into ingots of astragalus shape,[1] of which two were the proper load for a beast of burden, and taken by the natives to the island of Ictis, where they sold it to merchants, who carried it to Gaul, and sent it overland on pack horses to Marseilles and the mouths of the Rhone. This Ictis, which is described as an isle at high water and a peninsula at low water, must evidently be St. Michael's Mount, the only place in the tin-producing district which answers the description. It is useless to think of the Isle of Wight (Vectis), for not only is there no certainty that in historical days this island was connected with Hampshire at low tide, but also it is absurd to suppose that the Cornish tribes, well provided with harbours, would have sent their tin two hundred miles eastward to be shipped.

The best proof of the mercantile habits of the Celts of Southern Britain is that they adopted a coinage at least one hundred and fifty, and more probably two hundred, years before the Christian era. Their earliest coins are of gold—silver, bronze, and tin were not coined till much later—and are copied in a barbarous fashion from the well-known gold staters of Philip of Macedon, the first gold coinage which spread far into Europe. Since the money of the Southern Gauls and the Celtiberians imitated not this model but the coins of Marseilles and the other Greek colonies of the shore of the Gulf of Lyons, or else the *denarii* of the later Roman Republic, it is clear that the Britons must have got the originals which they imitated from another direction, and this direction was undoubtedly the course of the Rhine and Danube. Imitations of the money of the Macedonian kings, Philip, Alexander, and Lysimachus, were common among the barbarians of Thrace and Pannonia, and it must have been from thence that the models of the first British coinage came. When it is remembered that in the early years of the third century the south-eastern wing of the Celtic race was occupying the middle Danube, and devastating Macedon and Greece, we can easily see how the gold stater of Philip made its way in such quantities to their kinsmen of the North-West, that it became the most convenient unit of value for them to copy. It must have taken some generations, however, for

---

[1] It is curious to note that an ingot of astragalus shape, fitted with straps for carrying it, was the coin-type of the remote Illyrian mining town of Damasstium. No doubt the form was convenient for transport, as the splaying out at the corners prevented the straps from slipping.

the Philippic staters to travel to Britain, as is shown by the fact
that even the earliest of them are from fifteen to twenty grains
less in weight than the original Macedonian coin. The first British
pieces show a clear imitation of the head of Apollo, and the chariot
and driver, which formed the types of King Philip, but in the
course of ages the copy became more and more barbarous, till of
the face on the obverse only the laurel-wreath and some meaningless
lines survived, while of the chariot only one horse remained : the
charioteer and his vehicle had become a hopeless confusion of dots
and curves. By Caesar's time this typical British degeneration of
the Macedonian type had become more or less fixed, with varieties
of execution between the money of different tribes. Soon after his
day inscriptions giving the names of kings begin to appear, and
a whole new series of types, borrowed from the Roman contemporary coinage, was introduced into the island in rapid succession.
Of these pieces and the valuable historic evidence to be deduced
from them we shall have more to say in the proper place.

As might have been expected from a people advanced enough to
adopt a coinage, the Celts of Britain had attained to a very considerable degree of culture and civilisation. Their bronze, iron, and
gold [1] work was extremely artistic, in a style differing widely from
that of their predecessors of the Bronze Age. While chevrons and
other geometrical patterns, chiefly of straight lines, were the main
types of decoration alike of pottery and of metal-work in the
earlier time, Celtic art was distinguished by its preference for
graceful curves, and for patterns derived more or less closely from
foliage. Animal subjects were not unknown, though less common,
but scroll work inspired by vegetable forms was the typical ornament. Circles filled up with smaller curved designs, and branching
out into meandering patterns of all kinds, were also frequent.
The whole effect was usually very artistic. Enamelling with red
inlay was frequently used in metal work, and studs of coral and
other bright-coloured material were used to diversify the surface
both of small decorative ornaments and of larger objects, such as
shields or helmets.

Yet primitive barbarism lingered ; the practice of tattooing was
almost universally prevalent in Britain, as Caesar had occasion to

---

[1] Gold ornaments of the early Iron Age are, however, rare both in Gaul and
Britain.

remark; it survived among the remoter Goidelic tribes for centuries after the first Roman invasion, and so caused the Romans to call them the "Picti," in contradistinction to the conquered Britons, who had dropped the custom when they were taken into the pale of the general civilisation of the Roman world. A more horrid mark of barbarism was the survival of human sacrifices, which (as we have already seen) had certainly been practised by the remote fore-runners of the Celt. The custom was to immolate victims to the gods, or to the shades of the dead, by burning them alive in large wicker cages or frames, sometimes apparently as part of funeral ceremonies, sometimes as thank-offerings in the day of victory,[1] or as propitiatory offerings in the day of distress.

This brings us to the religion of the Celts, and to their famous priesthood, the Druids, whose central focus of power is said by Caesar to have been established in Britain. The Celts were poly-theists of the usual Aryan type, with a pantheon which seems to have differed much between tribe and tribe. This was the case with many another Aryan race—with the Greeks, for example, till the day when Homer and Hesiod popularised the system which was afterwards generally accepted, "and made regular the attributes and functions of the various divinities," as Herodotus remarks. This much is clear, that some of the deities most worshipped by the Celts of Gaul cannot be traced in Britain, while many gods made known to us by British inscriptions cannot be traced in Gaul. Caesar says that the Celts specially honoured a divinity whom he identified with the Roman Mercury, the inventor of arts, as well as Mars, Apollo, Minerva, and Dis Pater, the god of the shades, from whom, according to their Druids, they themselves were descended. It is not exactly easy to reconcile this short notice with the glimpses that we get of British deities from the dedications made to them in Roman times, or the scanty hints that can be gathered from early Celtic tradition preserved into Christian times. The British provincials, after the Roman conquest, behaved like most other barbarian subjects of the empire, and roughly identified their own local gods with members of the Olympian family wor-shipped by their conquerors. The most frequent of all such dedi-

---

[1] Boadicea in her day of victory over the Romans is recorded to have offered many human sacrifices to Andate, the goddess of victory in battle, with horrible details of torture. See Dio Cassius, epitomised by Xiphilinus, lxii. § 4.

cations are those of altars to a war-god, whose usual names or
epithets were Belutucadrus, Camulus, or Coccidius, and who was
equated with the Roman Mars. Then comes Sulis, a goddess to
whom the medicinal waters of Bath were sacred : she was usually, we
know not why, identified with Minerva. The Apollo of Caesar
seems in Britain to be represented by Mabon, a young god who was
connected with the sun, or perhaps was actually the sun. Dedications to Mercury, who, according to Caesar, was so prominent in the
Gallic pantheon, are not at all common in Britain, nor can we even
be sure of his local name—possibly he was the Lug who in Irish
mythology was the patron of smithcraft, music, and poetry, and
whose name seems to be compounded in some British local and
personal names, such as Luguvallium (Carlisle) and Lugotorix.
We see no signs of his having been one of the greatest gods on this
side of the water, whatever may have been the case beyond the
Channel. Jupiter, on the other hand, was very largely worshipped
in Roman Britain, but apparently he was the Roman Jove, "Op-
timus Maximus"; only one inscription among many scores in
Britain equates him with the Celtic Tanarus, a thunder-god who
was well known in Gaul. But there seems to be connection in
ideas between the two deities by means of the thunder alone—
Tanarus does not appear to have been the king and father of the
gods, like Jupiter. There was another British deity whose altars
have been found without any classical name added to his Celtic
title, Nodons or Nudens, whose temple overlooked the Severn
Estuary near Lydney. He seems to have been the lord of the sea
or the abyss, something between Neptune and Jupiter. To the
proper god of the lower world, whom Caesar calls Dis Pater, and
for whom, according to him, the Gauls had much reverence, there
are only two doubtful allusions in the epigraphy of Celtic Britain,
epitaphs in which Dis is mentioned in such purely classical connection that we feel no certainty that the erector of the monument
was thinking of the native god at all.[1] Many other deities are
known to us by name alone, such as Andate (Andaste),[2] of whom we

---

[1] C. I. L., vii. 154 and 250. "Omnibus aequa lege iter est ad Taenara Ditis"
and "Secreti Manes qui regna Acherontia Ditis incolitis," are the context words.
Taenarus and Acheron show that we have here mere classical "tags".

[2] Is this a misreading in Dio Cassius for Ancaste, a goddess to whom an altar
was discovered at Bitterne near Southampton (C. I. L., vii. 4)?

know no more than that she was identified with Bellona or Victory,
and was a war-goddess. In many parts of the country the local
deities of rivers, springs, and forests were worshipped—we know
that this was the case with the goddesses of the Dee and the Mersey
(Deva and Belisama), and of the spring on the Northumbrian wall
called, after the nymph, Coventina.

All the knowledge that we possess of the British gods, as will be
obvious, is woefully lacking in precision but it may be pleaded
that the actual beliefs of the Britons were equally vague, and that
the character of the deities varied indefinitely from tribe to tribe.
It is more important, perhaps, to know of their curious and well-
organised priesthood than of themselves. Among the Celts, says
Caesar,[1] "there are only two classes which are held in consideration
and honour, the Knights (equites) and the Druids. The latter are
concerned with all things divine, manage the public and private
sacrifices, and interpret sacred omens and religious scruples. Great
throngs of young men come to them to be trained, and they are
held in much awe by their pupils. For they make decisions on
almost all disputes, both private and public, and if a crime is committed, e.g., a murder, or if a lawsuit arises concerning heritages or
disputed boundaries, it is they who give the judgment. They name
the compensation or assess the penalty : and if any private person,
or even any community, will not accept their award, they interdict
them from taking part in the sacrifices. This is the heaviest
punishment that they can impose. Persons thus placed under
interdict are held impious and accursed, men quit their company
and avoid meeting them or speaking to them, lest they may come
to harm from the contagion of the wicked ; nor can the excommunicated plead in any lawsuit, or share in any public office. All the
Druids are under one arch-priest, who has the highest authority
among them. When he dies the man of most dignity among the
rest succeeds him : if several seem of equal worthiness the dispute
is settled either by the votes of the whole Druidical body, or (not
infrequently) by force of arms. At a certain season of the year they
hold a solemn synod at a consecrated place in the land of the
Carnutes [about Dreux] which is held to be the middle spot of Gaul.
Hither come from every side all who have controversies, and submit

---

[1] *Bell. Gal.*, vi. 13-14.

them to the decrees and judgment of the Druids. The system was invented in Britain, and from thence brought over to Gaul, as is generally believed; and even still those who wish to get the deepest possible knowledge of the Druidical training go to Britain to seek it. The Druids are free of military duties, and pay no taxes, having immunity from all service both in war and elsewhere. Attracted by these privileges, many young men come of their own accord to be trained by them, and many are sent by their parents and relatives. They are said to learn by heart enormous quantities of sacred poetry: some spend as much as twenty years in this training. None of their lore is permitted to be put down in writing, though in other matters public and private the Gauls are accustomed to use the Greek script. This prohibition seems to me to have two causes—first that the Druids do not wish their knowledge to be published to the common herd, and second that they imagine that those who trust to writing pay less attention to memory—as indeed may commonly be seen—so that, when they have got a thing committed to paper, they neglect the practice of learning by heart, and allow their memories to grow slack. The chief doctrine of the Druids is that the soul does not perish, but at death passes from one body to another,[1] and this belief they consider a great incentive to courage, since the fear of annihilation may be put aside. They hold many discussions concerning the stars and their movements, about the size of the world and the universe, about nature, and about the power and attributes of the immortal gods. . . . The whole nation of the Gauls is much given to superstition, for which reason those who are afflicted by a dangerous disease, and those who are involved in wars and dangers, either make human sacrifices, or vow that they will do so, and use the Druids as their agents at these ceremonies; for they think that the divine power cannot be conciliated unless a human life is paid for by a human life. They have public sacrifices ordained in this same fashion. Some tribes

[1] Two interpretations of this statement are possible: the one that the Gauls held the Pythagorean belief that the immortal soul went round many bodies—perhaps of beasts as well as of men, if there is an echo of Druidism in the strange passage concerning the transmigration of the soul of Taliessin in the early Welsh poem. The other is not that the soul of the dead man went into the body of some other person, but that it acquired a new spiritual body, in that land of happiness beyond the Western Ocean (Tier-nan-Oge in the Irish tradition) in which the Celts seem generally to have believed. The latter interpretation seems more likely.

make great images, whose limbs, woven of wickerwork, they cram
with live human victims, and then place fire below and slay them
by the flames. They consider that thieves and highwaymen and
other criminals are the sacrifices most pleasing to the gods; but
when the supply of such victims has failed, they have been known
to lay hands even on wholly innocent persons. . . . The Germans
are entirely different from the Gauls in these customs. For they
neither have any Druids to take charge of their religious business,
nor do they pay any attention to sacrifice."

From other authorities than Caesar we add to our knowledge
concerning the Druids the fact that they were given to augury and to
the choosing of lucky and unlucky days—a Gaulish bronze calendar
of this sort has actually been found.[1] Also that they reverenced
the mistletoe growing upon the oak (not a very common vegetable
combination), and that when it was found, the chief Druid would
sacrifice a white bull below the tree, before he ascended to cut the
mistletoe with a golden sickle.[2] Apparently the bush was considered
mysterious and divine because of its obscure origin and growth.

What are we to make of Caesar's surprising statement that the
Druidical lore had its origin in Britain, and that the deepest knowledge of it was in his day possessed by those who dwelt in the island?
Some modern historians have argued that if there was anything
specially strong and peculiar in the religious organisation of the
British Celts, as compared with that of their Continental kinsmen,
it must have owed its source to that racial element which was
stronger among the insular people than among the Gauls. They
explain that this element is the infusion of pre-Celtic blood, and
wish to regard the Druids as survivors of the medicine men or
wizards of the Bronze Age people,[3] who had somehow contrived not
only to continue their existence but to impose their power on the
conquerors. This is not absolutely impossible: the sacerdotal caste
of conquered races has sometimes obtained an influence over their
victors, like the Canaanite priests of Baal among the Jews, or—a

---

[1] At Coligny in the Department of the Ain, but made after the Roman Conquest, probably in the time of Augustus. See Sir John Rhys, *Celtae and Galli*, i.
4, etc.

[2] Pliny Senior, *Natural History*, xvi. 44, § 250.

[3] Perhaps ⸿ en of the Neolithic people. See Rice Holmes's *Ancient Britain*,
114-15.

more striking instance—the Christian priesthood who tamed the
Frank, Goth, and Burgundian in the fifth century of our own era.
It may also be conceded that the Druids, as remembered in Irish
and Welsh traditions of post-Christian date, are often represented as
magi, wonder-working wizards, who used marvels against St. Patrick
and his followers, as Jannes and Jambres did against Moses.

Nevertheless we have no sufficient evidence to link the Druids
with the pre-Celtic element in the population of Britain, and certainly the classical authors who touch upon the subject were convinced that Druidism was a typically Celtic institution, that it
prevailed everywhere from the Rhine and the Garonne to the
farthest coast of Britain.   Some of them thought that the conception of the transmigration of souls, which evidently formed an important part of the Druidical teaching, had been learnt first by the
Gauls of the South from Pythagorean philosophers, with whom they
had come into contact at Massilia or some other Greek colony of
the West.[1]   Possibly Caesar argued wrongly that Druidism originated in Britain, merely because he saw that in his own day it was
more severely dominant in the Island than on the Continent, whereas the fact may have been merely that the Celts of Britain had
been less influenced by external influences—Roman, Greek, or
German, or Ligurian—than their continental kinsmen, and so
may have preserved in a more intact shape a religion that had
been somewhat modified in the South.   How dangerous it would be
to argue that the place where any lore is most thoroughly studied
at a certain time is the place where it originated, may be exemplified
by an instance taken from an age seven centuries after Caesar's
time.   If a Chinese or an Arabian traveller or statesman had visited
Western Europe anywhere between 650 and 750, he would have
found Ireland the centre of Christian learning, and its monasteries
frequented by Frankish and English novices; it would have been
easy to deduce that Christian lore must have had its origin there.

In Tacitus's time the island of Mona (Anglesey) was the religious centre of British Druidism; whether this had always been
the case, or whether the cult had shifted its centre westward because of the oncoming Roman invasion, no man can say.   But
clearly Britain must always have had some central focus, corresponding to that for Gaul which Caesar noted as existing in the

[1] Diodorus Siculus, v. 28, § 6, and Timagenes quoted by Ammianus, xv. 9, § 8.

territory of the Carnutes. Very possibly it may have been among the prehistoric monuments of Salisbury Plain.

If arguments may be drawn from one branch of human activity to another, it is certainly probable that British Druidism may represent a survival of an original Celtic institution rather than a new discovery. Cæsar notes that the Britons were a stage behind their continental kinsmen in general development, with the exception of the newly arrived Belgic tribes on the south coast, who differed little from their neighbours beyond the Dover Straits. The difference was specially marked in military usages; while the continental Gauls had entirely abandoned the use of the war-chariot, it survived everywhere in Britain. The Romans of the third century before Christ had been well acquainted with the cars of the Gaulish chiefs, and triumphal monuments still recalled their shape. But since the days of Bituitus and Viridomarus the Gauls had abandoned the device, probably (as has been remarked) because they became acquainted with better breeds of horses in the South. In the northern island, where the undersized Celtic pony was still prevalent, the chariot remained, because the horses available were not fit to carry the fully armed warrior with ease. Even among the newly arrived Belgae chariots were still employed, and Caesar found that the flower of the host of Britain came out to battle like the chiefs who fought before Troy. Their tactics we shall have to describe when we are dealing with the campaigns of the first Roman invader.

This survival of primitive customs in Britain remains all the more striking because we know that the intercourse between the continental and the insular Celts was close and continuous. As we shall have occasion to note, when dealing with Britain at the time of Caesar's invasion, the two were so closely connected that the great pro-consul found the attack upon Britain a necessary corollary to the attack upon Gaul.

CHAPTER III

CAESAR IN BRITAIN (B.C. 55-54)

A VERY cursory exploration of Caesar's account of his earlier
Gallic campaigns suffices to show the close connection of the
Britons of the South and their relatives beyond the Straits of Dover
—a connection that was both political, commercial and religious.
Within human memory Divitiacus, king of the Suessiones, and for
a time suzerain over most of the continental Belgians—had extended
his power over some of the British states.[1] This empire, like all
Gaulish hegemonies, had been short and fleeting. But there were
still close personal connections between the Island and the Continent. Commius, whom Caesar had made king of the Atrebates,
the tribe between Somme and Lys, had great authority, as we are
assured, in certain British regions—presumably among others in
that occupied by the insular Atrebates along the south bank of
the middle Thames.[2] Gaulish exiles, who had made their own
countryside too hot for them, were wont to take refuge in Britain.[3]
British adventurers used to cross over in a similar fashion to Gaul :
Caesar remarks that in nearly every Gallic campaign he had found
Britons fighting among the ranks of his Celtic enemies.[4] How
close was the religious tie between the continental and the insular
Celts, we have already seen, when dealing with the vexed question
of the Druids. Gallic merchants and shipmen were well acquainted

[1] Caesar, *B. G.*, ii. 4.
[2] *Ibid.*, iv., 24. It would be invaluable to us to know whether other tribes kept
up the same touch as the Atrebates : *e.g.*, were the Menapii of South-Eastern Ireland (a Belgic colony sent out to Wexford by the Menapii of Picardy), in similar
correspondence with the mother state : or the Parisii of the Humber with the older
Parisii of the Seine, from whom we cannot doubt that they originally came ? Unfortunately surmise is all that is left to us : no evidence is forthcoming.
[3] *Ibid.*, ii. 14.   [4] *Ibid.*, iv. 20.

with the southern coast of Britain, and we can hardly doubt that
Britain, too, had its seafarers, who were equally conversant with the
shores of Northern Gaul.   Yet though in Caesar's war against the
Veneti in 56 B.C. that tribe is said to have sent for aid from Britain,
we cannot believe that the Britons had any fighting ships to lend:
the succour must have been given in men.   This Venetian war,
however, had, if we may trust Strabo, its origin and root in British
commerce.[1]   He asserts that the Veneti resolved to withstand Caesar
because they were, before the appearance of the Roman galleys in
the Atlantic, the main holders of the cross-Channel trade, and were
set on keeping off a new claimant for maritime supremacy in
those waters.   It was not therefore mere jealousy of the growing
power of Caesar in Central Gaul which led them to risk and lose
their national existence by an attack upon him, but a commercial
motive.

That same motive was also at the bottom of Caesar's attack
upon Britain.   It was not merely to punish the British tribes who
had sent auxiliaries to join the Veneti or the Belgae, nor to show
the Gauls that no enemy was safe from his sword, nor again to
dazzle the Romans by the report of victories over foes as remote
as those Iberians and Albanians whom Pompey had defeated in the
Caucasus, that Caesar first conceived the idea of crossing the
British Channel.   All these ideas were present in his mind, but he
had also a notion that profit might be made out of the subjection
of Britain.   It was believed to be fertile in gold, and Caesar must undoubtedly have seen many a British gold piece among the treasures
taken from conquered Belgae and other Celts, for (as numerous
finds show) staters from across the water were circulating freely in
North Gaul.   There was also the report of its tin trade to attract
him : he knew that tin was produced in Britain, though he wrongly
thought that it came from the inland parts of the island.[2]   He also
mentions the iron that was produced in regions nearer the coast, no
doubt the shallow mines of the Sussex Weald, which from the begin-
ing of the Iron Age to the eighteenth century were the best-known

[1] Οὐενετοὶ μὲν εἰσιν οἱ ναυμαχήσαντες πρὸς Καίσαρα· ἕτοιμοι γὰρ ἦσαν κωλύειν τὸν
εἰς τὴν Βρεττανικὴν πλοῦν, χρώμενοι τῷ ἐμπορίῳ (Strabo, *Geog.*, iv., 4, § 1).

[2] *In mediterraneis regionibus*, B. G., v., 12.   This curious blunder can only
arise from his having discovered, when he was in Britain, that it was not found in
those southern and eastern coast tracts which he himself visited; apparently he
argued that, if it came from a distance, it must have been from the inland.

British iron-field. It is curious to find him adding that for bronze the
islanders depended on the Continent, for the copper mines of Wales
and Cornwall were worked as early as the tin mines ; perhaps he was
misled by finding that southern articles of luxury in bronze were
eagerly sought by the Britons. It is certain that they made their
own ordinary bronze implements in enormous quantities and with
no small degree of art. Perhaps Caesar may also have heard of the
British pearls, which later Romans found so disappointing from their
bad colour—so that the British oyster was of better repute than the
gems which it sometimes sheltered. It is significant to find that the
only definite article of spoil which he is recorded to have carried
home from Britain was a breastplate adorned with pearls, which he
dedicated in the temple of Victory at Rome.

In dealing with all Caesar's wars of conquest, it is well to remem
ber that there were two very different classes of motive governing
his actions. On the one hand he was a great statesman and stra-
tegist, who was extending the Roman Empire to its natural geographical limits, and providing against further dangers, alike from
Gallic turbulence, and from the more perilous invaders from beyond
the Rhine, of whom Ariovistus was to be the last example for some
400 years. On the other hand, he was a Roman faction leader, at
the head of a most miscellaneous and unscrupulous following, who
disguised themselves under the name of the " Populares," the demo-
cratic party. The chiefs of that party, with few exceptions, were
greedy, self-seeking men, who had to be kept loyal by continual
payment. Caesar had to make money by his campaigns, or he
could not have kept his followers in good temper, or have continued
his policy of buying up the services of every young man of promise
who was for sale. It was necessary for him not only to make war
support war, but to have a surplus, with which he could continue
his purchases in the market where politicians were to be bought.
Hence he was anxious for plunder of all sorts, whether it took the
form of tribal hoards of gold and silver or of prisoners of war : the
most productive of all his sources of revenue was the sale of captured slaves : it was probably this prosaic and cruel motive which
lay at the back of his frequent orders for the demolition of whole
clans and nations. A general sale of the population, male and
female, of a tribe which had proved obstinate or treacherous,
enabled him to find the money both for shows which amused the

whole Roman populace, and for the purchase of individuals whose brains and activity were likely to be profitable to him.   We may be tolerably certain that the British expeditions of 55 and 54 B.C. were not undertaken merely because the adventurers of Britain had helped the Gauls, nor because the news of British triumphs would have an imposing sound at Rome, nor because the subjection of the insular Celts seemed a logical sequence to the subjection of their continental relatives, but also because Caesar believed that there was tangible profit to be got out of the expedition—a belief in which (as we shall see) he was woefully deceived.

The proconsul's first venture was on a small scale and in a tentative style.   The summer of 55 B.C. was already far spent, operations near the Rhine having extended over many months, when he made up his mind to cross the Channel, "thinking," as he writes, "that it would be very useful to him merely to visit the island, to get a thorough knowledge of the character of its people, and become acquainted with its topography. ports and landing-places". He began by collecting Gallic merchants and cross-questioning them as to the nature and resources of Britain: they apparently told him as little as they dared : such strange statements as that quoted above, concerning the production of tin in the Midlands, must have been false, to the clear knowledge of any far-travelled trader.   The Gauls had no interest in seeing the Roman intervene in a region where they themselves had till now enjoyed a monopoly of trade.   It is possible that some of the other improbable notes in Caesar may have been part of a set of tales told him by these untrustworthy informants, in order that he might be put off from his design by an exaggerated account of the savage nature of the islanders.   Such, for example, is that which tells that some of the British tribes were still in the horde stage, that "ten or a dozen men would have wives in common, often brothers with brothers or fathers with sons".   This was certainly not possible with the Celts, whether Brythons or Goidels, and we can hardly believe that there still survived in the remoter corners of the isle remnants of some pre-Celtic people still sunk in such barbarism, or that, if there had been, the merchants of the South would have had any knowledge of them.   Equally untrue was the statement that most of the people of the inland parts of the isle had no knowledge of cereals, and lived wholly on flesh and milk, as also that they

dressed in skins for want of linen or wool. Considering that we
have ample proof that corn was cultivated not only in the Midlands
but far in the North, even beyond Forth and Tay, and that all the
Britons were skilful weavers, we are driven to suppose that some of
Caesar's informants were trying to convince him that nothing profitable could be got out of the degraded savages whom they described
to him.

If this was so, they were unsuccessful. Caesar had made up his
mind to try the experiment. He collected two legions, the Seventh
and the famous Tenth, in the territory of the Morini (Picardy),
from which he had heard that the voyage to Britain was shortest.
He brought up ships, both galleys and transports, to the Dover
Straits, and arranged, as it seems, that the legions should embark
at Boulogne,[1] while the cavalry were to go on board eighteen
horse-transports, at a harbour a little farther up the coast (probably
Ambleteuse). A preliminary exploration of the shore of Kent was
made by a tribune named Volusenus, who coasted for five days
along the land opposite those ports, in search of spots suitable for
a landing. The Britons had been warned by Gaulish traders of
Caesar's designs, and were already under arms : Volusenus could
land nowhere, and had to content himself with such reconnoitring
as could be done from a safe distance. It was apparently during
the short time of his absence at sea that Caesar was visited by
envoys from several British communities, who announced that their
tribesmen were prepared to submit to the Roman people, and to
send over hostages. If this was done with the object of turning
Caesar from his design the plan failed : he merely commended their
friendly intentions, told them that he should be among them in a
few days, and sent them away, and in their company his dependent
Commius, the king of the Atrebates, who was to use his well-known
influence in Britain for the purpose of inducing his friends to make
their submission to the pro-consul. It was afterwards discovered
that this emissary was thrown into chains, and put in ward, the
moment that he had landed. The Britons had no intention of giving
up their independence without a blow.

Soon before midnight on the 25th of August a fleet of some

---

[1] Gessoriacum. For the question of Caesar's embarkation points during the
two British expeditions, see Rice Holmes's article on " Portus Itius," in the 2nd
edition of his *Caesar's Conquest of Gaul.*

eighty transports and a few war-galleys put out from Boulogne, carrying the two legions and a certain number of light troops— archers and slingers. The eighteen ships from the neighbouring harbour to the north were to bring over 500 Gallic cavalry. The whole expeditionary force must have been under 10,000 strong, as the legions had seen much service and had not been recruited up to full strength. Supplies for only a few days were taken, as Caesar intended to live on the country, whether he was received in a friendly or a hostile fashion. The wind apparently was favourable at first, but it very soon began to shift, and the cavalry trans- ports never got out to sea. The rest of the armament was off the cliffs of Dover by nine o'clock in the morning, the galleys close in- shore, the heavy transports straggling behind. The spot cannot be mistaken : Caesar describes it as "a place where the sea is so closely shut in by abrupt hills that a dart can easily be cast from the summit above on to the foreshore". Numerous armed natives could be seen on the heights. This was not the locality at which the expeditionary force could be safely landed, nor had Caesar any intention of doing so, as he knew from Volusenus's report that there was shelving beach instead of rugged chalk cliffs only a few miles away to the north. He waited till his slow-sailing transports had come up, and till the tide had begun to run eastward, and then in the afternoon bade the whole armament steer along shore in the direction of Deal and Walmer. The moment that his intention was visible the Britons on the cliffs above were seen streaming off for the same goal.

With the tide in their favour the Roman ships could sail faster than the British levies could march, and when Caesar bade his captains turn their prows shoreward to a point some seven miles north of Dover, only the chariots and horsemen of the Cantii were in sight, the tribal levies on foot were panting far behind. Still a fierce resistance was made to the landing : the transports had run aground some way from the shore, since the beach was gently shelving. The legionaries, when invited by their officers to leap into water from four or five feet deep, and to wade up for many yards to the land, hung back, daunted by the shower of missiles already playing upon them, and by the sight of hundreds of wild charioteers careering along the shingle and shouting their discor- dant war-cries. Caesar was obliged to order his war-galleys, on which the archers and slingers were serving, to push as near the shore as possible, and to cover the disembarkation by their shooting. Many of the Britons fell, and others drew back, so that the Romans were emboldened to plunge into the water and push forward. We are told that the standard-bearer of the Tenth Legion showed them the way, by pushing far ahead and challenging his fellow-soldiers to desert their eagle and betray their general if they dared. But when the legionaries began to wade up the watery slope in disordered groups, the boldest of the Britons came down to meet them, riding or even driving into the waves, and coming to hand-strokes with the invaders. Now that both were mixed together, the Roman archers and slingers could no longer let fly, for fear of harming their friends, so that they ceased to be of any assistance. But chariots are poor devices on a shingly beach, and when the British chiefs leaped down and fought on foot, knee-deep in the water, they were no better off than their opponents. Gradually the Romans formed into solid clumps and fought their way up the beach. When they felt firm ground under their feet, and could close up in some sort of regular array, the Britons began to draw off, and presently the whole band gave way, and rode, drove, or ran off towards the interior. There was no pursuit, because the Romans were utterly destitute of cavalry : the eighteen horse-transports had never come up. Whether the tribal infantry of the Britons arrived in time to take any serious part in the fighting is uncertain : they had seven miles to run, and must have arrived dead beat, long after the battle had begun. Caesar makes no mention of them, dwelling on the audacity and courage of the charioteers and horsemen alone.

That night Caesar entrenched a camp close to the beach, and hauled his galleys ashore : the heavy transports were anchored where they had run aground, the labour of hauling them up beyond high-water mark seeming to the proconsul excessive and unneces-sary. On the following day he was delighted to receive a deputa-tion from the enemy : the men of Kent, on whom all the fighting had fallen, for no one had yet come to their aid, were dis-heartened. They gave up their prisoner Commius, apologised for their resistance, which they ascribed to the hot-headedness of their young men, and offered to submit and give hostages. Caesar accepted their excuses, received their submission, and chose a certain number of hostages ; the rest were to be sent in within a few days.

It is probable that the Britons might have kept the terms if the powers of nature had not intervened. But on the morning of August 30, just as the belated horse-transports came in sight, a terrible north-easterly gale arose. The approaching ships were swept down channel, and ultimately came ashore after many perils, at various points on the coast of Gaul. As night came on the weather grew worse: many of the anchored transports were driven ashore, while the galleys which had been dragged up to the line of ordinary high-water mark, were not beyond the reach of the specially high tide accompanying the time of full moon. The sea, helped by the wind, washed over them and did them much harm. When the morning light came it was seen that many vessels of both classes had been broken up, and that most of the remainder had lost oars, spars, and tackle, and were in an unseaworthy condition. The Britons noting the effects of the gale, a line of wrecks and stranded vessels, thought that the powers of the air had come to their aid, and resolved to try once more the chance of war. No more hostages came in, and it was clear that trouble was impending. Caesar turned all hands to work to repair his fleet: twelve ships were given up as hopeless wrecks, and with their timber, metal fittings, and surviving tackle, he began to patch up the rest. Meanwhile the stores brought from Gaul were exhausted, and the legionaries had to forage for food, which they got by cutting all the standing corn for some miles inland from the camp.

Some few days later the Britons made an attempt to cut off the large foraging parties, supplied on this occasion by the Seventh Legion, which were abroad, hard at work with the reaping hook, at a long distance from the shore. They had a special good chance given them by the fact that the tribune in command had posted no outlying pickets to guard his fatigue parties, and had allowed the men to stack their shields and armour while they were at work. Suddenly a mass of British charioteers and horsemen swept down upon the reapers from under the cover of the surrounding woods, taking them wholly by surprise. Something like a panic took place, while the Romans were collecting in groups and running to their arms. Caesar is at some pains to explain the terrifying effect of a charge of chariots. The mere clatter and rush of wheels counted for something, even with veterans who were accustomed to face with serene confidence ordinary charges of infantry or cavalry. The agility of the British chariot-fighters was as great as their courage; "they could drive and turn their teams over ground of even the most steep and precipitous contours. They might be seen to run, balancing themselves, forward along the pole, and to stand on the yoke, and then to spring back into the chariot with ease." [1] Their tactics were "first to gallop round the enemy and hurl darts at him, which often put his line in disorder, and then to fall in among the intervals of their cavalry, when they leap down and fight on foot.[2] The charioteers meanwhile retire a little way from the battle-front, and draw up the cars in such a position that, if the warriors are oppressed by the superior numbers of the enemy, they can have a quick line of retreat to their vehicles. Thus they combine the mobility of cavalry with the stability of infantry." No doubt the Britons could have found no more favourable opportunity for a sudden terrifying swoop than that given them by the scattered half-armed soldiers of the Seventh Legion, surprised in the midst of their harvesting. They would probably have been cut to pieces if Caesar, on hearing a report that great clouds of dust were visible in the direction where the Seventh were foraging, had not hurried out with the two cohorts which were under arms as camp-guard, and ordered the rest of the Tenth to follow in haste. He arrived in time to rescue his endangered troops, and then retreated with them to his camp, "thinking that the conjuncture was inopportune for attacking the enemy and courting a pitched battle ".

There followed, after this narrowly escaped disaster, several days of heavy rain, which fixed the Romans to their camp, and deterred the Britons from making any further attacks. But auxiliaries from

---

[1] Apparently the object of this acrobatic feat was to get a good cast with the spear over the heads of the galloping horses. A Gallic chief (Bituitus) casting a javelin, with one foot standing on the pole of his chariot, seems to be represented on the coins of the Roman moneyers Aurelius Scaurus and Domitius Ahenobarbus (see Babelon's *Monnaies de la Republique Romaine,* i. 243, etc.).

[2] I take it that the *equites* of Caesar's sentence, " quum se inter equitum turmas insinuaverunt " means the British cavalry, because during this expedition Caesar had no horsemen at all. The meaning must be that the charioteers first made a demonstration, and then charged in company with their own horse, dismounting just before contact with the enemy's line, and running in on foot against foes who were expecting to meet only mounted men.

some of the remoter tribes joined the local levies during this interval, and their spirits grew so high that they were eager for another fight. When, on the first fine day, Caesar filed his legions out of his gates, and drew them up in battle order in the open, his challenge was at once accepted. The Britons charged in with vigour, but were repulsed after a sharp struggle, and fled in such disorder that a mere thirty mounted men under the Atrebatian Commius, all the cavalry that Caesar could produce, were able to cut down a considerable number of them—straggling footmen, it is to be presumed.

On the same evening envoys appeared again to ask for terms of peace. Caesar amused them with a discussion of details, announced that he should demand double the number of hostages that he had asked before, and said that they should be sent over to Gaul. But that same night he quietly embarked his whole force on his fleet, which was now in fair order, and set sail for Boulogne, which he reached after an uneventful voyage. It is clear that the expedition had been a failure: the army had not moved ten miles inland, it must have suffered appreciable losses in men, as it had in ships, and it had brought back no trophies—indeed it had absconded from Britain in a surreptitious fashion, which must have done much to destroy the effect of its victories in the three combats in which it had been engaged. The sole advantages to Caesar were that he had discovered a good landing-place, that he had learned the tactics of the Britons, and that he had found that they could be defeated, even if they were a more formidable foe than he had suspected when he first crossed the straits. One thing was clear—their celerity of movement made it useless to attack them with infantry alone: if the 500 horse, which had never got to Britain, had only come ashore with the rest of the army, something more considerable might have been accomplished. Nevertheless Caesar wrote a despatch to the Senate representing the campaign in such a brilliant light, that a "supplicatio" of twenty days was voted to commemorate his exploits. Of tangible result there was none, save that two solitary Kentish tribes, out of all who negotiated for peace, sent hostages over to Gaul in the winter, as they had undertaken to do.

But Caesar was not the man to accept a defeat: he was determined to repeat his invasion with a more formidable army and at a more favourable season of the year. He retired, as usual, to Cis-

alpine Gaul for the winter, to pick up the threads of his intrigues
with his supporters and enemies at Rome. But his legions were
left behind in Belgic Gaul, with orders to spend their time in
stationary quarters, in building a new fleet and repairing the old
one. The new vessels were specially designed for use as horse-
transports, and were all fitted with oars, for Caesar had been discontented with the slowness of his sailing transports during his last
voyage. The general shape of the ships was somewhat lower and
broader than had hitherto been customary, in order to facilitate
embarkation and disembarkation of horses and stores, and also to
permit of their running closer inshore, and being more easily hauled
up above high-water mark than the old type of transport had been.
The scale of the expedition was to be very large ; as many as 600
ships had been collected ; no less than 2,000 cavalry were to be
taken over, and the preliminary expenses were very heavy. But
everything was done to avert the chance of a second fiasco like that
of 55 B.C.

Some troubles among the Treviri, on the Moselle, kept Caesar
from commencing his second British expedition quite so soon as he
had expected, but by the middle of June he had concentrated a
very large army on the coast of the Channel, from which he selected
five legions and 2,000 horse, leaving the rest to garrison Northern
Gaul. The whole force that embarked must have been at least
25,000 men, when the light troops were counted in, or more than
double that employed in the preceding year. The Britons had
long warning of Caesar's intentions, but made no good use of it :
Cassivellaunus King of the Catuvellauni, the most powerful prince
of the South, and the natural leader for a confederacy, had been
engaged that spring in attacking his neighbours the Trinovantes
of Essex : he had occupied much of their territory, and slain their
king, whose son Mandubratius fled to Caesar, and promised to join
him with the wrecks of his tribe. Thus the invader was certain of
at least some assistance on his landing. His starting point seems
to have been Portus Itius (Wissant), the harbour of Boulogne
(Gessoriacum) not being large enough to accommodate so large a
fleet as that which had been collected for this expedition.[1]

On this occasion Caesar ran, once more, to the northward of
the Dover cliffs, and being apparently carried by the tide a little

[1] See Rice Holmes' *Caesar's Conquest of Gaul*, 2nd edition

farther than he intended, finally came ashore some five or six miles beyond the place of his former landing, not far from Sandwich (July 6-7, 54 B.C.).   No resistance was offered, and he was able to build a base-camp without molestation, at which he landed a great store of provisions, for this time he was resolved not to trust entirely to the resources of the country-side.   Not sufficiently warned by his former experience of the storms and tides of the Channel, he once more left most of his fleet at anchor, being apparently anxious to save the time which would have been required to drag the heavier ships ashore.   He then told off ten cohorts, under a tribune named Quintus Atrius, for the defence of his base, and advanced into the interior, taking, as it appears, the trackway in the direction of Canterbury, Rochester and London, which already existed, and along which population and food-resources lay thickest.   The men of Kent, aware of the formidable numbers of the Roman army, had no wish to engage in a pitched battle, till they had been joined by all the other tribes threatened by the invasion.   But they made some attempt to defend the fords of the Stour, and had occupied and covered with *abattis* the line of woods which lay above them.[1]   Their cavalry and charioteers were driven from the river after a skirmish, and fell back to the entrenched woodside, where more serious resistance was made.   But the Seventh Legion, advancing in column, and forming the *testudo* of locked shields to keep off the British darts, charged straight at the entanglements and cut their way through with no great loss. The Britons thereupon melted away among the trees, where it was useless to pursue them, and Caesar encamped for the night near the place of combat.

Next morning the Roman cavalry rode out in three directions, with infantry supports, to see whether the enemy was making preparations for further resistance.   They had not returned when Caesar received an urgent message from Atrius at the base-camp. A storm, not unlike that of the previous August, had caught

---

[1] Were the fords those of the Little Stour, three miles east of Canterbury, by Littlebourne and Bekesbourne, or those of the Great Stour, just beyond Canterbury, between Sturry and Thanington?   The distance given by Caesar, twelve miles from the base-camp by the sea, is in favour of the former river.   But the ground is better for defence on the Great Stour, and there seem to be some traces of entrenchments on the low hills above Thanington, which would form a very good position.   This was probably the battle-spot, as Caesar's estimate may have been rough.

the ships at anchor : many had been driven on shore and damaged, some had been sunk by collisions with each other. The whole armament was disabled. This was a hard but well-deserved penalty, to be paid for a neglect of the warning of the preceding year. Caesar, with a heavy heart, called back his cavalry and ordered the infantry to return to the coast. Inspection showed that forty ships had been destroyed, or damaged beyond possibility of repair. He was then forced to spend ten days in hauling up the uninjured vessels above high-water mark, a tedious business; while the military artificers of all the legions were turned to work on patching up the unseaworthy ones ; messages were even sent across to Gaul, to direct Labienus, who was left in command in Belgica, to forward all available shipwrights to aid in the repairs.

On the eleventh day only could Caesar resume his march, after leaving the same force as before, under the same officer, to guard the camp and protect the artificers. This delay had given the Britons time to collect in full force , King Cassivellaunus had called upon all his tributary chiefs and neighbours to march to the aid of the Cantii, and his levies had reoccupied the positions beyond the Stour, which Caesar had stormed twelve days before. There was trouble, however, preparing behind Cassivellaunus, for Caesar had sent his protegé Mandubratius, the exiled Prince of the Trinovantes, to land in the territory of his tribesmen, and to incite them to rise against their oppressors the Catuvellauni. But this diversion would only commence to affect the fate of the campaign after a space of some days.

Meanwhile Caesar found himself involved in a running fight, which seems to have lasted almost the whole way from the Stour to the Thames. On the first day the Gaulish cavalry, in advance of the legions, got involved in a long skirmish, and, pursuing too far after a small success, were charged again, when they were in disorder, and lost many men. On the same evening the enemy made an unexpected assault on the troops who were busy laying out and entrenching the usual camp. Their cavalry and charioteers drove in the outlying guard, and cut their way in a circle between the supports that came out successively to intervene in the fight, finally getting off with small loss after causing much confusion. In this fight fell the tribune Q. Laberius Durus, the only officer of distinction whom Caesar lost during his British campaign.

On the next morning the proconsul, finding no great force of the Britons in sight, sent out three of his five legions and the whole of his cavalry, under his legate Trebonius (afterwards destined to be one of his murderers), to sweep the countryside for food. The enemy had only been waiting for the Romans to scatter, and at a well-chosen moment suddenly emerged from the woods on all sides, in the greatest numbers that they had yet shown. They drove in the foraging parties and then boldly attacked the embattled legions : but to break the Roman infantry, when it was not caught unprepared, was beyond the power of the Britons. After a sharp fight they were repulsed with loss; Caesar then let loose his cavalry upon the routed mass, and bade his legionaries follow the horse as fast as they were able. The Britons, not daring to halt and turn upon the horsemen so long as the infantry was close behind them, were pursued and cut down for some distance—the loss, as we must suppose, falling rather on the tribal levies on foot, who could be easily overtaken, than on the swiftly moving charioteers. The chase was not pushed far enough to permit the enemy to turn and rend the cavalry, when they should have got out of touch of their supports.

This was a decisive defeat for Cassivellaunus, who made up his mind that it was useless to try another pitched battle at the head of the tribal foot-levies, who were hopelessly incapable of facing the legions. He sent them all home, and only retained the flower of his chiefs and their retainers, 4,000 chariot-fighters in all. With these he dogged the steps of the Romans as they marched from the neighbourhood of Canterbury, with the forest to their south and the Thames estuary to their north. Whether Caesar's advance followed the line afterwards marked out by Watling Street, past Rochester, or whether it took the " Pilgrims' Way," along the slope of the chalk ridge of the North Downs, it is impossible to say with certainty. But since he lays stress on the fact that he was marching through a populous district, and that he did as much damage as possible, by burning and wasting on all sides, it seems more probable that he took the former route, and not that along the untilled downs. The harm that he did, however, was limited by the fact that Cassivellaunus hung on to his flanks, and fell upon his raiders whenever they went far from the main body. The Gaulish cavalry could gain no mastery over the British charioteers, and had to stick close to their infantry supports, so that the

limit of ground overrun was bounded by the distance that the infantry could diverge from the line of march, in search of huts to
burn or crops to carry off. As the Britons had sent all their
women-folk and their cattle into the Weald, to be out of harm's
way, the devastation cannot have been very effective.

Caesar's objective was the territory of the Catuvellauni, whose
king was the head of the British confederacy, since he was convinced that if he could break the power of Cassivellaunus the other
tribes would sue for peace. That territory lay entirely north of
Thames, and seems (as we have already seen in a previous chapter)
to have extended from the Lea on the East to the Cotswolds on the
West, and from the Thames on the South to the Nen and the Warwickshire Avon. No serious pressure could be brought to bear on
the Catuvellauni by ravaging the boundaries of the men of Kent:
they must be sought in their own land. It was therefore necessary
to cross the Thames at the lowest possible point, and the nearest
ford to the sea appears in those days to have lain somewhere in the
neighbourhood of Kingston, possibly opposite Brentford, (though
the name of that place refers to a ford on the little Brent, not
on the Thames), possibly at Halliford, ten miles farther up the
meandering river.[1] The depth of the Thames has been so much
affected by the silting of twenty centuries, and the building of
locks and weirs, that it is impossible to make any certain affirma-
tion about its condition in Caesar's day. We only know that there
was one obvious and well-known ford, which was pointed out by
prisoners and deserters, and that Cassivellaunus had caused this
passage to be obstructed with stakes, and entrenched his army in
array behind it, so certain was he that this would be Caesar's point
of attack. The remnants of a large and elaborate stockade are
said to be found in the bed of the Thames opposite Brentford, and
these may mark the precaution of the Catuvellaunian king.

The defence of the ford, however, was a complete failure.
There must have been some miscalculation in the staking of the
river bed, since Caesar merely tells us that his cavalry was sent first
into the water, and that his infantry, following close by, plunged

[1] There is a whole literature dealing with the question as to where Caesar
crossed the Thames. The old view, from the time of Camden downward, was that
the passage was at Coway Stakes, near Walton-on-Thames. The statements in
the text above are those of the latest pronouncement on the subject, those of Mr.
Rice Holmes's *Ancient Britain*, pp. 692-98.

into the river, though it ran as high as their shoulders, and crossed
it in column with little delay.　Whether they pulled down some of
the stakes, or whether they eluded them by passing just above or
below, we are not told.　Nor would the words forbid the idea that
the cavalry may have swum the river at an unfordable point on
the flank, while the legions went straight at the ford a little later,
when the turning movement of the horse had already shaken the
enemy.　All that is definitely stated by Caesar is that the cavalry
was sent in first, and the movement of the infantry came a little
later.　But considering the fact that he has, in the preceding paragraphs, told us that all through this campaign the horse were liable
to be checked, and roughly handled, unless they were closely supported by the foot, it seems likely that the two arms worked together on this, as on other, occasions.

The retreat of Cassivellaunus was hasty, and can have been
accompanied by little slaughter of his men, yet Caesar had won
a great advantage by crossing the Thames.　He was now only
some fifteen or twenty miles from the boundary of the Trinovantes,
among whom his emissary Mandubratius had already penetrated.
The resentment of that tribe at their late conquest by the king of
the Catuvellauni was so bitter that they had risen at the summons
of their exiled prince, and were ready to join the Romans.　Their
ambassadors came at once to Caesar's camp, handed over to him
as many hostages as he required, and began to send him in great
stores of corn.　Moving across the Lea into their land, he procured
for himself a near and secure base in a friendly country.　A few
days later other tribes made their submission—the Cenimagni,
who seem to be the Iceni of later history, the inhabitants of East
Anglia, together with the Segontiaci, Ancalites, Bibroci, and Cassi.
These last four obscure septs, whose names never occur again in
history, may have been sub-clans of the Belgic population between
the Thames and the New Forest.　Possibly the Bibroci and
Segontiaci were sections of the Atrebates, who dwelt in Berks and
Surrey,[1] while the Cassi and Ancalites may represent fractions of
the Belgae proper of Hants and Wilts.　But this is wholly uncertain.

Cassivellaunus had yet one card to play.　While he himself
hung about the line of Caesar's march, he sent messages to the

[1] On some of the British coins of the next generation, belonging to Tasciovanus'
time, the inscriptions SEGO and CATTI occur.　Are these the tribal names of these
peoples ? or are they part of the names of Kings, such as Segonax or Cattigern ?

kings of Kent, begging them to make a vigorous assault on the
Roman base-camp near Sandwich, and so to call the invaders away
from the Thames, to the rescue of their comrades and their fleet
left behind on the shore. This plan met with the approval of the
Cantii, who were more irritated by Caesar's late ravages in their land
than tamed by their defeats. Under their four kings, Cingetorix,
Carvilius, Segonax, and Taximagulus, they assembled round the base-
camp and laid siege to it. But they were unable to crush the moderate force of ten cohorts and 300 horse which Q. Atrius had at his
disposal, and a sudden sally of the Romans scattered them with great
loss. Caesar specially records the capture of a chief of high birth and
importance, named Lugotorix, though he was not one of the kings.

Thus, since the diversion in Kent proved of no effect, Cassivellaunus had to face Caesar at the head of his own tribe alone,
since his tributaries had dispersed or surrendered. He was finally
reduced to despair by the capture of his chief stronghold, the
"Oppidum" of Verulamium—for this seems undoubtedly to be the
place whose storm is mentioned in the *De Bello Gallico*. A
British "oppidum," as we are here told, was simply a place of
refuge for folk and cattle, protected by woods and fenced round by
ditches and abattis. Though the fortress of the Catuvellauni was
a formidable specimen of its class, it was taken with no great difficulty, by a simultaneous attack on two of its fronts. An immense
amount of cattle and many prisoners were captured—no doubt the
whole of the families of the southern section of Cassivellaunus's
tribe had been stowed away for safety in Verulamium.

After this disaster the king sued for peace, being anxious to
get rid of Caesar at all costs. He made his overtures through the
Atrebatian Commius, and they were accepted. For the proconsul
was anxious to leave Britain : not much of the summer remained,
and the reports of trouble and disloyalty in Gaul were beginning
to disturb him. Indeed the great insurrection which broke out in
the next year but one was already brewing, and if the five legions now
in Britain had remained absent any longer, the revolt might have
started in the autumn of 54. Accordingly Caesar only insisted that
Cassivellaunus, like the other tribal kings, should make over many
hostages to him, and covenant that he would pay an annual tribute
to the Roman people. He was specially ordered not to molest the
Trinovantes and their newly chosen king Mandubratius.

Having received his hostages and an instalment of tribute, Caesar took his way back through Kent to his base-camp, and re-embarked for Gaul. He was obliged to make two trips, on account of the loss of ships and the number of slaves whom he was bringing back. For the surrender of the Britons had not secured them the restoration of their captives, from whose sale in Gaul and Italy Caesar hoped to make much more profit than was brought him by the moderate war-indemnity imposed upon the tribes. No attempt was made by the islanders to molest the second section of the army after the first had sailed; they were now thoroughly cowed. Indeed, but for the great revolt of the Gauls under Vercingetorix in the year 52, it is probable that the Britons would have continued to pay their tribute, and to observe the terms imposed upon them, for some time. But when in 52 all Gaul was aflame, and Caesar was fighting for life rather than empire, he had no thought to spare for the Britons, and they could do as they pleased without troubling themselves about his wrath. Following the two years of the Gallic revolt came the Roman Civil War, after a short interval, and Caesar's insular conquests pass out of our ken. Twilight descends once more upon Britain for nearly a century.

Thus Caesar's invasions, though fraught with important results for the future, had little importance for the present. He had shown the way to Britain, but had not left it open. On the whole the campaigns seem to have been considered rather disappointing by the practical mind of the average Roman. In one of Cicero's letters the matter is summed up by the prosaic reflection that there was practically no money to be got out of Britain, nothing but slaves; and these slaves were the roughest field hands for manual labour, "naturally there are not among them scholars or musicians," so that they were not valuable items in the Roman market.[1] And in the clash of the oncoming Civil Wars the memory of the projected conquest of the northern island passed out of the brains of the soldiers and statesmen of Rome. It was not till after Philippi and Actium, when the Mediterranean world had settled down under a single master, and internal wars had ceased, that the British Question began once more to flit at intervals before the imagination of the subjects of Augustus Caesar.

[1] *Ad Atticum*, iv. 16.   *Ad Familiares*, vii. 7.

CHAPTER IV

BRITAIN BETWEEN THE INVASION OF JULIUS CAESAR AND THE INVASION OF CLAUDIUS (B.C. 54-A.D. 43).

THOUGH Caesar's projected conquest of Britain came to such an abrupt and unsuccessful conclusion, he did not leave the island as he had found it.   When in 49 B.C. he crossed the Rubicon to engage in his great civil war with Pompey and the Optimates, he left Gaul behind him tamed, and organised into the shape of a Roman province.   So thorough had been his work that the newly subdued tribes made no endeavour to assert their independence during the absence of their conqueror, or even during the chaos that followed his murder by Brutus and his fellows on the Ides of March, 44 B.C.   There were one or two abortive Gallic risings during the long reign of Augustus, but they were so insignificant, and so promptly crushed, that it is clear that the nation as a whole had given up hope after the fall of Vercingetorix, and had fully accepted its new position as a part of the Roman Empire.

For the future, therefore, the neighbours of Britain across the Channel were no longer a weltering mass of Belgic and other tribes, sometimes united for a short moment in an uncertain league, or bowing before a common master (such as Divitiacus had once been), but more frequently engaged in unending civil wars.   Belgica, like the rest of Gaul, had become an orderly Roman province, kept down by the strong hand of the conqueror, and engaged in assimilating with a marvellous rapidity Roman customs and Roman civilisation.   The close touch between Gaul and Britain that had always prevailed did not cease for a moment, but Gaul having been transformed, Britain began to come under new influences.   The traders who came over to the island were in the new generation Gallo-Romans, and probably to a considerable extent Romans born, for no one was more daring than the Italian merchant in "pushing ahead of the flag". The frontier troubles of the Roman world, both under the republic and under the empire, were more frequently caused by merchants who got into trouble with barbarian peoples than by any other cause. The merchant question was to the Roman Government what the missionary question is to the British Government of to-day. Any exiles who now came over to Britain were fugitive rebels against the Roman Empire, not the mere tribal outcasts of old. Young Gauls who crossed the Channel to study in the schools of the British Druids were equally Roman subjects, engaged in keeping up a superstition on which the imperial authorities did not look with a favourable eye.[1] Similarly the British trader who crossed to the Continent found himself no longer among kinsmen living under conditions similar to his own, but was forced to notice and to ponder on the manifold activities of the Romanised cities that were springing up all over Gaul. The British exile, too, if he fled abroad with some hopes of returning to take up an old quarrel, found that he had to make his petition for aid not to a medley of tribal chiefs, but to the great central power of a world-wide empire. Such exiles, as we shall see, fled to ask Roman aid, not once or twice; but a century was to elapse before it was granted. Several times, however, in the early years of Augustus's reign there seemed to be an imminent prospect of the third invasion of Britain coming to pass. In the interval between Philippi and Actium, when he was still sharing the dominion of the world with Antony, he was in Northern Gaul with a considerable force, and intended, so it is said, to have turned it against Britain, if he had not been distracted by a rebellion in Dalmatia (34 B.C.). Then came the struggle with Antony, and it was not till some years later that the hands of Augustus were again free. The poetry of the post-Actian epoch is full of hints that the emperor may take up again his uncle's work—the best known of them is Horace's[2]

> Praesens divus habebitur
> Augustus, adjectis Britannis
> Imperio, gravibusque Persis,

---

[1] Suetonius, *Vita Claudii*. v. Druidarum religionem apud Gallos sub Augusto civibus interdictam, Claudius penitus abolevit.

[2] *Odes*, iii. 5.

lines that would not have been written unless the poet had believed that there was a great probability that the invasion of Britain was at hand.

In 27 and 26 B.C., when Augustus was for some time in Gaul, it was once more believed that a British expedition might take place. The explanation that he deferred it because of a revolt of the Alpine Salassi, who were after all an unimportant race, does not seem adequate.[1] Probably he had already in mind his great plan for giving the empire a scientific frontier along Rhine and Danube, which was to be the great work of his middle life, and saw that while this was unaccomplished the annexation of Britain would be a mistake, and a waste of power in the wrong direction. In his later years he had become too set on the principle "coercendi inter terminos imperii" to revive the scheme.

In Britain itself the old state of things continued : the tribal strife seems to have recommenced the moment that Caesar's back was turned. And we cannot doubt that the tribute which had been promised him ceased to be paid, either when the rebellion of Vercingetorix broke out in 52 B.C., or at least when the great proconsul went off to the civil wars in 49 B.C. The next development of local politics in Britain is to be traced from the evidence of coins alone—evidence very useful, but not always easy to interpret with certainty. But almost immediately after the time of Caesar's departure the coins of Britain begin to show inscriptions, which they had never borne before. Moreover, their types begin to change ; new devices drawn from the money of the Roman Republic commence to appear among the distorted copies of the Philippic stater, which had hitherto been the only model for all the issues of the island. What is more surprising is that the inscriptions seem all to be in Latin, not in Celtic—a fact which shows not only that new continental moneyers must have been imported, but that Latin must have been understood at the courts of the kinglets for whom the coins were struck.

The evidence of the coins of the period between Caesar's departure and the commencement of the Christian era seems clearly to show that the British states were coalescing into larger units, by reason of the conquest of the smaller by the more powerful tribes.

[1] Dio Cassius, liii. 25.

At the head of one of these incipient empires appears no less a
person than that Commius the Atrebate, of whom we have already
had to discourse. Though he had been given his kingship by
Caesar, he quarrelled with his benefactor and joined in the great
rebellion of Vercingetorix. Conscious that he was likely to have
little mercy from the Romans, he was one of the last chiefs to keep
up the standard of revolt. But after some hairbreadth escapes,
one of which is recorded at length by Frontinus in his *Stratagems*,[1]
he came to terms with Caesar's lieutenant, Mark Antony, by means
of intermediaries, for he had sworn never to look on a Roman
again.[2] He seems immediately after to have removed to a new
land, where he need never be offended by such a sight (51 B.C.).
This land of course was Britain, and he apparently retired, as was
natural, to his kinsmen the Atrebates of Berkshire, for soon after
we find gold coins struck in his name, which appear to come from
the lands south of Thames and west of Kent. But there are far
more numerous pieces issued by his sons, each of whom describes
himself on his issues as " Commii filius ". These princes were named
Eppillus, Verica (or Virica) and Tincommius. Their coins are fairly
common, and are found in Berkshire, Hampshire, Sussex, Kent,
and Surrey. Apparently the three brothers reigned simultaneously
over different portions of their father's realm, as the names of two
of them are often found on the same coin. Eppillus certainly held
the Atrebatian territory proper, since some of his money bears, besides his own name, the mint mark CALLEV, for Calleva (Silchester),
the well-known capital of the Atrebates. It may be regarded as
demonstrable to all probability that Tincommius must have been the
British king who is recorded to have fled to Rome, and to have
done homage to Augustus, on the famous " Ancyra Marble," the
long inscription in which the emperor records the history of his
reign. He claims to have sheltered two British exiles, Dubnovellaunus (of whom more hereafter) and TIM —, or TIN — (the name

[1] *Strategemata*, ii 13. Commius being pursued shorewards by the Romans
towards his ships, arrived to find them left grounded at low tide. Nevertheless he
ordered the sails to be hoisted, arguing that when his pursuers saw the canvas
stretched they would conclude that the vessels were afloat, and the escape complete.
And this happened, for when it was seen that Commius was apparently safe, the
Roman cavalry halted, and never came down to the beach. And so the king got
off. Frontinus plainly says that he was flying to Britain.

[2] " Ne in conspectum veniat cujusquam Romani." *B. G.* viii. § 48.

is broken across through its third letter). British proper names beginning with these letters are so uncommon that there is reasonable certainty that this must have been Tincommius, who may have been expelled either by his brothers or by some other foe. The coins of the Commius dynasty appear to range over the last half of the first century B.C. No later prince calls himself the son of Eppillus or Verica, so presumably the line ended with them; it is probable that they or their sons were crushed by Cunobelinus, the Catuvellaunian high-king who subdued all Southern Britain in the later years of Augustus's reign.

Contemporary with Commius and his three sons was, on the north of the Thames, a prince called Tasciovanus, who was evidently the king of the Catuvellauni, and very possibly the son and heir of Caesar's enemy Cassivellaunus.[1] This is indicated by the fact that his money is found scattered widely over Herts, Bedfordshire, Oxfordshire, and the other regions held by that tribe, but still more clearly by the name of Verulamium, found as mint-place on the larger number of his coins. The quantity of gold pieces that he issued testifies to his wealth, and the fact that, while his early money continues to copy the barbarised Philippic stater, the later pieces bear types borrowed from contemporary Roman denarii, proves that art and civilisation were progressing under his rule among the Catuvellauni. He had, however, a son much greater than himself, Cunobelinus, Shakespeare's Cymbeline, who ultimately became king of all South-Eastern Britain. There was another son named Epaticcus, whose comparatively rare coins come from the south side of Thames, Surrey and East Wilts, districts that he may perhaps have conquered from one of the sons of Commius. But he cannot have reigned long, and his dominions must have passed to his greater brother.

Cymbeline was the greatest prince of his time—in Roman authorities he is sometimes called simply *rex Brittonum*, as if he were supreme in the whole island. Certainly he conquered the Trinovantes of Essex, for their chief town Camulodunum (Colchester) appears as his chief minting-place. It seems probable that be may have driven out from this region that Dubnovellaunus

---

[1] This is suggested by the fact that in Tacitus, *Annals*, xii. 34, the Catuvellaunian King Caratacus says that his ancestors (majores) had repulsed Caesar. This ought to mean that his father, Cunobelinus, descended from Cassivellaunus.

whom Augustus mentions as an exile on the Ancyra monument, since coins of that prince, a little earlier in appearance than Cymbeline's issues, are found in Essex, though they also appear in Kent. Possibly Dubnovellaunus may have ruled on both sides of the Lower Thames before he was expelled by the Catuvellaunian conqueror. Cymbeline's money abounds all over Southern Britain from Kent to Gloucestershire, and seems to bear witness to the existence of a veritable empire, since no other coins which can be ascribed to the time contemporary with his later years are to be found anywhere on the South Coast, or the valley of the Thames. The limits of this power northward seem to be indicated by the fact that we have money belonging to the Iceni, the tribe which occupied the modern Norfolk and Suffolk, which from style and appearance must belong to Cymbeline's epoch. Presumably, therefore, they were not annexed to his realm. Since his issues are seldom or never found west of Wiltshire and Gloucestershire, it would seem a reasonable deduction that the Dumnonii of Devonshire and Cornwall were not in his sphere of influence, nor the Silurians of South Wales. It is, however, a notable fact that Cymbeline's son Caratacus, in the next generation, took refuge with the Silures and apparently acted as their chief commander : this suggests that his father may have had some power over them, though his coins are not found in their borders. And since this South Welsh tribe appears not to have used coined money at all, the fact that Cymbeline's issues are not found in their territory is not conclusive one way or the other.

Cymbeline's reign was very long, it extended at least from 5 A.D. to 40 A.D., and very probably may have begun somewhat earlier. It was clearly a time when wealth and civilisation were growing fast, as was but natural when the suzerainty of a single prince had put an end to the petty states and the constant tribal wars that went before. The wealth of Cymbeline is sufficiently vouched for by the enormous number of his gold coins that have been discovered, and which still continue to turn up every year. The growing culture of his court is indicated by the fact that, while his gold coins resemble those of his father Tasciovanus, and are still semi-barbarous, the silver and copper ones are beautifully struck, and bear a large variety of good classical types, evidently design:d by competent moneyers from the Roman Empire. On a few his own portrait appears—a head evidently imitated from that of Augustus, with the Latin inscription cvnobelinvs rex : more frequently we have mythological figures of the more fantastic sort, a centaur, a sphinx, a pegasus, or occasionally the figure of a divinity which appears to be a classical Apollo, Hercules, or Mars, though the subjects of Cymbeline may have recognised in them representations of their own local Celtic gods.   Oddly enough, the silver coins of this king are always more handsome and better executed than the gold.

The relations of Cymbeline with Augustus and Tiberius were evidently quite friendly—the imperial government made no attempt to restore by force of arms the princes who had fled to Rome from Britain—the Dubnovellaunus and Tincommius of the Ancyra Marble—and evidently recognised the accomplished fact, and left Cymbeline undisturbed.   A curious note in Strabo referring to these times deserves a word of comment.   " In our own days certain of the princes of Britain by their embassies and polite attentions have secured the friendship of Caesar Augustus, they have even put up offerings in the Capitol, and have made the whole island almost as it were native soil to the Roman.   They pay very moderate customs dues both on the goods which they export to Gaul, and on those which are sent to them from thence—which are mainly ivory, bracelets, necklaces, amber, glass vessels and such-like small merchandise.   So the Romans have no need to garrison the island, which would require at least one legion and some cavalry to enforce a tribute from them.   For the cost of keeping troops there would be at least as much as the tribute received, and if tribute were imposed the customs dues would have to be lowered, and moreover there would be some military risks when forcible subjection was taken in hand."   Strabo notes in the same paragraph that the exports of Britain were gold, silver, iron, skins, slaves, hunting dogs, and (what is more surprising) corn and cattle.   We should hardly have expected to hear of these two last staple commodities being imported into Roman Gaul from the still semi-barbarous island.

That Cymbeline made Britain οἰκείαν σχεδὸν τοῖς ῾Ρωμαίοις is exactly what we should have deduced, if Strabo had made no mention of the fact, from his coinage, with its Latin inscriptions and its neat classical devices.   That he was doing wisely for himself in keeping on good terms with the great empire across the Channel was obvious.   That he was doing ill for his successors in allowing the Romans free access to Britain, and permitting them to spy out all the resources of the island, was less visible at the time. But nevertheless it is evident that the Roman conquest, when it at last came, in the next generation, was rendered easy by the fact that the geography of Britain was now well known, and that its political factions were well understood, so that the invaders knew perfectly well who would be their friends and who their enemies. There must also have been a nucleus of Roman subjects, Italians as well as Gauls, settled in every important town of South Britain, and perhaps, we may add, a native commercial class, which for reasons of trade would look upon the conquest with equanimity.

It would be interesting to know whether the great Gaulish revolt of Florus and Sacrovir in 21 A.D., the eighth year of Tiberius, which was intended to be a national and religious protest against assimilation to Rome, got any support from Britain. On the one hand it seems to have been favoured by the Druids, and that priest-hood, still all-powerful in Britain, must have resented the disabili-ties which Augustus had imposed upon it in Gaul. Naturally the Continental Druids would have asked for help from their more fortunate insular brethren. On the other hand Cymbeline was set on keeping upon good terms with the Roman Government, and would be likely to do his best to keep his subjects from aiding the revolt. Unfortunately we have no hint whatever in Tacitus's narrative to enable us to come to any conclusion on the subject.

The end of the reign of Cymbeline seems to have been disturbed by the family troubles that generally vex the old age of a king in semi-barbarous countries. Adminius, who is supposed to have been his eldest son, rebelled against him, and had to be expelled by force of arms.[1] The exile fled to the court of the Emperor Caius Caesar (Caligula), who had succeeded to the throne of Tiberius in 37 A.D., and was now in the third year of his reign. That eccentric monarch, as Suetonius narrates, received him with glad-ness, and induced him to make a formal cession of his rights in Britain; after which he wrote a magniloquent letter to the Senate, stating that the whole island had become Roman soil. His mes-sengers were told to drive straight to the Forum in their travelling car, as if bearing in haste despatches of the highest importance; but they were also directed to see that the consuls should have collected

---

[1] This prince is probably *not* the Amminus or Amminius whose name is found on a few rare British coins. They seem from their style to be earlier than 35-40 A.D.

every available senator, and should have appointed the temple of
Mars as the meeting-place—which argued preparations incompatible
with the ostensible hurry of the proceedings. Then follows a much
stranger tale: Cymbeline having made no signs of taking his son's
proceedings seriously, the emperor massed troops somewhere on
the straits—apparently at Gessoriacum (Boulogne), "and then, as if
about to engage in warlike operations, drew up his force on the sea-
shore, with a display of balistæ and other military machines. No
one could know, or even form a conjecture, as to what he intended
to do : but suddenly he bade the soldiers to gather shells, and to fill
their helmets and their laps with them. 'These,' he said, 'are the
spoils of the Ocean, due to the Capitol and the Palatine.' And in
testimony to this triumph he erected a high tower, on whose summit a fire was to be kept burning at night, by way of a lighthouse,
to aid ships in the direction of their course." These antics recall
a much better remembered display on the same shore by a Gallic
emperor in 1804, where once again an "Army of Britain" was
reviewed in state, and then (instead of embarking) received a shower
of crosses of the Legion of Honour. Napoleon's review, like Caligula's, was afterwards celebrated by the erection of a lofty column.
Conceivably there was some political idea at the back of the earlier
monarch's manœuvres: but Suetonius will have it that mere insanity inspired them : the psychology of megalomania in all ages is
difficult to interpret, especially if we have no sufficient details left
us by the contemporary historians. Suetonius was writing three
generations after the famous review, and evidently thought that
madness explained all.

Caligula was assassinated in the following year (41 A.D.), to the
relief of the whole civilised world, and his uncle, the learned and
absent-minded Claudius, was forcibly extracted by the soldiery from
his hiding-place, and invested with the unexpected purple. The
new emperor was the James I. of Roman history, the wisest fool of
his age. Despite of the greedy parasites who surrounded him, the
Rochesters and Buckinghams of the Palatine, he made a much
better ruler than might have been expected. His domestic infeli-
cities and his frequent lapses into the grotesque only affected the
court and the city : for the empire he was rather a successful and
provident ruler. It was not for nothing that he had devoted long
study to Roman history and antiquities. He had a policy of his

own, and could justify it by apposite, if pedantic, quotations from the past. He was a kindly creature at the bottom, though his *morale* had been ruined by a youth and middle age spent in constant terror, under the inquisitorial eye of the gloomy Tiberius and the freakish cruelty of the mad Caligula. His long weak neck, his shambling gait, his eccentricities of speech, made him appear much more contemptible than he really was to those who were in daily contact with him. From sheer want of nerve or love of quiet, he would allow himself on occasion to be bullied by his worthless wives and his impudent freedmen. Yet he clearly had his views of imperial policy, and carried them out not without success. One of them was that the provinces were becoming so rapidly Romanised that large extensions of the franchise were practicable, and ought to be begun without delay. He carried them out with the best results. Another was that the times were ripe for a large addition to the number of colonies. A third was that moral reforms were necessary to save the ruling classes, and he tried to do something to deliver corrupt Rome from herself—only to be laughed at because his own wives and favourites were the very centres of her corruption. Among other humanitarian reforms he set himself to suppress Druidism in Gaul,[1] because of the cruelty of its rites, which even after Augustus had discouraged them, continued to be practised in secret. It may be possible that his crusade against the Druids partly tempted him into making his attack on Britain, in which he broke with the non-annexation policy that had prevailed during the later years of Augustus and the whole of Tiberius's reign. The priests of Gaul were encouraged and recruited by their insular brethren; it was necessary to strike at the central focus of the creed even if it lay beyond seas. No doubt there were other motives at the root of the invasion : from the mere political, as opposed to the religious, point of view it might seem anomalous to leave a section of the Celts in a state of liberty, in such close neighbourhood to their kinsmen who had become subjects of the empire. We know of no national Gaulish insurrection since that which had disturbed the commencement of Tiberius's reign, but it may be possible that subterranean heavings and convulsions were visible to the Roman government, and caused fear and suspicion. That Northern Gaul

---

[1] "Penitus abolevit," says Suetonius, "religionem dirae immanitatis."

was still capable of a great outburst was to be proved a quarter of a century later by the great rebellion of Civilis. Moreover at this particular moment the peace which had long prevailed in Britain under Cymbeline's rule had been ended by the death of that great king [41 A.D. ?]. Civil war had broken out among his sons, and it would appear that several of the races subject to the Catuvellauni were either already in revolt against the suzerain tribe, or were at least ready for it. The intervention of the emperor was solicited by Bericus, who seems to have been a son of Cymbeline driven out by his brothers, and we cannot help suspecting that it may also have been secretly solicited by the tribes which were found submitting to Rome the moment that the legions landed—the Boduni and Regni in the South-East, the Iceni in the East, the two former subjects, the latter perhaps foes of the Catuvellauni. An obscure sentence in Suetonius may perhaps mean that the victorious sons of Cymbeline, Togodumnus and Caratacus, had demanded, in terms that did not respect the dignity of Rome, the surrender of Bericus and other exiles.[1] Nor can we doubt that a policy of annexation must have been demanded both by the merchants from the Continent already domiciled in Britain, who had everything to gain from the end of Celtic independence, and from the great speculators and financiers of Rome, who were eager, as always, to extend the sphere of their operations. The moment that the conquest began they fell upon the island like a brood of harpies. In short, it is easy enough to find reasons why Claudius should have undertaken his expedition; his own general ideas on imperial policy must have fitted in with the private motives of his greedy advisers and favourites, who saw plunder everywhere, and with the ambitions of the whole mercantile class. Probably the wealth of the island, considerable as it was, was greatly overvalued, and the difficulty of its conquest minimised.

---

[1] " Britanniam tunc tumultuantem ob non redditos transfugas " is the phrase in Suetonius, in *Vita Claudii*, § 17.   This seems to be echoed by Orosius, vii. 6: Expeditionem in Britanniam movit, quae excitata in tumultum propter non redhibitos transfugas videbatur.

BOOK II
ROMAN BRITAIN

CHAPTER V

THE ROMAN CONQUEST OF BRITAIN. CLAUDIUS AND NERO
(43-69 A.D.)

THE third year of his reign had begun when Claudius made up his mind to undertake the conquest of Britain, and commis-sioned Aulus Plautius, a veteran who had been consul fourteen years before, and was now far on in middle age, to concentrate the troops that had been designated to form the expeditionary corps. The old legate was to organise the force and to lead it across the Channel, while the emperor himself was to follow a little later, and only to join the army when it was already on the road to victory. Since Claudius's own person and good fortune were to be risked, it was necessary to make the expedition too strong to fear any possi-bility of disaster. Four legions had been told off, three drawn from the Rhine, one from Pannonia ;[1] added to them was a body of auxiliaries, horse and foot, more than equal to the legionaries in number ; the whole army of invasion probably counted over 30,000 men, or about one-eighth of the entire Roman regular forces then in existence. It was a somewhat smaller host than that which Julius Caesar had taken over on his second expedition, but its task was not so hard as his, for he had been entering the unknown, while the troops of Aulus Plautius were seeking a country whose resources and geography had been thoroughly well explored by the all-per-vading Roman mercantile adventurer.

The moving of a Roman legion was no light matter ; ever since

---

[1] Their names are worth remembering, since two of them were destined to find a permanent home in Britain : These were the Rhine Legions, II. Augusta and XX. Valeria Victrix. The third Rhine Legion, XIV. Gemina Martia, went back to the continent after twenty-five years in Britain. The Pannonian Legion IX. Hispana was destined to perish in Britain, in the early years of the reign of Hadrian.

Augustus fixed the establishment and the cantonments of the regular army, its units had continued fixed down to the stations which he had appointed for them, with their dependants dwelling close by the camp in their " huts " (cannabae), and many time-expired veterans settled on allotments in the surrounding country-side. To disturb such a community was a serious matter, and one not to be undertaken without a clear necessity. Tiberius only shifted one legion during the course of his long reign. Hence when Claudius ordered no less than four corps to hold themselves ready for a move to Britain there was much murmuring and almost a show of mutiny. The measure which the emperor took for dealing with it—the despatch of his hated favourite Narcissus as a special commissioner to argue with the troops—was ill-advised, since the soldiers despised him equally as a civilian, a Greek and a freedman. But after insulting Narcissus, and indulging in a general riot, the legions returned to their duty and consented to depart, mainly (it is said) owing to their love and respect for the veteran, Aulus Plautius, who had been placed at their head.

The army sailed in three divisions, presumably from Gessoriacum, and came ashore without any hindrance save that caused by the uncertainties of wind and tide, which are said to have given rise to much trouble and anxiety. The Britons had not come down to the shore to offer opposition, though they had received ample notice of the expedition, owing to the long naval and military preparations on the opposite shore. We are told that they had believed that the sailing of the troops had been postponed owing to the mutiny, and were caught unprepared by the sudden arrival of the Romans.

The defence of Britain lay in the hands of Togodumnus and Caratacus, the two sons of Cymbeline, who ruled jointly over their father's lands, and seem to have preserved to some extent his hegemony over the lesser kings—Kent at least, which was no integral part of the Catuvellaunian State, was under their suzerainty. When Plautius first came ashore he found that the local Britons had retired into the woods of the Weald, and seemed inclined to avoid battle, and to do no more than hover on the flanks of the army and harass its foragers—the tactics that Cassivellaunus had used against Caesar a century before. There was no serious fighting till the Romans reached the line of the Medway, and before they got so far one local tribe had already made its submission. Where these

Boduni dwelt we cannot say, but since Plautius left a garrison to protect them, it is clear that they were dwellers in Kent or East Sussex. They are not to be confused, despite of the similarity of name, with the Dobuni of Gloucestershire.

Presently the Romans, following the great track that in all ages has led from Dover and Canterbury towards London and the passages of the Thames, reached the Medway in its lower tidal reaches somewhere near the site of Rochester. Here at last serious opposition was offered to them ; the two kings of the Catuvellauni had come out, with all their tributary princes, to defend the passage of the river, which seemed a formidable enough obstacle, with its great breadth at high tide, and its broad sheet of inaccessible mud flats, a still worse hindrance to crossing at low water. But Plautius had with him many auxiliaries from the army of Gaul, troops accustomed to operations in marshes ; mainly, as we may suppose, Batavian and other auxiliaries from the mouths of the Rhine. While Plautius made a demonstration with his main body against the front of the British position, a large force of these auxiliaries swam the river on his right flank, while the legate Vespasian—who was destined to become emperor a quarter of a century later—turned the other flank of the enemy by going far up stream with a second detachment The Britons were driven away from the river, but rallied on the ground beyond, where they offered battle again on the following day, and maintained the contest for some time on equal terms They surrounded and nearly captured Hosidius Geta, the legate of one of Plautius's legions, but were finally defeated with loss and forced to fly. They then retired behind the marshes of the Thames estuary, being still bent on fighting for their liberty. The second engagement must have taken place close to the site of London, since we find a bridge mentioned in the topography of the battle, and it is incredible that such a structure should have existed at any other point on the Thames estuary than that which was to bear the famous structure of later years. According to Dio's account the second combat bore much similarity to the first ; once more the Gallic auxiliaries swam the estuary at a point lower than that which the natives were guarding, while some of the legionaries forced the passage of "the bridge that lies a little way up stream ". The Britons were turned on both flanks and routed with heavy loss ; but the Romans also suffered, for they pursued the fugitives into a morass whose paths were unknown to them, and many soldiers perished in it.

Togodumnus, one of the two kings of the Catuvellauni, had perished in battle—whether in the first or in the second fight we do not know. But his surviving brother, Caratacus, rallied his levies and kept at least part of the confederacy together, and it was clear that there would be more engagements before Camulodunum was reached. At this moment Plautius halted, and sent for his master Claudius to conclude the campaign. Dio states that he did so because the campaign had been so fierce that he required the reserves—the Praetorian Guards, no doubt—which the emperor would bring with him. But it is equally probable that he waited in order that Claudius might have the glory of concluding the war, by winning the last decisive battle.

At any rate, the emperor came up in due course, bringing with him both the reserves and a large train, which included even elephants. He picked up the army on the Lower Thames, and then advanced on Camulodunum. Caratacus gave him battle somewhere on the road between London and Colchester, but was completely defeated. Not only did he lose his capital, but all his dominions were overrun, and he himself was compelled to fly into the West, with the wrecks of his personal following. All the tribes of south-eastern Britain, the Catuvellauni, Trinovantes and Cantii, were subdued, while other and more remote peoples did homage in order to save their territory from invasion. Among these latter were the Iceni of the Eastern Counties and the Regni of Sussex, whose kings, Prasutagus and Cogidubnus, were allowed to become "allies of the Roman people," and kept their thrones as vassals of the Empire. The province of Britain was formally constituted, and Camulodunum was fixed upon as its capital. Then Claudius returned to Italy, having, as we read with some surprise, remained no more than sixteen days in Britain—a time that seems hardly sufficient for the campaign in Essex, the capture of Camulodunum, and the submission of the British kings. He celebrated a triumph of great splendour on his return to Rome, and set up there an arch whose design is commemorated on many of his coins. The Senate voted the title of Britannicus both to Claudius and to his little son, the boy who was destined to be the victim of Nero twelve years later.

Aulus Plautius was left in command of the newly acquired

province, and ruled there for the next four years (43-47) with great vigour and success. He seems to have established a military frontier of considerable strategical merits, by conquering all the country south and east of a line drawn from the mouth of the Severn to the Wash. This advance involved a triple conflict—with the tribes of the south-west, those of the Lower Severn valley, and those of the Eastern Midlands. We know that the campaigns in the south-west were carried out by the legate Vespasian, the future emperor: of him it is recorded that "he fought thirteen battles with the natives, and added to the Roman Empire two powerful tribes, twenty towns (*oppida*) and the Isle of Wight, which lies near to the British coast".[1] The two tribes we may presume were the Belgae, whose territory extended from the Solent to Somersetshire, and the Durotriges of Dorset. The *oppida* would mean not so much towns as these fortified tribal camps to which Julius Caesar applied that designation. It may be taken as certain that the troops employed in these operations were the Second Legion and its auxiliaries, who always worked in Western Britain.[2] The fighting may often have been heavy, as Dio records that on one occasion Vespasian was surrounded by the enemy, and would have been slain, if his son Titus (possibly an error for his brother Titus Sabinus) had not rescued him from the Britons. How rapid and thorough was the conquest of the south-west may be judged from the fact that the lead mines of Mendip were being regularly worked for the Roman Government within six years of Plautius's landing. Two pigs of that metal, accidentally lost at the time of their casting, have been discovered, which bear the names of Claudius and his son Britannicus, and can be accurately dated to the year 49 A.D. On the other hand there is no trace of the extension of the Roman power over the Dumnonians, the inhabitants of the peninsula of Devon and Cornwall. Since there is no mention of trouble in the extreme south-west, and since no legion was left on guard in this quarter, it is clear that they must have made some form of submission. But few traces of Roman occupation west of Exeter can be found in the first century after Christ, and for some generations these remote regions seem to have been practically left to themselves. The great road system which was perfected in the second century stopped on the Exe, and it is not till the time of

---

[1] Suetonius, *Vita Vespasiani*, § 4; Eutropius, vii. § 19.
[2] See Haverfield in *Arch. Journal*, xlix. 181.

Constantine that signs of activity farther west become clear.   Apparently this had something to do with the decline of the old Cornish tin-trade, which was at a low ebb in the early empire, but revived in the third century.[1]

When the land up to the line of the Exe had been subdued, the Second Legion seems to have been drawn up to the line of the Lower Severn.   Its next regular station was to be to Isca (Caerleon) in the land of the Silures, beyond that river.   But it is not probable that it reached that advanced point during the governorship of l'lautius : Glevum (Gloucester) has been suggested by several specialists [2] as a likely abiding place for the legion, when the first work of subduing the Belgae was over.   There is, however, no proof whatever that it ever had its permanent camp at that place, and it moved on to Isca so early that, even if it was stationed for a few years at Glevum, it is unlikely that it would have left any memorials of itself behind.

Of the forward movement of the opposite, or eastern, wing of the Roman advance we have no record in the historians, and indeed we should have known nothing about the conquests of the south-west had not Vespasian, the man with a future, been in command in that direction.   It seems, however, that Aulus Plautius, after subduing the Catuvellauni, probably advanced the Roman frontier to the Wash.   The Iceni of the Eastern Counties having made an early and willing submission because of their dislike to their old enemies of the house of Tasciovanus, the natural front of the new province would be along the line of the rivers which cross England in a diagonal direction from south-west to north-east.   The empire of the Catuvellaunian kings seems to have reached beyond the Ouse, but never to have touched the Trent.   The Nen or the Welland would have been natural boundaries at which to draw the line of occupation.   But there is some reason to believe that Ratae (Leicester) found the extreme point of the advance, and that a detachment of Legion VIII. Augusta was there shortly after 43 A.D.[3] The locality is a very suitable one, since it covers the gap of plain-land, between the marshy lower course of the rivers which flow into the Wash, and that central forest of Britain which divided the basin

---

[1] See Haverfield on the Cornish tin-trade in *Mélanges Boissier*.

[2] Hübner, Furneaux, Panza.

[3] The only evidence, however, is tiles found there bearing the stamp of the VIIIth Legion, of which a " vexillatio " formed part of the invading army.

of the Severn and Avon from that of the streams falling into the North Sea. Its strategical importance was shown a little later by the fact that it became the only important town on the great Roman road which crossed the Midlands from Cirencester to Lincoln.

As to the central space of Britain, between Leicester and the Lower Severn, it is obvious that it cannot have been left wholly unguarded. It seems pretty certain that one legion remained behind at Camulodunum, to hold down the Catuvellauni, the old rulers of Southern Britain, as long as Aulus Plautius was governor.[1] Where the other legion lay, we have no means of determining. But as the front of the province was now drawn in advance of the Fosse-Way, which probably represents an early Celtic track from Cirencester to Leicester, running along the line of easiest passage through the Midlands, and avoiding the forest regions of Arden and Cannock Chase, we should expect to find the central legion on or just behind it. Durocornovium (Cirencester), appears rather too near the region in which the Second Legion was operating, yet there seems reason to believe that it was a very early military centre.[2] On the other hand, on purely strategical principles we should expect to find a legion somewhere in support of the line of the Fosse, and for choice on Watling Street, the line by which London is (indirectly) connected with Leicester, at some such point as Lactodurum (Towcester) or Bannaventa near Daventry. But this is pure hypothesis.

Aulus Plautius came back to Rome in 47, and was duly commended by his master "for having conducted and concluded the British War with honour". He was granted a triumph, which ended with a great gladiatorial exhibition in the Amphitheatre, at which many unfortunate captives fought and fell. His appointed successor was Publius Ostorius Scapula, a governor of whom we

[1] I think that this view, that of Hübner, is made pretty certain by the passage (Tacitus, *Annals*, xii. 32) where the author says that Ostorius Scapula in 49 found that: "Silurum gens non atrocitate non clementia mutabatur, quin bellum exerceret, castrisque legionum premenda foret. Id quo promptius venerit, colonia Camulodunum valida veteranorum manu deducitur, subsidium adversus rebelles et imbuendis sociis ad officia legum." This can only mean that Scapula wanted to move legions against the Silurians, and in order to get as many as possible available, collected a veteran colony at Camulodunum as a substitute for a legion up to that time quartered there. Probably this was Legion XX. of whom tombstones are found at Colchester.

[2] See Haverfield, *Archæological Journal*, l. p. 110. Many military tombstones have been found at Bath, some very early, but these seem merely to prove that convalescents went to take the waters, and sometimes died there.

know more than of his predecessor, because the gap in Tacitus's *Annals* which covers the early years of Claudius has now come to an end, and we have not any longer to depend solely on meagre scraps of Dio or Suetonius. Plautius had finished the conquest of the plain-land of Southern Britain, where population was comparatively thick, and where communications were easy. Perhaps the Roman government would have been content to halt, when this paying part of the island had been subdued. But this was impossible : the un-tamed and warlike tribes in the hills of North and South Wales— the Ordovices and Silurians, and the still more powerful and rest-less Brigantes, who held the whole North, from Derbyshire to the Solway, persisted in ravaging the borders of the new province. Probably they had been wont to harry their tribal neighbours in the plain from time immemorial, and would not desist even when the legions came to protect them. But a political aspect was lent to the war by the fact that Caratacus, the exiled king of the Catuvellauni, had taken refuge among the Silurians, and was leading their forays, having apparently not only been granted shelter by the tribe but also some share of military authority. His hope was to keep the war afoot, and wear out the Romans, in the expectation that his former subjects might some day rise to aid him.

Ostorius, on his arrival in Britain, had to face a dangerous series of these incursions, which at the beginning of the winter season were specially difficult to resist. But knowing that impunity would render the enemy more daring, and probably lead to a revolt inside the province, he called out his cavalry and light-armed cohorts, and set to work at once to hunt down the raiders. He surprised many bands, and drove them back to their mountains with heavy loss. He then announced that he should disarm all the provincials whose loyalty he suspected, and so pacify all the land that lies on this side of Severn and Trent.[1] These precautions roused a

---

[1] There is a disputed reading and a topographical difficulty here. The text says : " Detrahere arma suspectis, cunctaque castris Antonam et Sabrinam fluvios cohibere parat ". Some editors have substituted Aufonam for Antonam, thinking that the Warwickshire Avon was a likely line for a series of camps. But fortifications along the Avon would have nothing to alarm the Iceni, and it seems better to take Antona for the Trent, not as Mommsen did for the Shropshire Tern, whose ancient name is unknown, as is also that of the Trent. The ingenious emendation of cis Trisantonam for castris Antonam is very attractive, but the name Trisantona is as un-known as that of Antona in British geography, save as that of a small river in Sussex, in Ptolemy's description of the South Coast. See Furneaux's *Tacitus*, xii. 31, § 2.

general revolt in Eastern Britain, which was headed by the Iceni, who had been the allies of the Romans ever since their landing, and resented the proposed disarmament. They were joined by their neighbours, no doubt the Coritani between Wash and Humber, and the wrecks of the Catuvellauni, and offered battle to Ostorius on ground chosen by themselves, difficult of approach and fortified with earthern ramparts. The governor risked an attack upon the position, though he had no single legion with him, but only a mass of auxiliaries. His boldness was rewarded by a complete victory, in spite of the desperate resistance of the rebels [48 A.D.].

The Iceni seem to have been granted easy terms, as their state still appears under a vassal king for some years after this revolt. But the crushing character of the defeat induced all the neighbouring tribes "who had been hesitating between peace and war," to proffer their submission. It was probably at this moment that Ostorius pushed forward the frontier of the province, annexing the territory of the Coritani and Cornovii, and sending on the Legion lately at Ratae to Lindum (Lincoln), while the Fourteenth and Twentieth may both have been moved to Viroconium (Wroxeter) on the Middle Severn. This arrangement would be intended not only to hold down the newly won districts, but to oppose a solid force to the powerful tribes to whose border the province had now advanced—the Yorkshire Brigantes and the Silures and Ordovices of Wales. It was probably from the new base at Viroconium that Ostorius sent out in the following year (49 A.D.) an expedition against the Deceangi, who occupied the lands at the mouth of the Dee in Flintshire, Denbighshire and Western Cheshire, and possessed valuable lead mines. Probably they were a section of, or subject to, the powerful race of the Ordovices. While engaged in devastating their territory, and "not far from the Irish Sea," Ostorius was drawn back by the news that the Brigantes were on the move. But on his approach only a few of these enemies were met and routed—the bulk of the great Northern tribe had held back, and now offered or accepted terms of peace.

This left Ostorius free to continue the campaign against the tribes of the Welsh hills. He is said to have prepared for it by making sure of his base; the legions being now transferred westward, he thought well to establish a great colony of veterans at Camulodunum, to serve instead of a garrison for the provincial capital. The time-

expired veterans of his legions were settled there, and given lands
in the vicinity; this nucleus of war-tried soldiers was the first
Roman city in Britain : it was named Colonia Victrix, as some
inscriptions prove.   It would seem that Ostorius, leaving Eastern
Britain ungarrisoned save by the legion at Lincoln, took all the
other three off to his Western campaign.   The Second Legion was
brought up to Isca Silurum (Caerleon) from Gloucester, or whatever other place was its original headquarters : the Fourteenth and
Twentieth operated from the newly occupied base at Viroconium
on the Severn.

At the beginning of the ensuing series of campaigns, which
lasted for three years, the Silurians, the southern enemy, seem to
have taken the lead, with the untiring Caratacus at their head.
But when the governor had turned his attention to them, the
exiled king drew away into the territory of the Ordovices, and
transferred the main seat of the lingering war northwards.   Ostorius followed him, and after many vicissitudes of fortune, found
him offering battle in a very strong position, whose flanks were
covered by precipitous hills and its centre protected by an entrenchment of rough stones, while a river, hard to ford, ran along its front.
This was the last chance of Caratacus: we are told that he rode
along the line reminding the Britons of how his ancestors had
turned back Julius Caesar, pointing out to them the meaning of the
Roman yoke to men who had hitherto lived in freedom, and urging
them to save themselves and their families from tribute, slavery and
dishonour.   The warriors shouted their approval of his words, and
the Ordovices and Silurians bound themselves, each swearing by the
gods of their tribe, that they would conquer or die.

Nevertheless, the battle, after a very hard struggle, went in
favour of the Romans, who forded the river and stormed the entrenchments after a desperate struggle and with heavy loss.   Even
when their line had been pierced, the Britons rallied at the top of
the hill, but in a second combat they were again broken, and then
dispersed in all directions.[1]   The wife and daughter of Caratacus
were captured in the British camp, and some of his male relatives,
who had hitherto followed his fortunes, surrendered themselves.
But the king fled to the Brigantes, and tried to rouse them up to

[1] Cefn Carnedd, near Llanidloes, and Coxall Knoll, near Lentwardine, have
been suggested as probable sites for the battle.   No certainty is possible.

engage in the war. This tribe was at the moment ruled by a queen named Cartimandua—a strange phenomenon among a Celtic race. She had already resolved not to court war with the Romans, and instead of taking arms, seized Caratacus and handed him over in chains to the governor [50 A.D.].

Ostorius sent the captive and all his family to Rome, where Claudius made a great public spectacle of their reception. They were led through the Forum under a military guard to a high tribunal, where Claudius sat to determine on their fate. Caratacus is said to have displayed an undaunted spirit, to have told the emperor that he considered himself justified in having defended himself and his possessions to the last gasp, and to have added that his long resistance had made the Roman triumph all the more conspicuous in the end : " If I had been betrayed and captured when the war began, neither my fortune nor your glory would have been so notable : I might have been put to death without attracting much attention : but now, if you were to spare my life, I should be an example of Roman clemency for all ages ". Yielding, we may suspect, rather to his natural good nature than to this argument, Claudius granted Caratacus and his whole family their lives, and ordered their chains to be removed. Apparently the king ended his days as a pensioned exile in Italy ; history only preserves the anecdote that walking through Rome after his release and gazing at the splendour of its palaces, he exclaimed : " and yet the owners of all this must needs covet our poor huts in Britain "[1] [51. A.D.]

To the surprise of Ostorius the capture of Caratacus did not bring the war in Western Britain to an end. The Silurians became more active than ever after his disappearance from the scene, " whether it was that the Romans grew somewhat careless, thinking that they had finished the struggle by removing the king, or whether the enemy burst out into a more bitter passion of revenge from pity for the fate of so gallant a prince ".[2] At any rate the war took a turn for the worse after the year 51. The Silurians surrounded and well-nigh cut off a legionary force which had been left to build a fortress in their territory—perhaps the camp still visible at Gaer in Cymddu. The detachment was saved by reinforcements which hurried up from

[1] Dio Cassius, *Fragments*, 90.
[2] Tacitus, *Annals*, xii. 39.

he nearest garrison,[1] but a prefect, eight centurions and very many of the rank and file had been slain.   Not long after, this vigorous tribe routed a foraging force, and the cavalry supports which had been sent off to cover it, and were only checked by the arrival of more than one legion on the ground.   These fights were followed by a long wearing campaign "like a series of brigand raids in woods or marshes".   After two auxiliary cohorts, raiding incautiously, had been surprised and exterminated, Ostorius fell ill and died from fatigue, and the wear and tear of constant anxiety, "to the great joy of the enemy, who declared that if not a battle yet at any rate the war had made an end of this by no means despicable general".

Aulus Didius was sent out hastily from Rome to replace Ostorius, and arrived to find matters more unpromising than ever, a legion commanded by Manlius Valens having been defeated in open battle by the Silurians just before he landed.   The western war dragged on without any definite result, and he was also threatened with an attack from the Brigantes, among whom civil strife had arisen between the faction favourable to the Roman alliance, and that which wished for war.   Cartimandua, the Brigantian queen, who had given up Caratacus, had married a chief named Venutius, but she presently quarrelled with him, and murdered his brother and certain other of his kinsmen.[2]   He therefore flew to arms, and put himself at the head of the war party, while the queen appealed for aid to Didius.   Seeing that the triumph of Venutius would mean a Brigantian invasion of the Midlands, the governor lent her the services of a detachment from the legion at Lincoln, IX. Hispana, then under the command of Caesius Nasica.   The fighting began not too favourably for the Romans, but ended with a success, and apparently a peace was patched up between the contending factions, since Cartimandua and Venutius are still found reigning together more than fifteen years later.

[1] Possibly from Isca, but "castellis" seems to suggest smaller posts : we should expect "castris".

[2] A hoard of Brigantian coins dug up at Honley near Huddersfield, in 1893, contained a coin of Cartimandua, the on y one yet discovered.   The pieces were interesting, the early ones showing the name of an unknown king, Volisius, associated with one Dumnocoverus, while the later retain the name of Volisius but show on the reverse the name CARTI——.   These inscriptions suggest that Volisius was a king who associated with himself first a colleague (perhaps his son) named Dumnocoverus, and, after the death of the latter, Cartimandua who must surely have been his daughter and heiress.

Didius ruled for five years—the two last of Claudius, the three first of Nero (52-57). He is said by Tacitus to have been an unenterprising governor, being well advanced in years, and destitute of ambition, since he had already attained to all the honours to which a subject might aspire. He handed over the conduct of all his campaigns to his lieutenants, and thought that he had done enough when he retained what his predecessor had conquered. It seems that the frontier remained fixed, well-nigh [1] as Scapula had drawn it, on the line from Lincoln to the mouth of the Dee, and from thence to Isca—the Silurians and Ordovices retaining their independence, despite of constant raids directed against them from the base-camps on the Severn and Usk. The northern border would be kept safe through the friendship of the queen of the Brigantes.

Didius retired in 57 : his successor Veranius appeared in the following year, and announced that he was about to assume a more active policy. But he had only just commenced an attack on the Silurians, and ravaged their borders, when he died. In his will was found a curious pledge in which he promised the Emperor Nero that in two years he would guarantee the complete subjection of Britain. After some little delay he was replaced by Suetonius Paulinus, a general of rare merit, and very popular with the army and people, who called him the rival of Corbulo, his great contemporary, who saved the Armenian border and forced the Parthians to peace [59 A.D.].

Suetonius changed the front of the Roman advance, and took the land of the Ordovices in North Wales as his objective, partly in order to turn the flank of the Silurians and take them in the rear, but mainly because, as Tacitus tells us, the Isle of Mona (Anglesey), the farthest stronghold of the Ordovices, was the centre of the national religion of Britain, and the refuge of all rebels and deserters. It may have been now that the headquarters of one or both of the legions at Wroxeter were moved to Deva (Chester), on the estuary of the Dee, the natural base for all operations against North Wales, though the change may have been Didius's work. He built a flotilla of flat-bottomed boats on the Dee, with which he intended to carry his infantry across the Menai Strait : the

---

[1] Didius is said by Tacitus to have pushed forward a few forts, but to have done no more, but possibly Deva was made a legionary station by him, as there seem to be signs that it was already occupied not very long after A.D. 50, i.e., in the time of Didius rather than that of Suetonius.

cavalry was to swim across at low water. Apparently a year was consumed in these preparations, as it was not until the spring of 60 A.D. that the invasion of North Wales began. The governor took with him, no doubt, the whole or parts of the Fourteenth and Twentieth Legions, though a garrison must have been left at Deva to guard the base, while the Second Legion at Isca watched the ever-hostile Silures, and the Ninth at Lincoln was the only solid force left in Eastern Britain. The boats coasted along the rocky shore of North Wales parallel to the advance of the land army, and could have been used to turn the enemy's sea-side flank, if he had made any resistance during the march. But we are not told that the Britons attempted to hold the line of the Conway, or any other of the defensible rivers which flow into the sea between Deva and the straits. Their efforts were reserved for the defence of Anglesey, where the whole force of the tribe was concentrated to defend the ancient sanctuaries. " Along the shore was seen a dense line of armed warriors, while women were rushing about between the ranks garbed like the Furies, in black gowns, their hair flowing loose, and torches in their hands. The Druids were visible in the rear offering sacrifices to their gods, raising their hands to heaven, and calling down dire imprecations upon the head of the invader." At first the soldiery, on being thrown ashore, were somewhat impressed by the strange wild scene, and stood as if paralysed under the shower of weapons. But their officers called them on, and they began to exhort each other to have no fear of an army of women and fanatics. In the first charge they broke the Britons, and drove them back on the flames of their own sacrifices. There followed a great massacre of priests, warriors, and women alike; after which Suetonius bid his men cut down the sacred groves, and destroy the altars on which the Druids had been wont to offer human sacrifices, and to seek signs from heaven in the entrails of their victims. At this moment the governor suddenly received terrible news from the rear. All Eastern Britain, where no trouble had been known for more than ten years, had blazed up into sudden revolt.

The immediate cause of this explosion was the recent annexation of the subject-kingdom of the Iceni, in modern Norfolk and Suffolk. Its king Prasutagus had lately died, leaving no male issue, and the Roman government had resolved to put an end to the existence of his little state, though he had endeavoured to propitiate the young emperor, by naming him, along with his own daughters, as part heir to all his possessions. Apparently none of the male kin of Prasutagus dared to oppose the annexation, which might have been completed peacefully if the agents employed to carry it out had behaved with common decency and moderation. But the officers sent by the governor to take military possession of the kingdom, and the clerks told off by the procurator (who represented the imperial private estate (*fiscus*) in Britain) to investigate the personal property of Prasutagus, disgraced themselves by their violent and unrighteous doings. The realm, says Tacitus, was devastated by the centurions, the palace by the procurator's slaves. Many of the richest Icenians were stripped of their ancestral estates—the late king's relatives were treated as if they had been left as slaves to the emperor. The widowed queen Boudicca was arrested and scourged for offering opposition to the officials, and—worst of all—her two young daughters were violated by their ruffianly captors. The whole tribe of the Iceni sprang to arms to avenge these outrages, and were at once joined by the Trinovantes, who had their own special grievances to avenge. The most notable of these was that the owners of an immense area of land round the new colony of Camulodunum had been expropriated without compensation, in order to provide allotments for the veterans there established. Nor was this all: the settlers habitually subjected their surviving provincial neighbours to violence and insult, and the Britons could get no redress from the government. Instead of strengthening Roman influence in the South-East, as Ostorius had hoped when he founded it, the colony of Camulodunum had weakened it, by provoking the wrath of the surrounding population. Yet the colonists had not taken precautions against their aggrieved neighbours: the place was not provided with a ditch or wall, or a castle of refuge, and the only building in it capable of defence was the large and solid stone temple of Divus Claudius.

Other details are given us by Dio Cassius,[1] which enable us to comprehend more clearly the discontent of the British provincials. It was a very common thing for Roman financiers to persuade or compel tribal magnates to borrow money from them—a thing to

---

[1] In Xiphilinus, *Epitome*, xii. 2.

which the thriftless and ostentatious Celtic chiefs in Gaul, as well
as in Britain, were always prone. The celebrated Seneca, then
one of the two chief ministers of Nero, is said to have been the
greatest money-lender of all, despite of his philosophy and his ostentatious love of moderation and justice. At this moment he
had just called in loans amounting to 10,000,000 sesterces without warning. Hence scores of British landowners found themselves
threatened with bankruptcy, or even with slavery. At the same
time, the procurator of the imperial private *fiscus*, Decianus Catus,
was demanding the instant payment of much money which had
been given or lent by Claudius to prominent supporters of the
Roman cause.

Thus the exactions of the local officials conspired with the greed
of the financier to turn old friends into enemies. All the chiefs of
Eastern Britain, whatever their former politics, listened to the
appeal of Boudicca, when she pleaded her own wrongs, and region
after region rose, and placed its levies at the disposal of the injured
queen, who became not only the trumpet of sedition but the general
of the confederate army. For she rode in her chariot at the head
of the warriors, and put herself in the forefront of the battle.

On the outbreak of revolt among the Iceni the colonists of
Camulodunum at last saw their peril, and, since the governor was
absent on his Welsh campaign, applied for aid to the procurator,
Decianus Catus. He could only supply them with 200 men, but
the veterans and other settlers took arms, and began to think of
fortifying the town ; this project is said to have been hindered by
British residents who were in secret agreement with the rebels. At
any rate a sudden onslaught of the Icenian and Trinovantian levies
carried the place with a rush, and drove the garrison into the temple
of Claudius. This was besieged and stormed on the second day.
The whole of the settlers, Roman and foreign, were put to death
with cruel tortures ; even the women were stripped naked, mutilated
and impaled. Just after this disaster succour came over-late: Petillius
Cerealis approached, at the head of the Ninth Legion, the only solid
force of regulars which had been left in Eastern Britain, when
Suetonius went off to the west. The Britons turned upon him
and inflicted a complete defeat on his troops. The whole of the
legionary infantry was cut to pieces ; Cerealis escaped with a few
hundred cavalry alone. At once the whole of the neighbouring

tribes took arms to aid the victorious Boudicca ; the Roman and other foreign immigrants took refuge in the towns of Verulamium and Londinium. The Procurator Catus fled in despair to Gaul.

Such was the news which was brought to Suetonius, on the shores of the Menai Strait, immediately after he had achieved his victory in Mona. He started to fly to the assistance of the isolated Roman towns in the East, and set all the troops that could be spared from North Wales in motion. At the same moment he sent orders to Poenius Postumus, who was in command of the Second Legion at Isca, to bring up that corps to join him. [1]

A rapid rush across the island brought Suetonius to London, whose first definite appearance in British history dates from this year, though we know from its name that it must have been an old Celtic trade centre long before the Romans came to Britain. Tacitus calls it " a town which though not honoured with the title of a colony was very celebrated for the number of its merchants and the abundance of its resources ". But on reaching London the governor found the situation so much worse than he had expected that he dared neither to hold the town and stand a siege, nor to offer battle to the rebels. It is probable that his own troops had not yet come up in full force. Nor had he yet been joined by the expected Second Legion. Therefore he bade the citizens of London pack up their goods and retire under his protection. They mostly did so, but many, either from necessity or because they thought that they had friends among the Britons, refused to follow Suetonius. All these were massacred when Boudicca occupied the city after the legate's retreat. The sum of the Roman disasters was completed by the fall, about the same time, of the flourishing municipality of Verulamium, which was sacked and burnt with atrocities that rivalled those which had been

[1] The version of Suetonius's campaign here given is suggested by Professor Haverfield, who points out that Tacitus's narrative does not necessarily imply that the legate reached London with his whole field army about him, and that the "jam Suetonio quartadecima legio cum vexillariis, etc.," of *Annals*, xiv. 34, gives the force present at the battle only, and does not say that it had marched with Suetonius. It certainly seems easier to understand the general's abandonment of London and Verulamium if we believe that he had got ahead of his army. The "agmen" which Tacitus speaks of in xiv. 33, as accompanied by the fugitive Londoners, must on this hypothesis have been composed of the trifling garrison of London. The "infrequentia militis," which induced Suetonius to retreat, according to this paragraph, does not indeed square in well with the generally accepted idea that he had already 10,000 men with him.

perpetrated at Camulodunum. The ancient historians state, no doubt with exaggeration, that at Camulodunum, Londinium and Verulamium about 70,000 persons perished, when Romans, continental traders from Gaul and elsewhere, and friendly Britons were calculated all together.

Suetonius, as it seems, had now been joined by all the troops from the North-West, the whole Fourteenth Legion, some chosen cohorts of the Twentieth, and auxiliaries enough to make his total force up to 10,000 men. But Poenius Postumus had failed to bring up the Second Legion, and had disobeyed orders by shutting himself up in the camp of Isca, where the Silurians were no doubt threatening him. It was necessary either to fall back on Isca or Deva, the only points in Britain now in Roman hands, or to offer battle at once to the rebels. Probably the fact that his march was clogged by thousands of refugees from London, who would have made farther retreat slow and difficult, induced the governor to take the bolder course. He turned and faced the pursuing Britons in a narrow position where his wings and rear were covered with woods, so as to make flanking operations impossible. Boudicca and her horde encamped opposite him ; they are said to have been a vast host of more than 80,000 men, accompanied by thousands of waggons loaded with their wives, camp followers and provisions.[1]

Flushed by her unbroken series of successes, the furious queen had no thought of tactics, and resolved to overwhelm the Romans by the wild frontal rush of a multitude. She harangued the tribes to a pitch of frenzy, and then flung them forward on the Roman line. Suetonius received the headlong charge with his men halted, but when it was beaten off, took the offensive in his turn, and sallied out from his position with the legion in a dense column in the centre, the auxiliaries on each side of it, and the cavalry on the wings. Caesar's old saying that only the first rush of a Celtic army was to be dreaded once more proved true. When the Romans broke out upon the disordered multitude, and pierced its centre, the greater part of the British host gave way and fled. But many thousands were thrust back upon the waggon-laager of their own encampment,

---

[1] The battle spot is impossible to locate. Professor Haverfield suggests that if Suetonius had fallen back from London to pick up his army, or part of it, we must suppose the battle to have taken place somewhere along the line of the road London-Wroxeter (Watling Street), on which the troops must have been moving.

and were overtaken as they vainly strove to disentangle themselves from it. The Romans cut to pieces not only the flying warriors but the women and camp followers—the example had been set them by the enemy, who in the sack of three towns had spared neither age nor sex. An incredible number of Britons are said to have fallen— enough to avenge all their late massacres. Boudicca escaped for the moment, but took poison when she saw that the rebellion was doomed to failure.

Suetonius had now to reduce practically the whole island to submission, since the Roman authority had disappeared everywhere during the recent disasters. He was able to do so when his field army had been increased. The Second Legion came up from Isca —its disobedient commander had committed suicide to avoid a court-martial. From the continent there came over 2,000 legionary recruits to replace the lost infantry of the Ninth Legion, eight auxili- ary cohorts, and a thousand horse. Instead of going into winter quarters, the governor led his troops up and down the rebellious districts, wasting them with fire and sword. Yet the tribes, though suffering terribly from famine, were slow to make their submission. It was said that the new procurator, Julius Classicianus, the suc- cessor of Decianus Catus, had given the Britons secret counsel to the effect that the longer they held out the better terms would they get. This he did, we are told, from hatred of Suetonius, for whose recall he was intriguing at Rome, since he calculated that if the rebellion went on much longer the governor would be super- seded, as incapable of terminating the war. After a space Nero sent across to Britain his favourite freedman Polycletus, to make a report on the state of the province: it was apparently favourable to Suetonius, who was retained in command for a year longer, and succeeded in restoring order within the old boundaries of the pro- vince, though he was too busy therein to be able to pay any atten- tion to his original enemies the Silurians and Ordovices. But at the end of 61 he was recalled, on account of a new disaster which Tacitus vaguely describes as " the loss of some few galleys and their crews on the coast ". We are left uninformed as to whether the loss was by shipwreck or by capture at the hands of the enemy.

The next governor was Petronius Turpilianus (A.D. 61-63), a cautious man, who thought his duty was to restore the administra- tion of the province rather than to court further wars : " and so since he neither attacked the unsubdued tribes nor was attacked by them, he was able to cloke his want of enterprise with the honourable name of peace ". The boundaries of the province had returned to the position which they had occupied before Boudicca's rebellion, Isca, Deva and Lindum being held as the frontier strongholds, while the Brigantes, Ordovices, and Silurians retained their independence. Doubtless Petronius had enough to do in reorganising the shattered fabric of government within the old limits, and was wise to subordinate all else to that end. His successor, M. Trebellius Maximus, who ruled the province for the space of six years (63-69), a longer term than any previous governor had enjoyed, would appear to have been a man of a similar temperament. Tacitus, in somewhat contemptuous terms, remarks that he endeavoured to keep the province quiet by mere urbanity and good temper, but at the same time accuses him of meanness and parsimony, and states that he kept the soldiery in arrears of their pay. This makes it appear likely that Trebellius's way of keeping the Britons in good temper was to raise as little money from them as possible, even if military efficiency was thereby endangered. But it must be remembered that his power of resuming a forward policy and completing the conquest of Western Britain was seriously diminished by the fact that Nero, in 68 A.D., withdrew the Fourteenth Legion from Britain for a projected expedition on the Armenian frontier. This left the line facing the Silurians and Ordovices guarded by only two legions, the Second at Isca, and the Twentieth at Deva. It must be concluded from the fact that this removal was possible that either Petronius or Trebellius had patched up some sort of a formal peace with the mountaineers of Wales.[1] We learn without surprise that the rule of Trebellius was not unpleasing to the Britons, though we need not ascribe his popularity to the fact that the barbarians had " begun to look with less disfavour on the corruption of Roman civilisation," [2] as Tacitus unkindly puts it. Economic administration and courteous treatment are sufficient to account for the phenomenon. It is probable that more solid progress in the assimilation of the province was made in the years

[1] Tacitus only states that Petronius had made terms with the rebels, and says nothing about his dealings with the rest (*Agricola*, c. 16).

[2] Didicerunt jam barbari quoque ignoscere vitiis blandientibus (Tacitus, *Agricola*, 16).

61-69 than in all those which had gone before: in the more stirring times that were to follow the Britons of the south and east gave no trouble whatever, a sufficient sign that they were growing less discontented. Probably the prosaic but necessary work of road-making, and the improvement of towns, was going on apace, when all the resources of the province were no longer devoted to feeding an offensive war. It is quite likely that to this period belongs the development of the great highways of Britain—Watling Street (from London by Viroconium to Deva), Ermine Street (from London by Castor-on-Nen to Lincoln), the Fosse Way (from Exeter, Bath, and Cirencester, by Leicester to Lincoln), and the nameless but important road from London, by Silchester, to Cirencester, Gloucester, and Isca, which was the most important link between South-Eastern and South-Western Britain. All had no doubt been primitive Celtic trackways, which the conquerors straightened out, and converted into good metalled roads at their leisure. Less important arteries of traffic awaited construction or improvement at a later day; in some outlying or thinly peopled districts the Romans seem never to have cared to build proper "streets," and to have made shift to employ the old tracks during the whole period of their occupation of Britain. This was certainly the case in the extreme west, in the Dumnonian lands of Devon and Cornwall, where Roman milestones have been found, but no properly constructed Roman paved roads of the usual type. There were many regions of the Midlands which were no better served—where we find scattered traces of Roman habitation, but no metalled *chaussées*. The middle valleys of the Thames and Severn, were, down to the end, very badly served by the provincial road system. The east and west roads, from London to Bath and Gloucester, went by Silchester and Speen, many miles south of the Thames. There was no corresponding road at all on the north of the river: if a traveller had persisted in going from London to Gloucester through the South Midlands, his only chance would be to take the angular and circuitous route—St. Albans, Towcester, Bicester,[1] Cirencester. Similarly in the Severn Valley the obvious route—Gloucester, Worcester, Viroconium—does not seem to have existed, the north and south roads

---

[1] Or rather, to be more exact, not Bicester, but Alchester, which lies a mile or so from the modern town.

in this region running many miles away from the river, the one from Viroconium to Isca through Herefordshire, the other keeping along the slopes of Cotswold, crossing the Avon in its middle course, and joining Watling Street at Letocetum near Lichfield. The explanation is that the valleys of the middle Thames and Severn were mainly undrained areas of swamp and jungle, where there lived at most small communities of fishers and hunters. The population lay along the higher and drier ground, and there were as yet no towns to represent the mediæval Reading and Oxford, or Tewkesbury and Worcester.

The placid and economical Trebellius was still ruling when chaos commenced all over the empire at the death of Nero (68). Britain, however, suffered less from the civil wars of the "year of the three emperors" (69) than most other provinces ; its legions followed, at a distance, the motions of those of Gaul, and adhered to the cause of Vitellius, as did the governor. But Trebellius, being unpopular with the soldiery—however much he may have been liked by the provincials — had some unpleasant experiences. The turbulent legate of the Twentieth Legion, a certain Caelius Roscius, raised a sedition against him, and finally compelled him to fly out of the island and take refuge with Vitellius. For some time the three legates of the legions ruled Britain at their pleasure, but they all adhered to the same cause that the ex-governor had taken up, and after some delay detached 8,000 men, picked legionary and auxiliary cohorts, to join the army with which Vitellius invaded Italy. These British troops were too late for the first battle of Bedriacum, in which Otho fell, but found a notable and much-trusted part of the forces which, a few months later, contended on the side of Vitellius against Vespasian in the second North Italian campaign.

Meanwhile that indolent and short-lived emperor had sent Vettius Bolanus to take the place of Trebellius as governor of Britain, and had also restored to the island the Fourteenth Legion, which Nero had taken away from it, two years before, for his abortive Caucasian expedition. No doubt the garrison had been weakened to the verge of danger by the drafts sent to Italy, and troops to replace them were much needed. The Fourteenth Martia was the corps selected for that purpose, both because it had long served in Britain, and because it had taken the part of Otho in the late civil war, and was therefore not safe to leave in Italy when another contest was impending.

That struggle went against Vitellius, and after his death Vespasian was acknowledged as emperor in every corner of the empire. In Britain the governor, Bolanus, had done little or nothing to aid Vitellius, both because he was an unenterprising person, and because two of his legions had strong sympathies for the other side—the Second Augusta, because of its kindly memory of the time when Vespasian had been its legate in 43-47, and the Fourteenth, because it had always been opposed to the Vitellian faction. So little had Bolanus committed himself to the lost cause that the new emperor actually retained him in command for some months, although he had been appointed by his enemy and predecessor. He is said to have been an easy-going and not unpopular ruler, who shirked the task of imposing the necessary return to discipline upon legions which had got out of hand. The last note recorded of him is that he was compelled to send back to the continent the Fourteenth Legion, which had so recently returned to Britain.[1] The cause of this transfer was the breaking out upon the Rhine of the great Gallo-German insurrection of Civilis, a rebel of genius, against whom troops had to be concentrated from every corner of the empire. The Fourteenth Martia Victrix never returned to Britain, being replaced, when the war on the Rhine was over, by a newly-raised corps, the Second Adjutrix. But this happened after the supersession of Bolanus by Petillius Cerealis (70 A.D.), a hearty supporter of Vespasian, who had atoned by laurels newly won from the German rebels for his old defeat at the hands of Boudicca in 60 A.D. For this is the same Cerealis whose legion had been completely cut to pieces by the Iceni after the fall of Camulodunum.

[1] During its short second stay in Britain the Fourteenth Martia may have been at Lincoln, along with the Ninth Hispana, as a monument to one of its men has been found there. C.I.L., 187. A concentration at Lincoln may have been due to the impending trouble among the Brigantes, who were just about to take arms.

CHAPTER VI

CONQUEST OF NORTHERN BRITAIN.   CEREALIS AND AGRICOLA
(71-85 A.D.)

WITH the accession of Vespasian, or rather with the complete establishment of Vespasian's power in the North-West, after the crushing of the rebellion of Civilis, begins a new era of expansion and conquest in the history of Roman Britain. There had, as we have seen, been no considerable annexations made since the governorship of Ostorius Scapula, and no shifting of the legionary stations since the forward move to Deva.   The Ordovices and Silurians seemed to have won a permanent independence by their obstinate resistance : the Brigantes of the North had never been seriously attacked.   The new aggressive departure which begins with the governorship of Petillius Cerealis (71-74) may have been first provoked by movements on the part of the Britons, but it is clear that it continued long after any necessity for self-defence was over, and was part of a deliberate policy for bringing the provincial boundary up to the limits which the governor, or his master at Rome, considered natural and convenient.   Vespasian was in a much more sound and solid position than his predecessors, and being bred a professional soldier must have had all his ideas dominated by military considerations, in a way which could not be expected of Claudius or Nero. We cannot doubt that he would agree with a lieutenant who demonstrated to him that the continued existence of the independent Silurians and Ordovices, along the whole Western flank of the province, was a tiresome anomaly, and that if the Brigantes gave trouble, there was no reason for leaving them unmolested in their highlands.

The commencement of the new series of wars of aggression, which lasted from 71 to 85, was brought about by domestic strife

among the Brigantes. We find to our surprise that the divided
kingship among that tribe, which we have already noted in the
days of Ostorius Scapula, was still in existence. The queen-regnant
Cartimandua and her consort Venutius were still alive in 71, and
were engaged, as they had been twenty years before, in perpetual
quarrels. These came to a head when the queen, who must now
have been well advanced in middle age, publicly repudiated her
husband, and married his armour-bearer Vellocatus. Not unnaturally the insulted chief collected his followers and set to work
to expel his wife and her paramour from the land. Cartimandua,
as she had already done once before in 50 A.D., asked for aid
from the governor, pointing out that she had always been the
friend of Rome, and that Venutius was the head of the war party.
The governor—it is uncertain whether this was one of the last acts
of Bolanus, or one of the first of Cerealis [1]—sent some cohorts to
help her. But her party was so much the weaker, that the Romans
had to be content with bringing her away to a place of safety—
the kingdom fell to Venutius, who was the advocate of resistance
to Rome, and had no wish to patch up a peace, even when he had
got rid of his consort.

Hence open war with the Brigantes began, and did not cease
for many a year: the territory of that stubborn tribe was often
invaded, and several times subdued, but at the slightest opportunity
they were ready to revolt, and the periods of rebellion were so
numerous, and so long, that it is difficult to say that the annexation
of the land between Humber and Solway was really completed till
the reign of Hadrian, sixty years after the Brigantian wars began.
Even after Hadrian's death there was at least one serious revolt,
with which we shall have to deal in its due place. The legionary
troops available for the conquest of the North were the Ninth Hispana
at Lindum, and the Twentieth Valeria Victrix and the newly arrived
Second Adjutrix at Deva, each supplemented by a proper comple-
ment of auxiliary horse and foot. The bases from which they

---

[1] From the place in which the Brigantian civil war and the Roman interference
is first mentioned by Tacitus, in *Histories*, iii. 45, we should be inclined to put
them in Bolanus's time in the year 69-70. But from the way in which the same
incidents are related in the *Agricola* we should suppose that Petillius took up the
war, " terrorem intulit Petillius Cerealis, Brigantum civitatem, quae numerosissima
totius provinciae adgressus " (*Ag.* c. 17).

operated would make it certain that the invasion must have been
double, one column taking Lancashire as its objective, the other
Yorkshire. It is improbable that the whole garrison of Chester was
ever used against the Brigantes: probably one legion habitually
remained behind to watch the Ordovices.

The course of the operations is only known to us in the vaguest
outline : " the battles were many and sometimes cost much blood :
but the greater part of the Brigantian territory was either annexed
or devastated ". Presumably this implies that the plain of York
and the flat parts of Lancashire as far as the Ribble were added
to the province of Britain, while the valleys of the Pennine Range,
the stronghold of the tribe, were frequently invaded but never
properly subdued. There is no reason to suppose that Petillius ever
reached the Tyne or the Solway, but it is probable that the legion
Ninth Hispana was moved up from Lindum to Eburacum (York)
before the war had long been in progress, and that the foundation of
the capital of the Roman North on the site of a Brigantian village
dates from the year 71 or 72.[1] We have no trace of a similar advance from Deva to Mancunium, which would have been *per se*
equally probable. It is clear, however, that Petillius had begun, but
was far from completing, the task of subduing the Brigantes when
he was superseded by Sextus Julius Frontinus in 74. Of this governor
we have many eulogies as an officer, but he was an author also, and
has left behind him books on military stratagems and another
on the aqueducts of Rome which chance to have come down to us.

It can hardly have been of set purpose that Frontinus, with the
Brigantian war already on his hands, allowed himself to be drawn
into a new struggle with the Silurians. We cannot doubt that
it must have arisen from incursions into Roman territory on the
part of these mountaineers, at a moment when they conceived the
governor to be too busy elsewhere to pay much attention to them.
But Frontinus, apparently leaving the northern struggle undecided,
turned his main strength against the Silurians, and for several years
(75-78) devoted himself to their conquest. More fortunate in the
Welsh hills than Ostorius or Suetonius, he actually achieved his

---

[1] Inscriptions show us that II. Adjutrix was at Deva and IX. Hispana at
Lindum in the earliest years of Vespasian. We get later traces of IX. Hispana at
York, both in inscriptions and tiles : but none of II. Adjutrix, though it was in
Britain till about 85 A.D.

purpose, and we are told that the tribe was reduced to complete submission before he ended his term of government. The legion Second Augusta, which must have borne the brunt of the struggle with them, was not moved forward to any new garrison in the heart of their territory, but continued to occupy its old post at Isca. But no doubt some auxiliary cohorts must have been posted for a time in the inner Silurian territory, at forts such as the Gaer in Cymdu and Gellygaer in Glamorganshire, where there are traces of permanent Roman fortifications.[1] How early it was before the great military road from Gloucester to Isca was continued along the coast to Nidum (Neath) and Maridunum (Carmarthen) it is impossible to say. That South Wales was always considered a district that could not be left without a garrison is made clear by the fact that the Second Augusta remained there down to the fourth century. But whether its later task was to watch the Silurians, or rather to guard against possible pirate raids from Ireland, is not quite certain.

Frontinus was recalled in 78, and returned to spend a long old age in Rome, where he survived in high honour and office till the times of Nerva and Trajan. He was succeeded by Cnaeus Julius Agricola, the father-in-law of the historian Tacitus, whose biography of the great governor is a valuable yet a disappointing work for those interested in the history of Roman Britain. It might have given us all that we could wish to know about the geography and ethnology, the civil and military organisation, of the island-province. But unfortunately it consists in great part of vaguely epigrammatic laudations of Agricola : it contains no statistics, no accurate dates, very few proper names of the persons, Roman or British, with whom Agricola came in contact, and still fewer geographical names. There is a short sketch of the general topography of the island, but it is almost destitute of names. Incredible as it may seem, neither the Thames nor Trent, the Severn nor Dee, neither London nor Lindum, Eboracum nor Deva, Isca or Camulo-dunum, are mentioned in it, and the names of only three or four tribes appear in the whole work. Similarly there is a short note on the provincial history of Britain ; but it consists of little more than a list of the governors, to each of whose names a few epigram-

---

[1] The coins found in 1908 at the well-preserved fort at Gellygaer were mostly of Flavian date, and the last was a piece of Nerva, 96-98 A.D.

matic sentences of description are added. There is hardly a fact
included which is not already known to us from the *Annals* or the
Histories. The account of Agricola's governorship, though it takes
up many chapters, is almost equally barren of detailed facts ; in the
tale of his seven years of campaigning the only geographical names
that occur are the Clota and Bodotria estuaries (the firths of Clyde
and Forth), the isle of Mona, the river Tanaus, the names of the
tribes of the Ordovices and Boresti, one single harbour (Portus
Trutulensis) and Mons Graupius—the unidentified site of the
governor's great battle with the Caledonians. Apparently Tacitus
intended his father-in-law's biography to be a mere panegyric rather
than a serious historical work. The result of this paucity of names
is that we are kept wandering in unidentified wastes, not certain
whether we are on the Tyne or the Tay, or whether the vaguely
indicated enemy is the Brigantes or the Caledonians.[1] At the end
of the narrative comes a "purple patch" of wholly disproportion-
able length, concerning Agricola's battle at the Mons Graupius ; it
contains two orations of the most unconvincing and commonplace
type, by the governor and his shadowy foe Calgacus the Caledonian.
The details of the battle itself are hard to follow, but, as has been
truly said, "Tacitus was the most unmilitary of all historians," and
here is no more faulty than is his wont. He was as uninterested in
statistics and organisation as in military affairs ; his readers were to
be impressed by the noble character of Agricola, rather than instructed in the prosaic details of Agricola's work. Hence we have
much rhetoric and few facts. There is even some possibility that
Tacitus's fervent and uncritical laudation of his distinguished relative are intended to cover a magnificent and ambitious failure. It
might be urged that Agricola's expeditions were bold and far-
reaching rather than wisely planned, and that many of his conquests were no more than raids without result, so that Tacitus's
account of the campaigns of his family hero may be compared with
that of the trans-Rhenane wars of his other idol, Germanicus, in
which blood, money, and resources were lavished so as to win some
glory, perhaps, but no profit for the empire.

Be this as it may, we must accept with gratitude whatever the

[1] Most tiresome of all is his failure to give the names of the tribes between
Solway and Forth which Agricola fought and defeated, and his omission of any
details which would enable us to make out whether, as has lately been proved, the
governor built a regular line of forts from Tyne to Solway.

great historian has deigned to tell us about the events of the years
78-86, the time of his father-in-law's activity in Britain. It must be
premised that Agricola had passed the greater part of his official life
in the island. He had served as a young man on the staff of
Suetonius Paulinus, and had witnessed the revolt of Boudicca and
its repression. After an absence of some years he returned as legate
of the Twentieth Legion, towards the end of the time of Bolanus,
and took part at the head of that corps in the Brigantian war of
Petillius Cerealis, in which he is said to have won much distinction.
For these services he was promoted to the rule of the Gallic province of Aquitaine—a governorship of the third class, which he
held for somewhat less than three years. After this he was recalled
to Rome, given the consulship in 77, and then sent out to take
charge of Britain, a task very different in responsibility from the
management of the civilised and peaceful Aquitaine. But public
opinion and the will of Vespasian had pointed him out for the post,
as the man who had the best knowledge of the island among all his
contemporaries of suitable standing and seniority.

Agricola landed in Britain to take up his charge in the late
summer of 78, and had to engage in a difficult expedition before he
had been many days on shore. The Ordovices of North Wales,
untaught by the disasters of their Silurian neighbours, had raided
the Roman frontier just before his arrival, and surprised and exterminated a whole regiment of auxiliary cavalry. It was feared that
the recently subdued region might rise again, and that the trouble
might spread all over the West and North. Agricola therefore
mobilised a competent force, though the campaigning season was
nearing its end, and took in hand the subjection of the Ordovices.
He beat them in battle among their own mountains, for they had
refused to face him in the plain, and then pressed the pursuit with
unrelenting vigour as far as the Menai Strait. For the defeated
tribesmen, following the precedent of their fathers in the days of
Paulinus, had taken refuge in the sacred island of Mona. Agricola
had no such fleet with him as his predecessor had possessed, but
dared to attempt the forcing of the straits at low tide. His
auxiliary cavalry, with picked swimmers from all the cohorts, tried
the deep ford, which affords a dangerous and difficult passage, forced
their way across, and established themselves on the farther side.
The rest of the army followed as best it could, and the Ordovices,

cowed by the exploit, submitted without further fighting. Thus the tribes of North Wales, like those of South Wales, found themselves subdued, after a resistance which had lasted more than a quarter of a century since Ostorius had first entered their borders. We hear of no further trouble in this region, but since the legion Twentieth Valeria Victrix remained permanently fixed at Deva, we may conclude that Agricola and his successors thought it prudent to keep a solid force at hand, lest rebellion might break out once again in a land so well suited for defensive mountain warfare.

For two years after the conquest of the Ordovices Agricola devoted himself mainly to the reorganisation of the administration of the province. According to his son-in-law he was the most just and wise of rulers. "The Britons were capable of enduring the conscription, the land-tax, and all the other obligations of Roman subjects, if only abuses were avoided : it was abuses that they would not endure, for though they were so far tamed that they would yield obedience, they would not tolerate being treated as slaves. . . . Agricola paid the greatest attention to the public opinion of the provincials, having learnt by the experience of his predecessors that conquest followed by oppressive administration was of little profit: wherefore he resolved to extirpate the abuses that were the causes of rebellion." A most fruitful source of discontent had been the petty oppression and peculation of the clerks and freedmen of the governor's staff, and the officials of the *fiscus*, the imperial private exchequer. Against such offenders he conducted a long campaign, till he had purified the provincial civil service. Apparently the worst grievances of the Britons were to be found in the department of requisitions in kind, for the service of the army. The commissioners had been making illicit gains, by tricks of the same sort which we find Cicero detailing, when he describes the difficulties of his Cilician government, more than a hundred years before Agricola's day. One was to order the individuals or communities who had to supply corn to pay in their contributions at distant and inconvenient places, when they might just as well have been delivered near home. Agricola is said to have made the taxation much more tolerable, by redistributing the quota on a new and equitable basis, and accepting payments at the place and time most suited to the contributors.

At the same time he was doing his best to attract the Britons towards town life and the amenities of civilisation. " He thought that a nation accustomed to live in scattered hamlets and with little comfort, and thereby easily persuaded to war, might be lured to quiet and peace through the pleasures of life. He exhorted them in public, and aided them in private, to build temples, market-places and solid houses. He would praise those who fell in with his ideas readily, and chide those who hung back, so that rivalry to win his approval acted as a sort of compulsion. He induced the chiefs to allow their sons to be trained in the liberal arts, saying that though the Gauls were better educated the Britons had more natural talent. Hence it came that provincials who but lately refused to learn our tongue were found manifesting a desire to shine in Latin eloquence. The Roman garb even came with fashion, and the toga was frequently to be seen. By degrees the Britons began to appreciate those attractive instruments of social corruption, pillared colonnades, public baths, elegant banquets: all this the simple people called 'civilisation,' but it was really the token of their submission to the conqueror." It is interesting to find that at this very time educated Britons were already to be found in Rome, apparently in good society. Martial, writing in the days of Domitian, has many compliments for a lady named Claudia who "though descended from the painted Britons had the heart of a Roman," and was noted for her many accomplishments. She was the wife of a certain Pudens, so that intermarriage between the two races had already begun.[1]

But, while engaged in these peaceful tasks, Agricola was preparing to carry forward the Roman boundaries to what he considered a natural frontier. The present situation was an impossible one, since of the Brigantian territory half was conquered but the rest was unoccupied and independent. Its inhabitants were perpetually raiding the plains of Yorkshire and of South Lancashire, being still in possession of the mountainous district which separates these two lowlands, as well as of all the moors of the North. The deplorable parsimony of Tacitus with regard to local names prevents us from determining with accuracy what Agricola accomplished in 79 A.D. —the year of the death of Vespasian and the accession of the short-lived Titus. We are told that he collected a field force during the summer: " that he chose himself the sites for camps, and explored in person woods and estuaries: he left no part of the hostile territory

[1] Martial, *Epigrams*, v. 48 ; vi. 58.

undisturbed, but ravaged it all by sudden incursions. When he
had struck sufficient terror into the souls of the enemy, he wooed
them to submission by his clemency. By which policy many communities which had hitherto dealt with the Roman power as no more
than their equal, were induced to give hostages, and to abandon
their angry hostility. Their territories were encompassed with garrisons and forts, with such system and care as had never before been
displayed in any newly conquered part of Britain."

This vague language is most tantalising. The enemy seem to
be the Brigantian clans of the Pennine Range, Northumberland,
Cumberland and Westmoreland. The estuaries are presumably
those of Tees, Tyne and Solway. The "encompassing" of the
communities which surrendered must mean the placing of garrisons
and forts up both sides of Britain, along the lines where ran in
later days the two great roads from York to Newcastle and from
Manchester to Carlisle. As Agricola also drew a line of forts from
Solway to Tyne, where the Wall of Hadrian was afterwards to be
built, the Brigantes would be literally encircled on all sides. Even
the cross-lines across the Pennine Range, from Manchester to York
via Ilkley, and from York to Carlisle *via* Aldborough, Catterick
and Bowes, may have been originally selected as routes, and gar-
nished with forts and blockhouses, at this early date, so as to cut off
one community of the Brigantes from another.

But Agricola was not satisfied with the line of Solway and Tyne
as a frontier for the province, though it was a good natural boundary,
and though it coincided almost exactly with the northern limit of
the Brigantian territory. He had heard that there was a still shorter
line across the island, ninety miles farther to the north—that from
Clyde to Forth—and determined to advance to it—a bold resolve
when the Brigantes were still newly subdued, and when he had no
nearer bases than Eburacum and Deva. There can be no doubt
whatever that he took in hand during the next four years a task
that was too great for the resources that were at his disposition,
since, to be really safe, all the newly conquered northern tracts
required heavy garrisons, which he could not spare if he was to
provide himself with a sufficiently large field army. That he penetrated so far north as he did in 80-84 was only due to the fact that
the Brigantes were for the moment cowed : if they had taken arms
in his rear, as they did in later years while his successors were ruling

Britain, he would have found at once that his northern enterprises were premature and hazardous.

Favoured, however, by the temporary exhaustion of the Brigantes, Agricola accomplished marvellous feats in the third and succeeding years of his governorship. In 80 he started out to subdue the lands north of Tyne and Solway, "opening out new races, for he devastated the land of all the tribes that dwell as far as the estuary called Tanaus"[1] (apparently the Tay, remote as that may seem). So terrified were the enemy that they did not dare to assail the army, though it suffered dreadfully from bad weather. Hence Agricola had leisure for the building of forts. "Engineers took note of the fact that no other general chose defensive sites with such an unerring eye. No stronghold whose place he had selected was ever taken by storm, or evacuated on terms, or abandoned. The garrisons made frequent sorties : for each had been victualled with a full year's provisions, to guard against the danger of a long siege. So winter brought no anxiety, and each fort could take care of itself, contemning the enemy, who was reduced to despair. For the Britons had hitherto been wont to consider that they could win back in the winter all that they had lost in the summer : but now they were repelled in summer and winter alike. . . . The next campaigning season (that of 81) was spent in taking solid possession of the lands which had been already traversed. And if the courage of the army and the glory of the Roman name had but permitted it, a final frontier might have been fixed in Britain. For Clyde and Forth (Clota and Bodotria) running up far into the land from the two separate tidal seas, are separated by no more than an isthmus. This line was made safe with garrisons, and all the nearer sweep of land was grasped, the enemy being driven off, as it were, into another island."[2]

Here again, as in 80, we are lamentably hampered in our comprehension of Agricola's work by the want of detailed geographical names. The identification of the Taus (or Tanaus) with any other river than the Tay seems impossible, considering that we are told

[1] Or Taus in one MS. We know of no stream called Tanaus : some have suggested the Northumbrian Tyne, but that is too far south. The Tweed would be possible, but we do not know its ancient name : the Forth, which geographically looks most likely of all, had the name Bodotria, so cannot be meant.

[2] *Agricola*, § 22-23.

that in the year 81 lands previously traversed were firmly occupied, and a line drawn at Forth and Clyde. Therefore the campaign of 80 had gone at least as far as these estuaries ; and if the troops reached Stirling in a raid, why should they not have reached Perth ? That Agricola's routes in arriving at the isthmus were mainly along the eastern side of the Lowlands may be inferred from the fact that his exploration and conquest of Galloway were deferred to the year 83, and are narrated in a separate chapter of his biography. But since Carlisle had been occupied at the time of the surrender of the Brigantes, and must from the necessities of its situation have been a very important base when expeditions farther north were in question, we may suspect that Agricola's invasion was carried out in two columns. The right hand one must have advanced along the valley of the North Tyne, up which the later Roman road to the Forth was drawn, and would cross Cheviot so as to drop down into the valley of the Teviot near Jedburgh. From thence its progress would be under Eildon Hill, where the great camp of New-stead (Trimontium) was most certainly one of Agricola's chosen sites, and then across the Lammermuirs, descending on to the Firth of Forth at Inveresk and Cramond, both Roman stations of im-portance in a later age. Probably this line of invasion was taken by the Ninth Hispana, the York Legion, and its auxiliaries. Mean-while detachments of the two Chester Legions, Twentieth Valeria Victrix and Second Adjutrix, and their auxiliaries, starting from Carlisle, might fix their first camp in hostile territory at Birrens (Blatum Bulgium),—a considerable station in later days, at least, though we know not what it may have been under Agricola,—and then ascend the valley of the Annan, and after crossing the water-shed descend into Clydesdale.[1] This double line of invasion seems much more probable than a single advance from the Tyne to the Forth. Nor would it present any dangers, since we are told that the tribes of the Lowlands failed to combine, and never offered battle to the invaders. Among the numerous Roman camps in their territory it is difficult to separate those founded by Agricola from those of later days, but Raeburnfoot in Eskdale, New-stead, under Eildon, and Barr Hill, on the line between Forth

[1] Unfortunately there has apparently been no discovery of clearly Flavian date at Birrens, so the hypothesis stated here is unverified.

and Clyde, must surely have been of his selection, and certainly
also Cramond, Inveresk, Castlecary and Camelon, all south of the
line of the Forth. It is curious to find little trace, either from
Agricola's time or later, of either castles or lines of communication
along the coast of Northumberland, Berwickshire or East Lothian.
All expeditions to the north from the valley of the Tyne seem to
have avoided the shore, and to have followed the inland road from
Corbridge by High Rochester (Bremenium) to the central course of
the Tweed by Jedburgh and Newstead. It is strange that Tacitus
makes no mention of the names of the tribes whom Agricola met
between Solway and Forth, but they must have been the three
races whom Ptolemy places in this direction : the Otadini on the
east from Tyne to Forth, the Selgovae along the upper Tweed, and
the Dumnonii in the north, on both sides of the isthmus formed by
the two firths. The Novantae, in Galloway and along the Irish
Sea, would not be affected by these invasions of 80-81 A.D. There
are no signs that any of these were powerful or vigorous tribes, and
they may even, for all we know, have been vassals of the Brigantes.
It is at any rate clear that the Lowlands were thinly peopled,
though Ptolemy gives us the names of some dozen " cities " of one
sort or another among them. None of these had a future before
them : of the Lowland towns of mediæval Scotland—Edinburgh,
Glasgow, Ayr, Dumfries, Roxburgh, Berwick—not one seems to be
on a site indicated by the old geographer.

Agricola's next summer of campaigning (82) was dedicated to
the conquest of Galloway. " In his fifth year he started by going
on shipboard, and tamed by many successful combats tribes hitherto
unknown. He then garrisoned the part of Britain which looks out
on Ireland, more with a view to future operations than because
there was anything to be feared. For he considered that Ireland,
which lies in the midst between Britain and Spain, and is adjacent
also to the Bay of Biscay, might be made a flourishing and useful
part of the Roman Empire. Though smaller than Britain, it is
larger than any isle of the Mediterranean Sea. Its soil and climate,
the character and manners of its people, do not differ much from
those of Britain. It is easier of approach, and its harbours are
known through commerce and merchants. Agricola had sheltered
one of the Irish kings, who had been expelled in civil strife, and
kept him at hand in friendly guise, to use if opportunity offered. I

have often heard my relative say that Ireland could be conquered and held down by one legion, and a moderate contingent of auxiliaries. And its conquest would be useful with regard to the Britons, if Roman arms were everywhere, and independence were no longer visible in any direction." [1]

It is clear that no firm hold was established on Galloway; all that Tacitus seems to imply is that troops were placed at points on its coast, from which an expedition to Ireland could be easily conducted. It was well for the governor's reputation that such an attempt was never made, for his estimate of the force required to subdue and garrison the sister island was obviously far too low. It reminds us of Strabo's *obiter dictum* that Britain itself would require but one legion and some auxiliaries to hold it down. Four legions, and the corresponding contingents of non-legionary troops, were actually employed in Britain for thirty years before the frontier even reached Tyne and Solway! Ireland would have absorbed at least half that amount of troops, besides a large addition to the British fleet. If Agricola had invaded it with a smaller force, he would have been beaten off; if he had taken over all his field-army (which would really have been necessary) there is not the smallest doubt that the Brigantes and all their northern neighbours would have revolted. The governor would then have had to return, in a not very dignified fashion, and to repeat all his work of 80-82 over again. And his task would have been harder than before, because he would have lost his reputation for infallibility and invincibility. But he found other work to do, and the Irish prince who was to play the part of Adminius and Bericus was never utilised.

In his sixth year (83), instead of attacking Ireland, Agricola made himself busy north of the isthmus between Clyde and Forth, where he had so recently established his line of garrisons. His advance to that line had alarmed the tribes of the North, they had leagued themselves together, and were not only ready to defend their independence, but to take the offensive and threaten his lines of communication with his southern bases. Apparently conscious that the whole country behind him, as far as Yorkshire, might revolt, if the northern tribes burst into the Lowlands, the governor resolved

[1] *Agricola*, § 24.

to take the offensive himself, and give the enemy enough to do near home. His fleet was sent to coast around the headlands of Fife, and to explore the Firth of Tay : the land army marched parallel to its advance, in three columns, one of which kept in close touch with the naval forces. In this fashion the lands between Forth and Tay were overrun : the enemy was discovered after a time : "all the tribes that inhabit Caledonia "—a name now heard for the first time in Roman history—had united to form a single host. Their force was imposing, and was exaggerated by rumour to an innumerable multitude, so that many of the Roman officers advised their general to retire behind the Forth before he was compelled to do so. Agricola thought that he was strong enough to face the danger, and his confidence was justified by the event. The whole Caledonian host concentrated upon the column which consisted of the Ninth Legion, the weakest of the three divisions in which the Roman army was moving.[1] They attacked its camp at night, succeeded in bursting in, and were in a fair way to overcome its obstinate resistance when Agricola arrived at the head of the other corps, assailed them from the rear and inflicted on them a decisive defeat. The barbarians retired into their woods and marshes, disappointed, but still unbroken in spirit. Agricola then went into winter quarters, almost certainly in the region of the Earn and Lower Tay, where the great camps of Ardoch and Inchtuthill have yielded much evidence of first-century occupation.

The last of the great offensive campaigns of Agricola fell into the following year (84).[2] The soldiery are said to have started with the intention of "penetrating Caledonia, and finding the end of Britain, even if it were necessary to fight all the way". But it is hinted that their general's plans were more modest—though what his exact purpose was Tacitus will not tell us. He informs us that the fleet was sent up the eastern coast, to keep the natives uncertain as to his exact line of invasion, while the field army, now

---

[1] Weakest apparently because it had vexillations detached in this year for Domitian's German war, as a continental inscription shows.

[2] Tacitus makes no break between the sixth and seventh campaigns of Agricola, so that we cannot be sure where the winter-quarters come in. But since the battle speech in the seventh campaign alludes to the attack on the Ninth Legion as having taken place in the preceding year, the halt probably took place at the time indicated above.

strengthened by some British levies,[1] advanced till it reached the Graupian Mount, on which the Caledonians lay. The enemy had sent his non-combatants and cattle up into the remoter valleys, and the tribes had bound themselves at a solemn congress, accompanied by sacrifices, that they would not flinch from each other. Thirty thousand warriors are said to have been collected, not all foot (as might have been expected) but partly charioteers and horsemen.

The Graupian Mount cannot be identified. From the fact that it had been deliberately occupied by the enemy before the Romans came up, it must clearly have been some well-known position of strategical importance. Agricola, advancing from the valley of the Lower Tay, must have taken one of three lines, either that which follows the river and leads into Athole, past Dunkeld, "the gate of the Highlands," or the route more to the east which goes towards Aberdeenshire *via* Cupar Angus and Forfar, or else the coast road which, starting along the Firth of Tay, goes by Dundee and Arbroath towards the same destination, keeping south of the Sidlaw Hills. The Mons Graupius has been looked for in all these directions, since the older view that it was a general name for the range which divides the basin of the Tay from that of the Dee has been abandoned. Yet the ancient hypothesis, and a misreading of Grampius for Graupius, has imposed the wholly fictitious name of the "Grampian Hills" on modern geography books, which invariably mark the range that separates Aberdeenshire from Perthshire and Forfarshire with that designation. Something is to be said for each of the three routes named above: some spot north of Dunkeld would be a very natural place for the mustering of a Highland host, even at this early date, and if Agricola marched with the intention of fighting the enemy wherever he might be found, starting from his great base-camp at Inchtuthill, there are plenty of battle grounds up the Tay.[2]

[1] Presumably Southern Britons, as they were "longa pace exploratos" which could not include Brigantes or Ordovices or other recently subdued people. This is the only mention in Tacitus of British auxiliaries serving with the regular army (*Agricola*, § 29).

[2] For a long discussion of localities, ending in the selection of Delvine near Dunkeld, see Sir James Ramsay's *Foundations of England*, i. 71-75; General Roy, the first scientific investigator, pitched on Stonehaven, north of Montrose, arguing from the situation of real or supposed Roman camps. Mr. Skene contended for the neighbourhood of Blairgowrie, on the central route. But since modern explorations have shown that the great camp at Inchtuthill was Agricola's, and that he made a long march north, Delvine is much too far south. See George Macdonald, *Journal for Roman Studies*, 1919.

On the other hand the North British tribes seem to have been stronger and more numerous along the comparatively fertile and accessible lowlands of Forfarshire and Aberdeenshire than in the woods and moors of Athole, and a position somewhere about Cupar Angus best covers those regions against an enemy advancing from Perth. Yet again, Agricola had a fleet, and the temptation to keep in touch with it might well lead him along the coast-route by Dundee. In that case the natural position for the Caledonians to occupy would be somewhere north or south of Montrose. Yet since there is no mention of the vicinity of the sea to the battlefield in Tacitus, which even he would hardly omit in such a case, it seems safer to conclude that one of the two other routes was adopted by Agricola, and that the excursion of his fleet along the coast had been intended merely to distract the enemy. The student may make his choice between the valley of the Middle Tay and that of Cupar Angus as the situation of the Graupian Mount. Certainty is impossible.

The topography of the battlefield is as vague as its situation. We should gather from Tacitus that the Caledonians were arrayed at the point where the foot-hills of some considerable range touch the plain—their chariots and horsemen on the flat, their infantry in successive lines on the rising slope. The Romans were drawn up below them in front of their camp, with 8,000 auxiliary infantry forming the main line, 3,000 horse equally divided between the two wings, and the legionary foot (which consisted of the whole or the greater part of at least two legions) in reserve outside the camp. The whole force must have amounted to at least 16,000 men : it is improbable that the Caledonians can have put more in line, though they are credited with 30,000 men by Tacitus. But no Highland army throughout recorded history ever attained the historian's figure. A lively harangue is put into the mouth of Calgacus, the most noted of their chiefs, but it is obviously a rhetorical composition, as little to be trusted as any other set speech.

The operations are difficult to follow, but we gather that the Caledonians took the offensive, and that first the horse and chariots assailed the auxiliaries. As long as the fight was at arm's length, the long claymores and darts of the barbarians contended at no great disadvantage with the short sword and the lance. But when Agricola bade his infantry close, the enemy was driven back, their lack of armour and the inferiority of their long blades in hand-to-hand combat putting them at a great disadvantage. They then tried to get round the wings of the advancing auxiliaries, by throwing their reserves or rear lines upon the Roman flanks and rear. But the masses which attempted to execute this movement were charged and broken by Agricola's cavalry. The whole Caledonian army then sought refuge in some woods, which lay at the back of their position, and made pursuit difficult. Among the trees they turned upon the first of the victorious auxiliaries, and checked them : but on the approach of formed cohorts they gave way again, and melted off in small bodies through fastnesses where they could not be followed. Agricola lost one praefect of a cohort, a certain Aulus Atticus, and about 360 men; he estimated the loss of the enemy at 10,000 men, an impossible figure, though no doubt many Caledonians had fallen in the *mêlée*, before they could escape into the woods.

But the battle had not made the Romans masters of Caledonia : next morning they could see the smoke of many villages on the horizon : this meant that the enemy had burnt their abodes, and were going up into the mountains, in order to continue the war. Only one tribe, the Boresti, probably the people of Forfarshire, submitted and gave hostages. The season was now far advanced, and seeing that it was no triumphal march to Cape Wrath that awaited him, but the continuance of a campaign in the wilderness, Agricola took his army back to winter quarters somewhere nearer his base—presumably on the Firth of Tay. He directed his fleet, however, to undertake a daring voyage round the northern end of Britain, and to return by the Irish Sea and the Channel.[1] This was accomplished without disaster : the fleet touched at the Orkneys, where a landing was made and the submission of some natives received. It is said to have seen Thule a " land of snow and winter " in the far distance—apparently this must have been Foula or even Sumburgh Head at the south point of Shetland. Then coasting down the western side of Britain, past a hundred rugged isles, the galleys rounded Land's End, ran up the Channel, and reached Portus

---

[1] The account of this voyage is not given by Tacitus in its natural place, *Agricola*, § 38, where it is only said that the governor ordered the fleet to circumnavigate Britain. But the details are given in § 10. That this was the voyage in question is proved from Dio Cassius, xlvi. § 20.

Trutulensis [1] (a harbour whose site is unfortunately not identifiable) in time to winter.   This was, strangely enough, not the actual first passage of the Pentland Firth by Roman soldiers.   Tacitus records that in the preceding year, 83, a cohort of Usipii, untrustworthy German levies, who were quartered somewhere on the west coast of Britain (probably in Galloway), mutinied, murdered their officers, seized three ships, and coasted amid a thousand dangers [2] round the northern cape of Britain, from whence, striking across the North Sea, they reached Germany, only to be fallen upon by the Suebi and Frisii, who slew some and made slaves of the rest.   It was through certain captives, who were sold in the markets of the Rhine, that the Romans heard what was the end of the mutinous cohort.   Dio Cassius says that the story of their adventures had reached Agricola by the autumn of 84, and was the cause of his sending his fleet to make from east to west that passage of the Pentland Firth which the Usipii had already made from west to east.[3]

Before the campaigning season of 85 came round, and, as it appears, during the early months of that year, Agricola was recalled by Domitian, and probably superseded by one Sallustius Lucullus, who was certainly governor of Britain a year or so later.   Tacitus ascribes the sudden summons to Rome received by his father-in-law as caused by the emperor's jealousy for one who seemed to be acquiring a military reputation of a splendid and unique character. He says that Domitian imagined that every one was comparing the real victories of his legate with the hollow and fictitious triumphs which he himself had claimed over the Germans in A.D. 83.   "He feared above all things that the name of a simple citizen should be exalted higher than that of the sovereign : . . . to be considered the only great general is a prerogative of the emperor."

But though Domitian may have been both jealous and timid, he had good political reasons for recalling Agricola.   The great general had now been campaigning for seven years in Britain, and despite all his victories the end of the war still seemed far off.   It

[1] The fleet reached Portus Trutulensis "proximo Britanniae latere lecto omni," the "nearer" shore being the Channel coast, and that of the North Sea, probably this unidentifiable port was on the Firth of Forth, convenient to Agricola's army.

[2] They are said to have been driven to cannibalism from sheer famine during their long voyage.

[3] Xiphilinus, *Epitome of Dio*, xlvi. § 20.

must certainly have been most expensive both in men and in money, but this was not the worst. The emperor had matters on hand upon the continent, which seemed to him more important than the conquest of Northern Britain. His German war of 83 had been brought to a successful close, but it had ended in a forced annexation of great districts beyond the Rhine, for which garrison troops were badly needed. And it appears that in 85 new fighting began in Germany, while in 84 there seem to have been serious troubles on the Danube—at any rate in that year Domitian was saluted as *imperator* for the sixth and seventh time on account of victories in Pannonia or Moesia. Troops were so badly needed that a detachment (*vexillatio*) of the Ninth Legion was actually borrowed from Britain in 83, though Agricola was in the midst of his sixth campaign. Apparently in 85, just after his recall, the whole legion Second Adjutrix was hastily brought over and moved to the Danube, where it took part in the Dacian wars. There is good reason, therefore, to think that Domitian put an end to Agricola's aggressive campaigns in the North mainly because he could not afford to allow them to continue, when troops were required to guard much more vital points of the empire.[1]

Nor, despite of all the innuendos of Tacitus, does it seem that the emperor failed to show his appreciation of the great services which Agricola had done to the empire. Alone of all the generals of his time he was granted triumphal honours, and (no small favour under "the bald Nero") he retained his life and his high position till the day of his death in 93, surviving unmolested through eight years of a tyranny that was ever growing worse. Even his son-in-law does not pretend to credit the story that he died by secret poison administered by Domitian's orders, though (after his usual wont) he inserts the rumour in his biography.

[1] For a good note on Domitian's probable motives see Gsell's *L'Empereur Domitien*, 172-75.

CHAPTER VII

FROM DOMITIAN TO COMMODUS (85-180 A.D.)

WITH the recall of Agricola the progress of the Imperial arms northward stopped short. There was no immediate evacuation of the lands beyond Tyne and Solway, and several of their military stations show signs of having been held for many years. More than one of these were destroyed, rebuilt, and destroyed again, and by the beginning of the second century the North was completely out of hand. Nothing is clearer than that Agricola's Caledonian campaigns were only possible because the Brigantes kept quiet, and it seems that, soon after his disappearance from Britain, that unquiet race burst out into fierce and obstinate rebellion. The army of the province was not numerous enough to garrison every strategical point up to the Tay, and at the same time to provide a competent force for field operations. When Agricola was fighting at the Graupian Mount the line of communication behind him must have been desperately thin, for (as has been already said) there was no solid base nearer than Eburacum. The camps and castles on Tyne and Solway, on Forth and Clyde, were not self-sufficing centres of military strength, but newly-established strongholds in an enemy's country, which needed to be revictualled constantly, and to have every item of munitions of war, perhaps even of food, brought up from the distant South.

Whether the Brigantes flared up in insurrection the moment that Agricola had departed, or whether they waited till, very shortly after, one of the four British legions—the Second Adjutrix—was withdrawn to the Danube, we have no means of knowing. The later British wars of Domitian are not chronicled even in the unsatisfactory style in which those of his earlier years are preserved. Presumably the garrisons left by Agricola beyond Tyne and Solway were attacked by the Caledonians. The Brigantian rising may have been simultaneous with troubles further North or posterior to them: we have no authorities to tell us which was cause and which effect, any more than we have information as to the details of the strife.   All we know is that in the later years of Domitian there was bitter trouble in all the lands that Agricola had conquered, and that the Brigantes were perpetually in arms.   Juvenal speaks of the daily life of the professional soldie⸱ as being " to destroy the huts of the Moors or the castles of the Brigantes ".[1]   In another passage he guesses that the best and greatest news that Domitian would have liked to receive was that the Briton Arviragus (a Brigantian king, no doubt) might have fallen dead from his war-chariot.[2]   The evidence of archæology clearly proves that the hold of Rome on anything north of the Tees and Morecambe Bay in this period was precarious.   There are hardly any inscriptions that date before the year 120 north of York and Lancaster, and inscriptions are the best proof of settled and permanent occupation.   The evidence of the coins dug up at many fortified places — Brough on the Derwent, Slack by Huddersfield, Templeborough near Rotheram, Melandra Castle near Glossop, Castleshaw above Oldham—shows that garrisons had to be kept up, even at the south end of the Pennine Chain, from the time of Domitian down to that of Hadrian.   If the Peak district and the West Riding had to be held down by force, it is clear that things must have been far worse on Tweed or Tyne.   Yet recent excavation shows that far into the early years of the second century many of the Lowland forts were still held.   We must think of Sallustius Lucullus and Metilius Nepos, the two governors of Domitian's later years, as campaigning continually, and not always with success, on the moors and hills between the Ouse and Mersey, as well as on more northern ground.

It is noteworthy, however, that we have no evidence from the spade or from literary sources to show that troubles were prevalent in the other quarter where they might have been expected, the west side of Central Britain.   Indeed the occupation of some of the Roman forts in Wales seems to have ceased about the time of Trajan, as if they were no longer required for the keeping down of the population,[3] and legionaries drawn from the Welsh garrison of Isca

---

[1] *Satires*, xiv. 196.   [2] *Ibid.*, iv. 126.

[3] The last coin from the great fort of Gellygaer is of Nerva. See J. Ward on that station, in the recently published monograph dealing with it (1909).

Silurum were being freely used in Brigantian territory in Hadrian's day—a clear proof that they had no pressing work nearer home.

Indeed this was the period in which all Southern Britain was being rapidly and steadily Romanised, after the fashion set by Agricola. Wars had ceased out of the land south of Humber and Mersey, and the road-system and the commerce that followed it were penetrating all the province, save the remote south-western peninsula beyond Exeter, and the inaccessible hills of Mid Wales. It was now as Juvenal sarcastically remarked that "the fluent Gaul was giving lessons to the British pleaders, and that Thule was seriously thinking of hiring a professor of elocution". The towns were growing in size, wealth and splendour; Nerva made Glevum a colony (96-98), and probably Lindum attained the same dignity within the same generation. Glevum, which had long ceased to be a garrison town, must have gained its distinction purely as the commercial centre of the Severn Valley, whose fertile southern slopes are more thickly strewn with the remains of Roman villas than almost any other district of Britain. Lindum, also happily placed on a high road in the centre of a well-cleared district, evidently survived as an already existing town of importance when the legion which had been its garrison was moved on to Eburacum early in the Flavian period, perhaps about 80 A.D. Most of all must London have been growing in importance, though it never attained either colonial or municipal rank. But more objects of artistic merit and intrinsic value are dug up from the ruins of Roman London than from any other town in the province. We may guess that its public squares were better decorated than those of many places that had higher official rank, when we look on the splendid head of the bronze statue of Hadrian in the British Museum, almost the best piece of Roman work that has been found in this island. It was dredged up from the Thames, a beautiful fragment, probably dropped by some fifth-century spoiler, who had broken up the colossus purely for the sake of the fine yellow bronze of which it was composed.

The lesser towns of the south, centres of tribal commerce, or places happily placed at the junction of great high-roads, like Calleva or Corinium, or sought for other reasons like Aquae Sulis,[1] the spa frequented by so many invalids of all ages, were all steadily

---

[1] The earliest Bath inscription is as old as Vespasian.

growing in prosperity, and no doubt acting as centres for the
diffusion of Roman civilisation and the Latin tongue.

Nothing can be more definite and well marked than the evidence
that the higher civilisation of the conquerors destroyed within two
or three generations the lower national culture of the conquered.
Celtic art had a peculiar character of its own, which it is impossible
to mistake, and countless British finds bear witness to the fact that
it was alive and flourishing when Claudius crossed the Channel.[1]
But it could not stand against the world-culture of the Romans.
The Briton preferred the classical type when it was presented to
him, even in inferior and second-hand examples, to his own ancestral
work, just as the native artisan of India to-day is prone to cast
away the time-honoured patterns of the East and to copy the most
commonplace European models. On the whole it is true to say that
from the second century onwards there was hardly any Celto-Roman
art in Britain, but only Provincial-Roman art, an art that cannot
easily be distinguished from that which prevailed in other remote
and rough western parts of the empire, such as Lusitania or Armorica. Even the ordinary better-class crockery of daily life was imported from Gaul, or copied at first and second hand from the
Aretine ware of Italy itself. The careful archæologist detects a few
weak survivals of old Celtic tradition in the so-called "Castor
ware" of the East Midlands, or the pottery of the New Forest,
both of which show scroll work and returning spirals with affinities
to the pre-Roman style, and delight in conventionalised animal and
vegetable forms that are not copied from the usual provincial types
of the West. But such exceptions were survivals of an isolated sort
in an ocean of commonplace work, directly borrowed from the conquering race. Nor is it even the case that the towns, with their
partially immigrant population, shared in the monotonous culture of
the empire, but that Celtic life survived in the villages. Just as the
better houses in a south country hamlet copied the hypocausts and
tesselated pavements of the Roman, in poor style and with cheap
material, so did their inhabitants grow into using mean imitations
of Roman utensils, pottery, and metal-work. Rural Britain soon
grew to be provincial and not barbarous in its outer aspect, though

---

[1] For all these see Haverfield's "Romanisation of Roman Britain," in *Proceedings of the British Academy* for 1907.

it was but a poor province, and though the village people were as
far behind the southern Gauls of the open country, as the towns
people fell short of the inhabitants of Arles or Narbonne in wealth
and splendour. We must only except from this generalisation certain districts of Britain where the population was very thin, where
the great roads never penetrated, and where no towns arose to
diffuse civilisation around them, such as the Dumnonian peninsula
west of Exeter, Mid-Wales, and the wooded districts of the western
Midlands, where the whole land was covered by the vast forests of
which Arden and Wyre were the medieval survivals.

The Romanisation of exterior culture was accompanied by the
Romanisation of religion. Like so many other provincials of the
West, the Britons proceeded to make rough identifications between
their own divinities and the Romano-Greek pantheon of their conquerors. Mabon was identified with Apollo, Sulis with Minerva,
Belatucadrus with Mars, and so forth. In the process of time the
Celtic appellation became a mere epithet of the Divinity, or was
forgotten altogether. The larger half of the altars and shrines
discovered in Britain are simply set up to honour the ordinary gods
of the Roman world. But in some cases the native divinities lingered
on as objects of local worship, and we find all through the second
century dedications to forgotten powers with strange names such as
Nodons (or Nudens), Antenociticus, Ancasta, Cocidius, and Coventina
(this last a spring-goddess on the Northumbrian wall). So little
remains to us of the prehistoric Celtic mythology that we can
generally make no guess as to the character of these local survivors
from it. It is interesting to find that the well-known Roman practice of making divinities out of personifications of regions, virtues,
moral qualities, etc., was fully acclimatised in this province. Not
only Britain herself,[1] but Brigantia, the personification of the
North,[2] had altars and statues. Victory, Fortune, Peace, Bonus
Eventus, even Discipline (a deity not always worshipped in practice
by the British army) are adored by various votaries. Caesar-worship,
the most typical development of the religion of the Roman empire,
is found widely spread. The number of dedications to the divinity

[1] She is " Britannia Sancta " in a York inscription, C. I. L., 232.

[2] She is " Dea Brigantia" in some cases. She is found adored at Birrens
(Dumfriesshire), Addle (near Leeds), on the Irthing near Naworth, and elsewhere in
the North. Her statue is a Minerva-like figure with helm and shield.

of the emperor (*Numen Augusti*) or emperors, or to his or their
"genius" which are extant, is as great as that of the dedications to
any one of the old gods.   Equally characteristic signs of the cosmo-
politan nature of the pantheon of the Roman world are the number
of deities adored in Britain who are neither members of the orthodox
Olympian family nor survivors from Celtic heathendom.   Merchants
and soldiers from every land, Gaul, Spain, Germany, or Syria,
brought with them their devotion to strange divinities, Ricagam-
beda and Harimella, the Dea Syria, Mithras,[1] Contrebis, and all
manner of other aliens, and raised altars to them on the western
soil to which they had been led by the chances of trade or of military service.

Of the political organisation of Britain, outside the few towns
which had been granted the rights of a colony or a *municipium*,
we could till lately do no more than make speculations.   Inscriptions mentioning the *civitas* of the Catuvellauni and the Dumnonians had been found,[2] but they were too short to allow any
deductions to be made from them.   Fortunately a monument was
discovered at Caerwent in 1903 and another at Wroxeter in 1924,
which made it clear that Britain was, like Gaul, organised in large
cantons bearing the names of the old tribes.   The Caerwent inscription is put up in honour of an ex-governor, by decree of the Senate
"of the community of the state of the Silures".[3]   The Wroxeter
one is in honour of Hadrian, dedicated by the state of the
Cornovii.   If these western tribes in remoter corners of Britain had
regular cantons and senates, and were organised into "civitates,"
we cannot doubt that all the other regions of the south
were governed by similar institutions.   The Wroxeter inscription shows that these constitutions are as early as the reign of
Hadrian.   There is no reason why some, or all, of them may not
date back to the time of the governorship of Agricola, that
great organiser and innovator, who (as we have already seen)
trained Britain into civilised ways.   It is to be imagined that the
"civitates" of Britain were fairly large, that they represented units

---

[1] Mithras got a wonderful popularity in the third century, and was worshipped
not by Oriental immigrants only but by many a western citizen or soldier.   His
chapels have been found under the wall of Severus.

[2] C. I. L., 775 and 863.   Both found on the Northumbrian wall.

[3] "Ex decreto ordinis, respublica civitatis Silurum."   The governor's name, at
the head of the inscription, is unfortunately knocked away.

into which many of the smaller tribes of the first century had coalesced. It may be noted that in Ptolemy's statistical picture of Britain there are only seventeen tribes south of the line from Tyne to Solway, which represented in his day the boundary of the province. We do not find in him the names of the small tribes mentioned by Caesar, the Bibroci, Ancalites, Segontiaci, or Cassi, nor of Tacitus's Deceangi or Jugantes. It seems certain that the race had been gathering together into larger units since the day of Caesar: though whether this mainly came about owing to the wars of the house of Cunobelinus and its rivals, before the coming of Claudius, or whether it was the work of the Roman administrator a generation or two later, we cannot tell. But it is pretty certain that cantonal names of the second century, like those of the Belgae or the Cantii, and probably of the Atrebates also, represent several of the older and smaller units confederated together. Of the seventeen *civitates* some must have been immeasurably larger and more wealthy than others : some, the Cantii, Belgae, Iceni, had very large and well-peopled territory : others like the Durotriges of Dorsetshire, and the Atrebates of Berkshire, had narrow limits : others again like the Cornavii in the Midlands or the Dumnonii in the extreme south-west, represented very thinly peopled and poor districts. Yet, as the inscription quoted above shows us, there was certainly a *civitas* of the Dumnonii—and presumably, therefore, all the other tribes had each become a regular canton.

The North had yet to be reconquered rather than reorganised. The lands beyond the lines of Agricola's forts between Tyne and Solway had certainly been lost for some time when Hadrian came to Britain in the year 120. The Brigantes were in arms and had cut up a Roman force. We have only allusions to the disaster, but Fronto's statement that "a great number of soldiers were slain by the Britons in the reign of Hadrian"[1] must surely be put in juxtaposition with the fact that the garrison-legion of York, the IX. Hispana, suddenly disappears from the imperial muster rolls at this moment.[2] It was the rarest thing in the world in the earlier empire for a legion to be reduced : indeed this only happened as the result either of utter extermination (such as that of the XVII., XVIII., XIX.,

---

[1] Fronto, *De Bello Parthico*, 107. See Mommsen's *Roman History*, v. 171.

[2] It was still existing in Trajan's day, as an inscription at York dated in the year 108-109 shows. C. I. L., 241.

who fell to the last man in Varus's German disaster) or of disband-
ment for specially bad cases of treason and mutiny (the fate of the
old First Legion and certain others that joined Civilis in A.D. 70).
We can hardly doubt that the former was the case with the IX.
Hispana: that it must have been exterminated in some unrecorded
Brigantian battle. This, probably, was the reason why the emperor
crossed himself to Britain in 120, probably bringing with him the
Sixth Legion, which we know to have been transferred from the
Rhine to Britain at this moment. It replaced the vanished IX.
Hispana at York, and is found garrisoned there down to the last
years of the Roman dominion in Britain, when the famous *Notitia
Dignitatum* was drawn up about 400 A.D. An inscription found
in Italy gives us the information that detachments (vexillationes) of
three other Rhine legions (VII. Gemina, VIII. Augusta, XXII.
Primigenia), also came over to Britain for the "expeditio Britannica" of Hadrian, a fact borne out by the fact that a shield-boss
belonging to the second of these corps has been found in the Tyne
near Newcastle, and an inscription belonging to the last-named
exists at Abbotsford.

It is one of the saddest mischances of British history that we
have no detailed account of Hadrian's British expedition. The
man himself was a character of strange and fascinating interest—
by nature a dilettante and a man of pleasure, he was by the chance
of an intrigue placed at the helm of the empire. He rose to the
occasion, and made an admirable emperor, though the routine of
his work must often have been most distasteful to his wayward
spirit. The literary and artistic matters in which his real interest
lay had to be put behind him, while he was absorbed in questions
of frontier policy, taxation, or political organisation. But his in-
satiable and intelligent curiosity as to the world at large, and his
resolve that if things had to be done they must be done well, carried
him through twenty years of incessant travel and heartbreaking
toil, and at the end a grateful empire rightly honoured "Divus
Hadrianus," of the *animula vagula blandula*, that loved jests and
pleasure yet turned unwillingly but manfully to hard work.

On crossing the British Channel in the third year of his reign,
Hadrian, as his biographer Spartian informs us, "found many things
to put right in Britain"—the reorganisation of a depleted army and
the repression of the revolt of the Brigantes were but a part of his

work.   Yet no historian has thought fit to leave us a record of what
the emperor's jesting friend Florus called his "walking about Britain."
Only coins commemorate his review of the British legions, his
"advent," and his "restoration" of the province. The largest work
which he left behind him, as the memorial of his reign, was the great
wall between Tyne and Solway, which marked a determined and
successful effort to put an end to the disorders of the north.   It
was built after his departure, as the dating of the inscriptions found
on many points of its course indicate.   He left Britain, apparently, in
121 A.D., and the wall-inscriptions mainly date from 123-4, when
the governor Aulus Plaetorius Nepos was busy all along the chosen
line, with detachments of military masons drawn not only from the
VI. Victrix, the York Legion, and the auxiliaries of the North, but
from the other British legions, II. Augusta from Isca, and XX.
Valeria Victrix from Deva.   We cannot, however, doubt that the
wall was the emperor's own inspiration, and that he had surveyed
the ground on which it was to run, while he was present in person in
the British Islands.   Clearly he must have visited York, to inspect
the newly arrived legion, and to form his own views as to the best
way of dealing with the troublesome Brigantes.   And, once in Brigantian territory, he must have been drawn up to take a view of the
short line between Tyne and Solway, on which he must have found,
occupied or unoccupied, Agricola's forts, and to form his own conclusions as to their suitability as a base for operating against the
rebels.   The idea of shutting in these hillmen by drawing a line
of garrisons along their northern frontier certainly dated back to
Agricola, as we have seen in the last chapter . yet these garrisons
had proved inadequate to restrain Brigantian revolts, for the enemy
could pass between and around them, and could summon through
their gaps succours from the remoter North.   Though the country
between Tyne and Forth was, as far as we can judge, thinly inhabited,
it must nevertheless have owned a certain amount of untamed raiders,
and beyond Forth the Caledonians were both numerous and enterprising.   The design of Hadrian's Wall seems to have been to oppose
a very solid barrier to the peoples of the North—all its fortification
is turned in that direction—and at the same time to provide a chain
of garrisons which would be useful against the Brigantes; though the
main task of repressing the latter would fall upon the troops sown thick
in forts and castles among the strategical centres of the Pennine Chain

The works which fall into the period 121-124 and must be associated with the name of Hadrian are (setting aside the isolated castles south of the line from Tyne to Solway) (1) a great ditch between mounds, which archæologists have usually called the *vallum* though the *limes* would be a better name; and (2) a wall of good hewn stone running close on the northern side of the ditch, at a distance of not more than a few hundred yards from it; (3) between wall and *limes* runs a fine military road.

The *limes* is essentially a non-military work. It may mark the definite civil boundary of the province of Britain, and this was probably its object, but it cannot serve any end of defence. It consists of a deeply cut ditch, the earth of which has been thrown up into high banks on each side of the artificial hollow, probably with additional soil from remoter ground added. The bank on the northern side is the loftier of the two, and single: that on the southern side is double, there being a smaller mound on the very edge of the ditch, and a larger one some twenty feet further out. The central hollow itself seems to have been flat-bottomed, and with sides sloping outward at a rather obtuse angle, so that it averages fifteen feet broad at the bottom and thirty at the top. Its depth is only some seven or eight feet. It is separated by a berme, some twenty-five feet wide, from the northern mound. On the south side there is no berme, the smaller of the two banks running quite close to the edge of the ditch : this accumulation of soil may have been the result of a supplementary cleaning out of the ditch at some time after its original excavation. The engineer who was responsible for the first digging probably caused the earth to be carried twenty or thirty feet away from the edge of the ditch on both sides, lest it should slip back again. The cleaner of the ditch more carelessly threw his upcast all on to the southern side, and left it quite close to the brink. The mounds, it must be repeated, are wholly unsuitable as a line of defence either against the north or the south. They are rough deposits of excavated earth, not shaped away so as to give a sharp face either on one side or the other. Nor is there any trace of a road, either on the berme behind the northern mound or at the bottom of the ditch—the only places where a road could conceivably have run. There are no bridges and few marked crossing-places visible along the eighty miles of the *limes*. But where it lies close behind forts on the line of the Wall, which we are now about to discuss, it has generally been worn down or filled up. This seems to prove that the garrisons of such forts in later ages found it inconvenient, and either gradually trod it into non-existence, or deliberately threw rubble into it, in order to level it up for convenient egress.

(2) To proceed to the Wall. Much evidence was once produced to show that the solid stone structure now visible on the Northumbrian Moors is not Hadrian's original work, but a reconstruction by Severus.[1] It was argued that since Hadrian generally chose the best course possible, the later stone wall runs exactly on top of his structure : that there is only one short section where his work still remains intact, viz., in the stretch of between two and three miles, to the west of the fort of Birdoswald (Amboglanna), where the stone wall takes a curve further than usual from the limes, in order to obtain a rather better and more commanding slope. At this point we can survey a wall of sods, the rest of whose course lies buried below the line of the stone wall. We find that it was, like the later Clyde to Forth wall of Antoninus Pius, built of turf solidly laid in regular courses, and not of stone. Some support for the theory that Hadrian built a turf wall, and that Severus rebuilt it in stone, might be got from the one classical author who mentions the two walls together. Julius Capitolinus says that Antoninus Pius, " Britannos per Lollium Urbicum legatum vicit, alio muro cespiticio submotis barbaris ducto ".[2] This, translated in the most natural fashion, might mean that the first wall (Hadrian's) as well as the second (that of Pius) was a murus cespiticius, made of sods, like the western part of that traceable from Forth to Clyde. Many antiquaries have argued that Hadrian built a turf wall only, of which the above-mentioned three miles near Birdoswald is the only surviving trace, and that Severus replaced the structure by a solid wall of stone; several classical authors, indeed, attribute a stone wall to Severus, though none of those who do so state that he built it over a ruder line of Hadrian's date. Recent excavation, however, seems to lead to the undeniable conclusion that Severus was only a restorer, and that the stone wall, like the limes, was the work of Hadrian. The surviving fragmentary patch of turf wall would seem to be a sort of "first draft" which Hadrian's engineers

---

[1] Since I wrote this chapter in 1909 so much new evidence has come up, to show that Hadrian built the stone, as well as the turf, wall, that the controversy may be considered settled.

[2] Capitolinus, de Antonino Pio, c. 5.

promptly corrected, on finding a better line a few hundred yards to the north. Possibly there was a turf wall thrown up all along from Solway to Tyne, which was replaced by the more costly and permanent stone wall within a year or two.

Hadrian's Wall, then, a solid stone wall, strengthened with forts at frequent intervals, must be considered to be represented, both for direction and for character, by the existing structure, though Severus, and perhaps other builders, made many repairs. It runs roughly parallel to the *limes*, sometimes within a few yards of it, sometimes at a distance of as much as 500 yards from it. For the *limes* seeks the shortest and easiest course, since it has no military purpose, while the wall habitually diverges from the line of the *limes*, in order to seek higher and more defensible ground, wherever the latter is taken along localities unfavourable for defence against an attack from the North. At the highest point of its course, between Aesica and Procolitia (Great Chesters and Carrawburgh), the wall climbs to the edge of a steep ridge, with frequent cliffs along its northern face, while the ditch and mounds forming the *limes* pursue their even way at the south foot of the slope, at distances varying from 250 to 500 yards from the summit of the ridge. In short, the wall dominates the whole of the ground over which an attack from the North would come, while the *limes* would be completely commanded by an enemy established on the higher slopes of the ridge along which the wall runs.

The full length of Hadrian's wall is stated by his biographer Spartianus at eighty Roman miles, which fairly corresponds with the seventy-three English miles between Segedunum (Wallsend) on the Tyne and Bowness (Gabrosentum ?) on the Solway. The wall continues for some miles at each of its ends after the *limes* has come to an end. The latter stopped when it reached tidal water at the head of the Solway Firth; the wall was extended some way along the estuary, in order to prevent out-flanking by enemies who might cross the tidal flats at low water,[1] or come across the head of the firth in small boats. Hadrian's forts, many of them on sites already chosen by Agricola, seem to be the same fifteen visible

---

[1] See later, under the reign of Severus, for statements by Roman historians as to the way in which the uncivilized Briton or Caledonian would cross tidal marshes where the legionary could not follow him (p. 132).

to-day along the wall. In some cases they were certainly smaller than those which now exist, but the localities seem to have kept, even when structural additions were made by later builders. The considerable number of inscribed stones, bearing the names of the emperor and his legate Aulus Plaetorius Nepos, which are to be found along the wall, all appear to have come originally from the stone structures, gates, stores, official residences, etc., belonging to the forts. None of them, unfortunately, record the character of the building which they commemorated. The majority, however, state that the building, whatever it was, had been the work of a legion; several have the name of the legion from Isca, II. Augusta, or that of the Chester Legion XX. Valeria Victrix. More than one has been taken from its original place, in order to be used in building or repairing the stone wall under Severus, ninety years after it had been set up in Hadrian's time. The Romans had as little scruple in using up old material in this fashion as had the mediæval builders, who afterwards wrecked Severus's patchings in order to build churches or farm-houses.[1]

There are enough inscriptions belonging to the Antonine period along the line of Hadrian's Wall to enable us to say that, although the building of it was largely done by the legions, yet the garrisoning of it was handed over entirely to the auxiliary cohorts and *alae*. Indeed many of these units, first placed on the wall by Hadrian, seem to have retained their position there for a century, some for two centuries and more. The First Dacian cohort, whose name Aelia shows that it was raised, or at least honoured, by Hadrian, seems to have been at Birdoswald (Amboglanna) from its first coming to Britain down to the moment when the *Notitia Dignitatum* was drawn up about the year 400 A.D. Several others of the auxiliary garrisons can be traced back from the *Notitia* well into the time of the Antonines, and if we find them localised by 150 or 160 in the places where they still lay in 400, we may fairly suppose that their original placing goes back to the first builder of the wall himself. Other units which leave record of themselves on the Wall in the second century have been superseded by new-comers in the third. But on the whole, there was singularly

---

[1] See Professor Haverfield's paper on the Epigraphy of Hadrian's Wall in *Proceedings of the Society of Antiquaries*, for 1892.

little change in the composition of the army of Northern Britain from first to last.[1]

In dealing with the British army of the second, third and fourth centuries, we must guard ourselves against the natural idea, drawn from our knowledge of earlier Roman days, that the soldiery, whether legionary or auxiliary, were wholly alien to the population of the province. From the time of the Antonines onwards it is certain that both legions and cohorts were growing more and more closely connected by ties of blood with the provincials among whom they were quartered. The change had begun in the time of Vespasian. Down to his reign the recruits of the legions in the West had been largely Italians, all citizens born, the remainder being supplied by a *delectus* held mainly in the old senatorial provinces, which had long been incorporated in the empire, and had lost all national feeling, such as Baetica and Gallia Narbonensis. The men so drawn were of free birth, and received the citizenship on being enrolled : they mixed freely and without difficulty with the purely Italian element among their comrades. The legion was usually Roman in feeling, and alien to the district in which it was quartered. Such were the corps which fought in Britain under Aulus Plautius or Suetonius Paulinus. But Vespasian put an end to the levying of legionaries in Italy, and seems to have laid down the rule that only the Praetorian Guard should for the future be raised from the inhabitants of the peninsula. Legionary tombstones show that while plenty of Italians were serving in every western legion when Vespasian came to the throne, and for some years later, they had almost disappeared from the ranks by the end of the reign of his son Domitian.

So far as the inscriptions allow us to trace the nationality of legionary recruits after the change made by Vespasian, it would

---

[1] A bronze tablet found at Riveling near Sheffield (C. I. L., 1195) contains a list of cohorts and *alae* serving in the eighth year of Hadrian's Tribunician Power within Britain. There are twenty-one cohorts and six *alae*. Of their names those of three *alae* are lost. There remain three *alae* and all the twenty-one cohorts. Of these troops serving in 124 there still survive in the *Notitia Dignitatum*, compiled about the year 400, at least two *alae* and nine cohorts. After the wear and tear of nearly three centuries this is astonishing. Moreover there are several more units, whose names do not happen to occur in this tablet (since no soldiers belonging to them chance to have been granted privileges in it), yet which were certainly in Britain under Hadrian and still survive in the *Notitia*, *e.g.*, I. Aelia Dacorum, named above in the text.

seem that in the days of his dynasty, and in the following time of Nerva and Trajan, the policy was carried out of keeping the composition of the legions very heterogeneous. The *delectus* was carried out in different provinces every year, so that each corps was formed of strata (so to speak) of different provincials. A western legion would have all its recruits one year from South Gaul, and the next from South Spain. But in the time of Hadrian (a great innovator in all things) a new tendency comes to the front. We get a decided commencement of local recruiting, of the telling-off of the conscripts of each province to the legions quartered in it or near it. Nothing could better mark the complete absorption of old tribal nationalities in the common Roman name, than the fact that it had now become possible to think of levying homogeneous legions from the population of the provinces in which they were quartered. In Britain this plan was not carried out so fully as in Gaul or Spain, because the civilised Latin-speaking communities suitable for the providing of legionary recruits were few. But nevertheless the legions became largely Britonised in another way : an enormous proportion of recruits in the second and following centuries were provided from the legions themselves, by children born in the camp who took up their father's profession. And as the legionary almost invariably married a provincial wife, from the district in which he was quartered, his sons were semi-British. There was a danger, therefore, that as the proportion of locally connected recruits continued to grow, the legions would grow "particularist," and think of themselves as provincials rather than Romans. This danger did not happen in the days of the Antonines, but showed itself clearly in the following century, when each provincial army represented not merely a military but a racial unit, with a close *esprit de corps*, and a rancorous jealousy of the legionary armies of other provinces. This simple fact was at the bottom of all the civil wars of the third century.

If the legions grew Britonised from Hadrian's time onward, the case was far more so with the auxiliaries. Vespasian was the innovator in this branch of army organisation, as well as in the branch of recruiting for the legions. But his changes had not been in the same direction. Under the early empire, down to 69, an auxiliary cohort was normally both raised from the tribe whose name it bore, and quartered fairly near its recruiting centre. Batavians served

with the army of the Lower Rhine, Gauls with the army of the
Upper Rhine, Moors in Africa, and so forth.   But the great revolt
of Civilis, which gave so much trouble to Vespasian, showed that it
was dangerous to keep auxiliary cohorts garrisoned among their
own countrymen.   From that time the large majority of them
were sent to do duty far afield—Moors even to northern Britain,
Britons to Dacia, Syrians to the Danube.   This arrangement
rendered the preservation of the national character of each regiment
very difficult : instead of requiring recruits to be brought from
thousands of miles away, the local military authorities would be
tempted to accept eligible men who could be obtained nearer the
place where the cohort was quartered.   By the time of the Antonines the composition of the auxiliary regiments very largely ceased
to bear any relation to their titles.   Some corps kept up their
national recruiting better than others : in Britain it seems that the
Tungrian and Batavian auxiliaries were still mainly Tungrian or
Batavian in the third century.   But cohorts or *alae* brought
from much further afield, like Dacians, Thracians, or Moors, could
not be kept national, and got more and more filled up with local
recruits.   We have clear instances of Brigantians serving in their
own country in a cohort that was nominally Thracian,[1] and so forth.
When in the third century the empire was broken up for long
years into fractions dominated by different rulers, *e.g.*, in the long
" Gaulish empire " that lasted from 258 to 274, or the " British
empire " of Carausius and Allectus, which lasted from 287 to 296,
a cohort of Thracians or Moors garrisoned in Britain cannot have
had for many years a single recruit of its nominal nationality, since
Mauretania or Thrace were not in the hands of the usurping
emperor acknowledged in Britain.   The cohorts continued to exist,
but were completed with western, and mainly no doubt British,
conscripts.

Hence from the time of Hadrian onward the auxiliaries, even
more than the legionaries, began to be closely connected with the
province in which they were quartered, and to possess a provincial
particularist feeling, identical with that of the people among whom
they dwelt.

Hadrian reigned for seven or eight years after the *limes* and

---

[1] *E.g.*, One Nictovelius son of Vindex "nationis Brigans" in the second
Thracian cohort C. I. L. 1090.

the great wall from Tyne to Solway had been completed in 123-24.
The frontier stood still, at the line where he had drawn it, only for
a few years longer, for in 140-41 it was carried forward to the line
of Forth and Clyde by Lollius Urbicus, the governor of Britain
under Antoninus Pius.   What led to this advance it is difficult to
conceive: possibly the Brigantes were considered to have been
finally tamed; they had settled down into a more or less delusive
quiet, since the garrisons along the wall had encompassed them and
cut them off from any connection with the North.   On the other
hand, the tribes between Solway and Forth, the Otadini, Novantae,
and Selgovae may have been giving trouble, yet have seemed weak
enough to be easily subdued, since there is every sign that their
country was but thinly inhabited.   The way to tame them would
be to encompass them with another wall, just as the Brigantes
had lately been surrounded by the first wall.   Troops for the holding of the first line might seem procurable without danger from
the garrisons of the forts in Brigantia, and on the Tyne-Solway
wall, where the number of cohorts could safely be cut down if the
unruly tribe was truly broken in spirit.   What happened can only
be gathered from inscriptions—the only mention of the movement
in the historians is the single sentence in Julius Capitolinus which
has been already quoted.[1]   But the inscriptions show us that Lollius
Urbicus took detachments from all the three British legions, the
second, sixth, and twentieth, and a number of auxiliary cohorts
drawn mainly from the Wall-garrisons, and with them advanced
across the Lowlands, and seized the narrow neck from Clyde to
Forth, which Agricola had already discovered sixty years before,
"the place where Britain is narrowest from ocean to ocean," as the
geographer of Ravenna very correctly observes.   He then built a
wall, of turf only in its western part, with a ditch from Carriden
on the Forth, near Abercorn, to Old Kilpatrick on the Clyde, a
distance of a little less than 37 miles.   At least sixteen forts lay
along this line, at intervals from each other much less than those
between the fifteen forts on Hadrian's wall.   A great road was
constructed to join the new wall to its military base on the south.
It started from Corstopitum (Corbridge) on the Tyne, and ran to
Abercorn on the Forth, having dotted along it large permanent
forts at Habitancium (Risinghame) and Bremenium (High Ro-

[1] See p. 113.

chester) in Northumberland, at Newstead on the Tweed near Melrose (Trimontium ?), and at Inveresk and Cramond, on each side of Edinburgh. Apparently a corresponding highway for the western side of the Lowlands must have been begun, but it was never completed. For a very large permanent camp was built at Blatum Bulgium (Birrens) in Dumfriesshire, and a visible road connects this fortress with Luguvallium (Carlisle) and the Solway end of Hadrian's Wall. But north of Birrens there is no clear continuation of this track, as might have been expected, towards the western end of the wall of Lollius Urbicus. Traces of a road can be discovered along the course of the Clyde, the direction which a way from Birrens to Old Kilpatrick must have taken. But Roman remains of all kinds are not common in Lanarkshire, while they are found in considerable quantities all along the road through Northumberland, Tweeddale, and Lothian, on which Habitancium, Bremenium, and Trimontium lie. The conquest of the western Lowlands, the modern Lanark, Ayr, and Galloway, can have amounted to nothing more than the submission of the local tribe, the Novantae, who did not receive garrisons among them like those on the eastern side, the Otadini and Selgovae. Though several of Agricola's old camps north of the wall, such as Ardoch, were rebuilt and regarrisoned, nothing was done in the West. The complete occupation and settlement of the district on the Irish Sea must have been postponed till that on the eastern shore should have been thoroughly finished. And this time was never to come, for the forty years of the occupation of the Lowlands were not a period of quiet advance, but one of trouble in the rear. The large majority of the monuments found beyond the Cheviots may be dated to the years of Antoninus Pius following the conquests of Lollius Urbicus (140-161); there is hardly anything from the time of Marcus Aurelius (161-181); and absolutely nothing from that of Commodus.[1] Coins give the same evidence: the finds along the wall of Lollius Urbicus, and at the camps behind it, like Cramond, Newstead, and Birrens, consist of coins of the time of Trajan, Hadrian, and Pius in great quantities, of a certain amount of those of Marcus Aurelius, and barely one or

---

[1] Of course undated inscriptions are hard to attribute with certainty. But such seems to be the case. The large majority of the inscribed stones belong to the first building operations of Lollius Urbicus, in 140-41.

two of Commodus and his wife Crispina.[1]   Clearly the evacuation
of the region must be placed at the very commencement of the
reign of the unworthy son of the philosophic Marcus.

The reason why Roman conquest never bit deep in the Lowlands
would seem to have been that about the end of the reign of Pius,
in the governorship of Julius Verus (*circ.* 155-158) the last great
revolt of the Brigantes took place.   It is only recorded in a paren-
thesis in Pausanias's [2] description of the Peloponnesus, a very strange
place in which to find a notice of a purely British affair—and the
note which there occurs is very puzzling in its language.   Pausanias
says that Antoninus had to punish the Brigantes by annexing a
great part of their territory, because they had dared to make armed
incursions into "the Genunian part" (τὴν Γενουνίαν μοῖραν) which
was subject to the Romans.   If we did not know that the Brigantes
had been already taken completely into the Empire by the building of Hadrian's Wall many years before, we should have supposed
that what Antoninus did was to appropriate part of the lands of a
tribe which had hitherto not been fully subdued.   But considering
the situation of affairs in 155 A.D., this is an impossible rendering.
The term "the Genunian part" is equally puzzling: there is no
mention elsewhere either in historians, geographers or inscriptions
of Genunians.   And we are at a loss why they are called a "part,"
and of what they were a part—was it of the Brigantes themselves?
Or is the curious phrase a translation of some Caledonian local name
—since the Picts at a later time divided themselves into "parts"
each with the word Dal (which has that meaning) prefixed to it.[3]
And why is stress laid on "the Genunian part" being subject to
Rome—as if the Brigantes themselves were not also within the
empire?   The whole statement of Pausanias is a riddle, and all
that we can deduce from it is that the Brigantes attacked other
Roman subjects, whether north or south of Hadrian's Wall, and
were severely punished for it, by part of their territory being removed from the authority of the tribal *civitas* and put under some
other form of administration.   That the subjection of the Brigantes
did not take place without a severe struggle seems proved by the fact

---

[1] See Dr. George Macdonald's admirable article on the Roman coin-finds of
Scotland in *Proceedings of the Society of Antiquaries of Scotland*, vol. of 1917-18,
pp. 203-207.

[2] Pausanias, viii. 43.

[3] See for this hypothesis Rhys's *Celtic Britain*, pp. 90, 91.

that military building all round their territory can be traced in the governorship of Julius Verus, whose inscriptions show that he restored forts as far south as Brough in Derbyshire, and as far north as Newcastle-on-Tyne, Birrens in Dumfriesshire and Netherby at the north-east end of the Solway Firth.[1]

It would seem that the revolt under Pius was the last struggle of the Brigantes, and that (whether because of the partition of their territory, or because their spirits were tamed at last) they gave no further trouble. Some, if not all, of the garrisons in their southern limits were evacuated in the third quarter of the second century, no doubt because they were no longer required. Such small traces of civilised Roman life as are found in their land seem to commence about the same time. Probably York got a new lease of life when the country outside its own immediate circle of plain became safe and peaceful. Isurium (Aldborough), fifteen miles further up the Ouse, must have developed into the flourishing little town that can be restored from its remains, about the same time. Corstopitum (Corbridge) the northernmost town, as opposed to a mere military station, in Britain, may have made its start earlier, as being the base-depot for the road that led to Antoninus's wall, and well protected by the line of garrisons close in front of it. But it must have profited much by the submission of the Brigantes, since it would become the market-town of the northern members of the tribe, as Eburacum and Isurium were for those who dwelt farther south. Luguvallium (Carlisle) saw a similar change, but its remains have never been properly explored : a certain number of tombstones of civilians found in its cemetery prove that it was not a wholly military settlement.

But the pacification of Britain south of Hadrian's Wall was not followed by that of the regions north of it, by Clyde and Forth. And probably the last Brigantian War was precisely the circumstance that prevented the work of Lollius Urbicus from being completed. The troops on guard along Antoninus' Wall may have been in part recalled, and certainly no advance can have been made in the settling up of the Lowlands, while the land south of them was aflame. Nor did better times come with the accession of Marcus Aurelius (161 A.D.). In the reign of the philosopher-em-

[1] See Professor Haverfield's Note on the Brough Inscription (1903).

peror the Roman world began to show, for the first time, an alarming
lack of stamina and recuperative energy. Whether the famines and
pestilences which raged through the greater part of Marcus's time
were the cause, or only a symptom, of decay, it is not necessary to
decide. But it is clear that the time of advance was over. Britain
was one of the provinces where trouble began early : the new reign
had hardly started when we are told that a British war was impending, and that Aurelius had to send Sextus Calpurnus Agricola,
one of his best officers, to deal with it. This trouble must have
been caused by revolts of the tribes in the Lowlands, complicated
by irruptions of the Caledonians from the north, for it clearly did
not affect the region south of Hadrian's Wall. The name of the
second Agricola is found in several British inscriptions, but they do
not suggest trouble on this side of the wall—consisting mainly of
altars erected by some of the garrison troops at Carvoran, with a
dedication in honour of the emperor at Ribchester. Similarly the
traces of the next governor, Ulpius Marcellus, who may have been
ruling Britain about 165 or 170, do not imply disorder—an aque-
duct was put up at the fort of Chesters (Cilurnum), hard by the North
Tyne, bearing his name, and an altar at Benwell, another Wall-
station. This sort of record of building and peaceful religious
dedication does not suggest a time of strenuous warfare.

But in the parts north of Hadrian's Wall the case is different,
and there is strong suspicion that matters were not going on in a
satisfactory fashion. The numerous inscriptions from that region
which bear dates from the reign of Antoninus Pius have no successor from the time of Marcus, and his coins also are not found in
such profusion as those of his father-in-law. It is quite probable
that a distinct retrograde movement had already set in, and even
that the wall from Forth to Clyde may not have maintained consistently through the whole of Marcus's life-time. It is certainly
strange that not a single inscription from that line mentions his
name, though so many bear that of Pius.[1] The deduction would
seem to be that while Hadrian's Wall was safe in the period 161-
180, we cannot be sure that the northern wall was intact. But there

---

[1] But we must of course remember that most of these were connected with the
building of Antoninus's Wall, or of forts, so that Marcus, who had not to do such
building, would naturally be less commemorated.

is no reason to think that the whole of the Lowlands were lost at
this time ; even if the Wall was sometimes pierced, the road must still
have been open to it, and the great intermediate forts, Habitancium,
Bremenium, Trimontium were still held in force.   The crisis was
not to come till the next reign.

CHAPTER VIII

ROMAN PERIOD. COMMODUS TO CARAUSIUS (A.D. 180-296)

WHILE our evidence concerning the state of the frontier of the British province under Marcus Aurelius is fragmentary. and leads to the deduction that Hadrian's Wall and all that lay behind it was safe, but that there was perpetual strife and little progress north of that wall, we have decidedly clearer signs of disaster in the time of Commodus. Except at three or four iso- lated points, all traces of Roman occupation beyond the line of Tyne and Solway cease about the year 181. These exceptional spots are Habitancium (Risinghame) on the road from Corbridge, Bremenium (High Rochester) farther to the North on that road, and close under Cheviot, and on the western front Castra Exploratorum (Netherby) and Bewcastle, in front of Carlisle.[1] These were all firmly held down to a late date in the third century. But all north of them was clearly abandoned soon after the year 180. The ex- cavations at the more important Lowland stations, such as Newstead and the castles on the Antonine Wall, show that these fortresses were either stormed by an enemy or evacuated in dire haste by their garrisons. When inscribed altars are found choking the main well of a station, we may recognise either the mischievous hand of the triumphant barbarian, or the despair of a departing occupant, who never dreams of returning.

These are traces of the "British War" which filled the earlier years of Commodus, and for which he was most undeservedly voted the title of Britannicus by the subservient senate. It seems to have filled the years 181-87 A.D., and to have started with a

---

[1] At High Rochester, despite its advanced position, thirty miles in front of the Wall, important military buildings were being constructed, as we shall presently see, as late as the time of Alexander Severus, more than fifty years after the accession of Commodus.

disastrous Caledonian raid.   The short account of it in Xiphilinus's
Epitome of Dio Cassius is the only coherent narrative that is left
to us.   " Certain of the insular nations having crossed the wall that
divided them from the stations of the Romans, did dreadful damage,
and cut to pieces a certain general together with the division which
he commanded."[1]   Commodus sent against them a very aged officer.
Ulpius Marcellus, who had already been governor of Britain twelve
years before, in the time of Marcus Aurelius.   This grim and
severe personage, concerning whose austerity and sleepless vigilance
curious tales are told, is said to have inflicted many defeats on the
barbarians.   But the war undoubtedly went on after his time, and
ended with the abandonment of the wall of Antoninus and all the
stations of the Lowlands, and a retreat to the line of Hadrian's
Wall.   We have no information as to whether the Caledonian
invader was assisted by a rising of the Otadini and the other tribes
between the walls, a thing in itself most probable.   But the
Brigantes, though tamed only forty years before, do not seem to
have been tempted into insurrection.

The epilogue of the British war of Commodus was a series of
desperate mutinies on the part of the legions, who may possibly
have been goaded into sedition by the austerity of Marcellus.
There follows the astonishing statement that they sent a deputa-
tion of 1,500 men to Rome to demand the death of the Praetorian
Praefect Perennis, the rather inexplicable cause given for their
action by Lampridius is that " during the British war he removed
senators from military command, and substituted men of equestrian
rank for them, whereupon he was called the enemy of the army
and dragged out to be torn to pieces by the soldiers " [186 A.D.].
Helvius Pertinax, afterwards emperor, succeeded Ulpius Marcellus, and met with similar mutinies.   In one of them he was so
maltreated that he was left for dead upon the ground.   We are
told that he punished the soldiery in the most bitter fashion for
their outrages, and reduced them to order.   But Pertinax then
asked and obtained his own recall from the emperor, saying that
the troops would not settle down, on account of the intense hatred
that they bore him for restoring discipline.   Yet on his first
arrival the legions are said to have wished to make him emperor

[1] Xiphilinus, *Epitome of Dio*, lxxii. 8.

" since they wanted to set up an emperor at all costs, and thought him specially fitted for the post ". Despite his unimpeachable conduct, Commodus's informers are said to have tried to persuade their master to accuse Pertinax of treason. But he refused to listen, and when he recalled him gave him the honourable post of Director of the Corn Supply of Rome.

It was presumably Pertinax who brought the war to an end, since we are told that it was still going on when Perennis fell a victim to his unpopularity with the army. From 187 onwards the frontier is once more at Hadrian's Wall : the peace may probably have been accompanied by some vague admission of Roman supremacy by the British tribes just outside the wall. But it seems that the Caledonians must have made a southern advance, at the expense of these Britons, occupying some part of the land just south of the Forth, up to the Pentland Hills. Two of the subterranean dwellings or "weems" characteristic of the Picts have been found near Crichton and Newstead, with roofs partly composed of hewn stones from ruined Roman forts. And three Pictish "brochs," or round works, exist at Bar, Torwoodlee, and Edinohall. This implies a permanent Pictish occupation, not mere ravaging. Harried by Pict and Roman the unfortunate Britons between the two walls must have been in evil case.

A few years later (192 A.D.) we find the British province in the charge of D. Clodius Albinus, who may have been the immediate successor of Pertinax in command. He was of an ancient and wealthy family, had served with credit in his youth, and is said to have been good-humoured and liberal, qualities which gave him a popularity with the soldiery which neither Marcellus nor Pertinax could command. He was withal, rather ambitious, given to vainglory, but lacking in decision. On a false rumour of the death of Commodus reaching Britain, he is said to have harangued the legions in terms which were taken to hint at his willingness to make a grasp at the diadem. This was reported to the emperor, who sent out Junius Severus to supersede him. But Commodus died in real earnest, assassinated by his own courtiers, before Albinus was removed, and the latter found himself still in command of the British army during the chaotic year 193, which gave every opportunity for a man of energy. The senate, as it will be remembered, named Pertinax as Augustus, but the Praetorians slew him, put the empire up to auction, and sold it to the wealthy but incapable Didius Julianus. Thereupon the three great frontier armies of the Roman world each proclaimed its commander emperor, the Danube army acclaiming L. Septimus Severus, the Syrian army Pescennius Niger, and the British army the not-unwilling Albinus.

This triple nomination was destined to bring about an abnormal situation of affairs both for Britain and for the Empire. Severus, who succeeded in reaching Rome and slaying Didius Julianus before the other would-be emperors could even make a start, saw that he would have to fight both Niger and Albinus. But preferring to face them in detail, and fearing the fierce British army more than the Orientals, he sent to Albinus, offering to recognise him as his junior colleague, and to leave him complete control of Britain, in return for his alliance against Niger. The British pretender showed greater simplicity and a more halting ambition than had been expected. Apparently he thought that the Antonine practice of imperial adoption might be renewed, that he might be the Hadrian of the new Trajan, serve him loyally, and ultimately succeed to his throne. Accordingly he accepted with thanks the title of Caesar offered to him by Severus, and remained in Britain, where he ruled with some success, instead of crossing to Gaul and summoning the German legions to join him. This condition of affairs lasted for over three years, during which Albinus reigned in Britain alone, though his name was added to that of Severus in official documents and inscriptions throughout the west.[1]

But this compromise, which foreshadowed the British Empire of Carausius, only lasted till Severus had made an end of Pescennius Niger and the Syrians, and had then devoted another year to the reorganisation of the East. He had children of his own, whom he intended to make his associates in the imperial dignity, and by 196 the unfortunate Albinus had become unnecessary to him. The excuse made for attacking him is said to have been that it was discovered that many important senators had been sending him secret letters, bidding him seize Rome while Severus was still absent and busy in the East. But Albinus, whatever answer he may have made

---

[1] There is a notable one in the Museum at Mainz, but none, oddly enough, in Britain.

them, had taken no steps to break his contract with Severus : indeed we are told that he had shown himself indolent and easy-going, and displayed intense satisfaction in the title and state of Caesar.

Meanwhile Severus brought up the Illyrian army to the Western Alps, and then declared war on his colleague. Seeing that he must choose between defending Britain, or seizing Gaul and winning over its legions, Albinus took the bolder step. He declared himself Augustus, mobilised every corps that could be spared from the island, hastily crossed the Channel, and called upon the Gauls to join him. Some of the cities and many troops did so, but more hung back, prudently determining to join the victor, whoever he might be. But Albinus was able to push on to Lugdunum before he met with resistance. In front of that great city he was confronted by Severus and the army drawn from the Danube. Then followed the greatest battle between Romans that had been seen since Philippi, for the forces on both sides were larger than those which had fought under Otho and Vitellius at Bedriacum in 69. The fight was long and doubtful " for the Britons," says Herodian " are no whit inferior in courage or sanguinary spirit to the Illyrians ".[1] The wing of Severus's army in which he himself fought was completely routed by the charge of Albinus's legions, and the emperor had his horse killed under him, and had to fling away his purple cloak to escape notice. But at this moment, when the Britons seemed sure of victory, a fresh corps under one Laetus, which had been marching to join Severus, came suddenly upon the scene, checked the rout, and beat back the exhausted and disordered troops of Albinus. Their arrival decided the day : the British army fell back in complete disarray, and was pursued and slaughtered up to the very gates of Lyons. The victors pushed their way into the city along with the fugitives, and not contented with massacring their armed opponents, burnt and plundered the houses of the citizens. Albinus was taken alive in the city, and promptly decapitated by his captors, who took his head to Severus. Thus ended the first " British Empire," which had lasted over three years (193-97).

The whole of the garrison of Britain must have been completely disorganised by the departure of Albinus with its picked corps, and the destruction of many thousands of veterans at the battle of Lug-

---

[1] Herodian, ii. 24.

dunum. Severus paid some attention to the island after his victory :
to curb the power of future governors he divided the province into
two halves, "Upper" and "Lower" Britain, so that for the future
there were two co-ordinate and rival authorities in the island. The
probable boundaries of the two new units may be guessed from the
fact that Dio Cassius mentions that the Sixth Legion at York was in
Lower Britain, while both the Second Augusta at Caerleon and the
Twentieth Valeria Victrix at Chester were in Upper Britain. Lindum
(Lincoln) was—like York—in the Lower Province : so possibly the
boundary ran from the Mersey to the Wash. This note of Dio,
confirmed by numerous inscriptions, shows that Severus did not
disband the remnants of the legions which had pressed him so hard
at Lugdunum, but reconstructed the three corps, probably filling up
their depleted ranks with conscripts drawn from other regions than
those which had produced the men who fought so furiously against
him in 197. As to the auxiliary cohorts, we find a great number of
those which had served under Hadrian in Britain still existing in the
third century : but it is likely that some perished for ever on the field
of Lyons. Be this as it may, it is probable that for some years after
the civil war had ended the garrison of Britain was both under its
normal strength and in a disorganised condition. Nor can we doubt
that the old disease of mutiny, which had raged so severely under
Commodus, must have been seething under the surface, when the
troops were forced to obey the conqueror who had slaughtered
thousands of their comrades and slain their chosen emperor.

It is by the weakness and discontent of the British army that
we can best explain the disasters which befell the province in the
middle years of the reign of Severus. The troubles commenced by
incursions of the Southern Picts into the region of Hadrian's Wall.
These people are now (for the first time) called Meatae : the Epitome
of Dio gives us the information that by this date all the smaller
tribes of North Britain—the Boresti, Vacomagi, Taexali, etc., of
Tacitus and Ptolemy—had merged themselves into the two confederacies of the Caledonians and the Meatae, "of whom the latter
dwell close on the wall that divides the island in two" [no doubt the
turf-wall of Antoninus is meant] while the former possessed the
remoter regions of the North. In the time when Virius Lupus was
governor of Northern Britain (197-205 ?) the Meatae attacked the
province : the legate was resisting them, and had apparently won

some small successes,[1] when it was reported to him that the Caledonians were about to intervene, despite of the treaties which
were in existence with them—presumably agreements made either
by Pertinax or Clodius Albinus. Thereupon Lupus, with unseemly
haste, bought peace from the Meatae by giving them huge subsidies.
Of course no permanent quiet was secured by this cowardly policy.
In 205-8 we find Alfenius Senecio, the successor of Lupus, busy in
repairing the Northern fortifications,[2] and finally reporting to Rome
"that the barbarians were in a state of disturbance, overrunning the
country, driving off booty, and laying everything waste, so that
there was need either for large reinforcements, or even for an expedition headed by the emperor in person.[3]

Severus was at this moment free from foreign troubles, having
brought to a successful end his great Parthian war. His position
was quite safe at home, his mental vigour was undiminished,
though he had begun to be afflicted with violent fits of gout, and,
as we are told, he was anxious to find a good excuse for removing
from Rome his two young sons, Antoninus (Caracalla) and Geta,
who were beginning to alarm him by their dissolute life and unseemly addiction to the shows of the ampitheatre. Accordingly
he announced his intention of taking up in person the charge of
the Caledonian war, and of utilising it for the purpose of giving
the young princes their first experience of military life.

He carried out his promise with great energy, crossing Gaul
with unexampled speed, and arrived in Britain long before he was
expected, and that although his gout lay heavy upon him, so that
he had to be carried for many stages on a litter. The moment
that he reached Britain he began to make elaborate preparations
for a long campaign, calling up troops from all quarters—the Praetorians no doubt accompanied him—and he probably made large
drafts from the Rhine army. Hearing of his sudden arrival, and
terrified at the strength of the force that was being collected, the
Caledonians and their fellows sent ambassadors to Severus, begging

---

[1] αἰχμαλώτας τινὰς ἀπολαβὼν ὀλίγους, Xiphilinus. lxxv. 5. So there must have
been some small local captures.

[2] Inscriptions on the quarries overhanging the River Gelt show that they were
being worked in the Consulship of Aper and Maximus (207). An inscription at Bain-
bridge (C. I. L., vii. 269) shows buildings by the Sixth Nervian cohort under
Senecio's orders.

[3] Herodian, iii. 46.

for peace, excusing their past transgressions, and proffering all sorts of guarantees. The emperor deliberately wasted time before giving them an answer, in order that his preparations might be finished, but finally sent them away. He had never really intended to treat, being fully determined to complete the conquest of Britain, by carrying the boundaries of the empire up to the Northern Ocean.

We are told that among the preliminary measures of Severus was the construction of many bridges and causeways over marshy places, more especially over certain tidal swamps, where the rising and falling tide made passage difficult and dangerous for the legions, " though the barbarians were wont to wade through them and to traverse them immersed as high as the waist; for going naked as to the greater part of their bodies, they despise the mud. Indeed they have no proper knowledge of clothing, and wear collars and belts of iron round their waists and necks, thinking these the best of ornaments and a sign of wealth, as the other barbarians consider gold to be." [1]   It is difficult to locate this bridge and causeway-building, which (since it is described as preliminary to the actual campaign) must have been somewhere quite close to the frontier. The region about the head of the Solway Firth suggests itself as a possible place; but the Romans had already a solid road turning the head of the tidal sands of Solway, and going as far as Blatum Bulgium (Birrens) in Dumfriesshire, which is recorded as the Northern terminus of the British road-system in the Antonine Itinerary. The only other district where large tidal marshes could give difficulty is the estuary of the Forth below Stirling; but this seems a very advanced position for the Roman army to be occupying before the actual commencement of the war. Yet there is no other large stretch of tidal swamp on the east side of Britain beyond Hadrian's Wall, and recent excavation has shown that Severus certainly repaired and used as his chief base the old Roman station of Cramond in Lothian,[2] a convenient port for an expedition which probably utilised sea-transport on a large scale. It is quite conceivable that the Meatae had drawn back beyond the Forth.

Be this as it may, Severus commenced his advance in the spring of 209, and made two long campaigns, without desisting from his original plan of complete conquest: from the first to the last he

---

[1] Herodian, iii. 47.
[2] See especially Dr. G. Macdonald on " Roman Coin-finds " in Scotland.

never seems to have left the field, save to take up his winter quarters at York. The troops were probably, like those of Agricola, compelled to remain from October to March in camps established far within the enemy's territory. For if they had withdrawn behind the Forth, or to the shelter of Hadrian's Wall, the whole of their work would have had to be commenced *de novo* as each spring came round. We have no consecutive narrative of the war, but only a series of depressing pictures of its monotonous and deadly futility. "The army underwent indescribable labour in cutting down woods, levelling acclivities, making marshes passable, bridging rivers, but fought not a single battle, nor even saw an enemy in regular array. Occasionally the barbarians threw herds of sheep or oxen within reach of the soldiers, in order that they might be enticed to pursue them, and so worn out by fatigue. The army also suffered dreadfully from the rains, and whenever they were scattered in detachments ambushes were laid for them. Many men are said to have been despatched by their own comrades, when they were too worn out to walk any longer, lest they should fall alive into the hands of the barbarians. It is said that in one way or another 50,000 men perished." So far the epitome of Dio: Herodian in less dismal language gives much the same story. "The moment the army had passed the rivers and the earthen walls [1] which form the boundaries of the empire, there were numerous small affrays and skirmishes, and retreats on the part of the barbarians. But to them flight was easy, and they hid themselves in woods and mosses, having the necessary local knowledge. But all these things were adverse to the Romans, and served to protract the war."

But Severus was not a man who could easily be turned back from his purpose. Despite of all difficulties of weather and of territory, he forced his way to the Northern Ocean " until he drew near to the extreme end of the Isle of Britain," according to his biographer.[2] But it is improbable that in reality he got any

---

[1] The statement of Herodian that the boundary of the empire was protected at this time by ῥεύματα καὶ χώματα is very important. The χώματα no doubt are the two walls of Hadrian and Antoninus. The ῥεύματα must probably mean Forth and Clyde—since Tyne and Irthing cannot be called protections, nor Tweed or Eden.

[2] Certain traces of Severus's expedition are rare: what archæological evidence there is comes from Fife and the Lower Tay. The northern camps have not been properly explored.

farther than the eastern end of the Moray Firth, where the promontory of the Taexali (Kinnaird Head), with the land falling
away from it to west and south, may well have seemed to his army
the very end of the earth.   It is a sign of his active and curious
mind that he caused investigations to be made at this northernmost point of the explored world into the parallax of the sun, and
the length of the days and nights both in summer and winter.[1]
Doubtless he was set on verifying by actual investigation the calculations already made by geographers, such as Ptolemy, as to these
facts,[2] for one of the localities whose exact situation and whose
extreme hours of light and darkness had been calculated by the
Alexandrian scientist, was the " Winged Camp " in the territory of
the Vacomagi, a locality which, being somewhere in the north-east of
Scotland, must have been very near the last point of Severus's advance.   Possibly some unhappy corps of the imperial army had
its winter quarters for 209-10 fixed in bleak Aberdeenshire, and
came to know only too well the length of its winter nights.

As far as the evidence and the probabilities go, it would seem
that the main seat of Severus's campaigning was the eastern side of
the Highlands, that starting from his base in Lothian he worked
up the comparatively flat and easy country along the North Sea,
the land of the Meatae,—which was afterwards to be known as
Fortrenn,—leaving the Caledonians proper, in the recesses of Athole
and Badenoch and the remoter North, comparatively unmolested,
though no doubt raids may have pushed up past Dunkeld, "the
gate of the Highlands," into the valley of the Upper Tay, or up
Strathearn, or along the whole southern side of the Moray Firth.
He may have reoccupied the whole series of Agricolan and Antonine
camps which starts with that of Ardoch, ten miles north of Stirling :
there are others at Comrie, Strageath, Abernethy, Gask and Inchtuthill,[3] all in the basin of the Tay.   But the supposed traces of
Severus farther north, in Forfarshire and Aberdeenshire, need
verifying.

Awful as were the sufferings of the Roman army, Severus's steady
and undeviating advance, and his evident intention to persevere till
he should have finished his undertaking, ended by cowing the spirits
of the barbarians.   They sued for peace at the end of the second

[1] Xiphilinus, *Epitome of Dio*, lxxvi. 13.   [2] *Ptolemy*, viii. 2
[3] All these places show signs of several successive Roman occupations.   See
p. 98.

campaign, that of 210, not only doing homage and surrendering
arms, but consenting to cede a great tract of territory, presumably
the lands from Forth to Tay, where the Roman garrisons were now
securely established, as well as anything that they may have been
occupying south of the Wall of Antoninus. It was time, for the
emperor's sake, that the war should end ; he was now sixty-five,
his health had completely broken down, his fits of gout were growing more persistent and dangerous, and he had accomplished more
marches in his litter than on his horse. Not the least of his trials,
as we are told, came from the conduct of his eldest son. Geta had
been left in the South to govern Britain, but Antoninus had accompanied his father through both campaigns. Though showing a very
meagre interest in the war, he had been doing his best to court the
favour of the army, deprecating the labours which Severus was
imposing on the soldiery, tampering with the loyalty of ambitious
officers, and making open and indecent preparations for his father's
death, as his health grew worse and worse. He is even said to have
schemed to murder his unhappy parent, though we can hardly
believe the story that he drew his sword upon him as they were
riding to a conference with the Caledonian chiefs, and only sheathed
it when the staff, who were riding behind, uttered a unanimous
shout of horror. The tale must surely be either a sheer invention,
or a misrepresentation of some incident capable of misinterpretation
which actually happened.

Severus returned to York in the autumn of 210, leaving garrisons
behind him in the newly annexed districts, and rested there for the
winter His arrival in the city is said to have been accompanied with
many strange and unfavourable omens, but the worst was his own
broken form and haggard face. Yet his mind was still strong : he
is actually said to have quelled a mutiny from his litter, and to have
remarked to the repentant soldiery, pointing to his swollen limbs,
" that they should remember that it is the head and not the feet
which commands ". But his health steadily grew worse, the effects
of the late campaign conspiring with the undutiful conduct of
Caracalla to bring him low. At midwinter the last blow was given,
by a report that the Meatae had attacked the garrisons, and that
the Caledonians were joining them Severus swore that they
should be punished, and began to make preparations for a new
campaign in March, warning the soldiers, as it is said, that no

quarter should be given on this occasion. But the excitement was too much for him, he had to take to his bed and to delegate the task of marching against the Picts to his son, who showed no relish for it. A few days later he died (Feb. 4, 211) : his end is said, probably without good grounds, to have been hastened by physicians suborned by his unworthy heir.

No sooner was Severus dead than Antoninus proceeded to patch up a peace with the Caledonians and Meatae. He withdrew every garrison that had been left in the North, and they in return gave some hostages and some easy promises of homage. Then he departed for Rome, there to slay his brother, and reigned with brutal tyranny for six years, till he was overturned and slain by the rebel Opelius Macrinus (217).

It might have seemed that all the work of Severus was wasted, since under Caracalla the line of Roman defence was drawn back to where it had stood at the death of Commodus ;—the wall from Tyne to Solway once more forming the frontier, with its outposts at Bremenium, Castra Exploratorum, etc. But this was not so, Severus left as legacy to his successors a vastly improved boundary, having repaired Hadrian's Wall, which obviously had been broken in many places by the Caledonians in the recent wars, in such a thorough style that several historians, neglecting the work of his predecessor, ascribe its actual building to him. It may seem strange that the emperor who had designed to add all Caledonia to his realm should have devoted attention to a structure which would have lain right in the midst of his dominions, and would not have guarded any frontier, if his plans had been carried to a successful conclusion. Yet there seems no reason to doubt that the stone wall of Northumberland was repaired and rebuilt with care by Severus. "The chief glory of his reign," writes Spartianus, a writer who had good authorities before him, and wrote only three generations after this time " was the wall which he drew right across the isle of Britain, from sea to sea." The same statement is made by Aurelius Victor, who copies Spartianus's very words ; Orosius adds some details, " he thought fit to divide the conquered part of the island from the untamed tribes without by a wall : and so he drew a great ditch and a most solid wall, furnished with frequent towers, for a distance of 132 [a misreading for 82] miles between sea and sea." Eusebius makes the same miscalculation. A similar statement is found in Eutropius, with the opposite blunder of a calculation of the wall at 32 instead of 82 miles, as also in Cassiodorus. It is impossible to ignore all this evidence, though much of it is late. Yet the results of the most modern excavation prove that the core and main bulk of the present stone wall between Tyne and Solway was undoubtedly the work of Hadrian. It suffered many dilapidations, and was thoroughly patched up by Severus, but it is curious that so many authorities should have treated him as its original builder. Its repairer he was, undoubtedly : inscriptions from his age have been found, and in some places forts have been rebuilt on modified plans. Often the filled-up ditch has its bottom filled with a muddy deposit, which implies the accumulation of many years, while above this mud is the gravel and *débris* thrown in to level the surface, when the new fort was constructed. The wonderful remnants of the stone wall, which we follow as it charges steep ravines or soars above the very edge of precipitous crags, with its great forts and numerous mile-castles and turrets, must be assigned, therefore, to the reign of Hadrian, no less than the earlier turf wall which may, however, have preceded it. Severus's repairs were many and important, obvious enough to the third century observer.

If we ask why Severus cared so much for the wall, if he intended to conquer all Caledonia, the reply seems to be that the commencement of the work dates back to before the time of his personal visit to Britain. He arrived in 208, and probably late in the year : but inscriptions show that the wall-quarries were being energetically worked in the consulship of Aper and Maximus (207),[1] long before his landing in Britain, as well as in that of Faustinus and Rufus (210), the year of his second Caledonian campaign.[2] Conceivably an attempt to reconstruct Hadrian's shattered structure was one of the defensive measures taken in hand by the governor Alfenius Senecio, before the war grew so dangerous that he implored the presence of his master in Britain. Yet we cannot suppose that it was finished before Severus's arrival. Did the emperor employ the large army which he collected in 208 upon the completion of the wall, as we know that he employed it during the winter of 208-9 on the building of roads and causeways through tidal marshes? If this work was well advanced towards completion before the actual campaigning began, it is quite conceivable that, when the Caledonians had made their submission

---

[1] C. I. L., vii. 912.　　　　[2] *Ibid.*, 871.

in 210, Severus may have thought it worth while to utilise the services of the greater part of his army, which must have returned from the north in that autumn, in finishing the structure, even though it would be a superfluous precaution in case the conquest of Caledonia turned out to have been successful and permanent. We know that emperors, when they had a very large army collected, and actual campaigning was not on hand, often employed its energies upon building work, on the principle that idle hands always find mischief. It may be remembered that Probus, two generations later, tried precisely this expedient on the Danube, till he worked his army so hard that a mob of soldiers suddenly burst out into mutiny and killed him. Conceivably the sedition that Severus is said to have suppressed in the autumn of 210 may have been caused by precisely the same sort of discontent at forced labour. But all this is hypothetical: whatever his reasons, we must believe that Severus lavished much work on the wall which still remains as the chief wonder of Northern England.

There seems every reason to believe that the measures taken by Severus for the defence of Britain were more effective than those which were employed by other third century emperors for the protection of the Rhine and Danube frontiers. It would not be sufficient to argue from the silence of historians concerning serious troubles in Britain that none such occurred: for the annals of the time between Severus and Constantine are short, and scrappy in the extreme. Only those who have read the miserable stuff served up by the *Scriptores Historiae Augustae*, and the later epitomists, understand how little is known of the third century. We get trifling personal anecdotes instead of continuous history, and often events of serious permanent importance have to be inferred because they are not narrated. But this much is clear, that throughout the decades in which the defence of the outworks on Rhine and Danube was being broken down, the British frontier left by Severus was maintained. The *Limes* beyond the Rhine was broken up and evacuated: Dacia was lost for ever: but the garrisons on the wall from Tyne to Solway stood at the end of the century exactly where they stood at its beginning. We find inscriptions on the Wall, showing building or repairs, which date not only from the reigns of Elagabalus and Severus Alexander, when chaos had not yet come, but from the darker times after the house of Severus had disappeared.

Most striking of all is it to discover, at the remote outposts far north of the Wall, records of elaborate constructions of edifices which were rather luxuries than necessities. At Netherby there was a riding school (Basilica exercitatoria equestris) erected in 222. At High Rochester (Bremenium), the most northern point of all, a Ballistarium, or storehouse for military machines, dates from the same period (219-22). If the advanced posts were thus adorned, the Wall, far behind them, must have been absolutely safe. On it are found the names of the unfortunate Gordian III.[1] and his murderer Philip,[2] and, what is more surprising, those of ephemeral rulers like Gallus and Volusian,[3] and the Gaulish usurpers Postumus and Tetricus. During the existence of the so-called Gallic Empire under Postumus and his successors (258-74 A.D.) Britain, whether with enthusiasm or not we cannot say, acquiesced in all the proclamations of new monarchs on the Rhine, and showed no wish either to cling to the legal emperor at Rome, or to set up provincial pretenders on its own account. On the whole it is probable that the adherence of the island to the secessionist empire was willingly given, for in the later attempts of the West to break loose from Rome, after Tetricus had made his tame submission to Aurelian, the Britons are found taking a leading part in the particularist movement. This was the revolt of Bonosus and Proculus, of whom the former was the son of a British father and a Gallic mother. He may be noted as the first pretender of British blood who made a grasp at the imperial diadem. These two conspirators are said to have expected to obtain assistance from all the Gauls and Britons and even from the Spaniards. They proclaimed themselves emperors at Cologne, and maintained themselves for some time, indeed there seemed to be some chance that they would be as successful as Postumus had been twenty years before. But when the legitimate emperor Probus came up against them he was joined by all the Trans-Rhenane Germans, whom the usurpers had vainly supposed that they had won over to their alliance. Bonosus and Proculus were defeated and slain, but not even

---

[1] Under whom there seems to have been repairing done just south of the wall, a military store, etc. at Lanchester (Co. Durham) restored (conlapsa restituit) and a bath and Basilica built (balneum cum basilica a solo instruxit) at the same place. C. I. L., vii. 445-6. Three or four military units become *vexillatio* or *numerus Gordianus* in his time, at High Rochester, Ribchester and Lanchester.

[2] Who gives his name as an honorary title to the Cuneus Frisiorum at Papcastle.

[3] Their names are found in a dedication at Penrith.

then, if we are to believe Zosimus and Zonaras, did Probus finally recover Britain. Another pretender, whose name is not given, was set up in the island : he fell by treachery not by force of arms. For one, Victorinus the Moor, who had formerly been the rebels' friend and patron, pretended to flee from Probus as if in danger of his life. But when he had been welcomed in Britain, he took the opportunity of secretly murdering his host at night, and returned to report success at Rome. Thereupon the rebellion came to an end, and the province returned to its allegiance (277 A.D. ?) It is recorded that Probus sent over to Britain, no doubt organised in military units— *cunei* or *numeri*—all the Vandal and Burgundian warriors whom he captured in his German campaigns. They are said to have been intended to act as a counterpoise to the local troops, with whom they could have no community of feeling.

There is no reason to believe that during all the years of murder and civil war which lie between the death of Severus and the accession of Diocletian Britain was to any great extent molested by her old enemies the Caledonians, while domestic turbulence no longer took the form of tribal rebellion against the Roman imperial system as a whole, but rather that of adhesion to usurpers who were not recognised in the capital. The century was probably quite a prosperous period for Roman Britain. The laudatory description of the province which we get at the end of the period from the Panegyrist Eumenius is sufficient proof that it was in a flourishing condition.[1] It would have been fruitless to write of its lively seaports, its wealth in corn and cattle, its numerous mines, its large revenues, if all had been laid waste either by the barbarian or by civil strife. All the disasters of the empire during the third century had come from invaders who arrived by land, and since Britain was protected against its only land neighbours, the Caledonians, by Hadrian's Wall, it escaped the misfortunes of Gaul, Dacia and the Balkan Peninsula.

But at the very end of the century traces of danger from the side of the sea at last appear, and against such a danger the island had not yet been secured. There had always been a *Classis Britannica*, as inscriptions show, but it was a small affair, and insufficient

---

[1] " Terra tanto frugum ubere, tanto lecta numero pastionum, tot metallorum fluens rivis, tot vectigalibus quaestuosa, tot accincta portibus," Eumenius writes in 296.

to guard the whole of the North Sea and the Channel. For reasons which we cannot fathom,[1] the Franks—the newly-formed league of German tribes on the Lower Rhine—and the more distant Saxons began to take to the sea and to act as pirates in the last years of the third century. Why they had not done so before is a problem as difficult to solve as the similar question as to why the Scandinavian Vikings did not start on their great raids before the age of Charlemagne. Perhaps the recent disasters of the empire had encouraged them to feats of unprecedented boldness : perhaps the Ocean flotilla of the Romans had been allowed to sink into practical non-existence during the existence of the ephemeral Western state founded by Postumus. At any rate, we find that, about the time of the accession of Diocletian, the coast-lines of Northern Gaul and Eastern Britain were beginning to be infested by Frankish and Saxon pirates. The evil does not seem yet to have bitten deep, and the enemy were mere raiders in open boats, not owners of a properly constructed war navy. But the nuisance became serious enough to require special attention, and Maximianus Herculeus, the colleague of Diocletian in the Western half of the empire, was forced to strengthen, or perhaps to create, naval forces for the discomfiture of the pirates. This command was practically the same which was afterwards known as the "Countship of the Saxon Shore," for in the fourth century the tracts on both sides of the Channel exposed to the pirates received the name of *Littus Saxonicum per Gallias* and *per Britannias*. The count had in the end not only the charge of the fleet but that of certain fortified ports and sea-coast castles, but whether this arrangement existed from the first we have no opportunity of knowing.

To command the fleet destined to cope with the pirates Maximian appointed one Carausius, an experienced officer of North-Gaulish blood,[2] who is called both a Menapian and a Batavian.

---

[1] But not solely as Zosimus would have it, because they were fired by ambition to copy the great sea raid of the escaped Frankish cohort from Pityus (i. 66).

[2] He is called Menapiae civis by Aurelius Victor, whence many of our own earlier writers ascribed his origin to the British Menapia (St. David's), arguing that if he had been a Gallic Menapian the author would have styled him civis Menapius. But the fact that Eumenius, a contemporary, calls him *Bataviae alumnus* would seem to make it clear that he was really a Belgian. And the evidence for Menapia as a town is not clear. If he had come from thence Carausius would more probably have been called Civis Demeta.

The new admiral commenced his career with marked success, destroyed many of the marauding Teutons, and recovered much plunder from them. But he was presently accused before Maximian of being less anxious to prevent the raids than to catch the raiders, when they were laden with spoil. And the proceeds of his captures were said to benefit himself and his crews, rather than the imperial exchequer, or the robbed provincials. It was even hinted, with or without justification, that he had a tacit understanding with some of the Franks. Learning that the emperor intended to seize him and perhaps to execute him, Carausius took the bold step of appealing to his followers to join him in rebellion. He proclaimed himself emperor and landed in Britain, where he was joined at once by a legion and many auxiliary cohorts.[1] Apparently an appeal for insurrection was seldom made in vain to the turbulent soldiery of the province. Ere long the whole island came over to his standard, with much enthusiasm ; for while some of the coins which he struck to commemorate his accession show emblems and inscriptions witnessing to the " concord of the army," others represent Britannia herself welcoming Carausius with the inscription EXPECTATE VENI, as if she had long been yearning for a saviour.[2] The type is unique in Roman numismatic history, and despite of the habitual flattery to which the mints were prone in choosing designs, must surely have had some real provincial feeling behind it.

Carausius reigned in Britain for over seven years (286-93 A.D.), apparently with great success and with undisputed sway. He increased his fleet by building many more galleys, raised new levies to strengthen his army,[3] and hired a great force of barbarian mercenaries from the Franks. But his ambition was not merely to be Emperor of Britain but to reconstitute the old " Empire of the Gauls ". He had a hold beyond the Channel, owing to his possession of Gessoriacum (Boulogne), which was one of the arsenals of his fleet, and he tried from thence to extend his power all over Gaul. He

[1] " Occupata legione Romana, interclusis aliquot peregrinorum militum cuneis," says Eumenius. But there is no reason for supposing that the legion was taken by surprise or the cohorts "surrounded" in any physical sense. The Panegyrist is merely lavishing abuse on the usurper.

[2] Sometimes Britannia bears a sceptre, at others a long caduceus, and at others, again, a military standard.

[3] Eumenius tells us that he conscribed Gaulish merchants, perhaps mainly seafaring traders, and that all his recruits were " ad munia nautica eruditi ".

seems to have been for some time in possession of a considerable tract of its northern coast, for it is pretty clearly proved that he had a mint at Rotomagus (Rouen) during part of the early section of his reign, and he was tampering with the loyalty of the legions of the Rhine army, who had not forgotten the old times between 258 and 274 when they were independent of Rome.[1] But his wider schemes proved unsuccessful: he failed to extend his power in Gaul, the troops on the Rhine did not join him, and he lost all his possessions beyond the Channel save the single town of Gessoriacum, which he maintained for several years. Yet his naval power was too great for Maximian. The emperor built a new fleet to attack him, but it was repeatedly beaten through the unskilfulness of the untrained sailors, who proved unable to endure the fogs and cross-currents of the Channel.[2] After several repulses Maximian and his colleague Diocletian, who had many other troubles on hand, stooped to the necessity of making peace with Carausius, and acknowledged him as their colleague, while he undertook to desist from his designs on Gaul. The peace was marked by the issue from the mint of London of numerous coins struck in honour of Diocletian and Maximian, and of others representing the busts of the three emperors side by side, with the legend CARAVSIVS ET FRATRES SVI, and the reverse PAX AVGGG, "the peace of the three Augusti" [289 A.D.].

After this Carausius reigned for several years in great prosperity. His large fleet kept the province safe from the Saxons, and his coins commemorated a "Victoria Germanica" which must refer to some triumph over them. With the Franks he had made peace, and kept many of them as auxiliaries. The Caledonians must certainly have been kept in due check, since milestones with the name of Carausius were erected just behind Severus's Wall—a certain proof that law and order were safe in that quarter. A sign

[1] The mint at Rouen seems to be conclusively proved by Mr. Percy Webb's articles on the coins of Carausius in the *Numismatic Chronicle* for 1907-8. The tampering with the Rhenish troops seems inferable from the fact that Carausius struck a considerable amount of money marked with the crests or emblems of these legions—First Minervia, Thirtieth Ulpia, and two or three more. As they were not actually under his command, the move must have been intended to appeal to them to join the other Western legions. It is notable to find that Victorinus, Carausius's predecessor, in a similar usurpation, did exactly the same thing twenty years before, striking coins in honour of legions which were outside his sphere of influence.

[2] Eumenius, *Panegyricus Constantio Caesari*, c. 3.

of care for trade and commerce was the restoration of the silver coinage, which had ceased to exist throughout the empire for many years, having been replaced first by half-alloyed pieces and then by mere silvered bronze. While the rest of the empire was using this depreciated stuff, Carausius issued a large coinage of pure silver denarii. It was only some years later that Diocletian copied him by issuing a similar reformed coinage for the rest of the Roman world. If the care of the usurper for other economic needs was as enlightened in other respects as in this, he may well have been justified in placing the legends UBERITAS AVG. FELICITAS TEMPORUM and RESTITUTOR SAECVLI on his money. We know from similar evidence that he celebrated secular games, though how he managed to find a centenary anywhere about the year 290 A.D. it is hard to see, since the Emperor Philip had conducted the last games of the sort with great pomp less than fifty years before, in 248 A.D.[1] Probably almost equal importance was attached to the ceremonies at which Britain put up the "Quinquennial" and "Vicennalian" Vows for the safety of its Caesar. But Carausius was not destined to see twenty years of power; his reign was to last for less than eight.

In 292 Diocletian and Maximian, having put down the rest of their enemies, thought it time to turn their attention once more against the British usurper. War was declared on him, and the charge of it was given over to Constantius Chlorus, the Caesar whom Maximian had just adopted as his junior colleague. Under his auspices the struggle took an indecisive turn, for though he succeeded in recovering Gessoriacum, the one foothold which Carausius had retained upon the Continent, he was utterly unable to obtain command of the seas. While the Channel was held by a fleet superior both in force and in efficiency, nothing could be accomplished against the insular realm.

When the renewed war had been some two years in progress, and showed no signs of coming to an end, Carausius was basely murdered by one Allectus, of whom we know nothing save that he was the underling (satelles) of his victim. But since the assassin was not crushed at once by an enraged soldiery, it is probable that he was holding some great office under Carausius which had

---

[1] Perhaps he reckoned from Domitian's secular games of 88 A.D., counting Philip's celebration as incorrectly calculated, just as Domitian had ignored the celebration by Claudius.

made it possible for him to secure the favour of at least some part of the army. He may even have been his designated successor, since we know from numismatic evidence that Carausius had nominated a "Princeps Juventutis," a title only given to persons who had been formally nominated as heirs and colleagues by the reigning emperor.[1]

It is much to be regretted that we know so little in detail concerning Marcus Aurelius Carausius,[2] the first sea-king of British history. His numerous and often well-executed coins show him to have been a broadly built, bull-necked, square-headed man, well advanced in middle age—he must have been considerably over forty, by his portrait, at the moment of his usurpation. Of his designs and ambitions we have all too little evidence, but it seems clear that those who have represented him as a mere "particularist," a British patriot, are in error. Not only did he make a serious effort to conquer Gaul, but he may have even aimed at the sovereignty of the whole empire. One of his most frequent coin-types is that of RENOVATIO ROMANORVM, surrounding the Roman wolf and twins, a clear sign that he wished to be regarded as a Roman reformer, not as a British separatist. Other coins are struck in honour of ROMA AETERNA. Though he honoured some twenty gods and goddesses.[3] there was only one of them who was local and provincial—Hercules Deusoniensis, a divinity worshipped on the Lower Rhine.[4] And this worship may have been part of his propaganda for an appeal to the sympathy of the Rhine legions. The first person who had commemorated that divinity was Postumus, the founder of the "empire of the Gauls". Carausius thrice assumed the title of Consul, and probably took up all the other usual attributes of imperial authority: it is likely that he kept some sort of a senate to vote and ratify his behests. It is most unfortunate that inscriptions from his reign are practically non-existent: a single long commemorative dedication might give us a clearer conception

[1] No emperor seems to have taken the title for himself, after he had become Augustus. It was reserved for " Caesars," heirs designate and colleagues.

[2] Carausius had a fourth name, which began with MAVS—and was evidently Gallic in character. But the inscription from which we get it does not give it in full. No doubt it was his original proper name, and Aurelius only an assumed one.

[3] Including Jupiter, Apollo, Mars, Sol, Hercules Pacifer, Diana, Neptune, Oceanus, Venus, Vulcan, besides Victory, Fortune and many other half-abstractions.

[4] Possibly Carausius had learnt to worship this local god in his own youth, for he came from the region where this form of Hercules was venerated.

of his constitutional status and political ambitions than all his numerous coins, from whose types we have to reconstitute them for lack of literary evidence.

Allectus appears to have been a man inferior in every respect to the master whom he had murdered : certainly he lacked his courage and his military skill. Probably his throne was from the first a tottering one, since his predecessor must have left behind him many friends and admirers. We have a hint that he was obliged to rely almost entirely on his barbarian mercenaries, for when he had to fight for his life and crown he took the field with them almost alone, presumably because he could not trust the legions. According to the story of his enemies the British provincials found that their persons, their families and their property were exposed to the rapacity of a licentious foreign soldiery, and yearned to be quit of the " tyrant " at the earliest possible opportunity.

This much is certain, that the fall of Allectus was sudden and ignominious. He reigned for some three years, during which his enemy Constantius was occupied in building large fleets at all the harbours of Northern Gaul. Apparently he made no attempt to take the offensive, and to destroy these armaments before they grew overwhelmingly strong. In the third year (296) Constantius sailed for Britain, with his fleet divided into two great sections, one of which issued from Gessoriacum, the other from the mouth of the Seine. Allectus's own vessels, which were still numerous, were lying off the Isle of Wight waiting for the latter division ; but a chance fog hid from them the course of their enemies, who were carried farther down channel than they had intended, but came to shore quite unopposed—presumably somewhere west of the island. The praetorian praefect Asclepiodotus, who commanded this squadron, burnt his boats, after the manner of Agathocles, and pressed inland. Meanwhile Allectus, abandoning his fleet and his fortified ports, hastened to throw himself between the invaders and London, with a force composed only of his marines [1] and his Frankish mercenary

---

[1] The marine troops must evidently be the " veteres illius conjurationis auctores " who, according to Eumenius, were the only troops, over and above the Franks, whom Allectus took out to the battle. Probably the usurper was at Portchester looking out for the arrival of the expedition from the Seine, for we are told that on hearing of Asclepiodotus's landing " classem portumque deseruit ". If the fleet was " apud insulam Vectam in speculis," its base must have been Portchester or possibly Clausentum (Southampton).

troops. He was beaten, after a fight in which, according to the
prejudiced testimony of his enemies, he displayed military incompetence verging on insanity.[1] He himself perished unnoticed in
the rout, for he had thrown away all his imperial insignia save one
garment.[2] The downs for many miles were thickly sprinkled with
the bodies of the Franks, easily recognised by their barbarous dress
and long red hair, but very few Roman citizens fell, for Allectus
had shrunk from putting his legions in line, no doubt because he
mistrusted them.[3] The engagement must have taken place somewhere on the road from Salisbury and Winchester to London, and
possibly near Woolmer Forest, where an enormous hoard of copper
coins of Carausius and Allectus was found some forty years ago,
evidently a hastily buried regimental treasury.

Constantius himself meanwhile, who had sailed from Boulogne,
had apparently come ashore unopposed in Kent,[4] while one division
of his squadron, going farther north than it had intended, in that
same fog which had favoured the landing of Asclepiodotus, ran into
the mouth of the Thames. This detachment, reaching London,
found the town in a state of confusion, for the surviving relics of
Allectus's mercenary array of Franks had fled thither, and were
plundering the citizens, preparatory to embarking in their own boats
and fleeing to the Rhine-mouth. Vast numbers of the robbers
were slaughtered in the streets, to the great pleasure of the Londoners, who were glad to be rid of the usurper and his unruly
auxiliaries. It was not unnatural, therefore, that Constantius was
welcomed with enthusiasm when he appeared in person. The whole

---

[1] In modum amentis properavit ad mortem, ut nec explicaret aciem nec omnes
copias quas trahebat instruxerit. Eumenius, *ibid.*

[2] "Ipse vexillarius latrocinii, cultu illo quem vivus violaverat sponte deposito,
vix unius velaminis repertus est indicio." So he had kept one imperial garment,
presumably the purple tunic below his cuirass.

[3] Adeo ut nemo fere Romanus occiderit, imperio vincente Romano, *ibid.*

[4] This may be gathered from the fact that Allectus is said to have been
avoiding Constantius when he attacked Asclepiodotus. "Te fugiens in tuorum manus
incidit." Probably the usurper was merely striking at the nearer enemy. Starting
from Gessoriacum, Constantius must have come ashore somewhere in Kent or
Eastern Sussex. We are told that the squadron on the Seine only put to sea when
it heard that the Caesar had already sailed from Boulogne. We should guess that
the northern expedition must have reached Britain first; yet it had no fighting to
do, or Eumenius would have said something in praise of his master's valour, instead
of merely commemorating his good fortune.

province returned to its allegiance with alacrity, and the Caesar found no further operations necessary, since even the barbarians beyond the Wall sent him submissive messages and kept quiet. "He had no reason to go further, unless he had wished to explore the boundaries of Ocean himself, which Nature has forbidden."

The triumph of Constantius and his entry into London are commemorated by a famous medallion of gold, discovered at Arras when that city was being rebuilt after the Great War. This immense coin represents the Cæsar on horseback received at the gate of the city—whose name is duly written above—by a kneeling lady with a turreted crown, evidently representing the genius of London. Below we see the Thames, with a galley upon its water. The inscription around is RESTITUTORI LUCIS. This unique and most interesting coin gives the first known pictorial representation of London.

CHAPTER IX

THE ROMAN PERIOD—DIOCLETIAN TO HONORIUS (296-410)

THE defeat and death of Allectus brought Britain once more into the general system of the Roman Empire, and enabled Diocletian to subject it to the same reorganisation which he was already carrying out in the remaining provinces. He had divided the Roman world into four portions, two of which (the East, and Italy with Pannonia and Africa) were governed directly by himself and his senior colleague Maximianus Herculeus, while the other two (Gaul with Spain, and the Balkan Peninsula) [1] were administered by the two junior emperors, the Caesars Constantius Chlorus and Galerius Maximianus. Britain, of course, fell into the share of Constantius, and looked for the future to Trier, the capital of the western section of the empire, instead of to Rome, as the administrative centre from which it was to be governed. Constantine completed and modified Diocletian's arrangements, and in the fourth century we find Britain a "diocese" of the "Praefecture of the Gauls". Each of these dioceses consisted of several old provinces: the British one being composed of the two units "Upper" and "Lower" Britain which had been created by Severus, just as, e.g., the Spanish diocese was formed by the union of Lusitania, Baetica and Tarraconensis. Inside the diocese wholly new subdivisions were created, much smaller than the old provinces. Those of Britain were four in number, Britannia Prima and Secunda, Maxima Caesariensis and Flavia Caesariensis. A fifth was added in 369 when Valentinian made certain northern tracts of the diocese, lately recovered from the barbarians, into the province of Valentia. We are unfortunately wholly without information as to the situa-

---

[1] Galerius, however, did not get Thrace, which went with the East, while Constantius had the outlying province of Mauretania Tingitensis in Africa.

tion of these units. The sole facts preserved about them are that
Corinium (Cirencester), as is shown by an inscription found there,[1]
was in Britannia Prima, and that Valentia was in the North.[2]

The essential core of the system of Diocletian and Constantine
was the division of military from civil power in each section of the
empire, with the object of preventing provincial insurrection headed
by viceroys who were also commanders-in-chief—the disease of the
third century. Accordingly the *vicar* or governor-general of the
diocese of Britain, was a civilian, who was at the head of all the administrative and financial machinery, but had not direct control
over the military officers who commanded the troops of Britain.
Under the vicar were four other civilian governors for the four
provinces, a *consularis* in Maxima Caesariensis, three *praesides*
in Flavia Caesariensis and the two Britanniae. The troops on the
other hand were entrusted to three commanders, the *Comes Britanniarum*, the *Dux Britanniarum*, and the *Comes Littoris
Saxonici*, all of whom reported directly to the Praetorian Praefect
of the Gauls, and not to the vicar. The title of *comes*, it must be
remarked, was in the fourth century superior to that of *dux*, quite
contrary to the usage of the Middle Ages. The *Dux Britanniarum* commanded in the North, having under him the garrison of
the Wall: the Count of the Saxon Shore was in charge of a fleet,
and of the coast-garrisons from the Wash to the Solent: he was the
successor of Carausius for all intents and purposes. The *Comes
Britanniarum*, who was the senior officer of the three, was probably
in command of the other two: his own troops formed a small reserve
army, which could be brought up to aid any threatened point in
time of need. We do not know where they were normally cantoned:
perhaps a large proportion of them may originally have been in the
West Midlands and South Wales, where down to the third century
two legions had been stationed at Chester and Caerleon. But our
only list of the stations of the British army is that in the *Notitia
Dignitatum*, an official directory drawn up about 400 A.D. Vast
changes must have taken place between the fall of Allectus and that

---

[1] See p. 183.
[2] The boundaries shown in all old and (alas!) some new atlases are taken from
the ingenious forgery of Professor Bertram, an eighteenth century Dane, who foisted
on the learned world a catalogue, fathered on the chronicler Richard of Cirencester,
of roads, towns and provinces in Britain manufactured by himself.

date.   Yet it is curious to find that even in 400 many of the old
arrangements of the third century still subsisted.   The Sixth Legion
was still at York, and of the regiments in the North about half
were those which had been there ever since the time of Antoninus
Pius.[1]

It was probably to a great extent in consequence of the division
of military from civil authority, introduced by Diocletian, that for
more than fifty years after the fall of Allectus Britain was vexed by
no further insurrections.   Perhaps the unhappy memory of the last
years of the "British Empire" under Allectus had cured the soldiery
and the provincials alike of seditious tendencies.   But something
also must be allowed for the fact that during the early years of the
fourth century the island was more frequently the residence of an
emperor than had ever been the case before.   Both Constantius and
his son Constantine the Great were resident in Britain for long
periods, as was natural with Caesars who only ruled the West, and
had no concern with troubles on the Danube or the Euphrates.   It
was during a stay in Britain in 306 A.D. that the former emperor
contracted his last fatal illness, and it was at Eburacum that he
expired a short time after.   He had been joined just before he
crossed the Channel[2] by Constantine, who had up to that moment
been retained as a hostage by Constantius's colleague Galerius
Valerius Maximianus.   A chance allusion in Eumenius tells us that
the elder emperor's last journey was not caused by absolute military

[1] So slightly changed is the garrison of the Wall in the *Notitia*, when compared
with its garrison in the time of Severus, that Mommsen started a theory that the
list in the *Notitia* was not a genuine directory to the cantonments of the British
army in 400, but a screed copied from some much earlier document, to hide an un-
sightly gap in the military organisation of the empire, caused by the destruction of
the British garrisons in the recent disastrous wars with Pict, Scot and Saxon.   This
theory will not hold water for a moment.   Though there is certainly a much greater
similarity between the army of 200 A.D. and the army of 400 A.D. in Britain than in
any other province, we yet find in it regiments whose nomenclature belongs distinctly
to the reign of Honorius.   Not to speak of the *Equites Honoriani Seniores*, whose
title dates these clearly enough, we have a regiment of Taifalae, a tribe never mentioned till the late fourth century, and several numeri with names like Defensores,
Directores, Solenses, Victores Juniores Britanniciani, Catafractarii Juniores, which
have the stamp of the post-Constantinian epoch.   Still there is a wonderful survival
of old regiments, and a lack of new ones with the grotesque names common on the
Continent, like Ursi, Exculcatores, or Seniores Braccati.

[2] Ad tempus ipsum quo pater in Britanniam transfretabat, classi jam vela.
facienti, repentinus tuus adventus illuxit,—Eumenius addressing Constantine in 310

necessity "he was not seeking British trophies, as the vulgar believe: he was not set on annexing the woods and marshes of the
Caledonians and the other Picts, nor the neighbouring Ireland, nor
distant Thule, nor the Fortunate Isles—if indeed they exist ".   But
another, if a later authority,[1] tells us nevertheless that Constantius
made a campaign against the Picts, and gave them a severe chastisement, returning to York to die immediately after—perhaps from
fatigue or disease contracted during his expedition [July 25, 306].
The chance that the emperor died at Eburacum caused that city to
be the place where his son Constantine was proclaimed his successor,
much to the vexation of Galerius, who had not intended that he
should inherit his father's share of the empire.   But the young
prince assumed first the title of Caesar, and afterwards that of
Augustus, which Galerius had intended to confer on his dependant
the Illyrian Severus.

The story that Constantine was born in Britain has no foundation: at the moment of his birth (274) the usurper Tetricus was
reigning in Britain and Gaul, while Constantine's father, a nephew
of the legitimate emperor Claudius Gothicus, was following the
fortunes of Claudius's duly elected successor Aurelian.   Equally
destitute of foundation is the legend that Constantine's mother
Helena was a British princess, the heiress of a mythical King Coel.
These are late Celtic tales, and we must believe the fourth-century
historians who tell us that the first Christian emperor was born
" ex obscuriori matrimonio," if not that Helena was the daughter
of a Bithynian innkeeper, whom Constantius had picked up while
campaigning in the East.

Immediately after his proclamation Constantine crossed over to
Gaul, to guard his father's old dominions from the grasping hand
of Galerius.   How many times he returned to Britain, before he
began the great series of campaigns which ultimately made him
master of the whole Roman world, we do not know.   At least one
such visit is mentioned in the statement of the chronicle of Eusebius
Pamphilus that "after he was firmly seated in power, and had seen
to the peoples in his father's share of the empire with benevolent
care, . . . he passed over to the British tribes, which lie within,
on the very borders of Ocean, and put them in order ".   And again

---

[1] The anonymous chronicler whose excerpts about Constantius, Constantine and
others are found at the end of the history of Ammianus Marcellinus.

we are told that "at the commencement of his reign the Britons who dwell along the Western Ocean were subdued by him ". This must probably refer to campaigning north of the Wall, on the borders of the Irish Sea. But it is hard to believe that any proper annexation of the Western Lowlands can have been made by him.[1] Probably the Selgovae and Novantae, or the tribes who had succeeded to the former holdings of these peoples, did him homage and gave hostages. If there had been any serious fighting or notable victories in Britain, in the period of Constantine, it would almost certainly have been recorded on the coinage—that public gazette of the Roman Empire. But while the chastisement of Franks, Alamanni and Sarmatians,[2] and the valour of the Gaulish and Illyrian armies are recorded on the money of Constantine and his elder son Crispus, there is no mention of British victories Perhaps it is not without significance that the favourite type of the London mint during the middle period of the reign of Constantine is Beata Tranquillitas—though it must be owned that the same inscription appears also on the coinage of Trier, which was quite close to the site of the Frankish wars.

Archæological and literary evidence, however, join in suggesting that the period between the fall of Allectus and the middle of the fourth century was probably the most prosperous epoch which the British provinces ever knew. The general laudation of the fertility and wealth of the island in which the Panegyrists indulge is corroborated by such practical evidence as the fact that Constantius collected masons and artisans for the rebuilding of the Gallic Autun in Britain, "quibus illae provinciae redundabant". We find milestones of Constantius and his son, testifying to the care for, and repairing of, the old roads, on the most exposed edges of the land, e.g., on the highways just south of Hadrian's Wall and the coast of South Wales. The London mint was pouring out enormous quantities of money from the time of the

---

[1] It is well, however, to remember that after the abandonment of Britain by the Roman Government in the reign of Honorius, we seem to find the British tribes of the Lowlands merged with those on the Wall, and acting together in union. See also pp. 189 infra, concerning the general Coroticus, who bore sway in those parts in the middle of the fifth century. It is possible that the campaigns of Constantine led to a more real exertion of suzerainty north of the Wall than had been existing before.

[2] FRANCIA DEVICTA, ALAMANNIA DEVICTA and SARMATIA DEVICTA are all found about 320 A.D.

arrival of Constantius in 296 down to the later half of Constantine's reign. Why it was closed somewhere at the end of the lifetime of the latter emperor it is impossible to say ; but this was the case,[1] and no more coins were issued there save during the usurpation of Magnus Maximus nearly fifty years later. The agricultural prosperity of the island is vouched for by the fact that it was sending corn to the provinces of the Lower Rhine even in the time of Julian (360 A.D.) when evil days had once more begun to dawn upon the empire. But the greatest and most widespread mass of evidence concerning the tranquillity of the province comes from the use of the explorer's spade. Of the countless Roman villas of Britain that have been excavated, nearly all seem to have been occupied, and many to have been built, during the Constantinian epoch. The mines of Mendip, which had apparently been neglected for more than a century, were being worked with energy in the first half of the fourth century. The few traces of Roman occupation in Cornwall and Western Devon belong mainly to the same time ; they only begin in the late third century. The more important of them, four milestones and an ingot of tin stamped with the imperial marks, come from the days of the descendants of Constantius Chlorus.[2] The majority of the coins dug up in the extreme south-west also belong to this epoch. We should know much more of the administration of Britain if the practice of marking every new building with a dedicatory or commemorative inscription, so universal in the second century, had continued into the fourth. But the historical inscriptions of this age can be counted on the fingers of one hand, if milestones are set aside. The two most important, the Cirencester dedication alluded to in a later page (see p. 183), and the Yorkshire inscription near Whitby, are later than Constantine—one seems to date from Julian, the other from Honorius. It is not correct to ascribe this silence of the fourth-century officials and soldiery of Britain to the introduction of Christianity, and the consequent cessation of the erecting of altars to the gods, or to the genii of the cohorts and legions.

---

[1] The date can be fixed at somewhere about 335 A.D., because of the absen e of coins of the sons of Constantine with the title of Augustus, which was conferred on Constans and Constantius II. in 337.

[2] See Professor Haverfield's papers in *Proceedings of the Society of Antiquaries*, 1900, and *Numismatic Chronicle* of the same year.

There is, as we shall see, reason to believe that Britain was still predominantly pagan down to the end of its connection with the Roman Empire. A more potent cause was the increase of the barbarian element in the army; the "cunei" and "numeri" of Germans from beyond the frontier, who formed an ever-growing proportion of the garrison of Britain, did not commemorate themselves or their gods as the old auxiliary cohorts had done. But it is curious to find a noteworthy lack of ordinary sepulchral inscriptions of private persons in the fourth century ; there are a very few Christian tombs—the small number need not surprise us— but it is much more surprising to find a lack of those of the ordinary heathen type, which ought to have been set up by the hundred during a period which seems to have been one of considerable prosperity. Conceivably the fourth century tombs, like the fourth-century public buildings, lay on the surface-stratum of Roman Britain, and were handiest for the Saxon spoiler, or the medieval seeker after hewn stone, to destroy or to carry away. The memorials of earlier days may have escaped in greater numbers because they were already buried below later Roman work.

When Constantine died in 337 Britain fell into that share of the empire which he left to his eldest son, Constantine II. But that ill-fated prince died early, slain in battle with his younger brother Constans, whose dominions he was endeavouring to annex (340). All his lands fell to the victor, who reigned over the whole West from 340 to 350. It is in his time that we have the first note of renewed danger from the barbarians reported from Britain. The Picts seem to have made a sudden and dangerous assault on the districts along the wall, perhaps assisted by the Scots, an enemy of whom we have not heard before, but of whom we shall have much to tell. It seems likely that they actually burst through the Wall, though of definite evidence for this disaster we have only the fact that Corstopitum, the largest town behind it, shows signs of having been burnt at a date after the death of Constantine (337) and before the time of Julian or Valentinian (360). The books of the history of Ammianus Marcellinus which deal with the reign of Constans have unhappily perished. We only know from allusions, in a later part of his work, that Constans went in person to Britain,

---

[1] Yet it is curious that the London mint put Christian emblems on its coins before those of Trier, Lyons, or Arles. See *Corstopitum* Report, 1910, pp. 51-2.

and imposed terms of peace upon the invaders.[1] The line of the
Wall was restored and regarrisoned. From another source we know
that the danger had been so fierce and sudden that the emperor
crossed the Channel at midwinter to bring prompt help.[2] A large
bronze medal of Constans, commemorating his embarkation at
" Bononia Oceanensis," seems to refer to this abnormal voyage.
Its date was apparently 343 A.D.

Constans, though a prince of some vigour and merit, perished
suddenly and miserably, in strife with the rebel Magnentius. This
person was the second usurper of British blood who wore the purple,
Bonosus (as we have already remarked) being the first. He had
served with distinction in the guards under Constantine the Great,
and had been made a count and entrusted with the command of
two legions by Constans. Having slain his master in Gaul, he was
recognised as emperor by both Britain and Spain, and ruled them
for three years (350-53). He made his brother Decentius his Caesar
and colleague, and these two Britons were obeyed at Rome as well
as in all the West, till Constantius, the last surviving son of Constantine, came up against them with the armies of Illyricum and the
East, and beat them in three desperate battles, one at Mursa in
Illyricum the other two in Southern Gaul. After his last defeat the
usurper committed suicide, to avoid falling into the hands of a foe
who had his brother's blood to avenge, and was known for his calm
and deliberate cruelty. Magnentius had met with many supporters
in Britain, as was natural considering that he drew his origin from
her, and had been notably helped by Gratianus, once local commander-
in-chief (comes Britanniarum). After his fall Constantius sent
into the island one Paul the notary, a secret spy and inquisitor
whom he often employed on matters of police, bidding him seek out
all traitors and send them to Rome. Paul did his work in such a

---

[1] Speaking of the events of 360 Ammianus (xviii. 2), says that Julian was disturbed by the fact that the Picts and Scots *rupta quiete condicta* (terms had therefore
been imposed upon them) were again wasting the lands near the *Limes*, and that
the Caesar doubted whether he ought not to go at once against them, " as we have
already related that Constans went". But he did not do so.

[2] Julius Firmicus " hyeme (quod non factum est aliquando) saevientes undas
calcastis sub remis vestris . . . insperatam imperatoris faciem Britannus expavit " ;
he adds, " vicistis hostes, propagastis imperium ". So the empire was in some
sense extended ; probably by terms of submission being imposed on a new enemy,
the Scot.

reckless and cruel fashion, arresting and imprisoning multitudes of innocent persons, that Martinus the *vicarius* (governor-general) of Britain openly withstood him. Whereupon Paul presumed to declare the vicar himself a traitor, and came to arrest him. This so enraged the governor that he drew his sword, and tried to cut down the notary ; but having missed his blow and failed to slay Paul, he suddenly turned his weapon against himself before he could be seized, and escaped capture by suicide. We are told that his fate moved universal pity, as he was the justest and most kind-hearted of men. Paul brought back to Constantius a multitude of chained captives, who suffered the scourge and the rack. Some were finally put to death, others sent into exile.

We hear nothing more of Britain for seven years, but in 360, when Constantius was still emperor and his cousin Julian was ruling as his lieutenant in Gaul, troubles of the same kind that had been seen in the days of Constans broke out in Britain. The Picts and Scots broke the peace imposed upon them seventeen years before, began to ravage the lands about Hadrian's Wall and caused a panic throughout the island. The Pict is but the Caledonian under a new name; the Scot deserves a word of further notice. The Romans applied the name to all the inhabitants of Ireland, but the Scot proper was the *Scuit*, the " man cut off" or " broken man," [1] who was to the other Goidels what the Viking was to the Danes four hundred years later. The name was not national, nor often used in Ireland itself.

It was applied in a particular sense, however, to a tribe in the extreme north-west of Ireland, in the modern county of Antrim, who seem to have been exiles driven out of lands farther west and south by other peoples. Their country was called Dalriada, a name that was afterwards transferred to that district of the Highlands, across the water in North Britain, which was destined to be colonised by these Scots. It is curious to find that just south of the Irish Dalriada there was another small territory held by a fragment of the Picts, who, at some unknown date, had found their way to Ireland. Moreover somewhere in the fourth century, as we must suppose, another section of the Picts established themselves on the north shore of the Solway Firth, in the modern shires of Kirkcudbright and Wigtown, intruding among the British Novantae and

---

[1] *Not*, I think, the " tatooed man " the explanation of Isidore of Seville.

Selgovae, who held that territory at an earlier time.[1] These Picts were known as *Niduarii* from their dwelling on the west bank of the Nith (Nidus)[2]. They were certainly lodged there before the end of the fourth century, as the Christian missionary Ninian was working among them at that date. It seems more probable that they were an offshoot of the Irish Picts of Ulster, than that they had pushed south from the Highlands behind the Forth, and settled beyond the Britons of the Clyde Valley, whom the Northern Picts never succeeded in conquering.

Such a settlement in Britain would be quite in keeping with what is known of other Irish movements at this time. For there seems to be no doubt that another Hibernian tribe, the Desse or Daesi, thrust out of their old home in County Meath by their neighbours, passed over into Britain and settled in the land of the Demetae in South Wales, where in the fifth century they were occupying the districts of Gower and Kidwelly.[3] As we know that this region was securely held by the Romans in the time of Constantine, whose mile-stones and road-building can be traced along its coast, we must suppose either that the immigrants were received as peaceable settlers by the imperial government—a thing common enough in that epoch—or that they came later than 340, and that their movement was part of that general assault on the Roman borders in Britain of which we get the first trace in the reign of Constans. It is even conceivable that their arrival formed precisely the crisis which drew Constans to Britain in midwinter, and that their submission to him after some fighting was the " extension of the empire " on which Julius Firmicus congratulated that emperor.

But whatever was the character of the first coming of the Irish to Britain, and whatever was the cause of their arrival, it is certain that by the year 350 A.D. they had commenced that series of de-

[1] Ptolemy, writing in the second century, knows of no tribe save Novantae and Selgovae in the Western Lowlands.

[2] But apparently earlier Novius, as in Ptolemy.

[3] See Bury's *Life of St. Patrick* (p. 14) and the long passage concerning the Desse in Zimmer's *Nennius Vindicatus*, pp. 84-89. But I cannot agree with the conclusions made by the latter that the Irish immigrants came as early as the third century, and remained in possession of Demetia permanently, till they were absorbed by their Brythonic neighbours. The definite statement in the *Historia Brittonum* that they were expelled by Cunedda's family is too strong, and Zimmer omits the tale of Urien Reged and his conquest of these Goidels of South Wales.

structive raids which was to last for about a century. As was the case with the Vikings 400 years after, the first attacks seem to have been sporadic and tentative, but after a time the number of the invaders increased, and their fleets were led not by mere adventurers but by tribal chiefs, and even by the high-kings of Ireland themselves, of whom two Niall (*circ.* 405) and Dathi (*circ.* 425) are recorded in the earliest annals of their island as having perished beyond seas —one in the British Channel, the other in Gaul. The front of the Irish invasion was from the Solway Firth to the Bristol Channel,[1] the poorest and most rugged face of Britain, yet one where plunder sufficient to tempt the pirate was to be got, in favoured districts such as the lowlands about Carlisle, the lower valleys of the Dee and Mersey round Deva and Mancunium, the south coast of Glamorgan, and most of all the rich and well-peopled plain of Gloucester. We may reasonably attribute to the Scots the destruction of the many Roman villas of the Constantinian epoch on both sides of the Severn mouth, which evidently came to an end by burning. It was apparently in this region that one of their bands captured, along with other prisoners, the boy Patricius, who was destined to become the Apostle of Ireland—but this was in the year 405, long after the date which we have now reached.[2] It is highly probable also that it was the Scots who made an end of Deva, and even of Viroconium, whose destruction may have come early, for its ruins have yielded no coins later than the year 380.[3] But the coast of Cumberland, south of Hadrian's Wall, was certainly another focus of Scottish raids. It must have been against them that a guard was kept by the numerous auxiliary regiments whom the *Notitia* records as placed from Gabrosentum at the mouth of the Eden to Morecambe Bay, with reserves among the Westmoreland Hills The Scots and Picts are often found acting together: it must have been in this region that they would most easily meet, the one coming down from the Highlands, by way of the Clyde and the

---

[1] The iron-bound northern coast of the thinly peopled Devon and Cornwall cannot have tempted them.

[2] See Bury's *Life of St. Patrick* for an elaborate argument to prove that the Saint must have been carried off from the region of the Severn Mouth rather than that of the Clyde.   His birthplace was Bannaventa, which must probably be one of the two Banwens of Glamorganshire.

[3] But the site is so imperfectly explored, that this deduction would be dangerous. If sacked in 380, Viroconium might surely have been restored.

Annan, the others coasting along Galloway, and ready to outflank the line of the Roman Wall by landing south of it and taking it in the rear.

In the series of invasions, growing every year more serious, which began in 360 A.D., we first hear of the Picts and Scots alone. They ravaged the lands along the Wall, and so attracted the notice of the Caesar Julian who, being distracted by dangers on the Rhine, refused to cross to Britain, but sent over his *magister equitum*, Lupicinus, with four regiments of German and Illyrian auxiliaries. But the death of Constantius II. and his own accession to the throne seem to have distracted Julian's attention from Britain, and two of the newly landed corps were withdrawn to the East. It does not seem, however, that the raids on the North can have been very serious as yet, for Julian was not only able to ignore the military needs of Britain, but to draw great stores of corn from it for the devastated Rhine provinces,[1] and even to cut down certain of its military expenses, " which were nominally spent on the soldiery, but really went into the private purse of the governors ".[2]

During the short three years during which Julian ruled as sole emperor after the death of his cousin Constantius, we have no further notice of Britain: all the attention of the historians was drawn to his vain struggle to arrest the progress of Christianity, or with his Persian wars. It is not till the " Apostate " had perished, and his short-lived successor Jovian had followed him to the grave, that in the reign of Valentinian we again are permitted to get a glimpse of insular affairs. In 364 we are told by Ammianus that Britain was being harassed by the joint assaults of four enemies. Not only were the Picts and Scots on the war-path, but the province was also being attacked by the Saxons—an enemy of whom we have heard nothing since the day of Carausius—and also by the Attacotti "a warlike race of men ".[3] Who those last invaders can have been is somewhat of a puzzle. They are only mentioned at this particular date, and save Ammianus no ancient author names them except St. Jerome, who vouchsafes the startling information

---

[1] See Julian's Letter to the Athenians, 360 A.D. Such exports were not unusual. Previous drafts of corn from Britain are mentioned in 358 by Zosimus, iii. 5.

[2] ἣ τοὔνομα μὲν ἦν στρατιωτικὴ, τῷ δὲ ἔργῳ πρόσοδος τῶν ἡγουμένων (Libanius, *Oratio Parentalis in Julianum Imperatorem*).

[3] Ammianus, xxvii. 8.

that they were a British tribe who practised cannibalism! who, when they carried off swineherd and swine together, preferred a steak from the human rather than the porcine captive.[1] The saint states that he himself had seen certain of these monsters in Gaul. This is quite possible, for the Roman army, when the *Notitia* was drawn up, contained no less than four regiments of Attacotti. But that any British tribe at this date should have been given to cannibalism is incredible, all the more so one out of which the Romans were raising many auxiliaries. The fact that the Attacotti are called Britons is sufficient proof that they were neither Irish nor Saxons. They are also carefully distinguished from the Picts by Ammianus: we are therefore driven to believe that the name must represent some of the Brythonic tribes between the Walls of Hadrian and Antoninus, disguised under a new designation, which perhaps represents a temporary confederacy. Seeing that we find them serving in considerable numbers in the Roman army a generation later, this seems a probable explanation; the land between the Walls would be a very natural region from which to enlist auxiliaries.

When mentioning the Picts on this occasion, Ammianus takes the opportunity of stating that they were at this time divided into two leagues or sections, the Dicaledonians and the Verturiones. The former seems to represent the Northern tribes, who dwelt along the so-called Ducaledonian Ocean : the latter appears to be a new name for the Southern Picts or Meatae, of whom we heard in the time of Severus. Their designation is connected with the later Fortrenn, the title given by the Britons to the region to the north and east of the Tay.

The assault of Picts, Saxons, Scots and Attacotti upon Roman Britain is ascribed to a "conspiracy" among the four barbarian races, so that it would appear that they were deliberately acting in unison and playing into each other's hands. Their attacks grew more frequent and formidable as the years of Valentinian's reign went on, till in 367 A.D. we learn that the whole defence of Britain was shattered, owing to two simultaneous disasters, Nectarides, Count of the Saxon Shore, being defeated and slain by the pirates of Germany, while Fullofaudes the "dux Britanniarum" or commander of the Northern garrisons, at York and on the Wall, fell into an ambush and perished —no doubt at the hands of the Picts. The defence of the Wall

---

[1] Jerome, *Adversus Jovinianum*, ii. 201.

was broken down, many of the surviving troops disbanded themselves, and the barbarians came flooding into the Midlands. The emperor Valentinian, after sending in quick succession three generals to Britain, who accomplished nothing, gave the command of the province in 368 to Count Theodosius, an experienced officer of Spanish extraction, and the father of a better-known son of the same name, who was destined to wear the purple some twelve years later.

Theodosius was allowed to take with him the Batavians and Heruli, the best auxiliary troops in the Gallic army, and the Jovii and Victores from the imperial guard. So far south had the barbarians spread, that he was forced to make London the base of his first operations—presumably therefore York and Chester had been evacuated by their legions and had been sacked by the enemy. We are told that the invaders offered no opportunity of a pitched battle to Theodosius, that they were scattered over the country in numerous bands, each intent on its own particular raid. His only difficulty was to locate them, since their movements were rapid and uncertain. But by means of the information furnished by captives and deserters he succeeded in hunting down and destroying many parties, and cleared the southern parts of the province of them. He then increased his force by offering free pardon to all deserters who should return to their standards, and calling in many disorganised detachments, who had retired into remote corners of the province, and had there been living at free quarters.

It was apparently in the next year (369) that Theodosius, with an army that had been strengthened both in numbers and in efficiency, cleared the North, right up to the Wall, and reoccupied many cities and forts which, though they had suffered damage of all kinds, were capable of restoration. At the same time he had to crush the beginnings of a provincial rebellion ; one Valentine the Pannonian, a political exile, was detected tampering with the soldiery—no doubt with the disorganised bands which had only lately returned to their allegiance,—in order to induce them to declare him emperor. He was detected in time, captured, and executed, along with two or three of his confidants ; but Theodosius refused to make any further inquiry into the plot, lest by arresting many conspirators he should cause general distrust, and give occasion for provincial tumults to break out.

This being done, he repaired and re-garrisoned the Wall and the camps behind it, and restored the old course of civil and military administration, wherever it had been swept away. He made one change, we are told, by abolishing a frontier institution called the Arcani. These were a body of men, evidently Britons, who had been stationed far out beyond the *Limes*, for the purpose of discovering by constant explorations, and reporting to headquarters, any signs of movement on the part of the Picts or other neighbours.[1] They were accused and convicted of having repeatedly given notice to the enemy of the movement of Roman troops, in return for bribes. Such treason would be almost inevitable if the Arcani were mere Britons of the frontier—Brigantes or Otadini—who were near kinsmen of these hostile tribes between Solway and Clyde who were now known as Attacotti.

The work of Theodosius was evidently very thorough. We are told that he not only cleared the land of invaders, but pursued them out to sea. " He followed the Scot with wandering sword, and clove the waters of the Northern ocean with his daring oars." " He trod the sands of both tidal seas " (the Irish and the North). "The Orkney isles dripped with the blood of the routed Saxon." There must be much exaggeration in these lines of Claudian—we can hardly believe that Theodosius reached the Orkneys, or that the Saxons would have chosen these islands as their refuge : and our suspicion turns into certainty when we read that slaughtered Picts lay thick in the fabulous Thule. But nevertheless the poet must have had some facts on which to base his hyperbolical account of the naval exploits of Theodosius. There need be no doubt that he reorganised the fleet no less than the army—there are two naval regiments marked on the *Notitia* as lying on the North-west coast,[2] and the whole establishment of the " Saxon shore " was restored, which must have included, as of old, a squadron of ships no less than the land troops registered as belonging to it. All this must represent the re-arrangements of Theodosius, for all that had existed before him had been swept away for the moment.

---

[1] Arcanos, genus hominum a veteribus institutum, paullatim prolapsos in vitia a suis stationibus removit, aperte convictos acceptarum promissarumque magnitudine praedarum allectos, quae apud nos agebantur aliquotiens barbaris prodidisse. Id enim erat illis officium, ut ultro citroque per longa spatia discurrentes, vicinarum gentium strepitus nostris ducibus intimarent (Ammianus, xxviii. 3).

[2] The Barcarii Tigridenses and Cohors Ælia Classica, at Arbeja and Tunnocellum.

Having completed this work of reorganisation, Theodosius returned to his master Valentinian, who received him as if he had been some dictator of the old days of Rome, a Furius Camillus or a Papirius Cursor, and gave him the important post of *Magister Equitum Per Gallias*. The emperor also decreed that the newly recovered Northern province of Britain should be named Valentia, in allusion to his own name. Conceivably it was also at this same time that Londinium was given the honorary title of Augusta; but this may have been the work of Constans, twenty years before.[1] It is in error that some historians have supposed that Theodosius added a new province to the Roman Empire, and that " Valentia " means the land between the Walls of Hadrian and Antoninus. The words of Ammianus are clear : " Theodosius restored the province that he had *recovered*, which had been lost to the barbarians, to its ancient state, so that it had once more a legitimate ruler, and was afterwards named Valentia by order of the emperor, who had as it were triumphed over it." There is no extension of the border implied in these words.

It would seem that Britain had a rest for some ten or fifteen years after the victories of Theodosius, and that the great general himself was dead—slain in Africa by orders of the cowardly Valens, who suspected him of aiming at the crown—before troubles once more began. The only note that we have in these fourteen years (369-83) is that Valentinian transferred over to Britain a certain king, Fraomar, chief of the Buccinobantes, a section of the Alamanni ; the territory of this race had been so devastated that they were moved wholesale to serve as a " numerus " of military settlers on this side of the Channel, no doubt in some region that had been depopulated by the late incursions of Picts and Scots (371 A.D.).

The awful defeat of Adrianople (378) in which the Goths slew Valens, the Emperor of the East, and so for a time got possession of all the inland of the Balkan Peninsula, had no effect in the West. Here matters seem to have been fairly quiet, under Gratian, the son and successor of Valentinian (375-83). But the woes of Britain recommenced with civil strife; Gratian, though a youth of many

---

[1] Ammianus in naming the city calls it " Londinium, vetus oppidum quod Augustam posteritas appellavit ". This is the first mention of the new name. It was still Londinium in 330. The coins of Magnus Maximus (383-88) and the *Notitia* (400 ?) both call it Augusta.

merits, was unpopular with his soldiery, who accused him of loving barbarians over-much, and neglecting his military duties for the chase. An insurrection against him was headed by Magnus Maximus, a Spanish officer of mature years,[1] who had seen much service in Britain under Theodosius, and was still in office there fifteen years after. We are told by Orosius that the legions invested him with the purple almost against his will, and that he was " an energetic and just man, and would have been well worthy of the title of Emperor if he had not come to it by breaking his oath of allegiance ".[2] Zosimus, however, who, like Orosius, wrote little more than thirty years after the insurrection of Maximus, declares that he was the secret instigator of the revolt, having conceived a great hatred for Gratian, because he had not received the promotion which he thought his due.[3] Apparently, therefore, he was not Count of the Britains, commander-in-chief in the island, but must have held some subordinate military post, such as that of duke, or Count of the Saxon Shore.

Magnus Maximus seems to have reigned for some short time in Britain alone, where he opened the long-disused mint of London,[4] and repelled an incursion of the Picts and Scots, who probably saw an opportunity for raiding presented to them by the outbreak of civil war.[5] But in the same year that saw his proclamation he concentrated the picked corps of the British army, and crossed into Gaul. He had already been tampering with the officers of the Rhine legions, which came over to his cause en masse. Gratian started to fly to Italy, but was murdered at Lyons by one of his own officers, who wished to commend himself to the usurper by this treacherous deed. Spain submitted to Magnus Maximus immediately after, without fighting, and he thus became master of the whole West. Valentinian, the younger brother of Gratian, still reigned at Rome, but was too young and weak to revenge his brother's murder. His ministers patched up a peace with Maximus, which lasted two years. In the third the usurper resolved to cross the Alps with his British

---

[1] As he had a son almost grown up to manhood, and had been already an officer in 368, he must have been at least forty when he rebelled.

[2] Orosius, vii. 34.   [3] Zosimus, iv. 35.

[4] Where a few coins were also struck in Theodosius's name.

[5] For this campaign we have only the evidence of Prosper Tiro, who misdates it, placing Maximus's rebellion in 381 and the Pictish War in 382.

and Gallic legions (387).   He was almost unopposed, and Valentinian
and his family fled to Constantinople, to throw themselves on the
mercy of Theodosius the Younger, the son of the murdered general,
who had been reigning in the East since 379.

It seems clear that the depletion of the British garrisons by
Maximus, at a moment when the Picts were already on the move,
marks a stage in the final ruin of the province.   It is, at any rate,
taken as a starting point by Gildas and the *Historia Brittonum*,
who date from it the beginning of the end.   Many of the displaced
troops never came back.   Maximus, who had inherited from his
predecessor a German war on the Rhine, and also feared the latent
hostility of the Emperor of the East, kept his army concentrated in
the South, anxiously expecting hostile moves on the part of Theodosius, the protector of the young Valentinian II.   The war which
he had dreaded came at last in 388 : after much hard fighting in
the passes of the Eastern Alps the Gallic and British legions were
defeated by the Eastern army, and Maximus, falling into the hands
of the victor, was beheaded at the third milestone from Aquileia
(388).   His son and colleague Flavius Victor was murdered soon
after by Count Arbogast, who had been left in comn.and in Gaul,
and thought that his submission to Theodosius would be received
more kindly if accompanied by the head of the unfortunate Caesar.
The British home-garrisons, left without a leader, and probably engaged in an uphill battle with the Picts and Scots, returned to
their allegiance, and found themselves the subjects of the young
Valentinian II., to whom Theodosius now handed over the dominions
of the whole Western Empire.   But this young prince was murdered only four years later by Arbogast, the same ruffian who had
put to death Flavius Victor, and had thereby won undeserved
pardon and promotion.   Another civil war followed, in which the
ever-victorious Theodosius put down Arbogast, and his puppet the
pretender Eugenius.   But this virtuous and hard-working emperor
died in the next year, leaving the Roman world to be divided between his two young sons, Arcadius and Honorius (395).

The latter, an unhappy boy of eleven, was the tool or victim of
a series of unscrupulous ministers throughout his life, and when he
reached full age showed neither courage nor capacity.   The few
acts in which he was personally concerned prove that he lacked all
his father's good qualities, and was cowardly, treacherous and un-

grateful. But during the first years of his minority the Roman
frontiers were still maintained with more or less success by the great
general Stilicho, whom Theodosius had left as a legacy to his son,
and who acted as regent in the whole West. As authority for the
activity of this energetic (if selfish and grasping) personage in Britain
we have only the verses of his panegyrist Claudian. But after
allowing for a due percentage of flattery and exaggeration, we can
extract a certain amount of definite information from his lines.
Evidently the lands on this side of the Channel were, at the end of
the reign of Theodosius, in a condition of perpetual war. The
province of Britain is introduced, speaking in the first person, " I
was perishing at the hands of the neighbouring tribes, when Stilicho
took up my defence : the Scot was stirring up the whole of Ireland,
and the sea foamed with his hostile oars : it is Stilicho's work that
I no longer fear the darts of the Scot, nor tremble at the Pict, nor
look out along my line of shore for the Saxon, who might arrive
with every shift in the wind ".[1]   In another poem, written a few
months earlier, Rome says, " what is my strength, now that Honorius
reigns, recent events show : the sea is more quiet now that the
Saxon is tamed, Britain is secure now that the Pict has been
crushed." [2]   There must have been enough truth in this to permit
Stilicho, who was no fool, to accept it as genuine praise. Evidently
a serious effort had been made both to beat off the maritime incursions of Scot and Saxon, and to stop the inland raids of the Pict.
Whether Stilicho himself visited Britain we cannot say : he was
certainly busy in Gaul for long periods, and may well have crossed
the Channel. But Claudian only speaks of his care and providence :
he does not definitely declare that he beat off the raiders in person.
These poems date from the year 399, and the dating of the pacification of Britain by the fact that Honorius is emperor, shows that
it cannot have taken place earlier than 395.[3]   Presumably, there-

---

[1] *In primum Consulatum Stilichonis*, ii. 247.

[2] *In Eutropium*, i. 391-93.

[3] I cannot follow Professor Bury's view that Stilicho's activity in Britain may
possibly date from the reign of Valentinian II. (*Life of St. Patrick*, p. 327). His
whole argument hinges on the statement that Claudian in the *In Eutropium* " em-
phasises a defeat of the Picts *and does not refer to the other foes of Britain* ". But
this is not so : Claudian says :—

" domito quod Saxone Tethys
Mitior, et fracto secura Britannia Picto ".

fore, the province had been enduring perpetual raids ever since Magnus Maximus took away great part of its garrison in 383, during the twelve years during which it gave its allegiance to Maximus himself (383-88), to Valentinian II. (388-92), to Eugenius (392-94) and to Theodosius the Great (394-95). It is obvious that neither Maximus nor Eugenius, whose whole interest lay in their contest with the Eastern Empire, can have had much attention to spare for Britain. And the reign of the boy Valentinian II., which was notoriously a time of chaos and decay, is equally unlikely to have seen any amelioration in the state of the island. But Stilicho evidently reorganised its defences very thoroughly during the first four years of Honorius.

The result of his rearrangements must be the state of things shown in the *Notitia Dignitatum*, a document which, though it dates from the very last period of the Roman Empire in Britain, is yet the only complete summary of its military and civil organisation that we possess. It evidently belongs to the date 400-402 A.D., and probably to the earlier rather than the later of those three years. The first thing notable in it is that the army of Britain had suffered less change than those of most of the other frontier provinces during the fourth century. The great change instituted in the defence of the empire by Diocletian had been the division of the troops into a sedentary frontier army, on which fell the ordinary work of protecting the *limites*, or the river banks on the border, and a movable field-army formed out of an enormous imperial guard, and so called "palatine" legions or regiments. But this second force, which acted as a reserve for the "limitary" army, did not go out with the person of the emperor only, as the old Praetorians had done, but was sent in smaller or larger detachments whenever there was abnormal pressure on any section of the border. On the Continent there were many provinces where the Palatine army was as numerous as the frontier guard: this was specially the case in Gaul and on the Danube. But in Britain the central reserve, which was commanded by the *Comes Britanniarum*, the senior military officer on this side of the Channel, only included three regiments of foot

He does therefore mention Saxon as well as Pict: and we cannot draw the conclusion that the lines in the *de Consulatum Stilichonis* do not refer to the same events as those in the *In Eutropium*. There is no proof that Stilicho ever worked under Valentinian II. : probably Theodosius always kept him under himself.

and six of horse. The bulk of the local army was under the *Dux Britanniarum*, whose rank was below that of the Count, and was devoted entirely to the protection of the Northern regions. The headquarters of the Dux was undoubtedly York, where the Sixth Legion still remained on guard. Yorkshire and Lancashire, to use modern terms, had three cavalry and ten infantry regiments of auxiliaries, scattered about in cantonments which were evidently designed to protect the whole country-side against sudden incursions of enemies from the sea. But the greatest accumulation of forces was on the line of Hadrian's Wall, which, from Segedunum at the mouth of the Tyne to Uxellodunum on the Solway Firth, was garrisoned by no less than twelve regiments of foot and four of horse. Close behind the Wall, all at its western end, in Cumberland and Westmoreland, were six more infantry and one more cavalry regiments, probably intended to guard against raids by the Scots from the water-side rather than to support the landward defence against the Picts. Thus the *Dux Britanniarum* had in all one legion, twenty-eight auxiliary regiments of foot, and eight units of horse under his control, a full two-thirds of the garrison of Britain.

The third military commander in Britain was the Count of the Saxon Shore, whose sphere of office extended from Branodunum, on the eastern side of the Wash, to Portus Adurni on the Solent. Besides his fleet he had one legion, the Second Augusta—the corps which had been lodged at Isca Silurum in older days, and had been responsible for the peace of South Wales—as also two regiments of horse and six of foot. The legion lay at Rutupiae (Richborough in Kent): the two cavalry regiments were both in Norfolk, one at Branodunum (Brancaster), the second at Gariannonum on the mouth of the Yare. The other garrisons of the count were Othona in Essex, Reculver at the mouth of the Thames Estuary, Dover and Lymne on the Straits, Anderida (Pevensey) in Sussex, and Portus Adurni, which seems to be Portchester, hard by Portsmouth.[1] Evidently all this display of force was for the benefit of the Saxons, whose beat must have extended from the Wash to Southampton Water. They habitually ran down the Frisian coast as far as the mouths of the Rhine and Scheldt, and then turned to right or left.

---

[1] That Portus Adurni is not Arundel, and that the name Adur for the river there is an eighteenth century antiquarian invention, have been conclusively shown by Professor Haverfield. (*Proceedings of Soc. of Antiquaries*, 1892).

There was another *Littus Saxonicum* in Gaul, whose defence was independent of that of South-Eastern Britain.

The notable thing about the map of military Britain furnished by the *Notitia* is that no provision whatever seems to be made for Wales or the South-Western regions round the Severn mouth, unless indeed the *Comes Britanniarum* was in charge of the West. But no localities are given for the garrisoning of the very modest force—three regiments of foot and six of horse under that officer, —and it seems more likely that his headquarters were at London, and that his duty was to support the Northern and Eastern garrisons in time of special danger. The legion once at Isca Silurum— Second Augusta—has (as we have already seen) shifted its garrison to Richborough in Kent. The legion once at Chester (Twentieth Valeria Victrix) has disappeared entirely from the imperial muster-roll.[1] No auxiliary regiments are found south of Lancashire or west of Portsmouth. Yet we know that the Scots had been marauding all down the Western coast of Britain, and in 405 an Irish king is recorded to have perished in the British Channel. What had become of Wales and the West Country? Is it conceivable that the Roman Government had handed over the charge of it to its own inhabitants? It will be noted in the next century that these were precisely the parts of Britain which appear as organised kingdoms at the time of the Saxon settlement, and made the longest stand against the invaders. Or had the Scottish raids bitten so deep between 383 and 400 that the West was a wreck not worth protecting? The *Historia Brittonum*, a work of the seventh century, tells us that all North Wales was in the hands of the Scots shortly before the year 400, and till they were expelled by the British chief Cunedda. In South Wales, too, immigrants from Ireland, perhaps the already-mentioned Desse, were in possession of Gower and Kidwelly. Did Stilicho give up the reorganisation of this ravaged land as hopeless? Yet even such a hypothesis would not account for the want of troops in the region of Gloucester and Somersetshire, which

---

[1] Mr. Hodgkin's ingenious hypothesis that the Twentieth Legion had been moved to Italy to reinforce Stilicho against the Goths, but had not yet arrived there, and so escaped mention in the *Notitia* altogether, is not convincing. It might have gone to the Continent with Magnus Maximus and have been destroyed in one of his defeats. Or the same fate might have befallen it when Eugenius and Arbogast fell. Or it might have been destroyed by the Scots anywhere between 368 and Stilicho's reorganisation.

had been one of the most prosperous and thickly-peopled parts of
Roman Britain. It seems impossible that Stilicho should have
placed 30,000 men on Hadrian's Wall and in Yorkshire, while
leaving the Midlands wholly uncovered on the Western side, where
the invasions had been many and dangerous during the last generation. It is difficult to come to any safe conclusion on the fragmentary evidence that lies before us : yet, if some hypothesis must
be framed, it seems quite possible that the Dumnonii and the Demetae and the Silurians may have taken arms for themselves, with the
aid and approval of the provincial government, and that Western
Britain was already defending itself. If we take the legend of
Cunedda as genuine history, we gather from it that British tribal
levies from the North, under British leaders, had saved North Wales
from the Scots before 400 A.D., *i.e.*, ten years before the formal abandonment of Britain by the imperial government. For Cunedda's exploits are placed "146 years before the reign of King Mailcun," [1] and
that prince certainly died in 547, so that his "reign" falls about
the period 530-47, and Cunedda's reconquest of Wales would be
somewhere about 385-401. Cunedda can have been no barbarian,
his father and grandfather bear ordinary Roman names, Æternus
and Paternus, though he himself is said to have come from "Gododin," the land of the Otadini, just north of the Wall. Is it conceivable that the Roman defence of Britain about the year 400 had
as one of its essential factors the maintenance of the West by British
chiefs, heading native bands which formed no part of the imperial
army ? Thus, at least, some sort of an explanation for the want of
troops on the side of the Severn might be made out.

The fact that the local army of Britain was steadily growing more
British, through the third and fourth centuries, sufficiently explains
its bitter particularism and its chronic mutinies at the end of that
period. There was no desire to "cut the painter" and break loose
from the empire; the province and army gloried in the name of
citizens and Romans. But there was evidently a strong feeling of
local self-assertion, and a wish to kick against any authority which
disregarded British opinion or sacrificed British interests. Usurpers
who promised "felix temporum reparatio," the catchword of the

---

[1] *Historia Brittonum*, M. H. B., 75 and 56. The phrase is "CXLVI annis ante
quam Mailcun regnaret" : so we must date, not from his death in 547, but from his
floruit some years earlier.

century, were always certain of a following. Weak or unlucky
emperors, who could be accused of neglecting the defence of the
province, commanded no loyalty or respect.

The end of the Roman power in Britain took place amid a very
debauch of disorder and military mutiny, all the more inexcusable
because it broke out at a moment of acute danger to the empire,
when all citizens and soldiers should have held together with
redoubled loyalty. In 402-3 began the attack of Alaric and the
Visigoths upon Italy, the first serious stroke of the barbarians at
the heart of the empire. To meet it Stilicho was obliged to recall
one of the two British legions, no doubt accompanied by a considerable body of auxiliaries. The corps recalled was probably the Sixth
Victrix, as Claudian describes it as " that legion which is stretched
before the remoter Britons, which curbs the Scot, and gazes on the
tattoo-marks on the pale face of the dying Pict." [1] This would not
suit the Second Augusta, which lay in Kent, and had the Saxons as
its special care.

Stilicho beat Alaric out of Italy (402-3) after winning the
tremendous battle of Pollentia. But no troops came back to
Britain, for a second, but wholly distinct, barbarian invasion, that of
Radagaisus supervened. It penetrated further into Italy than the
Goths had done, yet was finally defeated, with the destruction of
Radagaisus and all his host, in 405. But Stilicho was holding back
a flood of many waves, and one was no sooner checked than another
came swelling up at a fresh point. On January 1st, 406, a new host,
composed of a confederacy of Suevi, Vandals, Alans and Burgundians, crossed the Middle Rhine, sweeping the frontier guard before
them. They penetrated deep into Gaul, almost cutting the line of
communication between Rome and Britain. [2]

This moment was chosen by the British army as a suitable one
for a fierce and prolonged mutiny—as if Stilicho had not done all
that was humanly possible to save the empire. But he had done
nothing of late for Britain, and this was evidently resented. In the
autumn of 406 the troops in Britain saluted one Marcus as emperor.
But he was murdered almost as soon as he had been exalted

---

[1] Claudian, *De Bello Gallico*, 416. But it is not certain that *legio* in Claudian
need mean a definite legion. He sometimes uses it for troops in general.

[2] I am taking here the sequence of Chronology in Zosimus, vi. 3, not that of
Prosper Tiro.

to the purple.   The mutineers then elected a certain Gratianus, who
is described as " municeps ejusdem insulae," and was therefore certainly a Briton, to rule over them.   But he reigned only four
months, and was then assassinated.   The third head of the insurrection was a soldier named Constantine, also a Briton, of whom we
are told that he was a person of low origin, and had nothing to
recommend him save his name.   At any rate he was a little more
capable than his predecessors, for he succeeded in keeping alive for
more than three years after his election (407-11).   If Constantine
had confined his energies to reorganising the defence of Britain, and
keeping the island secure against Pict and Scot, we might have
understood and pardoned his conduct and that of his partizans.
Instead of doing so, he exactly copied the policy of Magnus Maximus.   He collected as much as could be spared of the provincial
army, crossed to Boulogne, and appealed to the troops in Gaul to
join his standard.   This they did, as their predecessors had done in
383.   Great districts of Central Gaul were in the hands of the barbarians, but both the wrecks of the Rhine-army, and the troops as
far as Aquitaine on the one side, and as Lyons and Vienne on the
other, acknowledged him as emperor.   He promised much, and he
was at hand, while Stilicho was far away and was held responsible
for the late disasters on the Rhine.   Again, something might be
said in defence of Constantine and his friends, if they had set themselves in a whole-hearted way to the expulsion of the Vandals and
Burgundians from Gaul.   Instead of taking this task in hand,
Constantine sent his son Constans and part of his troops to attack
Spain,—which for a time they subdued,—while he himself bickered
on the Lower Rhone with the generals of Honorius.   The war
between the British usurper and the legitimate emperor went on for
three years, with many rapid changes of fortune : but in the end
the cause of Constantine fell : his son was murdered by one of his
own generals—Gerontius, another Briton,—who wished to try Caesar-
making on his own account, and nominated an obscure person, one
Maximus, as emperor in Spain.   Constantine, after much fighting,
was besieged and captured in the city of Arles ; he was taken to
Ravenna and executed (411).   The remains of his army were never
sent back to Britain, but went to form or to reinforce a Britannic
element in Gaul, of which we must speak later.[1]   Before the death

[1] See pp. 236-7.

of the usurper, indeed, Britain had ceased to form part of the Roman Empire.

The clearest account of what happened is that given by Zosimus, " Gerontius (the traitor in Spain) stirred up against Constantine the barbarians who were in Gaul (the Vandals, Burgundians, etc.). Constantine could make no head against them, because the greater part of his army was in Spain. And the barbarians from beyond the Rhine (evidently the Saxons) ravaging everything at their pleasure, put both the Britons and some of the Gauls to the necessity of making defection from the Roman empire, and of setting up for themselves, no longer obeying Roman laws. The Britons taking up arms and fighting for their own hand, freed their communities from the barbarians who had set upon them. And the whole of Armorica and certain other provinces of Gaul imitated the Britons, and freed themselves at the same time, expelling the Roman officials and setting up a constitution such as they pleased. This defection of Britain and certain of the Gauls took place during the usurpation of Constantine, the barbarians having attacked them because of his neglect of the empire.[1]" The date to be assigned to this last revolt of Britain is apparently 409-10, the third and fourth years of the usurpation of Constantine, since the great incursion of the Saxons in Britain is fixed to those years by Prosper Tiro, in his annalistic notes—" in the fifteenth year of Honorius and Arcadius [409], on account of the languishing state of the Romans the strength of Britain was brought to a desperate pass. In the sixteenth year of the same emperors [410] the Vandals and Alans wasted all that part of the Gauls which had already been ravaged by the Saxons. The usurper Constantine kept up a hold on what remained."

The Britons, though they had taken up arms for themselves, did not conceive that they had thereby given up all connection with the empire. Indeed, they could plead formal justification for their conduct, since Honorius, involved in war with Constantine, and at the same time seeing Italy overrun by Alaric and his Visigoths, " sent letters to the communities of Britain bidding them defend themselves " (410 A.D.). They had done no more ; and if they expelled certain officials, as would seem to be implied from Zosimus's narrative, this by no means implied a complete repudiation of

---

[1] Zosimus, vi. 6.

the imperial authority. Possibly some new obscure Caesar may have been invested with the purple, but we have no mention of the fact.[1] More probably the new government theoretically acknowledged Honorius as emperor, and the sole outward sign of the event so often miscalled "the Departure of the Romans," was the expulsion of the Vicar and Praesides whom the usurper Constantine had nominated three years before. So far as there was any " departure " at all, it was that of Constantine and his field army in 407. No doubt he took with him the sole surviving legion (Second Augusta) the picked German *numeri*, and a certain number of the best of the other auxiliaries, who, whatever the names of their corps, must have been mainly Britons by birth. But it is quite certain that he cannot have taken off the whole garrison of Britain. He had been nominated emperor by the local army because the Britons considered themselves neglected. If he had proposed to celebrate his accession by evacuating the whole island, he would undoubtedly have perished at once, like his ephemeral predecessors in revolt, Marcus and Gratian. He left behind him in 407 most undoubtedly both a civil administration and a garrison, which subsisted till 410, when the indignation of the provincials that their nominee had failed both to conquer the whole West and also to bring better times to Britain, caused them to abandon his cause, and establish a provisional government of their own.

All our misconception of the meaning of the events of 410 may be traced back in the end to the tirades of Gildas, who wrote merely from oral tradition, and 130 years after the events which he is describing. It is from him that we derive the unhappy idea that in the fourth century the "Britons" and the "Romans" were two distinct nations, the one subject to the other, and the wholly erroneous notion that the local army was alien and non-British. His account of the events between 383 and 410 is entirely unhistorical. Magnus Maximus, he says, took away every armed man from Britain in 383, and left the province "entirely ignorant of military usages" to the tender mercy of the Pict and Scot. The Britons sent legates to Rome to beg for an army, and promised to be more loyal to the empire if only they were succoured. A legion was sent, which routed the barbarians out of the land, and then, for the defence of the province, bade the Britons erect a wall from sea to sea, which they did,

[1] For this possibility of τυράννοι see Procopius, *Bell. Vand.*, i. 2.

making it of turf. The legion then returned with great triumph
to Rome: whereupon the Picts and Scots reappeared in a worse
temper than before. This induced the Britons to send a second
embassy to the Romans: the latter " profoundly moved by the
tragic history, flew swift as eagles to the rescue," and made a great
slaughter of the barbarians. But they then declared that they
could not be worried any longer by having to make such laborious
expeditions, and that they should return home, leaving the islanders
to defend themselves. They bade the Britons accustom their hands
to the use of spear, sword and shield, and as a final legacy to them,
built a stone wall from sea to sea to replace the first wall of turf,
and also erected a series of castles along the sea coast "and then
they said good-bye, as never intending to return ". There followed
a third series of Pictish and Scottish inroads, against which the
Britons made as ineffective a resistance as before ; these continued
till the third consulship of Aetius (or Agitius as Gildas calls him),
i.e., till the year 446, when a third appeal to Rome was made, but
this time to no effect.

It is hardly necessary to criticise this rubbish. What attention
need be paid to a writer who thinks that the Walls of Hadrian and
Severus and the castles of the Saxon shore were all built some time
after the rebellion of Magnus Maximus in 383? The whole narrative is nonsense: there was a continuous garrison in Britain down
to 410: the Britons formed a large portion of it, and were excellent
troops. It is hopeless to endeavour to find a historical basis for
the "first devastation" in the years between 383 and 388, or for
the "second devastation " in the years between 392 and 395. The
only thing proved by the whole narrative is that by 540, even
learned men in Britain (Gildas passed as such, and was called
"Sapiens" by admiring posterity) were ignorant of all the details
of the provincial history of their own country.

CHAPTER X

CHRISTIANITY IN BRITAIN DURING THE ROMAN PERIOD

THERE is no doubt that individual Christians, perhaps even small communities of Christians, were to be found in Britain as early as the second century after Christ, though their proportion to the whole population of the province would seem to have been very small. Even in Gaul it was not large in the age of the Antonines, and only the partly-Greek towns of the Rhone Valley contributed martyrs, nearly all with Greek names, to the roll of the victims of M. Aurelius's persecution. Among the many hundreds of religious monuments, civil and military, strewn about Britain from the second to the early fourth century, all are purely pagan. Yet there is no reason to doubt the statements of Tertullian—writing in about 208 A.D.—or Origen—writing in about 230 A.D.—that the Christian religion had an appreciable number of converts in the remote province of the extreme north-west,[1] although many of its wilder regions may not yet have heard the Gospel preached.[2] The legend of King Lucius and the missionary Fagan is a blunder of the sixth century, caused originally by a confusion between the local names Britannia and Britium: for the letter of Lucius to Pope Eleutherus seems genuine, but the king ruled in Edessa, not

---

[1] Tertullian, *Adv. Jud.* vii. Cui enim et aliae gentes crediderunt? Parthi . . . Gaetulorum varietates, et Maurorum multi fines, . . . et Galliarum diversae nationes, et Britannorum inaccessa Romanis loca, Christo vero subdita . . . ut pote in quibus omnibus locis populus Nominis Christi inhabitet. Origen, *Homil.* vi., *in Luc.* i. 24. Virtus domini Salvatoris et cum his est qui ab orbe nostro in Britannia dividuntur.

[2] Origen, *Comm. series in Matt.* xxiv. § 39. Non enim fertur Evangelium praedicatum esse apud omnes Ethiopas . . . quid autem dicamus de Britannis aut Germanis . . . quorum plurimi nondum audierunt Evangelii verbum.

in Britain, and Birtha (Britium) was his citadel.[1] It is hardly necessary to allude to the later and wilder legend, which made " Bran the Blessed," the father of Caratacus, a Christian convert long before the first century of our era had run out. This was a pious imagining of some patriotic Celt of the later Dark Ages.

It is clear that Gaul as a whole was hardly permeated by Christianity till the beginning of the third century, and that Britain was far behind Gaul. But in the long peace for the Christian community which followed the persecution of Severus and lasted practically unbroken till that of Decius and Valerian—a period of forty years—the new religion pushed northward and westward with greater power. There seems no reason to doubt the existence of the small number of British martyrs whose names appear in the earliest martyrologies, all the more so because these documents are purely continental in character, and show none of the vast array of Celtic saints whose dates belong to the time after 409, when connection between this island and the surviving Roman dominions on the continent ceased. The very early martyrology which is wrongly known by the name of St. Jerome, but which was apparently constructed on a fifth century foundation,[2] gives precisely three names which are drawn from Britain [3]—the latest is that of Saint Patrick (*obiit circ.* 461) the other two are given as martyrs of the old pre-Christian time. They are Augulus, Bishop of Augusta (London) and Alban, the saint who was long after to give his name to Verulamium, the place where he suffered.

It is strange that we know nothing of Augulus, whose name is repeated in many later martyrologies, but the fact that his see is called Augusta shows that the name was taken down somewhere between 340 and 410, for London was officially styled Londinium down to the later part of Constantine's reign,[4] and was only known as Augusta

---

[1] This seems to have been clearly proved by Dr. Harnack. The earliest trace of the Lucius-letter in connection with Britain, is in the original form (drawn up about 530 A.D.) of the Liber Pontificalis, in which a sentence about Eleutherus and the letter appears. The first British mention is in Nennius.

[2] Its latest possible date seems to be 630, but the bulk seems to be sixth century notes on fifth century foundations.

[3] Besides one or two more wrongly ascribed to Britain, such as Faustinus and Juventia (really of Brixia), Timotheus (really a Mauretanian), and Socrates and Stephanus.

[4] As is proved by his large coinage at the London mint, all signed P. Lon. The only coins giving P. Avg are those of Magnus Maximus and Theodosius.

in the second half of the fourth century—perhaps the honorary title was bestowed by Constans during his visit to Britain in 343. When the city next emerges from the darkness that follows the year 410 it is London once more. The legend of Augulus and his martyrdom is one of the many things that perished in the Saxon invasion. Of Alban's existence our knowledge is decidedly more certain, since Saint Germanus is recorded to have visited and honoured his grave in 429 ;[1] his cult, therefore, was well established at Verulamium in the early fifth century, when men were still alive who might have spoken with those who remembered the Diocletian persecution. It hardly needs the evidence of Gildas, writing in the middle of the sixth century, to establish his name and fame.[2] Unfortunately the details of his life, how he served as a soldier, contrived the escape of a Christian missionary,[3] converted one of his guards, and dried up a stream on his way to execution, are late additions to the mere fact of his martyrdom, to which no attention can be paid. But there must have been something special and striking in his fate to account for the fact that he was honoured above all Romano-British saints in the early fifth century. Julius and Aaron of Caerleon do not appear in the earlier martyrologies, and, if they are found in later ones, probably owe their place to Gildas, who records their fate in a few words. If the *Book of Llandaff* can be trusted for its own day, we might believe that there was an estate near Caerleon which served as an endowment for a church dedicated to them. But this *territorium Julii et Aaronis* may conceivably be an invention of a ninth century forger, bent on proving ancient ecclesiastical property to have existed, where land was in dispute in his own generation. There are many doubtful passages in the compilation.

An attempt has been made to discredit the tradition of these martyrs, one and all, on the ground that Constantius Chlorus, into

---

[1] The visit is recorded in Constantius's *Life of Germanus*, a work written apparently within thirty years of Germanus's death.

[2] Gildas, *Hist.*, § viii.

[3] This Amphibalus, whom Alban is said to have set free, is believed by many to be a stupid invention by a scribe who took " dimisso amphibalo " to mean " having sent off Amphibalus " instead of " having laid down his cloak ".

[4] Statements in the Anglo-Saxon Chronicle and elsewhere, which put the British martyrdoms down to the year 286 A.D. are erroneous ; this is merely the first year of Diocletian. The persecution did not begin till 303, and from 287 to 293 Britain, under Carausius and Allectus, was not under Diocletian's control.

whose section of the empire Britain fell, along with Gaul and Spain, is declared by Eusebius [1] to have shrunk from carrying out the persecution ordered by Diocletian. Lactantius, too, definitely states that the Caesar only so far complied with the orders given by his seniors as to order the destruction of churches, while declining to authorise bloodshed.[2] But we have definite proof that the proconsul Dacianus, who ruled in Spain under Constantius's authority, sought out and put to death many Christians, whether his immediate superior approved or no. If this was so, the same may have been the case in Britain, and the only effect of the tolerant mildness of Constantius may have been that the victims were few instead of many—as indeed we should judge to have been the case from the shortness of the list of names preserved. It must be remembered also that Diocletian's edict was only issued in February, 303, and that persecution in the West ceased with his abdication in 305. [3] The statement in the pseudo-Hieronymian Martyrology and many other later documents of the same kind, that Alban was only one of 890 British martyrs—the rest, save Augulus, being anonymous—may be disregarded.

Whatever was the strength of the British Church in the time of Diocletian, we find it as a well organised and rapidly growing body in the early years of Constantine the Great. As early as 314 three bishops from Britain appeared at the Council of Arles and signed its decrees—Eborius of York, Restitutus of London, and Adelphius, probably of Lincoln.[4] The West was scantily represented at Nicaea (325), and certainly no British prelates were present at that greatest of Councils. But we are distinctly informed that Britain, along with Spain and Gaul, accepted its decisions respecting the condemnation of Arianism and the celebration of Easter. The same would seem to have been the case with regard to the Council of Sardica (343) : though not represented there, the insular Church hastened to accept the decision which acquitted Athanasius, and the

---

[1] *Hist. Eccl.*, VIII. xiii. § 12.

[2] *De Mortibus Persecutorum*, xv., xvi.

[3] *Cf.* Stubbs and Haddan, *Councils*, vol. i. pp. 6-7.

[4] He appears as " Episcopus de civitate Colonia Londinensium " in the list in the Corbie Codex, as " ex civitate Colonia " in the Toulouse Codex. Colonia by itself would probably mean Colchester; but Londinensium looks like an error for Lindumensium. But it *might* stand for Legionensium (Caerleon), or be merely a careless repetition.

saint gratefully records the fact.[1] Sixteen years later, however, at least three British bishops were counted among the four hundred fathers who sat at the Council of Ariminum, which was hurried by Constantius into decisions of doubtful orthodoxy. The way in which they are mentioned shows that some at least of their sees were very poor. "Three bishops alone," says Sulpicius Severus, " all Britons, had no private means, and drew an allowance from the public funds, refusing to live on a collection made for them by their colleagues ; for they thought it more proper to draw on the exchequer rather than on the charity of individuals. I have heard Bishop Gavidius making invidious reference to this choice of theirs ; but I differ from him, and think it was creditable to those bishops to be so poor that they had no private means."[2]

There may, of course, have been many more bishops from Britain at Ariminum besides these three indigent persons. But internal evidence would lead us to conjecture that the whole British Church was probably very poor in the middle of the fourth century. There seems every reason to believe that the main bulk of the population in this remote province of the West remained pagan till a much later date than was the case elsewhere. Nothing else can explain the total lack of large churches and fine sepulchral monuments which we find in Britain ; there is nothing on this side of the Channel to compare with the magnificent Christian sarcophagi which stand in rows in the Museum of Arles, or with the fourth century basilicas that are to be found all around the Mediterranean. The few churches whose ruins have survived from Roman Britain are all small and plain. If the Christians of Calleva found the diminutive church lately discovered there sufficient for their needs, they must have been but a few hundreds in a population that would seem to have numbered perhaps 2,000 souls. In that same town a temple of Mars [3] was found, which must have been used down to the end of the existence of the place, for the remains of the god's statue and of a dedicatory inscription were found beneath the fragments of the roof. If Calleva had become completely Christian before the days of its evacuation, the image of Mars would not have been left on his pedestal to meet the incoming Saxon.

[1] Athanasius, *Hist. Arian.*, *op.*, i. 360.
[2] Sulpicius Severus, *Hist. Sac.*, ii. 41.
[3] Apparently some odd local British form of the god, as the broken attributes are abnormal.

It is, of course, quite possible that the greater towns, such as York, London, or Colchester, had more splendid buildings, but no trace of them has been discovered.[1]   The small number of Christian sepulchral inscriptions is equally notable, though such have been found at Carlisle and Lincoln and elsewhere.   It is very strange that a religion which was first publicly tolerated and later encouraged by the government for nearly a hundred years before the fatal year 410 A.D. should have left so few records in stone behind it.   It may perhaps be suggested that Christianity, as elsewhere in the empire, was strongest in the great towns during the fourth century, and that the sites of the great towns remain the most unexplored portion of Roman Britain, because they are still covered with buildings which it is impossible to remove in a systematic way for regular exploration.   The places which have been well excavated, such as Calleva, Viroconium, Venta Silurum, or Corstopitum, were small towns which perished entirely, or where the modern representative of the old Roman town was so small that it never covered any large portion of the old area, or even grew up outside it.   In such localities the churches might either be small stone structures, since nothing larger was wanted, or even wooden edifices, of which no trace would remain.   A hint as to the prevalence of wood is given by Bede's mention of St. Ninian, the apostle of Galloway, which states that the saint (*circiter* 400-410) attracted some notice by building his church " de lapide, insolito Brittonibus more," [2] but Bede lived far too long after the break-up of the Roman Empire to enable us to draw a sure inference as to what methods of building were common in Britain when Honorius reigned.   His words can only be taken as clear evidence that the Celts of his own century seldom or never reared stone churches.

The existence of a vigorous British Christendom in the fourth century is sufficiently proved by literary evidence which it would be absurd to attempt to minimise.   But without that literary evidence we should have gathered little information about it from archæological research.   It must be borne in mind that secular inscriptions and secular buildings of fourth century date are singularly rare in

---

[1] That ruins of Roman churches, capable of restoration, existed above the surface in the end of the sixth century is shown by Bede, i. 26.

[2] Bede, *Hist. Eccles.*, iii. 4.

Britain, no less than ecclesiastical ones. Probably the hand of the invader at the moment, and of the thrifty stone-appropriator in the Middle Ages, fell heaviest upon the most recent buildings of Roman Britain, simply because they were upon the surface, while the remains of the third and second centuries were to a great extent buried beneath them, and so escaped notice and destruction. But even this fact does not wholly account for the extraordinary lack of fourth century archæological material.

Probably the most interesting inscribed relic of the days when Britain was ceasing to be pagan and becoming Christian, is the little pedestal of a statue of Jupiter at Cirencester, on which Septimius the *Praeses* of Britannia Prima proclaims in execrable verse that he has renewed and replaced the column and image of the God, which had been reared by the piety of the ancients.[1] This must surely date from the reign of Julian, the only period in the century, after Constantine had turned away from the old faith, when a governor could have dared to make his boast of restoring a pagan monument. It is unfortunately quite unique in character. Roman governors of the fourth century seem to have been as chary of erecting or inscribing anything as their predecessors of the second century were lavish in so doing.

It has been observed, somewhat cynically, that schisms and heresies are proofs rather of the vigour than of the weakness of a Church, and that nothing bears greater testimony to a dearth of true spiritual life than a dead level of orthodoxy. The British Church clearly did not fall under this condemnation, since it produced in the very last days of the Romans a heresiarch, whose teaching not only proved powerful in his own lifetime but maintained its influences for many generations after his death. This was the celebrated Pelagius, a British monk who is first heard of in the pontificate of Anastasius (398-402), and whose personal activity falls into the first quarter of the fifth century. He was presumably, therefore, born somewhere about 370 or 380 in the time of Valens and Gratian. He taught not in his native country, but in Rome itself, his special doctrine

---

[1] Signum et erectam prisca religione columnam
Septimius renovat, Primae Provinciae rector.
As Britannia Prima was a creation of Diocletian, who only got possession of Britain in 297, the inscription must be fourth century. And it must belong either to its very earliest years or to Julian's time. The character favours the later date.

that "original sin" is a vain invention. It is not naturally en-
gendered in every man of Adam's race by reason of his descent from
a guilty progenitor. On the contrary, sin is a personal and not an
inherited failing: men do evil and become hateful to God by their
own individual fault: they "follow Adam" it is true, but of choice,
not of necessity. This doctrine shocked the fathers of the fifth
century mainly for two reasons. Firstly it seemed to imply that
Christ did not necessarily live and die to redeem *all* men: for if
original sin was not universal in the human race, there may have
been individuals who had no need of redemption. Secondly—and
here the objection became more practical—if man is not necessarily
sinful, and is capable of perfection through his own virtue, there is
a danger that all self-righteous and overweening persons may claim
to be impeccable. And from this state of mind to mere anti-
nomianism there is but a step, for saints of this description, in all
ages, have been found to abuse their supposed sinlessness in the
most scandalous fashion. This was not, however, the case with
Pelagius himself, who is recorded to have been a monk, a man of
austere life, and one who shunned controversy so far as it was possible for an innovator in doctrine to do so. He did not himself see
that the assertion of Free Will was incompatible with a belief in the
Atonement. But his opponents grasped the fact, and were never
tired of urging it. The rival doctrine, which St. Augustine taught
in an extreme form a few years later, to the effect that man is con-
genitally sinful, and that God's grace alone, not any deliberate
choice of his own, can secure him salvation, did not commend itself
to every one. Pelagius gained many followers, and his views spread
all over the West: these were specially welcomed in Britain, where
they were introduced by one Agricola the son of a Pelagian bishop
named Severianus.[1] The earliest recorded works written by Britons
are those of the heresiarch himself, and of a British bishop—his see
is unknown—named Fastidius, who is said to have been at least a
semi-Pelagian. The tracts of the latter, which are mentioned by
St. Jerome, have been preserved. So have fragments of Pelagius's
own Commentary on the Epistles of St. Paul, the oldest book known
to have been written by a Briton.[2]

Yet if the Christian Church of Britain was vigorous enough to

---

[1] Prosper of Aquitaine, *op.*, i. 399.
[2] See Dr. Souter in *Proceedings of the British Academy*, 1906.

make new sallies in dogma, and to indulge in controversies that
lasted for several generations, it is at the same time almost certain
that it had not yet succeeded in converting the heathen of the rural
parts of the province, who may still have formed the larger half
of its population at the moment when the Roman domination
ceased. We find that when in 429 A.D. the Gallic bishops Germanus and Lupus crossed to the now independent Britain, to confute
the disciples of Pelagius, they had to baptise converts by the thousand. There is no reason to suppose that the catechumens were
merely heretics asking for a second baptism.[1] It seems more likely
that the same phenomenon was seen in Britain as on the Continent,
that the turmoil of the barbarian invasions gave the death-blow to
lingering paganism. When the Roman State fell, the Christian
Church was the only living power left in the West, and seems to
have completed, in those years of chaos and misery that make up
the fifth century, the conversion of the heathen remnant. Christianity was a better religion for those who had to suffer and endure
than moribund polytheism. And the Church supplied the sole
organisation round which the Romanised provincials could rally,
when the State had been destroyed. Who could have faced the
incoming Frank or Saxon with inspiration drawn from the worn-out
faith of Mars and Jupiter?

[1] To baptise such would have been contrary to the custom of the time.

BOOK III

THE ANGLO-SAXON INVASION

CHAPTER XI

THE ANGLO-SAXON INVASION (410-516 A.D.)

FROM the landing of Julius Caesar down to the year 410 the history of Britain can be traced with a fair amount of continuity, though—as we have seen—it is full of dark corners. But for more than a hundred and fifty years after the obscure revolution that followed the Edict of Honorius which bade the British communities "defend themselves," there is a sheer break in the sequence of the narrative. We know what was the condition of the island in 410, and we know what was its condition in the end of the sixth century. But of the stages of the transformation, by which the Roman provincial Britain of Honorius became the Anglo-Saxon Britain of Aethelbert and Aethelfrith, we have little certain knowledge. There is a complete solution of continuity in the tale ; six generations pass by in which we have but the scantiest glimpse of what was going on in the island.

There is only one literary document of some length which belongs to this period, the " Liber Querulus " of Gildas, and that, as we have already seen, is full of notorious errors concerning the earlier part of this Dark Age, and for the remainder of it gives us little more than denunciations in vague language, borrowed from the Prophets of the Old Testament, which reprove certain British kings contemporary with the author. We shall have to ascertain, in due course, how much of solid fact can be elucidated from these jeremiads. To supplement the hysterical periods of Gildas we have three historical narratives belonging to a much later age. The first is the *Historia Brittonum* or *Volumen Britanniae* of an anonymous author who wrote, somewhere about the year 685, a compilation which—mixed with other and later material—has come to be known by the name of Nennius, a ninth-century redactor of the little work. The second narrative is that of the Venerable Bede, who wrote, about 730, his excellent and scholarly *Ecclesiastical History*, in which he endeavoured to construct a sketch of the early history of Britain from Gildas, combined with the traditions of his own English ancestors, and some small help from writers of the latest Roman period. The third source is the Anglo-Saxon Chronicle, whose earlier section was compiled by the order of King Alfred in the very end of the ninth century. Its annalistic entries covering the fifth and sixth centuries are largely derived from Bede, but are supplemented by many statements, more or less credible, drawn from independent English tradition, of which the greater part are concerned with Alfred's own forebears, the royal house of the West Saxons.

The most cursory examination of the narratives of the *Historia Brittonum*, and of the Anglo-Saxon Chronicle, proves that both abound in doubtful matter,—as might indeed be expected when we reflect that they were written so long after the events which they purport to record. In especial, the earlier of the two, the *Historia Brittonum*, contains many chapters which are clearly not history at all, but wild legend, full of dragons, enchanted castles, and fires that fall from heaven. That there remains in them a residuum of acceptable fact, when all the errors have been cleared away, our historians agree. Unfortunately, the precise amount of that residuum is hard to settle.

In addition to the four sources which we have named, a certain amount of scattered information may be gathered from other quarters. Some short but useful glimpses of fact may be found in certain early lives of saints—especially from those of Patrick and Germanus. A note or two may be taken from early councils of the Cambro-British Church. There are some entries which seem trustworthy in Irish chronicles, drawn up at a much later date. There are a handful of fifth and sixth century inscriptions on the west side of Britain. A very few mentions of insular affairs occur in continental historians, such as Prosper and Procopius. But the total amount of external material for checking or correcting the statements of Gildas, the *Historia Brittonum*, Bede, and the Anglo-Saxon Chronicle is lamentably small. The spade, so useful in the

Roman period, helps us little here: the Teutonic invader has left us no inscriptions earlier than the year 600: his British enemies hardly any, and those of the shortest. Saxon graves of the pagan period give us a good deal of information concerning the social life and culture of the incoming race, but not definite history: in that respect they can only be used like the barrows of the Britons who lived before Julius Caesar.

We left the Roman province of Britain suffering under the simultaneous assaults of the Pict from the North, the Scot from the West, and the Saxon from the side of the Eastern Sea. These invasions certainly did not grow less fierce and continuous when the provincials were abandoned by the central government of the Roman Empire, and told to shift for themselves. We might have expected that the whole island from sea to sea would have fallen a prey to them within a few years—as Spain fell to the Visigoths in this same period, or Northern Gaul to the Franks a little later. But no such complete catastrophe occurred: the British provincials defended themselves with unexpected resolution, and even a century and a half after the time of Honorius they still retained half Britain unsubdued. The Pict and Scot were beaten off, with singularly little loss of territory on the part of the defenders, on the West and North. The Saxons and their kinsmen made many conquests, yet after great successes at the beginning were brought to a stand, and never completely achieved the enterprise that they had begun.

One would naturally have supposed that of all the districts of Britain that most surely doomed to conquest by the barbarians would have been the Northern region, about and beyond Hadrian's Wall, which had never been properly occupied by the Romans since the time of Commodus, and which had been reclaimed for the empire in name alone by the elder Theodosius. Here the Pict and Scot were near neighbours on the North and West, while the East coast was exposed to the raids of the Saxon. Yet in this borderland of the Britons, through which Pictish invasions must have swept on innumerable occasions, in order to reach the more desirable plunder beyond the Wall, and to which the keels of the pirates from beyond the North Sea came early and often, the resistance offered to the external enemy was fierce and successful. The Picts won nothing more than a small strip of land to the south of the Firth of Forth,[1] from the neighbourhood of Stirling to that of Edin-

[1] They may even have been holding it since the third century.

burgh, the "Manau" or "Manau Gododin" of the British poems
and chronicles. The other Pictish settlement in the Lowlands,
that in Galloway, where lay the "Niduarian Picts," was, as we have
already seen reason to believe, the prize of an earlier invasion from
Ireland, before the Roman power had been broken in Britain, and
not a land subdued in the time of chaos that followed the year 410.
The Scots seem to have devoted their chief energies to the seizure
of regions farther North and South—the isles and peninsulas of
Argyleshire on the one side and Wales on the other.

The Teutons won something more than the Picts or Scots, as their
settlements on the East coast from Lothian to the Humber seem to
have begun early, and always to have been increasing. But at first
they were mere scattered patches on the shore, and it was long before
they were united into that Northumbrian kingdom which began to
threaten the independence of all the Northern Britons only in the end
of the sixth century. At the earliest return of historical twilight we
find them still weak and divided, while the Britons were holding
their own, and had even got possession of lands beyond the Wall of
Antoninus. The strong rock of Alclyde, "the fort of the Britons"
(Dumbarton), on the northern shore of the Firth of Clyde, was
reckoned not merely as their outpost but as their capital. The successful resistance of the people of the land between the two walls
to their invaders may be ascribed to either—or both—of two causes.
It is clear that they had never been absorbed into the area of Roman
civilisation like their kinsmen farther South, and military vigour
went hand in hand with comparative barbarism. But it is also
possible that they may have rallied at the first around the wrecks
of the old trained garrison of Hadrian's Wall. Indeed their first
leaders may have been the captains of the auxiliary cohorts, which
were not withdrawn when the last legion sailed South, to aid the
much-vexed Honorius or the usurper Constantine III. We have
one glimpse of the state of the Lowlands somewhere about the year
450 A.D. St. Patrick wrote in the later years of his long life [1] his
"Epistle to the Christians subject to Coroticus," from which most
suggestive deductions may be drawn. This chief appears as ruling
the land that lies opposite Ulster in the most vigorous style. The
saint speaks of him as a Christian Briton whose power depended on

[1] See Bury's *Life of St. Patrick*, pp. 195 and 303, where the date 459 A.D. is
suggested.

the bands of his soldiers (milites), a word that seems to imply trained troops and not merely tribal levies, when used by one who was a Roman citizen by birth. He also possessed a fleet, and had used it to carry out a raid—retaliatory no doubt—against the Scots on the other side of the North Channel. In this expedition his men had surprised, and carried off as slaves, some of Patrick's newly-baptised converts, " with the sign of the cross still fragrant on their foreheads ". It was a case, no doubt, of the "stork among the cranes "; all Scots were pirates, and fair game in the eyes of the soldiers of Coroticus. But the most striking point in the denunciation of Coroticus, for preying on his Christian brethren, is that we are told that part of his expeditionary force had consisted of heathen barbarians, both Picts and Scots. The former may have been some of those Picts of Galloway, who had been partially converted by St. Ninian some fifty years before; some of them had relapsed into heathenism, or had never deserted it. But to find Coroticus possessed of a Scottish contingent is more surprising. Had he hired them from the settlement on the Argyle coast, or were they simply broken men, like those numerous Danes of five centuries after who readily took service with a Christian employer? At any rate Coroticus was sufficiently energetic, and (we must suppose) sufficiently wealthy to maintain barbarian auxiliaries, and it was they, and not his own native soldiery, who had slain some and enslaved others of Patrick's disciples. The saint wrote his epistle not to the chief himself, to whom he had already made application in vain, but to the whole Christian community subject to him, including his soldiers, though these last he declares to be " no fellow-citizens of mine or of the pious Romans, but fellow-citizens of devils, on account of their evil deeds, men who ally themselves with Scots and apostate Picts ". All of Coroticus's subjects who retain a spark of Christian feeling are bidden to bring pressure to bear upon the "tyrant "—Patrick calls him neither king nor general—in order that he may release his captives. They are asked to see that the letter gets to his hands, and then, unless he repents, to boycott him and his soldiers, to deny them the participation of hearth and board, to take no gift from them, and to refuse obedience to their orders until the prisoners are set free. Whether any of the Christians of North Britain tried this somewhat perilous experiment on the tyrant we know not. The darkness descends again for nearly a century on the

land between the two walls.[1] But it would seem that Coroticus succeeded in maintaining his power till his death, and passed on his
authority to his descendants. For in the genealogies attached to
Nennius in the Harleian Manuscript he appears, under the name of
Ceretic Guletig, as the ancestor of the sixth century kings of
Strathclyde,[2] Rhydderch Hen, Elfin, Clinog, Eugenius, and the rest,
down to that Beli King of Alclyde, whose death is recorded under the
year 722 A.D. The family would seem to have had many branches,
who followed each other on the throne of Alclyde in a very irregular line of succession. Probably several princes of the house were
often reigning at once, under the suzerainty of one of their kinsmen,
and the hegemony often passed from one to another cousin. One
of the line, Rhydderch Hen, son of Tudwal, is recorded in Nennius
as taking a prominent part in the struggle with Hussa, the son of
Ida, the first great Anglian king of Bernicia, about the year 580.
He was no doubt the same as the Rodarcus, son of Totail, King of
Alclyde, who is found in Adamnan's *Life of Columba* sending to
Iona to beg the saint to prophesy in his behalf.

The house of Coroticus were not the only family of hard fighters
that was produced in the land between Hadrian's Wall and the Firths
of Forth and Clyde. It must be remembered that from this same
region came that Cunedda, the son of Aeternus and grandson of
Paternus, whom we have noted in a previous chapter as descending
from the North, in the latest years of the fourth century, to deliver
Wales from the invading Scots, who had crossed from Ireland to the
lands about the Menai Straits and the foot of Snowdon. If the date
given by the *Historia Brittonum* and the sequence of the later
Welsh genealogies be approximately correct, Cunedda had come
down with his eight sons and his army, from "Manau Gododin"
on the Forth about 390, long before the final departure of the
legions under the usurper Constantine III.[3] We cannot tell whether
he left Manau because he was driven out by incoming Picts, abandon-

---

[1] A wild Irish legend (see *Tripartite Life of St. Patrick*, ed. Whitley Stokes,
p. 498) tells that Coirthech, King of Alclyde, refused to listen to the saint's pleading,
that Patrick cursed him, and that he was therefore turned into a fox by miracle in
the presence of his retainers, and never was seen again.

[2] Whereas the later set of genealogies in the Hengwrt MS., which gives the
Bonhed Gwyr y Gogledd, or "families of the men of the North," wrongly takes back
this family to Maxim Guletig, *i.e.*, the Emperor Magnus Maximus.

[3] See chapter ix. pp. 170-71.

ing a region which could no longer be held, or whether he went as
the vassal and ally of Rome, to face in behalf of all the Britons that
wing of the barbarian invasion which seemed at the moment the
most dangerous.   But at any rate "he expelled the Scots with much
slaughter from those regions (North Wales), and they never returned
again to inhabit them".   The other, or South Welsh holding of
the Scots, about Gower and Kidwelly, was finally reconquered by the
house of Cunedda, and reincorporated with West Britain, though
a strain of Goidelic blood no doubt survived there, and some princely
families of South Wales, even long after, traced themselves back to
Irish ancestors on one side of their genealogy.[1]

But while it is clear that Northern and Western Britain beat
off the Pict and Scot, after a long struggle and many vicissitudes of
fortune, the history of Southern and Eastern Britain is very different.
This, as we have already seen, was the most thickly settled and
highly organised part of the island, a region where Romanisation
had been complete and thorough.   Though often harried on the
coast-line by the Saxons before 410, it was still a wealthy and
civilised land when we lose sight of it in that fatal year.   A century
later the eastern side of it, from the extreme north to Southampton
Water, was occupied by a number of petty Teutonic kingdoms,
while the western side of it was still held by the Britons, who were
engaged in an obstinate defence of the South-West and the Midlands against the invaders.

When and how did the kingdoms of the Saxons, Jutes and
English come into existence?   Gildas gives us almost dateless
rhetoric: the *Historia Brittonum* an elaborate legend full of
marvels, miracles and folk-lore tales.   Bede and the Anglo-Saxon
Chronicle supply us with a rationalised version of the hysterical
paragraphs of Gildas, supplemented with ancestral memories of the
invaders, written down centuries after the epoch to which they are
supposed to belong.   Most modern writers follow in the footsteps of
Bede and the Chronicle; and the legend of Vortigern and Hengist,
fixed down to the years following 447 or 449 A.D., appears in every
history of England.   That there is every reason to suspect its details we must now proceed to demonstrate.

When in 410 Honorius bade the Britons "defend themselves"

[1] See Zimmer's *Nennius Vindicatus*, and E. B. Nicholson's *Dynasty of Cunedda*.

the message must have been delivered to the magistrates of the tribal
cantons into which the province was divided, and to the commanders
of those cohorts and *numeri* which still survived out of the old garrison. "Vicar" and praesides there were none, since these governors
had been expelled shortly before, when the Britons threw off their
allegiance to the usurper Constantine. Perhaps the most obvious
course for the islanders to take would have been to proclaim another
local emperor : but it is clear that they did not do so. We must
therefore suppose that they organised some sort of a provincial
league, as did their neighbours on the opposite coast of Gaul, the
Armoricans, about the same time. Since self-protection against
the Saxon, Pict and Scot was their most obvious need, they must
surely have appointed some military magistrate to take charge of
their defence, and there are indications that such a person existed
some generations later, and had taken up the title as well as the
duties of the *Dux Britanniarum* of the later empire. Probably
a vague suzerainty on the part of Honorius was still recognised in
theory, for till a much later date the Britons regarded themselves
as "*cives*," citizens of the empire, and the term is still used for
them in the work of Gildas, written more than a hundred years
after this period, though he at the same time blames them for
"casting off rather than cherishing the name, manners and law of
Romans." What was the inner organisation of the British communities in the earlier period of their independence we can only
guess : presumably in the larger towns, like Londinium, Camulodunum, Eburacum or Lindum, regular municipal government continued for some time to exist. In the remoter districts where towns
were few, and the canton rather than the city was the unit of civil
life, something like the old pre-Roman tribal chieftainships were soon
re-established. For there were plenty of old and wealthy British
noble houses, some wholly Romanised, as the names of their members
show, others less so, round whom it would be natural for the
peasantry to rally, in a time of unfortunate war and perpetual invasion. Such nobles would in many cases have held office, civil or
military, before the break up of the empire : the not unfrequent
Britons like Magnentius, Gerontius, Gratian Municeps, and others,
who occur in the pages of Ammianus and Zosimus, must have been
persons of this sort. Starting from the condition of magistrates or
local magnates, they and their descendants became in the course of

a generation or two real tribal chiefs. To Gildas[1] they had become
reguli, tyranni, even *reges.* The process must have been assisted
by the fact that in the West of Britain a clear and definite kingship was being set up by Cunedda and his sons, who, after expelling
the Scottish invaders of Wales, had established real military monarchies on a small scale therein. Similar phenomena were not
unknown elsewhere in the Roman Empire. Not to speak of Syagrius
and Aegidius in Gaul, who only just failed to build up a native
kingdom on the Seine in the end of the fifth century, there was a
prince named Masuna in Africa, who in the sixth century declared
himself "Rex Romanorum et Maurorum" and held out for some time
with that strange title in the recesses of Atlas. We have already
noted the parallel case of Coroticus, in the extreme north of Britain,
though that chief evidently had not assumed any royal style, and
was presumably no more than a military magistrate. If guessing
is permitted, we may think of Britain in the early fifth century as
a loose confederacy of communities, in which the municipal element
was progressively growing weaker and the monarchical element
stronger.

It is a curious fact that while the few notices of Britain which
come to us from the continent in the first half of this period seem
to make the Saxons the chief enemy of the island, Gildas speaks
more of the Picts and Scots during the early fifth century, and only
begins to enlarge on the ravages of the Teutonic invaders after some
time has elapsed. Something may perhaps be allowed for the local
standpoint of the informants: the so-called Prosper, writing in
Gaul, thought most of the face of Britain which looked toward his
own land. Gildas, a West Briton whose outlook embraced only his
own half of the island, had received a tradition which told more of
the invaders on that side than of those who wasted the Eastern
regions. Be this as it may, the Gaul tells us, under the years 409-
10, of the "strength of Britain being brought low" and the Saxons
being engaged in devastating Gaul also, and then in 441 assures us
"the Britons after having been long vexed with various disasters
and ill chances down to this moment, are now reduced to subjection
by the Saxons". This can, at the most, only have been true of some
parts of the Southern and Eastern coast, but even in respect to this

---

[1] Gildas, § 10.

limited part of the island, his statement is absolutely contradicted
by Gildas, who makes the first permanent conquests of the Teutonic
invaders to date from some years after the third consulship of
Aetius [446 A.D.] and then to fall far short of that complete success
of which Prosper speaks. For the years before this Saxon settlement Gildas speaks only of the Picts and Scots as invaders, "races
differing from each other in part as to their manners, but alike in
their delight in bloodshed, and in their preference for covering their
villainous faces with hair, rather than their immodest middles with
raiment"—the first recorded hit at the kilt. According to him the
Britons, after suffering disasters for a long series of years from Pict
and Scot, at last turn to the unhappy idea of calling in the Saxons
to save them from the Northern enemy. To judge from his narrative this would be the first appearance of the Teutonic invaders—
which as we know is absurd, since they had given Carausius occupation nearly two centuries before, and had been among the chief foes
of Stilicho in 395.

Clearly Prosper and Gildas contradict each other. It remains
to be seen what more can be gathered from less obvious sources. Of
these the most useful is the life of St Germanus, Bishop of Auxerre,
by Constantius, a biography written in the last quarter of the fifth
century, and therefore long before the time of Gildas. Germanus
was twice in Britain, and his doings there have fortunately been
recorded by his disciple. He first crossed the Channel in 429, along
with his friend Lupus, Bishop of Troyes, as a deputation sent by
the Gallic Synods to preach against the Pelagianism, or semi-
Pelagianism, which was invading the Christian Church of Britain at
the moment. We may omit his miracles, which take up much space,
but profit us little for historical inquiries. But when they are
extracted, we have some solid political information. Britain seems
to be still mainly under municipal, not regal, governance : there is
no mention of a king, though we hear of "a man of tribunician
rank," and are told that the supporters of Pelagianism included
wealthy magnates arrayed in splendid apparel. It is most important to note that the synod at which Germanus and Lupus refuted
the heretics was held at Verulamium, where the Gallic bishops venerated the tomb of St Alban. The heart of South-Eastern Britain,
therefore, was still intact, and the walls and shrines of its cities
were still standing. But we also learn that the island was being

harassed at the moment by a joint invasion of Picts and Saxons, who were not merely co-operating in a general way, the one from the land-side, the other from the sea, but were concentrated in a single host "driven into one camp by their common necessity, they undertake war against the Britons with conjoined forces ". The invasion must, of course, have taken place somewhere considerably to the north of the region which Germanus had been visiting, presumably in York-shire or the North-Midlands, but the locality of the conflict cannot be identified. It was certainly *not* Maes-Garmon (the field of Ger-manus) in Flintshire, where Welsh antiquarians have placed it : that is too far to the West, and not on any reasonable line for a Picto-Saxon invasion.

The Britons—no mention is made of a king or even of a single general—terrified by the exceptional strength and violence of the raid, sent for Germanus and Lupus to their camp : the step was not destitute of practical wisdom, since the former had been a great man of war in his youth, and had held the high military post of *Dux* of the Armorican region before he became Bishop of Auxerre. The bishops strengthened the hands of the British army, and induced many thousands of them, who were still heathen, to be baptised before the day of battle. Germanus then selected a defensive position for them, a narrow plain bounded by mountains, on whose slopes many of the Britons were hidden away in folds of the ground, so as to lie on the flank, or even the rear, of an enemy pushing along the central valley. When the Picts and Saxons had advanced far up the level ground, making for the troops visible in front of them, Germanus gave the signal for a general attack, by bidding the whole army raise the war-cry " Hallelujah," and display itself. The shout was repeated by the ambushed forces all along the hillsides, and the barbarians saw themselves surrounded, as it were, and threatened on every side. Whereupon, instead of attacking, they wheeled round and fled down in the valley in disorder, casting away their arms, and making no resistance when they were pursued and cut down by the oncoming Britons. Many were drowned at the fords of a river which lay behind their line of flight. The " Halle-lujah Victory," a rout without a battle, saved Central Britain for at least some years from a repetition of the Pictish and Saxon invasion.

Clearly, however, the results of this well-concerted affair would only be temporary. We have an account of a second visit of

Germanus to Britain in 447, when he came accompanied by Severus, Bishop of Trier, once more set on the task of combating Pelagianism, which had raised its head again in the island. Unfortunately there are no political or military facts preserved in connection with his second mission, whose narrative deals only with his conflicts with heresy. Yet, if there is any truth at all in Gildas, he must have been in Britain just at the moment of its greatest distress, since in the preceding year (446) fell the third consulship of Aetius, to whom, according to that dreary author, was sent the doleful letter called the " Groans of the Britons ": " The barbarians drive us to the sea—the sea throws us back on the barbarians : we have only the choice between the two methods of death, whether we should be massacred or drowned ". Moreover, six years before falls the date given by the so-called Prosper as that of the " falling of Britain under the domination of the Saxons ". There can be little doubt that the state of the island must have been much worse in 447 than at the time of Germanus's first visit in 429. Conceivably he was sent for to act as a saviour from the barbarians once more, as well as a champion of orthodoxy. If so, his second appearance had less happy results than his first. He returned to Gaul, to die there in the next year, and the state of Britain grew progressively worse.

It is curious to find that Gildas makes no mention whatever of Germanus, thus showing once more the shortness of his historical perspective. The *Historia Brittonum*, on the other hand, has only too much about the Gaulish Saint, but its narrative is mainly wild legend. The chief work of Germanus, according to this strange book, was to protest against the wickedness of a certain Vortigern, who seems to be represented as king of the whole island, and as reigning from somewhere about 425 down to at least 455. He was not only a tyrant and murderer, but the friend and patron of the Saxons, to whom he betrayed the Britons, and a notorious evil liver who kept many wives, among whom was his own daughter. Germanus harried him from place to place, " following him with all the British clergy, and upon a certain rock prayed for his sins during forty days and forty nights ". Finally, fire fell from heaven and devoured the wicked king in his castle of Caer-Vortigern on the Teifi, together with all his wives and his retainers, male and female. An almost similar fate fell upon another prince of equally deplorable

manners called Benlli, the imprecations of Germanus in the legend
having the same power as those of Elijah in the Book of Kings.

In this wild fashion do we get our first glimpse of Vortigern, a
personage who appears in every normal history of England as the
immediate cause of the Saxon invasion. It may be granted, however, that he is probably to be identified with a certain unnamed
king, spoken of by Gildas, who (with all his faults) is a better
authority for the sixth century than the *Historia Brittonum*.
According to the " liber querulus " the Britons having failed to get
any help from Rome in 447, after their last appeal in the third consulship of Aetius (or Agitius as Gildas calls him), took to defending
themselves, not without some success. " Kings were elected, not by
God's ordinances, but such as showed themselves more fierce than
other men : and not long after they used to be slaughtered by those
who had anointed them, not after any examination of their true
merits, but because others more cruel still were elected. And if
any one of them seemed milder than the others, and in some degree
more regardful of the truth, the anger and weapons of all men were
turned against him, as if he were the undoer of Britain." The island
is in a state of elective despotism, tempered by assassination, when
a new invasion of the Picts and Scots is announced. "Then all the
councillors, together with their haughty king, are so blinded that,
devising a succour (say rather a destruction) for their country, they
introduce into the island those ferocious Saxons of accursed name,
hateful to God and man, bringing—as it were—wolves into the
sheepcote, in order that they may drive back the races of the North.
. . . The cubs from the lair of the barbarian lioness arrive in three
cyuls (keels) as they call them, that is three warships, with a
favourable wind and with omens and prophecies favourable, for it
had been foretold to them, by their own best seers, that they should
hold the land to which they were directing their prows for three
hundred years, and for half of that time, a hundred and fifty years,
should frequently devastate it. They land first on the eastern side
of the island, by the orders of the unlucky King of Britain, and fix
their horrid claws therein, nominally about to fight in defence of our
country, but more really for its destruction. Their mother-land,
learning of the success of the first band, sends over in more numerous companies these dogs of mercenaries, who come across on their
ships to unite with their base-born comrades. From that time the

seed of iniquity, the root of bitterness was planted among us, and
the poisonous growth, as we deserved for our demerits, sprang up
on our soil with rank-growing stalks and leaves.   The barbarians
introduced among us as our soldiers, and ready (as they falsely
boasted) to brave every danger in behalf of their worthy hosts, ask
for regular pay.   It is given, and for some time stops, as the proverb
goes, the dog's maw.   Presently, however, they complain that their
monthly wages are not supplied in sufficient quantity, deliberately
making out a colourable case against their employers, and say that
more profuse maintenance must be given, or they will break their
agreement and ravage the whole island.   Nor is there long delay :
the threat is followed by its execution.   For the conflagration that
started in the east, the due punishment for our previous sins, was
spread from sea to sea, fed by their sacrilegious hands ; it blazed
across every city and region, nor did it stay its burning course until,
after devastating almost the whole surface of the island, its ruddy
tongues licked the Western Ocean."   Gildas then describes in moving terms the destruction of a civilised community by reckless and
ignorant barbarians.   " Every colony [1] is levelled to the ground by
the stroke of the battering ram, the inhabitants are slaughtered
along with the guardians of their churches, priests and people alike,
while the sword gleamed on every side, and the flames crackled
around.   How horrible to behold in the midst of the streets the
tops of towers torn from their lofty hinges, the stones of high walls,
holy altars, mutilated corpses, all covered with livid clots of coagu-
lated blood, looking as if they had been crushed together in some
ghastly wine-press !   And there was no grave for the dead, unless
they were buried under the wretched ruins of their homes, save the
bellies of birds and beasts of prey—with reverence, be it spoken, of
the blessed souls (if indeed there were many found) which were carried at that time by the holy angels to the height of heaven. . . .
Of the miserable remnant some flee to the hills, only to be captured
and slain in heaps : some, constrained by famine, come in and surrender themselves to be slaves for ever to the enemy, if only their
lives might be spared—and this was the best that was granted,
others wailing bitterly passed overseas."

A remnant, however, as Gildas tells, continued to resist among

[1] *Omnes columnae* should clearly be *omnes coloniae*, for which indeed there is
some MS. authority (Gildas, 24).

woods, mountains, and crags by the sea, till the first rush of the
invasion was over, and many of the barbarians had retired to their
homes laden with plunder.   These desperate patriots rallied under
the leadership of Ambrosius Aurelianus, " a modest man, who alone
was courteous, faithful, strong and truthful, and alone of the
Romans was left alive, in the turmoil of this miserable time.   His
relatives had won the purple, and had fallen in the civil wars of this
age : his descendants still survive in our own day : they have degenerated much from their ancestor's virtue, but still make head and
challenge the triumphant barbarian to battle : God has granted them
victory according to our prayers."   From the time of Ambrosius
onwards, sometimes the citizens, sometimes the enemy, have been
successful, " down to the year of the siege of Mount Badon, which
lies near the mouth of the Severn, the year of the last and not the
least slaughter of these ruffians, which was the forty-fourth (as I
know), with one month elapsed, since it was also the date of my own
nativity.[1]   But even now our cities are not inhabited as they were

[1] The date of the battle of Mount Badon is one of the most puzzling points in
the chronology of the English invasion of Britain.   The Latin of Gildas in the
above-quoted sentence is very peculiar and obscure.   It runs : " Ex eo tempore
[the time of the appearance of Ambrosius Aurelianus] nunc cives nunc hostes vince-
bant, usque ad annum obsessionis Badonici montis, ₁qui prope Sabrinum ostium
habetur], novissimaeque ferme de furciferis non minimae stragis, quique quadra-
gesimus quartus, ut novi, oritur [or orditur] annus, mense jam primo emenso, qui
jam et meae nativitatis est ".   Most commentators take this to mean that the battle
was forty-three years and one month before the date at which Gildas wrote.   Now
internal evidence proves the *Liber Querulus* to have been written about 545-46, since
Maglocunus, the tyrant whom he most denounces, is recorded as dying in 547 in the
Annales Cambriae.   But that same compilation gives the battle of Mount Badon as
taking place in 516, which is only thirty years before.   Of course it is a late work,
yet it represents the received traditions of the Welsh.   Some students have wished
to make out that the date of Maglocunus's death is wrong, and that of Mount Badon
correct, running the former on to the year 560, so as to get the forty-four years' interval from 516 correct.   But this seems dangerous, because the tyrant is recorded
to have died in the " Great Mortality," and the famous plague which swept from
Persia over all Europe can be accurately dated from Procopius and other sources to
543-44 in Constantinople and Italy, so that it might naturally ravage Britain in 547.
If this date, therefore, is certain, and Gildas's words are taken in the usual sense, the
battle of Mount Badon and the birth of Gildas ought to have fallen somewhere between 500 and 503, according as the *Liber Querulus* was written two, three or more
years before the death of Maglocunus.   Mommsen prefers this explanation, fixes the
battle in 500, and throws over the date of 516 given in the *Annales Cambriae* as
simply wrong.
    But we have another curious note to make.   Bede, copying Gildas otherwise

of yore, but lie in ruins, deserted and wrecked, our foreign wars having ceased, but not our civil strife." Gildas then proceeds to denounce five British kings of his own day for their evil life and perpetual turbulence. It is notable that they all dwell on the western side of Britain, one in Damnonia, one in Demetia (South Wales), one in Venedotia (North Wales), the other two, as it seems, respectively on the Severn and on the southern shore of the Bristol Channel. But of these princes more hereafter.

It will be observed that this narrative, though vague and lacking in names and dates—Ambrosius Aurelianus is the only person specifically named in the fifth century, and the year of the battle of Mount Badon the only epoch fixed—contains little that seems impossible or even unlikely. It thereby differs *toto caelo* from the wild tale of the *Historia Brittonum*. There is nothing improbable in the story that the Britons hired barbarian auxiliaries—their Roman predecessors had done so a hundred times. The only error of im-

almost word for word, about the battle of the *Mons Badonicus*, says that it took place *quadragesimo circiter et quarto anno adventus eorum (hostium) in Brittaniam*, as if he had a manuscript before him which had contained these words, " adventus eorum," in the middle of the clumsy sentence of Gildas. As he seems to place the advent of Hengist somewhere about 447-49 this would make the battle fall in 493 Some foreign commentators (*e.g.*, La Borderie *Rev. Celtique*, vi. 1-13), accept this view.

Yet another suggestion has been made. Mr. E. B. Nicholson, wishing to keep both the dates in the *Annales Cambriae*, 516 for the battle, and 547 for the death of Maglocunus, as correct, makes the forty-four years run *from the appearance of Ambrosius Aurelianus* counting forward, not from the date of the writing of the *Liber Querulus* counting backward. This ingenious explanation would make the appearance of Ambrosius fall about 472—a date against which there is nothing to say—and leave 516 for the battle and the birth of Gildas ; but Gildas would have written his book at the age of about thirty, instead of about forty-four. The *Annales Cambriae* gives Gildas's death under the year 570 : if we take Mr. Nicholson's hypothesis he was then fifty-four : if Mommsen's, he was about seventy : if Bede's, he would be about seventy-seven.

If we accept 472 for the date of the appearance of Ambrosius, it must clearly have been not that prince but some other leader who led the Britons to victory forty-four years later, in 516. This allows space for the campaigns and successes of Arthur, if we accept the existence of that much discussed personage, as I am inclined to do. It may be remarked that if Ambrosius was alive and fighting in 516, and if Gildas wrote the *Liber Querulus* in 545, only thirty years after, it is a little surprising to find the latter describing the princes of his own day as the grandsons rather than the sons of Ambrosius—they have degenerated *avita bonitate* not *paterna bonitate*. But if Ambrosius flourished 472-500 the generations seem to fit in better. Mr. Nicholson's hypothesis, therefore, is well worthy of consideration.

portance seems to be that the Saxons are represented as new visitors, whereas we have seen reason to believe that their attacks had been continuous ever since the Roman Empire began to grow weak.   It is possible, also, that Gildas gives too much the impression that Britain was under one king only about the year 450, by talking of a single *superbus tyrannus*, when really Vortigern (or whatever his name may have been) was at most the chief among several contemporary dynasts.   But in one respect his narrative seems to fit in with archæological evidence in a way that the ordinary received tale of the Saxon conquest fails to do.   He represents the disaster to civilised Britain as being sudden and fearful, as a conflagration that spread from sea to sea in a short time, and then retired from a great part of the area that it had devastated, leaving irreparable ruin behind.   Much of the island was liberated by Ambrosius, but it was never restored to its old state of wealth and culture.   This is precisely what we should guess from the condition of the old Roman cities when they are excavated.   In hardly one of them, even in those of the West Midlands, do we find any trace of a continued occupation by civilised Romano-Britons going on for many years after 410.   Nearly all, so far as we can see, show signs of having been burnt or deserted at a comparatively early date, and never inhabited again, even though their sites were not permanently occupied by the Teutonic invaders till the sixth or seventh century. There is no satisfactory evidence for the existence of an independent British Colchester, London or Lincoln, or even of a survival of York, Chester or Wroxeter.   The only known exception to this general rule is Calleva (Silchester), where a single post-Roman inscription in Ogham letters has been found, commemorating a certain Ebicatus : it seems to belong to the second half of the fifth century. But there are strong reasons for supposing that Calleva was evacuated by the Britons before that century was over.   It is quite possible to believe that the date 441, given by the so-called Prosper as that of a complete domination of the Saxons in Britain, really represents a moment when the invaders seemed to inundate the whole south and east of the island, though they ultimately lost their hold on great part of it.

The *Historia Brittonum* gives a much longer account of this period, but one that does not at all square with the narrative of Gildas.   Since, however, it was compiled not earlier than 685, while

Gildas was writing in 545, the later book can have no authority when it conflicts with the earlier. Moreover Gildas gives a possible series of events, while the *Historia* is replete with wild miracles and obvious folk-tales. Told shortly, for what it is worth, the version of this strange book runs as follows.

About forty years after the death of the tyrant Magnus Maximus, *i.e.*, about the year 428, Vortigern reigned in Britain, and was distracted between three fears, that of the Picts and Scots, that of the Romans, and that of Ambrosius [apparently a competitor for his throne, but clearly not the Ambrosius who flourished in 472-500]. To him came three ships from Germany, in which were the brothers Hengist and Horsa, exiles, and their war-band. Vortigern gave them the Isle of Thanet to live in, and hired them as allies against the Picts and Scots. About this time St. Germanus came to Britain and wrought many miracles, especially the portentous destruction of the tyrant Benlli by fire from heaven. [Here then we seem to be in 429, the time of Germanus's first visit.] After a time the Britons grew weary of paying their Saxon auxiliaries, and began to quarrel with them, but Hengist persuaded the king to retain them as his guard, and even to send for sixteen more ships'-crews of his countrymen. With this second party of the strangers arrived the daughter of Hengist, a girl of surpassing beauty, with whom the king fell desperately in love. He was so infatuated with her that, to buy her hand from her father, he gave him the whole region of Kent, though that was at the moment the patrimony of a certain British prince called Guoyrancgon. At the same time Hengist persuaded his son-in-law to enlist more mercenary bands, headed by his son Ochta and his nephew Ebissa, to whom he allotted for settlement the lands near the Great Wall. They came with forty ships, sailed around the coast of Pictland, devastated the Orkneys, and seized several tracts lying beyond the *Mare Frenessicum* [whatever that may be—possibly the estuary of the Forth] as far as the boundary of the Picts. Hengist meanwhile with his own band occupied great part of Kent.

At this moment the evil life of Vortigern, who had just added polygamy and incest to the list of his offences, drew down on him a second visit from St. Germanus. He was cursed by the saint and all the British clergy, and felt himself so insecure that he fled into the mountains beyond Severn, where he purposed to build himself

an impregnable castle. Here follows a wild tale about a mysterious
boy, certain wizards, two dragons, and some *ex-post-facto* prophecies
about the fate of Britain. The boy, whom the king had at first
intended to slay, revealed himself as Ambrosius, the son of a Roman
consul, and showed such marvellous knowledge that Vortigern fled,
and built, in another spot than that which he had chosen, his refuge-
castle of Caer-Vortigern.

Meanwhile, the king being apparently disgraced and discarded,
the Britons took as their leader his son Vortimer, a hard-fighting
hero, who fell upon Hengist and the Saxons, and after four general
actions drove them out of Kent, and even from their original grant
in the Isle of Thanet. The battles seem all to be placed in Kent—
the first on the Darent (*flumen Dergwentid*), the second " at the
ford which is called in their tongue Episford, but in ours Rithergabail.[1] There fell on the one side Horsa and on the other Categirn,
the second son of Vortigern and brother of Vortimer. The third
conflict was at the Inscribed Stone, which stands on the shore of the
Gallic Sea : there the Saxons were forced to flee on board their keels,
and were entirely driven out of Britain." [2] But Vortimer died no very
long time after his last victory, and when he was gone Hengist and
his Saxons came back in force. Vortigern, who seems to return to
power on his son's death, was ready to receive them on friendly
terms, because of his affection for his Saxon wife. A conference was
arranged between 300 deputies on each side, who were to come un-
armed ; but in the midst of the proceedings the Saxons, who had
hidden daggers in their boots, fell upon and massacred the British
delegates, all save the king, whom they held to ransom. As the
price of his life Vortigern ceded them the regions afterwards known
as Essex and Sussex.

Thoroughly discredited among the Britons, Vortigern fled after
this last disaster to his own special dominions beyond the Severn.
He was pursued thither by St. Germanus, who came to give him
once more a spiritual castigation. The king avoided him, slinking
from place to place, till he reached his stronghold of Caer-Vortigern
on the Teifi, where the saint blockaded him, as it were, praying and

---

[1] This in the *Saxon Chronicle* appears as Aegelsthrep (Aylesford) and as a victory
for Hengist, under the year 455.   Rithergabail means " the ford of the horses ".
[2] Lapis Tituli is perhaps Stonar, near Deal and Richborough.   Evidently there
was a large Roman inscribed monument near it.

fasting for three days outside the castle gate. On the fourth night fire descended from heaven and destroyed the king, his harem of wives, the castle and its garrison. " But others say that he was not thus slain, but wandered as an outcast from place to place, banned by every one, till he died of a broken heart." His third son, Pascentius, succeeded to the heritage of two regions, Builth and Vortigerniaun, and ruled there under the suzerainty of the celebrated Ambrosius, who was afterwards chief among the kings of Britain. And Fernmail, his descendant in the tenth generation, was reigning there when the last recension of the *Historia Brittonum* was made in the year 820, " the fourth year of King Mermin," who reigned from 816 to 844.

Meanwhile Hengist the Saxon died, and his son Ochta came from the northern side of Britain to the kingdom of Kent, and from him descend the kings of the Kentish men. The Saxons "increased in multitude and grew in Britain " till they were checked, not, as we should expect from Gildas, by Ambrosius Aurelianus, whom the *Historia Brittonum* only mentions incidentally, but by Arthur, a new name to us, though it is destined to be so famous in British story. Of him we are told that "he used to fight against the Saxons in company with the kings of the Britons, but was himself *dux bellorum*," a title which seems to descend from that old Roman *dux Britanniarum*, of whom mention has already been made. Arthur defeats the Saxons in twelve battles, most of whose names present difficulties of identification, though the tenth of them is that of Caer-Legion, *i.e.*, Chester, and the twelfth, that at *Mons Badonis*, is clearly the same as the victory of *Mons Badonicus*, of which Gildas speaks. Of it we are told "there fell in that one day 960 men before the assault of Arthur, and no one felled them save he alone". No cessation of the Saxon attack is mentioned as following the battle of Mount Badon, though Gildas has told us that forty years of comparative peace were won by it. But the *Historia* merely says that "routed in all these battles, the enemy sought succours from Germany, and were increased in numbers without intermission, and they brought over kings from Germany, to reign over them in Britain, down to the time when Ida came to be king, who was son of Eobba, and was the first king in Bernicia ".

Quite at variance both with Gildas and the *Historia* is the tale told by the *Anglo-Saxon Chronicle*, which represents the conquest of Eastern Britain as having been made, not by one wide-spreading incursion, led by Hengist, but by the separate enterprises of many different war-bands, Saxon, Anglian and Jutish, who worked very slowly forward, and conquered small patches of territory at long intervals of time. According to this narrative, only put together at the end of the ninth century, the course of the invasion was as follows :—

First, in 449 Hengist, a Jutish adventurer, with his brother Horsa, landed in the Isle of Thanet, at the summons of Vortigern, who offered them land in the south-east on condition that they should fight against the Picts. They drove off the northern barbarians, but soon quarrelled with their employer, and were for twenty years and more fighting to win the mastery of the land of Kent; Hengist proclaimed himself king in 455, and after many victories drove the Britons as far back as London in 457. But his subsequent battles were in Kent, and the last mention of him, in 473, does not imply that he had won any more than the single district where his descendants are found reigning a century later.

Secondly, in 477, Aella, the Saxon, and his three sons land on the South coast, establish themselves in Sussex, and in 491 besiege and take Anderida, its chief town. Their efforts do not extend beyond the forest of the Weald, the limit of the later South-Saxon kingdom.

Thirdly, in 495 Cerdic, another Saxon adventurer, and his son Cynric, land somewhere on Southampton Water, and after many battles with the Britons, all apparently in Hampshire, are hailed as kings in 519. A second contemporaneous invasion in the same region is made by one Port, who lands with his sons "at the place which is called Portsmouth," slays many Britons and makes a settlement. The relations of this certainly fictitious person (who is no more than the eponymous hero of Portsmouth) with Cerdic are not explained. But in 530 Cerdic conquers the Isle of Wight, and in 534 he dies. Since nearly twenty years later (552) the West Saxons have not yet occupied Salisbury, which they win in that year, it is clear that Cerdic's kingdom is conceived as covering no more than Hampshire, with, conceivably, parts of Berkshire and Surrey.

Fourthly, we are given a short notice of the establishment of an Anglian kingdom north of the Humber by Ida, who began to reign

in 547, lived twelve years longer, and fortified the royal stronghold
of Bamborough.

Fifthly, we get a mention of Aella, the first king of the other
Northumbrian kingdom of Deira, who is said to have received recognition as king in 560.

No statements are made in the *Chronicle* as to the foundation
of the other primitive Teutonic States in England, such as those of
the East Saxons, East Angles and Mercians.

The great irruption of the invaders into Central Britain is said
only to begin in 571, when, under the West Saxon king Ceawlin, the
grandson of Cerdic, a great battle is fought at Bedford, and the
four towns of Aylesbury, Lenbury, Bensington and Eynsham, all
north of Thames and south of Bedford, are taken.   Clearly, then, the
Chronicle conceives that the Britons were still holding the South-
Midlands more than a hundred and twenty years later than the supposed date of the landing of Hengist.   The first penetration of the
Saxons to the western side of the island follows a few years later,
with Ceawlin's victory at Dyrham, in South Gloucestershire (577),
after which he took from the Britons three cities, Gloucester, Cirencester and Bath.

It is clear that this ninth century narrative, evidently composed
from the ancestral memories of the invaders, with no direct help
from Gildas or the *Historia Brittonum*, and much from Bede,
contrasts in the strongest way with the version of the Saxon conquest given by the fifth and sixth century writers.   Nor can we
doubt that when they come into collision we must trust the earlier
rather than the later authority.   In a similar way Gildas must give
way when he comes into conflict with the *Vita Germani*, which was
written sixty years before his time.   And the *Historia Brittonum*
must be rejected when it conflicts with Gildas, whose testimony is
good for the sixth century, in whose very commencement he was
born, though it is not to be trusted for the early fifth century, of
which he clearly had only a knowledge in outline.   Indeed the
Historia can only be used with discretion and doubt for any history
earlier than the eighth century, in whose end it was first compiled.

Putting the whole of these authorities, whose weight varies so
much, into historical perspective, the version of the Saxon invasions,
which we are forced to construct, must run somewhat as follows :—

Down to about the year 429, the time of the first visit of

St. Germanus, Britain was assailed by Pict, Scot, and Saxon simultaneously, but, though suffering severely, more or less held its own. The heart of the Romanised Eastern and Southern Britain was still intact, but local kingships were beginning to spring up both in the West and the North, and these were Celtic rather than Roman in character : in fact a kind of Celtic revival was in progress, as is shown by the fact that the recorded names of princes are often non-Roman—e.g., Cunedda, Coroticus, and a little later Vortigern. A side-light on this movement may be got from the unique fifth century Ogham inscription at Silchester, which proves that barbarism was making its way towards the eastern side of the island. As already stated, it gives the name of Ebicatus written in the rude Celtic character common in Ireland, but rare in Britain, which begins to be used about this period. Apparently the words are in a Goidelic dialect, and Ebicatus may conceivably have been a visitor or immigrant, and not a citizen of Calleva.

Somewhere in the middle of the century, the Pictish invasions, checked for a moment at the " Hallelujah victory " of 429, grew again so dangerous that the Britons hired Saxon or Jutish mercenaries against them. We must conclude, from Gildas's mention of a "*superbus tyrannus*" and *consiliarii*, that there was at this moment a federation of kings and cities over which one prince held some sort of suzerainty or presidential power. And there is no reason to doubt that this was Vortigern, though his name is not given by Gildas. We must conceive of him as being a king of South Wales, since his descendants were reigning in Builth and Radnorshire when the *Historia Brittonum* was written, and the site of his castle was remembered to have been on the Teifi. There is no reason for distrusting this pedigree—and Vortigern was not an ancestor so creditable that any one would wish to claim him, unless there was good reason for so doing. The names of his predecessors in the pedigree, Vitalis (Guitaul), Vitalinus (Guitolin), Bonus, and Paulus, show that they must have been Romanised British nobles. He was clearly not " King of Britain," but one of many kings, who whether by election, or by force of arms, enjoyed a preponderance over the rest.

That Teutonic mercenaries, when they had accomplished the task of fighting for which they had been hired, often turned against the hand that fed them, is a well-known phenomenon of the fourth and fifth centuries, all over the Roman world. I see no reason to doubt that Gildas's story concerning the breach between the British king and his mercenaries may be true.   And we may allow that the chief of the Teutons was named Hengist, not so much because the *Historia Brittonum* says so, nor even because the English remembered him as founder of the Kentish kingdom, when Bede wrote in the eighth century, or when the *Chronicle* was compiled in the ninth, but because we have a much earlier authority for the fact. This is the anonymous " Geographer of Ravenna" who, describing the world a century before the *Historia*, and writing in a region where British or English legends were equally unlikely to penetrate, says that " the race of the Saxons, coming from Old Saxony, under their prince Anschis settled the island of Britain some time back ".[1]

What followed the breach between the Britons and their dangerous employés must have been something much more resembling the tale of Gildas than that of Nennius or the Anglo-Saxon Chronicle.   That is to say, we can hardly doubt that the Saxons swept with fire and sword all over Eastern Britain, and even as far as the Western Sea, during the course of a comparatively few years. They sacked all the great cities, probably with details of horror as great as those detailed in the lurid paragraph of Gildas quoted above.   They massacred, drove out, or enslaved the whole population, and firmly established themselves all down the length of the shore from Northumberland as far as Southampton Water.   How far to the West these ravages may have extended it is impossible to say ; we have the definite statement of Gildas that " the conflagration which started in the East, did not stay its course till, after devastating almost the whole island, its ruddy tongues licked the Western Ocean ".   This may mean, and probably does mean, nothing more than that the farthest raids of the Saxons touched the Bristol Channel, or the estuaries of Dee and Mersey.   The area of permanently conquered territory can not have reached nearly so far.   But there is no reason to doubt that there came an end, somewhere about the middle of the fifth century, to all the Romano-British states, municipal or monarchical, along the eastern side of Britain.   When Gildas wrote, his list of surviving British kingdoms seems to include nothing that lay east of the basin of the Severn, and of the line drawn from its southern edge to the English Channel across Wiltshire.

---

[1] For Mr. Chadwick's idea that Anschis = Oisc, see *Origins of the English Nation*, p. 47, but those who take it as a form of Hengist are more numerous.

He seems to have no knowledge of the eastern side of the island.
Yet he tells us that since the year of his own birth, early in the sixth
century, nothing more had been lost to the barbarians, and the
Britons had been comparatively free from foreign—if not from
domestic—strife.   The victory of the *Mons Badonicus* and the
rally headed by Ambrosius Aurelianus had saved the West but had
not recovered the East.   London and Camulodunum, Lindum and
Eburacum, were lost for ever.

We are forced to conclude that, starting before the year 441,
which the so-called Prosper gives as the date of the overrunning of
Britain by the Saxons, the wave of invasion swept in one (or at the
most two) generations up to the central watershed of England, and
was then checked by the rally of the Britons.   The devastated
eastern half, which had once been the most populous and civilised
part of Roman Britain, remained with the invaders; the western
half had crystallised into a number of native States, which maintained their independence, but had lost in the time of chaos nearly
all traces of the Roman culture, which had never bitten deep on the
western side of the island, save in a few isolated districts like the
Valley of the Lower Severn.

There seems no reason whatever to doubt the historic existence
of Ambrosius Aurelianus, whose grandsons " much degenerated from
their ancestor's virtue " were still reigning in some part of Britain
when Gildas wrote about 545.   The genuine tradition concerning
great historical figures extends with ease over a period so short as
sixty years, which must be about the interval between the exploits
of Ambrosius and the date of Gildas's book.   The other great British
hero whose name falls into this period has caused much searching of
heart to historians.   Is it possible to believe in Arthur, " *dux
bellorum* " and victor of Mount Badon, as he is described in the
Historia Brittonum ?

Arthur is not mentioned by name in Gildas, nor in Bede, nor in
the Anglo-Saxon Chronicle.   The chapter dealing with his twelve
battles in the *Historia* was not written till 685 at the earliest—a
date nearly two centuries later than his supposed exploits.   Hence
some historians frankly reject his historical existence : he has been
called " a hero of romance, a pure myth," to whom the exploits of
the real Ambrosius have been wrongly transferred.[1]   His origin has

[1] Ramsay, *Foundations of England*, i. 125.

been sought in the remotest antiquity, he is a Celtic "culture hero" or early divinity, brought down into historical times by some strange error of tribal memory. Or he is "the ideal champion of his race, belonging to all the Celts who spoke a Brythonic language from Morbihan to the Caledonian Forest". He is called "a popular creation, localising himself readily here, there, and everywhere, in the domain of the race in whose imagination he lives".[1] His name has been resolved into something mythological, and he disappears into a sun myth or a racial totem—Art-ur, the "bear-man"—in the writings of certain exponents of folk-lore.

I must confess that I am not convinced by these arguments, and incline to think that a real figure lurks beneath the tale of the *Historia Brittonum*. The name was un loubtedly Roman, like that of most British princes of this period : leaving out of count the numerous Artorii in the Classical Dictionary who had no connection with this island,[2] we know of one who held high command in Britain in the third century, and went, at the head of "Vexillations" of horse and foot, from the legion at York and other garrisons, to put down an insurrection of the Armoricans. This C. Artorius Justus, whose monument has been discovered in Illyria,[3] may have left numerous relatives or freedmen in Britain. At the same time, any Celtic-speaking provincial may have confused the purely Latin name with the Art = bear root in his own language. It is to be found several times in centuries later than the fifth : there was a South-Welsh prince named Arthur, son of Peter, whose name appears in the Harleian genealogies, during the seventh century. As to the fact that Arthur is not mentioned by name in Gildas, we may point out that the same is the case with Constantine, the last usurping emperor in Britain, with Germanus, Vortigern and Hengist. Indeed, the only two names that occur in the fifth century portion of the *Liber Querulus* are those of Aetius ("Agitius" as Gildas prefers to call him) and Ambrosius Aurelianus. It is even possible that Arthur is alluded to in that hysterical work, though he is not named, in one of its most obscurely-worded paragraphs.[4]

[1] Rhys, *Celtic Britain*, 236-37.
[2] Besides Augustus's physician, and the person censured by Juvenal, there are a considerable number of Artorii in C. I. L. inscriptions.
[3] C. I. L., Illyria, No. 1919.
[4] Gildas, as Mr. Nicholson of the Bodleian pointed out to me, calls one of the contemporary princes whom he abuses, a certain Cuneglassus, "ab adolescentiae

Nor is this enigmatical hero to be found in the *Historia Brittonum* alone. His name is associated with very many sites both in North and in South-Western Britain, and, though this fact may not prove his existence, it certainly does not disprove it. It is safer, on continental analogies, to look for a real personage dimly remembered, distorted, or even wrongly localised, behind such place-names, than to deny his historical character. The memories of Brunehaute, Charlemagne or Roland, even when attached to spots or works with which those undoubtedly real personages had apparently no connection, testify to a genuine memory of their existence and greatness. Probably "Arthur's Seat" and "Arthur's Oon" and such like, must be considered as bearing similar evidence. It may be added that Arthur is repeatedly mentioned in the earliest Bardic poems of Wales—whatever may be the date of the shape in which they survive. When Celtic scholars will agree to assign a fixed age to those ancient relics, we shall be better able to judge of their value as corroborating the *Historia Brittonum.* Meanwhile, the allusions to Arthur which occur in them seem to belong to the earliest stage of their compilation, and have no trace of the later Arthur-legend which grew popular in days after Nennius, and was ultimately put into literary shape by that most unconscientious person Geoffrey of Monmouth in the twelfth century. As in the *Historia,* he seems to be merely *dux bellorum,* a military chief, not a king—still less a supreme high-king of all Britain, such as tradition afterwards made him. Meanwhile historians still await a satisfactory estimate of the exact worth of these poems from a competent critic, who must be at once a Celtic philologist and a sound historian. If the decision is in favour of an early date, we cannot hesitate to accept the Arthur of the *Historia Brittonum* as a well-established historical person. If it places the poems very late, we are thrown back on what information we already possess concerning him, and I am inclined to think that this alone suffices to take him out of the region of myth.

annis multorum sessor, aurigaque currus receptaculi Ursi". Can this possibly mean that Cuneglassus, who is spoken of as no longer young, had been in earlier days the charioteer, or, to use late-Roman phraseology, the *comes stabuli* of some king whom Gildas calls the " bear "=Arth ? It is puzzling, however, to see that Cuneglassus is also himself called " Urse," unless that word be a mistaken duplication from the immediately following Ursi.

CHAPTER XII

THE SETTLEMENT OF THE CONQUERORS. THE EARLY KINGDOMS
(516-570)

WHEN the first triumphant inrush of the Teutonic invaders of
Briton was arrested by the resistance made by Ambrosius
Aurelianus, and finally checked at the battle of the *Mons Badonicus*, the survivors settled down, not into one single State, like the
Franks in Gaul or the Visigoths in Spain, but into many. The
same phenomenon was seen four hundred years later, when the
Danes of the " Great Army," who had been acting for many years
as one compact war-band, broke apart into many sections, after they
had been taught by Alfred's sword that all England was not to
be theirs.[1] The moment of settlement was a moment of political
disruption.

The first invasions must have been led by many chiefs in succession, of whom Hengist was the first and very probably Aella the
second. The tradition preserved by Bede[2] that an " imperium "
over all the bands of the invaders, from the Humber southward to
the Gallic Sea, was possessed by Aella the founder of the South
Saxon kingdom, then by Ceawlin a West Saxon, then by Aethelbert of Kent, then by Raedwald the East Anglian, is clearly a
memory of the fact that the Saxons, Jutes and English worked
together against the Britons. The view that each war-band stuck
to the narrow piece of coast on which it had landed, without paying
attention to what was going on to right or left, is an erroneous deduction from the entries of the Anglo-Saxon Chronicle. They do
not necessarily bear such an interpretation, and, if they did, it must

---

[1] We might add, as a parallel in a nearer time, the fate of the Lombards in Italy,
who broke up into the states of Benevento and Spoleto, besides the larger northern
kingdom, after failing to conquer all Italy.

[2] *E. H.*, ii. 5.

be remembered that they come from a document of the late ninth
century, which (as we shall presently see) has little authority for
the history of the sixth.   It is incredible that the "imperium" of
Bede means a territorial domination over all the newly established
insular states, held by chiefs who owned such small realms as Sussex,
Kent, or even East Anglia.   But taking the word in its classical
military sense, a sense which Bede was scholar enough to appreciate,
there is no reason to doubt that a league of war-bands might be,
from time to time, captained by a chief whose own following was not
the largest contingent in the host.   The settlement that he occupied as a permanent holding might, therefore, be comparatively
small.

Down to the check at the *Mons Badonicus* it is quite probable
that we ought not to speak of separate Teutonic kingdoms as existing in Britain.   The fluid mass of invaders may have crystallised
into solid units only when there was, for a time, no more land to
be won, so that it became necessary to take stock, so to speak, of
that which was still at their disposition.   The disruption of the
conquering host into petty kingdoms with definite boundaries is a
phenomenon of the early sixth century, and was practically complete
by its end.   Concerning their foundation we have in some cases a
certain amount of information, but in others none.   Exactly similar
was the history of the Danish "Great Army" in the ninth century,
of which we shall tell in due course.

One thing is clear : the invaders had been no homogeneous mass
of "Saxons," as we should have gathered from the narratives of
Gildas and the *Historia Brittonum*.   Their own account of their
origin, as given by Bede, must be accepted, for this is one of the
matters on which tribal tradition does not go astray in a mere
two hundred years.   "The immigrants came from three very
powerful nations of Germany—Saxons, Angles and Jutes.   From
the Jutes are descended the people of Kent and the Isle of Wight,
and those also who, dwelling in the province of the West Saxons, are
to this day called the Jute-folk, seated opposite to the Isle of Wight.
From the Saxons, that is from the land which we now call Old
Saxony, came the East Saxons, the South Saxons and the West
Saxons.   From the Angles, that is from the region which is now
called 'Angulus,' and which is said to have remained from that
day till now depopulated, lying between the boundaries of the Jutes

and Saxons, came the East Angles, the Mid Angles, the Mercians, and all the race of the Northumbrians who dwell north of the river Humber, and the remaining English tribes." [1]

The Saxons, Jutes and Angles are old acquaintances of those who have read Tacitus's *Germania* and Ptolemy's *Geography*. The former had dwelt in the second century to the north of the river Elbe, in what is now called Holstein, "on the neck of the Cimbric Chersonesus," as Ptolemy puts it. They owned also "the three islands off the mouth of the Elbe," whatever that may mean. Tacitus, oddly enough, makes no mention of the Saxons, and from Ptolemy to the third century they escaped the notice of Roman historians, because they were far away from the wars of the Rhine frontier. But in that third century fell the period of the building up of the great confederacies which formed the later German nations. And just as the Franks on the Lower and the Alamanni on the Upper Rhine suddenly appear as new composite units, superseding many older and smaller tribal entities, so it is with the Saxons farther north. They evidently coalesced with the Chauci, the most numerous of the North German races, who occupied all the land between the Elbe and the Ems, in the modern province of Hanover. The confederacy took the Saxon not the Chaucian name, and we find Zosimus calling the Chauci "a part of the Saxons," in the fourth century.[2] Apparently the Saxons, though the smaller tribe, had, by conquest or by peaceful means, taken the greater part in building up the union, and imposed their name on it. From 286 A.D. onwards we find them perpetually mentioned by the Roman historians as pirates infesting the North Sea, as we have seen already when dealing with the history of Carausius and Stilicho. Hence came the establishment of the two naval governments of the *Littus Saxonicum per Brittanias* and *per Gallias*, whose fleets and harbour-forts were destined to cope with the marauders. With the break-up of the Roman power in Britain and Northern Gaul, during the miserable reign of Honorius, the defence of the North Sea and Channel ceased, and the Saxons could not only ravage for the future but settle down where they pleased. It was not only in Britain that they won themselves a holding; a section of them seized part of the north coast of Gaul, between the

[1] Bede, i. 16.
[2] Zosimus, iii. 6. See Bremer's *Ethnographie der Germanischen Stämme*, 124.

mouth of the Seine and the Peninsula of the Cōtentin, where they are found in the fifth and sixth centuries under the name of the *Saxones Bajocassini* [1] (from Bajocae, now Bayeux, the chief centre of the settlement). They were presently subdued by the Franks, and incorporated in the Merovingian realm. It seems likely that there was another small Saxon settlement on the coast of the Dover Strait behind Calais, where a group of place-names of purely Saxon type covers a small compact region. But no traces of these colonists appear in historical records : unlike the Saxones Bajocassini they did not attract the notice of Gregory of Tours.

The Jutes are the second Teutonic tribe named by Bede as taking part in the conquest of Britain, and to them belonged, by common repute, the exiled chief Hengist, who hired himself out with his war-band to Vortigern, and afterwards led the first great raids of the piratical confederacy. The Jutes are a much more obscure people than the Saxons. They are apparently first found in Tacitus, as the Eudoses, one of a group of seven small tribes (of whom the Angles and Varini were others) dwelling together some-where far to the north beyond the Langobardi. The historian has nothing of interest to say about these races, save that all seven joined in the common worship of an earth-goddess named Nerthus, whose sanctuary was on an island [2]—but whether it lay in the North Sea or the Baltic there is no indication. Indeed, all Tacitus's geography in this part of the *Germania* is vague to a degree. Since, however, the Varini and Angles, who are mentioned along with the Eudoses, were certainly seated in the Cimbric Peninsula, there can be little doubt that the Jutes also were already dwelling in Jutland, the land where they have left their name, as early as the year 100 A.D. Ptolemy, however, has no mention of them, and it is not indeed for several centuries that we again come upon them, under the names of Eutii, Euthiones, or Eucii, in connection with the Franks. Venantius Fortunatus, the last Roman poet of Merovingian times, tells us that his patron Chilperic had defeated the Dane, the Euthio and the Saxon, and some forty years earlier a letter of King Theudebert to Emperor Justinian states that the Saxons and Eucii [3] had recently

---

[1] *Gregory of Tours*, v. 26, and x. 9.

[2] Alsen off the east coast of Schleswig ? (see Furneaux's note to the *Germania*).

[3] Or perhaps the Saxones Eucii, the phraseology is obscure. It is quite possible that the Merovingians considered the Jutes as Saxons, just as the Britons most cer-tainly did.

submitted to him. That the Frankish power ever reached to Jutland in any effective way seems unlikely : but since Fortunatus mentions the " Euthio " between the Saxon and the still more remote Dane, there can be no doubt that the races had been in collision. And since we know that Danes under Hygelac (Chrocolaicus) invaded the Frankish northern borders by sea in 515, and were defeated by the son of King Theuderic, we may perhaps suppose that the Jutes also had been attempting settlement in the same direction. If they came to Britain, they could far more easily come to the lands of the Rhine-mouth. Objections have been raised on philological grounds to the identification of Bede's *Jutae* with the Euthiones or Eutii,[1] owing to the initial J of the name. But the balance of opinion seems to be in favour of regarding them as a North-German folk, closely akin to the Angles, who were afterwards subdued by the Danes, and amalgamated with their conquerors, so that their language and customs ceased to be German and became Scandinavian. That the old English had no doubt that the Jutes of Kent and the Wight came from Jutland, is sufficiently shown by the fact that the chronicler Ethelweard says, that the Cantuarii and " Uuhtii " of England derived their origin from the Gioti, and that the Angles dwelt between the Saxons and the Gioti.[2] King Alfred in his translation of Bede, calls the Jutes of the earlier writer Geatas,[3] but in his *Orosius* renders " provincia Jutorum " by Eotaland.[4] Eotas, Gioti, Geatas and Jutae were clearly in the minds of Alfred and Ethelweard interchangeable forms. But the G initial and the form Geatas were apparently caused by a confusion of the inhabitants of Jutland with the Goths of Sweden. The older Scandinavian name for the Jutlanders seems to have been Iotar or Jotar, the later Danish form was Jyder—neither of which should be identified with the Gautar across the water in the Scandinavian Peninsula, who were the real Geatas or Goths.

The Angles give less difficulty to the inquirer. They are named by Tacitus along with the Eudoses and Varini, among the seven tribes who lay beyond the Langobardi, *i.e.*, north of the Elbe, and worshipped Nerthus in common. They were therefore already in the

---

[1] See Bremer's *Germanischen Stämme*, 122 ; Chadwick's, *Origin of the English* 103-5, and Müllenhoff's *Beowulf*, 13, 19.

[2] Ethelweard, Preface to book i.

[3] Alfred's *Bede*, 1, § 15. [4] Alfred's *Orosius*, 1, § 19.

Cimbric Peninsula at the end of the first century A.D. Ptolemy mentions them as the Angeiloi, but apparently makes a hopeless confusion as to their geographical position, since he says that they are an inland tribe lying to the *east* of the Langobardi, and stretching northward to the Middle Elbe. Apparently his points of the compass have got wrong, and having once placed them east of the Langobardi instead of north, he is forced to consider them as lying in Brandenburg instead of in Schleswig. Their real position is clearly given by Bede—as above quoted—lying between the Saxons and the Jutes, and also by King Alfred when he says that "north of the Saxons lies the land called Angle, and Sillende (another district of the modern Schleswig) and some part of the Danes". Ethelweard is still more definite, " Old Anglia is situated between the Saxons and the Gioti, having a chief town which in Saxon is called Sleswic, but in Danish Haithaby". Here lies to this day the square peninsula called Angeln, between the Schleswig and Flensburg fiords.

It must not be supposed, however, that the territory of the numerous race who settled all the north-eastern coast of Britain was limited to the narrow bounds of the modern Angeln. It undoubtedly extended over all Schleswig, some of the Danish isles,[1] and possibly also over part of Jutland in the fifth and sixth centuries. It is not unlikely that the Angles may have amalgamated with themselves some of the other small tribes whom Tacitus mentions as leagued with them in worship of Nerthus—the Reudigni Aviones, Suardones and Nuithones. The Angles must have been sharing in the maritime expeditions of the Saxons in the fifth century, for, though their name is not on record in the historians, yet we find a corps of Angli among the Teutonic mercenary regiments of the Notitia Dignitatum. Evidently, therefore, they had gone south in considerable numbers, and were occasionally enlisting in the imperial army—which can only have happened through sea voyages. It seems possible also that somewhere about the sixth century they had settlements on the Lower Rhine—just as the Saxons had on the north coast of Gaul. The evidence for this, however, is only an early code of laws called the *Lex Angliorum et Werinorum, hoc est Thuringorum*, which has been attributed to various dates

---

[1] Certainly Fünen at least. See Bremer, *Germanischen Stämme*, 119.

between the sixth and ninth centuries. The Thuringi of this code are evidently the people on the Lower Rhine, more generally known as Thoringi, who, as we know, were annexed to the Frankish empire in the sixth century. The Werini are the Varini of Tacitus, neighbours of the Angles in the Cimbric Peninsula, who had apparently shared in this southward move of some part of the race. Conceivably this settlement on the Lower Rhine may have been the stepping stone of the Angles on their way to Britain, though it is equally possible that all the colonists came directly from their Cimbric home to our island. We have independent evidence for the existence of the Varini in the Netherlands from Procopius (*circ.* 550), who tells us a long tale concerning their relations with the Franks "from whom they are separated only by the Rhine". But he unfortunately makes no mention of the Angles as being settled with them in that region. We have therefore no other evidence for their existence in the Low Countries than the title of the code cited above.[1]

Bede is apparently correct when he says that the old home of the Angles in Schleswig was completely deserted in his own day. The Anglian name disappears from the Cimbric Peninsula just when it becomes widely spread in Britain, and we have little trace of any inhabitants save Danes and Saxons in this region after the sixth century. Very nearly the whole race had migrated to Britain. Thus only, indeed, can we account for such a phenomenon as the conquest of the entire coastland from the Firth of Forth to the mouth of the Stour by a tribe whose original home was of such limited dimensions.

Along with the Jutes, Saxons and Angles it can hardly be doubted that fragments of other tribes reached Britain. The invaders were a mixed multitude led by chiefs of several races, and there is good reason to believe that their hosts must have included small bands from the neighbouring tribes of the coastland of the North Sea—especially from the Frisians. Procopius, in his curious account of Britain, speaks of the invaders recently

---

[1] Some authorities wish to place the Angles and Varini of the code in the Thuringia of Central Germany, not the Thoringia of the Netherlands, where names similar to those of Angles and Varini "Engelin" and "Werinofeld" are found as small districts on the Unstrut and Saal. See Chadwick, 110-12, but *cf.* for the other view Bremer, 120-21, whom I follow.

established there only as Angles and Frisians, omitting not only the Jutes but also the Saxons. Yet none of the historical kingdoms of England traced themselves back to a Frisian ancestry. It is probable that stray Varini and Heruli, if not Franks also, may have been among the settlers, since all were more or less seafaring, and all were at hand to profit by the weakness of the Britons, after the removal of the Roman fleet from the Channel.

That the settlements of the Teutonic invaders developed into many small states, and not one powerful kingdom like that of the Franks in Gaul or the Ostrogoths in Italy, is easily to be explained. The settlers were of at least three separate races, and each racial element was composed, not of a king migrating at the head of the whole body of his subjects, like Alaric or Theodoric, but of many war-bands under many chiefs. These obeyed, no doubt, the general whom they had chosen from time to time to head their confederacy, the Hengist or Aella of the moment, but they were not a compact or homogeneous host. Even the Angles, who appear to have migrated practically *en masse* to England, seem to have been led, not by any single prince representing the old royal house that had ruled in Angeln, but by many chiefs of varying descent. In the pedigrees of the kings of the later states of East Anglia, Bernicia, Deira and Mercia,[1] which are undoubtedly the oldest surviving fragments of Anglian historical memory, we do not find that all the founders of the states start from the same series of ancestors, as would have been the case if all had deduced themselves from the old kings of the Angles. On the contrary, though all ultimately get back to the god Woden, the inevitable forefather of all Teutonic kings in Britain, whether Anglian or Saxon, they reach him by four separate lines of descent, which have no single name in common, save that the Deiran and the Bernician lines both purport to start from Baeldag, son of Woden. It is curious to note that the West Saxon royal house, which one would have supposed likely to own a perfectly distinct descent from any Anglian line, claimed three ancestors, Woden, Baeldag and Brond, identical with the initial names in the Deiran list as given in the *Historia Brittonum*. But Woden and his immediate descendants being clearly mythical, we can only deduce that the Anglian royal houses had no real connection with each other

---

[1] All to be found at the end of the *Historia Brittonum*.

that could be traced. Otherwise they would have had a number of common ancestors, ending in the generation falling before the date of the invasion of Britain.

The kingdoms which were certainly in existence about the year 550 seem to have been the following :—

(1) Kent, whose kings claimed to descend from Hengist, though their family name of Oiscings was taken not from him but from Oisc, who is called his son both by Bede and the *Saxon Chronicle*, though the *Historia Brittonum*, says that Octha was the son of Hengist, and Ossa (apparently a corruption of Oisc) was the son of Octha. The settlers in this region were wholly or predominantly Jutes, which accounts for the fact that the Kentish dialect had marked peculiarities, which differentiated it from the speech of the Saxons to the west and the Angles to the north. The kingdom of the Oiscings never extended over any tract of territory much larger than the modern county of Kent, but it is likely that parts of Surrey may have belonged to it in the sixth century, since the dialect of that region shows some, if not all, of the Kentish peculiarities. Yet the name "Surrey," the "southern region," must surely have been imposed on this thinly-peopled and much-wooded district by invaders who entered it from the North, rather than from Kent.

But the strength of the Oiscings in early days must have depended, not on the exact amount of territory occupied by their own Jutish war-band, but on their personal influence as generals of the combined Teutonic invaders of South Britain. It is thus alone that we can account for the fact that Aethelbert (560-617) was reckoned by Bede to have held the *imperium* of all Britain south of Humber, and was certainly granted homage and tribute by his immediate Saxon neighbours, and even by remoter Anglian dynasts farther to the north.[1]

(2) A State even smaller than Kent was founded upon the narrow sea-coast between the chalk ridge of the South Downs and the woods of the Weald on the one side, and the water of the Channel on the other. This, the least important of all the Teutonic states of Britain, was inhabited by a people who claimed to be of Saxon descent, and to trace their origin from the war-band of a chief named Aella who had landed in this island a whole generation after Hengist and the Jutes. Yet Aella, according to Bede, had been reckoned

[1] Bede, *E. H.*, ii. 3.

the first of all those princes who held the *imperium* of Britain ; we must conclude, therefore, that he had been the chief commander of the whole Saxon swarm in the last quarter of the sixth century, and probably was the leader who had to face the rally of the Celts under Ambrosius Aurelianus. As was the case with Kent, the smallness of the personal war-band which followed the predominant chief of the moment did not prevent him from holding authority over confederates who brought larger forces to the field. But when Aella was dead his descendants became unimportant, because none of them was vigorous enough to assert a predominance over his contemporaries. To win such a position became, of course, a task increasingly difficult for the master of a very small war-band, as the other states of Britain crystallised into permanent units.

(3) To the north of the estuary of the Thames we find in the second half of the sixth century the kingdom of the East Saxons, occupying very much the same territory that had once been held by the British Trinovantes, but in addition Middlesex and probably the Eastern borders of Hertfordshire. Neither the royal lists in the *Historia Brittonum* nor Bede give us any tradition concerning the origin of this kingdom nor the name of its founder. But later genealogies, preserved in writers of a much less remote antiquity,[1] show us that the Kings of Essex had compiled an ancestry for themselves going back to Woden through his son Seaxneat—a Saxon war-god. It is notable that the first king of the East Saxons in Britain is made to be a certain Aescwin, who was the grandfather of Saebert, the undoubtedly historical personage who was reigning when St. Augustine landed in Britain in 597 A.D. Working on some rough computations of generations, the pedigree-makers placed the date of Aescwin's assumption of the kingship in 527. This puts the origin of the kingdom so late that we are tempted to conclude that it only formed itself out of certain sections of the general swarm of Saxon invaders, when the defeat of the *Mons Badonicus* had brought invasion to a stand, and forced the surviving war-bands to divide up among themselves so much territory as they still retained. For the fertile and thickly-peopled lands along the coast, between the great Roman towns of Londinium and Camulodunum, must have been

---

[1] But the lists at the end of Florence of Worcester and Henry of Huntingdon undoubtedly represent genuine Saxon traditions, and date back four or five centuries before these chroniclers.

among the very first conquests of the Saxons in the middle of the
fifth century.   Whether Middlesex, the land of the Middle Saxons,
was ever a separate State we cannot tell ; it certainly was under the
power of the East Saxon king Saebert in 604, when London was
chosen as the site of the bishopric founded to serve his dominions.
Surrey, "the South region," must also have formed part of the
first Saxon settlement in this direction—as has already been observed [1]—though its later history was not connected with Essex but
with Kent and the West Saxons.   East Hertfordshire was a part of
the Essex bishopric of London from the tenth century onward, and
was probably included in it from the first ; but it is not absolutely
certain that the boundaries of the See of London may not have been
varied in the confusion that followed the Danish invasions.

(4) Another realm which must have been created on the break-
up of the great confederacy of Saxon invaders which followed the
disaster of the Mons Badonicus was that of the West Saxons.   The
early history of this realm, as has been remarked in the last chapter,
seems to have been wholly confused by the entries between the years
495 and 530 in the Anglo-Saxon Chronicle.   These meagre and
inexplicable paragraphs inform us—firstly, that two "ealdormen,"
Cerdic and his son Cynric, came to shore with five ships at the place
called Cerdics-ora in 495, and there fought against the Welsh on
that same day.   Secondly, that in 501 Port, with his sons, Bieda
and Maegla, arrived with two ships, at the place that is called
Portsmouth, landed there and slew a young British prince of high
nobility.   Next, in 508, Cerdic and Cynric fought and slew a king
whose name was Natan-leod, and who had 5,000 men with him.
Since then the district has been named Natan-lea as far as Cerdicsford.   We are then surprised to find that "in 514 the West Saxons
came to Britain with three ships, at the place that is called Cerdicsora, and Stuf and Wihtgar fought with the Britons and routed
them".   In 519 Cerdic and Cynric " obtained the kingdom of the
West Saxons, and in the same year they fought with the Britons at
the place called Cerdicsford : and from that time the royal line of
the West Saxons has reigned ".   In 527 Cerdic and Cynric fight
against the Britons at the place called Cerdicslea.   In 530 the same
two kings conquered the Isle of Wight, and slew many men at

[1] See p. 221.

Wihtgarabyrig. Finally, in 534, Cerdic died and his son Cynric became sole king : and they gave the whole Isle of Wight to their two nephews,[1] Stuf and Wihtgar. Finally, Wihtgar dies in 544 and is buried at Wihtgarabyrig.

The first strange fact that we note in this narrative is that there is apparently a duplication of the incidents. Cerdic and his son arrive in 495 at Cerdicsora, but in 514 "the West Saxons" arrive at the same Cerdicsora under Stuf and Wihtgar. In 509 Cerdic and Cynric slay Natan-leod in the district near Cerdicsford : in 519 they fight again at Cerdicsford and "obtain the kingdom". When we reflect that Cerdic lands in 495 with a son who is full grown and able to act as his colleague, i.e., at an age that cannot be less than forty, and probably is more, and that he then proceeds to fight and conquer for a period of thirty-five years (495-530) we cannot but be confirmed in our suspicion that there is something wrong with the chronology. The whole of the incidents are confused and suspicious.

But this is not all : the Port who lands at Portsmouth betrays to the first glance that he is an eponymous hero created from the name of the Roman harbour, *Portus Magnus*. Similarly Wihtgar is clearly the eponymous hero of the people of the Isle of Wight, the Wihtgaras ; but the name of the Isle has been Icht, or, in Latin, Vectis, for centuries before the Saxon invasion began. The prince got his name from the Isle, not the Isle from the prince.[2] Finding ourselves in the company of mythical persons of this sort we begin to notice that Cerdic, too, is only mentioned in connection with places whose titles are compounded with his name, Cerdicsora and Cerdicsford and Cerdicslea. Can it be possible that he is a creation of the same species as Port and Wihtgar ?

The next development of the puzzle is even more serious. Many modern philologists tell us that Cerdic (Ceretic, Certic) is not a Teutonic name at all, but Celtic.[3] We know of three or four

---

[1] *Nefan*, however, is a vaguer word than nephew.

[2] Wihtgar certainly and Port possibly are real Saxon names. But the coincidence of the two being made to come to the localities Portsmouth and Wight, whose Roman names were Portus Magnus and Vectis, is wholly incredible. But see Stevenson in *Eng. Hist. Rev.*, xiv. 44.

[3] But see Stevenson's article, p. 34, quoted above. The assertion that the Welsh name Ceretic (or Coroticus) could not lose its stressed second syllable, seems to be disproved by the fact that Cerdic of Elmet has lost it in the *Historia Brittonum* written by a Celt, as also by the modern form Cardigan for Cerétigiaun.

British characters of the name. The first is a person in the *Historia Brittonum*, who is said to have been Vortigern's interpreter, "and no one save he among the Britons could understand the tongue of the Saxons ".[1] The next is one of the many descendants of the great Cunedda, from whom the district along the West coast of Wales got its name of Ceredigiaun—the modern Cardiganshire. A third is Cerdic, Prince of Elmet, in the early seventh century, who was conquered by the Northumbrian King Edwin. A fourth is that Coroticus, to whom St. Patrick wrote—for the name is the same, and in the genealogies this dynast appears as Ceretic Guletic. What right has a Saxon ealdorman descended from Woden to this purely Celtic name? It may be urged that one of the historic kings of Wessex bore a Welsh name, Ceadwalla, in the late seventh century. But at that time the Saxons had been two centuries in Britain, had become Christians, and had begun to intermarry with the Welsh kingly families. Cerdic, the invader of 495, if he ever existed, must have been born about 450, in days when such intimacy with the Britons and the borrowing of a name from them seems almost incredible. A wild suggestion has been made that the founder of the Wessex dynasty may have been a Briton, no less a person than Vortigern's Saxon-speaking interpreter, the Cerdic of the *Historia Brittonum*. It is suggested that he may have known the tongue of the invaders because he consorted much with them, being perhaps a kinglet who made himself strong by hiring a Saxon bodyguard. If he sided with the Saxons in the long wars, he might have survived, and started a lineage and a kingdom that was at once Celtic and Teutonic. A parallel might be cited in that Domnal Kavanagh, the son of Dermot McMurrough of Leinster, who adhered consistently to the Norman invaders of Ireland in the twelfth century, and founded a great baronial family, which for all intents and purposes became Anglo-Norman and ceased to be Irish. But this is pure speculation. It is safer to regard the existence of any Cerdic as founder of the West Saxon realm with deep suspicion.

There remains the most fatal objection of all to the early history of the kingdom of Wessex, as related by the Anglo-Saxon Chronicle. The lands where Cerdic, Port, Stuf and Wihtgar are

---

[1] *H. B.*, 37.

found as conquerors in this narrative are described by Bede, an
authority far older and better than the Chronicle, as not Saxon at
all but Jutish.   We are distinctly told by him, as has been already
pointed out, that the Isle of Wight and the lands opposite it on
the mainland had been settled by Jutes, and that even in his own
day the people on the mainland north of the Solent were called the
Jute-folk (*Jutorum natio*).[1]   If this was so, we have no room for
West Saxon conquerors, such as the alleged Cerdic and Cynric,
in this direction.   Moreover, Bede's statement that Wight was
originally independent of the West Saxons is borne out by the first
definite mention that we get of it in genuine history.   Wulfhere,
King of Mercia, about the year 681, gave to Aethelwalch, king of
Sussex, "two provinces, *viz.*, Wight and the land of the Meonwaras,[2] which last is in the realm of the West Saxons".[3]   Some
years after Ceadwalla, King of Wessex, slew Aethelwalch and conquered Wight, which, we are told, was down to that time "entirely
given over to heathenism," though the West Saxons had been converted to Christianity forty years before, in the time of King Cynegils and the Bishops Birinus and Agilbercht.   Ceadwalla made a
horrible massacre of the inhabitants of Wight, and settled the island
again with men of his own nation.   Moreover, he took pains to exterminate its royal house, by hunting out and executing the brothers
of Arwald, king of the island, who had hidden themselves in the
"provincia Jutorum," *i.e.*, the Hampshire coastland, opposite to
Wight.   All this narrative seems to prove that the island was
originally unconnected with the West Saxons, and had a people of
a different race from them, as well as a royal house of its own.   Nor
need we doubt that the case was originally the same with the
Jutes of the Hampshire coast, though Bede is ready to regard these
"Meonwaras" and other Jute-folk as forming a part of Wessex in
680.   Archæology corroborates this.   All early Teutonic grave-relics
of Wight and of the opposite coast resemble those of Kent : they are
not of Saxon type.

But if Cerdic is a doubtful figure, and if the coastland of Eastern
Wessex was Jutish soil in the sixth century, whence came the origin
of the West Saxon state ?   We are almost compelled to conclude

[1] See Bede, i. 237.
[2] South-East Hampshire, where the name is still preserved in the hundreds of
East and West Meon and Meonborough.
[3] Bede, *E. H.*, iv. 13.

that the original nucleus was formed from those parts of the earliest Saxon swarm which did not coalesce into the other kingdoms of Sussex and Essex, *i.e.*, from war-bands seated west of Middlesex, in Berkshire and North Hampshire, and perhaps holding also some small settlement north of Thames. We shall see reason to believe that Ceawlin, the first historical king of the West Saxons, started from this centre, since his first recorded actions were the driving off of the men of Kent from Surrey, and the conquest of the regions about Buckingham, Bedford and Oxford. When the first " bishop-stool " was created in West Saxon territory, after the conversion of king Cynegils, it was placed at Dorchester-on-Thames, in Oxford-shire, and in nearly every other case in Britain we find that the first bishop was established close to the court of the king.[1] The deduction would seem to be that the royal dynasty of Wessex may have had its favourite residence on the Thames rather than in the South. Winchester may have taken the place of Dorchester only when South Hampshire and the Wight had become West Saxon soil. It may be noted that the name West Saxons suits a people seated on the Middle Thames quite as well as a people seated in Hampshire, according to the accepted tradition. It gives also a far better meaning to Middlesex, which on this hypothesis is actually between the East and the West Saxons, while most maps show it lying between the East Saxons and Anglian tribes seated in the South Midlands.[2]

Ceawlin, as has been already said, is the first king of the West Saxons of whose existence we can be sure. Bede mentions him as next after Aella among those monarchs who held an "imperium" over all Britain south of Humber. The Wessex genealogy which makes him son of Cynric and grandson of Cerdic may have been compiled at a very much later date. The Anglo-Saxon Chronicle fixes his accession at 560; whether this be correct or no, he was certainly the leader who renewed the attack on the Britons which had ceased since the disaster at the Mons Badonicus in 516. Gildas, writing apparently in 545, says that his countrymen had lost no

---

[1] This is not a necessary deduction. But certainly the king must have had much royal demesne about Dorchester.

[2] For the arguments for and against this hypothesis see Sir Henry Howorth in *Eng. Hist. Rev.*, xiii., answered by Mr. Stevenson in the same periodical, xiv., and a summary in Chadwick's *Origin of the British Nation*, pp. 20-33.

more territory to the Saxons since that fight, which was about thirty years back when he wrote the *Liber Querulus*. Apparently if he had written a generation later he would have had to unsay his boast. Ceawlin's victory at Deorham—only ten miles from Bath (577)— undid the work of the earlier battle, and marks the commencement of the second great advance of the Saxons. Of this more anon.

The West Saxons had a tribal name besides the more ordinarily used appellation drawn from their geographical position. This was Gewissae ; it does not seem however to have been an early designation orought by them from Germany, but merely means the "allies" or " confederates," a sufficiently good name for a body of war-bands, leagued together originally for some temporary need. We might even suspect that it implies a mixed origin in the composition of the host, which may have included other elements besides the purely Saxon. An ancestor called Gewis was inserted in the pedigree of the Wessex kings to act as the eponymous hero of the tribe.[1]

(5) North of the settlements of the East Saxons and the West Saxons we find the Angles established, all along the east coast of Britain, before the year 550. The southernmost of their kingdoms was that of East Anglia, a State composed of two sections, the North-folk and the South-folk. There are indications that this division may have implied the existence of two original[2] petty kingdoms : but they seem normally to have acted as a single unit, and to have obeyed a single king, in later times, and the royal house of the Wuffings ruled over both. The state must have come into existence among the earliest of the Teutonic kingdoms of Britain, but we know nothing about its early history. Wuffa was the grandfather of Raedwald, who was reigning in East Anglia about 600-618, so that his date cannot be put earlier than 550-70. The genealogies at the end of the *Historia Brittonum* state that Guecha (Wehha) father of Wuffa was the founder of the kingdom :—if his existence may be accepted, the East Anglian settlement must have coalesced into a State somewhere about 520 : this is one of the many indications which tend to make us fix the epoch immediately after the battle of the Mons Badonicus as that of the crystallising into permanent units of the Anglian and Saxon war-bands. The territory

---

[1] See Müllenhof, *Beowulf*, p. 63.

[2] Bede tells us that when Sigebert ruled East Anglia his relative and successor Ecgrice " partem ejusdem regni tenebat" (*E. H.*, iii. 18).

of the East Angles was compact, and well marked by natural boundaries ;—like that of their predecessors in the land, the British Iceni. It extended westward only to the edge of the great marshland which then, and for many centuries after, surrounded all the lower course of the Ouse from Huntingdon northward to the sea. The Isle of Ely, in the midst of this fen, was reckoned part of East Anglia.[1] Cambridge on the other hand seems to have been considered outside the borders, and to have belonged to another Anglian tribe. Southwards the boundary was formed by the East Saxons, whose march lay along the estuary of the Stour.

The only East Anglian king who ever attained to importance during the early history of the state was Raedwald, who according to Bede held the *imperium* over South Britain for a few years in the first quarter of the seventh century, having superseded Aethelbert of Kent in the position of dominance, though the latter survived his loss of power for some years.

(6) North and west of the East Angles lay three or more kingdoms inhabited by men of the same race—those of the Lindiswaras, the Middle Angles, and the Mercians. The settlement of the former, in the lands between the Wash and the Humber, around the old Roman city of Lindum—which gave the district its modern name of Lindsey—must have belonged to a date as early as that of East Anglia or Essex. But the same may not necessarily have been the case with the inland kingdoms of the Mercians and Middle Angles. Indeed the question as to how far the first devastating rush of the invaders carried them in this direction, during the second half of the fifth century, is the hardest point to settle in early English history. The East Midlands, the Valleys of Trent, Ouse, and Nen, had been one of the less important and less populous districts of Roman Britain ; there was apparently no important town west of Verulamium or Lindum, or east of Corinium, Viroconium and Deva. The resisting power of the Britons must have been very weak in all this region ; on the other hand, it might be argued that the thickly wooded and often marshy plain may not have been so attractive to the Saxon or Angle as certain other lands. If we could only trust the early entries of the Anglo-Saxon Chronicle, we should be obliged to conclude that the Midlands fell at a very late date into

---

[1] Bede, iv., 19. " Est autem Elge in provincia Orientalium Anglorum."

the hands of the invaders, for Cuthwulf, the West Saxon, is described as fighting with Britons at Bedford in 571, and capturing immediately after "Lygcanbyrig and Aeglesbyrig, Benesingtun and Egonesham," which are undoubtedly four places in Oxfordshire and Buckinghamshire, *viz.*, Limbury and Aylesbury, Bensington and Eynsham. I must confess that this entry seems to me wholly untrustworthy. That the Britons could have been holding as late as 571 places like Bedford and Aylesbury, in a region where archæology has recently discovered scores of early Teutonic graves, containing relics of the 5th and 6th century style, and of Saxon rather than Anglian character, seems contrary to all probability. But this is not all ; we are not merely dealing with probabilities ; Gildas, writing about 545 A.D., over twenty years before the alleged conquests of Ceawlin in this direction, gives us a picture of a Celtic Britain which does not extend anywhere towards the east coast, and indeed would seem to stop short at the eastern watershed of the Severn Valley. We are forced to conclude that the existence of British principalities in the South-East Midlands about the year 571 is simply incredible. Yet Ceawlin is undoubtedly a historical personage. Bede vouches for him—as a great conqueror, and the practical founder of the West Saxon kingdom. One way out of the difficulty alone remains, Ceawlin may have fought at Bedford, and have subdued Aylesbury and Eynsham, but the idea that his enemies were *Britons* may have been a misconception of the Wessex annalist who compiled the Chronicle in the ninth century. So many entries begin with " This year King X fought with Britons at Y," that for once the words " with Britons " may have slipped in unadvisedly. The preceding entry in the Chronicle introduces Ceawlin contending, not with Britons, but with Teutonic neighbours, as beating King Aethelbert at Wibbandun and driving him back into Kent in 568. Granting that this means that he was endeavouring to establish a hegemony over all the Teutonic principalities, what is more likely than that his next move would be to turn northward against smaller Saxon or Anglian communities, seated beyond Thames, on the Thame and the Ouse and the Evenlode ? They are added to the West Saxon league of " Gewissae "—" confederates ". Perhaps they even give the conquering nucleus that new name. It is when they have been attached to Ceawlin's original war-band that the king becomes strong enough to require homage from East Angles or East Saxons, and to acquire, in Bede's phrase, the " imperium " of South Britain. Only when this is his own does he start campaigning against the Britons in 577, and put an end to the comparative peace from external invasion which they had been enjoying for more than half a century.

It may therefore be permitted to us to attribute the overrunning and settlement of the whole of the Midlands, north and south, to a date nearly a century earlier than the conquests of Ceawlin. And Bensington and Eynsham, Bedford and Aylesbury, may be taken as the central villages of small Saxon tribal communities, rather than as Welsh strongholds.   Their names certainly suggest that this must have been the case : not one of them was an old Roman town, such as might have been the capital of a British king.   Indeed Bensington is but three miles from an old city—Dorchester-on-Thames—whose name shows its Roman origin, and whose walls would certainly have been the residence of a British prince if such a person had existed in Oxfordshire about 571.   A Teutonic settler, surely, would have been the only person who would have deserted this site for the adjacent Bensington, whose name shows its origin. The name of the whole group of settlers was " Chilternsaetas," [1] men of Chiltern, in the seventh century.

We may suspect Saxons far north of Thames, but farther away, along the courses of the Nen and the Welland, as well as in all the land that lies beyond them, the first colonists were Angles.   In Bede's time the whole of the region from the borders of Essex as far as Leicester was known as the land of the Middle Angles, while the lands in the basin of the Trent, from the boundary of Lindsey as far as the Welsh frontier, were called Mercia, the "march land ". The former then included the modern shires of Cambridge (minus the Isle of Ely), Huntingdon, Bedford, Northampton, Leicester : the latter was composed of Nottinghamshire, Derbyshire, Stafford-shire, part of Warwickshire, and the eastern strip of Shropshire. The Middle Angles apparently consisted of a group of sub-tribes, of whose names that of the Gyrwas (Gyrvii), on the borders of the Fenland (Cambridgeshire, North Northamptonshire, South Lincoln-shire) is the only one that survives in written history.   But it is pretty certain that a number of other small units, whose names are

[1] This tribal name, though not found in Bede, occurs in the celebrated " Tribal Hidage," which is undoubtedly a seventh century document.

232 THE SETTLEMENT OF THE CONQUERORS [A.D. 550

recorded in the curious early document called the "Tribal Hidage"[1] also belonged to the Middle Angles—such as the Arrosaetna, on the Warwickshire river Arrow, the Faerpings and the Spaldings.

Bede calls the land of the Middle Angles a kingdom,[2] but we have no trace of its having a king, or indeed of its having formed a homogeneous unit of any sort, till Penda of Mercia made his son Peada ruler of the whole district about the year 653. It is quite probable that down to that date it was but a loose confederation of neighbouring tribes, each with a local prince.[3]

The Mercians, on the other hand, seem to have coalesced into a monarchy at a comparatively early date, and we have for them a royal genealogy of the usual sort, going back to Woden and his son Wihtlaeg. The progenitor whose name was preserved in the patronymic of the house was a certain Icel, from whom they were called Icelings. Icel was said to be the fifth in ascent from Penda, the first king of Mercia concerning whom we know anything tangible. As this prince reigned from 626 to 655, the founder of the family ought, if there is anything of truth in the pedigree, to have been living somewhere about the year 500 or a little earlier. The date is sufficiently probable, but we have no external evidence to support it, save that it is possible that a Crida whose death is recorded in the Anglo-Saxon Chronicle under the year 593 may be the Mercian King Creoda, who was great-grandson of Icel and grandfather of Penda. But the Chronicle is of no great authority in the sixth century, and moreover its Crida may not be the Mercian Creoda.[4] The Mercians are described by Bede as being divided into two sub-tribes—the North and South Mercians—by the river Trent; but there is little reason to think that there were ever two distinct kingdoms among them.[5] On the other hand the Pecsaetan—or dwellers in the land of the Peak—in North Derbyshire, seem to be treated in the "Tribal Hidage" as a separate unit from the Mer-

---

[1] For an account of this interesting seventh century list, see Mr. Corbet's article in *Proceedings of the Royal Historical Society* for 1900.

[2] *E. H.*, iii. 21.

[3] The Gyrvii had certainly such a ruler in the seventh century, see Bede, *E. H.*, iv. 19.

[4] There is a mysterious Creoda in the West Saxon royal pedigree in certain versions. See Plummer's A. S. C. ii. pp. 4-6. But his date would not suit.

[5] The only reason for thinking of such a possibility is the mention by Bede of a Cearl king of the Mercians who does not appear in the royal genealogy.

cians proper, though their region is always counted a part of
Mercia in historic times.   It may only have been annexed by King
Penda at the same date that he conquered the various sections of
the Middle Angles on the other—the southern—side of his realm.
The Pecsaetan are, however, the only tribe whom we seem to find
owning a separate identity in the North-Western Midlands, and
the Mercians under the house of the Icelings were probably from
the first one of the more considerable Anglian States.   Their realm
must have included all the lands bounded by the Mountain of
the Peak district on the North, and the Forest of Arden on the
South, and extending to the Severn Westward.   But Chester
itself (Deva) was still in the hands of the Britons, and was first
taken from them in 616[1] not by the Mercians but by an invader
from another quarter, the Northumbrian king, Aethelfrith.

It may be convenient to state at this point, before passing on
to consider the settlements of the Angles north of Humber, what
we know of the Celtic kingdoms of Southern and Western Britain, at
the time (550-70) at which we have arrived while dealing with their
Teutonic enemies.   Here we have to help us the works of Gildas,
an absolutely contemporary writer, since he composed his *Liber
Querulus* while Maglocunus (Mailcun) was the most prominent
British king, and that prince died in 547 of the "yellow plague,"
the famous pest which, starting in Persia in 542, devastated the
empire of Justinian in 543-44, and then spread slowly westward all
over Europe.   In 545, when Gildas seems to have composed his
book, the British kingdoms are described by him as being still
practically unmolested by the Saxon or Angle, as had been the
case ever since the battle of the Mons Badonicus.   But they are
not therefore prosperous; city life had almost ceased; "the towns
of my fatherland are not inhabited as of old, but to this very
moment they lie deserted and ruinous, though foreign wars (if not
civil wars) have ceased".[2]   The kings are entirely given over to
family feuds and inter-tribal strife.   Since the generation which
helped Ambrosius Aurelianus to check the Saxon died out, all ideas
of public duty have been forgotten both by the lay and the ecclesiastical rulers of Britain.   The bishops and clergy are given up to
simony and self-seeking; the kings, when not occupied in murdering

---

[1] Not 617, see Plummer, Bede, ii. p. 77.   [2] Gildas, 26.

their relatives, or robbing their neighbours, are prone to commit
every crime in the calendar, from marriage with a deceased wife's
sister to harbouring highway robbers, and giving flagrantly unjust
decisions in their courts of law. "Britain has kings, but they are
tyrants; she has judges, but they are godless: they strike down
and prey upon the innocent alone. They give shelter and patronage
—but only to robbers and criminals. They have many wives—but
all of them adulteresses or prostitutes. They often take oaths, but
always break them. They make vows but almost immediately
perjure themselves. They wage wars, but only unjust wars on their
own countrymen. They may hunt down thieves in the countryside,
but they have thieves at their own tables, whom they love and load
with gifts. They distribute great alms, but heap up a greater mass
of crimes in their realms. They sit in the seat of judgment, but
rarely seek for the rule of right decision." The quotation might
be continued to a weary length. The important thing in Gildas,
however, is to note the names and dominions of the five kings on
whom he descants in detail, when he has finished his long general
preface.

The first is Constantine of Damnonia, who has divorced his
legitimate wife, and has planted a "slip of the vine of Sodom" in
his heart. He has also lately murdered two young boys, his near
relatives, in a church, before the very altar, though a certain abbot
cast his cloak around them to give them protection. The second is
Aurelius Caninus,[1] apparently the descendant and successor of
Ambrosius Aurelianus, whose heirs (as Gildas has previously observed) still lead out the Britons to war, though they have sadly
degenerated from the virtues of their ancestor. This young prince
has "rolled as deeply in the mud of parricide and adultery as Constantine, or even deeper". His territories are not named, but must
certainly be that portion of South-West Britain which was not
embraced in Damnonia—the as yet unconquered regions between
the Severn mouth and the Dorsetshire coast, where the West
Saxons had not penetrated in 545. Perhaps Bath, Gloucester and
Cirencester, which yet existed in some diminished shape as inhabited
towns, were his strongholds. They are mentioned thirty years later
in the Anglo-Saxon Chronicle as British "chesters" The third

[1] Or Conanus, apparently the well-known Celtic name Conan, famous in
Brittany.

king censured is Vortiporius, ruler of Demetia (South Wales), " a
man spotted like the leopard with crimes and evil living," the
worthless son of a good father, whose hair has grown grey in a long
reign of craft and cruelty. The fourth is Cuneglassus, who is
described in the curious terms, already referred to in a previous
chapter, as having been in his youth " the driver of the chariot of
the den of the Bear ".[1] He has lately driven away his wife in order
to wed her sister, who had taken vows as a nun, thus doubly vio-
lating the precepts of the Apostle. His dominions are not specified,
but he is certainly the Cinglas, son of Eugenius and descendant in
the fourth generation from Cunedda, who occurs in the oldest
Welsh genealogies.[2] His realm must be sought for on the borders
of Mercia, in the northern parts of the basin of the Severn, in what
was later called the region of Powys.

Lastly, we have the greatest king of all, Maglocunus (Mailcun),
" the dragon of the island," as he is called by Gildas, because he
ruled his North-Welsh kingdom from a royal residence in Anglesey.
This prince was evidently the dominating personage in Britain when
Gildas wrote ; as many paragraphs are devoted to him as to all the
other wicked kings taken together. He has deprived many other
tyrants of their lives as well as of their realms. He started by dis-
possessing his own uncle, and after him made havoc of many more.
But when incontestably the greatest lord of Britain, he was suddenly struck with penitence, devoted himself to religious studies,
abdicated his throne, and became a monk, after what Gildas owns to
have been a real spasm of remorse and consciousness of sin. " Oh
what an abundant flame of heavenly hope would have been kindled
in the hearts of desperate sinners, if thou hadst but remained in
that blessed estate." But a short experience of monastic life had
disgusted Maelgwyn : he " returned like the dog to his vomit,"
resumed his crown, called back his followers and started on a second
career of conquest, accompanied with much evil living. He is particularly reproached with having murdered his nephew and taken
his widow to wife, after clearing a way for her by slaying the spouse
whom he had married before his monastic episode. It breaks the
heart of the preacher to see the renegade monk once more the
greatest and the most boisterous of kings, " first in mischief, strongest

[1] See p. 211-2.   [2] See Zimmer, *Nennius Vindicatus*, p. 307.

in malice as well as in power, more liberal than others in giving, more licentious in sinning, strong in arms but stronger in working his own soul's destruction ". He is threatened with all the torments of the damned, in language of a violence which would surely have secured Gildas's instant execution if he had shown himself within the realm of North Wales. Indeed, the virulence of his denunciation in dealing with all the five kings whom he takes to task is so extraordinary, that we might well believe that the *Liber Querulus* was written, as tradition relates, outside this island, while the author was residing in the monastery in Brittany of which he was the founder.

That Britain had not yet lost all traces of her Roman civilisation is shown by the fact that Gildas quotes Virgil and Philo, and seems to show a knowledge of Claudian and Juvenal, as well as of Jerome, Orosius and other Christian writers with whom we are not so surprised to find him acquainted. His style is obscure and euphuistic, after the manner of Cassiodorus and other sixth-century writers— indeed it is often quite hard to make out what actual meaning his bombastic phrases are intended to convey. But he has no historical perspective, and all that he narrates of events beyond his own memory needs careful study before it can be accepted. Yet for the affairs of 545 his book, so far as it goes, is of absolutely primary and incontestable authority. He is the only source from which we know of the cessation of the Teutonic invasion between 516 and 570, after the Badonic battle, and from him alone can we judge with some degree of certainty what was the boundary between Briton and Saxon about the year 545, and what was the internal state of the British kingdoms.

One of the most extraordinary gaps in the narrative of Gildas is his omission to say what was going on to the north and south of the limited area on which he sheds a fitful light. One of the great phenomena of the fifth century had been a wholesale emigration of Britons to Gaul. Gildas gives no hint of this save in the single sentence in which he says that "some sought regions beyond the sea, groaning under the sails, by way of rowers' song, 'Thou has given us as sheep to the slaughter, O God, and scattered us among the Gentiles' ".[1] But the Britons appear in Gaul by no means in the character of scattered sheep, but rather as warlike bands seeking

[1] Gildas, § 25. *Cf.* also the curious note in Procopius, *Bell. Goth.*, iv. 20.

settlement by force of arms. If the *Historia Brittonum* can be trusted, the first emigrants were the British auxiliaries of the usurper Magnus Maximus, "who gave them many lands from the pool that is on the crest of Mons Jovis [the great St. Bernard] as far as the city which is called Cantguic [Quentovic, south of Boulogne], and they are now at the Western Promontory, that is Crucoccident [Cape Finisterre, in Brittany]. For the Britons of Armorica, who lie beyond the sea, who went forth on the expedition of Maximus the tyrant, since they could not come home, devastated all Western Gaul, slew off all the males, and took their widows and daughters as consorts." This is, of course, like all the early narrative of the *Historia Brittonum*, very doubtful stuff. There is no reason why the first British settlement in Armorica should not have begun as early as 383, with the arrival of the troops of Magnus Maximus in that region. But at the same time we have no trace in contemporary continental sources of such immigrants. On the other hand, we have clear proof from the Roman writers of the late fifth century that, from about 460 onwards, Britons were numerous north of the Loire. The first tangible mention of them seems to be that a certain Mansuetus, "bishop of the Britons," attended a council at Tours in 461. There is no indication that he was a Briton of the island, and as, immediately after, we find great masses of his countrymen on the spot, it seems safe to conclude that he was their representative. In 469 we find in the letters of Sidonius Apollinaris [1] the statement that one Arvandus had been accused of treason before the Emperor Anthemius, for having incited the Visigoths to attack "the Britons situated beyond the Loire". In the same year we find that Anthemius solicited aid from these Britons, and that their King Riothimus came to join the imperial army with a force of 12,000 men. [2] This number, even if exaggerated, shows that there was a large colony already established in Armorica. Riothimus reached Bourges, and was apparently at that city for some time, as Sidonius wrote several letters to him, complaining of the conduct of his soldiers, who had been tempting away the slaves of the neighbouring Gallic proprietors. [3] But the Visigoths finally came up against Riothimus and defeated him at Deols in the

[1] Sidonius, *Epistolae*, i. 7.
[2] Jordanes, § 45.
[3] Mancipia, Britannis clam sollicitantibus, abducta, *Epistolae*, iii. 9.

department of the Indre, so that he was forced to fly.[1] He thereupon disappears from history, but his countrymen remained seated in
Armorica, as is shown by plenty of later notices.

It seems probable that, whether the soldiers of Magnus Maximus
made the first settlement in Armorica or not, the development of a
British colony in that peninsula was mainly caused by the great
Saxon assaults in Britain about the middle of the fifth century.
That the exiles came largely from the South-British lands affected
by the ravages of Hengist and Aella seems probable. But there
also must have been many West-Britons among them to account
for the transference of names like Domnonie (Damnonia) and Cornouailles, from the island to the continent; and that this was the
predominating strain among the immigrants is made clear by the
fact that the Britons of Armorica spoke Celtic and not Latin. If
they had mainly come from the south-eastern regions, they would
have spoken Latin and not Celtic.

It is always unsafe to lean too heavily on dates or facts drawn
from the lives of saints, written long centuries after their death.
But it is worth while noticing that the period assigned by legend
to the coming of the British monastic missionaries to Armorica is
the fifth century, and its later half, just as we should have expected
from the more trustworthy facts to be gleaned from contemporary
secular writers. St. Samson, who founded the bishopric of Dol, is
said to have landed somewhere about 448. St. Machutus (St. Malo)
seems datable to somewhere about the year 450. St. Brieuc
falls a little later, apparently about 485. St. Paternus, the
patron of Vannes, was consecrated between 461 and 470.[2] We
may recognise in these holy exiles the fugitives of Gildas, who
crossed the ocean to the continent ingeminating psalms. It is a
pity that he has told us nothing of their warlike countrymen who,
like Riothimus, emigrated with their swords in their hands, and
plunged fiercely into the wars of the dying empire in Western
Gaul.

But strange as it may be that Gildas says so little about the
lands beyond the Channel, it is far more strange that he gives no

---

[1] Jordanes, 45; Gregory of Tours, ii. 18. From Jordanes' mention of ships and
disembarkation with regard to Riothimus, some modern authors would make him an
insular Briton. But see La Borderie, *Histoire de Bretagne*, i. 251-52.

[2] See La Borderie, pp. 203-4 and 295-307 for all this dating.

information as to the condition of affairs in North Britain, in the
parts beyond the realm of Mailcun. A struggle was going on between Briton and Angle north of the Humber, while in the south
and the Midlands the invasion had come for a time to a standstill.
For this northern conflict we are driven to use the *Historia Brittonum*, which begins, about the year 550, to give us information
which can be accepted with gratitude, and differs entirely from its
wild tales of Vortigern and St. Germanus and other fifth-century
worthies. With the aid of the *Historia*, supplemented with caution
by names from the earliest Welsh genealogies, and with still
greater diffidence by entries in the much later *Annales Cambriae*,
some sort of a sketch of Northern Britain in the sixth century may
be made out.

Our last knowledge of these regions was obtained from St.
Patrick's letter to Coroticus.[1] When we once more get a glimpse of
the lands between Humber and Forth we find several British states
in existence, and still more kings, the lands owned by a dynastic
group being apparently shared or held in common by three or four
of its members. The main principality, comprising Clydesdale as
its central nucleus, but with its capital at Alclyde, north of the
Firth, on the rock of Dumbarton, seems to have been in the hands
of the descendants of Coroticus, or Ceretic Guletic, as the genealogies call him. South of it was another state called Reged,[2] which
seems to represent the modern Cumberland with so much of Northumberland as had not yet been conquered by the Angles. Possibly [3]
the name Redesdale preserves a memory of this forgotten realm.
It is probable that the Picts of Galloway—the Niduarii—were
subject to their British neighbours but still had sub-kings of their
own. The kingdom which centred at Alclyde seems to have included neither the west coast of the Lowlands nor the shores of the
Firth of Forth. Kyle, Carrick and Cunningham, the three districts
of the former region, may represent ancient principalities—Coel,
Carawg and Canawon—which appear vaguely in the earliest Welsh
poetry. On the east the Angles seem to have had an uneasy lodgment
upon the shore of Lothian, but the western section of that region,
the plain of Manau, was still in the hands of the Picts, who had

---

[1] See p. 189.
[2] Not to be confounded with the South Wales Reged in Glamorganshire.
[3] See Cadwallader Bates, *History of Northumberland*, p. 52.

moved southward into it in the fifth century, and held the lands
between the Carron and the Avon. South of Reged there were
other British states ; we only know the name of Elmet, which comprised all, or great part, of the West Riding of Yorkshire. There
must have been at least one more principality west of Elmet, along
the Irish Sea, but its very name is forgotten. South Lancashire, on
the other hand, seems to have gone along with Chester and the lands
by the Dee, which together formed a region named Theyernllwg, and
were more closely connected with North Wales than with the kingdoms farther up the Irish Sea.

While Alclyde, and probably a presidency over the other
North British States, seems to have been in the hands of the house
of Coroticus, there was another many-branched family in possession of much territory. This was the line of Coel the Old, who (if
the Harleian genealogies count for anything) lived four generations
before 550, *i.e.*, somewhere about the year 430. They held Reged
and many other lands. In the war with the Angles that filled the
third quarter of the sixth century, we find three "kings" of this
house, representing three separate lines, Urbgen (or Urien), Gwallawg, and Morgant, joining with Rhyderch of Strathclyde in resisting the advance of the Angles. But these houses were as prone
to civil war as their kinsmen farther south, whom Gildas abused
so strenuously.

By the time that the sixth century had passed its middle year
the Angles had long been established on the coast line from
Lothian to Spurn Head, all along the shore of the two regions
which were to be called Bernicia and Deira—names of uncertain
derivation, the latter probably adapted from the Celtic Deifyr, the
former perhaps originating with the dim ancestor Bearnoch who
appears in Northumbrian genealogies. The first landings on the
Yorkshire and Northumbrian coast must have started in the very
beginning of the Saxon invasion—we may believe, if we like, that
there may be something in the tale in the *Historia Brittonum*
that Hengist's kinsmen Ochta and Ebissa were granted land near
the border of the Picts, at the same time that the Jutish chief himself was established by Vortigern in Kent. Nothing is more probable, though nothing is more impossible to prove. Long before,
it will be remembered, Saxon allied with Pict had already been
trampling down the northern parts of Britain, in the days of the

"Hallelujah Victory". We may take it for granted that all the Romano-British towns in the North-east—York, Corbridge, Aldborough and their smaller sisters—perished long before the year 500 was reached—very probably even before the year 430.[1]

The genealogies appended at the end of the *Historia Brittonum,* which are shown by internal evidence to have been compiled not long after 685, give us lists of the two Anglian royal houses of Bernicia and Deira, which go back, as usual, to Woden. But in each case the prince who is credited with establishing a kingdom comes long after the first ancestor who is brought to the shores of Britain. The Bernician kingship starts with Ida, whose date is fixed by Bede at 547,[2] a year which works in well with the data in the *Historia.* The Deiran kingship begins a few years later, in 560, with Aella. But in the Deiran genealogy in the *Historia* it is Aella's predecessor in the fifth generation, one Soemil, of whom it is said that "iste primus separavit Deur a Birneich". Taking the usual calculation of thirty years for a life, Soemil must have lived somewhere not long after 410, *i.e.,* in the very first days of the Teutonic ravages in Britain, and his "separating of Deira from Bernicia" must mean the carving out a principality for himself from the loosely compacted Anglian settlement. There is no reason to doubt the real existence of the persons intervening between Soemil and Aella, for two of their names Uxfrea and Iffi are found among later members of the royal house of Deira, the son and grandson of the good King Edwin.[3] Edwin would very naturally bestow the names of his own grandfather and great-grandfather on his descendants. Similarly in the more northern Anglian settlement where Ida is reckoned the first "king," we must believe that at least his father Eoppa and his grandfather Ossa, and probably remoter ancestors also, were settled in Britain. Ossa Cyllelawr, "Ossa with the knife," appears in the earliest Welsh traditions— whatever their worth may be—as the opponent of British kings in the North, even of Arthur himself.

Be this as it may, there must have been a full century between the first establishment of Anglian settlements on the coast between Forth and Humber and the establishment of the "kingdoms"

---

[1] Though many of them, like Corbridge, emerged as royal " vills " in the Northumbrian period.

[2] Bede, *E. H.*, v. 24.   [3] Bede, ii. 14-20.

of Bernicia and Deira. We must suppose that (like the Middle Angles) these original settlers were planted in small communities, ruled by ealdormen who did not attain to the royal title. Indeed William of Malmesbury, late though his date and weak his authority, was practically right when he wrote that the Northumbrians for nearly 100 years were content with "duces," who took no kingly title and ruled each in his own corner,—though we may doubt his additional statement that they paid a general homage to the king of Kent.[1]

Ida, according to the *Historia Brittonum*, reigned for twelve years (547-59) and fought long and fiercely with the Britons, whose chief leader at the moment was a king called Dutigern. We are told that Ida joined to his kingdom of Bernicia the great stronghold of Dinguardi, *i.e.*, the rocky promontory crowned by a fortress, which later generations were to know as Bamborough. But as yet it bore only its Celtic name, for Queen Bebba, from whom its new English denomination of Bebbanburh was to come, was the wife of Ida's grandson Aethelfrith. Ida had twelve sons,[2] of whom no less than five succeeded him on the throne. The list of these short-lived kings, Adda, Frithwulf or Frithwald, Hussa, Theodric and Aethelric is given in different order by the *Historia Brittonum*, the chronicle appended to Bede's history, and the later authorities [3]—a fact which may point to a division of the kingdom between them. More than one of them, it would seem, fell in battle with the Britons, as might have been guessed from the shortness of their reigns, of which the whole only make up thirty-three years (559-93).

Against the sons of Ida the British princes fought long and

[1] W. M., i. 44.

[2] See the Bernician genealogy in *Historia Brittonum*. But I am unable to follow the order of reigns of the five sons there set forth.

[3] According to the genealogy annexed to the More MS. of Bede we must add another son, Clappa, who reigned a single year immediately after his father Ida. But he does not appear in the *Historia Brittonum* or its appended genealogy, though Florence of Worcester and other late authorities give him. The order of succession presents immense difficulties. Our earliest source, the *H. B.*, first gives the order—Adda, Aethelric, Theodric, Frithwald (or Frithwulf), Hussa. But it then goes on to say that Urien fought Hussa, and also fought Theodric and was murdered after he had shut up his enemy in Farne. So according to this version of the tale Theodric is apparently the later of the two; but Aethelric was certainly the last of all, since it was he who annexed Deira after the death of Aella in 588, and passed on the crown to his son Aethelfrith.

courageously. This seems to have been a time notable for vigour in the Britons of the North. The *Historia Brittonum* tells us that it was then that the great bards flourished, Talhaern and Aneurin, Taliessin and Bluchbard (Lluwarch). Poems attributed to several of them are still extant, and celebrate the exploits of the very princes whom the *Historia* gives as their contemporaries, Urbgen (Urien Reged) and his son Owen, Rhyderch and Gwallawg. If only we could be sure that the poems had not suffered fatally in transmission, or had not been entirely rewritten at a later age, we should have much lyrical detail for the story of early Northumbria.

Urien Reged was the most notable of the British champions. According to the *Historia Brittonum* he fought against Hussa and Theodric with frequent success. He shut up the latter prince for three days and three nights in the Isle of Metcaud (Lindisfarne), having literally driven the Angles into the sea. But while he was on this expedition he was murdered by contrivance of King Morgant, his kinsman, from envy, "because he excelled all other British chiefs in warlike capacity". Later tradition had much to tell concerning the assassination of Urien, by the traitor Llovan Llawdivro, the tool of Morgant, on the sands of Aberllew.[1] Owen, son of Urien, took his father's place, as leader against the Angles, but with less success. He was slain by Theodric "the burner" (Flamddwyn) as the Britons called him. After this the defence seems to have slackened, and the Celts retired to the interior, leaving the kingdom of Bernicia a stronger state than it had ever been before.

Aethelric, the last survivor of the sons of Ida, not only ruled Bernicia but got possession of Deira also on the death of Aella, whose daughter Acha he married to his son Aethelfrith. Aella had no male heir save his infant son Edwin, who was carried off into safety and exile by faithful adherents, and was harboured first by Cadvan, King of North Wales, if Welsh tradition may be trusted, and afterwards, as it would seem, by English neighbours south of Humber. Aethelric reigned for five years over Bernicia and Deira united, and left the double crown of Northumbria to his son Aethelfrith [593-617].

---

[1] The poem xii. in the Red Book of Hergest, whatever its date, is full of details of Urien's murder. Aberllew is apparently on the Low, the stream that enters the sea opposite the Isle of Lindisfarne.

With this prince we may be said to emerge from the twilight of history, in which we have hitherto been wandering. For the future we have Bede to guide us, instead of the meagre and confused notices of the *Historia Brittonum*. Aethelfrith was already reigning at the moment when Augustine's mission to Kent began, and his story is intimately associated with that of Edwin, the first Christian hero of Northumbria, of whom the *Ecclesiastical History* has so much to say. Of him more must be told in a later chapter.

It is curious to find that archæology gives us little help as to the early fortunes of the Bernician kingdom, though it is so useful for the history of Southern Britain. The Anglian invasions began early in the north; yet we find little or no trace of 5th century settlement, and very sparse indication of 6th century occupation, in Lothian and northern Northumberland. It looks as if Ida's principality round Bamborough had been a small affair, and as if the subjection and settlement of the lands by Tweed and Forth had come only in the time of his grandson Æthelfrith or not many years before. These indications tally well with the Celtic legends of a very fierce and prolonged struggle during the 6th century.

CHAPTER XIII

THE SECOND ADVANCE OF THE INVADERS. CONQUESTS OF CEAWLIN AND AETHELFRITH (577-617 A.D.)

SOME twenty years before the union of Bernicia and Deira under Ethelfrith had enabled the Angles of the North to commence a new series of conquests, the Saxons in the South had at last found the leader who was to enable them to resume the westward march which had been stayed two generations back, at the Mons Badonicus. This leader was Ceawlin, the third king, according to Bede, who asserted an *imperium* over the whole of the petty States that had been established by the first invaders. His domination was evidently created by force of arms the first fact recorded of him is that in conjunction with his orother, Cutha[1] (or Cuthwulf, to use the longer form), he fought in 568, with Aethelbert, King of Kent, a young prince who had come to the throne three years before, defeated him at Wibbandun, and drove him back into his own realm. The battle-place is apparently the suburban Wimbledon in Surrey; the victory must have put that region for the moment into the hands of the West Saxons. It is probable that it may also have forced the men of Kent, and perhaps those of Sussex too, to become subject-allies of Ceawlin. The next exploit of the West Saxons was an invasion of the regions north of Thames in 571; Cuthwulf, the king's brother, fought a battle at Bedford, and immediately afterwards conquered the four towns of Aylesbury, Limbury, Bensington and Eynsham. We have already seen that these successes must almost certainly have been won over Teutonic and not over British neighbours,[2] despite of the mention of

---

[1] Cutha is only a shortened " hypocoristic " form of Cuthwulf. Later chroniclers, not knowing this, made them distinct persons.

[2] See p. 231.

the latter as enemies in the Anglo-Saxon Chronicle. The result
of the campaign was to make the " Chilternsaetas," the people of
the Chilterns, subjects of the West Saxon state. They remained
united to it for more than a century ; certainly they were by race
Saxons, not Angles ; so that the union would be easy and natural.
We may suppose that Essex and East Anglia yielded, not long
after, the homage which gave Ceawlin the "*imperium*" of which
Bede speaks. At any rate, he was able six years later to begin a
great invasion of Western Britain. Presumably it was at the head
of a confederate host, not of his own tribesmen only ; a large force
must have been required to undertake an enterprise which no Saxon
king had essayed for sixty years.

Ceawlin struck at the point where the belt of British states
lying across Western Britain was narrowest, between the Upper
Thames and the Bristol Channel. Advancing, as we may presume,
by the old Roman road from Silchester to Bath, he met the united
forces of three British kings at Deorham (Dyrham) a few miles to
the north of the last-named city. His adversaries are named by
the Anglo-Saxon Chronicle—Conmail, Condidan, and Farinmail.[1]
One of them was, no doubt, the ruler of the British realm immediately attacked, that which occupied parts of Gloucestershire,
Somersetshire and Wiltshire, and which had lately been the holding of the heirs of Ambrosius Aurelianus, whom Gildas mentions
thirty years before. His allies must have been kings either of
Damnonia or of the British states along the Severn or immediately
beyond it.[2] Whatever may have been the dominions or the military
strength of his enemies, Ceawlin defeated and slew all three (577).
The consequence of his victory was the complete conquest of the
land between the Somersetshire Avon and the Forest of Arden,
with its three cities of Bath, Gloucester and Cirencester, all of which

---

[1] Condidan is apparently the Roman name Candidianus in a Celtic form. His
identification with a Cynddylan whose elegy is found among the Bardic poems (Skene,
i. 311) is not properly made out, and the poem is too late. Farinmail (Fernmail,
Fernvael) is a known name in Welsh genealogies ; a prince of the house of Vortigern bearing it was reigning on the Upper Wye some generations later, and is
mentioned in the *Historia Brittonum*. Conmail is apparently equivalent to Cynvael,
also a known royal name. But the Welsh records do not give us any trace of
dynasts bearing these names about the year 577.

[2] There is no reason to suppose that the three kings ruled each over one of the
three cities, Bath, Gloucester and Cirencester, as is often assumed.

seem to have been surviving in some sort of decayed existence at the moment. The region was at once settled up by Teutonic colonists : they appear in subsequent history as the race of the Hwiccas,[1] whose name still remains on their eastern and western boundaries—in Wychwood, the forest that divided them from the Chilternsaetas, and the Wych—the northernmost pass of the Malvern Hills. Their territory embraced all Gloucestershire east of the Severn, most of Worcestershire, and the southern and larger part of Warwickshire. They were probably a mixed multitude, mainly Saxon but partly Anglian, as was Ceawlin's army. They were so far from being homogeneous with the West Saxons that they never became amalgamated with them, and within two generations after their first settlement appear as a distinct sub-kingdom with *reguli* of their own. Whether the seventh and eighth century rulers of the Hwiccas claimed a descent from the West Saxon royal house we cannot tell—the early links of their genealogy are lost.[2]

This was the greatest conquest that the Saxons had made for three generations, and it must have exalted Ceawlin's power to a high pitch. We are told that he continued his campaigns against the Welsh, presumably pushing up the Severn, or across it in the direction of South Wales. But seven years after the victory of Deorham he seems to have met with a decisive check ; he and his brother, Cuthwulf, fight with the Britons in 584 "at the place which is called Fethanleag". There Cuthwulf was slain, and Ceawlin "after taking many towns and spoils innumerable, returned wrathful to his own land". Fethanleag cannot be identified ; nothing serious can be urged in favour of putting it at Faddiley in Cheshire, or at Frethern in Gloucestershire, the two sites that have been suggested. It is probably the name of a wood or a district rather than a place.

Then occurs a gap of six years in West Saxon history, after which we get, to our surprise, the notice that in 590 Ceolric,[3] the

---

[1] This at least seems the easiest and most probable way of accounting for the appearance of the Hwiccian tribe. Their dialect seems to be Saxon rather than Mercian. But we have no definite mention of them till a century later.

[2] Their names such as Eanfrith, Osric, Oswald, Eanhere, mentioned by Bede, and living 650-700, and the later Oshere, Aethelhere, Aethelweard, Aethelric, for the most part suggest a Northumbrian rather than a West-Saxon origin. Aethelweard, however, is a name of the West Saxon house.

[3] Called in a tiresomely syncopated form Ceol in most MSS. of the Anglo-Saxon Chronicle.

son of Cuthwulf, was set up as king, and that in 591 "there was a great slaughter in Britain at Woddesbeorge, and Ceawlin was expelled". This seems to mark the end of his *imperium,* since Aethelbert of Kent was held to be the dominant king in South Britain very soon after. The obvious suggestion is that first some of Ceawlin's own people revolted against him and chose his nephew as king, and that his subject-allies then aided the rebels in crushing their former lord. We can hardly doubt that Aethelbert must have been the mainspring of the movement. There is no reason to subscribe to the view that Ceolric had been proclaimed king by the newly settled Hwiccas, or that the Britons had anything to do with the affair. The locality of the battle Woddesbeorge, or Wodnesbeorge as some manuscripts have it, was apparently Wanborough near Swindon in North Wiltshire. But to argue from its position that Hwiccas or Britons must have been involved in the slaughter is most dangerous.[1]

Ceawlin, though his *imperium* had certainly been shattered, though his vassals had all fallen away, and though he may even possibly have been deprived of his kingship over the West Saxons themselves—for the word "expelled" (*utadriven*) suggests even this—survived two years more and perished in 593, probably in civil war with Ceolric. The crown passed away for nearly a hundred years from his house, and stayed from 593 to 685 with the descendants of Cuthwulf; Ceolric (591-97) and his brother and successor Ceolwulf[2] (597-611) can have made no attempt to maintain Ceawlin's lofty position. They were more or less subject to the *imperium* of Aethelbert of Kent, and probably retained only those conquests of their uncle which were made before 577. The Hwiccas even may already have broken loose and started a principality of their own.

---

[1] The narratives of Ceawlin's fall in Guest and J. R. Green, are pure hypothesis. Mr. Stevenson doubts the identity of Woddesbeorg and Wanborough.

[2] Terrible confusion is caused in the early West Saxon history by the fact that the shortened form Cutha was often used in the chronicles for Cuthwulf, brother of Ceawlin. Many later writers supposed them to be different persons, and gave Ceawlin two brothers. But Ceawlin had also a son, Cuthwine, whose name was likewise shortened to Cutha, and got in that shape into some of the West Saxon royal genealogies (as in that of Ceadwalla under the year 685 in the A. S. C.). To make things worse it seems that Cuthwine had a son, Cuthwulf, and he too appears as Cutha in a still later genealogy, that of Aethelwulf (under the year 855 in the A. S. C), unless, indeed, Cuthwine and the third Cutha in this passage are a stupid reduplication.

All that is recorded of these kings is that in 607 Ceolwulf fought with the South Saxons—a weak enemy—with no recorded result and the utterly impossible statement that he also "fought and contended incessantly against Angles, Welsh, Picts and Scots," an entry which looks as if it rather belonged to the name of Ceolwulf of Northumbria (729-37), for how could a king of Wessex have fought with Picts or Scots in the early seventh century? The son of Cuthwulf was clearly an unimportant subject-ally of the King of Kent. He would have left more of a name behind him if he had ever conducted great northern campaigns. Perhaps the confusion arose because Ceolwulf of Northumbria was, like his Wessex namesake, the son of a "Cutha".[1]

Aethelbert meanwhile was now at the height of his power; "he had extended his dominions as far as the great river Humber, by which the southern Angles are divided from the northern".[2] That is to say that he was undisputedly suzerain over all the Teutonic states of Britain save the united realm of Bernicia and Deira, now held by Aethelfrith, the one king who could vie with him in power. His name was so great that, first of all the insular sovereigns, he had been granted the hand of a daughter of the famous Merovingian house—Bertha, the child of Charibert, King of Paris—and this though he was a heathen. The house of Hengist was once more predominant in Britain, as it had been at the moment of the first invasions, and Ceawlin's western conquests seemed only to have been made in order that his supplanter's empire might be the broader.

Meanwhile the King of Northumbria was adding to the Anglian territory as much as Ceawlin had won for the Saxons of the South. Aethelfrith was a great and ruthless conqueror. "In that day," as Bede relates, "he was the strongest of kings, and the most greedy of glory. He harried the race of the Britons more than all the other chiefs of the English : so that he might be compared to Saul, King of Israel [who was a head and shoulders taller than all his contemporaries] but for the fact that he lacked knowledge of the true faith. He conquered more lands from the Britons than any other ealdorman or king, and either drove out their inhabitants and

---

[1] He is so called in his genealogy in the A. S. C., *sub anno* 731. As a matter of fact his father was named Cuthwine, like the son of Ceawlin.

[2] Bede, i. 25.

planted them afresh with English, or subdued them and made them tributary " [1] (593-617).

It seems clear that the accession of strength which had come to the house of Ida by the annexation of Deira had given the Northumbrians a preponderance over the Celtic neighbours which they had never enjoyed before. Aethelfrith pushed his conquests right across the Pennine range to the shores of the Irish sea, over-running the kingdom of Reged and driving the petty kings of the house of Coel to the north and west. It seems that the Britons in their despair called in fresh aid from the north, for in the year 603 we find Aedan, son of Gabran, king of the Dalriad Scots, the newly established kingdom of Irish settlers on the coast of Argyle, marching against Northumbria with a very great army. Anglian tradition said that he was called in by Hering, son of Hussa, the Bernician king who had reigned thirty years back.[2] Very possibly Hering had been rejected because of his tender age, according to Teutonic custom, when his uncles, Frithwulf, Theodric and Aethelric, were successively elected kings, in the thirteen years that followed Hussa's death (575-88). Now he is said to have brought do.n the Scots to back his claim, promising, no doubt, the aid of a faction among his cousin's subjects. But it is almost certain that Aedan must also have been invited to march against Aethelfrith by the vanquished Welsh princes, who had suffered from the new conquests of the Angles. For he is said to have collected "immense" forces, which could surely not have been furnished by his own small realm on the coast of Argyle, even though he was also, as we know, aided by adventurers from Ireland. It must be remembered that Aedan was a Christian ; he had been baptised and anointed by St. Columba, who had come from Ulster to Iona about 565, and had completed the conversion of the Dalriad Scots, which had been begun by earlier Irish missionaries. Aedan appears to have been a very vigorous and enterprising prince. He had cast off the connection with Ireland, which his ancestors had kept up, and with it the tribute that they had been wont to pay. He had fought long and successfully with the Picts, and had even directed maritime ex-peditions against the Orkneys and the Isle of Man. In 603 he must have been far advanced in age, as he had been reigning since

---

[1] Bede, *E. H.*, i. 34.   [2] Anglo-Saxon Chronicle, *sub anno* 603.

574, and in 596 had many sons old enough to take the field in war. Clearly he was the one prince in Northern Britain to whom all the enemies of Aethelfrith, whether Northumbrian malcontents or Celtic kinglets, might look for succour.

But the attempt of the Scot to beat down the rising power of the grandson of Ida was doomed to failure. The hosts faced each other at Degsastan, apparently Dawston in Liddesdale,[1] on the frontier of the Bernician realm, and on land which the Angles can only lately have won. The fight was hard, and Aethelfrith's brother, Theodbald, fell with his whole following.[2] But the fortune of the day was with the Northumbrian king; the allied princes of the North were smitten with a great slaughter: the few put to flight the many, and Aedan fled homewards with only the wreck of an army, leaving dead on the field his ally Maeluma, son of Baedan, King of Ulster, and many other chiefs. "This fight of Aethelfrith's," wrote Bede in 730, " was in the year 603, after the incarnation of Our Lord, after he had completed the eleventh year of his reign, which in all covered twenty-four years. It was also in the first year of the Roman Emperor Phocas.[3] And from that day onward no king of the Scots in Britain has ever dared to come to open battle with the race of the English."

The victory of Dawston must have confirmed Aethelfrith in the possession of the upper valleys of the Tweed and its tributaries, as far as the watershed of the Clyde, and, no doubt, of the land round Carlisle and the west end of the Roman Wall also.[4] It is curious to find that he did not then proceed to make an end of the British kingdom of Elmet, in the hills and woods of the West Riding, for this state, as we know, survived into the next generation. It is,

---

[1] Mr. Plummer suggests, however, in his edition of Bede, ii. p. 66, that Daegsastan may be only a corruption of " aet Aegdanes Stane," at Aedanstone, in which case we may have to look elsewhere for the battle-site.

[2] For the narrative of the battle, see Bede, i. 34, and the entry in Tighernach's Irish Annals.

[3] Quite correctly dated, as it would seem, for Phocas came to the throne in November, 602, so that the fighting season of 603 would fall into his first year. But the Ulster annals give 605 and Tighernach 606 for the battle. Welsh legend ascribed the defeat to Aedan's treachery or cowardice, and he is recorded in the Triads as one of " the three great traitors of the Isle of Britain "—which seems hard.

[4] It has been suggested that the " Catrail," the long boundary ditch, from the Tweed southward across the lands toward Solway, may mark this delimitation between the Angles and the Britons. But this is very doubtful.

however, highly probable that Aethelfrith may have compelled its king Cerdic to do him homage and pay him tribute. But his last and greatest expedition was directed further to the south, against a region broader and more fertile than the mountain valleys of Elmet—the lands between Ribble and Dee, which were still in the hands of the Britons. These formed, in the early seventh century, part of the kingdom originally known as Theyrnllwg, of which the later Powys was the surviving remnant. It then extended from the Ribble to the Upper Wye, and from the Clwyd to Cannock Chase, and had been for a century the connecting link between the Britons of the North and those of the West.[1] Its ruling sovereign at the moment was Brocmail, son of Cincen, a descendant of that Catell, who appears in the *Historia Brittonum* as first founder of this kingdom, in the days of Vortigern and St. Germanus. To aid Brocmail in the defence of this all-important central isthmus of the British territory came his neighbour and overlord, Cadvan, King of Gwynedd, and Selim, son of Cynan, a prince whose dominions it is impossible to identify, but who may have been a kinsman of Brocmail, and a sub-king of some part of Powys. According to the Harleian genealogy he was Brocmail's grandson.[2]

The forces of the invader and of the Welsh princes met near the site of the old Roman Deva, the " city of the legions," which may already have been the "waste chester" that we read of in ninth century annals. For there is no sign that it was a living city, or the capital of Theyrnllwg, as we should have expected. No story of the sack of a great and wealthy town ends the history of Aethelfrith's campaign in Bede, or is hinted at in the later legends of the Welsh. Indeed, the chief incident that is recorded concerning it seems to imply that Deva, though the strategical centre of the district, was no longer its spiritual centre. " Aethelfrith," says Bede, " being about to give battle, saw the priests of the Britons, who had come together to pray to God for their soldiery, standing apart in a place of safety. He asked who they were, and for what they had assembled in that place. Now the most of them were

---

[1] According to Welsh tradition the limits of Theyrnllwg were " from the Forest of Derwent to the Aerfen (Dee). [See Guest's *Origines Celticae*, ii. 49].

[2] According to the legend (*H. B.*, 35) he was a serf who was given the blessing by the saint that he should become a king, and that kings should never fail from his seed. In the Triads, he is one of " the three kings in Britain who were born serfs ".

from the monastery of Bancor, in which there is said to have been
so great a number of monks that, the monastery being divided into
seven parts, with a ruler over each, none of those parts contained
less than three hundred persons, who all lived by the labour of
their hands.   A great part of them came to this battle, after
having celebrated a fast of three days, to pray along with the rest,
having Brocmail appointed as their escort, to guard them from the
sword of the barbarians while they were intent on their prayers.
And when Aethelfrith heard of the cause of their coming he said :
' If they cry to their God against us, they too are our adversaries,
though they bear no weapons, since they oppose us by their imprecations'.   So he ordered them to be first attacked, and then
destroyed the rest of that unlucky army, not without much loss in
his own ranks.   About 1,200 of those monks who came to pray are
said to have been slain, and only fifty to have escaped.   Brocmail
and his men had turned their backs at the first charge, and left
those whom he should have guarded unprotected to the mercy of
the sword." [1]

This tale seems to be corroborated, at least in part, by the
fact that the Irish annals call the battle " the slaughter of the
Saints ".   Selim and another king called Cetula (Catell ?) are said
to have been slain in the fight, though Brocmail escaped inglori-
ously [2] (613 A.D.).

It might have been expected that the victory of Chester would
have given permanent possession of the lands between Ribble and
Dee to the Northumbrians.   This, however, was not to be the case :
Aethelfrith probably annexed the region, but it did not stay with
his successors.   He was destined to fall in battle only four years
later, and if the conquered region did not then revert to the
Britons, it certainly did so at the death of his successor Edwin
in 633, when Cadwallon of Gwynedd destroyed for a moment the
whole power of Northumbria, and ravaged it as far as Hadrian's
Wall and the Firth of Forth.   The lands about Chester and the
mouth of the Dee were destined to form part of Mercia, not of

[1] Bede, *E. H.*, ii. 2.
[2] The tale of the monks of Bangor (of course Bangor Iscoed, not Bangor-on-
Menai) is told by Bede *apropos* of the prophecy said to have been made by St.
Augustine, that if the British clergy would not join in preaching Christianity to the
English nation they would be punished by receiving death at English hands (see
p. 269).

the more northern English realm, and their permanent occupation
was by settlers from the valley of Trent, not from the valleys of
the Ouse or Tyne.

Meanwhile we must leave Aethelfrith, the last but one of the
great heathen kings of the English race, in order to turn back to
the history of Aethelbert of Kent, to whose court the missionaries
of Roman Christianity had come when the Northumbrian conqueror
was but commencing his eventful reign.   The heir of Hengist had
already bowed his knee before the Cross when the heir of Ida was
slaughtering the servants of Christ in ignorant hostility before the
walls of Deva.   The second epoch of the history of the Teutonic
settlers of Britain had begun before the first was well finished.
The period of the conversion of the English overlapped that of
their great conquests.   But Ceawlin and Aethelfrith between them
had finished the more important part of the work of settlement.
The lands which were to be added to the area of permanently
settled Saxon or Anglian soil after 613 were but of limited extent
compared to those which had already been occupied.

CHAPTER XIV

THE CONVERSION OF THE ANGLO-SAXON KINGDOMS (597-671 A.D.)

WITH the year 597, when Aethelbert of Kent had already enjoyed for some years a predominance over all the kingdoms south of Humber, while Aethelfrith, ruler of the united realm of Deira and Bernicia, was supreme north of that estuary, begins the second period of Anglo-Saxon history.

Sometime in the spring of that year there landed in the Isle of Thanet, at Ebbsfleet or possibly at Richborough, the mission of some forty persons headed by the priest Augustine, which Pope Gregory the Great had sent forth from Rome about ten months before. It is impossible to omit the pretty tale which explains Gregory's interest in the English race, though Bede, its first narrator, gives it only as an *opinio*, a tradition or ancient report.[1] Long before Gregory had been consecrated to the Roman bishopric, perhaps about 585-88, he had seen in the slave-market beside the Tiber a group of youths exposed for sale, notable for their fair complexions, their attractive faces, and their abundant hair. " When he saw them he asked from what region or land they had been brought. He was told from the Isle of Britain, whose inhabitants were all of that aspect. Again he asked whether these islanders were Christians, or still wrapped in the errors of paganism. He was informed that they were heathens. Then he drew a long sigh and exclaimed : ' Alas ! that beings of a such a fair countenance should be in the grip of the Author of Darkness, and that such a graceful exterior should enclose minds destitute of grace within !' So he asked again what was the name of this nation. The reply

---

[1] There is a letter of Gregory's to one of his agents in Gaul, ordering the purchase of English slaves. See Haddon and Stubbs, *Councils*, iii. 4.

was that they were called Angles. 'Good,' he answered, 'for they
have the faces of angels, and such should be co-heirs with the angels
in heaven. But what is the name of the province from which they
have been brought?' He was told that it was Deira. 'Good
again!' he said, '*De ira eruti*—snatched from God's wrath, and
called to Christ's mercy. And how is the king of their land
called?' The answer came that he was named Aella. But
Gregory, playing with the name, exclaimed: 'Then ought Alleluia,
the praise of God our Creator, to be sung in the realm of Aella'."
The legend tells that he immediately went to his bishop (Pelagius II.) and offered himself as a missionary for the conversion of
the English, but that he was unable to carry out his desire " because
the citizens of Rome could not bring themselves to allow him to
depart to such a distance from their city ".[1] When, however, he
was elected bishop himself a few years later (590) he was able to
start by proxy the work which he was prevented from discharging
in person.

The mission to England was but one of many enterprises which
Gregory the Great took in hand. The activity of the founder of
the medieval papacy was all-embracing: his emissaries strengthened
the hands of the pious Reccared, newly converted to orthodoxy, in
Visigothic Spain. They won peace from Agilulf the Lombard, who
seemed at this time destined to make an end of the Roman empire
in Italy. Gregory was the familiar correspondent and adviser of
the able if unscrupulous Austrasian queen, Brunhildis, who was
vainly endeavouring to maintain the crumbling royal power among
the turbulent Franks. He started the as yet half-conscious attempts of the Roman see to free itself from the political supremacy
of Constantinople, by his contest with the Emperor Maurice and
the patriarch John the Faster.[2] The papacy was to be the heir of
the empire in the West, and the missionary invasion of England
was in a very true sense the reclaiming for the world-power which
was to replace the empire, of the province which had been lost
under Honorius. Apostolic zeal is none the less real though it be
combined with statesmanship, as it was in this case.

[1] The date of the legend is fixed to the years 585-88 by the fact that Gregory
only returned from a very long stay in Constantinople in the former year, while
Aella died in the latter.

[2] Yet we must allow he does not always show independence in his correspondence with Maurice, and addresses the cruel usurper Phocas in adulatory terms.

A glance at the internal condition of Italy in 590-96 suffices to explain why the mission of Augustine only went forth six summers after Gregory had been elected to fill the papal throne. The period of the commencement of his episcopate was one during which the Lombards were ravaging the remnant of imperial Italy with special vigour and success. They had closed in on Rome itself, and actually laid siege to the city in 593 : though turned back, they continued to occupy Tuscany and much of Umbria ; it was still possible for some time that they might reappear, to sack Rome, or to turn it into the residence of a duke or a royal " gastaldus ". The twenty-seven years during which—as Gregory complains in one of his letters—Rome had lived in terror under the shadow of the Lombard sword, were only just over when the missionary band destined for Britain was despatched. Indeed formal peace was only obtained in 599, when Gregory negotiated with King Agilulf a *modus vivendi* not only for his own city but for all the surviving imperial territory in the peninsula. Augustine and his party must have passed in 596 through towns and fields still black with recent burning, and have suffered perils by the way from half-hostile Lombard war-bands, for though King Agilulf had ceased to advance he had as yet consented to no definitive treaty.

The character of Gregory, saint and statesman, is sufficiently well known to us, not so much from his biographers, as from his own books and letters. Augustine is a more shadowy figure: he was a man of mature years and had been a monk in the monastery of St. Andrew on the Caelian Hill, of which he was prior at the moment of his despatch to Britain. Gregory says that he had been well trained in monastic discipline,[1] " was filled with a knowledge of Holy Scripture, and endowed with good works by God's special grace ". The story of his mission shows that he was zealous, persuasive, untiring and ascetic, but suggests at the same time weak points in his temperament—the two opposite faults of a certain want of self-reliance and of an occasional lapse into self-assertion. Of the latter we shall hear more hereafter. The former seems to be indicated by the curious fact that he and his party actually halted at Aix or Arles on their way to Britain, " seized with a sudden fear at the idea of proceeding to a barbarous, fierce and unbelieving nation ". Augustine returned to Rome, bearing the

[1] *Epistles*, XI. iv. 66.

request of his companions that they might be excused so dangerous and uncertain a mission. But the resolute Gregory sent him back, with orders to proceed at all risks, and letters commendatory to many Gallic prelates who were to help the travellers on the way (July, 596). Very early in the following year the whole band crossed the Channel, apparently from Boulogne: they had, as it seems, passed through Autun and Metz on their northward progress.

They landed in Thanet, " an isle of about 600 families according to the English manner of reckoning, separated from the mainland by the river Wantsum, which is about three furlongs broad, and is fordable only in two places". Ebbsfleet is the traditional point of their coming ashore, though something may be urged in favour of Richborough, despite of the fact that the site of that old Roman port cannot be described in strict accuracy as lying in the bounds of Thanet; it was apparently in those days isolated on a little island of its own.[1] The party was permitted to land without hindrance, and Augustine was allowed to announce his arrival to Aethelbert, who bade him remain in Thanet till he himself should have leisure to take counsel concerning him.

English heathenism does not seem to have had any firm hold on its votaries. Apparently it had lost vitality on being transplanted from its original continental birthplace. Religions which are bound up with local ceremonies and institutions, such as those which Tacitus describes as being common to the Angles and their neighbours, are indeed wont to grow weak when they are divorced from their old connection. A very few generations had sufficed to destroy the faith of all the other Teutonic races, which had taken part in the great migrations of the fourth and fifth centuries. If the invaders of Britain adhered longer to the faith of Woden and his fellows than did other kindred races, it was because their conditions differed from those of the Frank or the Goth. They had well-nigh exterminated the earlier Christian inhabitants, instead of receiving the whole provincial community to surrender and homage. Their religion, like their language and their social customs, had survived in a way that was unknown on the continent. They had erected temples containing rude idols in spots specially consecrated;

[1] See the excursus on Augustine's landing-place in Mason's *Mission of St. Augustine.*

we hear now and then of priests, though there is no evidence that the class was numerous or powerful.   There is absolutely no indication that they formed an organised body, able or willing to combine in defence of the old faith.   Indeed, on the only occasion where a heathen priest is recorded to have taken a prominent part in religious discussion with the Christian missionaries, he was on the side of innovation.   The speech of this Deiran high priest, recorded in Bede, seems to hint that his position was not a very important one.   "No one," he is made to say, "has applied himself more diligently to the worship of our gods than I; and yet there are many who receive greater favours from their king, and are more preferred than I, and more prosperous in all their undertakings. Now if the gods were good for anything, they would rather forward me, who have been more careful to serve them.   If on examination we find the new doctrines which are now preached to us better and more efficacious, let us receive them without any delay." [1]   It seems probable that in matters religious the king, as the general representative of the nation in its dealings with the powers of heaven, was more important than any priest of any individual god.

Nothing can be more striking in the narrative of the conversion of England than to note the toleration displayed to the emissaries of Christianity, even by those rulers who remained themselves impervious to its teaching.   Penda of Mercia, who was to a certain extent the champion of the old religion, and put down the Northumbrian kings who had abandoned it, was yet no persecutor.   "He did not obstruct the preaching of the Word among his people, if any were willing to hear it, but on the contrary hated and despised those who, when they had once received the faith, he saw not living up to its works.   He would say 'these are wretched and contemptible men who despise the commands of the God in whom they believe'." [2]   It is a notable fact that in the long history of the English missions, which lasted for three-quarters of a century between Augustine's landing and the conversion of the last heathen in the Sussex Weald, there is not a single record of martyrdom. The preachers of the new faith were sometimes hunted away, but never, as far as we know, put to death.   If any had suffered, it is absolutely certain that their fates would have been recorded in

[1] Bede, *E. H.*, ii. 13.   [2] *Ibid.*, iii. 21.

moving words by the conscientious Bede. This contrasts strongly
with what happened in Frisia and continental Saxony, where several
notable martyrdoms took place.

It appears probable that the English had been impressed by the
fact that their powerful neighbours across the Channel, the Franks,
had long ago abandoned their native heathenism. This was the
only race with whom they had much to do in the way of friendship
and commerce, and it seems clear that the insular kings looked up
to the Merovingian royal house, and that Aethelbert had been considered fortunate to win the hand of one of its daughters. It must
not be forgotten that close kinsmen of the English, the Saxons of
Bayeux and on the Picard coast, were subjects of the Franks, and
had shared in their conversion. Nay, some of the Merovings had
even claimed a certain suzerainty over the English in general,[1]
though we have no proof that it was ever admitted. Augustine
brought with him Christian interpreters from the Frankish realm;
it is almost certain that they must have been descendants of some
of the Saxons settled beyond the Channel.

That any predisposition which the English may have felt
towards Christianity came from their connection with the Franks,
and not from intercourse with the Britons, is certain. The English
had from the first spared a certain number of the conquered Britons,
who became the base of the servile class among them, those of
whom Gildas speaks as " coming in, worn down by famine, to hold
out their hands to the enemy, accepting perpetual slavery that they
might not be slain forthwith—the best terms that they could
obtain ". But it is certain that they were but a remnant, and exercised no influence on their masters ; it is not even clear that they
preserved their Christianity after a generation or two. The unconquered Britons of the West and North made no effort to convert
their adversaries, a refusal not very unnatural in itself, which is
perpetually used as a source of reproach to them by Bede[2] and
other English writers. Even 150 years after the first invasion they
were still as bitter as ever against the incomers ; the only reference
to the English that can be detected in the surviving notes of the
proceedings of British church-councils is a clause in the canons of
the Synod of Lucus Victoriae (569 A.D.), imposing a penance of

---

[1] Procopius, iv. 20.   [2] Bede, *E. H.*, i. 22, and other places.

thirteen years on any man who shall have acted as guide to "the barbarians," or a penance for life if the barbarians, so helped, shall have done any serious damage on their raid.[1]   It is certainly strange that no improvement of the relations between the two races, resulting in missionary effort on the part of the British clergy, should have taken place during the long halt of the Saxons, between the battle of Mount Badon and the advance of Ceawlin—a period of sixty years.   We find that exiled Anglian princes were during the period of their paganism occasionally entertained at the courts of British kings, as happened with Edwin, the son of Aella, and his nephew Hereric.   And the Celts were even politically leagued on occasion with Angles, as in the case of Hering, the son of Hussa.[2] But such communication as these relations involved does not seem to have led to any attempt at conversion.   Not one solitary legend survives to hint at such an endeavour; the British Church, as a whole, contrasted strongly throughout its independent history with the daughter Church of Ireland in its lack of missionary enterprise. It appears to have exhausted the greater part of its energy in the multiplication of monasteries and the practice of minute asceticism. Those who are interested in the details of the monastic life may find many strange ordinances in the fragments of Gildas's tract *On Penitence* and the canons of the *Sinodus Aquilonalis Britanniae.* If we may judge from these documents, no amount of rules and no seclusion from the world was wholly sufficient to prevent strange lapses from the rules of ordinary morality among the British clergy.   The common punishment for all offences, great and small, was a longer or shorter diet of bread and water and the repetition of a smaller or greater number of Psalms.[3]   The Welsh Church seems to have been in its organisation a legitimate descendant of the Roman provincial Church of the fifth century : it had regular diocesan bishops, whose dioceses were coterminous with the kingdoms, and was not ruled by tribal abbots and non-territorial bishops like the Irish Church.   The earliest indications seem to show that there were probably five bishoprics west of Severn, four of which

---

[1] Si autum evenerit strages Christianorum, et sanguinis effusio, et dira captivitas, residuo vitae paenitentiam agat, relictis armis (Stubbs and Haddan, i. 118).

[2] See p. 250.

[3] See the texts in Stubbs and Haddan's *Councils and Ecclesiastical Documents,* vol. i., pp. 110, 120.

survived as the sees of Bangor, St. David's, St. Asaph and Llandaff; a fifth at Llanbadarn, which took in the greater part of the modern Cardiganshire and Brecknockshire, was merged in St. David's not long after 700. In South-Western Britain there were at least two more, one probably comprising Cornwall, the other the more eastern parts of Damnonia. Farther north, St. Ninian's bishopric of Whithern (Candida Casa), for the Galloway Picts, goes back to the fifth century, and St. Kentigern's bishopric of Glasgow to the sixth. But it is extremely probable that there were other British sees between Clyde and Mersey whose memory has perished.

Aethelbert of Kent was certainly acquainted with the existence of Christianity, and not indisposed to give its missionaries a friendly welcome, but this was due to the fact that he had been wedded for many years—as has already been mentioned—to a Christian spouse, Bertha, the daughter of Charibert, the Merovingian King of Paris. She had brought over with her many dependants of her own religion, including a certain Luithard, a bishop,[1] who acted as her chaplain, and her husband had permitted her to utilise the old Roman Church of St. Martin, on the east side of his royal town of Canterbury, as her chapel. Pope Gregory, in a letter to her, which has been preserved,[2] gives her a gentle admonition that she might have done more for the faith; but at least she appears to have predisposed Aethelbert in its favour, and when Augustine appeared in Kent she exercised all the influence that she had in his favour.

A few days after the arrival of the mission the king came to Thanet, and bade Augustine appear before him and state the cause of his coming. The interview, as Bede tells us, was held in the open air, because there was an old superstition that witchcrafts and deceptions might be practised within four walls, but not beneath the sky. But the strangers were permitted to approach in processional order, singing litanies, and marching under a silver cross and a banner consisting of a panel-picture of the Saviour. Augustine was invited to seat himself and to explain his mission. He spoke, through his interpreters, with great fervour, setting forth the blessings of Christianity in this world and the next. The king replied that "his words and promises were fair, but because they were new and unproved, he could not give his adhesion to them,

---

[1] He is said to have been Bishop of Senlis.
[2] Gregory's *Epistles*, xi., ind. iv., No. 29.

abandoning all the beliefs that he and all of his race had held from time immemorial. Yet since the missionaries were evidently desiring to communicate to others things that they sincerely believed to be good and profitable, they should be given a fair trial. They should receive daily food from the royal store, and might preach where they would, nor should any hindrance be put in the way of their making converts." Probably Aethelbert was already prepared to go farther than he said, and gave this cautious answer, rather for the benefit of his chiefs and councillors sitting around, than because he himself had any objection to a faith of which he must long have known the main characteristics by means of his wife.

At any rate Augustine was treated with a kindness much greater than had been promised him. He was invited to Canterbury, lodged close to the royal dwelling, and permitted to preach, to pray, and to celebrate the sacraments, in the old church which had already been granted as a chapel to the queen. Aethelbert frequently attended at his services, and held private conference with him. There was evidently no resisting power in Kentish paganism : the missionaries were not only unopposed, but welcomed everywhere. On Whitsunday (June 2), 597, less than three months after Augustine's landing in Thanet, the king was baptised, and after him great numbers of his subjects great and small. The royal convert presented to his teacher an adequate residence in Canterbury, and certain permanent endowments. It is interesting to find that Aethelbert bade Augustine not only to build but also to *repair* churches wherever he might please.[1] This seems to suggest that a considerable number of Roman ecclesiastical buildings must have been standing in a more or less ruinous condition. Had they been used by a subject British servile population all through the last 150 years ? Or were they merely wrecks which could be identified as churches by their form ? Lacking, as we do, all trace of a Christian subject population in Kent, it is safer to accept the second alternative.

Augustine had been told by Gregory that, if his mission should prosper, he must get himself ordained a bishop, as the first step towards giving the English Church a definite organisation. When all seemed going well, he repaired to Gaul, and was consecrated by

[1] Bede, *E. H.*, i. 26.

Virgilius,[1] Bishop of Arles, probably late in 597. He promptly returned to Kent, and then sent two of his companions to Rome, not only to bear the tidings of his success, but to lay before the Pope a number of questions relating to problems which were beginning to trouble him. Some of them were questions of the same sort which often beset missionaries of to-day in Africa—problems as to the recognition of heathen marriages, the distribution of alms, and the punishment of crime among converts. Others related to ceremonial. But the most important of them all was the request for a definition as to Augustine's position with regard to the Bishops of Britain, by which was clearly meant the Celtic Church of the West. It is not quite certain whether Gregory fully understood the problem, or even realised that there was an existing Church in Britain, bitterly hostile to the English, converted or unconverted.[2] He replied : " All the bishops of Britain we commit to your charge, that the unlearned may be instructed, the weak be strengthened with per- suasion, the perverse corrected by your authority ". But he was at the same moment arranging that Augustine should consecrate an English hierarchy, and it is quite possible that it was to this alone that he was referring. If he had known of the difficulty that was arising as to the relations of the English and the Welsh Churches, he would probably have written at great length on the problem, as he did on several other of the questions that were submitted to him.

It is a clear sign of the inadequate knowledge that Gregory possessed of the state of Britain that when, in 601, he sent over many priests to England to aid in Augustine's mission—among them Mellitus, Justus and Paulinus, all destined in the future to be archbishops—he made them the bearers of a letter in which he set forth a scheme for the division of the island into dioceses, which was wholly impracticable. They bore a *pallium* for Augustine, with which he was to invest himself on taking the title of Archbishop of London ; he was to consecrate twelve bishops as suffragans to himself, and a thirteenth as Archbishop of York, who, " when that city and its neighbourhood receive the Word of God," was to con- secrate another twelve to be subject to himself. This arrangement could not be carried out, firstly, because it would have been unwise

---

[1] Not Aetherius, as Bede wrongly says. The latter was Archbishop of Lyons.
[2] See Mason's *Mission of St. Augustine*, p. 79.

for Augustine to desert his patron Aethelbert of Kent, and to transfer his residence to a city of he comparatively unimportant king of Essex ; secondly, because the mission, satisfactory though its progress was, did not convert all England at one sweep. It was twenty-four years before York saw an archbishop, and nine centuries before the English Church counted as many as twenty-four dioceses—a total not reached till the reign of Henry VIII. Augustine himself only lived long enough to ordain two suffragans, Justus for Rochester and West Kent, Mellitus for London and the kingdom of the East Saxons. For Kent and its subject state of Essex were the only two realms which seemed sufficiently settled in their Christianity to justify the appointment of a bishop, and even in these—as we shall see—there was a period of reaction. King Saebert of Essex, the nephew of Aethelbert, was the only one of that monarch's vassals who followed the example of his suzerain, by giving a prompt adhesion to the new religion. He was a zealous convert, and joined with his uncle in the foundation of St. Paul's, London, as the cathedral of Bishop Mellitus ; that Aethelbert took part in it shows that his authority over Essex was much more than a nominal hegemony. Raedwald of East Anglia, a more powerful vassal, would not go so far ; he was baptised during a visit to Canterbury, but on returning home, " seduced by his wife and certain perverse teachers, he tried to serve at the same time Christ and his former gods. For he had in the same temple an altar to Christ, and another small one in which he used to immolate victims to devils."[1]   On what logical principle Raedwald worked, whether Christ was introduced into the heathen pantheon, according to the experiment once made by Alexander Severus of old, or whether Woden and Frey were treated as vassals and demiurges of Jehovah, it is interesting but useless to speculate. At any rate, this scandalous trimmer in religion got no bishop granted him from Canterbury.

The only important events which are recorded concerning the later period of Augustine's seven-year archiepiscopate are his unfortunate conferences with the Celtic bishops in the year 603, which started the bitter strife between the English and the Welsh Churches which was to endure for several centuries.   When the

---

[1] Bede, *E. H.*, ii. 15.

conditions of the meeting are taken into consideration, it is perhaps hardly wonderful that the Roman missionary and the Welsh clergy could come to no agreement. The question of obedience was the really fatal point. The British Church had governed itself, according to its own lights, for the last 150 years, and during that long period had practically no relations with any other Christian body save the daughter community in Ireland. When Augustine came, with his letter from Gregory, which placed him at the head of all the insular churches, it was hardly wonderful that the Celts saw no reason to accept as their overlord this stranger, who had been but a few years in Britain, and had made a few thousand converts in districts very far from their own border. The Britons refused to surrender their autonomy, but they made their fight, not on the question of recognising the authority of the Roman pontiff, but on a number of matters of ecclesiastical custom and ritual, which served to mask the real heart of the controversy.

The conferences were held at the place afterwards called Augustine's Oak, " on the confines of the West Saxons and the Hwiccas," apparently Aust on the Bristol Channel, a very convenient place for Welsh delegates crossing from Gwent or Glamorgan by the well-known old Roman passage.[1] Augustine, as we are told, began by brotherly admonitions to the " bishops and doctors" who had come to meet him, urging that they should undertake in common the labour of preaching the Gospel to the English. But he showed little tact if, as Bede seems to state, he raised at the same time the question of their differences from the continental churches, especially—the head and front of their offence —their habit of keeping Easter at a different date from the Romans and the other Western Christians. The project for mission work among the English provoked no enthusiasm among the Welsh ; they disliked the enemies who had robbed them of two-thirds of Britain so bitterly, that they could not feel any deep concern for Saxon souls. But this, of course, it would have been scandalous to state in so many words. The insinuations against their orthodoxy, on the other hand, offered fine fighting ground. " After a long dis-

[1] Bede, E. H., ii. 9. Some commentators have argued that the first conference may have been not at Aust, but at some place such as Cirencester or Malmesbury more exactly on the confines of the two peoples. But Aust answers fairly well for both.

putation they would not comply with the entreaties, rebukes, or exhortations of Augustine, but preferred their own traditions before all the churches in the world."

The Paschal controversy, on which the dispute mainly hinged, was in its essence a comparatively simple business. Down to the year 458 the whole of the Churches of the West, from Italy to Britain, had calculated Easter in a rather loose fashion, determining the Paschal Moon by a cycle of eighty-four years attributed to Sulpicius Severus (*circa* 410) but really going back to the Council of Arles in 314. In 458, however, the Roman Church began to use a new system of computation, the 532 years cycle of Victorius of Aquitaine; and this again was replaced in 525 by the decidedly more correct Alexandrine cycle of Anatolius, also of 532 years, a change which had the additional advantage of bringing the Roman reckoning into harmony with that of Alexandria and all the other orthodox churches of the East. These changes had been gradually copied by all the continental Churches in touch with Rome. But the British and Irish Churches, cut off from the rest of Christendom by the intervening wedge of English heathenism, had continued to employ a form of the 84 year cycle, attributed to Sulpicius Severus. They were now so devoted to it that they utterly refused to make a change, on the authority of Roman or other foreign calculators ; they considered their own system good enough after its long hallowing by tradition. They were also, it may be suspected, incapable of following the astronomical and arithmetical arguments against it. It resulted that their system was to count as Easter Day the Sunday which fell next after the Spring Equinox, between the 14th and 20th days of the moon. The latest Roman system took Easter to be the Sunday which fell next after the Spring equinox, between the 15th and 21st days of the moon.[1] A considerable discrepancy of dates naturally resulted. That any communities of Christian men should have refused each other communion, on points of dispute of which this mere mathematical problem was the most important, seems sufficiently deplorable. But the root of the matter was not, it is clear, the Paschal cycle, but the determination of the British Church

---

[1] It is clear that the Welsh were *not* " Quartodeciman " heretics of the old type. Bede expressly acknowledges this (iii. 17), though Aldheim insinuates it, somewhat unfairly. The British Church did not insist on the number 14. See the excursus on the controversy in Plummer's edition of Bede, vol. ii. pp. 348-55.

to preserve its autonomy; if it chose to make its calculation on an antiquated system, it would do so, despite all argument. This was patriotic obscurantism, no doubt; but on the whole more blame attaches to Augustine for insisting that the Britons should abandon a system which was, after all, Roman and very ancient, in order to take up the new one. If only the new English and the old British Churches could be got into friendly communication, for the common purpose of missionary work among the heathen, the greater would of necessity end by absorbing the less. It is clear that the Apostle of England showed himself lacking in tact and pliability, if the Celts were lacking in common Christian missionary zeal.

The first abortive conference at Augustine's Oak was followed by a second, to which there came many more representatives of the British Church, seven bishops (as Bede gives the tradition) and many learned monks, of whom Dinooth, Abbot of Bangor Iscoed was the most notable. But the arguments were as unfruitful as those at the earlier meeting, and the controversialists parted denouncing each other as schismatics. Bede gives a legend—surely British in origin—to explain the breach. Some of the Welsh delegates, on their way to the conference, sought advice of a certain anchorite of great sanctity. "If Augustine is a man of God follow him," said the hermit. "Our Lord said, 'Take My yoke upon you and learn of Me, for I am meek and lowly of heart'. If, therefore, Augustine is meek and lowly of heart, it is to be believed that he has taken upon himself the yoke of Christ, and offers the same to you. But if he shows himself stern and haughty, it appears that he is not of God. Contrive that he arrive first at the place of conference; if at your approach he shall rise up to meet you, hear him submissively. But if he shall show you that he despises you, by not rising up to greet you, let him be contemned." The story runs that the Welsh bishops tried this plan, and that Augustine, as it fell out, received them sitting on his throne, as a superior meeting inferiors. "Whereupon they flew into a passion, charged him with pride, and contradicted all that he said."[1] The incident is, no doubt, mere legend, but it contains this much of truth, that the key to the whole quarrel was that the Roman Church treated other Churches as subjects and inferiors, and that the British Church was proud and sensitive, and rejected all notion of inferiority.

[1] Bede, *E. H.*, ii. 10.

The breach, if Bede may be followed, took the form of an ultimatum by Augustine, requiring the Welsh delegates to reform their custom of keeping Easter, to adopt the Roman details in the sacrament of baptism,[1] and to join at once in missionary work among the English. Minor divergencies of ritual he would not insist upon. The Celts answered that they consented to no one of his three points, and that they did not acknowledge him as an archbishop. Thereupon Augustine departed, with a threatening prophecy that "if the Britons would not preach the Way of Life to the English nation, they were likely to find death from the English sword". This vaticination was considered to have been fulfilled a few years after Augustine's death, by the great slaughter of the Welsh princes and clergy by the heathen King Aethelfrith of Northumbria, at the battle of Chester (613 A.D.).

From this time onward the breach between the newly founded English Church and the old British Church seemed irreparable, and the relations of the Roman mission with the Irish Church were hardly better. A few years after Augustine's death we find Archbishop Laurentius, his successor, complaining that an Irish bishop, one Dagan, refused when passing through Canterbury not only to eat with him, but even to enter the same dwelling. Three generations later St. Aldhelm records that the priests of the Welsh not only refused to join in any act of worship with an English cleric, but regarded him as so deeply polluted that they would not use a dish or cup which he had touched, but would break it, or at least solemnly purify it with ashes or sand, and cast any food partly eaten by him to dogs or swine. The English retorted by treating all British or Irish bishops as schismatic, and called the peculiar Celtic tonsure, in which the whole front of the head instead of the crown alone was shorn, "the tonsure of Simon Magus". So far was the conversion of some of the English kingdoms from having any effect in bringing out better relations between Christian Celt and Christian Teuton, that we shall find the Welsh king Cadwallon deliberately leaguing himself with the heathen Penda of Mercia against the Christian Edwin of Northumberland, and after Edwin's death ravaging Deira with peculiar atrocity, in company with the

---

[1] What was the particular divagation of the Welsh Church from common practice in baptism is not clear. Perhaps a neglect of subsequent confirmation, or of the trine immersion. See Plummer's Bede, ii. pp. 75-6.

pagan Mercians. It was to be many generations before a better
state of things was gradually reached. National hatred was far
too strong to be affected by theoretical brotherhood in Christ.

On Augustine's death (May 26, 604) he was succeeded as
Archbishop of Canterbury by Laurentius, one of his original companions, and the person who carried his queries to Gregory and
brought back the answer in 601. He had been consecrated as his
spiritual father's coadjutor not long before, " lest upon his decease
the state of the Church might falter, if it should be destitute of a
pastor, though but for one hour". We know little of him, save
that he was an indefatigable worker, and made some attempt to
renew the negotiation with the Welsh Church, which had failed so
lamentably in his predecessor's time. It had, as might have been
expected, no effect. In the twelfth year of his archiepiscopate died
King Aethelbert (February 24, 616) who had ruled Kent for the
long period of fifty-six years, and had raised it, during the central
portion of his reign, to a predominance over the other English
kingdoms which it was never again to enjoy.

It would seem, however, that in his old age his power was
beginning to slip from him, for we are told that, while he yet lived,
Raedwald, King of East Anglia, once his vassal, had begun to
assert himself, and to claim the primacy for his own tribe. Whether
this king, the man who devised the strange compromise between
Christianity and heathenism already mentioned, had rebelled against
his suzerain and freed himself from homage by force of arms, or
whether Aethelbert's former hegemony insensibly slipped from him,
we do not know. But for a few years Raedwald was reckoned
chief king among the English ; his domination extended over a wider
area than that of his predecessor, for in 617 he overcame and slew
Aethelfrith of Northumbria, the victor of Chester. The cause of
their strife was that the East Anglian king had harboured Edwin,
the exiled son of Aella of Deira, whose dominion Aethelfrith had
long possessed. After striving to get the young prince delivered
up to him, first by bribes and then by threats, Aethelfrith declared
war on Raedwald, but was surprised, as we are told, before all his
army had assembled, and slain with all his followers on the banks
of the Idle, in North Mercia. Raedwald then placed his *protégé*
Edwin on the Northumbrian throne, not only restoring to him his
own kingdom of Deira, but gaining for him Bernicia also, which

was properly the patrimony of the house of Ida. Aethelfrith's
four sons escaped, and spent many years as wandering exiles. Like
Edwin, however, they were destined one day to come to their own.

The period which began with the death of Aethelbert and the
predominance of Raedwald was one very unfavourable to the infant Church of England. Aethelbert's son and successor, Eadbald,
had never been baptised, and immediately on his accession scandal-
ised Archbishop Laurentius by wedding his father's young widow, a
second wife whom Aethelbert had espoused in his extreme old age,
after the death of Queen Bertha. This caused an open breach
between the king and the Christian community among his subjects;
the archbishop lived for a long time under daily expectation of
misusage or exile. But open persecution was never seen in England
during the age of the early missions. Eadbald contented himself
with ignoring the protests of Laurentius, and signifying his dis-
pleasure. Many fair-weather converts fell away, but the Church
was not openly molested. Yet the general outlook was unpromising. Saebert, King of Essex, died very soon after Aethelbert, and
his sons, Seaxred and Saeward, were pagans at heart, though during
their father's lifetime they had seemed to acquiesce in the establishment of Christianity within his realm. They expelled Bishop
Mellitus from London, and proclaimed that the worship of the old
gods was once more permitted. Yet here again we hear neither of
martyrdom nor of actual persecution. The two princes of Essex in
the very next year quarrelled with Cynegils, King of the West
Saxons, and were slain by him in battle (617). But Sigebert, the
son of Saeward, who succeeded his father and uncle, was also a
heathen, and the Church which had been planted among the East
Saxons became almost or quite extinct.

The exiled Bishop Mellitus and Justus, Bishop of Rochester, so
much despaired of the situation that they fled over seas into France,
lest worse things might befall them. Laurentius of Canterbury, so
Bede's story runs, would have followed them, if he had not been
reproved and chastened by St. Peter in a dream. He resolved to
remain, and shortly afterwards things began somewhat to mend.
King Eadbald was visited with a succession of temporary fits of
insanity, which his uneasy conscience ascribed to his rejection of
Christianity and its laws. He put away his wife, abjured the worship of idols, and sought peace with the archbishop, by whom he

was shortly afterwards baptised. Justus was recalled to his bishopric of Rochester, and the church of Kent began once more to flourish. But Eadbald did not possess his father's authority over the other kingdoms, and twenty-five years after Augustine's first coming, Christianity was officially recognised in Kent alone. Laurentius died in 619, and was followed in succession at Canterbury by Mellitus (619-24) and Justus (624-27), both elderly men who had worked under St. Augustine. The spread of the new faith seems to have made no progress during their short archiepiscopates. But their successor, Honorius (627-53) was destined to see times of better omen and greater prosperity.

The new advance was due to a political change, which once more placed a convert zealous for the new faith at the head of the English kingdoms. Raedwald of East Anglia died within a year after his great victory over Aethelfrith of Northumbria, and since his son Eorpwald was a man of no mark, the short predominance which he had won for his state passed away, never to return. The most able and enterprising of the surviving princes of England was that Edwin of Deira whom Raedwald had restored to the throne of his fathers, after the destruction of Aethelfrith. In the course of a few years he asserted over the rest of the English states that same sort of loose suzerainty which Aethelbert and Raedwald had enjoyed before him. We have no details of his earlier wars, but it is certain that before 626 he had reduced the Mercians and East Angles to homage, and was about to assail Cynegils and Cwichelm the joint kings (father and son) of Wessex. Nor was it the English alone who felt his sword : he had taken up the task which had been begun by his predecessor and enemy, Aethelfrith, of harrying the Britons of the North and West. He annexed the little Celtic State of Elmet or Loidis, in the Yorkshire West Riding, which had probably already been made tributary by Aethelfrith, and expelled its king Cerdic. It is quite possible that other expeditions of Edwin against the less remote British States may belong to his earlier years, though, if we accept Bede's rather vaguely worded narrative of his conquests, we must place them all in the time after 626.

It is certain, however, that the period of his greatest activity and power was after his conversion to Christianity. How this came to pass is narrated at great length in Bede's *Ecclesiastical History*. Edwin having lost his first wife made overtures to King

Eadbald of Kent, to ask for the hand of his sister, Aethelberga. From the political point of view, the match offered many attractions to Eadbald, since it would ally him to the most powerful monarch in England. But he doubted whether he ought to give a Christian princess in marriage to a heathen. The Northumbrian, however, promised that his wife should be allowed to keep her own faith, and to bring with her priests, along with any other retinue that she might desire. This concession settled the matter, and Aethelberga was accompanied to the North by one Paulinus, who was to act as her chaplain. In the hope that much might come of his mission, Archbishop Justus ordained him a bishop before his departure (July, 625).

Paulinus was a man of tact as well as of zeal, and while labouring among the queen's court found means to commend himself to the king. Edwin cannot have been wholly ignorant of Christianity, since, during his years of exile, he had spent a certain time at the court of Cadvan, King of North Wales. He was apparently already well disposed to listen to the missionary, when a narrow escape from death brought his hesitation to a crisis. On Easter Day, 626, he received an ambassador from Cwichelm, king of Wessex, whom he was apparently threatening with war. The envoy, one Eumer, was a desperate and devoted follower of Cwichelm, who had suborned him to assassinate Edwin. When received in state by the Northumbrian king, Eumer, while pretending to deliver his message, suddenly drew a dagger and dashed at Edwin, who would have perished if a faithful thegn, named Lilla, had not thrown himself between them and received the thrust. " Yet the wretch struck home so fiercely that he wounded the king through his retainer's body." [1] He was then cut down, fighting so hard that he slew another thegn ere he was finally despatched.

On the same night Aethelberga bore to Edwin her first-born child, a daughter. The king at first gave thanks to his own idols, but afterwards listened to Paulinus, when he assured him that his own and his queen's happy deliverance were both the results of Christian prayers. He vowed that if the god of Aethelberga would grant him that his wound might heal, and that he might take vengeance on Cwichelm, he would accept the new faith. And as a pledge of his promise he allowed Paulinus to baptise his little

[1] Bede, *E. H.*, ii. § 6.

daughter, whom he consecrated to Christ. This child, Eanflaed, was afterwards destined to wed King Oswiu, and to be the ancestress of the second Northumbrian royal house.

When healed of his wound Edwin conducted a furious campaign against the two kings of Wessex, whose land he devastated till they craved his pardon and did him homage. That he did not pursue them to the death was perhaps the first mark of Christian pity in his heart. On returning victorious to his own land he informed Paulinus that he would redeem his word, but that he must first confer with the council of his wise men, and hear their opinions. The narrative of the proceedings of this meeting, as given by Bede, gives clear proof of the weakness of English heathenism. The outworn creed had come to be despised by its votaries, because it did not satisfy their moral aspirations, or their sense of divine justice, or their desire for knowledge of the other world. "The soul of man," said one old councillor, "is like a sparrow, which on a dark and rainy night passes for a moment through the door of a king's hall : entering, it is for the minute surrounded by light and warmth and safe from the wintry storm ; but after a short spell of brightness and quiet, it vanishes through another door into the dark storm from whence it came. The life of man is a moment visible ; but what goes before, or what comes after, we know not. And if this new doctrine can tell us something about these mysteries, by all means let us follow it." Less poetic in imagery and less noble in thought, but more practical in its appeal to common-sense, was the curious speech of the pagan high-priest, Coifi, which has already been alluded to in an earlier paragraph. The ancient gods, he said, have no care for those who have served them most faithfully. Their loyal worshippers fare no better than other men. He had himself been for a whole lifetime their most diligent servant, but had won neither special favour from his king nor worldly prosperity. The more carefully that he sought for truth in his old religion the less did he find it. "And I freely confess that in the new preaching I seem to find the truth I sought, when it promises us the gifts of life, salvation, and eternal bliss. Wherefore I advise, O king, that we abjure and give to the flames those temples and altars which we have hallowed without receiving any fruit from them."

In short, the whole Witan gave an active or passive assent to the king's wishes, and Coifi the priest himself took the lead in destroy-

ing the great temple at Godmundingham, the chief sanctuary of
Deira, which lay not far from York to the east, beyond the river
Derwent. The king, with many of his nobles and a countless multitude of the commons, was baptised on the following Easter Day,
and the oratory which was built for him became the first church of
York, and the cathedral of Paulinus, who assumed his episcopal
title from that town, as Gregory had ordained in his letter to
Augustine a quarter of a century before. So great was the fervour
of the first conversion that Paulinus is recorded to have spent
thirty-six continuous days at Adgefrin (Yeavering, near Wooler)
in baptising in the river Glen the multitudes of Bernicians who
flocked to him, desirous of admission to the king's new faith. Among
the Deirans also the conversions were very numerous; tradition
records similar great baptismal gatherings at Catterick (the old
Roman Cataractonium) on the Swale.

Edwin was anxious that his vassal kings should join him in
casting away heathenism, and his efforts were very successful. Eorpwald, King of East Anglia, the son of his old benefactor Raedwald,
was the first to conform (628). He was murdered shortly afterwards by a pagan; but his cousin Sigebert, who finally succeeded
to his throne, was a very zealous Christian. He had spent some
years among the Franks across the Channel, where he had been
baptised, and called in a bishop, Felix of Burgundy, whom he
established at the port of Dunwich, which became the religious
centre of East Anglia. There Felix taught and baptised with much
success for seventeen years. In the sub-kingdom of the Lindiswaras,
south of the Humber, which seems at this moment to have been
directly subject to Edwin, Paulinus himself made a long missionary
tour. He set up a stone church in Lincoln city, and baptised there
Blecca, who was its high-reeve (*praefectus*). The report of his good
work made such an impression at Rome, that Pope Honorius raised
him to the dignity of archbishop, and sent him a pallium, thus
making him the equal of his own namesake, Honorius of Canterbury, to whom he sent the same gift shortly after.

While Edwin was aiding and forwarding these missions he was
at the same time extending his political power. The six years after
his conversion appear to have abounded in offensive wars: the most
striking of his expeditions was an attack by sea on Man and Anglesey—the last naval enterprise but one that is recorded on the part

of any king of the Heptarchic period. He is said to have reduced them both to homage.[1] The expedition against Anglesey seems to be connected with a general assault on North Wales; we are told in the Welsh chronicles that in 629 he besieged Cadwallon, King of Gwynedd, in the isle of Glannauc[2]—Priestholm, opposite Beaumaris—and there are some indications that Cadwallon was shortly afterwards an exile in Ireland.[3] If this were so, it would seem that Edwin drove him out, and set up for a time in his stead princes who were prepared to do homage to Northumbria. By this supposition we can best account for Bede's very clear and definite statement that Edwin " received under his dominion all the borders of Britain that were provinces of the English or of the Britons—a thing which no king had ever done before ".[4] We may connect with this general expansion of his kingdom the building, or rebuild-ing, of his great castle on the rock, far to the north in Midlothian, the Edwinsburgh which was to be the nucleus of the future capital of Scotland. We have also to fit into his general policy a cam-paign in the south. The Anglo-Saxon Chronicle records under the year 628 that Penda, King of Mercia, who was at this time one of Edwin's vassals, fought with the West Saxon kings, Cwichelm and Cynegils, at Cirencester, and came to a treaty with them after the battle. This seems to show that the two kings of Wessex had tried to reassert themselves, after their discomfiture by Edwin in person before his baptism, but were defeated by the Mercian : the treaty probably involved the cession of the lordship over the Hwiccas of the Lower Severn Valley, which may have passed at this moment from Wessex to Mercia. At any rate, this is the last mention for many years of the appearance of any kings of the house of Cerdic in Gloucestershire.

To Edwin's last years, 630-33, we may refer the picture of the prosperity of Britain which Bede records. " There was such perfect peace that, as was said in the proverb, a woman with her new-born babe might walk through the island, from sea to sea, without receiv-ing any harm. Moreover, the king took such good care for the good of his people, that at every fountain by the highway he set up

---

[1] Bede, *E. H.*, ii. 9.
[2] *Annales Cambriae*, sub anno 629.
[3] See Rhys's *Celtic Britain*, 132.
[4] Bede, *E. H.*, ii. 9.

stakes, with brass cups chained to them, for the convenience of travellers.   And no man would touch them save for their proper use, either for the dread that they had of Edwin or for the affection that they bore him.   His dignity was so great that banners were borne before him, not only in battle, but when in time of peace he rode with his officers through town and countryside.   And when he walked on foot through the streets of towns that sort of ensign which the Romans called *tufa* was in like manner carried before him."   Some have seen in this ceremonial a claim of Edwin to take up the old Roman dignity of the *dux Britanniarum*, or even of the emperor himself, which might be claimed, without too much presumption, by a monarch whose suzerainty was owned over every foot of land which had once formed part of the old province of Britain.

But Edwin's greatness was to have a disastrous end.   Cadwallon of Gwynedd returned from Ireland and raised rebellion against him. He was joined by Penda of Mercia, the greatest of the English vassal kings, and one who was a staunch adherent of paganism. This prince was a man of marked character : he had succeeded to the Mercian throne at a very advanced age—he was fifty, we are told—in the year 626, but had from the first shown himself able, ruthless and ambitious.   He had no scruple in joining with the Welsh, the old enemies of his nation, and in their company advanced towards York.   Edwin, apparently cut off from the succours of his other subject allies, gave him battle at Heathfield (Hatfield, near Doncaster), but was utterly defeated and killed, along with his eldest son Osfrid (Oct. 12th, 633).   All his army was slain or scattered, the city of York fell into the hands of the victors, and for many weeks the whole of Deira was cruelly devastated.   The Christian Cadwallon, we are told, showed himself a more pitiless enemy than the heathen Penda.   He aimed at nothing less than exterminating the whole nation of the Northumbrians, and his Welshmen spared neither women nor children, and took no captives. Indeed, he intended to make the whole land Celtic soil once more, and cared nothing that the tribe whom he was trying to extirpate were Christians.

Aethelberga, the wife of Edwin, fled to her native Kent, accompanied by his infant family and Archbishop Paulinus.   Their two sons died young, but Edwin's daughter Eanflaed survived to wed his

worthy successor, Oswiu. The Deirans rallied for a moment under
Osric, the cousin of Edwin, and his nearest adult male relative; but
the Bernicians called back from exile Eanfrid, the eldest son of
Aethelfrith, and the representative of the house of Ida, which
Edwin had driven out. Both Osric and Eanfrid reverted to
paganism, though the one had conformed during his cousin's reign,
and the other had been baptised by the Irish monks of Iona during
his exile. Apparently they judged that the conversion of Edwin
had brought him ill luck, and that the Northumbrians would fight
better against the Christian Cadwallon in the name of their old
faith. Indeed the conduct of the Welsh king had estranged many
new converts and led to a widespread reversion to paganism. Hardly
one [1] of Paulinus's missionaries had remained behind, when their
leader fled, and Christianity seemed almost extinguished in the land
But the days of the two apostate kings were few and evil. Osric,
at the head of his Deirans, beset Cadwallon as he lay encamped at
York; but he was slain in a sally of the Welsh after a reign of only
six months. Eanfrid that same autumn (634), after being defeated
in battle, came with twelve of his thegns to offer homage to the
conqueror, but Cadwallon refused to grant him grace, and ordered
him to be beheaded.

The Bernicians, thereupon, saluted Oswald, the next brother of
Eanfrid, as their king. This prince, unlike his predecessor, was a
devout and zealous Christian; he rallied his countrymen for one
more battle, and set up as his standard a great wooden cross, under
which, on the banks of the Deniseburn, near Hexham, he gave
battle to Cadwallon.[2] He was completely victorious, though his
army was a mere remnant, much outnumbered by the enemy. The
Welsh king was slain, and with him perished the hope of the Celts
that they might once more recover the north. Many reckoned him
the last high-king of Britain, and dated the end of the Celtic
supremacy at his death.

The victorious Oswald not only became undisputed monarch of
all Northumbria, but claimed to succeed to Edwin's superiority
over the other English kings. Bede reckons him the sixth who

---

[1] Bede only mentions one, James the Deacon, of whom he has much to tell.

[2] The spot of victory was called the "Heavenfield" (coelestis campus) by the
Northumbrians, Bede, iii. 2. The Deniseburn has been identified by mention in
a Hexham charter: it runs into the Tyne south of the Roman Wall.

enjoyed "imperium" over the whole land. But there is surely
exaggeration in this view of his position, for during the eight years
that he reigned (634-42) he never succeeded in making an end of
Penda of Mercia, though he may possibly have concluded a truce
with him for a time. That ancient heathen, indeed, seems to have
been very powerful during Oswald's earlier years, since we know
that in 635 he fell upon East Anglia, and slew in battle its two
kings, the pious Sigebert and his successor, Egrice. Sigebert, we
are told, had retired to a monastery after three years of reign,
handing over his kingdom to Egrice, his cousin. But on the
approach of Penda, his former subjects insisted that he should lead
them to battle, though he refused to bear arms, and would carry no
more than a wand, lest any man's blood should be upon his head.
His prayers availed them nought, and both he and Egrice were
slain.

Whatever may have been the case with Mercia, however, it is
certain that Oswald exercised a certain supremacy over the West
Saxons, for it is related that when the aged king, Cynegils, was
baptised, Oswald was present at the ceremony, and confirmed the
gift of the town of Dorchester-on-Thames to the Church, which the
ruler of Wessex made as the first-fruits of his conversion. Since
Wessex and Mercia were generally at war, it would have been
very natural for Cynegils to seek the aid of Northumbria, though
it could only be obtained by doing homage, or even by embracing
Christianity. The missionary who baptised the King of Wessex,
and received Dorchester as his place of abode, was one Birinus, of
whom we only know that he came to Britain by the advice of Pope
Honorius, having vowed to work in some region where no other
preacher had been before him : wherefore he went neither to Canterbury nor to York, but selected Wessex, as a virgin field. Whether
he was an Italian or a Frank we do not know. He is recorded as
a zealous teacher, and a consecrator of many churches, during his
sixteen-years' episcopate. But his time was troublous, since not only
was Wessex often wasted by war in his days, but Coenwalch, the
younger son of Cynegils, had not been baptised with his father, and
when he came to the throne (643) remained for some years a
heathen, till he learnt Christianity, in the moment of defeat and
exile, at the court of the pious Anna, King of the East Angles.
On his restoration he took Birinus as his teacher, and when he died

(650) placed at Dorchester in his stead a Frankish bishop named Agilberct.

The glimpse of Oswald's activity in the south fits in well with all that we know of his life. He was busy for the faith in every direction. But his inspiration came not from Rome, like that of Aethelbert and Edwin, but from Iona, where he seems to have assimilated the enthusiastic, ascetic, and emotional Christianity of the Irish monks. His main guide and helper was the Scot Aidan, who had come down to his aid, when the first bishop sent to him from Iona proved a stumbling-block to converts, on account of his tactless severity. Aidan won all hearts by his humility, sweetness, and lack of self-assertion; he was the most charitable of all men both in act and in thought, and found in the king a kindred spirit. Bede's touching story of their friendship is well worth quoting. The Lenten fast was just over, and Oswald and Aidan were sitting together, about to commence their Easter feast, when the official charged with the king's alms came in to whisper that he had distributed all his resources, but that many starving poor were still waiting outside the royal gate. The king, without a moment's hesitation, sent out his untasted meat to be distributed among them, and then ordered the great silver dish which had stood before him to be cut up into pieces, and distributed among the most necessitous. Aidan, moved to tears, seized his master's right hand, and cried, "May this hand never perish!" Northumbrian tradition added that the saint's blessing took such effect that when Oswald's hand was lopped off, in the battle which brought him death a few years later, it remained incorruptible, and was preserved entire and unshrunken for centuries in the church of St. Peter at Bamborough. It may be noted that even Welsh tradition remembered the king as "Oswald Lamngwyn," "Oswald of the fair hand," in the days when the *Historia Brittonum* was compiled.

But Oswald's piety and zeal did not save him from the same fate which his predecessor Edwin had encountered. He fell in strife with Penda of Mercia, who was apparently once more leagued with the Welsh—for the site of the battle was Maserfelth, better known in later history as Oswestry (Oswald's tree) [1] on the border of Powys, north-westward from Shrewsbury; and in the Welsh

---

[1] The local traditions and dedications of Oswestry seem to corroborate the statements of the *Vita Oswaldi* as to the identification.

records the field bears the name of Cocboy. It seems quite clear that
such a spot can only have been the meeting-place of the armies if the
Welsh were concerned in the matter; either Oswald must have been
marching against the Welsh, and have found Penda already joined
with them on their frontier, or he must have heard that they were
about to concentrate, and have hurried forward to give them battle,
before they should attack his own dominions by way of Cheshire
and Lancashire.   No ordinary struggle between Northumbria and
Mercia could conceivably have been fought out at such a spot as
Oswestry (Aug. 5, 642).

The Northumbrian king's death was in unison with his life; it
is recorded that when he saw the battle lost, and the remains of his
host surrounded, his last thoughts were for them, and not for himself, "Lord, have mercy on the souls of my army," were his dying
words.   The victory was apparently an expensive one to the
Mercians, as we are told that Penda's brother Eowa, the ancestor
of many later kings, fell there with countless others.

The first result of the disaster of Maserfelth was to break up
the Northumbrian realm; the same result followed that had been
seen after Edwin's fall at Heathfield.   The Deirans, once more
reverting to the house of Aella, took as their king, Oswin, the son
of that Osric who had been slain by Cadwallon in 634.   The Bernicians acknowledged Oswy (Oswiu) the younger brother of Oswald
as their lord.   This state of things lasted for seven years, and
while it endured Northumbria was powerless before King Penda.
The situation, however, differed from that of 633-34, in that both
the new kings were zealous Christians; there was no reversion to
heathenism, and Aidan and his priests did not have to flee away, as
Paulinus had done after Edwin's death.   The Irish mission seems to
have bitten more deep into Northumbria than that which had
started from Kent.   Bede, though deploring the fact that Aidan
was in communion with the schismatic Church of the West, and not
with Rome, cannot find terms sufficiently high to praise his character and his influence.

For thirteen years after his victory over Oswald, Penda of
Mercia seems to have enjoyed as great a pre-eminence over all the
other kingdoms as Aethelbert or Edwin had ever possessed, yet he
is not reckoned in the list of kings who owned the *imperium* by
Bede, perhaps because he was a heathen and an enemy of those

Christian kings whom the historian so much admired. But the
recital of his acts shows that his power extended into every corner
of England. He repeatedly harried all Northumbria, as far as
Bamborough, whose walls were only delivered from his assault,
according to tradition, by the prayers of Bishop Aidan. He fell
upon his old enemies of Wessex, over whom Coenwalch, the son of
Cynegils, was now reigning (645), and drove the king out of this
realm, setting up in his stead petty chiefs who became his vassals.
The East Anglians suffered equally at his hands; he descended
upon them in 654, and slew in battle their king Anna, the third
Christian prince of the house of Wuffa who perished at his hands.
Aethelhere, the brother of Anna, was compelled to become his
vassal and tributary. It seems probable that Oswy also must have
made submission to him during some part of the early years of his
reign. For thus only can we understand the fact that the Mercian
king's daughter Cyneburh was wedded to Oswy's son, Alchfrid,
while Peada, Penda's eldest son, took to wife, Alchflaed, daughter
of Oswy. This double marriage must have marked a temporary
peace between the Christian and the heathen princes, which can
hardly have come about on any other terms than that the former
should do homage to the latter.

It is noteworthy that Penda's political supremacy by no means
put an end to the rapid spread of Christianity during the middle
years of the seventh century. He himself was so far from being a
persecutor that he made no objection when his son Peada was baptised, under the persuasion of his Bernician bride. He was wont to
say that he despised not Christians but bad Christians, and, though
he rejected the new faith him-elf, did not count all its adherents as
his necessary enemies. The final and definite conversion of several
of the English kingdoms falls into his day of supremacy. Coenwalch, King of Wessex, when he won back his kingdom, in 648, after
three years of exile, openly adhered to Christianity, though he had
rejected it in the day of his father Cynegils. He brought over the
seas a Frankish bishop named Agilberct, whom he installed in the
see of Dorchester, which his father had created, and afterwards set
up another bishop of Saxon birth, named Wini, at Winchester.
Essex, where the Church seemed to have been extinguished by the
expulsion of Mellitus in 617, and where several heathen kings had
reigned since the death of the pious Saebert, was won back to

Christianity in the reign of Sigebert the Good (650-60), who was converted by the personal influence of Oswy, whom he used—as we are told—often to visit in Northumbria, presumably to concert common political action against Penda. He brought back with him to London, as his bishop, Cedd, a brother of the better known St. Chad, who was consecrated by Oswy's bishops of the Irish line (653). Of Sigebert the curious tale is told that he was ultimately murdered by two nobles of his own kindred, " who being asked why they slew him, had nothing better to answer than that they hated him, because he was too apt to spare his enemies, and easily to forgive the wrongs that had been done him ".[1] Christian ethics did not appeal at once to all the English; it is indeed marvellous that they took so strong and early a grip upon the majority of them.

It will be noted that more than one of the bishops named above was of English blood. The surest sign of the firm establishment of the Church was that it had become possible to fill its higher ranks with well-trained and learned native priests. The first bishop of English parentage was Ithamar, consecrated to Rochester in 644, a Kentishman; the second, Thomas, a Gyrwa by birth, bishop of the East Angles in 647; the third, Cedd, already named; after that year native bishops became the rule and not the exception, and Canterbury, the highest see of all, received in 655 its first archbishop born within the isle, Frithonas, or Deusdedit as he renamed himself, a South Saxon. Between him and the first Norman archbishop in the eleventh century, Robert of Jumiéges, there was only one primate who was not an Englishman.[2] This, however, was one of the greatest of all the archbishops, that Theodore of Tarsus (668-90) of whom we shall have much to tell hereafter. Whether trained in the school which St. Augustine had started at Canterbury, or in the monasteries of the Scots, the early native bishops of the seventh century seem to have kept a high level of life, and to have been most worthy pastors of the new Church. There is only one of them, Wini of Winchester, of whom any evil is told; he is said to have lapsed into the sin of simony, by purchasing for money the see of London from King Wulfhere.[3]

This happened, however, some years after the date which we have reached—the time when Penda was exercising his domination

---

[1] Bede, iii. 22.   [2] Odo, Edmund's archbishop, was however an Anglo-Dane
[3] *Ibid.*, iii. 7.

over most of the English kingdoms. That hegemony probably extended over the Britons of Wales also, since we find that Welsh princes are named among his auxiliaries. But whether Cadwallader, the son of Cadwallon, and the rest, marched as the allies or the vassals of Penda, it is not possible to determine with certainty. Oswy's first endeavours to maintain his independence from the Mercian were certainly unsuccessful. In 651 he slew Oswin of Deira, under circumstances that reflected no great credit on himself,[1] but he did not thereby succeed in uniting Southern Northumbria to his own Bernician realm. The Deirans chose as Oswin's successor Aethelwald, son of St. Oswald, and refused to submit to Oswy. The new king called in Penda, and by doing homage to him preserved himself from his uncle Oswy.

What was the cause of the last war between the Mercian and the Bernician kings we do not know, but possibly Penda resented Oswy's religious dealings with Essex and his other southern vassal states, and detected a political meaning beneath them. At any rate, in 655 he marched against Bernicia at the head of all his auxiliaries, English and Welsh—thirty kings or kinglets are said to have been seen in his host. Their strength was so overwhelming that Oswy fled to the far North, took refuge in the insular castle of Giudi or Judeu, on the Firth of Forth, and sent his royal treasure as a peace-offering to the invader, a sum so great that it was remembered in Welsh legend as " the ransom of Judeu". But Penda refused to accept it,[2] saying that he had come to make an end of Oswy and his men, not to take tribute. Whereupon the Bernician vowed that if the pagan would not accept his gift, it should be offered to one who would accept it, the God of battles. He marched out to fight, with his son Alchfrid, at the head of an army which did not amount to one-third of the forces of the confederacy opposed to him, and met Penda on the banks of the river Winwaed, whose identification is not quite certain.[3] There was

---

[1] Oswy, we are told (Bede, iii. 23), invaded Deira in such force that Oswin dared not face him, but disbanded his army and hid himself. He was betrayed to his rival by a treacherous host, and promptly put to death. This was considered the sole blot on Oswy's otherwise blameless reign.

[2] So Bede, iii. 24; but the *Historia Brittonum*, cap. 65, says that Penda took the treasure, distributed it among his auxiliaries, and went on nevertheless to fight.

[3] If Giudi or Judeu is the castle on the Firth of which Bede speaks elsewhere (i. 12) —Inchkeith, or less probably Dunbar or Edinburgh—it is very strange that

division and treachery, however, in the Mercian host. Catgabail, one of the Welsh kings, withdrew his contingent in the darkness of the night before the meeting, " whence he was afterwards called Catgabail Catguonmed " (battle-eager battle-shunner),[1] and Aethelwald of Deira drew apart, and did not engage at the moment of the general advance. Evidently Penda's auxiliaries, Welsh and English, had endured his domination long enough, and had little heart for the fray. This may account for his unexpected defeat; he fell himself in the forefront of the battle, and with him Aethelhere, King of East Anglia, and many Welsh princes. So ended this vigorous and warlike old heathen, who is said to have been nearly eighty years of age when he died the warrior's death. He is often treated as a mere hindering force in the evolution of English history; but this seems a misconception. It is useless to asser' that he prevented Northumbria under Edwin and Oswald from establishing a permanent hegemony over all the English states. The same chance was given to the northern realm under their successor Oswy, and after initial successes, as notable as those of the two earlier kings, he failed in the task, just as they had done, though no Penda opposed or slew him. The fact was that the English states were not yet ripe for close union. But Penda accomplished something positive, in that he at least built up a larger Mercia, as a permanent unit which survived him. The attempts of Oswy and other kings to break it up, and resolve it into its former component parts, failed, because a cohesion had been created which defied the destroyer. This cohesion was undoubtedly the result of the quarter of a century of victorious campaigns fought out in company, to which Penda had led his subjects.

For a few years after the battle of the Winwaed Oswy was supreme in England. He re-annexed Deira to Bernicia,[2] and added also to his immediate dominions not only the lands of the Lindiswaras about Lincoln, but North Mercia—the region north of Trent

---

the battle should have taken place at Winwedfield, near Leeds, the place usually identified with the Winwaed. We should have expected it to be within the bounds of Bernicia, and probably very far north, on the Tweed or in Lothian. Yet Bede says that Oswy "concluded the war *in regione Loidis*," which seems to bring us to Leeds. Possibly, when his overtures were rejected, he took the offensive in despair, and advanced into Deira to meet Penda and his auxiliaries.

[1] *Historia Brittonum*, cap. 65.

[2] What became of Aethelwald, last separate King of Deira, we do not know.

in the modern Derbyshire and Nottinghamshire. To his son-in-law Peada, the Christian son of Penda, he left Southern Mercia, south of Trent; but when this pious prince was murdered—by domestic treachery it is said—in 656, it would seem that Oswy annexed this remnant of the original Mercian realm, and held it for three years. He must at the same time have been enjoying a suzerainty over all Eastern England : Sigebert of Essex was certainly his vassal, and no doubt also Aethelwald of East Anglia, who had succeeded Penda's friend Aethelhere, who fell with his master at Winwaed field. Nor is there any reason to suppose that Coenwalch of Wessex, an old enemy of Mercia, refused his homage. Indeed, the wars of this prince against the West Welsh of Damnonia, which cover a period that begins before Penda's fall and ends long after it, may be closely connected with an alliance with Oswy, since all the Welsh were certainly Penda's allies. In 652 Coenwalch fights at Bradford-on-Avon; in 658 "at the Pens" (*aet Peonnum*), *i.e.*, at Pen-Selwood, in the same direction, on the borders of Wilts and Somerset. The second battle must have been a considerable victory, as we are told that the Britons were driven beyond the Parret (Pedrida). Yet it does not seem that the borders of Wessex were extended to that limit, the conquest of Mid-Somersetshire being reserved for one of Coenwalch's successors. The kingdom does not seem to have made much permanent or considerable growth westward between the conquests of Ceawlin and those of Ine.

There is much greater difficulty in making out the political condition of the country north-west of Wessex in Oswy's day. We have seen [1] that the land of the Hwiccas, on the Lower Severn, was probably taken from King Cynegils and annexed by Penda in 628, after the battle of Cirencester. What was its fate when that great king fell and his realm was broken up ? We have no definite statement on the point in Bede or elsewhere; but we find *reges*, or *subreguli*, of the Hwiccas starting at a date not later, and probably somewhat earlier, than 661. They have purely Northumbrian names—Eanfrith, Eanhere, Osric, Oswald, Oshere, Aethelric—a fact which makes it highly probable that Oswy set up a younger branch of his own house in Hwiccia in 655, which was sufficiently well established there to survive the ultimate extinction of his power as overlord in Central England.

[1] See p. 276.

This cutting short of the Northumbrian supremacy began in the year 659, with the rebellion of the Mercians, under Wulfhere, a younger son of Penda, who had lived in exile or obscurity till this moment. He is said to have been proclaimed king by the three *duces* (ealdormen) of the Mercians—Immin, Eafa and Eadbert— and to have recovered all his father's dominions, even as far as the Humber, for Lindsey was certainly in his power a little later. His reign of seventeen years seems to have been occupied in a long war with Oswy, who strove strenuously, but without success, to maintain or recover his grasp on the Midlands. But so far was he from success that Wulfhere not only reconstituted the old Mercian realm, but won a supremacy over all the minor kings of the South and the East. He is found in 665-66 not only recognised as suzerain by the rulers of Essex, but actually appointing a Bishop of London without their consent being asked. As to Wessex, he wrought terrible havoc upon it, and did his best to destroy its unity. Aethelwalch of Sussex, the remotest of all the Saxon kingdoms, is recorded as his vassal a few years later.

The strife between Mercia and Wessex is said in the Chronicle to have begun in 661, two years after Wulfhere's accession. The Mercian began the campaign by defeating Coenwalch at Posentes-byrig, which seems to be Pontesbury in Shropshire, not far south of Shrewsbury. The locality of the battle seems to suggest that Coenwalch must have been advancing, in company with Eanfrith, the King of the Hwiccas, to execute a diversion in favour of their ally or suzerain Oswy. For unless the host of Wessex had advanced across Hwiccia, it could not have reached the neighbourhood of Shrewsbury. The defeat must have been complete, as Wulfhere is found immediately after devastating Ashdown, the ancient name for the region of West Berkshire. A nephew and a cousin of Coenwalch are recorded by the Chronicle to have died at this conjuncture, perhaps slain in opposing the invader. But the advance of the Mercian army was not stayed ; in the same year, 661, it is recorded that Wulfhere laid everything waste as far as the shore of the Channel. He then, to cut short the power of Wessex, made a present of the Jutish land of the Meonwaras, on both sides of Southampton Water, to Aethelwalch, King of Sussex, who was his vassal and godson. This region must have been, since Ceawlin's time at least, attached by direct or indirect subjection to Wessex. At the same

time, Wulfhere made Aethelwalch suzerain over the *subregulus* of
the Wight, where the Jutish royal house was still subsisting.[1]

This blow at Wessex was followed by a depression of the power
of the house of Cerdic that lasted for a whole generation; it was
not for twenty-five years that the lost land on Southampton Water
was recovered. Apparently the West Welsh of Damnonia were
encouraged to make strenuous attempts to win back what they had
lost; in 667 [2] we hear of a second battle of Mount Badon, between
Coenwalch and the Britons, and fighting at Bath implies that the
Celts were in Saxon territory. Nor was this all; when Coenwalch
died in 672 his realm seems to have lapsed into anarchy. The
Chronicle tells us that Seaxburh, his widow, reigned for one year
after his death. Such an event, unparalleled among the old English
dynasties, seems only explicable on the idea that she must have
ruled as regent for an infant son whose name has perished. Bede,
on the other hand, says that on Coenwalch's decease the *subreguli*
of Wessex "took upon themselves the kingdom, and dividing it
among them held it for ten years".[3] We have during this period
a mention of two kings—Centwine, brother of Coenwalch, and
Aescwin, his distant cousin, a representative of the house of Ceolwulf—who may have been either rivals or else two royal ealdormen,
who in a time of general confusion successively took upon themselves the kingly title. It is impossible to reject Bede's distinct
statement that Wessex reverted for ten years to a state of divided
rule, recalling the earlier anarchy that seems to have prevailed after
Ceawlin's fall in 591. Possibly Wulfhere supported one claimant
against the others: at any rate the Chronicle relates that he fought
with Aescwin in 675 at "Biedanheafde" (a spot that cannot be
identified), and apparently defeated him. Obviously it would be to
the Mercians' interest to keep Wessex weak and divided. A few
years later (682) we hear of Centwine fighting with Britons, and
driving them "to the sea": presumably this implies that the

---

[1] See Chronicle, *sub anno* 661, and Bede, iv. 13. Bede's "not long before
681" seems to mean twenty years.

[2] The second battle of the Mons Badonicus is only recorded in the *Annales
Cambriae*. It is placed under 665, but the *Annales* are one or two years in arrears
at this time, as is shown by the fact that they place the Great Comet of 678 under
676, and the plague of 684 under 682. The death of Oswy in 670 is put to 669, one
year wrong only.

[3] Bede, *E. H.*, iv. 12.

Damnonians had again taken advantage of the weakness of Wessex in order to invade it, but were driven back to the shores of the Bristol Channel. Certainly no advance of the Saxon border is implied, as some historians seem to have inferred. This was a time of chaos, not of growth.

The last eleven years of Oswy (659-70), after the rise of Wulfhere, must have been a time of diminished power for Northumbria, but it does not appear that its internal strength and prosperity had much suffered. Oswy seems still to have been considered the greatest king in Britain, even though he was no longer its undisputed master. There is no sign that his realm suffered, like Wessex, from Mercian invasions. Allied to Earconbert of Kent, and to Coenwalch of Wessex and his successors, he was strong enough to keep Wulfhere in check, though not to subdue him. The most important event of his later years had nothing to do with battles or with secular politics, yet was of the highest moment for the future history of England. This was the celebrated Synod of Whitby (664), at which he and the whole Northumbrian nation abandoned their connection with the Church of Iona, and put themselves into communion with Canterbury and Rome.

Oswald and Oswy, as will be remembered, had been themselves converted and baptised at Iona, and had brought down with them to Northumbria, when they became kings, Aidan and Finan, the Scottish preachers to whom the second and effectual evangelisation of Bernicia and Deira was due. The survivors from Edwin's earlier Roman mission were few. What Bede calls "the episcopacy of the Scots among the English" lasted for thirty years, and Oswy "having been instructed and baptised by them, and being perfectly skilled in their language, thought nothing better than what they taught". In his old age, however, he fell under other influences; his wife, Eanflaed, the daughter of Edwin, had been reared in Kent, and steadfastly adhered to the Church in which she had been brought up: and his son, Alchfrid, whom he had made under-king in Deira, was of the same persuasion, owing to the teaching, as we are told, of Wilfred, Abbot of Ripon, who had been trained at Lyons and Rome, and held the Scots in contempt. The queen and prince had sufficient influence with Oswy to induce him to put aside his predisposition in favour of his original teachers, and to undertake a serious inquiry into the relations of the Irish and the Roman

Churches. He was, as we are told, a sincerely religious man, and had long been vexed by the continuous friction caused by the divergent views of the two bodies of mission workers, both of whom he readily supported. For he was on friendly terms with the East Anglian and West Saxon kings and bishops, who held to the Roman allegiance, though his own clergy in Northumbria, and the teachers whom he had sent out into Mercia and Essex, were of the other confession. At his own court the absurd sight of two Easters kept in continuous weeks was sometimes to be seen, "for on the day when the King, having ended his fasting, was keeping the Paschal Feast, the Queen and her retainers would be still fasting, and celebrating Palm Sunday".[1] It is quite possible that Oswy had already made up his mind to conform to the ceremonial and accept the suzerainty of Rome, in order to secure unity for the English Church, before he summoned the synod of Whitby. But he allowed a prolonged discussion of the points at issue before he declared his decision. On the one side appeared his own bishop, Colman the Scot, and Cedd, who had been consecrated in Northumbria bishop of the East Saxons, with many of their clergy. On the other, was Wilfred, Abbot of Ripon; Agilberct, Bishop of the West Saxons, who chanced to be on the spot as a visitor; James, the last survivor from Paulinus's mission, and several others. The discussion was of a polyglot sort, for neither Agilberct nor Colman had a mastery of the English tongue, and Cedd had to act as interpreter.

The main topic over which the arguments ranged was, according to Bede, the usual point in dispute between Rome and the Western Churches—the much-vexed question of Easter, though no doubt the tonsure and the other minor divergencies had their place. Colman is said to have claimed for the Irish and British usage an immemorial antiquity, derived originally from the practice of St. John the Evangelist, and hallowed by the sanction of Columba and other saints. Wilfred, who spoke for the other side, quoted the authority of the Council of Nicaea, and contrasted the dignity and learning of the Apostolic See and the Continental Churches with the "rustic simplicity" of a small community in a remote island, which lacked the culture needed to understand the new calculations which had been adopted everywhere else. Rome was greater than Iona,

[1] Bede, E. H., iii. 25.

Peter than Columba, and Wilfred concluded by quoting the oft-misused text—" Thou art Peter, and upon this rock I will build My Church, and the gates of hell shall not prevail against it, and to thee I will give the keys of the kingdom of heaven ".[1]

Oswy, we are told, found a way to end the discussion by asking Colman whether the text was correctly quoted, and when the Scot owned that it so ran, declared that " if the keys of heaven are given to Peter, and he is the door keeper, I will not oppose him, but obey his decrees, lest when I come to the gate of heaven there be none to open to me, the guardian of the keys being my adversary ". The king's words are not to be taken literally, or counted a mark of naïve superstition and barbarous cunning, but were rather a humorous way of putting the fact that the authority of the whole Western Church weighed heavier than that of the Celtic remnant in the far West. He closed the controversy by announcing that he should conform to the Roman usage, and place himself in communication with the Church of Rome. Cedd, and the majority of the English priests of Northumbria, followed the example of the King, and conformed. But Colman, with his Scottish clerks, shook the dust of England from their feet, and retired to Iona. Oswy replaced him by one Tuda, " a good and religious man, who, though educated and ordained bishop among the Scots, yet kept the Catholic time of Easter ".

Thus ended the chance that Teutonic Britain might be permanently divided into two Churches, the one in communion with Rome, the other with the Celtic peoples of the West. Nor can it be doubted that Oswy's decision was in every way beneficial to the English. The connection with the Papacy was fraught with dangers and difficulties in the future ; before the next generation was over the first of those innumerable appeals to Rome, which were to cause so much trouble throughout the Middle Ages, had been made. But for the present the advantages of the decision made at Whitby were clear and decisive. It was more profitable for the infant Church of England to be in touch with the bulk of Western Christendom than with the Scots alone, if it was to be an active and useful limb of the great Christian community. The Celtic Church produced many great saints and many devoted missionaries, but it was always lacking in order and organisation.

[1] Bede, *E. H.*, iii. 25.

Fervour and ascetic self-sacrifice are essential virtues for those who have to build up a Church, but for those who have to administer a Church already solidly constituted, tact, practical wisdom, and a broad charity of spirit are also necessary. The Celtic Church put before it as its highest aim the extension of the monastic ideal, as is sufficiently shown by the fact that the great tribal monastery was the centre of religious life, while the bishop was a comparatively unimportant personage, inferior to the abbot in status, and only necessary because he alone could make priests or consecrate sacred edifices. But all mankind, even in the most ideally pious nation, could not be swept into monasteries. Nor is the perfection of the individual soul by ascetic rules the sole aim of Christianity. As an organisation for the spiritual government of a mixed community the Celtic system left much to be desired. Its influence for good was much diminished by its narrow ideal. Most of all was it noticeable that it had no effect whatever as a unifying force for the nations among which it prevailed. The greatest blessing for Ireland would have been political consolidation, to put an end to its innumerable tribal wars. Absolutely nothing in this direction was accomplished by its Church; instead, the great monastery of each sept became a centre of its local particularism. Ireland, for want of a proper episcopal organisation, was from the ecclesiastical point of view a group of disconnected and independent monasteries. How invaluable, on the other hand, the Roman organisation proved to England as a unifying influence will be shown in the next chapter. It was in Church Synods that the representatives of the English kingdoms first learnt to take peaceful counsel together; a common obedience to the primate taught them in due time the reasonableness of a common obedience to a single high-king.

Almost the first historical notice that we get in England after the Council of Whitby marks a laudable common interest between North and South as to the state of the Church. Only a few months after its end a great pestilence swept over the island, in which died both Archbishop Deusdedit, the first native primate, and Earconbert, King of Kent, a very religious prince who showed his zeal for the faith by destroying the few surviving idol temples in his realm, and fining men who would not keep the Lenten fast. We are told that the appointment of a successor for Deusdedit was a common concern to Oswy and to Ecgbert, the new King of Kent, and that "with the consent of the Holy Church of the English nation"[1] (presumably after a synod of some sort) they chose in common one Wighard for primate, and sent him to Rome, to receive consecration and the pallium from Pope Vitalian. But the archbishop-designate died not long after he had delivered his credentials, a victim to a pestilence which raged in Italy no less than in England (665), and the Pope sent back in his stead the last and greatest of the foreign primates, the celebrated Theodore of Tarsus, who did not reach Canterbury for more than three years after his predecessor's death. Of him there is much to tell hereafter.

Oswy's later years are said to have been troubled by dissensions with his eldest son, Alchfrid, whom he had made under-king in Deira. But whether they came to open war, and whether Alchfrid died before his father, or was thrust into exile, we are not informed. It is only certain that when Oswy died, on February 15, 671, he was succeeded by his second son, Ecgfrith, and not by his natural heir. It would seem that we must connect with this strife between the old king and Alchfrid the beginnings of an ecclesiastical dispute, which was to vex Northumbria for many a year. Tuda having died in 664, Alchfrid designated as bishop his teacher and confidant, Wilfred, Abbot of Ripon, the successful controversialist of the Synod of Whitby, and sent him over seas to be consecrated by his old friend, Agilberct, once bishop of the West Saxons but now established at Paris. Wilfred was duly ordained to the office, at Compiègne in a great meeting of Frankish prelates, but he tarried some time before returning. Whereupon Oswy, either because he had now quarrelled with his son, or because he was irritated by Wilfred's long absence,[2] nominated another bishop, Chad (Ceadda), the saintly brother of Cedd, the bishop of the East Saxons. This holy man was consecrated by Wini, the bishop of Coenwalch of Wessex, assisted by two Celtic prelates who had conformed to the Roman method of keeping Easter.[3] Thus from 665 onward there were two rival bishops of Northumbria, but Chad was in possession, while Wilfred tarried at Canterbury, where he made himself useful by performing episcopal functions during the long vacancy of the

[1] Bede, *E. H.*, iii. 29.

[2] Eddius, Wilfred's biographer, says that Oswy was worked upon by secret enemies of Wilfred, old allies of Colman, who told him that the Church would suffer from the unreasonably long absence of its designated pastor.

[3] Presumably Damnonian bishops, certainly not Welsh.

see that fell between the death of Wighard and the arrival of Theodore of Tarsus.

Of Oswy's end we know no more than that, two years before his death, he was reconciled by Theodore of Tarsus to Wilfred, and allowed him to return to his see (669), while Chad, who showed wonderful humility of spirit, and refused to stand out for his own cause "judging himself never to have been worthy of the episcopal office," was compensated by being transferred to the bishopric of Mercia, then vacant. This transaction proves that Oswy and Wulfhere must at the moment have been at peace, for otherwise the southern king would never have allowed a Northumbrian prelate—however great his personal sanctity—to be thrust upon him. The reconciliation of Oswy and Wilfred seems to have been complete, since we are told that in his last year of life the king determined to make a pilgrimage to Rome, and begged the bishop to accompany him. All arrangements had been made, and a large treasure spent, when Oswy's failing health prevented the expedition from starting, and not long after he died. He still seems to have been regarded as the most important king in Britain, though he had never recovered the lands beyond Humber, which Wulfhere had torn from him. On the other hand we are told that he was still, when he died, supreme not only over Deira and Bernicia, but over a great part of the Picts. By this, Bede seems to mean not only the Niduarian Picts of Galloway, but some at least of the northern Picts beyond Forth. The connection seems to have come from the marriage of Oswy's brother, Eanfrith, to a Pictish princess, in whose right "Tolargain Mac Anfrith," the Northumbrian king's nephew, reigned for some years over Pictland.[1] On Tolargain's death in 657, Oswy seems to have asserted and maintained a domination over the lands immediately north of Forth, though another Pictish prince, Gartnaid, son of Donnel, reigned in the farther Highlands. A certain Bernhaeth, who appears as Ealdorman (*dux*) or *subregulus* about 670-72 was probably Oswy's lieutenant for the part of Pictland which he retained under his power. Along with this region

---

[1] It must be remembered that the Picts adhered to the ancient, but in these latter days abnormal, custom of preferring the female line of succession to the male in the kingship (Bede, *E. H.*, i. 1). There does not seem in the whole series of Pictish kings to be a case of son following father; the succession would normally go to nephews on the female side.

there can be no doubt that Oswy was also supreme over the Welsh kingdom of Strathclyde—perhaps it was actually annexed to Bernicia, since no names of kings of Alclyde appear between 658 and 694, and we are distinctly told that Oswy and his son, Ecgfrith, owned Britons as well as Picts among their subjects.[1]

[1] Bede, iv. 26.

CHAPTER XV

THE BALANCE OF POWER. MERCIA, NORTHUMBRIA AND WESSEX, (671-709)

AT the moment of Oswy's death in 671 the future development of the English States was still a matter on which prophecy would have been difficult. It might, however, have been foreseen that a permanent domination of Northumbria over the southern kingdoms was improbable. The failure of Edwin and Oswald to hold the "imperium" which they had won counted for comparatively little; but that of Oswy, whose opportunities were greater than those of his predecessors—for all Mercia had been for three years crushed beneath his feet—was conclusive. The shattered Mercian realm had reunited itself under Wulfhere, despite of all difficulties, had reasserted its independence, and won back its border as far as the Humber. Nay more, it had established a suzerainty over Essex, Sussex and East Anglia, and had almost annihilated the ill-compacted West Saxon state, which had fallen into chaos and anarchy. It looked as if the future was with Mercia, whose central position gave it a unique facility for dealing with its enemies in detail. Northumbria had no such geographical advantages, and the other States were too small and weak to vie with the realm of the house of Penda. Moreover, Mercia might still grow at the expense of the Welsh, a chance denied to all the other English states save Northumbria and Wessex. Indeed it would seem that expansion in this direction was actually taking place in Wulfhere's reign. In the third quarter of the seventh century we find a new district beyond Severn in the hands of the English, with a *sub-regulus* who was the vassal of Mercia, and (a little later) a bishop of its own. This was the land of the Magesaetas or Hecanas, which comprised the modern Herefordshire, with South Shropshire and the Forest of Dean. This annexation may have been made by Penda, but it is unlikely, as he was the ally of the Welsh, and had their aid in all his wars, from Heathfield down to the day of his death at the Winwaed. It was more probably the work of Wulfhere, whose brother, Merewald, is recorded to have been the first alderman or sub-king of the Hecanas, the founder of the abbey of Leominster, and the father of the two sainted nuns Mildred and Mildgyth.[1]

This sub-kingdom of the Magesaetas was the last considerable patch of territory won from the Welsh of the Severn valley by the English. There were small modifications of the boundary in the eighth century in favour of Mercia, but no great addition was made. The extent of the district is indicated by that of the see of Hereford, whose first bishop died in 688; it included the land between Wye and Severn from the Bristol Channel northward, and at its northern extremity reached the Severn on each side of the Wrekin, though Mercia proper was reckoned to include some small portion of the land south of that river, in the immediate neighbourhood of Pengwyrn, the Welsh town which had changed its name to Shrewsbury (Scrobbesbyrig). The Magesaetan boundary westward was not that of modern England[2]; the Welsh still held rough lands like Clun Forest and Ewyas. The dialect of Herefordshire seems to show that the settlers were not pure Angles, but included Hwiccian elements.

It seems probable that the whole Mercian realm, as held by Wulfhere, consisted of the original nucleus on both sides of Trent with which Penda had started in 626, increased by the subject provinces of the Magesaetas, Hwiccas, Gyrwas and Lindiswaras,[3] each governed by a local prince, whose status is indicated by the fact that his title fluctuates between *subregulus* and *dux*, *i.e.*, between king and ealdorman. It remains uncertain whether the

[1] I see no reason to doubt the existence of Merewald, king of the "West Angles," West Mercians, or Hecanas, as he is called in various places. He is not named by Bede, but occurs in the Mercian genealogical table preserved by Florence of Worcester, and is mentioned as the husband of Eormenburh, daughter of Eormenred, King of Kent, in the sketch of the Kentish royal house in the same author. But his best warrant is that he is always given as father of St. Mildred, a well-known saint whose convent was in the eighth century the glory of Thanet.

[2] So at least we may conclude from the boundary of the diocese of Hereford.

[3] The names of Lindiswara princes recorded in Florence of Worcester's genealogies suggest Northumbrian origin, like those of the Hwiccas.

West Saxon district north of Thames, the land of the Chilternsaetas, round Dorchester, Aylesbury and Eynsham, was in Wulfhere's hands. The deplorable state of Wessex at the time renders this highly probable. If so it must have been lost again by Mercia at some subsequent date, since the kings of the house of Ceawlin were in possession of it again in the early eighth century. Surrey was certainly under Wulfhere's influence.

But great and powerful though Mercia was in the year 671, Northumbria was still strong enough to renew the struggle for supremacy, and, if the lands of its British and Pictish vassals north of Solway are taken into consideration, its whole empire was no less in extent than that of the southern kingdom. Ecgfrith, the son and successor of Oswy, seems to have resolved to take up the struggle in which his father had failed. After putting down, in the very commencement of his reign (671-72), a rising of the northern Picts,[1] he turned three years later to attack Wulfhere, probably leaguing himself with Aescwin of Wessex, whose unsuccessful campaigns against the Mercians have been already narrated, and with Lothere of Kent.[2] If his ally failed, Ecgfrith himself seems to have been more successful, as he recovered the province of the Lindiswaras,[3] and held it from 675 (or perhaps a little earlier) till 679. We are even told by one almost contemporary writer that the Northumbrian expelled Wulfhere from his whole kingdom, a statement which can hardly be accepted.[4] But it is certain that the Mercian king died in 675, the year of his last battle of "Biadanheafod," and was succeeded by his younger brother Aethelred.

Apparently this prince continued the war with Ecgfrith and his allies, for in 676, the year after his accession, we are told that he cruelly ravaged Kent, burning many monasteries and the cathedral and city of Rochester.[5] But the struggle did not come to a head

---

[1] This rebellion and the victory of Ecgfrith and his *subregulus* Bernhaeth are told in some detail in the life of Wilfred, by Eddius, § xix.

[2] Bede, *E. H.*, iv. 12.

[3] See p. 304.

[4] The war betwe en Ecgfrith and Wulfhere must have commenced later than 673, since in that year the Northumbrian king was present at Archbishop Theodore's great synod, which was held at Hertford. Clearly Ecgfrith could not have been at that spot if he were at war with Mercia, nor could a synod at which bishops from all the states were present have been held in time of war.

[5] A. S. Chronicle, 676, and Bede, *E. H.*, iii. 12.

till a great pitched battle was fought on the Trent in 679. It was evidently a victory for the Mercians, since a story told by Bede shows us that Aethelred's army had possession of the battle-field,[1] and Aelfwin, Ecgfrith's brother, is recorded to have been slain. But the Northumbrians if beaten were not disheartened, "and there was every reason to expect more bloody war, and a more lasting enmity between those kings and their fierce nations". Peace, however, was unexpectedly brought about by the mediation of Archbishop Theodore, who was equally respected by both parties. The Mercians paid a heavy *weregeld* for Aelfwin's death, but Ecgfrith, on the other hand, surrendered the province of Lindsey, so that the balance of profit was on the side of Aethelred. The treaty seems to have included Ecgfrith's allies of Kent and Wessex, "and peace continued long after between the kings and their kingdoms".[2] Indeed it was to be thirty-five years before we have another record of war between the two chief powers, Mercia and Northumbria—an interval unparalleled since the first strife between the greater English States began, in the time of Edwin and Penda, and not to be repeated again in their later history. During this long time we shall find Northumbria entirely occupied with northern wars against the Celts, and Wessex striving both with the Damnonians and with her smaller Teutonic neighbours, Kent and Sussex. But as far as we can judge, a real balance of power had been created, and no king disturbed it by grasping at the "imperium" which Edwin or Penda, Oswy or Wulfhere, had exercised over his neighbours.

Into the earlier part of this long peaceful interval fell the major part of the activity of the great primate Theodore of Tarsus (669-90), though, as we have already seen, he had been busy at his work of organisation ever since he arrived in England. To the same period belongs the chequered career of the Northumbrian prelate Wilfred, whose grievances and triumphs fill such a disproportionate space in Bede's history, and are set forth at even greater length by his biographer Eddius.

Theodore, whose career was far more important than that of Wilfred, deserves a careful study. He had been, as it will be re-

---

[1] *E. H.*, iv. 22. A Northumbrian noble, left for dead on the field, is captured by Aethelred's soldiers and sold as a slave.

[2] Bede, iv., xxi.

membered, nominated to the primacy by Pope Vitalian in 668, after the death at Rome of the archbishop-designate Wighard. He was a Cilician by birth, and a monk by training : apparently he had been driven westward, with many other refugees, by the first irruptions of the Saracens into his native district. It seems that Vitalian selected him for a difficult post, which had already been refused by two other notable men, because of his unusual combination of learning, saintliness of life, and practical wisdom. The one doubt as to the wisdom of the appointment was caused by his age—he had reached his sixty-sixth year; but his vigour was unbroken, as was sufficiently shown by the fact that he survived his appointment by twenty-two years, most of which were spent in active and trying work. Theodore was ordained in 668, and sent off in company with the Abbot Hadrian, an African monk excellently skilled in Greek as well as in Latin literature, who was his helper throughout the whole of his career. It was to the fact that the archbishop was a Greek by birth, and the abbot a Greek scholar, that Canterbury became and remained for some generations a centre of Greek learning, and that the Hellenic tongue was well known in England when it was almost unknown in the other Western Kingdoms.[1] Their arrival in England was, however, delayed by the suspicions of Ebroin, the Frankish mayor of the Palace, who feared—as we read with some surprise—that Theodore, since he was a Greek, might be acting as an emissary of the Emperor Constans II., and designing to stir up the Kings of England to attack the Merovingian realm for some obscure Byzantine object.[2] After a long detention in Gaul the archbishop only reached Canterbury in 669.

The work of Theodore's long and green old-age was the organisation of the English Church on a permanent and well-ordered basis. Hitherto it retained something of its original missionary character, though all England was now converted, save the insignificant kingdom of Sussex, and the Jutes of the Isle of Wight, whose remoteness and obscurity was still keeping them out of the movement which had swept over the rest of the island. Even in this last dark corner

---

[1] Bede, *E. H.*, v. 20.

[2] The idea was not so strange as it seems at first sight. In 668 Constans was in Sicily, and deeply interested in West European politics. He had lately been to Rome, which had not been visited by any emperor since Romulus Augustulus, and was altogether an abnormal and disturbing influence in the West.

there were Christian kings and Christian teachers, though the bulk of the people still clung to the old faith.

Down to the arrival of Theodore the English States had (with the exception of Kent) possessed but a single bishop each, and he in all cases retained something of his original status as the king's chaplain : the sees were generally established in the royal cities, and the bishop was very often at his master's side. Churches in the country side were comparatively few. The bishop's priests seem to have habitually lived near him, and to have gone out in summer for long tours to baptise and to preach. The piety of wealthy laymen generally took shape in the founding of a monastery, rather than in the establishment of anything like a localised parochial system. Indeed there would seem to have been a great lack of priests in the country-side, the majority of persons who felt a vocation for holy orders preferring to enter a religious community. Immense districts like Wessex, Northumbria or Mercia could not be adequately served by a single bishop, whose duties at court as a member of the king's council of *sapientes* must often have interfered with his normal avocation as the shepherd of the vast flock entrusted to him. Nor could the people be kept in the daily course of Christian life, in any adequate fashion, by an itinerant clergy whose visits to any particular village must have been few and far between.

The whole Church had entered the Roman obedience in consequence of the Synod of Whitby, but the union had never been brought to practical working, because Archbishop Deusdedit had died just after the union was accomplished, and the primacy had been vacant ever since. Theodore had to start his career by claiming the allegiance of the regions which had been lately in the Irish communion—Northumbria, Mercia and Essex. In all of them the actual condition of the Church was irregular—Chad was holding the See of York, but by a doubtful title, his predecessor Wilfred being in exile at Canterbury. Wini, Bishop of Wessex, had been expelled from his own land, but had bought the See of Essex from King Wulfhere, and was residing in London in simoniacal possession of it. Jaruman, Bishop of Mercia, was lately dead (667) and that immense kingdom had no spiritual head. Rochester was also vacant. Boniface of East Anglia, indeed, was the only bishop in England who was in legal and undisputed possession of his proper see, and he was aged and infirm.

Theodore's first duty, therefore, was to assert his primatial authority, by restoring order among the subject sees, and filling up the vacancies. His task was rendered easy at the point where most trouble might have been expected: Chad, the meek and saintly occupant of the Northumbrian bishopric, consented without difficulty to resign his place to Wilfred. Nor did he make the least objection when Theodore suggested that his consecration had been irregular (since Celtic bishops had taken part in it), and insisted on reordaining him before he transferred him to the vast diocese of Mercia. Chad moved southward in obedience to the orders of his superior, and established himself at Lichfield, which henceforth became the spiritual centre of the kingdom. Wilfred moved back to York, and presided with great energy over the affairs of the northern realm for the next nine years. Boniface of East Anglia resigned, on account of bodily infirmity, and Bisi was ordained to his place. The vacant Rochester was filled up by the nomination of a certain Putta, "more addicted to simplicity of life than to activity in worldly affairs," whose docility was probably his best recommendation to Theodore. Coenwalch, King of Wessex, was allowed to choose as his bishop Lothere (Eleutherius), a nephew of the earlier occupant of the see, Agilberct, whom he had imported from Gaul. Wini at London seems to have been left undisturbed, though his election had been simoniacal.

Thus, within two years after his arrival, Theodore had restored order to the episcopate; each of the existing sees had been duly provided with a bishop, and all had acknowledged the primacy of Canterbury. But the great archbishop's designs aimed at something further; he had come to the conclusion that many of the tribal dioceses were far too large for practical administration, and it was his desire to cut them up into smaller and more wieldy units. To this opposition might be expected; the actual tenants of the sees might object to surrender the importance which they enjoyed through being each the sole spiritual ruler of a kingdom. And the princes might prefer to have at hand a single bishop established at their court, rather than several bishops scattered round their realms. The unity of the State seemed to be strengthened by the unity of the bishopric ; and the appointment of separate bishops for the sub-kingdoms might seem to favour decentralisation and local particularism, which an imperial king of the type of Oswy or

Wulfhere might fear. That such objections existed is shown by
what occurred at the Synod of Hertford (Sept. 24, 673). This was
the first meeting of the united English Church, and was summoned
by Theodore to confirm the arrangements which he had already
made, and to establish a general system of organisation for the
whole island. Its acts, preserved by Bede, give interesting information as to Theodore's aims. They provide that no bishop shall
trespass in the diocese of another, that monks shall not wander at
their will from monastery to monastery, that a priest shall not quit
his diocesan without letters dismissory, that a convocation of the
whole Church should be held once a year at "Cloveshoch"—an
unknown locality probably in some central position near London.[1]
There were some clauses dealing with the canonical celebration of
Easter, and with the rules for lawful marriage and divorce. All
this was passed without objection; but Theodore's ninth proposi-
tion "that more bishops be made, as the multitude of believers
increases" was not ratified, but for the present passed over, evidently because objection, whether from clerical or from lay quarters,
was offered.

The projected annual synods at Cloveshoch were not held,
probably because of the outbreak of war between Northumbria and
Mercia in 675, which set all England in confusion for some years.
But before it began, Theodore had taken the first step in dividing
up the great tribal bishoprics. In 674 when Bisi of East Anglia
resigned on account of infirmity, two sees were created, one at Dunwich for Suffolk, the other at Elmham for Norfolk. It is probable
that a quarrel between Theodore and Winfrith, the successor of
Chad as Bishop of Mercia, recorded in the following year, may have
been due to the resistance of that prelate to the carrying out of a
similar division in his own vast diocese. The archbishop ended by
deposing his suffragan, who retired to the continent—perhaps in
order to make an appeal to Rome.[2] But Sexwulf, his successor,
held the undivided Mercian see for some years; the war had broken
out, and Theodore probably thought that he had better not meddle
with Mercia while it was in progress. But before it was over he
obtained a great triumph in Northumbria. King Ecgfrith had

[1] Perhaps Cliffe-at-Hoo. Two notable synods were held at this place in the
eighth century.
[2] See notes to Plummer's edition of Bede, ii. p. 167.

quarrelled with his bishop, Wilfred, and, to revenge himself, espoused eagerly the archbishop's plan for splitting up the broad tribal
bishoprics; for no better means could be devised for humbling a
masterful man, who rejoiced in the breadth of his sphere of authority,
than to take from him the greater part of his diocese. The origin
of the strife between Ecgfrith and Wilfred is said to have dated for
some years back, when the latter had supported and encouraged the
Queen Aethelthryth (St. Audrey) in her determination to retire
into a nunnery, contrary to her husband's wish. When she had
taken the veil (672) Ecgfrith married again; his second wife,
Eormenburh, is said to have been a bitter enemy of Wilfred, and to
have stirred up the king against him, accusing him of pride, per-
versity, and an over great love of getting lands for the Church.
There was probably some truth in the accusation, for Wilfred was
undoubtedly a great lover of state and dignity, a very stiff-backed
adversary, who always stood upon his rights, and a great founder of
churches and monasteries. He has been compared in character, and
not inaptly, to Becket.

When Ecgfrith invited Theodore to York, and explained that
he was willing and indeed eager to fall in with his plans for dividing the Northumbrian diocese, the primate expressed his pleasure,
and proposed that it should be split into four parts—Wilfred should
keep York and Deira, but there should be two new Bernician sees
at Lindisfarne and Hexham, while the newly conquered district of
the Lindiswaras should form a fourth diocese. Wilfred's consent
was neither asked nor obtained, but at a meeting of the Northumbrian Council the division was proclaimed as an accomplished
fact. The injured prelate protested, and asked that reasons should
be shown for his humiliation. The king and primate replied that
no personal charge was made against him, but that the change was
made for the benefit of the Church—and this was true enough.
Wilfred announced that he should appeal to the Pope, and left the
kingdom without obtaining permission from either his spiritual or
his temporal suzerain.

This appeal and departure Theodore regarded as contumacious,
and Ecgfrith as treasonable. The primate, though he owed his
appointment to Pope Vitalian, was not inclined to welcome Roman
interference when his own authority was questioned. He therefore declared Wilfred deposed, and consecrated Bosa as bishop of

York, at the same time that he made Eadhaeth bishop of Lindsey, and Eata bishop of Bernicia. Ecgfrith is said to have taken
measures to secure that Wilfred should never see Rome ; according
to Eddius he induced his friend, Ebroin, the Frankish mayor of the
palace, to send myrmidons to kidnap or slay the exile. But Wilfred's ship was driven out of its course by storms, and he landed in
Frisia instead of in Neustria, and made his way from that heathen
land to Italy among many dangers. In 679 he reached Rome, and
laid his complaint before Pope Agatho. The pontiff thought that
he had been harshly treated, but at the same time held that Theodore's scheme for dividing up the Northumbrian diocese was wise
and necessary. After some delay he sent the exiled bishop back to
England, with letters in which a compromise was set forth. Wilfred
must be restored to his see, and the intruding bishops must resign ;
but when matters had been regularised in this fashion, Wilfred must
acquiesce in the division of his diocese, and name bishops for Lindsey
and Bernicia, whom Theodore should then consecrate. Before his
departure from Rome, Wilfred took part in the Council of 680,
which denounced the Monothelite heresy ; his signature as Bishop
of York is appended to its acts.

Returning in triumph to Northumbria, Wilfred presented the
papal letters to King Ecgfrith. But to his surprise and dismay the
monarch declared that he had probably bought them for money
and shut him up in prison. This was exactly the same line of conduct that William the Conqueror or Henry II. would have pursued,
in the days when seeking and importing bulls from Rome had become a well-known offence to temporal rulers. The three intrusive
bishops are said to have supported their master. After nine months
however, Ecgfrith released his prisoner from the castle of Dunbar,
and expelled him from the kingdom. Unable to tarry in Mercia,
because the Northumbrian king and Aethelred were now reconciled,
Wilfred made his way to Sussex, where the local prince Ethelwalch [1]
was a Christian, but the bulk of the tribe were still heathen.[2] This
king gladly received the exile, and begged him to take up missionary
work in his realm. In this task Wilfred was usefully and most successfully employed for six years (681-86). The starting of his career

[1] See p. 287-88.
[2] Though, oddly enough, an Archbishop of Canterbury, Deusdedit, and Damian
bishop of Rochester had been Sussex men.

as a preacher is said to have been much helped by the fact that he taught the barbarous people of the coast the art of sea-fishing, with which they were hitherto unacquainted, and by the providential chance that a great drought, which had ruined their crops, ended in a pleasant rain on the day upon which he held his first great public baptism. " By such benefits the bishop gained the affections of all, and they began to expect celestial profit when he preached, because by his ministry they had already received temporal profit." [1] Within six years the men of Sussex had all been converted, and Wilfred had founded, by the king's liberality, a monastery at Selsey, which became the seat of a new bishopric. Nor did his missionary work end here: in the first days of his exile he had befriended one Ceadwalla, a member of the West Saxon royal house, who had been outlawed and was living the life of an adventurer. When in 686 this prince cut his way to the throne of Wessex, and conquered the Jutes of the Isle of Wight, which was absolutely the last region in England to remain heathen, he made a gift of a quarter of its land to Wilfred, and gave him the charge of converting such of its people as he had not massacred. They were instructed and baptised by Wilfred's nephew Bernwine and his priest Hiddila. Thus the great bishop's banishment from the North turned to the advantage of the remotest and most barbarous South.

Archbishop Theodore, meanwhile, had, since Wilfred's fall, proceeded most successfully in his design for multiplying the English Episcopate. In 681 he had, with Ecgfrith's approval, established a second Bernician see at Hexham, and a bishopric for the Picts subject to Northumbria, both in Manau and beyond Forth, with its local centre at Abercorn in West Lothian, not far from the end of the Wall of Antoninus. Apparently he had succeeded in persuading King Aethelred to part the vast diocese of Mercia at an even earlier date, perhaps immediately after that pacification of 679 in which he had borne the part of mediator. But the details of the cutting up of Bishop Sexwulf's unwieldy domain must have taken some time to carry out. When completed they stood as follows: Sexwulf kept Lichfield and Mercia proper, Leicester became the seat of a bishop of the Middle Angles; the territory of the Hwiccas became the see of Worcester; Lindsey, now just recovered from Northumbria, received a new Mercian bishop who dwelt at Sidnacester (Stow). The

[1] Bede, *E. H.*, iv. 13.

land of the Chilternsaetas, recently conquered from Wessex, as it
seems, became another diocese, whose bishop was placed at Dorchester-on-Thames, the original religious centre of Wessex. But
when this land was won back by the house of Cerdic the Mercian
bishopric ceased. Finally, some years, as it seems, after the
establishment of the rest of the new creations, the Magesaetas
beyond Severn were organised into the bishopric of Hereford.[1]

Before the completion of these arrangements, Theodore held the
second of his great Synods, at Hatfield, on September 17th, 680, at
which not only bishops but abbots and " many venerable priests and
doctors " were present. Its object was to acknowledge and confirm
the proceedings of the Council held at Rome six months before,[2] by
anathematising the Monothelite heresy, and proclaiming the complete adhesion of the English Church to the orthodox doctrine of
the West. We are not informed that any notice was taken at the
synod of the difficulties turning on Wilfred's exile : he must at this
moment have been crossing Gaul on his way homeward, if he had
not already been cast into prison by King Ecgfrith. Theodore, in
either case, had no intention of restoring him to York.

Meanwhile secular affairs must once more attract our attention.
The peace between Mercia and Northumbria had left Ecgfrith free
to turn his attention to the lands over which he exercised, or at least
claimed, imperial suzerainty in the far North. The trouble in this
direction seems to have been caused by a Pictish prince, Bruide (or
Bridei), son of the daughter of King Talargain, and therefore a distant kinsman of Ecgfrith, since Talargain was son of Eanfrith, the
brother of Oswy, who had married the heiress of the royal line of the
Picts. Bruide (672-93), who seems to have held at first only the extreme northern regions about the Moray Firth, was a warlike
prince, who encroached on the territories of the southern Picts who
had submitted to Northumbria, probably while Ecgfrith was engaged
in his four-year Mercian War. He seems also to have allied himself
with Fearcha Fada, a king of the Dalriad Scots, and to have made
war with his help on the Strathclyde Britons, who were vassals of
Ecgfrith. Possibly they obtained assistance from the Scots of Ireland

---

[1] The idea that Putta, the exiled Bishop of Rochester, became first Bishop of
Hereford, as early as 676, seems to be a mistake (see Plummer's *Bede*, ii. 222).
We have no certain Bishop of Hereford before Tyrhtel, consecrated in 688.
[2] See p. 305.

also, for thus only is it easy to account for an almost inexplicable action of the Northumbrian king in 684.[1] In that year, as Bede and the *Ulster Chronicle* both tell us, Ecgfrith sent a fleet under his ealdorman Beorht (or Beorhtred) across the narrow seas, and ravaged the plain of Breg, the lands between Liffey and Boyne, "miserably wasting a harmless nation, which had always been friendly to the English, insomuch that not even churches and monasteries were spared".[2] This is the last indication that the kings of Northumbria were wont to keep war-ships in the Irish Sea, as in the days when Edwin had conquered Man and Anglesey half a century back. Indeed these two notices are the only proof that remains to us to show that the English had not yet wholly forgotten the seamanship of their piratical ancestors.

Chroniclers, Saxon no less than Celtic, were wont to regard the disaster which fell upon Ecgfrith in the following year as the vengeance of heaven for the devastation of the churches of Ireland. In the spring of 685 he entered Pictland, and ravaged all the land till he had passed the Tay. King Bruide "made show as if he fled, and drew him on into the straits of inaccessible mountains," but turned to bay behind a morass called Linngaran "the pool of the cranes," near Dunnechtan (Dunnichen by Forfar). There Ecgfrith fell in battle, with all his nobles and the greater part of his army, on Sunday, May 20th, in the fifteenth year of his reign and the fortieth of his age. His death is said to have been seen in a vision by St. Cuthbert, the anchorite whom he had drawn from his hermitage only a few months before, to rule over the see of Lindisfarne. Cuthbert, who had warned Ecgfrith not to undertake the expedition, was seized with a trance as he stood admiring the Roman walls of Carlisle, exclaimed that "even now the conflict was perchance decided," and sent to warn the queen to depart at once to York, and await the worst of news, which came only two days later.

The battle of Nechtansmere, as the English called the fight, was a fatal blow to Northumbria, which on Ecgfrith's death not only lost the greater part of its northern empire, but seems to have started on a permanent decline in strength and vitality. The kingdom

---

[1] The only other explanation suggested is that the Irish were harbouring Ecgfrith's illegitimate brother Aldfrid, whom he had driven out of the realm (see Plummer's *Bede*, ii. 260).

[2] Bede, *E. H.*, iv. 26.

showed no signs of recuperative power : it made no serious attempt
hereafter to vie with Mercia as the leading power in England, and
in the next generation fell into a state of faction and civil war, from
which it was never destined to emerge. The immediate result of
the disaster was that the Picts of the north recovered not only
their complete liberty, but all the lands which Oswy had annexed
beyond the Wall of Antoninus, while the Scots of Argyleshire, and
great part of the Britons of the Lowlands ceased to pay the tribute
which they had been wont to yield.[1] The Strathclyde Welsh,
apparently, revolted, but not the dwellers about Carlisle ; nor did
the Niduarian Picts of Galloway get free, as is shown by the fact
that Northumbrian bishops continued to rule the see of Whiterne
for another hundred years. Trumwine, however, the Bishop of Abercorn, withdrew to Whitby with many other fugitives from Lothian,
so that apparently Manau, no less than the parts beyond Forth,
had been evacuated. Bede, writing the fourth book of his history
forty-six years after Nechtansmere, makes special note that nothing
that was then lost had been recovered down to his own day.

Ecgfrith's successor was his half-brother Aldfrid, an illegitimate
son of Oswy, who had long been in exile, first in Ireland and then
at Iona. He was a gentle and learned prince, who had been
destined for the Church, and though he had refused the tonsure
had learned in a monastery to love books and scholars. During
his reign of twenty years (685-705) he kept peace so far as he
might, leaving Mercia alone, and making no attempt to interfere in
the contemporary troubles of the far south, where war was afoot
during his early years, though an ambitious king might have sought
to turn the struggle in Wessex, Kent and Sussex to account. It is
clear that the Picts must have occupied Aldfrid's main attention;
probably the struggle on the borders of Lothian went on during
the greater part of his reign, though of it we have only one notice
in the Chronicles, viz., that in 698 [2] the Picts slew in battle Beorht
(or Beorhtred), the ealderman, the leader who had ravaged Ireland
fourteen years before at Ecgfrith's behest. But that this disaster led
to no further loss of territory seems to be shown by Bede's state-

[1] Bede, iv. 26.

[2] So in the Chronicle appended to Bede, but the Anglo-Saxon Chronicle says
699. Tighernach agrees with the former, calling the ealderman Brechtraig, the son
of Bernith (Bernhaeth).

ment that Aldfrid "nobly retrieved the state of a kingdom that
had been ruined, though it was now less extensive than of yore ".
The best token of his peaceful disposition is that, the moment he
was firmly established on the throne, he made peace with Bishop
Wilfred, and invited him to return from Sussex to Northumbria.
The matter was settled on the lines suggested by the papal letters
of 680—Wilfred took the diocese of York, the intrusive Bishop
Bosa resigning, but the new sees of Lindisfarne and Hexham
remained in existence, so that Bernicia was never reunited to Deira
as to its ecclesiastical organisation.   Archbishop Theodore took a
large part in arranging the matter : he had no personal objection
to Wilfred, with whom he was openly reconciled at a meeting in
London, but was determined that the old system of unwieldy tribal
bishoprics should not be restored.   Hence the return of Wilfred to
the new and narrower see of York did not displease him.   This is
the last act of the great primate which is on record ; he died in
690 at the age of eighty-eight, and was buried at Canterbury, in
St. Peter's, among his predecessors.   He was never formally canon-
ised—most probably because of his long quarrel with Wilfred, who
had won the hearts of the clergy both in his own day and in succeeding times.   But he had done far more for the welfare of Christendom
than many saints, "for to say the truth, the English churches
received more advantage during the time of his pontificate than
they had ever done before ". [1]   He has sometimes been credited
with the origin of the parochial system of England, as well as of
the localised episcopate.   This is an exaggeration.   No doubt he
encouraged the building and endowment of churches by lay landowners, but the system had begun before his time, and was not
completed till long after it.   His *Penitential*, the only written
work from his hand that has come down to us, speaks of local
divisions each administered by its own priest, but it is probable
that such were still the exception rather than the rule.   His real
memorials are the Diocesan Episcopate, and the school of Greek
learning which he left behind him.

Theodore's last years must have been saddened by the outbreak
of war in South Britain, where for a time all had been peaceful
after his great pacification of 679.   The first stirrer up of trouble

[1] Bede, *E. H.*, v. 9.

was that Ceadwalla who has already been mentioned in connection
with Wilfred. He was a descendant of Ceawlin, none of whose
house had held the supreme power in Wessex since 592, though his
father, Coenbert, is called a *subregulus*. His name, which is purely
Welsh, and that of his brother Mul, "the half-breed," seem to suggest that their mother must have been a Celt. At first we hear of
Ceadwalla as an adventurer, lurking with a war-band in the forests
of Chiltern and Andred,[1] then as a pretender to the throne of
Wessex. Possibly he may have received aid at first from Lothere,
King of Kent, since he was certainly the foe of that prince's chief
enemy. We read that in 684 Lothere had expelled from his realm
the son of his predecessor, Ecgbert—one Eadric—who seems to
have been reigning up to that moment as his colleague, or perhaps
as sub-king of West Kent.[2] Eadric took refuge in Sussex, and
raised an army there, apparently by the help of King Ethelwalch.
He then attacked Lothere, who was mortally wounded in the battle
which followed (Feb. 5, 685). The majority of the Kentishmen
then submitted to him. But a few months later Ceadwalla burst
into Sussex and slew King Ethelwalch, as has already been related.[3]
Two ealdormen, Bercthun and Andhun, rallied the South Saxons and
drove him off, and then (as it would appear) recognised Eadric of
Kent, who had won his throne by the aid of their countrymen, as
king of Sussex also.

We next hear of Ceadwalla as attacking his kinsman Centwine,
the King of Wessex, and forcing him to retire into a monastery.
Having thus won the throne, he engaged in a desperate war with
Eadric, being, as Bede says, *strenuissimus juvenis*, and as cruel as
he was ambitious. There probably lurks below the meagre tale of
his rise much unrecorded fighting, since Ceadwalla had as his enemy
not only the king of Sussex and Kent, but probably Aethelred of
Mercia also. For when an outlaw in Chiltern he must have been
trespassing in that monarch's newly won conquests from Wessex,
and when he achieved the kingship he seems to have won back all
the land of the Chilternsaetas. Sussex, too, whose king he had
slain, and whose lands he had wasted, had been vassal to Mercia
since the days of Wulfhere.[4]

---

[1] Eddius.
[2] They issued together a code of Laws, from which we shall have occasion to
quote later on.
[3] See p. 306.   [4] See p. 287-88.

In 686 Ceadwalla fell upon Sussex for the second time, slew Bercthun, the ealdorman, and devastated the whole realm. He then conquered the regions which Wulfhere had given over to Sussex twenty years before—the Isle of Wight and the land of the Meonwaras, to the north of Southampton Water. The former at least of these Jutish districts seems never before to have been in West Saxon hands. The conqueror dealt very harshly with the pagan men of Wight, slaying many, and planting a settlement of West Saxon colonists among them. The cruelty of his tender mercies may be judged from the ghastly anecdote in Bede, which tells how he captured the two brothers of Arwald, King of Wight, and was about to slay them, when a certain abbot, Cynebert, begged that they might not be sent to the other world as heathens, destined to certain damnation. Ceadwalla thought over the matter, and granted Cynebert a few weeks to instruct and baptise them. They were then beheaded, " joyfully enduring temporal death, through which they did not doubt that they would pass to everlasting life ".[1]

Having conquered Wight and crushed Sussex, the West Saxon king extended his invasion to Kent, where he apparently tried to set up his brother Mul as king, relying probably on help from the faction which had once backed Lothere and resisted Eadric. Perhaps the brothers counted some Kentish strain among their female ancestors, to justify the claim. And fate seemed at first to favour the project; in the autumn of 686 Eadric died, apparently by natural death, since he is not said to have fallen in battle. It seems that for a moment Mul was recognised as king by at least some part of Kent.[2] But it was but for a moment; in 687 his subjects beset him by a sudden rising, and he with twelve of his thegns were burnt alive, presumably in some palace or stronghold in which they had striven to defend themselves. Ceadwalla was soon back in arms to avenge his brother; he ravaged Kent cruelly from end to end, and then his devastating career came to an unexpected termination. We read, to our surprise, that in a sudden moment of contrition and agony of spirit, he laid down his blood-stained sword, resigned the throne which he had so hardly won, " and quitted his crown for the sake of Our Lord and His everlasting Kingdom, desiring to go to Rome to obtain the peculiar

[1] Bede, iv. 16.
[2] See Plummer's notes to Bede, ii. 265.

honour of being baptised in the Church of the Holy Apostles, and hoping that, laying down the flesh as soon as he should be baptised, he might immediately pass to the eternal joys of heaven ".[1]   It is strange to find that Wilfred's friend had not been baptised already ; presumably, like Constantine the Great, he had been deferring a ceremony which would impose upon him moral obligations that he dreaded. Some unrecorded, but horrible, incident of the devastation of Kent may have so preyed upon his conscience that he felt a sudden impulse to put ambition under his feet, and to flee from further bloodshedding. If his conduct with regard to the two Jutish princes from Wight was a fair specimen of his career, such incidents must have been many. His desire was granted him ; having abdicated in the autumn of 688 he had reached Rome by the following Easter, was there baptised by Pope Sergius, and died ten days after, on April 20, 689, aged only thirty.

His short and stormy career seems to have left permanent results behind it. Sussex seems never again to have enjoyed complete independence; apparently the race of native kings had ended with Ethelwalch, and the later *subreguli*, whom we occasionally meet, were subject to Wessex,[2] and sometimes (as it would seem) princes of the royal house of Cerdic. This was certainly the case with Nunna (710), the next South Saxon prince whose name has survived; he was the kinsman as well as the vassal of the King of the West Saxons. It seems clear that Ceadwalla also left his mark behind him by winning back the land of the Chilternsaetas from Aethelred of Mercia. The Mercian bishopric of Dorchester-on-Thames ceased about 685, and the region is found in West Saxon hands when next it comes into sight. Kent seems to have come very badly out of the wars; there was chaos in the land for two years after Ceadwalla's abdication, and it was not till 694 that Wihtraed, brother of Eadric, appears firmly established as sole ruler, after a struggle with certain "dubii vel externi reges," of whom Swebheard, King of Essex, seems to have been one.[3]

---

[1] Bede, *E. H.*, v. 7.

[2] Or to Mercia, when the latter, as in Offa's day, had stricken down Wessex for a time.

[3] But see Plummer's *Bede*, ii. 177 notes. Wihtraed was claiming kingship in 692, but the A. S. Chronicle puts his accession in 694, when no doubt he became sole ruler of Kent.

In Wessex itself, Ceadwalla was followed by Ine, son of Coenred, who was also a descendant of Ceawlin, but a very distant relative to his predecessor. The house of Cuthwulf, which had reigned from 592 to 685 continuously, wí apparently extinct, and all the later kings of the Gewissae come from Ceawlin's branch. Ine appears to have been a man of mark, who not only maintained his realm with the enlarged limits which Ceadwalla had won, but increased it as none of his predecessors had done since the day of the battle of Deorham. His long reign of thirty-eight years (688-726) contrasts strongly with the ephemeral rule of the five kings before him, none of whom had kept his throne for over nine summers. He was the first prince of his house, since Ceawlin, who gave any promise of winning that supremacy over the neighbouring states which was ultimately to fall to the kings of Wessex, when both Northumbria and Mercia had been tried and found wanting.

But since Ine's reign extends far into the eighth century, we must defer a consideration of it till we have dealt with the careers of the kings of the two great Anglian realms who were reigning when he came to the throne in 688.

Of Aethelred of Mercia there is comparatively little to tell. The later years of his life did not correspond to that triumphant beginning in which he had avenged Wulfhere, and restored the boundary of Mercia on the Humber, by winning back the region of Lindsey. He certainly lost the authority over Southern England which Wulfhere had asserted, and the rise of Ceadwalla permanently cut short his power. As far as we can judge he must have been a peaceful and pious prince ; the few notices that we have of him show that he was reckoned a dear friend of Archbishop Theodore, and a founder of bishoprics and monasteries on a large scale, though early in his reign he had been an evil neighbour to the prelates and monks of Kent. It is therefore surprising to find in the Saxon Chronicle, under the year 697, the meagre and inexplicable statement "in this year the Southumbrians slew Ostritha, the Queen of Aethelred," which is slightly enlarged in the epitome appended to Bede, by the note that the murder was done by "the chief men (*primates*) of the Mercians". This would seem to point to civil strife and palace revolutions, of which we have no other trace. Ostritha may have been the leader of a political party, but we know no more about her than that she had shown her piety by translating the bones of her kinsman St. Oswald to the abbey of Bardney. Her death did not involve the deposition of her husband, who reigned for seven years more, till in 704 he abdicated his throne, and retired into the monastery of Bardney, of which he and his wife had both been great benefactors; he died some years later as its abbot. Sigebert of East Anglia had set the example of resigning the crown for the cowl half a century before, and Centwine of Wessex had copied it—not apparently by his own free will—in the next generation. But Aethelred appears to have been, like Sigebert and Ceadwalla, an instance of genuine world-weariness, on the part of a conscientious man who felt that he was too old or too weak to cope with the rough political problems of his day. He was succeeded by his nephew Coenred, the son of his predecessor Wulfhere, though he had left an heir of his own, Ceolred, who was to mount the Mercian throne a few years later, for Coenred reigned only from 704 to 709. Apparently he reigned in peace, and certainly he was as pious as his uncle; we have no note of him save that he did not think it beneath him to rebuke and argue with those of his servants who lived an evil life.[1] Bede merely tells of him that "having for some time nobly governed the kingdom of the Mercians, he did a yet more noble act by quitting his throne and kingdom, and going to Rome, where he was shorn and ordained a monk by Pope Constantine, and abode to his death (five years later) near the relics of the Apostles". He made over the crown before his departure to his cousin, Ceolred (709-16), a prince of very different character, warlike, licentious and boisterous, who seduced nuns, plundered churches,[2] and opened a long war with Wessex, of which we shall have much to tell hereafter.

Meanwhile Aldfrid of Northumbria survived the abdication of his old enemy Aethelred by a year, dying peaceably at Driffield on December 15, 705. The later part of his reign had been disturbed by a new quarrel with Wilfred of York, who does not seem to have been able to agree even with a prince whom all writers agree in praising for his learning, meekness, and piety. We are told that the trouble arose from Aldfrid's wishing to take from Wilfred his

[1] Bede, *E. H.*, v. 13.
[2] Our chief notice of him is from an unexpected source, a letter of Boniface, the great English apostle of Germany, who lived in the next generation, so is a good authority.

abbey of Ripon, which he held along with the see of York, in order
that he might found a new bishopric there. The king seems to
have held that Deira, like Bernicia, ought to be divided into two
dioceses, according to the scheme of Archbishop Theodore, which
Wilfred could not bring himself to accept. He departed, or was
expelled, from his see of York, and removed to Mercia, where King
Aethelred gave him the bishopric of Leicester, which chanced at
that moment to be vacant. He administered it for no less than
eleven years, before he was permitted to return to Northumbria.
Naturally he made an appeal to Rome, as he had done before in
678; but though Pope John VI. decided that he had been wrongly
expelled, and sent bulls in his favour to Aldfrid, he was not restored.
In 702 the king called a council at Estrefeld (Austerfield) to which
came Archbishop Bertwald of Canterbury, and many other prelates.
It seems to have ended by an offer made to Wilfred that he should
return to Northumbria, if he would resign the see of York and keep
his old abbey of Ripon alone. This meagre compensation was of
course refused with scorn, and Wilfred went once more to Rome, to
plead his cause in person, though he was now so far advanced in
years that the long journey was almost fatal to him (703-4). The
reigning pope, Sergius I. reaffirmed the judgment that had been
given in his favour, and wrote to Archbishop Bertwald bidding him
assemble a synod and do justice to the exile. The primate declared
himself disposed to carry through the matter; but King Aldfrid,
though pious, was obstinate, and nothing had been accomplished
when he died in 705. There was a short time of trouble after his
decease; his son, Osred was only eight years old, and the reign of
a child was a thing unknown in Northumbria. Eardwulf, a distant
relative whose lineage is unknown, seized the throne, but held it
for only two months, when he was expelled by the ealdorman
Bertfrid and other magnates, who had resolved to make the experiment of crowning the child, Osred. Immediately afterwards Bertfrid, who was now practically in charge of the realm, assembled a
council on the Nidd, to which came Bertwald the primate, and all
the bishops of the North. The ealdorman and the archbishop being
both friendly to Wilfred, a compromise was finally negotiated, by
which he received back not his old bishopric of York, but Hexham,
a see of much inferior dignity; however his famous abbey of Ripon
and his other possessions were restored to him. With this arrange-

ment Wilfred was fain to be content, though he regarded himself
as having been very harshly treated.　He held his new see for four
years, and died at Oundle in October, 709, while on a visit to
Mercia to confer with King Ceolred.　His misfortunes, his undaunted spirit, his lavish patronage of monks and monasteries, and
his excellent missionary work in Sussex secured him the title of
saint.　But there can be no doubt that his troubles were largely of
his own making, and that his haughty bearing and unconciliatory
disposition were the real cause of his long strife with men of such
excellent character as Archbishop Theodore and King Aldfrid.
The origin of the whole matter lay in his resistance to Theodore's
very necessary and profitable scheme for cutting up the unwieldy
tribal bishoprics, to which no plea of "vested interests" was a
sufficient objection.　Even at that early date his repeated appeals
to Rome were resented by the rulers both of Church and of State.
But there is no reason to impute blame to him for them, for he had
indubitably received hard treatment, and there was no other
tribunal to which he could apply for justice.　His best title to
kindly remembrance, over and above his conversion of the South
Saxons, is his zeal for church building, to which he applied all his
energy and wealth in the day of his greatness.　The foundations of
his great minster at Hexham survive, to show the comparative
magnificence of his designs, in an age when architecture was in its
infancy.

CHAPTER XVI

THE EIGHTH CENTURY, 709-802—THE MERCIAN DOMINATION

IT has often been remarked that while on the Continent the seventh century was the most miserable period of the Dark Ages, in England the eighth century has that unenviable distinction. While abroad the Merovingian royal house was sinking into senility under a long succession of shortlived and impotent kings, while the Visigoths of Spain were preparing themselves for servitude to the Moor by incessant murder and civil war, while the Lombards were losing their chance of building up a national kingdom of Italy, the English were still a strong and vigorous race. The impulse of conquest was not yet lost, while the introduction of Christianity had brought with it a higher moral standard and broader aims. Kings like Edwin and Oswald, Oswy and Aldfrid, contrast very favourably with their continental contemporaries. The chronicle of this island, though full enough of battle, murder and sudden death, is not a mere list of horrors, like the history of the Merovingians, as detailed by Gregory of Tours and the meagre annalists who followed him. Most of all is it to be noted that the English Church, for the first hundred years of its existence, was the most creditable branch of seventh-century Christendom, as much above its Frankish, Visigothic or Lombard sisters in learning and godliness as in energy and missionary zeal. With the commencement of the eighth century we begin to find a change for the worse ; it looked as if the experiment of putting the new wine of Christianity into the old bottles of English tribal life had led first to effervescence, and then to a settling down into turbid decay. It took some generations for the process to become complete ; for the first third of the eighth century the English Church might still be called learned, disinterested, and zealous, and the English kingly houses still produced on occasion men of vigour and piety. This was, indeed, in one sense, the Golden Age of Anglo-Saxon England, when scholar-kings like Aldfrid and Ceolwulf of Northumbria reigned, when the school of Greek learning started at Canterbury by Theodore and Hadrian was still flourishing, when Aldhelm and Bede were writing, when Abbot Ceolfrid was causing the *Codex Amiatinus* to be engrossed, and Caedmon the poet was but recently dead. Bede's work, if it were the only thing surviving from the period, would give us a very high idea of contemporary English culture. He was an author of a degree of merit to which no other historian of the Dark Ages attained. Procopius, writing in Constantinople—the centre of all learning—is the only wielder of the pen who can be compared to him in the space of five centuries. It is only necessary to name the other chief annalists of the West—Gregory of Tours, Isidore of Seville, Paulus Diaconus— in order to realise how far Bede excelled in breadth of view, power of arranging sources, and critical faculty. He is a model to later ages for his admirable habit of citing his personal authority for each statement, and his anxiety to get his chronology correct. Here indeed was a real historian ; and the wonder grows when we find that his *Ecclesiastical History of the English People* was only one among very many works of theology and scholarship which engrossed his busy life. And he was no isolated phenomenon, but only the best example of a race of literary men which flourished for at least two generations, and left heirs in Alcuin and other scholars of the next epoch.

But a Golden Age is too often the result of the good work of a previous generation, rather than the start of a continuous period of activity destined to endure. While Bede was still writing, the signs of deterioration were already visible; he himself saw and noted them, and the last paragraph of his continuous narrative ends in a note of doubt and foreboding concerning times "so filled with commotions that it can not yet be known what is to be said concerning them, or what end they will have ".[1]

Evil days were at hand, and it may be said that save for the single great figure of Offa of Mercia among laymen, and save for the great missionary Winfrith (Boniface), the apostle of Germany, among clerks, the rest of the eighth century is a period of dulness

[1] *E. H.*, v. 23, § 2.

and gloom.[1]   Boniface, writing about 745 to censure a contemporary monarch, remarks that the evil began with the two young kings Osred of Northumbria and Ceolred of Mercia, of whom the former reached man's estate in 714 and the latter ascended the throne in 709.   Both were dissolute youths, tyrants, murderers of their noblest subjects, ravishers of nuns, plunderers of monasteries. Both died violent and terrible deaths.   But it is not single sinners, even in the highest places, who break down a well-established system of morality, or ruin a State or a Church.   A general decay of energy and a general lapse into ill-living comes from general causes, though particular instances may point the moral.   If we have to search for the reasons of the decline of the English kingdoms in the eighth century we find them to be many and various.

The first was one which worked not only in England, but in all the Teutonic kingdoms of Western Christendom—the want of an established rule of succession in the kingship.   This was quite as deadly to the Visigoths of Spain and the Lombards of Italy as to the English.   When a kingdom is still in the making, living by the sword, and always in danger from external foes, the rule of the " survival of the fittest " among its rulers may do comparatively little harm.   It is absolutely necessary that the sceptre should be in the hands of the most competent fighting man, or the State may be extinguished.   But, in a kingdom which has won its way to a condition of permanent solidity, nothing can be more dangerous than that any descendant of Woden, more or less remotely connected with the reigning royal line, should think it possible to make a grasp at the crown.   In all the English kingdoms the number of princely houses which claimed an ancestry going back to the original founder of the state was enormous.   A glance at the genealogical trees of the houses of Cerdic or Ida, of Penda or Aesc, is absolutely bewildering.   The succession often moved about in the most unexpected way from one branch to another.   Any adventurer of the royal blood who had won fame in war might upset a reigning king who was weak or unpopular.   No ancestor of Ceadwalla of Wessex had won the crown for a century, yet he apparently dethroned Centwine with ease.   The worthless Osred of Northumbria was

---

[1] Bishop Aldhelm and the scholar Alcuin, the friend of Charlemagne, can hardly be mentioned along with the other two, though the latter is worthy of remembrance as the last flower of English learning.

murdered and followed on the throne by Coenred, who descended
from Ida in the sixth generation, but had no nearer kinship to his
victim ; and Coenred was followed by Osric, his equally remote
relation, to the exclusion of his brother Ceolwulf. The same was
the case in Mercia, where the kings of the later eighth century
descended from three separate nephews of Penda in succession.
When the crown might be grasped by any successful leader of a
war-band, civil war tended to become endemic ; nearly every king
" slew the slayer and must himself be slain," or at least be deposed,
tonsured and relegated to a monastery. For, as at Constantinople
during the same age, the milder type of usurper contented himself
with making his predecessor a monk, while the more ruthless type
slaughtered him.

The second cause of trouble was nearly connected with the first :
the weakness of the monarchy arose, to a great extent, from the fact
that when the age of conquest was over, and no more soil was won
from Briton or Pict, the king ceased to have an illimitable power
to endow his personal retainers, who were the core of his army, with
the land which they required to maintain them. The royal demesne
was no longer increasing, and it had actually begun to diminish in
a notable way. Not only had much been given to the members of
the *comitatus* of each successive king, which did not come back to
the crown, but remained with the grantee's family, but much more
had been spent in lavish endowment of the Church.[1] Bede, though
a monk himself, makes in his Epistle to Archbishop Ecgbert (734)
a strong protest against the way in which monasteries were swallow-
ing up all the available land, with the result that there was not
enough to provide for the fighting men needed for the defence of
the realm against the " barbarians ".[2] It is true that he is mainly
thinking of ill-regulated monasteries, which kings and ealdormen were
too wont to endow rather as a comfortable refuge for the old age of
themselves and their relatives, than as houses for the service of God.
But even the better sort of monastic establishments were in that
age multiplied beyond all rational necessity. In this comparatively
peaceful time, as Bede remarks, " multitudes of the Northumbrians,
both noble and simple, laying aside their weapons, incline to devote

---

[1] For the way in which this came about and estates got alienated to lay as well
as clerical occupants see the notes on *bocland* in chapter xviii., *infra*.

[2] *Epistola ad Ecgbertum*, § 11-12.

both themselves and their children to the tonsure and monastic vows, rather than to exercise themselves in the studies of war. What will be the end of it the next generation will see."[1]   The kings in all the states without exception set the example.   Sigebert of East Anglia, Centwine of Wessex, Aethelred of Mercia, have already been mentioned: Ceolwulf of Northumbria, just when Bede was writing his history, was the first, and by no means the last, example in the Northern Kingdom.   Where the retirement was voluntary, and not forced, the king who took the cowl naturally made ample provision from his royal property for the house which he destined as the retreat of his declining years.   The private monasteries are said to have become an intolerable abuse; when a great man founded such a place of retirement he not only lived there as a law unto himself, but filled it with relatives, some of whom were quite young men, who (save that they were not married) behaved in every way like laymen of a low type, spending their time in idleness, drinking and gluttony, listening to minstrels and buffoons, and not unfrequently lapsing into carnal lusts.   This was all the more easy when, as in some cases, the founder built a double monastery for men and women, taking charge of the first himself, while his wife presided over the others. St. Aldhelm tells us that he had met gay young nuns, who insisted on wearing garments of purple or scarlet trimmed with fur, and paid so much attention to their toilette that they habitually used curling tongs for their hair.   These young people, male and female, frequently got into trouble—as might have been expected.   But when pious fathers devoted sons or daughters to the cloister at their birth, or while they were still in the nursery, without any reference to their vocation, what else could have been expected?   The only wonder is that so many of these royal and noble recluses, who had not chosen their own lot, developed into saints: the number of royal abbesses in the English Calendar is surprising, and the cases of scandal much fewer than might have been expected.

The number of members of the great houses diverted into a monastic life for which they had no aptitude, was not the sole bad effect of the multiplication of religious houses.   We are told that the scions of the military class, sons of ealdormen and thegns, who would in an earlier age have done fighting-service for their own king, found that they could get no endowment from him at home,

[1] E. H., v. 23.

and wandered abroad to seek service as adventurers, as members of
the *comitatus* of a foreign prince, or as pirates. Those who stopped
landless at home were the obvious tools of every aetheling who was
meditating a snatch at the crown.

The curse of the land, in short, was that there were too many
"aethelings," *subreguli*, and ealdormen of royal blood, and too few
landholders of moderate status. The king was not strong enough
to hold down the nobility, unless he was a man of exceptional ability
and energy. It was exactly the same phenomenon which was seen
at the same time both among the Visigoths of Spain and the
Franks of Gaul. But the fate of the English was to be different
from that of either Goths or Franks. They were not destined to
be completely overwhelmed by the infidel, like the one, nor to find
salvation in setting a race of "mayors of the palace" to supersede
a decadent royal line, like the others. The Visigoths perished because
they were too few to leaven an alien subject-population; in England such a population hardly existed, save to a small extent in the
lands most recently conquered from the Welsh. The Franks fell
under the dominion of the great mayors because the Merovingian
kings had become utterly effete. The English royal houses never
sank so low; they continued to produce capable men from time to
time, till at last one dynasty, that of Wessex, prevailed over the
rest because it chanced, in the ninth and tenth centuries, to give
birth to a succession of monarchs of more than average ability for
several generations, who fought down barbarian invasions as dangerous as those which overwhelmed the Visigoths and bid fair at one
moment to overwhelm the Franks also.

The one aspect of the eighth century which gave some promise
of better things for the future was a marked tendency towards a closer
union between the various tribal units. It seems clear that local
particularism was growing less militant, partly because some of the
kingdoms and sub-kingdoms lost their royal lines in the civil wars,
and gradually learnt to endure rulers of alien origin, but much more
because, under the influence of the Church, all the races of England
were commencing to regard each other as brethren and countrymen,
rather than as neighbours only less to be hated than the Welsh or
the Picts. The much-ramified royal houses had intermarried with
each other to such an extent that members of one had generally a
female descent from one or more of the others, which would make

them less intolerable as rulers, if they chanced to conquer or even to inherit another crown. This was the way in which Kent ultimately got united to Wessex—the father of Ecgbert of Wessex had actually reigned as a *subregulus* in Kent, probably by a female descent. The union of Deira and Bernicia had certainly been facilitated by the fact that Oswy, the heir of Ida, married the daughter of Edwin, so that all his descendants had Deiran as well as Bernician royal blood in their veins. It seems certain also that the lesser kingdoms by the end of the eighth century were so far losing their particularism that they acquiesced more easily in accepting as sub-kings relatives of one of the greater royal houses, who were from time to time placed over them by some conqueror who had achieved a general "imperium" (as Bede would have called it) over his neighbours. Local patriotism died hard, but it was distinctly on the decrease in this age, though the union of all the kingdoms would undoubtedly have taken a much longer time to achieve but for the Danish invasions, which taught Angle and Saxon that servitude to the heathen Viking could only be avoided by combination.

But of all the unifying influences there can be no doubt that the Church was the most powerful. At her frequent synods kings and ealdormen no less than bishops from all the realms habitually met, to debate on equal terms for the common benefit of all England. The advantages of the presidency of a single archbishop must have been a perpetual object lesson, to teach that there would be equal profit in the suzerainty of a single secular ruler. Indeed during the second half of the eighth century, while Offa of Mercia was reigning (757-96), there was a distinct approach to national unity, and if only he had been succeeded by heirs of equal ability a kingdom of All-England might have come into existence under the Mercian royal house. But his male line died out with his only son, who survived him only four months, and when distant collaterals succeeded to his throne the other kingdoms broke loose, and England reverted to disunion and anarchy for a generation, only to be reunited by Ecgbert of Wessex.

Proceeding with our early eighth century annals, we note that although the long peace between Northumbria and Mercia was still to endure for another generation, so that no question of a claim of either to dominate the whole island arose, yet each of the two greater kingdoms had foreign wars to vary its domestic troubles.

In Northumbria, Osred, who succeeded in 705 as a mere boy of eight, seems to have been for many years under the tutelage of the ealdorman, Bertfrid (son of the Beortred who had served as general to both Ecgfrid and Aldfrid). This nobleman is described in 710 as defeating the Picts "between Haefe and Caere," apparently the rivers Avon and Carron, just south of the Firth of Forth ; Finguine, the leader of the Picts, was slain, and no doubt the frontier of Northumbria in Lothian was made secure for some years. A few years later we find Osred governing for himself, though no more than seventeen or eighteen years old. He is said by Archbishop Boniface to have been a youth of precocious wickedness, godless, cruel and debauched, who provoked his subjects until they rose upon him and slew him, "so that he lost his glorious kingdom, his young life, and his lustful soul by a contemptible and vile death" (716). He is said in the Anglo-Saxon Chronicle to have been slain "South of the Border," but whether this means the border against the Picts, by Forth, or the border against the Mercians, by Humber is not made clear. The chief of the conspirators who slew him was one Coenred, a very distant relative, since he descended, not from the line of Aethelfrith, which had occupied the Bernician throne ever since 593, but from another branch of the house of Ida, which had never before risen to royal power. He was apparently merely an ambitious aetheling, who saw his opportunity in the unpopularity of his master ; at any rate he was saluted as king and reigned for two years, to the exclusion of Osred's brother Offa and his first cousin, Oslac (the son of that Aelfwin who fell at the battle on the Trent in 679) to one of whom the crown should have fallen if any regular rule of succession had existed. This was the commencement of that series of murders and *coups d'état* which make the history of Northumbria for the next hundred years a miserable record of blood and treason. Coenred died, apparently by a natural death, in 718 : he left a brother, Ceolwulf, but this prince was thrust aside for a time by one Osric, who was as remote a kinsman to Coenred as the latter had been to Osred, since he descended from a third branch of the house of Ida, of which we only know that it had never before been counted royal.[1] He reigned eleven

---

[1] So at least the genealogy in Florence of Worcester, through Alric, Bofa, etc. In Simeon of Durham, however, Osric is called " filius regis Alfridi," but is this Aldfrith who died in 705 ? See notes in Plummer's *Bede*, ii. 337-38. Bishop Stubbs wished to identify him with the Hwiccian sub-king, Osric, son of Alchfrid.

years (718-29), but hardly a single fact has been preserved concerning him, save that he bequeathed his crown to Ceolwulf, the brother of his predecessor.[1]   But the transaction was ill received by many of the magnates, so that Ceolwulf's reign began—as it was to end —with dire commotions.   A rival king was raised up against him : but whether it was some one of the house of Ecgfrid, the old reigning line, or whether it was his own cousin, Eadbert, who ultimately became his successor, we are not told.   Several of the chroniclers inform us that he was taken prisoner, forcibly shorn, and immured as a monk in the monastery of Lindisfarne in 731.   Yet some inexplicable revolution drew him from his retirement in less than a year, and he had a second reign from 731 to 737.   Apparently he was a pious king and a lover of scholars ; probably he was, as often happens with princes of such a type, too feeble for the times in which his lot was cast.   Bede informs us that Ceolwulf was not only a diligent student of the Scriptures, but an industrious student of the actions and sayings of all ancient men of renown, and that he had often desired that a chronicle of England should be written "to excite the attentive hearer to imitate that which was good, and to shun that which is harmful and perverse" through following the tale of the past.[2]   Hence it was to him that the *Ecclesiastical History of the English People* was dedicated.   He had ample time to study it in his old age, for his later reign ended even as his earlier ; in 737 he retired to Lindisfarne for a second time—abandoning in despair the care of a troublous realm which was too much for him. He survived there till 760, in what, it would seem, was a not too comfortless seclusion, for we are told that "when this king became a monk, licence was given to the brethren to drink wine and beer ; for down to that time water and milk alone had been permitted to them, according to the rule of St. Aidan".[3]   Of his reign two events only are recorded, besides a general notice of commotion and civil war.   The first is that he procured the pall of an archbishop for his cousin, Ecgbert, who was then holding the see of York— Wilfred and all the other successors of Paulinus had been no more

---

[1] Bede, *E. H.*, v. 23.   The Chronicle of Ethelweard, ii. 13, says that Osric was slain or murdered (*occiditur*), but this seems incredible when compared with Bede's way of naming his death.

[2] Bede, *E. H.*, book i., preface.

[3] Simeon of Durham, ii. 102.

than bishops. The second is that he established a new diocese, seated at Candida Casa (Whiterne in Galloway) for the Niduarian Picts, who were still subjects of Northumbria, though their northern neighbours the Strathclyde Welsh had been independent ever since the battle of Nechtansmere.

Meanwhile the history of Mercia had remained for a whole generation entirely disassociated from that of Northumbria, but inextricably mixed with that of Wessex. Ceolred (709-16), the contemporary of Osred and his rival in turbulence, lawless cruelty and evil living, was apparently drawn into war with Ine of Wessex, because the latter had made his kingdom so strong that it had now become—what it had never been before—a serious rival of Mercia, and a competitor for the supremacy in England, south of the Humber. Ine (688-726) had succeeded to the throne when his distant relative Ceadwalla went on his famous pilgrimage to Rome. Our first notice of him is that he continued or resumed the war with Kent which his predecessor had begun, and brought it to a successful conclusion, since he received from King Wihtraed and his subjects the enormous war indemnity of 30,000 gold *solidi*, each of 16 *nummi*, which is equivalent to 3,750 pounds,[1] as compensation or weregeld for the death of the West Saxon prince, Mul, the brother of Ceadwalla, whom the Kentishmen had burnt seven years before. Nor was this all; Sussex, which had been in the hands of Wihtraed's brother, Eadric, fell under the power of Ine, who there established his kinsman, Nunna (or Nothelm) as *subregulus*. This least of the Saxon kingdoms seems to have been for the future habitually dependent on Wessex, and its rulers are as often styled *duces* (*i.e.*, ealdormen) as kings. It is probable that in consequence of Ine's victories not only Sussex but also Kent and Essex yielded him some sort of homage. But the only proof of this is that in his famous code of laws of 693 he styles Earconwald of London "my bishop," along with Haedde of Winchester. The phrase seems to imply definite suzerainty over London and its district.

Having established his borders in a satisfactory fashion in the East, Ine would appear to have turned his attention towards the

---

[1] So Ethelweard: the best texts of the Anglo-Saxon Chronicle say simply " 30,000," with no name of coin added. But probably Ethelweard and Florence of Worcester are right in making it *solidi*, or *mancuses* as these gold pieces were afterwards called. They weighed 65·6 grains, and eight equalled a pound.

Damnonian Welsh. His wars with them must have begun early in his reign, for Exeter was English before 700. But the only entry concerning them in the Chronicle is that in 710 Ine and his vassal Nunna fought against Gerontius (Geraint) of Damnonia, beat him and won from him much land. Taunton was occupied and fortified as a royal burgh to guard the newly acquired district,[1] which extended even to the Exe.[2] The growth of the West Saxon kingdom had already been marked by the division of its territories by Ine into two bishoprics, instead of the one at Winchester which had hitherto served for the whole realm. On the principle introduced by Theodore a new see was created for the parts west of Selwood, in Dorsetshire and Somerset, with its seat at Sherborne. St. Aldhelm, the learned Abbot of Malmesbury, was its first bishop (705-9).

Our most precious information as to the early part of Ine's reign is given not by the meagre entries in the Chronicles, but by the text of his code of laws of 693,[3] already alluded to above. Its interest lies in the proof which it gives that, just about the time when Ine's conquests were beginning, the western parts of the realm of Wessex contained a large subject population of Welsh, who had settled down as landed proprietors, small and great, and were so far amalgamated with their conquerors that they sometimes became royal officials, and served in the king's *comitatus*, though they retained a separate name and status. Evidently the old days when conquest implied extermination were long over, and a favourable *modus vivendi* for the Celt had been devised. That the system was successful is shown by the fact that in a few generations, West Somerset and East Devon had become entirely English. Of this Code we shall have more to say in its due place.

In 715, five years after Ine's campaign against King Gerontius, we find him engaged in war with Ceolred of Mercia. We cannot

---

[1] Ine is mentioned as having built it *some time back* in 722, so there can be little doubt that it arose after the campaign of 710, or even earlier.

[2] The main evidence for believing that Exeter now came under Ine's hand is that the great missionary Bishop Winfrith is recorded by Willibrord to have been educated at Exeter by an abbot named Wulfhard. Unless the city was English it is hard to see how this could have happened. And as Winfrith was born before 690, Ine must surely have been fighting with the Welsh much earlier than 710.

[3] So to be dated by the mention of St. Earconwald, Bishop of London, who died in that year. For details about this Code see Chapter xvii. *infra*.

be far wrong in concluding that while the pious and peaceful Coenred had endured the rise of Wessex without offering opposition, the fierce and violent prince who succeeded him had resolved to check it, and to win back for Mercia the supremacy over the whole South which Penda and Wulfhere had held in an earlier age. The Mercian king entered Wessex, evidently through the land of the Hwiccas, and engaged in a great pitched battle at " Wodnesbeorg," apparently the same spot, somewhere in North Wilts, where Ceawlin had fought and failed 130 years before. The result was perhaps indecisive—certainly not in favour of the Mercian. But the war would probably have continued if in the next year Ceolred had not perished. His end was sudden and awful—St. Boniface, writing only thirty years later, tells us that while he was feasting in state among his nobles, he suddenly became possessed by an evil spirit, burst out into boisterous madness, and died raving, without being able to receive the last sacraments of the Church. Presumably an attack of *delirium tremens*, consequent on a long course of evil living and hard drinking, is implied (716).

Ceolred's sudden death was followed by the accession of one Aethelbald to the Mercian throne. He was a young aetheling, whom Ceolred had exiled and persecuted, probably not without good cause, for the record of his career shows that he was violent and ambitious. His kinship to his predecessor was very remote, since he descended not from Penda, but from that king's brother Eowa, who had fallen at the battle of Maserfeld nearly a century before. In all probability his rise was accompanied by civil war and commotion, which prevented him from continuing the struggle with Wessex which was on hand. It seems also likely that he may have had trouble with the Welsh, as two battles in Glamorgan, at Garthmaelog and Pencoed near Bridgend, are recorded in the Cambrian Annals early in his reign. In both, as it is said, the Britons were victorious, and their enemies can only have been the Mercians.[1] It seems, at any rate, certain that Ine of Wessex found no hindrance from Aethelbald in the last years of his reign. The Anglo-Saxon Chronicle, always interested in the acts of the house of Cerdic, gives a number of notes concerning him, but they are all occupied

---

[1] This note is under the year 721 both in the *Annales Cambriae* and the *Brut y Tywysogion*. They are noted along with a battle in Cornwall in which Rodri Malwynog, a king of Wales, took part. Was this against Ine ?

with civil wars in the South, not with any struggle with Mercia.
In 721, as we read, Ine slew the aetheling Cynewulf, apparently a
domestic rebel.   In the following year another aetheling, one Ealdbert "the exile," raised Sussex and Surrey against him, but was
beaten and expelled.   In connection with this incident we are told
that Aethelburh, Ine's consort " razed Taunton, which her husband
had previously built ".   This puzzling entry has been interpreted as
meaning that, while the king was busy elsewhere, some of his enemies
seized Taunton, which Aethelburh took and destroyed, fighting in
her husband's behalf.¹   Three years later, we are told that Ealdbert
returned to the charge, once more found harbourage and assistance
among the South Saxons, and was for a second time defeated by
Ine : on this occasion, however, he failed to escape, and was slain in
battle.

Three years later Ine, now an elderly man, for he had reigned
thirty-seven years, copied the example of his predecessor Ceadwalla
by laying down his crown, and going on a journey to Rome " desirous to spend some time of his pilgrimage upon earth in the
neighbourhood of the holy place " (728).   He was accompanied by
his wife, who (according to a late version of the story) had spared
no pains to persuade him to the step.   Apparently they survived
for some time, in pious seclusion, near the tombs of the Apostles.²

Before starting on his voyage Ine had made over his crown to
his distant kinsman Aethelheard, who was also the brother of his
wife Aethelburh.   But the succession was not undisputed; an
aetheling named Oswald, a descendant of another branch of the
house of Ceawlin, also aspired to the throne; probably he was some
relative of the Ealdbert and Cynewulf whom Ine had slain, and was
supported by their faction.   He kept up civil war for two years,
till Aethelheard slew him in 730.   By this strife all the work of the
last thirty years was undone, and Wessex lost its predominance in
the South and sank very low.

It was, no doubt, Aethelheard's misfortunes which tempted
Aethelbald of Mercia to fall upon him.   This prince was now firmly

---

¹ So Henry of Huntingdon interpreted the story, and he seems for once to be
right, though there is no sign that he had anything to go upon save the mysterious
words of the Anglo-Saxon Chronicle.

² William of Malmesbury, we know not on what authority, says that Ine
" plebeio amictu tectus clam consenuit cum uxore " (i. 39).

seated upon his throne, and had his hands free for conquest. He was the greatest fighting man of his day, vigorous, unscrupulous and untiring: apparently he was not without his virtues, since St. Boniface, who sent him a letter of bitter rebuke for his misdoings, grudgingly concedes that he had a liberal hand and was a lover of justice. But he was an enemy of the Church and a notorious evil liver. The Mercian successfully invaded Wessex, defeated Aethelheard, and besieged and took the royal town of Somerton (733)—probably the place of that name in Somerset, not the one in Oxfordshire.[1] Yet it is likely enough that the region around the latter, the land of the Chilternsaetas, now lapsed once more into Mercian hands. Wessex, it would appear, became tributary to Aethelbald, and remained so during the rest of the life of Aethelheard and part of that of his successor Cuthred. Indeed the victor now became suzerain of all England south of Humber, and was, as Bede shows, as powerful as any of the great holders of the "imperium" who had preceded him.[2] Of all the English states only Northumbria was wholly free from his overlordship, and this exception he was determined to make an end of. The King of Northumbria was now Eadbert, the cousin of Ceolwulf, to whom that feeble monarch had resigned his crown, when he retired for the second time to the cloisters of Lindisfarne (737).[3]

We have now arrived at a period when the invaluable history of Bede at last fails us. His last chapter ends in 731, and he died on May 26th, 735. For the future we get no aid from his innumerable character-sketches, his illustrative anecdotes, and his careful record of dates and sources of information. We are now following the Anglo-Saxon Chronicle as our main source of information, and this work was drafted more than a century later, and was primarily concerned with the history of the house of Wessex. It can be supplemented to some slight extent from the short annalistic chronicle appended at the conclusion of Bede's fifth book, from the two Welsh Chronicles, the *Annales Cambriae* and the *Brut y Tywysogion*—both too late to be completely trustworthy—

---

[1] A victory in Somerset seems better to account for the complete collapse of Wessex than one in Oxfordshire.   [2] *E. H.*, v. 23.

[3] The Anglo-Saxon Chronicle wrongly ascribes Eadbert's accession to 738, and so makes Aethelbald attack Northumbria in the last year of Ceolwulf. But there is no doubt that the war began after the latter king's abdication.

and with equal caution from Ethelweard, a tenth century chronicler full of errors, and from Simeon of Durham, whose twelfth century book preserves the remnants of a lost Northumbrian history. Nor are the biographies and letters of certain saints—notably Boniface the English apostle of Germany and Alcuin without their value. Yet the whole period 730-8 0 is very dark and difficult of comprehension. For many of the English kingdoms we have hardly a note—the succession of kings in East Anglia from 793 onward is lost, and that in Kent and Essex very imperfectly known. Even where we have some sort of a continuous narrative, as in the cases of Mercia, Northumbria and Wessex, the bare facts only are before us. The local colour of the times, the causes and meaning of events, is hard to determine, and deductions are hard to draw. It is curious to note that while on the Continent the blackest darkness of historical knowledge lies between 600 and 750, in England it is from 730 to 850 that the obscurity is thickest. To put things shortly, the age of Charlemagne fell ninety years before the age of Alfred, and in each case the bright period casts a certain light on all sides of itself. But outside that radius things are dim and often inexplicable.

But to resume—Eadbert of Northumbria was the strongest monarch who had sat on the throne of Oswy and Ecgfrid for many years, so that Aethelbald's attack on him, which broke up the sixty years' peace that had reigned on Trent and Humber since 679, might be reckoned unwise and hazardous. But the Mercian had chosen his moment with care, when Eadbert, but newly invested with the crown, was occupied in a war with the Picts. This stab in the back, " an impious fraud " as the continuator of Bede calls it, in his Northumbrian patriotism, enabled Aethelbald to lay waste a considerable part of Deira, before his adversaries' forces could be disentangled from the northern war and brought to bear against him (740). But when the full force of Northumbria stood at bay under a capable king it was still too strong for the Mercian invader. We hear of no conquests made by Aethelbald, and since two years later we find him occupied by a Welsh war, while Eadbert has returned to his northern campaigning, it is clear that a peace had been patched up, after one or at the most two summers of war. The power of the two kings was too nicely balanced to encourage either in further strife; the union of England was to come neither by Mercia conquering Northumbria, nor by North-umbria conquering Mercia.

The northern wars of Eadbert were apparently brought about by new combinations among the Celts of Scotland. In this region there was at the time a great warrior, Aengus, king of the Picts, who had put down many competitors, and then turned upon his neighbours, the Dalriad Scots and the Strathclyde Britons. The former he harried to extremity, slaying their king Alpin and driving his family to take refuge in Ireland, and it would seem that the latter also were suffering from his sword. Whether Eadbert in 740 was defending the borders of Lothian against Aengus, or suppressing a rising of his own subjects, the Galloway Picts, is not clear. But it is probable that the latter was the case, for Aengus and Eadbert are soon after found in close alliance for many years, endeavouring to make an end of the Strathclyde Britons, old enemies of both. In 744 we get a note that the Picts were attack-ing Strathclyde, apparently with indecisive results.[1] But in 750 an attack upon that realm was made by the Picts and the North-umbrians at the same moment, no doubt by friendly arrangement. The northern inroad was beaten off; in a battle at Mugdoch (Mocetauc, Maesydog) in Dumbartonshire the Britons routed the invaders and slew Talargain, the brother of Aengus. But Eadbert at the same time ravaged all their southern borders, and added the region of Kyle to his kingdom, with other lands—perhaps the adjacent Carrick and Cunningham. In 756, however, the co-operation was better managed—Eadbert and Aengus joined their armies, overran Strathclyde together, and besieged and captured Alclyde its capital, which made formal surrender to the allies (August 1st, 756). Apparently Aengus stripped off the northern border of the Britons, beyond Clyde, while Durmagual, son of Tudor, the King of the Welsh, did homage to Eadbert for the rest of his dominions. We are told that the Northumbrian army suffered heavy losses while returning from Alclyde to Newburgh in the valley of the Tweed,[2] but this did not prevent Eadbert from

---

[1] For all this see Skene's *Celtic Scotland*, i. 292-96. But it is impossible to follow that author in all his deductions. Of the details, the continuator of Bede only mentions the war in 744 and the conquest of Kyle by Eadbert. Simeon of Durham gives the alliance of 756 and the capture of Alclyde. The rest comes from the *Annales Cambriae* and the Irish Chronicles.

[2] Simeon of Durham, *sub anno* 756.

keeping the overlordship of Strathclyde, which seems to have continued in vassalage for some years to Northumbria, till the domestic troubles of that kingdom caused it to lose all its outlying dependencies in the latter part of the eighth century.

After a reign that seems to have been in every way successful, and which forms the last bright spot in the Northumbrian annals, Eadbert, in 758, followed the example of Aethelred and Ine and the numerous other princes who retired to a cloister to finish their days. Unless he was in extreme old age, which does not seem to have been the case, for he survived nine years as a monk at York, his abdication can only be styled criminal,[1] for the domestic commotions and strife for the crown, which he had put off for twenty-one years, broke out with redoubled vigour on his disappearance from the scene. The time of absolute chaos began with the murder of his son and successor Oswulf, "slain by those of his own household," apparently in a palace conspiracy, after he had held the throne for less than a year (July 25th, 759).

Meanwhile we must turn back to Aethelbald of Mercia, of whom nothing has been said since he turned back from his ineffectual attempt to overrun Deira in the year 740. The energy which he could not employ to good effect upon Northumbria seems to have been turned aside upon the Welsh. In 743 we find him accompanied by his vassal, the King of Wessex—Cuthred had now succeeded to his kinsman Aethelheard's crown, and also to his obedience to Mercia—to harry the Celts. The details of the campaign are unrecorded, but it was presumably successful, since Aethelbald is found continuing in full power, and maintaining his supremacy over all England, south of Humber, for nine years more. His long reign, however, was destined to end in defeat and gloom. In 750 we are informed[2] that Cuthred rebelled against him; the same year bears the note that the Wessex king fought against "Aethelhun the proud ealdorman," possibly one of his own nobles set up against him by Aethelbald; we are told, though on late authority, that they contended *pro aliqua invidia reipublicae*.[3] But it was not

---

[1] There is a curious tale that his abdication was so much dreaded that his vassals offered him untold lands if he would only consent to postpone it.

[2] By Simeon of Durham only, while the A. S. Chronicle gives the note about Aethelhun.

[3] Ethelweard, i. 14.

till 752 that the war came to a head, at a great battle fought by
Burford in Oxfordshire; presumably Cuthred was advancing to win
back the old West Saxon district of the Chilternsaetas. The King
of the Mercians was completely defeated, and lost not only the
territory in dispute but his supremacy over Southern England. He
survived for five years longer, but with diminished power, and probably among civil dissensions, for his end was that he was "miserably murdered at night by his own bodyguard" (*a suis tutoribus*)
at Seckington in 757. Treason on the part of the thegns of the
royal *comitatus* was such a rare thing—this case and that of
Oswulf in 758 just narrated are almost unique—that it is probable that Aethelbald, soured by defeat, had goaded his followers to
desperation by a course of tyrannical acts. The throne fell to
Beornred, a distant relative, who may either have been already in
arms against the old king, or have been the contriver of the assassination plot. But "he held the kingdom for a little while and
unhappily". Before the year was out he was defeated and expelled
by Offa, the son of Thingferth, Aethelbald's cousin[1] and natural
heir. This prince was destined within a few years to raise the
Mercian realm to an even higher level of imperial power than
Aethelbald had achieved, but at the beginning of his reign he had
much to set right and restore. It appears that his opportunities
of greatness originally came from the temporary collapse of the
West Saxon kingdom, under the successors of Cuthred, the victor of
Burford.

After that successful campaign Cuthred, as it seems, had made
peace with Mercia on favourable terms, and turned his energy
against the Damnonians, who may have taken the opportunity to
assail him in the rear while he was engaged with Aethelbald. We
are assured that he was victorious, and it is quite possible that he
may have won some territory on the side of Devonshire. But in
the following year (756) he died, to the great detriment of Wessex,
which at once fell into times of trouble. His successor was his near
kinsman,[2] Sigebert, who, unhappily for his subjects, was a reckless

---

[1] Grandson of his first cousin, to be exact. See the Tables in Searle.

[2] He was *propinquus* (or *maeg* in Anglo-Saxon Chronicle). Here begins an error
of two years in the Chronicle, which goes on for a century and causes vast confusion
in dates till the middle of the ninth century, when right figures recommence after
851. See Plummer's *Bede*, ii., ciii.

and cruel tyrant; the West Saxons endured him for a year, when sedition broke out and the witan declared him deposed, and gave the kingdom to Cynewulf the aetheling, who represented another branch of the royal house, though his descent from Cerdic and Ceawlin is not preserved. But Sigebert maintained himself in Hampshire "until he murdered the ealdorman who longest remained faithful to him," one Cumbra by name. After this Cynewulf drove him out of his small remaining dominion, and chased him into the forest of Andred. There he lurked, until he was slain by a certain swineherd, who slew him to avenge ealdorman Cumbra, his late master, at Privetsflood (Privet, Hants). It would seem that these domestic troubles broke the power of Wessex, which under Cynewulf does not appear as an aggressive state, and for many years made no attempt to check the restoration of the Mercian *imperium* under Offa. Indeed till Cynewulf came into collision with that great king in 777, we have no information about his reign, save that he fought incessantly with the Damnonian Welsh, probably rather to defend lands already won, as we should gather, than in order to extend his borders westward, for his realm was clearly in a weak condition. It is possible that the aetheling Cyneheard, the brother of the deposed Sigebert, was giving trouble all through Cynewulf's time, though it was only at the end of a rather long reign of thirty-one years that the king fell a victim to the aetheling's hatred (786).

While this obscure monarch was reigning in Wessex, Offa was restoring the glories of Mercia. His first recorded campaigns were against the Welsh; in 760 he defeated them in front of Hereford; since this was the capital of the Magesaetas, and lay well within the border of their territory, we must conclude that the Celts had been the aggressors. It does not appear that the King of Mercia made any attempt to avenge himself for some years, though when the chastisement did come it was heavy and unsparing. In the early section of his reign it was rather in Southern England that he was active. Between 760 and 777 he apparently conquered one after another all the minor States. We know that by 771-72 he was so far master of the South that he was able to dispose of land in Sussex, by charters to which Ecgbert of Kent and Cynewulf of Wessex set their hands in consent, evidently as vassals. Probably their submission was at first uneasy, for Offa is found beating the

Kentishmen at Otford, near Sevenoaks, in 774, and then three years
later in collision with Cynewulf, who fought him at Bensington
near Dorchester-on-Thames in 777,[1] but was utterly defeated.
The town was taken, and with it all the land of the Chilternsaetas
was annexed to Mercia, for the last time; it never went back to
Wessex until, in common with other Mercian lands, it became
subject first to Ecgbert, the great unifier, and then to his grandson,
Alfred the Great.

With the battle of Bensington, active opposition to Offa in
South England seems to have come to an end, and for the remainder
of his reign—nearly twenty years—he ruled with undisputed sway
over vassals who had been taught obedience. The state of the
smaller kingdoms seems to have been in some cases peculiar—
several kings reigning in them at once under Offa's supremacy.
This would be well suited to the suzerain's ends, as it would keep his
subjects weak. In Kent, from 760, with or after Eardwulf and
Alric the last certain descendants of Hengist, there were reigning
at different times, as charters show, Sigered who called himself
"*rex dimidiae partis provinciae Cantuariorum* (about 760-62);
Ecgbert II., whose dates run between 765 and 779; Heahbert whose
floruit is about 775; and Ealhmund, a prince of West Saxon blood
who signs as *subregulus*, about 784-86.[2] Apparently as many as
three of them must have coexisted simultaneously in the one small
kingdom. There are some signs of a divided kingship in East
Anglia also, but here, in the very end of his reign (793), Offa took
the high-handed step of slaying the ruling prince and annexing his
realm to Mercia. There was evidently something particularly
atrocious about this business, as the young king Aethelbert was
reckoned a saint, and became one of the more popular names in the
English Calendar. Later legends told how he was lured to Offa's
court by the promise of the hand of his daughter, Aelfthryth, and
then murdered by the contrivance of Queen Cynethryth. Cynewulf of Wessex (757-86), who was contemporary with the greater
part of Offa's long reign, came to an evil end in circumstances which
throw a lurid light on the troubled condition of his realm during
the Mercian supremacy.

---

[1] The dates 774 and 777 in the Anglo-Saxon Chronicle are apparently, as usual
in this period, two years out.   [2] Concerning whom, see p. 388.

The entry concerning his death in the Anglo-Saxon Chronicle is too characteristic to be omitted. It is written at such unwonted length, and with such picturesque detail, that we must suspect it to be some fragment of a heroic poem which the Chronicler thought too good to be lost. Cynewulf "purposed to expel from his realm the aetheling Cyneheard, brother of his predecessor Sigebert," apparently a pretender to his throne, rather than an overgrown subject. The aetheling was in arms with a small body of his followers, when he heard that the king was near him almost unattended. For Cynewulf was intending to visit a lady dwelling at Merantun (Merton in Surrey) who was his mistress. Therefore he had left the greater part of his retinue behind him, and took to Merton only a few of his most confidential attendants. While he was sitting alone with the lady in her bower, Cyneheard and his men rode suddenly up to the homestead, poured into the courtyard, and rushed in straight to the king, who snatched up his sword and fought for his life at the door, till noticing the rebel prince in the rear, he charged out upon him, and wounded him, but was immediately encompassed and slain. The thegns of Cynewulf, alarmed by the screams of the lady, came rushing out of the hall just in time to see their master fall. The aetheling cried to them that the king was dead, and that all of them should have not only their lives but rich endowment, if they would take service with him. But the outraged retainers laughed him to scorn, attacked him, and were slain every man, save one, "and he a hostage, a Welshman, and sore wounded". Next morning the house where the slaughter had taken place was beset by the main body of Cynewulf's retinue, under Osric the ealdorman, who had heard of the king's death during the night. Through the barricaded doors the aetheling offered them "their own choice of lands and money if they would take him as king, and showed them that he had with him many of their own kinsmen, who would be true to him". But the besiegers cried out that no one was dearer to them than their lord, and that they would never follow his murderer, and they bade their kinsmen who were within to quit the aetheling and depart. Then Cyneheard's men answered "that they were no more minded to quit their lord than your companions yesterday, who fell with the king". Whereupon the ealdorman and his band assaulted the gate, and after hard fighting won their way in, and slew the aetheling and all who were with him, save one man who was Osric's godson, "and he was wounded in several places".

The tale illustrates well enough the old English ideal of chivalry, the boundless fidelity due from the sworn member of the war-band to his lord. But it also bears eloquent witness to the uncertainty of a kingship under which any ambitious prince could hope to buy over the chief officers of his master by lavish offers. Doubtless many another such adventurer as Cyneheard thus won the crown; similar scenes had another end in the cases of Osred and Aethelbald. The uncertain law of succession was a curse to the land, and was to remain so for many a year more.

Cynewulf was succeeded by one Beorhtric, of whom we know nothing more than that "his right paternal kin went back to Cerdic": he was apparently no close relation either to the dead king or the aetheling who had slain him. He reigned sixteen years (786-802), and was evidently a quiet vassal to Offa, whose daughter, Eadburh, he married. Wessex legend related that this lady was the instrument of her husband's death; she much hated a young thegn whom Beorhtric favoured, and prepared poison for him in a cup, which the king, coming in by chance, took up and drank. She fled to France, and was sheltered for a time by the Emperor Charlemagne, who gave her a nunnery as endowment. But she there lived such a scandalous life that she was expelled, and died an outcast in the streets of Pavia. So Asser tells the tale, having learnt it (as he says) from the mouth of the unlying Alfred himself, two generations after the tragedy.[1]

Offa's later and more serious invasions of Wales all belong to the second period of his reign, when South England was already subdued. The first was in 778, when we are told that he devastated all South Wales. In 784 comes his second spoiling of South Wales, which befell at Midsummer, and is said to have been provoked by previous incursions of the Celts into his own land. It was apparently after this that he drew from sea to sea the great earthwork that still preserves his name. "He caused a dyke to be made

---

[1] Asser says (§ 18) that the story of Eadburh's evil doings and end was told him by Alfred, and corroborated by the witness of several English travellers, who had seen her begging her bread in the capital of Lombardy when they were young. He adds what seems to be a mere folk tale, concerning a humorous offer which Charlemagne made to marry the lady when first she arrived in his dominions. It is told of other persons in other ages.

as a boundary between him and Wales, to enable him to withstand more easily the raids of his enemies, and that is called *Clawd Offa* from that time till this.   And it extends from the southern to the northern sea, from opposite Bristol at one end, to above Flint on the other, between the monastery of Basingwerk and Coleshill."[1]
To describe its course more exactly, we may say that it follows the east bank of the Wye from its estuary as far as a point seven miles west of Hereford, and then turns north-west past Kington, Knighton and Montgomery to the Severn near Welshpool.   From thence it strikes across Denbighshire, by Chirk and Ruabon, till it reaches the mouth of the Dee five miles north of Mold.   In this part of its course much that is now reckoned Welsh, in the counties of Montgomery, Denbigh and Flint, is marked as Mercian ; farther south, on the other hand, it leaves as Welsh much in Herefordshire that is now reckoned English—all the region of Ercyng (Irchenfield) and the Golden Valley.   Since Hereford had been an English town for more than a century,[2] it seems that the boundary had not been moved forward in this direction.   But in the north the advance was considerable, and placed all the lowlands north of the great bend of the Severn in Mercian hands.   Offa's last Welsh invasion, which included a devastation of Rhuveniog (West Denbighshire) in 795,[3] was probably caused by an attempt of the princes of Gwynedd to rebel, and win back some portion of the lost lands, when they thought that their conqueror had grown old and feeble.   The Dyke, as has often been pointed out, is not a work defensible along its whole length, but rather a boundary line, in the style of the first Roman *limes* in Northumberland, intended to mark clearly the border between Mercia and the vassal Welsh, which the latter could not overstep without definitely trespassing on their suzerain's land and challenging him to war.

From 777, the date of the battle of Bensington, down to his death in 796, Offa ruled England south of Humber with a completeness of authority which none of his predecessors had enjoyed for such a long period of years.   On the continent he seems to have been regarded as monarch of the whole English nation—Pope Hadrian I. formally addressed him as *Rex Anglorum*, Charlemagne

---

[1] *Brut y Tywysogion*, p. 843
[2] See p. 297.
[3] *Annales Cambriae, sub anno* 795.

dealt with him almost as an equal. Normally their relations were friendly, and at one time there were long negotiations for the marriage of one of Offa's daughters to Charles the Younger, the eldest son of the great Frankish king. We are told that they failed because Offa wished to secure in return the hand of one of Charlemagne's daughters for his son Ecgferth, which was refused him—for the Frank would never allow his daughters to marry, a thing that caused much wonder and scandal then and thereafter. The coolness that ensued soon passed over, and in 786 Charlemagne, when returning in triumph from his great victory over the Avars on the Danube, sent to Offa some of his trophies, gold, swords, and embroidered garments, as testimonies of his regard and friendship. We have a good deal of incidental information regarding the relations of the great king of the Franks and the overlord of Southern England from the letters of the English scholar Alcuin, who, though he had settled down on the continent and become a member of Charlemagne's court, never ceased to remain in close touch with his native country.

Not the least important side of Offa's life was his ecclesiastical policy, in which he evidently took a deep interest. He was a very zealous builder and benefactor of monasteries—like all the better kings of his age: St. Alban's was undoubtedly one of his foundations, and perhaps the house on Thorney Island near London, which Edward the Confessor developed into the Abbey of Westminster, was another. But in one respect he was a poor friend both to the Church and to the unity of England. He seems to have resented the fact that the primate to whom all his bishops owed obedience was placed at Canterbury, outside the limits of his own realm, and designed to break up the ecclesiastical union of Southern England by creating a new archbishopric within his own borders, which should be independent of the successors of St. Augustine. This was a retrograde step, and unnecessary also, considering that Kent had been politically subject to him for many years, and had made no attempt to get free since the battle of Otford in 774. But Bregwine and Jaenbert, the archbishops of Offa's central years (761-93) were not Mercians by birth, and probably were not so subservient as the great king desired. At anyrate he determined to have a primate of his own, dwelling under his own eye at Lichfield, who should rule over all that lay between Thames and Humber.

This plan was carried out, with the consent of Pope Hadrian, in 786: perhaps the papacy acquiesced in the scheme merely to please the king, perhaps, however, because archbishops ruling over smaller areas were less likely to give trouble and assume an independent attitude than those whose sphere of influence was conterminous with a whole national or imperial unit. At any rate the papal legates, George and Theophylact, visited England, and after being hospitably entertained by Offa, executed a sort of visitation of the whole country. George went north to York, and in company with Archbishop Eanbald held a provincial council for Northumbria, at which Alcuin (then in England) chanced to be present. Theophylact visited Mercia and its subject kingdoms. Then in the following year (787) both the legates were present together at the Council of Chelsea. Its first business was to discuss and assent to twenty decrees concerning details of church-governance, which were proposed under papal authority. One provided for the holding of two provincial synods every year; another ordered the bishops to carry out annual visitations of their dioceses; a third and most excellent clause gave the bishops the duty of inspecting monasteries, to see that their rule was duly kept. One of the greatest ecclesiastical troubles of the Middle Ages, the independence of religious houses, who so often defied the diocesan, would have been prevented if only this arrangement had continued. But undoubtedly the most important part of the proceedings was the carrying out of Offa's scheme for the cutting up of the Archbishopric of Canterbury: the plan was vehemently opposed, so that the meeting is called in the Anglo-Saxon Chronicle "the contentious synod".[1] But Offa, backed by the legates, was far too strong for Archbishop Jaenbert and his friends, and the matter was carried through. Higbert of Lichfield was designated as primate of all the lands of Mercia and East Anglia, seven dioceses in all, while Canterbury was for the future to have authority only over the Bishops of Rochester, Selsey, Winchester, London and Sherborne. Pope Hadrian sent the archbishop his pall, and Offa in gratitude promised to send every year 365 gold "mancuses" to Rome, to be used for alms and supplying the lights in St. Peter's. This donation was probably the origin of the well-known " Peter's pence" of which so much is heard in later history. Chance has pre-

[1] Under the erroneous date 785. But all the years in this part of the Chronicle are two years out, as has been previously noted.

served a single specimen of Offa's "mancus," which we find to our surprise was copied not from any late Roman coin, but from the *dirhems* of the Saracen Caliphs. It bears on both sides a blundered Arabic inscription, across which the words OFFA REX are engraved in large characters. This was a most exceptional piece of money; there had been a little gold coined in England at an earlier date, very small pieces copied from the Frankish *tremissis*, but it had long gone out of currency, and the striking of this larger coin was abnormal; there is nothing to compare it with in the Heptarchic age except a *solidus* of Archbishop Wigmund of York (837-54)—an equally rare issue, and equally notable in its type, which presents a full-face bust of that prelate, in a style far better than that of other contemporary coins English or continental. Offa is much better remembered for his silver than for his gold coins; he was the first king who discontinued the old *sceatta* and adopted the Carlovingian *denarius* or silver penny.

The humiliation of the see of Canterbury was only destined to last for sixteen years, as after Offa's death and that of his son Ecgferth, Coenwulf, the next king of Mercia, forced Higbert to resign, and restored his rights to Archbishop Aethelheard. His political reasons for doing so will be explained in their due place, and he had to do with a primate who was a Mercian by birth and a loyal supporter, and not with a more or less open enemy, such as Jaenbert had been in the time of his predecessor.

Offa died in the summer of 796,[1] still undisputedly supreme over all Southern England, in great amity with Charlemagne, and full of years and prosperity. His dynasty might have become permanent rulers of all the smaller States if it had but continued. But Fate intervened; his only son Ecgferth died in the flower of his youth only 141 days after his father, and with him the line was extinct. An heir was sought by the Mercian witan in one Coenwulf, a very remote relative, since he descended from a brother of Penda different from that Eowa from whom came the line of Aethelbald and Offa. His reign will be dealt with elsewhere, for just ere he came to the throne the great central dividing line of old English history was reached,—in Offa's thirty-sixth year (793) the first Danish raid on

---

[1] July 26th, according to Simeon of Durham or 28th according to the Anglo-Saxon Chronicle.

this island had taken place, and the new age of the Viking invasion had begun.

Before turning over this new leaf, it is necessary to dispose of the history of the unfortunate kingdom of Northumbria during the years that correspond to Offa's long reign. We had followed it no farther than the death of Oswulf, the son of that Eadbert who had laid down the crown against his subjects' desire in 758. This short-lived prince was slain after a reign of less than a year by conspirators among his own thegns (July 25, 759). The place of the murder was " Mickle-Wongton," apparently Great Whittington near Corbridge. Eleven days later one Aethelwald, nicknamed " Moll," was elected "a sua plebe," as the continuator of Bede puts it— a phrase which seems to hint that it was rather the popular voice than the will of the *sapientes*, the greater councillors, which placed him on the throne. He was supposed to have been the instigator of the murder of Oswulf : his descent is uncertain ; the statement that he was an illegitimate brother of Eadbert, and so the uncle of Oswulf, whose death he was accused of contriving, is certainly wrong.[1] His election, however, was not undisputed. The son of the late king was still a mere child, but the aetheling Oswine, apparently a younger brother or cousin of Oswulf, took up arms against Aethelwald, and found much support in Bernicia. However, " King Moll " went northward against him, brought him to action at Eildon Hill, near Melrose, on the Tweed,[2] and there scattered his army. The aetheling was left on the field mortally wounded (Aug. 6th, 761). This victory, however, only gave Aethelwald four years of troubled and uncertain kingship, in which the chroniclers find time to note the " mickle winter " of 763-64, which lasted from December to March, two years of " a great tribulation of mortality, several grievous distempers raging, but more especially the dysentery," and disastrous fires which destroyed York, Doncaster and other places. Aethelwald was apparently regarded as an unlucky sovereign, and " fires seen in the air lasting almost the whole night " [aurora borealis or a shower of meteors ?] on January 1st, 765, were considered ominous of more trouble to come. It took

---

[1] It has been suggested that he was a descendant of his namesake, Aethelwald the son of Oswald, who was Sub-King of Deira during Penda's ascendency. But see Haddan and Stubbs, iii. 395-96, and Cadwallader Bates, *Northumberland*, p. 76.

[2] The Anglo-Saxon Chronicle calls the battle-spot "Eadwin's Cliff ".

the shape of a turbulent meeting of the Northumbrian witan at
Finchale (Winchanheal), near Durham, in the following autumn, at
which the king was deposed and, much against his will, tonsured
and sent into a monastery. The chaotic rule of succession in the
North is sufficiently shown by the fact that although Aethelwald
himself had a son, and Aelfwald, the heir of his predecessor Oswulf,
still lived, the *sapientes* went out of their way to elect and crown
one Alchred, the head of a line which claimed to descend from
Ealric, one of the younger sons of Ida, though none of his ancestors
had ever worn the crown, and their royal descent seems not to have
been unquestioned (Nov. 3rd, 565).[1] Thus at this time there were
no less than three separate races contending for the Northumbrian
throne, and their representatives succeeded each other in chaotic
alternation.

To strengthen his elective title to the throne Alchred took as
his wife Osgeofu, daughter of the murdered Oswulf, but it availed
him little when her brother was alive to claim the throne. A
curious letter of the royal pair to Lull, Bishop of Mainz, the successor of St. Boniface, has been preserved, in which they set forth
that the state of affairs both in Church and in State is troubled and
unsatisfactory, but that they accept it as a divine dispensation.
Rebellion was apparently rife; at any rate, in 769 the royal town
of Catterick "was burned by Earnred the tyrant, and the wretch
himself, by God's just judgment, perished by fire within the same
year". We have no knowledge which of the contending lines
claimed him as a member, but he was clearly an unsuccessful pretender to the throne. Yet Alchred was not destined to close his
eyes in peace; his rule evidently gave little satisfaction, and at
Eastertide, 774, "by the counsel and consent of all his subjects,
deposed by a combination of the royal house and the princes, he
changed his majesty for exile". Aethelred, the son of Aethelwald
Moll, was elected in his place, but got no secure footing. The
banished monarch first seized Bamborough at the head of a few
faithful adherents, and, when evicted, then fled to Cynoht, King of
the Picts, the successor of Aengus, who seems to have kept up his
predecessor's friendship with Northumbria. There he died in exile,

---

[1] "Prosapia Idae regis exortus, *ut quidam dicunt*," says Simeon of Durham,
though the genealogies in Florence of Worcester give all the links.

but his son Osred remained as a pretender to the throne, which he was one day to enjoy for a short space.

Aethelred, the son of Moll, was apparently one of those princes who in a time of trouble think murder the sole remedy for all evils; the recipe has been known to succeed, but only when its employer was a man of genius—like Chlodovech the Frank or Ivan the Terrible—and this was evidently not the case with Aethelred. His whole record is one of blood, culminating in 778 in the simultaneous slaying by treachery (*fraude*) of three ealdormen (or highreeves, as the Anglo-Saxon Chronicle calls them)—Eardwulf of Bamborough, Cynewulf and Ecga. This apparently was too much for his subjects, and he was expelled a few months later, "and compelled to turn to the tone of sorrow and to utter pitiful complaints". For eleven years he remained in exile, waiting for a second chance for a snatch at power, which was ultimately to be granted him, much to the detriment of Northumbria, for he was in every way evil, an adulterer and a profaner of sanctuary, as well as a murderer.

The witan, on the expulsion of this wicked prince, gave the crown to Aelfwald, son of Oswulf, attracted perhaps not only by his descent from Eadbert, the last successful king in the land, but by his personal virtues. He was a pious and just monarch, "men called him God's friend," and miracles attested his sanctity. He ruled for nine years (779-88), a long period as Northumbrian reigns went, in this period of chaos; his four predecessors had only filled twenty-one years among them. It was also, as it seems, a period of comparative quiet: we have no mention of civil war, and the best remembered incident of the time was the visit to Northumbria of the papal legate George Bishop of Ostia, who held (as has been already mentioned) a provincial council at Finchale (786), when with the consent of the king, Archbishop Eanbald, and the other prelates of the North, those same twenty decrees were promulgated which were afterwards laid before the Council of Chelsea. But not even blameless life and general popularity could save a Northumbrian king in this age from the common fate of his race. Aelfwald was "miserably murdered by his ealdorman Sicgan at Scythleccster near the Wall,[1] on September 23, 788, as the result

---

[1] Apparently Chesters, near Chollerford.

of a conspiracy". He was buried with much wailing in Hexham Abbey, and a light was seen to shine for many nights, so the tale went, over the spot where he had been slain; a chapel was afterwards built upon it.

Aelfwald left two infant sons, Aelf and Aelfwine; they were too young to reign, and the witan chose the exile Osred, son of Alchred, to take the crown. But the evil days had begun again; after a reign of somewhat over a year (788-90), the new king was "circumvented by the wiles of his princes, arrested, deposed, and forcibly tonsured in his city of York". More fortunate than his predecessor, he got off for the moment with his life, and succeeded soon afterwards in escaping to the Isle of Man. The crown fell to Aethelred, the cruel son of King Moll, in whose interest the conspiracy had been managed. He returned to the throne, which he had lost in 779, in no wise improved by the bitterness of prison and exile.[1] He took the young sons of the saintly King Aelfwald out of their sanctuary in York Minster with false promises of safety, and sent them away to be secretly drowned in Windermere.[2] Another of his crimes had a curious end: he ordered that the aetheling Eardwulf should be put to death; his assassins led out their prisoner before the gate of the monastery of Ripon, and there slew him, as they supposed. His body was taken up by the monks, and placed under a tent outside the church, for burial on the next day. But after midnight the supposed dead man was found alive, and seeking sanctuary at the altar; he had been only wounded and had come to himself after a swoon of many hours, and crawled into the church. He was apparently assisted to escape by the brethren —certainly he fled into exile and survived to become King of Northumbria sixteen years after.

In 792 the exiled king, Osred II., made an attempt to recover his kingdom, being invited to return from his refuge in Man by a faction of nobles, who told him that the rule of Aethelred had become unbearable. He landed secretly in Northumbria and raised his standard, but his followers flinched from him, and he was cap-

---

[1] We know of the imprisonment from Alcuin, who was visiting England at the time, and says that he "de carcere processit in solium, et de molestia in majestatem" (*Mon. Alc.*, p. 170).

[2] "De ecclesia principali per promissa fallaciae abducti, miserabiliter perempti sunt a rege Ethelredo in Wonwaldremere" (Simeon of Durham). This seems to imply drowning.

tured by the king, who immediately ordered him to be beheaded. This seemed to make Aethelred's throne secure, despite of all his cruelties, and he was honoured with the hand of the great Offa's daughter, Aelflaed, a sign that the ruler of the South regarded him as a neighbour whose friendship was worth securing.

But a disaster was impending over him of a different kind from any that had gone before. It was no wonder that the spring of the fourth year after his restoration (793) was filled with dire prodigies—showers of meteors, perpetual thunderstorms, fiery dragons seen in the midnight sky, and such-like—for in the summer occurred the first great Viking raid that penetrated to England. It was wholly unexpected, since the struggle between Charlemagne and the Danes, which precipitated the outbreak of this pest, had apparently roused little interest on this side of the North Sea. An attack from the side of the sea by a foreign enemy was a thing which never had been seen, since the first of the Angles settled in Bernicia and Deira. Hence the terror aroused was dreadful, when it was reported that a squadron of pirate vessels from the Pagan North had descended upon the island sanctuary of Lindisfarne, sacked its church, plundered its treasures of gold and silver, slain some of the brethren with the sword, drowned others, and carried off a remnant as slaves. It was at first hoped that this was an isolated and abnormal phenomenon; but in the next spring the heathen appeared again, and plundered Jarrow, the monastery where Bede had lived and died. It was some consolation that on this occasion they did not escape unscathed: their leader—traditionally said to have been the famous Ragnar Lodbrog[1]—was captured and put to a cruel death; later generations said that the Northumbrian king cast him into a pit filled with adders. Many of the Danish ships were cast on shore by a violent north-east wind, and of their crews some were drowned and others taken and slaughtered. King Aethelred was not the man to spare an enemy of any sort.

But his blood-stained reign was just at an end. In the seventh year of his reign, on April 18th, 796, he was slain at Corbridge by conspirators, who proclaimed as his successor one Osbald, an aetheling who was also an ealdorman. We know nothing of his ancestry. But his party had miscalculated their strength. After reigning only twenty-seven days he was driven out by a faction

[1] An error: Ragnar's sons were harrying England eighty years later. See chapter xxi.

headed by Eardwulf, the ealdorman of whose miraculous escape from death at Ripon we heard a little while back. Three kings reigned in a year, and Charlemagne, who had been an ally of the cruel King Aethelred, expressed his high disgust, and declared that the Northumbrians were worse than their pagan enemies the Danes. The kingdom had indeed sunk to the very depths of degradation. It would seem to have been at this time that it lost its long-preserved suzerainty over the Galloway Picts, whose last recorded English bishop was consecrated in 791, and apparently died or withdrew from his see about 803. There are some signs that the border against the Strathclyde Welsh was also receding. The only wonder is that Offa of Mercia never seems to have thought it worth while to assert his supremacy over the decadent realm. Perhaps he considered that the turbulent and faction-ridden king-dom was safer as an impotent neighbour than as a troublesome vassal-state. It is clear that he might have had it as his own, by assisting one faction against another, at any time that he chose during the last twenty years of his reign. But he preferred to keep on terms of friendship with the *de facto* king of the moment : the only case in which he seems to have committed himself to anything more, was when he gave his daughter's hand to the cruel king Aethelred. When his son-in-law was murdered he made no attempt to avenge him ; but this may have been because he was already sickening for his final illness : the Northumbrian tyrant died on April 18th. Offa expired on July 26th, 796.

Having once reached the commencement of the Viking raids, we must consign the remainder of the miserable annals of the Northern kingdom to the chapter which deals with the struggle between Dane and Englishman. The troubles of Northumbria were to be protracted for another seventy years, under a succession of seven kings, whose record is quite as miserable as that of the last age, though one of them, Eanred (808-40), succeeded in prolonging his reign for the unprecedented term of thirty-two years, through no great merit of his own. Nothing short of the extermination of all the branches of the house of Ida by the sword of the Danes could teach these misguided Northumbrians wisdom. They finally found themselves the servants of the stranger, and only achieved a kind of freedom when, in company with their conquerors, they were absorbed into the new kingdom of All-England, through the annexation of the whole North by the great kings of the house of Wessex—the descendants of Alfred—in the middle of the tenth century. Melancholy as is the whole later history of the Heptarchic kingdoms, that of Northumbria certainly constitutes its most depressing page.

CHAPTER XVII

THE SOCIAL ORGANISATION OF THE EARLY ENGLISH KINGDOMS

ANY attempt to give an account of the social and political organisation of the Teutonic kingdoms in Britain during the first two centuries of their existence must necessarily proceed by the method of working backward.   Contemporary records there are none : but starting from the very moment of the conversion of the Jutes of Kent to Christianity, we find a long series of codes of laws, charters, and other instruments, which cast a light on the previous condition of the English peoples.   And information no less precious is to be elicited from the literary documents of the early Christian period, and most especially from the long and detailed *Ecclesiastical History* of Bede, who is almost as valuable for the social facts which he records incidentally, in the course of his countless anecdotes and divagations, as for his political narrative.   The process of working backward has its dangers, particularly when the nation and the state have just passed through a period of rapid development and transformation, caused by the introduction of Christianity.   But these dangers of this method are no whit greater than those which lie in the way of those who have taken the opposite course, and have endeavoured to reconstruct the social organisation of the Early English kingdoms by working forward from the picture of the second-century Teutonic tribes contained in the *Germania* of Tacitus.   The Roman author gives a sketch mainly derived from his knowledge of the races just beyond the Rhine, on the frontier of the empire.   He sometimes errs from misconception, and sometimes seems to be more set on pointing a moral than on supplying an accurate analysis of facts. More than three hundred years passed between the time when he wrote and the settlement of the English on the coast of Eastern Britain, and in that long period all the Teutonic tribes had gone through many new experiences. We do not even know how far his picture of the German states, if correct in the main for the frontier peoples whom he had seen, would have served, at the moment when he published his book, for a description of the remoter races, dwelling by the Elbe or the Eider. Caution, in short, is necessary on either hand: it is even more dangerous to argue that a second-century institution was still unchanged in the sixth century, than to deduce that a social fact observable in the early eighth century was already existent in the days of Ida or Ceawlin. Still, within certain limits, argument and deduction are possible, and it is only by their use that we can make any statement with regard to the dark space between Hengist and Aethelbert.

The first problem that confronts us, when we face this most problematic age, is one on which most of the constitutional difficulties of Anglo-Saxon history ultimately depend. Was the conquest of Britain carried out purely and solely by the personal warbands of individual chiefs—*duces, heretogas, ealdormen,*—or was it to any extent a settlement of tribes and families, as opposed to a settlement of individuals dependent on their chosen war-lords? Looking at the mere probabilities of the case, we should be inclined to accept the former alternative, and to think it probable that the first Teutonic communities in this island must have been started by the gift of land, with or without servile dependants dwelling upon it, by a conquering king to the members of his *comitatus*, the sworn followers whom he was bound to maintain in return for their loyal service in battle. The nucleus of the invading hosts was undoubtedly composed of such retainers, and in most cases it is clear that the English settlements were not made by races migrating *en masse*, and carrying the whole tribal community and its customs with them, but by parties, larger or smaller, conducted by adventurous leaders. The main body of the Saxons and the Jutes certainly remained behind in their old continental sites, whatever may have been the case with the Angles,[1] of whom we have seen reason to believe that the majority emigrated, and left that gap behind them, in the "Angulus" in Schleswig, which Bede describes. Fragments of a race, who had left the ancestral home at various dates and under many leaders—as did the Saxons at

[1] See pp. 217-18.

least—and who formed many settlements, not under the old tribal
king, but under princes representing younger branches of the royal
house, might be expected to organise themselves as new military
states, dependent on their chiefs, rather than as tribal groups.   In
short, we should expect to find reproduced in Britain the state of
things which certainly prevailed among the Frankish conquerors of
Gaul, where the royal power was all-important, and the settlers
regarded themselves as the sworn liegemen of the conqueror who
had parcelled out among them the lands of the Roman provincials,
not as a mere tribal community owing a traditional allegiance to
its ancestral monarch.   We have seen reason to believe that the
war-bands which invaded Britain were decidedly more heterogeneous
in blood than the Franks, and have noted that the first names of
the English states are not drawn from old designations of sub-tribes
in Germany or the Cimbric peninsula.   When they are not purely
local (like East-Saxons, Mercians, or Mid-Angles) they are either
borrowed from the Celtic lands recently conquered (like Bernicians,
Deirans, Lindiswaras, Kentings) or obviously designate a new and
artificial unit like Gewissae "the confederates".[1]   It is impossible
to point out a single name for the peoples of any Anglo-Saxon
kingdom or sub-kingdom which was clearly in use on the continent
for an already existing community before the invasion began.

Notwithstanding all this, we are confronted with the stubborn
fact that the social organisation of the English states, when first we
can visualise them with some approach to detailed accuracy, in the
seventh century, does not seem to have been the simple military
monarchy that we should have expected.   We should have looked
to find an all-powerful king, surrounded by subjects who derived
their endowment from him, and who only differed in importance, one
from another, in proportion as they had received a greater or
less share of his bounty.   Among such a community "nobility by
service," i.e., the differentiation of rank according to the scale
on which the settlers had commended themselves to the king's
liberality, and approached more or less nearly to his person,
might have been expected to prevail.   And as a matter of fact nobility by service—as we shall see—did ultimately become the main
feature of the Anglo-Saxon social system.   But just where we

[1] See pp. 228, 230.

should have looked for it in its most marked shape, in the earliest document available, the Kentish laws of the seventh century, we find in fact something different.

The first document in which the ranks and classes of one of the Teutonic kingdoms of Britain is set forth is the short Kentish code known as the "Laws of Aethelbert". This compilation, which dates from a few years after the king's conversion to Christianity, is followed at a distance of two and three generations by later Kentish laws issued by his descendants,—Eadric, Lothere, and Wihtraed. Like other early codes, the Kentish laws deal mainly with fines to be imposed for the various degrees of breach of the peace, from homicide downward, and are largely devoted to the setting forth of the exact compensation due for injury to members of each class in the state. The notable point about them is that they divide the population of Kent into three classes, *eorls*, *ceorls*, and *laets* (besides slaves who stand apart in the reckoning) *i.e.*, nobles, freemen, and tributary dependants, a partition apparently corresponding very nearly to the threefold classification found in the continental codes of several North-German tribes. For example, the Frisian laws give the division into *nobiles*, freemen, and *liti*. So do those of the Old Saxons by the Elbe. The code of the Thuringians (*i.e.*, the Netherland Thoringi, as we have seen reason to believe[1]) has a similar division, but calls the noble *adalingus*. While agreeing with these, the Kentish laws show a sharp contrast with the Frankish codes, where the only legal distinction between persons (outside that between Frank and Roman) is that the king's ministers and henchmen, the *comites*, *antrustions*, etc., are estimated at a value far greater than that of the ordinary Frankish freeman. There is little trace of birth nobility in the Merovingian realm, where the king alone is the source of all power and honour.

In Kent, on the other hand, as in Frisia or Saxony, birth-nobility certainly existed. And it seems probable that the same may have originally been the case in other English kingdoms. The Eorls of the Kentish codes find their parallel in the *nobiles* of Bede's *Ecclesiastical History*. In the account of the great baptisms in Northumbria in 627 (ii. 14) the *nobiles* among the converts are as carefully distinguished from the *regii viri* (the king's thegns and

[1] For these " Angli et Werini, hoc est Thuringi," see p. 219, in chapter xii. above.

other ministers), as in another passage they are from the "*privati*" or ordinary freemen (v. 23).   Similarly when Bede in another chapter (iii. 30) contrasts the "optimates" with the "plebs" of the East Saxons, the only natural way to understand his phrase is to think of the nobly-born as distinguished from the merely free-born, not to imagine that we are confronted with royal retainers as opposed to the ceorls.   So too when in the *Historia Abbatum* [1] he tells us that Benedict Biscop was *nobili stirpe gentis Anglorum progenitus*, he is most evidently referring to ancestral blood ; Benedict has been a member of King Oswy's following, but it was not this but his *stirps* that made him noble in Bede's eyes.   Similarly the unfortunate King Oswin, whom Oswy slew unrighteously,[2] is said to have been so kind *nobilibus suis atque ignobilibus* that even from other states *viri nobilissimi* would frequently come, with the request that they might be allowed to join his household. They were not ennobled by adhering to him, but were already "*nobilissimi*," obviously by blood.   The Kentish codes would have called all such people *eorlcund*.   Indeed the term *eorl* was so well known as the title of the well-born, as opposed to *ceorl* the ordinary man, that the jingle "eorl and ceorl," as expressing the whole body of the king's free subjects, continued to be used for long generations after the cross-division into persons belonging, or not belonging, to the nobility of service had become the dominant fact in social life.   It was employed even by Alfred in the ninth century [3] in general phrases, though long before his time the other form of classification had become the really important one for all practical dealings, both between man and man, and between the state and the individual.

It seems then that a clear distinction between the nobles by birth and the mere freemen existed in the English kingdoms so far as we can trace them back, and that the former had marked and manifest superiority by reason of their status, quite without reference to their relations to the king.   A Kentish eorl in Lothere's time had a *weregeld* of 300 gold *solidi*, while the death of a mere ceorl could be atoned for by a fine of 100 *solidi* only—and so in all the scale of valuations.

Nor is this the only sign that the king's favour was not the

---

[1] *Hist. Abbatum*, cap. i.   [2] *E. H.*, iii. 14.
[3] As in Laws, v., Swa we eac settath be eallum hadum, ge ceorle ge eorle, etc.

sole factor in differentiating social privilege in Early England. The family group appears as an important feature in all legislation. The individual, eorl or ceorl, is not merely a unit whose welfare concerns himself and the state alone : he is a member of a *maegth*, or kindred, organised in a joint association for mutual protection, and liable also to take up the responsibility for all the misdoings of its component personages. This family group is not an artificial invention, but a band of actual relatives, whose pedigree is carefully traced out to the fifth and sixth generation. It is by no means a mere gathering together of individuals for police purposes, like the frank-pledge groups of a later age, nor even a body which any stranger can easily enter by the fiction of adoption, like the old Roman gens. It is very jealously guarded by those who, in virtue of their birth, have a right to belong to it.

These two phenomena which we have just noted, the existence in the earliest organisation of the old English states of a hereditary nobility, and of a powerful and important system of family groups allied for purposes of self-defence and mutual responsibility, are by no means what we should have expected to find in kingdoms newly established by military adventurers. A war-band following a chief to a settlement over seas would, we should have supposed, be composed of individuals drawn from many families, and only connected by their common allegiance to the heretoga or ealdorman to whom they had bound themselves. And within the war-band birth would have been of little importance, compared with the favour of the chief, the source of all honour and endowment. But since these two phenomena are observed, we are forced to make certain deductions. The first is that the original settlers must have been to a much greater extent than might have been supposed, drawn from particular kindreds and families, who retained their mutual ties, despite of their having individually made themselves over to the king or ealdorman as members of his *comitatus*. The second is that a considerable number of noble families must have taken part in the original settlement—enough to be able to assert their old privilege of status, both against the king and against the other members of the war-band, who were but " ceorlish " in descent. In short, the population of a newly-founded English kingdom—Kent, Bernicia, Sussex, or what not—must have been much more of a section sliced off from the whole of the continental tribe which had sent it forth, and much less of a mere *comitatus*, than might have been expected.

This we could understand well enough in the case of the Angles, where (as has been already stated) the bulk of the race seems to have migrated, so that eorl, ceorl and tributary dependant would naturally come over together, with their old status and rights. It is more surprising in the case of the Jutes and Saxons, where only a moderate part of the old tribe abandoned its Continental home. But our evidence is very strong for the Jutes of Kent, since it is their code which is the oldest, and in it the position of the noble-by-birth is particularly well marked. A suggestion has sometimes been made that all the nobles of an early English kingdom may have derived their rights by inheritance from the original royal stock, of which they would represent younger branches. But though it may be granted that some of the royal houses, especially that of Wessex, had countless ramifications, and though individuals descended from *subreguli* or *aethelings* may have been an appreciable element in the nobility, it seems difficult to believe that they were its sole members. It seems indeed that while connection with the royal line was carefully remembered and highly esteemed, it was not the ordinary qualification for nobility. Bede speaks of *viri de regio genere;* the Anglo-Saxon Chronicle was careful to speak of persons " whose right paternal kin went back to Cerdic," though their ancestors had not reigned for many generations (*e.g.*, King Beorhtric [1]). In Northumbria we have a special note of surprise in the same authority when Aella was chosen as ruler, because he was "ungecyndne cyning" a king not of royal blood.[2] Such facts are just what we should *not* find if all *nobiles* had originally been aethelings.

We must take it then that in the early English kingdom the two phenomena of birth-nobility and family-groups were clearly displayed. It has been suggested that the easiest way of accounting for the existence of something like tribal kingdoms with a well-marked social stratification by birth, where centralised military monarchies might have seemed the natural form of settlement, can best be discovered by supposing that when some adventurous king and his *comitatus* had made the first lodgment, free tribes-

---

[1] A. S. C., under the year 784.   [2] *Ibid.*, 867.

men were invited in to strengthen the new community. The chief, finding his war-band too few to settle up what he and they had won, may have offered liberal terms to powerful eorls of his own tribe, and to whole family-groups of ceorls, if they would come over the water to his aid. They would stipulate for the perpetuation of their old privileges in their new homes, so that the state, when formed, would be much less autocratic in constitution than might have been expected. This is pure hypothesis, but we have to account somehow for the phenomena before us. And thus does it seem easiest to explain the preponderance in most parts of Eastern England of the family settlements which are its characteristic development. For it is impossible to regard the typical village names of those regions, all the Effinghams and Walsinghams, the Tootings and Wokings, the Whittingtons and Bridlingtons, as anything but the original homes of powerful *maegths*.[1]

The normal holding of the ceorl who formed part of one of the large kindred-settlements was the *hiwisc*, or in later phrase the *hide*, the amount of land which was considered competent to support a free household. Hence Bede and other early authorities use *terra unius familiae* as the equivalent for a hide, and a large estate may be called equally the land of five hides or of five families. The hide must not be conceived as consisting of a precise number of acres : soils are of unequal fertility, and the amount necessary to maintain a household would differ in area. Nor does it consist solely of arable land in the stripes dear to the early Teuton. To supplement them grazing ground in the common meadow is required, moreover there are rights over the wood of the common waste of the settlement. For the typical free settlement of an English *maegth* consisted first of the large arable fields divided up into narrow strips, of which each household possessed several, next of the almost equally prized meadow, which was hedged off into appropriated lots in summer, but thrown back into common in winter, and lastly of the undistributed waste, from

---

[1] Kemble's view on this point still stands, despite of much criticism. See also Vinogradoff, *Growth of the Manor*, 140, who finds Kemble's theory " conclusive," " the constant recurrence of these forms is sufficient to convince us . . . that the occupation must have been effected largely by connecting the territorial division with a kindred ". For a statement of the contrary view see Mr. Stevenson in *Engl. Hist. Rev.*, xiv., 1894.

which the whole community would draw its wood supply, and on which it would pasture its swine, or even turn out its cattle for rough grazing at some seasons.

The normal method of agriculture was the "three-field system," with a rotation of wheat, barley or oats, and in the third year fallow—to allow of the exhausted soil regaining some measure of its fertility. In the last year the field was left unfenced, and the cattle of the community picked up what they could from it, when they were neither on the waste, nor being fed with the hay that had been mowed from the meadow. There seem to have been exceptional cases in which the strips of the arable were not permanently allotted to different households, but were distributed, by lot or otherwise, to different holders in different years. But this was an abnormal arrangement: usually the proprietorship of the strips in each field was fixed.[1] And the usual arrangement would be that the fully endowed ceorl's household had just so much arable in its various strips as a full team of oxen could plough.

The king's *comitatus* appears clearly enough in the Kentish Laws, but in a less prominent way than we should have expected. Apparently there are already two classes of persons comprised in it. These are the *gesith* (later called *comes*) who is the superior of the two, a regular member of the king's war-band, already endowed with landed estates, and the thegn (*minister* as he was afterwards called) who was still the household servant of the king, and in many cases not yet a landholder by his master's bounty. There are only two allusions to the class, both in the latest additions to the code, those made by Wihtraed in 695. In one place the member of the royal following is called a "gesithcundman,"[2] a term that we shall meet more frequently when dealing with the Wessex code of Ine. In the other place he is styled a "king's thegn" (*cyninges theng*[3]). The superior status of both is shown by the fact that the *gesithcundman* is fined twice as much as the ceorl who commits the same offence, while the thegn is given the privilege of clearing himself from an accusation by his own oath at the altar, while the ceorl similarly accused has to bring forward four men of his own class to make oath for him.

There is one more element to take into consideration when

---

[1] See Vinogradoff, *Origin of the Manor*, 174-75.
[2] Wihtraed, § 5.   [3] *Ibid.*, § 20.

dealing with the social organisation of the earliest English kingdoms. Besides "eorl and ceorl" and besides the mere domestic
slave (*theow, esne*) who existed in this island as in every other
home of the Teutons, we find already existing in the code of
Aethelbert, a third class not enjoying complete freedom, yet
certainly not merely servile, the *laets*. Their name at once suggests
the *litus* and *lazzus* of the Continent, and we cannot fail to see
in them tributary dependants of alien blood. But a difficult
problem at once crops up : are these persons the descendants of the
old Romano-British peasantry, taken over along with the lands
which they cultivated, by the Teutonic conqueror ? At the first
glance this would seem to be their most probable origin, and the
analogy of the similar class in Gaul would serve us well. But a
second thought reminds us that the *lazzus*, a similar tribute-paying
person of inferior status, crops up also among the Saxons and
Frisians, in lands where there is no question of a survival of Roman
provincials. In Saxony or Frisia he must have been the descendant of conquered tribes or of emancipated slaves. What are we
to assign as his origin in Kent ? We know from the moans of
Gildas that a certain proportion of the old British population had
survived the Conquest—the people whom (in a passage already
quoted) he describes as "going, worn out by famine, to the enemy,
and surrendering to them on the condition that they would serve
them for ever, if only they were not slain at once, for this was the
best privilege that they could obtain ". This passage alone would
almost by itself suffice to prove the perpetuation of a certain
amount of British population in Eastern Britain. And when we
find a considerable class of tributary peasants existent in Kent in
the year 600, it is tempting to recognise in the *laets* of Aethelbert's
code the descendants of the broken provincials of whom Gildas
wrote. Yet on the other hand it is only fair to plead that *laets*
may also have come over from Germany, along with the eorls and
ceorls, in whose company they must already have existed on the
Continent. And if the surviving British population in Eastern
Britain had been numerous, it is hard to explain why the English
tongue won such a complete victory over the speech that preceded
it, in direct contrast to what happened in Gaul, where the debased
Romance dialect of the conquered overcame the old Frankish
speech. Moreover, as has been already pointed out in an earlier

chapter, it seems hard to believe that if the Romano-British peasantry had survived as the base of the agricultural population in
Kent and elsewhere, we should have no trace whatever of Christianity surviving also. Yet the narrative of the conversion in
Bede most distinctly implies that Augustine found no pre-existing
Christian population within the English states, and that Queen
Bertha and those of her household were the only baptised persons
whom he met on his arrival in Britain. It is true that the missionaries received permission from Aethelbert not only to build
places of worship where they pleased, but to repair old Roman
churches where they found them.[1] But the whole tenor of the
story implies that these last were ruins, not live churches with
congregations composed of British *laets* and served by a surviving
British clergy. Are we then to conclude that Christianity had
become extinct among the tributary subjects of the old English
kings? Or must we be driven still further, and doubt whether
the *laets* were Britons at all, accounting for them as immigrants
from Germany along with the eorls and ceorls among whom they
lived? In either case the problem presents great difficulties.

One thing, however, is certain. About ninety years later, when
the West Saxon King Ine drew up his code about the year 693, not
only was there a considerable tributary population in his realm—as
there seems to have been in Kent in the days of Aethelbert—but
this population was British in blood, so much so that a member of
it is invariably called a *Wealh ;* no such non-national term as *laet*
appears in this king's laws. It has sometimes been suggested that
this fact is only the reflection of the recent conquest of mid-Somersetshire, in which the West Welsh had just become Ine's subjects,
and that the whole code is the settlement-charter of a newly subdued
region. But if the Anglo-Saxon Chronicle can be trusted Ine's
Damnonian campaigns belonged to his middle years (710), while
the date of his code is fixed at some period before 693 by the appearance in its preface of Bishop Earconwald, who died in that year.
On the other hand there are reasons for thinking that Ine had
already won land as far as the Exe by 690,[2] so the problem is left
still unsettled.

As to the proportion in which the old provincial population

[1] See p. 263.   [2] See p. 328.

endured, the only deduction that can be made is that, as has been already said, the English tongue prevailed everywhere in Eastern and Southern Britain.   This shows that the surviving stratum of Romanised Celts cannot have been nearly so thick as in Gaul—not to speak of Spain or Italy.   Even in the vocabulary of husbandry and servile industry the number of loan-words to be discovered in the old English tongue is by no means large.   Indeed the language seems to have been far more affected by borrowings from Latin in the sphere of Church life, after the conversion, than by those from either Celtic or Latin in the sphere of domestic life made in the earlier centuries.

In short, the base of the state in seventh-century England must have been the *ceorl*, the small freeman, rather than the *laet* or *Wealh* of tributary status.   And long before the Norman conquest the surviving alien population seems to have been absorbed in the conquering race in all districts save the extreme West.

Ine's Laws are interesting as showing the full development of the "nobility by service," which is so slightly touched upon in the Kentish codes.   To the West-Saxon king the primary distinction among his subjects (putting the *Wealhs* aside) was not that between " eorl and ceorl," but that between those who belonged to his personal following and those who did not.   The former, as in the Kentish laws of Wihtraed, are called *gesithcund*, whatever their rank or status, and this term is used in normal contradistinction to the ceorl.   The *sithcundus homo* and the *cyrlisus homo* balance each other in many paragraphs of the Latin translation of the code. A gesithcund man might be holding land by the king's grant, or not ; in the latter case he is evidently one of the domestic retinue, who has not attained sufficient importance to be endowed with an estate.   " If a gesithcund man with land neglects the summons to war, let him pay 120 shillings ; " says the code, " if he owns no land, 60 shillings ; but let the ceorlish man pay 30 shillings for his *fyrdwite* " (fine for evasion of military service).[1]   Apparently the gesithcund men were not in full permanent and hereditary possession of the land which the king has given them : it was held purely on condition of service.   One law lays down that " if a gesithcund man wishes to depart, he may take with him only his reeve, his smith,

1 Ine, § 51.

and the fosterer of his children ".[1] The rest of the dwellers on his
land must be left behind. It seems also that by accepting the land
from the king he binds himself to bring it under cultivation, and to
people it, for another law says that " he who has twenty hides of
land must leave twelve hides of settled land (*gesettes londes, terrae
vestitae*) if he wishes to depart ; he who has ten hides, six ; he who
has three, one and a half hides of settled land ".[2] A very curious
paragraph gives the rate of rent at which estates were let out to the
king's men. " Whoever has ten hides shall pay yearly ten jars of
honey, 300 loaves, twelve *ambers* of Welsh beer (mead) and thirty
of clear beer, two fully grown oxen or ten wethers, ten geese, twenty
fowls, ten cheeses, a full *amber* of butter, five salmon, twenty
measures of fodder, and one hundred eels." These provisions presumably fed the king's domestic retinue in his constant journeyings
around his realm.

It is important to note that the royal following included men of
Celtic blood, as well as the English *gesithcund* men. Among the
statements of the *weregeld* of each rank—the sum due as compensation for manslaughter—we find the valuation of " the king's horse-
Wealh who can do him service as messenger " : he is reckoned at
200 shillings, which should be compared with the counting of the
ordinary Welsh landholder at 120 shillings,[3] and of three classes of
Englishmen at 1,200, 600 and 200 shillings respectively. The fact
that the " horse-Wealh " is in the king's service has raised his value
by 60 per cent., and equated him with one of the third and lowest
category of the superior race.

Another point of obvious significance in Ine's law is that the
gesithcund man of the superior class with his 1,200 shilling weregeld
is worth six times the ceorl with his 200 shilling valuation. In the
Kent of Lothere and Wihtraed, one generation before, the eorl had
been worth no more than three times the ceorl. The relative esti-
mation of the ordinary freeman to the great landowner has evidently
fallen in the interval.

The piece of information which we should have been most glad
to discover in the laws of Ine is, most unfortunately, withheld from

---

[1] Ine, § 63.   [2] *Ibid.*, § 64-66.

[3] We find, however, from law 24 that there were exceptional Welsh subjects of
the king who had as much as five hides of land, and these attained to a weregeld of
600 shillings, that of the second class of English.

us, *viz.*, the proportion in which the population of Wessex about the year 693 was divided between free ceorls living on their hides of land in the old fashion, dependent peasants living on the land of the king's gesithcund men, and tributary Wealhs. From the amount of attention devoted to the rights and liabilities of the second-named class we should suppose that it must have been very large. But whether it, as yet, formed a majority of the whole race of the West Saxons we are not in a position to say. At any rate we may be sure that what may be called the elements of feudalism were already well established in the land. Wessex was full of great landowners holding ten or twenty hides from the king, and working those hides by the labour of peasant families, English or Welsh, who paid them rent and service, just as they paid these same dues to the king. The lord was already entitled to share, along with the king, in the weregeld of his dependants if they were slain. He was already responsible in some degree for their good conduct: in the case of theft, for example, if the dependant (geneat) escaped with his plunder and had no kin pledged for him, the lord would have to pay up the fine and compensation for his crime.[1] We seem to detect two classes amongst the peasantry on the estates of the gesithcund men : the one get their dwellings and probably their outfit of cattle, etc., from him : the other have taken up land under him, but apparently have dwellings and stock of their own. Both might, as it seems, migrate with their lord's permission ; but if they passed into another shire clandestinely they were liable to be reclaimed, and sent back charged with a fine of sixty shillings.[2]

Among the paragraphs, however, of Ine's code which deal with dependents settled on the land of a lord, there are a considerable number of others concerning the other sort of community " where ceorls dwell having meadow land in common, and other land (*i.e.*, tilled land) in shares " : here we recognise the old free village that had started with the settlement of a *maegth*.[3] There are many rules laid down about the duties of hedging in fields so as to prevent trespass of cattle, and of making no more than moderate use of the common wood. The man who in greed felled too many trees might be fined as much as sixty shillings : the same penalty fell on him who by carelessness set the wood ablaze, " for fire is a thief ".

[1] Ine, § 22.   [2] *Ibid.*, § 39.   [3] *Ibid.*, §§ 40-44.

In these sections there is, of course, no question of payment or compensation to any one but the injured persons, there being no lord to claim a share. If, for example, cattle have done damage because some of the community have well fenced their fields and others have not, the owners of the unfenced shares have to compensate those who have taken proper precautions, and have suffered because their neighbours had not done the same.[1]

Notwithstanding all this, we are undoubtedly driven to the conclusion that Ine's Wessex was a state in which the free ceorl was not nearly so important, when compared to the landholder belonging to the kingly comitatus, as he was in Kent. The only evidence forthcoming for the other two kingdoms which grew great at the expense of the Welsh, Northumbria and Mercia, would seem to point to the conclusion that their social organisation was more similar to that of Wessex than to that of Kent. It may very likely have been the case, on the other hand, that East Anglia, Essex, and Sussex, where the conditions of settlement were more similar to those of Kent, and where extension at the expense of the Britons became impossible at an early date, showed the opposite phenomenon. But here we have no evidence at all : not a single law has survived from these kingdoms, nor have we even a series of charters to replace them. Once more we have come upon one of the numerous gaps in Anglo-Saxon history—gaps which are as frequent in social as in political annals.

[1] Ine, § 42.

CHAPTER XVIII

THE POLITICAL ORGANISATION OF THE EARLY ENGLISH KINGDOMS

HAVING dealt, so far as is possible, with the social organisation of the early English kingdoms, we must turn to their
political organisation.   The governmental machinery by which
the people of Kent, eorls, ceorls and laets, were ruled in the time of
Aethelbert and his descendants is passed over in the most surprising fashion in the Kentish codes.[1]   There is a clear indication of
the existence of a council of wise men in the prologue to Wihtraed's
Dooms.   The king has gathered " an advisory assembly of his great
men "[2] at Bersted and, as we then read, " every rank of churchman
spoke, in unison with the loyal folk :[3] and the great men resolved,
with the assent of all, to add to the rightful customs of the men of
Kent these following laws".   Beyond Bertwald, Archbishop of
Canterbury, and Gebmund, Bishop of Rochester, no one of the
" great men " is named.   That there were present a great many
of the ordinary ceorls must be inferred from the allusion to the
" loyal folk ".   But how far their approval to the new legislation
was asked or given is not clear from the phrase that the great men
enacted it *mid ealra gemedum* " with the assent of all ".   This
may or may not imply that the laws were formally submitted to
the whole crowd of men of Kent.   The gathering itself is called a
gemot.[4]

The only other allusions to any public assembly in the Kentish
laws occur, one in the Code of Aethelbert, where in the first clause
it is stated that there is a double fine for breaking the peace of the
" *Maethel*," the other in Lothere's law, where it is called " *Medle* ".
This is apparently the local assembly akin to the Frankish *Mallus.*

The preamble to Ine's code is in a quite different form.   He

---

[1] Ine, § 42.   [2] Eadigra geheahtendlic ymcyme.
[3] Mid þy hersuman folcy.   [4] Wihtraed, § 5.

states that he has published it "with the advice and counsel of
his father Coenred (a *subregulus* who never attained to the royal
crown), of his two bishops Hedde of Winchester and Earconwald of
London, of all his ealdormen, of the senior wise men of his kingdom (*thaem ieldstan witum minre theode*), and of a great assembly
of clergy ". There is no allusion whatever to the presence of any
general body of the freemen of the West Saxon kingdom, or of
their assent to the legislation, though the code is stated to be "for
the profit and better governance of our folk ". The impression
given to the reader by this, as by so much more, of Ine's termino-
logy, is that Wessex was a state in which the royal power was in a
much more advanced condition than in Kent, and in which the
smaller freemen counted for far less. But what of the greater ?
What was the relation of a Saxon king to the assembly of notables
who gave him advice—the *sapientes* or *consiliarii*, who composed his Witan ?

The constitutional position of the Witan and its relations with
the king on the one side, and the general assembly of the freemen
of the tribe on the other, have long been debated upon. In the
days when "primitive Teutonic freedom" was the watchword of
historians, it was usual to write as if there existed a regular system
by which the power of the king was limited, by his being obliged
to act by the counsel and consent of his "wise men," while the
ultimate legislative power lay in the hands of the whole body of
freemen, who had to confirm any laws or ordinance laid before
them. In this view there is something of misconception and much
of exaggeration. The Witan, so far back as we can trace it, is an
assembly of royal nominees, not a body of hereditary peers with a
right to advise the king. And we look equally in vain for any
sign that it was a representative body, which could speak in behalf
of the people. In the seventh century, when we get our first view
of it, as in the later times when documents grow numerous, it
appears to have consisted of the ealdormen, who governed under the
king the various units of his realm, of the archbishops and bishops,
and of a limited number of other councillors.

It would seem that these last constituted a definite and re-
cognisable class. There is a law of Ine which lays down a precise
fine for breaches of the peace, in the houses of such persons. If
any man brawls in the house of an ealdorman or of any other

"exalted wise man" (*othres gethungenes witan*) he has to pay a certain fixed and heavy fine.[1] Clearly then it was known who was and who was not of this status. Presumably they were gesiths or thegns of the greater sort, with ample landed endowment. But whether in Kent at the same time independent "eorls" of great landed wealth might not have sat among Wihtraed's "great men" it would be dangerous to speculate. At any rate this was not the custom in later centuries, when among the signatures of members of the Witan, annexed to some deed or charter, we can distribute all among four classes—(1) members of the royal family; (2) archbishops, bishops, abbots and other clergy; (3) ealdormen; (4) king's thegns (ministri) and other officials. There is no category of wise men of lay status who do not belong to the "nobility of service". Ine's code does not give us the smallest indication that this was not already the case in his day : there is no allusion whatever to great men who enjoy inherited eminence, and are not members of the body of *gesithcundmen*.

Since, then, the council was a council of nominees, its function was to advise rather than to guide or restrain the king, and a headstrong ruler might ignore its advice at his own peril, without committing a constitutional solecism. At the same time the Witan was not without its importance. If a king grew unpopular, deservedly or not, there were always members of the royal house in existence, who would naturally be members of the Witan, and who in unison with the other councillors would apply to him the most stringent check—resistance and rebellion. A tyrannical ruler could not rely, beyond a certain limit, on the loyalty of his dependants. We need only recall the cases of Aethelbald of Mercia, and Oswulf and half a dozen more Northumbrian kings "slain by those of their own household". This might be called mere "despotism tempered by assassination". But there are distinct cases where the unpopular ruler seems to have been formally deposed, and where the Witan are spoken of as carrying out or at least assenting to the deposition. Such was that of Sigebert of Wessex (A.D. 755) of whom it is said that his kinsman Cynewulf and the West Saxon Witan deprived him of his kingdom for his unjust doings.[2] Equally clear is the instance of the Northumbrians, Alchred who in 774 was

---

[1] Ine, § 6.   [2] A. S. Chronicle, *sub anno* 755.

dethroned by the counsel and consent of all his subjects [1] and
Osbald who in similar terms is recorded to have been deposed in
796. The same no doubt was the case in 765 with that king
Aethelwald, "qui regnum Northanhymbrorum amisit in Winchanheal III Kal. Novembris," Finchale being one of the regular
meeting-places of the Northumbrian Witan. For if the fall of Aethelwald had been the effect of mere rebellion and tumultuary violence,
it could not be said to have happened on a particular day and at a
particular place. Clearly some sort of definite form of deposition
must have been carried out. It would be mere playing with words
to say that the proceedings of the Witan in such a case were not
constitutional. For the word constitutional in all times, early and
late, save when a fixed framework of laws exists to define the polity
of a state, means little more than "habitual, and generally accepted
by the nation". If Witans on many occasions declared kings deposed, and deposition actually ensued, it is surely quibbling to say
that the action had no legal validity, and was only a form of
rebellion.

The Witan had also its part to play in another sort of case,
where the question was not one of the deposition of a tyrannical or
unpopular king, but simply one of the regulation of the succession
to the crown. In many, probably in most, cases a king who had
reached middle age, and had sons of his own, would get his natural
heir recognised as his successor-designate during his lifetime. Often
he gave him a sub-kingdom to rule, by way of starting him in the
necessary training, as did Penda or Oswy. Sometimes a king who
was setting his house in order, either because of age and infirmity,
or because he wished to enter the religious life, would commend a
relation who was not his son to the Witan and his subjects at large.
This happened in the case of Aethelred of Mercia, who resigned in
favour of his nephew Coenred (704); while Coenred in his turn went
on pilgrimage to Rome in 709, after handing over his sceptre to his
cousin the worthless Ceolred. So, too, we read in Bede how Osric
of Northumbria, "successorem fore Ceolwulfum decrevisset, fratrem
illius qui ante se regnaverat, Coenredi". Clearly the will of the

---

[1] Concilio et consensu omnium suorum, regiae familiae et principum destitus
societate, exilio imperii mutavit majestatem. Simeon of Durham, 774.

[2] For a lucid statement of the opposite view, denying any such power to the
Witan, see Chadwick's *Anglo-Saxon Institutions*, 362-65.

reigning king was in such instances the main factor in the determining of the order of succession, and he took measures, before his
death or abdication, to get his subjects to recognise the heir whom
he preferred. Probably the Witan went through some ceremony
of taking the successor as lord and doing homage to him.

But in other cases the order of succession was determined in a
less smooth fashion. If a king who had no designated heir fell in
battle, or if an unpopular king was deposed, some one had to be
set in his place. In many cases a pretender might make a mere
snatch at the crown with the aid of his relatives and dependants,
like that Osbald who " a quibus principibus ipsius gentis in regnum
est constitutus," [1] only to be deposed immediately after by the
Witan of Northumbria. But in others there seems to have been
something like a definite election. Aethelwald Moll of Northumbria
(759) is said, by the contemporary annalist who continued Bede's
history, to be " a sua plebe electus," and the same is implied of his
son Aethelred, when the Anglo-Saxon Chronicle says that " the
Northumbrians drove out Alchred from York at Easter-Tide and
took Aethelred to be their lord ".[2] For the taking of a prince to lord
must surely have been something more formal than the recognition
of a *de facto* king who has won the crown already by arms. When
Ine of Wessex is " functus in regem," and Ecgbert, a century later,
" in regnum ordinatur," some sort of an election seems equally implied. In each of the two latter cases the throne was vacant, and
the late king had left no heir. Later cases, where the phrase
" elected as king " [3] is used, sometimes with the addition that the
Witan is definitely stated to do the electing, may be found in the
Anglo-Saxon Chronicle under the years 924, 1016 and 1043. But
in all cases we cannot doubt that the wise men, and not any tumultuary meeting of the folk, must have been the body which made the
choice.

Passing on from the Witan to the other governmental machinery
of the early English realms, we are surprised to find in our earliest documents, the Kentish codes, no allusion to ealdormen (though
they certainly existed in Kent in the eighth century and later, and

---

[1] Simeon of Durham, 796.

[2] Florence of Worcester paraphrases this by " in regem levaverunt," a clear
allusion to the old Teutonic elevation of a newly elected sovereign.

[3] Gecoren to cinge, or gecear to cynge, or, as very definitely in Ethelweard, iv.
4, " a primatibus electus".

are repeatedly mentioned in the Chronicle) or to any royal officials
save the king's wicgerefa, or town-reeve, before whom, as is casually
mentioned in a law of Lothere, the vouching for the honesty of a
bargain may be made.[1]   He appears again (but called gerefa only)
in Wihtraed's laws,[2] as the person to whom any one who has a
charge to bring against one of the king's slaves ought to make his
complaint. We have mention of the king's retainers, as has already
been stated in the preceding chapter, both as his *gesithcundmen*
and as thegns. We hear also of his smiths and other servants, but
there is a sad want of detail as to actual officials.

Ine's code gives us much more information in this respect. It
clearly mentions the ealdorman as governor of a "shire" under the
king—the thirty-sixth law is to the effect that an ealdorman who
lets go a captured thief or hushes up a robbery, shall "lose his shire"
unless the king grant him pardon.[3] As early as 755 we have a
definite mention of a Wessex ealdorman by name and title, *viz.*,
of that Cumbra who ruled "Hamtunscire" for King Sigebert, and
was so ungratefully treated by him.[4] In that century and the next
we are able to account for all the later shires of Wessex as already
in existence, and there is no reason to doubt that all save Devon
were created before Ine's time. But as to their origin speculation
only is possible. Some have supposed that they represent the successive local units created by each advance of the Wessex border
against the Welsh—that Wiltshire, Dorsetshire, Somersetshire
were formed by bodies of settlers called Wilsaetas, Dornsaetas,
Somersaetas, from the regions in which they took up their abode,
and the names lend themselves to this hypothesis. A later view
is the shires represent, more or less, the realms of the numerous *subreguli* who parted the West Saxon realm among themselves on
several occasions in the seventh century. A plausible explanation
for Berkshire, at least, is that it represents the principality of 3,000
hides which King Coenwalch granted to his nephew Cuthred "in
Ashdown".[5] The ealdorman, under this hypothesis, would be a
royal official administering what had been once the realm of a *sub-*

---

[1] Lothere, § 16. This often-quoted passage does not seem to presuppose a
Kentish wic-reeve in London, as some suppose, but only provides that a bargain
made in London should be vouched for before the nearest wic-reeve.

[2] Wihtraed, § 22.   [3] Ine, § 36.   [4] See p. 336 above.

[5] See Chadwick's *Anglo-Saxon Institutions*, p. 287, etc.

regulus from its most important centre.   But again it is suggested that the shire names may be traced back to districts administered from important royal " vills," Hamton and Wilton, Dorchester and Somerton, which last obscure place was perhaps of some note in the seventh and eighth centuries.[1]

Be this as it may, we find in Ine's laws besides the ealdormen a person called the shireman,[2] who has generally been identified with the shire-reeve or sheriff of the tenth century. He appears as a legal official before whom accusations have to be enrolled. It seems hard to believe that he is not an early form of the sheriff, and in the later days of the Anglo-Saxon monarchy the two terms shireman and sheriff were certainly used indifferently for the same official.[3] He is apparently in Ine's time the most important of the king's reeves, or local stewards and bailiffs, having not a single estate, nor a single town, under him, but a large district, wherein he would be responsible for all the royal finances derived from litigation and taxation, no less than from the king's landed property. Every royal estate had certainly a minor reeve (gerefa), and probably every town also : we have seen already that Kent had " Wicgerefas " or town bailiffs when Wihtraed, Ine's contemporary, was publishing his " dooms "; and in later centuries we have definite mention of Wessex " Wicgerefas," *e.g.*, at Winchester and at Bath, who seem to have been persons of some importance.[4] It is noteworthy that in the other English kingdoms which were large enough to require administrative ealdormen, Mercia and Northumbria, we seem to have no trace of an early shire system. In Mercia there were ealdormen who governed districts for the king, but these all seem to be much larger than the Wessex shires. Indeed the ealdormen whose local *habitat* is ascertainable seem to have ruled the old sub-kingdoms, in succession to the *subreguli* who died out in the eighth century. We have definite mention of

---

[1] Outside Wessex, Winchcombshire and the later Liberty of Bury Saint Edmunds are examples of which documentary evidence survives. See the Charters in Thorpe.

[2] Ine, § 8.

[3] Mr. Chadwick, in the work cited above, p. 231, disputes this. He apparently thinks that Ine's *shireman* is the ealdorman, and that the later sheriff only came into existence in the tenth century.

[4] Sufficiently so to have their deaths mentioned in the Chronicle, as in 906 and 897.

ealdormen of the Hwiccas, and of Lindsey; presumably Mercia proper, the Magesaetas beyond Severn, and the Middle Angles were ruled by others.   Possibly the Gyrwas and the Chilternsaetas formed separate units also.   The charters of the great Mercian kings, like Offa and Coenwulf, are signed by a good many *duces*, but many of them were clearly not the rulers of Mercian districts, but came from Kent, Essex, and other regions which were vassal to the greater kingdom but not incorporated in it.   If the statement in the Anglo-Saxon Chronicle under the year 827 [825] could be taken as strictly meaning what it says, when it states that King Ludecan was slain by the East Angles "and his five ealdormen with him," we should be obliged to conclude that there were precisely five administrative districts in Mercia when its vassal kingdoms had shaken off the yoke—presumably Lindsey, Mercia Proper, Hwiccia, the Middle Angles, and the Magesaetas. But it is not certain that the possessive pronoun "his" can be pressed to this extent; for Ethelweard's chronicle translates what is evidently the same original into "et quinque duces cum eo," not into "cum suis quinque ducibus".[1]   Moreover, in late ninth century Mercian charters, issued after the Danes had occupied all the eastern part of the kingdom, we sometimes seem to find three or even four ealdormen signing.   It is hard to find territories for them all, unless we suppose that there was an ealdorman for the Chilternsaetas, or whatever name we apply to the Mercian district lying north of the Middle Thames. [2]

As to Northumbria, there were certainly ealdormen therein,[3] but we get no visible trace of a shire system.   If there were permanent local divisions, it seems that they were under *praefecti* (as Bede calls them) or high-reeves as the Anglo-Saxon Chronicle prefers to name them.   One family of such high-reeves can be traced at Bamborough for several generations, and its last members seem to have exercised as much power as a *subregulus* after the break-up of the Northumbrian kingdom before the Danish invaders.[4]   It

---

[1] Ethelweard, iii. 2.   He makes the strange error of putting Beortwulf instead of Ludecan.

[2] But possibly Aethelred, then ruling with quasi-regal power, had kept no region immediately under himself, and the other three ealdormen were those of Hwiccia, the Magesaetas, and Old Mercia (or such part of it as obeyed Aethelred).

[3] See A. S. C., 684 and 778.

[4] For this race of Eardwulfs and Ealdreds, see Cadwallader Bates' *History of Northumberland*, 85-94.

is notable that Simeon of Durham calls *duces* three notables whom the Chronicle styles high-reeves, all murdered by King Aethelred I. in 778. The Chronicle distinctly gives them local titles " Eardwulf high-reeve at Kingscliff," etc. If there existed a regular system of administrative division in the seventh and eighth centuries, it was certainly swept away by the Danes in the ninth.

Another class mentioned by Ine, of whom we would gladly know more, are certain judges (*deman* in the Saxon original, *judices* in the Latin version) who are named along with the shireman. They seem to be royal officials, but what was their status or the extent of their sphere we are unable to say. When so much of justice consisted in the administering and accepting of oaths of compurgation, and while " the suitors were the judges," the position of the presiding official at a court is a perplexing one to realise. Conceivably this *judex* was the " doomsman " of a hundred, though of the existence of that territorial unit we have no mention in Ine's Law, nor indeed till the time of Eadgar, more than two centuries and a half later. Yet it would be dangerous to deny that hundreds existed in all the early English kingdoms.[1] The idea of the unit of a hundred households supplying a hundred warriors was very early, and current in most or all Teutonic lands. If it is alluded to in Tacitus and found current as far as Scandinavia when historical times begin, it is no very perilous hypothesis to believe that it existed in seventh- or eighth-century England.[2] It has indeed been suggested, with great plausibility, that the reason why all early calculations of the area of districts were made in round numbers of hundreds, both in narratives such as Bede's history and in statistics such as the " Tribal Hidage," already alluded to,[3] is that the notion of the hundred in households or hides as the national primitive unit was well established.[4]

---

[1] See Vinogradoff, *Origin of the Manor*, pp. 144-45, and notes 30, 31. Ethelweard makes " Wuextan dux " in 802 read *centurias provinciae Wilsaetum.*

[2] Among the Franks there was no shire-court, but only what was practically a hundred-court. If the English had shire-courts always, and only introduced the hundred-court in the tenth century, their line of development was abnormal.

[3] See p. 231.

[4] Mr. Chadwick, though conceding that " the distribution of the nation according to hundreds of hides goes back in principle to early times " (*Origins*, p. 244, etc.), will not allow that there were actual administrative divisions, in the sense of the Doomsday Book hundreds, before the tenth century.

It is of course unfortunate that Ine and his councillors, when setting forth their code, were not intent on furnishing posterity with constitutional information, but on formulating in detail the precise penalties of various crimes. Their dooms mainly consist of clauses dealing, on a scale which the modern student finds minute and irritating, with the valuation of offences against life, person, and property, and the machinery by which those offences shall be dealt with. But this is equally the case not only with the Kentish laws, but with all the continental codes—Frankish, Lombard, Saxon, etc., of the Dark Ages. The most striking feature in Ine's legislation is the employment of the system of compurgation for the decision of all manner of cases. Instead of dilating on the fashion in which witnesses should be called and examined, Ine takes it for granted that the normal decision in the shire court will be made according to the scale on which the defendant will bring oath-helpers to vouch for him. The man who is known to be a bad character will be unable to collect compurgators, and will presently fall into the most unpleasant position. "The ceorlish man who has been several times accused of theft, and is then again taken in cattle-stealing, clearly guilty, shall have his hand or his foot cut off." [1] When the accused is not a notorious offender, and when his guilt in the particular charge laid against him is not clear, he will be able to get his lord, if he is a dependant, or his kindred and neighbours, if he be a free villager, to swear for him. Their swearing power is elaborately defined according to their rank, and is stated in terms of hides, as if credibility increased in exact proportion with the extent of landed property which a man enjoyed —a strange hypothesis to the modern mind. " A man accused of gang-robbery shall clear himself by the oath of 120 hides, or pay up." [2] " A royal tenant, if his weregeld valuation is 1,200 shillings (*i.e.*, if he is a freeman of the highest class among the *gesithcundmen*) may swear for 60 hides, if he is a regular communicant." [3] " If any man is accused of having stolen cattle, or harboured stolen cattle, then he may swear himself off the charge by the oath of 60 hides (*i.e.*, by the oath of one or more persons whose valuation comes to 60 hides) if he be oath-worthy." If the accuser is an Englishman the charge must be rebutted with twice as strong swearing : if only

[1] Ine, § 37.   [2] *Ibid*, § 14.   [3] *Ibid*., § 19.

a Welshman, the sixty-hide oath is enough."[1] If a man be accused
of homicide, and wishes to rebut the accusation by oaths, then, in
every body of oath-helpers that he produces, out of 100 hides of
swearing there must be an oath by a man of the royal following
with 30 hides,[2] whether the slain be *gesithcund* or *ceorl*. Such
are the curious provisions which continually meet the student
who runs through the laws of Ine. If the practical working of
the system be considered, it is clear that a first offender who had
devoted relatives, or a lord who valued his service, must have found
it easy to swear off a charge. But it would grow progressively
more difficult to collect oath-helpers to the required amount when
accusations began to be repeated, so that the habitual offender
would ultimately reach the stage of finding no one to swear for him.
At the best, the system was equivalent to letting off the man who
had a good local reputation : at the worst it must have amounted
to giving an opportunity for all unscrupulous families or lords, on
whom an oath sat lightly, to cover the misdoings of their connections. One may guess what must often have taken place in Wessex
by picturing to oneself the results that would follow to-day, if
compurgation prevailed in the West of Ireland for the crime of
cattle-driving !

   The offences on which Ine dilates at greatest length are homicide, theft—especially of live stock—gang-robbery, and brawling,
a list which gives the impression that his realm cannot have been
a happy residence for persons of peaceful disposition. Brawling
was clearly liable to break out anywhere, even in the vicinity of
the royal person. "If any man fights in the king's house, he is
liable to lose all his goods, and his life is at the king's disposal : if
any man fights in Church, he shall pay 120 shillings, if in an
ealdorman's house, 60 shillings to the ealdorman and 60 more to the
king. But if he fight in the house of a tax-paying man (*i.e.*, an
ordinary freeman) or a smaller peasant, the 120 shillings go to the
king and six only to the householder."[3] Gang-robbery evidently
prevailed on a very large scale : for, says Ine, "We call men thieves
if the party did not exceed seven persons; if it was between seven

----

[1] Ine, §§ 46-47.
[2] If this is the meaning of the curious phrase stating that 30 hides of the oath
must be provided by a person with a "king's oath" (Ine, § 54).
[3] Ine, § 6 (3).

and thirty-five it is a band (*hloth*), but if over thirty-five then we call
the gathering an army (*here*) ".[1] Owing to the public danger caused
by such felonious assemblies, the amount of penalty (or of compurgation) was heavily increased above that of mere theft when the larger
numbers were reached.

The influence of the Church is to be traced throughout all the
early laws, in those of Kent no less than in the later code of Ine.
It expresses itself in the high valuation given to ecclesiastical persons, and the severity with which injuries due to them are punished.
He who stole goods from the king paid ninefold value of what he had
taken, but he who stole " God's and the Church's goods," twelvefold.[2]
Theft from a priest cost ninefold, from an ordinary ceorl only threefold. The bishop's word, like that of the king, is indisputable, even
without an oath.[3] A priest can clear himself from an accusation by
standing before the altar of his church and asseverating " veritatem
dico in Christo, non mentior," when ordinary laymen would be
obliged to bring oath-helpers.[4] But the most notable feature of all
is that the state intervenes from a very early date to punish purely
ecclesiastical offences. Wihtraed lavishes the heaviest penalties on
every man, free or unfree, who is caught secretly worshipping the
pagan gods : he even enforces Sabbath rest with the enormous fine
of 80 shillings. Ine goes so far as to punish with a penalty of 30
shillings the man who has not had his child baptised within thirty
days of its birth, and to inflict a crushing fine on the negligent
person who has omitted to pay his church-scot.[5] The privilege of
sanctuary, destined to lead to so many abuses in later ages, was
already known. " If a man who has incurred the death penalty
flee to a church, let him keep his life and make [pecuniary] compensation according to the law : if he has incurred corporal punishment and so flee, let the chastisement be forgiven him."[6]

Ine's law shows the Church possessed of much land, and mentions abbots and abbesses with servile dependants. This is only
what we should expect from our reading in Bede, where the kings
are found, from the very foundation of Christianity, lavishing large
estates upon the missionary clergy, and later founding monasteries
on the most splendid scale. Two or three generations of liberality
such as that of Aethelbert and Edwin caused Church-land to

---

[1] Ine, § 13.　　[2] Aethelbert, § 1 and § 4.　　[3] Wihtraed, § 16.
[4] *Ibid.*, § 18.　　[5] Ine, § 2 and § 4.　　[6] *Ibid.*, § 5.

become an appreciable part of every realm in England. The habit spread from the kings downwards, till already Bede, in 730, was growing frightened at the enormous growth of the number of religious houses—many of them ill-managed, and unworthy of their name. But this tendency and its consequences have been dealt with elsewhere : [1] it never ceased till the Danish invasions swept over the land and destroyed monasteries by the score, so that a new monastic revival was required in the tenth century, when the land had once more settled down to peace.

From another point of view the growth of Church property is of high importance in English constitutional history, as being the main instrument in the breaking up of the old land-holding system of the original settlers, and its conversion into a more modern and individualistic type. It seems to be proved that the land divided up on the first conquest of a British region, and held according to the tribal rules of family inheritance, was called *folkland*, whether it went to king, to eorl or to ceorl,[2] as being held by *folkright*, national custom. The later Latin term for it seems to have been *terra publicae juris*, or (more clumsily) *reipublicae jure conditionis*.[3] Such land, whether owned by king or ceorl, could not be alienated from the family or devised by will, the proprietor being nothing more than a life-owner. It passed on his death to his heirs automatically, according to the rules of the tribal custom. It was subject to all the usual obligations to the state, military and fiscal—the *trinoda necessitas* of sending warriors to the host (fyrdfare), repairing of forts (burhbot) and work on roads and bridges (bricgbot), the obligation to entertain the king and his retinue on his progresses, and to pay his tax (gafol), etc. When once a region had been divided up, even the king could not permanently alienate the royal estates held as folkland, though he might distribute them as life-maintenance to members of his following. But the death of either the grantor or the grantee would bring the land back into

[1] See p. 321.

[2] For Folkland and its meaning, see Vinogradoff in *English Historical Review for* 1893, with additional explanation in the *Growth of the Manor*, pp. 142-44 and 244-45, and in *Mélanges Fitting* (1908).

[3] The very important term *folkland* only occurs, oddly enough, three times in documents : the odd Latin translations of it quoted above only once each, in two charters of Coenwulf of Mercia. Thorpe, *Dipl.*, 57, 58. See Vinogradoff's views in the places mentioned in the last note.

the royal domain, or the king could terminate the grant at his good pleasure if his gesith or thegn had displeased him.

The first serious objection to this ancestral system, as it appears, came when the kings of the seventh century wished to endow churches and found monasteries, a desire in which their ealdormen and thegns soon came to participate. To alienate land during the grantor's life was all that was in his power, so long as *folkright* prevailed. To render permanent endowments possible, however, a new device was soon found—this was the institution of *bocland*, land held by a "book," *i.e.*, a charter, instead of by folk-right. Such estates could only be created by a formal act of the king and his Witan, royal land as well as private land having to be freed from the old restrictions by a charter, since the king was (after all) only a life tenant of his own domain. Presumably the consent of the kindred ought to have been obtained in each case, for they had a clear interest in the land alienated by the creation of such a grant. "The proper course was to obtain the consent of the interested relations of the actual holder"[1]—though it is not clear that this was always done. The immediate result of the invention of *bocland* was the rapid diminution of the royal domain, not only when the king transferred lands in his own actual possession to a bishopric or a monastery, but also when he gave leave for royal folkland, in the temporary occupation of one of his ministers or officials, to be treated in the same way. This last form of liberality was very tempting both to the thegn and to the king, since the former was alienating to the Church land which was not permanently his own, while the latter was not making any new grant out of land in actual possession, but only consenting to part for good with an estate which was already in the hands of some one else—though it would ultimately have returned to the crown, and have been available for the rewarding of another generation of thegns. The pernicious effect on the royal revenue became even more marked when the king, on giving away a piece of royal domain or permitting other persons to make similar grants, added to the charter a clause exempting the newly-made bocland from a greater or lesser part of the services and taxation which it owed the state—occasionally it was let off even the *trinoda necessitas*,

[1] Vinogradoff, *Growth of the Manor*, pp. 143, 209.

the common obligation incumbent on all land under normal conditions.

These facts make it easy to understand the dismay with which far-sighted and statesmanlike minds, such as that of the Venerable Bede, regarded the wholesale alienation of "*bocland*" to the Church, which had been going on for a century in Northumbria when he wrote. How was the king to maintain an adequate revenue, or provide for endowment of his military retainers in the future, if all the royal domain was being gradually given away, and much of the private land once held under *folkright* being freed from more or less of its dues to the state ?

It was not long before it was discovered that if "*bocland*" could be made for the Church, it could also be made for private individuals. No boon could be greater to landowners than to give them leave to turn folkland into bocland, since they thereby became its actual owners, instead of merely the life tenants of what was bound to pass to their kin on their decease. For one of the main characteristics of the new tenure was that land held by it was alienable by gift or by will. Hence many favoured subjects of the king were anxious to get their estates chartered into *bocland* by the king and Witan, in order that they might be free to deal with them according to their desires. In the course of a century or two the larger part of the land of England had passed from family ownership into real private ownership in this fashion. It is interesting to note that, in most of the great eighth and ninth century wills which have been preserved, the bocland in the possession of the testator enormously exceeds the land of which he is possessed on other tenure.[1] King Alfred, at the end of the ninth century, seems to have been displeased by the way in which the kindred was suffering from this tendency, and in the forty-first clause of his code expresses his opinion that *bocland* which had been received from kinsmen ought not to be left outside the family. Probably he had lay public opinion at his back, as gifts to the Church were still the most frequent incident by which such land was being alienated. But it is clear from many instances that it was also being sold, or left in inheritance to those who were not the actual nearest kinsmen.

It has been suggested that another undesirable result of the wholesale creation of bocland was that it contributed to that depres-

[1] See Vinogradoff, *Growth of the Manor*, p. 247.

sion of the ceorl which characterises the later centuries of Anglo-
Saxon period.   As long as he was seated on royal folkland as
a rent-payer (gafolgelder) he would be better off than when
that folkland had been turned into bocland, and passed to a
monastery or a great thegn.   For thus he ceased to be in direct connection with the king, and became subject to a territorial lord, lay
or spiritual.   But of this depression we must take account in its
proper chronological place.

BOOK IV

THE DANISH INVASIONS

CHAPTER XIX

THE EVE OF THE STORM. RISE OF ECGBERT OF WESSEX
(A.D. 796-834)

THE first descent of the Scandinavian raiders upon the coast of Britain had fallen, as we have already seen, three years before the death of King Offa, when "the heathen men lamentably destroyed God's church at Lindisfarne with rapine and slaughter" in 793. Their second and less successful incursion at the mouth of the Wear had been in the following spring. Somewhere about the same time, as we may suspect, had occurred their first appearance in the southern parts of England, when, in the days of King Beorhtric of Wessex, those "three ships of the Northmen out of Haerethaland" came ashore near Weymouth, and slew Beaduheard the king's reeve of Dorsetshire, who would fain have taken stock of them, because he knew not who they were.[1]

But after these isolated incursions there is a gap of thirty years and more, before the raids of the Scandinavians began to come fast and furious, and forced the English to turn at last from their civil wars in order to face such a danger as they had never known

[1] This incident is often dated under 787, but wrongly, for the Chronicle only puts it under that year because it is speaking of King Beorhtric, " *in whose days* first came three ships," etc. This does not mean that 787 is the date of the event there recorded. It may have happened at any time between 787 and his death in 802. Probably it was about 793-94 or the chronicler could hardly have alluded to it as the *first* Danish raid, even though he was a Wessex man, mainly interested in the history of his own kingdom.

before.[1] These thirty years are a period of high importance, since in them the Mercian supremacy over Southern England, which had seemed so well established in the days of Aethelbald and Offa, reached its end, and the royal house of Wessex came to the front. Possibly the ascendency of Wessex might have been no more permanent than that of Mercia, if the second and greater series of Danish invasions had not recommenced, and struck down one after another all the English kingdoms save that over which the line of Cerdic and Ceawlin was reigning. But the long series of princes of more than average ability which that house continued to produce in the ninth and tenth centuries gave Wessex a chance which her rivals did not obtain. It is quite possible to argue that if weaklings had ruled in Wessex during the first century of the Viking invasions, while Mercia had continued in strong hands, or Northumbria had at last fallen under the control of a king of exceptional ability, the Midland or the Northern kingdom, and not the Southern, might have become the centre of resistance to the Northmen and the nucleus of the kingdom of All-England. The personal character of the reigning monarch was the main factor that settled with which of the great kingdoms the hegemony should reside all through the seventh and eighth centuries. The same was the case at the commencement of the ninth, and the fact that Ecgbert of Wessex and not some Mercian or Northumbrian king was the leading figure in England at the moment when the stress of the great raids commenced, had no small part in determining the future history of the whole island. The circumstance that the far greater personality of King Alfred appeared, at the later period when the attack of the Vikings reached its culminating point, finally settled the matter, and gave the house of Wessex its great future. But the position from which Alfred started had been secured for him by Ecgbert : if the grandfather had been a nonentity the grandson would not have had the chance of becoming the saviour of England, and the progenitor of the great line of monarchs who beat off the Dane and united all the heptarchic realms in one.

At the commencement of the ninth century, however, it would have been impossible to foresee any such future for the house of

---

[1] Meanwhile, as we shall see in the next chapter, they had been pressing heavily on Ireland, and had even been seen in Wales. But there is no allusion to their appearance on the English coast.

Wessex. The death of Offa did not bring the Mercian supremacy to an immediate end. That great king died, as has been already mentioned, in July, 796, and was followed to the grave within twenty weeks by his only son, the short-lived Ecgferth. But his remote cousin Coenwulf, who then succeeded to the Mercian throne, was a prince of sufficient energy and ability to maintain his predecessor's claim to supremacy in Southern England, though it was at once contested. It seems that East Anglia, which had been annexed by Offa after the murder of Aethelbert in 793, made no attempt to throw off the Mercian yoke for some time. But in Kent, which had been equally under Offa's hand in his later years—under-kings therein are not visible after about the year 790—there was a national rising the moment that the conqueror was dead. A certain Eadbert, whose nickname (we know not why) was Praen, "the Pin," proclaimed himself king in 796, and maintained his independence for two years. Eadbert is said to have been an apostate monk ;[1] very probably he was a member of the old Kentish royal house who had been forced into a monastery by Offa, and took the opportunity of the great king's death to throw off his cowl and replace it by the diadem.[2] There had been a precisely similar case among the Franks eighty years before, when Chilperic II., one of the last of the Merovingians, emerged from the cloister—where he had taken refuge under the name of Daniel—to contend for the rights of his house against the great Charles Martel. But Eadbert fared even worse than Chilperic ; after he had reigned two summers the King of the Mercians came down upon him in overwhelming force. Coenwulf had apparently been hindered from asserting his power at an earlier date by a rising of the North Welsh against him. In his first year the *Annales Cambriae* note a battle at Rhuddlan, which seems to mark the beginning of the trouble. In 798 the Mercians slew Caradoc, King of Gwynedd, and with his death the revolt seems for a time to have ended, so that Coenwulf's hands were free. When he appeared all Kent was cruelly wasted, "pene usque ad internecionem,"[3] and

[1] The troubles in Kent apparently began even before Offa's death, and had caused some correspondence between Offa and Alcuin. See Haddan and Stubbs, *Councils*, iii. 496.

[2] Eadbert is said by a very late authority (Florence of Worcester) to have been the brother of Aethelbert II., who had died in 762. This may be an error ; but he undoubtedly claimed to represent the old royal house.

[3] Simeon of Durham, 798.

Eadbert himself was taken prisoner, after lurking for some time in hiding. The conqueror put out his captive's eyes and cut off his hands, an atrocity for which there is hardly a parallel in English history. Apparently the cruel mutilation was at once special chastisement for an apostate cleric and an acknowledgment of the fact that, by reason of his clerical status, his life at least was sacred.

Coenwulf after this atrocity, which estranged the hearts of the conquered race from the Mercian supremacy more than anything which had gone before, proceeded to crown himself with his own hands as King of Kent. But after this assertion of his power he shortly afterwards handed over the government of the little realm to his brother Cuthred, who reigned therein as sub-king from 798 till his death in 806. He relied entirely on the protection of Coenwulf, for the men of Kent were only waiting for their chance to revolt again, in favour of any pretender who did not represent the hated overlordship of the Mercian house. But the day of revolt was not to come even on Cuthred's decease: he was succeeded by one Baldred, who was perhaps his kinsman and certainly a nominee of Coenwulf. For the Mercian signs Kentish charters for ten years longer, and thought so little of his vassal that he did not allow his name to appear on them even as witness. The best testimony that we have to the existence of the insignificant Baldred are his rare and interesting coins, on which he duly describes himself as REX CANT.[1] He reigned from 806 to 823, and nought is known of him save the years of his accession and his deposition.

Of Coenwulf, it is to be confessed, there is not very much more to be discovered. It is worth while noticing, however, that he undid the work of his great predecessor Offa in creating the separate archbishopric of Lichfield. This he did, perhaps, because he felt that Canterbury was now as much his own as the Mercian see, but more probably for reasons of personal gratitude to Archbishop Aethelheard, who then occupied the old metropolitan chair. For in 796 that prelate had refused to acknowledge the pretender Eadbert Praen, and had excommunicated him as an apostate priest.

---

[1] It is worth mentioning, as showing the complete supremacy of Mercia over Kent, that Cuthred's moneyer Duda, and Baldred's moneyer Tidbert, both struck, undoubtedly at Canterbury, coins for Coenwulf, on which he is called REX M. (*i.e.* Merciorum). They are quite different in appearance from the coins of the Anti-Mercian pretender, Eadbert Praen.

Whereupon the men of Kent drove him out in wrath: there is a letter of Alcuin surviving, in which the scholar prays the nobles and people to recall him from the Continent and restore him to his see. But it had no effect: Aethelheard was only brought back by Coenwulf's sword. In 800 the Mercian wrote to Rome, asking Pope Leo III. to consider again the rights of the see of Canter-bury, and enclosing a petition from Aethelheard and some of his suffragans. In the following year the archbishop was summoned to meet the Pope, and made the voyage to Italy. His plea was heard and granted on January 12th, 802, and when he returned to England in 803 a synod was held at Clovesho, in which the arrangements made in 787 were solemnly revoked, and all England south of Trent once more submitted to the jurisdiction of Canterbury. Higbert, the first and only Archbishop of Lichfield, seems to have resigned not only his pallium but his bishopric. He is apparently the Higbert *Abbas* who signs the proceedings of the Council, while one Ealdwulf ratifies them as Bishop of Lichfield.

A few years later Coenwulf may have regretted his dealings with Offa's old friend, for when Aethelheard died in 805 he was succeeded by a primate Wulfred, who seems to have been a Kentishman born, and an opponent of the Mercian supremacy.[1] For six years (814-20) the king and the archbishop were more or less at strife. Coenwulf seized many of Wulfred's estates, and wrote to accuse him to the Pope. The latter, however, seems to have taken the other side, as was natural in a quarrel between clerk and layman. But Coenwulf was near at hand and Pascal I. was far off: his support and that of the Emperor Lewis the Pious availed Wulfred little, when the Mercian king summoned him to a Witan at London in 820, and offered him the choice between submission and exile accompanied by the confiscation of all his goods. The primate yielded, gave up some more of his estates, and had to disguise as far as he might his hatred for his overlord. Before his death he was to have an opportunity of showing his real feelings towards the Mercian domination.

Besides his long quarrel with the archbishop we know little of

---

[1] It has been pointed out that all the coins of Aethelheard and his predecessor Jaenberct bear on their reverses the names of the Mercian kings Offa and Coenwulf, as acknowledgment of their supremacy, while those of Wulfred have the archbishop's name alone, and DOROBERNIA CIVITAS on the reverse, with no king's name. See Hunt's *History of the English Church*, p. 249.

Coenwulf's doings save that he made war on Northumbria about the year 801-2. It was apparently not his fault that hostilities broke out, for we are told that King Eardwulf attacked him, because he had sheltered northern exiles, and that he fought in self-defence. We should rather have expected him to have taken the offensive against the distracted Northumbrian realm, where kings continued to succeed each other with bewildering rapidity, and civil war was endemic. But after some indecisive campaigning Coenwulf allowed himself to be persuaded to peace by his bishops, and there was no more trouble between Mercia and Northumbria during the joint existence of the two kingdoms.

It is probable that Coenwulf's attention during his latter years may have been mainly taken up by wars with the Welsh. We hear nothing of trouble in this quarter from 798 to 815, but it would appear that he was busy with invasions of Wales between 816 and his death in 821. The English chronicles have no mention of them, but the *Annales Cambriae* note that in 816 "the Saxons," *i.e.* the Mercians, overran Rhuveniog (Denbighshire) and carried their devastations as far as Mount Ereyri (Snowdon). In 818 Coenwulf wasted all the provinces of Demetia (South Wales), and the war had not ceased at the time of his death—which is said to have taken place at Basingwerk, in Flintshire, obviously while he was on a Welsh expedition—since in 822 his successor is recorded to have stormed the castle of Conway and annexed the greater part of Powys. Since Coenwulf is found active both in North and in South Wales, it is probable that he was carrying on the policy of Offa, and endeavouring to retain by the strong hand the homage of all the Celtic kingdoms—a task rendered easier at this period by a long civil war between Howel and his brother Cynan, rival kings of Gwynedd.

His addiction to wars of invasion against the Welsh seems to prove that Coenwulf's authority in England was practically undisputed. It appears that not only Kent but East Anglia, Essex, and Wessex were all under his hand, and more or less quiescent in their servitude. But already in the last-named kingdom the prince was on the throne who was destined to make an end of the Mercian supremacy in the days of Coenwulf's successors. In 802, as has been already recorded,[1] died Beorhtric, King of Wessex, accident-

[1] See p. 339.

ally poisoned by his wicked wife, the daughter of Offa. In his place the men of Wessex chose his distant relative Ecgbert, son of Eahlmund and a descendant of Ingild the brother of Ine. For nearly twenty years the new king remained the vassal of Coenwulf, but he was all the time watching for the opportunity which came to him in late middle age.

Ecgbert was a man of wide experience and a chequered career. Though he was of the West Saxon royal house,[1] and though his ancestral estates lay in Hampshire,[2] it would seem that he had Kentish connections also. For his father Ealhmund is almost certainly identical with the prince of that name who about the years 784-86 had reigned as sub-king in Kent, along with Alric, as a vassal of Offa. Presumably, therefore, Ealhmund had either by marriage or by his maternal descent some claim sufficient to get him accepted by part of the men of Kent as their ruler.[3] That he was allied to the old royal house of Aethelbert is implied by the statement in the Anglo-Saxon Chronicle that the kingdom of Kent was " wrongly forced away from Ecgbert's kin" while it was under the hand of the kings Cuthred and Baldred, whom Coenwulf the Mercian set up. It is very possible that Ecgbert himself may have reigned for a short time as his father's successor, for there are some Kentish coins known of an " Ecgberht Rex," whose moneyers, Udda and Babba, also struck pennies, the one for Offa and Coenwulf, the other for Eadbert Praen. Their dating suggests that Ecgbert may have ruled for a short time somewhere about 790-96.[4] If so, he did not keep his Kentish sub-kingdom long. It is recorded in the Anglo-Saxon Chronicle that he was " driven out of England before he was king by Offa King of Mercia and Beorhtric, the King of the West Saxons, who helped Offa because he had his daughter

---

[1] This is disputed by Sir Henry Howorth (see Numismatic Chronicle of 1900, pp. 67-87) who would deny the authenticity of his pedigree in the Anglo-Saxon Chronicle, and believes his ancestor Ingild to be an invention. According to this view he was Kentish on the male side, and West Saxon only on the female side.

[2] He grants lands in 828 to his reeve Wulfheard, twenty-two hides on each side of the river Meon, "which had come to him by inheritance" (Birch, C. A. S., 377).

[3] Henry of Huntingdon, who is too late to be trusted, says that Ealhmund was close of kin to Eadbert Praen.

[4] See British Museum, *Anglo-Saxon Coins*, vol. i., and Sir Henry Howorth's article in *Num. Chron.*, for 1900, quoted above.

to wife, and Ecgbert abode in Frankland for three years ".[1] This
juxtaposition of names makes it seem possible that Ecgbert had
been urging claims in virtue of his royal West Saxon blood, which
had caused Beorhtric to bring down upon him his mighty father-in-
law, who expelled him from his Kentish sub-kingdom. Since Offa
died in 796, Ecgbert's expulsion cannot be later than that year,
and the latest period assignable for his exile in the realm of Charles
the Great is the three years 796-99.[2] How he contrived to return
to England in or before 799, and where he abode between that time
and the death of Beorhtric in 802 we cannot say. Nor is there
any evidence of how he spent his time in Frankland : the Count
Ecgbert, who was one of the best-trusted fighting men of Charles
the Great, cannot be the West Saxon exile, for his name keeps
occurring in Frankish history long after the son of Ealhmund had
returned to England.

This much, however, is certain, that on the decease of Beorhtric
the men of Wessex chose Ecgbert king, apparently without any
internal opposition. But there was trouble from outside. On the
very day that his election took place the Mercian ealdorman
Aethelmund made an incursion from the land of the Hwiccas into
Wiltshire, crossing the Upper Thames at Kempsford. To meet
him there came out Weoxtan, ealdorman of the Wilsaetas, with all
the men that he could raise. There was a great fight, and both
the ealdormen were slain, but the Mercians were defeated. Was
this an act of unlicensed brigandage on the part of Aethelmund
against a country which was for the moment without a king ? Or
was he acting by the orders of his master Coenwulf, who may have
wished—too late—to interfere in the choice of the Wessex Witan ?
The latter seems the less probable, since, if Coenwulf had resented
Ecgbert's election, he would have been strong enough to strike a
second time, avenge his slain ealdorman, and dethrone the newly-
chosen king. Since he tolerated Ecgbert as a vassal for many
years, he must have disavowed the action of Aethelmund.

[1] There is no justification for reading thirteen years instead of three for the
time of Ecgbert's exile, and taking it down to 802. The figure in the Anglo-Saxon
Chronicle is supported by all the minor authorities which copy from it.

[2] But it is conceivable that he might have been driven out by Offa and
Beorhtric in 793, and have returned in 796 to support the revolt of Eadbert Praen,
if the latter was indeed his kinsman. This does not help us with regard to what
he was doing in the years just before 802.

Between this stirring incident on the day of his accession and
the thirteenth year of his reign we have absolutely no information
about the fortunes of Ecgbert, who must apparently have remained
biding his time as long as Coenwulf lived. But in 814[1] we find
him, no doubt with his suzerain's permission, prosecuting vigorous
war against the West Welsh of Damnonia, whom his predecessors
had left unmolested for many years. He "laid waste the land
from East to West," and apparently compelled its king or kings to
do him homage, as he evidently regards 814 as an important year
in the growth of his power. For his charters of 826 are dated
"in the twenty-fourth year of his kingly power, and the fourteenth
since he obtained his suzerainty". [Anno regis Ecgbercti XXIIII.,
ducatus autem sui XIIII., Birch 390-91-93.] The word *ducatus* can
have no reference to the Bretwaldaship or primacy over all England, which he did not achieve till 829-30. The only conceivable
meaning that can be attached to it is that he had become a suzerain
over other princes, and these can only be those of Damnonia.
It seems very probable that he annexed what remained of Devonshire to his dominions at this date, leaving only Cornwall to the
native kings. But he was still far from being his own master ; it
was not till the death of the strong-handed Coenwulf that the
rise of Wessex to independence and domination became possible.

The last great King of Mercia died, as we have already seen, in
the year 821, apparently while he was on an expedition against the
North Welsh. The Anglo-Saxon Chronicle simply adds that he
was succeeded by Ceolwulf, who was his brother, and Ethelweard
and all other annalists confirm the fact. But there is a strange
legend, first to be found in Florence of Worcester, who no doubt
got it from some slightly earlier source, that Coenwulf left a son
named Kenelm (Coenelm), who was only seven years old, yet was
acknowledged as king. After a few days only of reign the boy was
murdered by the contrivance of his elder sister Cwenthryth (Quen-
drytha), abbess of Winchcombe. The tale is told at some length,
but with miraculous details, including a dove with golden wings
and an English letter dropped on the altar of St. Peter's, concerning

---

[1] Not 815 apparently, as we should have expected from the Anglo-Saxon
Chronicle being two years out in this part of its reckoning. For it is fixed as
the same year when Archbishop Wulfred returned from Rome, and that was 814.
See Stubbs and Haddan, iii. 577 ; Kemble's C. D., ccvii.).

the secret murder, which remove it into the realm of ecclesiastical
fiction.   Yet Kenelm became a favourite saint in the Middle Ages;
the place where his body was hidden in a brake was a well-known
haunt of pilgrims ; the expiatory chapel where they prayed was in
the Clent Hills near Halesowen in Worcestershire.   Roger of Wendover records a distich concerning the boy current in his own day :—

> In Clent coubethe Kenelm Kynebearn lith
> Under thorne haevedes bereaved,

and other late authorities have commemorated his fate under his
saint's day, July 17th.   The whole tale may be neglected ; Cwenthryth (whose eyes fell out by God's judgment, according to the
legend) is found four years after, litigating with Archbishop
Wulfred at one of the councils of Clovesho.   Perhaps her quarrel
with the primate was the cause why later generations fathered a
folk-tale upon her, for the legend of St. Kenelm is no more.

Ceolwulf was probably elderly when he ascended the throne—
his brother had reigned twenty-five years—and certainly incapable,
for the Mercian supremacy crumbled under his hands in less than
two years.   The first notice that we have of him is as continuing
Coenwulf's Welsh war, storming the castle of Diganwy (Conway)
and overrunning most of Powys in 822.   But from such affairs he
was called off, as it seems, by the rebellion of Beornwulf, one of his
late brother's ealdormen, and presumably a member of one of the
numerous branches of the Mercian royal house.   There was apparently civil war for two years,[1] and then Ceolwulf was deposed and
banished (823).   It would seem that the vassal states meanwhile
had cast off their dependence on Mercia.   The Welsh were certainly
in arms, and probably also the East Angles and the men of Wessex :
one or the other may have slain the two ealdormen, Burghelm and
Mucca, who are recorded by the Anglo-Saxon Chronicle to have
fallen in 824, the year after Beornwulf's accession, in a notice which
is all too short for lucidity.   But Aethelweard speaks of them as if
they had been put to death at a synod which the Mercian king held
at Clovesho in that year [2]—perhaps misinterpreting the Chronicle,
which was almost his only source for this period.

---

[1] For Beornwulf in charters of 825 (Cod.-Dipl. Sax. 220), speaks of the *third* year
of his reign, *i.e.*, he claims to be king since 822, while Ceolwulf was not driven out
till 823.

[2] Anno transacto facta est synodos magna in loco qui Clovesho nuncupatur, et
ibidem duo duces interimuntur Burghelm et Muca (Aethelweard, iii. § 2).

But Beornwulf's third year (825) was the critical one: in this year he and Ecgbert of Wessex fought a battle which was to turn the whole course of English history, and to register the fall of Mercia as an imperial power.   The first entry of the Chronicle, however, in that summer deals with the activity of Ecgbert in another quarter. He is recorded to have gone forth once more against the West Welsh, who perhaps may have been stirred up against him by Beornwulf.   Two casual grants of lands by him made at "Credian-treow" (probably Crediton), "quando rex exercitum Gewissorum movit contra Brettones," [1] give the date of the expedition as being in August.   Its central point was a complete defeat of the Dam-nonians at "Gafulford," which is generally interpreted as Camel-ford in Cornwall, but is not identifiable with certainty.[2]   It sealed the fate of West Devonshire, which remained embodied for ever in a Wessex shire: possibly the occupation of large estates in Cornwall as personal inheritance by the family of Ecgbert dates from this same conquest.   But their seizure may equally well go as far back as the king's first Damnonian campaign in 814, or have been made only as a punishment for the later revolt of the West Welsh in 835.

We get on to certain ground, however, when we read that im-mediately after his victory at Gafulford Ecgbert had to fight Beornwulf, who had invaded Wessex, and had penetrated as far as Ellandune [3] in the north of Wiltshire.   It looks as if the Mercian had taken advantage of the absence of the king and army in the extreme West, in order to strike at the heart of the realm of the West Saxons.   Perhaps indeed he had stirred up the diversion in Damnonia for that very purpose.   But if so his design was defeated. The army of Ecgbert was victorious and "the brook of Ellandune ran red with gore, stood dammed with battle-wreck, grew foul with mouldering corpses," [4] as some forgotten West Saxon poet sang.

---

[1] Kemble, *Corp. Dipl.*, 1033, 1035.   Cridiantreow, if not Crediton itself, is some other place on the river Creedy.

[2] Some identify it with Galford in the parish of Lew in West Devon.

[3] Probably the place now called Wroughton, near Malmesbury, not Allington, near Amesbury.   The former was till recently also known as Ellingdon.   See Mrs. Story Maskelyne's paper in *Wiltshire Archæological Magazine* for December, 1900. The identification is fixed by the Annals of Winchester (1277) speaking of the battle-spot " Ellendune " as *nunc manerium Prioris Wintoniensis*, which Wroughton *was*, and Allington was *not*.

[4] This scrap only comes as a quotation in Henry of Huntingdon, but clearly represents an old poem.   " Ellendune rivus cruore rubuit, ruina restitit, faetore tabuit."

This blow seems to have been fatal to the Mercian supremacy, which fell at once. Ecgbert sent forth without delay an army commanded by his eldest son Aethelwulf, Wulfheard, his ealdorman, and Eahlstan of Sherborne, the first fighting bishop in English history. This force was directed on Kent, while the king himself, no doubt, kept the defeated Mercians in play on the Thames. The expedition was completely successful : Baldred, the vassal-king who had ruled so long at Canterbury, fled away, because his people all deserted him. The men of Kent, as also the men of Surrey, and the South Saxons and the East Saxons, submitted to the invaders with joy, " because formerly they had been wrongly forced away from Ecgbert's kin." This statement of the Anglo-Saxon Chronicle is clearly correct enough as to Kent, where Ecgbert's father, Eahlmund, had once ruled, as also for Surrey which had long been part of the realm of Wessex, while among the South Saxons we know that Nunna, the kinsman of Ine, had once ruled, and probably others of his house after him. But the note as to the East Saxons is puzzling : we do not know that they had ever been connected with Wessex, and their king, Sigered,[1] who now submitted to Ecgbert, represented the old royal line of Saebert and Aescwin in direct descent. He was to be the last of his house who held the petty crown of Essex : three years later (828) he died, and had no successor, either because his family was extinct, or because Ecgbert found it safe to abolish the royal name, which had been borne by so many princes in succession, none of whom for many years had been really his own master.

It seems that Kent, at least, joyfully accepted liberation from the Mercians ; Archbishop Wulfred, who had so long been oppressed by Coenwulf, led the whole people to accept the new overlord. To indulge the national feeling Ecgbert named his son Aethelwulf sub-king of Kent, where he ruled under his father, apparently with success, from 825 to 839. Sussex, however, where the royal name had been disused for more than fifty years,[2] was not similarly indulged ; it became a mere shire of Wessex.

" At the same time," the Chronicle adds, " the King of the East

---

[1] It is quite possible that this is the same person who, with the title of *Dux* only, had been signing charters of Ceolwulf of Mercia in 822 and of Beornwulf in 824.

[2] The last sub-king of Sussex who called himself *Rex* was Aethelbert, who reigned *circ.* 774. After that we have only *duces*, ealdormen.

Angles and his people sought the alliance and protection of Ecgbert, for dread of the Mercians." This is the first mention of the eastern realm that we have had since Offa slew the unfortunate Aethelbert and annexed his dominions in 793. Since there is no trace of East Anglian kings during Coenwulf's reign, we are driven to believe that there must have been a rising in that quarter during the troubled time of Ceolwulf, and that some prince claiming to represent the old house must have taken advantage of the civil wars in the Mercian realm to proclaim himself king, in or about the years 822-23. There is little doubt that this was the Eadwald whose coins recommence the East Anglian series, in which there has been a gap since the death of Aethelbert. These pieces are very rare, so that the reign of the prince who restored the kingly title in the East must have been short.[1]

Immediately after the note as to the alliance of the East Angles with Ecgbert, we find in the Chronicle the statement that Beornwulf of Mercia turned himself against them, and was slain by them in battle. This must have been very late in 825, as after the August of that year we have to find room for the Ellandune campaign, and for Ecgbert's conquest of Kent, before coming to the disastrous end of the Mercian king at the hands of the East Angles.

The Mercians after this series of disasters chose as their king one Ludecan (or Ludican as he spells himself on his coins), who had been one of Beornwulf's ealdormen, and is said on late authority,[2] but with high probability, to have been his kinsman. He reigned for less than two years (end of 825 to middle of 827), evidently engaged in war both with Ecgbert and with the East Angles, as he vainly endeavoured to reassert the supremacy that his predecessors had enjoyed. His end was even more disastrous than that of Beornwulf: we read that in 827 he was slain in battle "and his five ealdormen with him" as he strove to avenge the death of Beornwulf on the East Angles. Such a slaughter evidently represents a most bloody defeat, involving the extermination of the vanquished, for Mercia did not count more than seven and perhaps only five ealdormanies within its borders.[3]

---

[1] See British Museum, *Anglo-Saxon Coins*, i., lxi. I should date them conjecturally at 822-28. The first writer who called attention to this line of inquiry was the Rev. Daniel Haigh in his *Coins of East Anglia*.

[2] Florence of Worcester.   [3] See p. 373.

This cutting short of the Mercian power was purely for the benefit of Ecgbert : he was now at the head of a league of all the minor states against the old suzerain, and found an opponent quite inadequate to face him in Wiglaf (who was chosen to fill the empty throne of Ludecan), a prince quite as obscure as his two predecessors. Ecgbert marched against him, no doubt at the head of a confederate army, in 829, and drove him completely out of his realm. " He conquered all the kingdom of the Mercians, and all that lies South of Humber." Moreover—and here it is not the Chronicle that gives us the information, but the actual coins that the conqueror struck— he actually annexed Wiglaf's realm, and took the title of King of the Mercians. No enemy of the great central state had been in the position to treat it so since Oswy slew Penda, and had uneasy pos- session of his heritage for three years, some hundred and sixty years before. Hence, not unnaturally, the West Saxons hailed their king as " Bretwalda," and claimed that he was eighth in that series of holders of the " imperium " of Britain which had begun with the shadowy Aella and ended with the great Northumbrians, Edwin, Oswald and Oswy. Ecgbert's power extended as far as that of the proudest of them, for at the end of his Mercian campaign he led his army to Dore (in Derbyshire, on the road to the North), where King Eanred of Northumbria came and offered him obedience and allegiance, " and with that they separated ".

Such homage had been demanded and received by earlier kings, and might have meant no more in the end than the ephemeral submission that had been granted to Edwin or Oswald. But the situation in 829 differed—though no man perhaps could have guessed it at the time—from that which had repeatedly been seen in the seventh century. A new power was about to appear in Britain, and to dash to pieces all the states which might have asserted them- selves against Ecgbert's heirs, when he himself—now a man well stricken in years—should have disappeared from the scene. It was the sudden recommencement of the Danish inroads that was to vary the conditions under which the English states had hitherto existed, and to prevent the rivals of Wessex from reasserting them- selves.

Meanwhile Ecgbert seems to have reorganised the subject realms immediately after the last of them had done homage to him as " Bretwalda ". After holding the Mercian crown himself for about a year, he permitted Wiglaf to return to his old kingdom and to reign there as his vassal during the remainder of his life (830-39). But in the other subject kingdoms no such policy was pursued; after the death of Sigered, the last King of Essex of the old line, no successor was allowed to take the crown of that petty kingdom, which was henceforth an ealdormany subject to Wessex, and generally attached for administrative purposes to Kent. In East Anglia, on the other hand, Ecgbert seems to have installed as sub-king his own younger son Aethelstan, when Eadwald died, and this prince ruled there until his father's death (829-39).[1] We have no means of knowing whether there survived, either in Essex or in East Anglia, any representatives of the old royal lines, or whether their extinction was the opportunity which Ecgbert took to unite all the South-East in a single group of provinces, immediately subject to his own house. It was but the carrying out of the same system which Coenwulf had used when he made his brother Cuthred king in Kent, and (as we have seen at a much earlier date) the *subreguli* of the Hwiccas probably owned their origin to a similar act on the part of the great kings of Northumbria.

It was shortly after Ecgbert had attained the position of Bretwalda that the ravages of the Danes began once more in the year 834. Before commencing to deal with them it may be well to recur to the isolated history of the kingdom of Northumbria, which has only been carried down to the date of the murder of the tyrant Aethelred on April 18th, 796.

The death of that strong-handed prince was followed by disturbances as violent as any of those which had troubled the Northumbrian realm during the last seventy years. An ealdorman (*dux et patricius*) named Osbald was the first to profit by Aethelred's murder. He was saluted as king by certain nobles of his own

---

[1] This is a fact recorded nowhere in the Chronicle, but the coins of an East Anglian king, Aethelstan I., obviously the successor of Eadwald and the predecessor of Aethelweard, and dating from about 829 to 839, if we draw deduction from the moneyer's names, are not uncommon. That this is Ecgbert's younger son, who was afterwards King of Kent, is demonstrated with some approach to certainty in the recently published *Corolla Sancti Edmundi*, and by Sir Henry Howorth in the *Numismatic Chronicle* for 1908, pp. 222-65. This Aethelstan has got confused with his nephew of the same name, son of King Aethelwulf, the chronicler Aethelweard having been followed in the blunder by Florence of Worcester and others. But Aethelstan, son of Ecgbert, is clearly vouched for by MSS. D, E, and F of the Anglo-Saxon Chronicle.

kindred, but only twenty-seven days after was disowned by the
Witan and driven into exile.   He fled to take refuge with the King
of the Picts,[1] while that Eardwulf who seven years before had
escaped by miracle from the sword of the executioners at Ripon [2] was
recalled from exile and crowned at York on May 20th, 796.   After
he had reigned two years, the faction which had murdered Aethelred and backed Osbald rose against him, under the leadership of an
ealdorman named Wada.   But Eardwulf defeated them with great
slaughter at Billinghow, near Whalley, and drove them out of the
kingdom.   Yet he got no rest thereby ; his reign was one of battle,
murder and sudden death.   "To detail at length the events, the
ends and the modes of each of these wars is forbidden us by reason
of their terrible prolixity," sagely remarks a chronicler whom they
had wearied out, " but the race of the Angles was hard by nature and
proud, and so it came that it was perpetually worn down by these
intestine struggles." [3]   Simeon of Durham's notices of this time are
mostly accounts of executions wrought by Eardwulf's orders.   In
799 he caused the ealdorman Moll—presumably some descendent of
King Aethelwald Moll—to be slain ; and also apparently another
ealdorman named Ealdred, who had been the actual murderer of
King Aethelred.   In 800 his guards arrested and put to death
Alchmund, son of King Alchred, who seems to have been plotting
or practising rebellion at the head of a band of exiles.   In the
following year he waged against Coenwulf of Mercia the last
recorded war between the two great kingdoms, because—as we read
—the Mercian had entertained rebels fleeing from his sword.[4]   But
peace was quickly patched up between them : Northumbria was to
perish by its own sword, not that of its ancient enemy.   In 803 the
old Northern Chronicle preserved in the pages of Simeon of Durham
comes to an abrupt end, and our knowledge of all that went on
beyond the Humber grows dim for many years.   Three years later
we learn—with no details given—that Eardwulf was "expelled by
his own people " : all his slaughtering had not sufficed to extirpate
the hostile faction.   One Aelfwald was proclaimed king in his stead,

---

[1] But afterwards became a monk, returned to Northumbria, and died at York
an abbot in 799.
    [2] See p. 387.   [3] Henry of Huntingdon, iv., *sub anno* 798.
    [4] Perhaps the ealdorman Wada was one of them.   There is some mention of
him in the Correspondence of Pope Leo III. and Charles the Great in 808.

no doubt as the representative of the party which had supported
in succession Alchred, Osred and Osbald ; but his parentage and
claims to the throne have not been preserved.   He reigned two
years only (806-8), obscurely but certainly not happily, for he
was deposed, as it seems, under circumstances unparalleled in English history.   Eardwulf had fled after his deposition to the court
of Charles the Great, and from thence to Rome.   He was favourably received at both, and returned to England in 808, accompanied
by a papal legate and two abbots sent by the emperor.   These
clerics entered into negotiations, as we are told, with the Northumbrian Witan, and persuaded them to receive back their old
king.   Aelfwald II. abdicated without making any resistance, and
the exile was restored, to reign for two years more, and then to die and
leave the crown to his son Eanred, whose accession—by some
miraculous chance—does not appear to have been celebrated by the
usual civil war.   He seems to have been made his father's colleague
at the time of his return to England.

It is strange that no account of Eardwulf's restoration occurs
in any English chronicle.   The facts recorded above, concerning the
papal and imperial interference in Northumbrian affairs, are only
to be found in the Chronicle of the Frank Einhard, and in a series
of papal letters ranging over the year 806-8.   Possibly the native
English writers resented this foreign influence and deliberately
neglected to mention it, from a dislike to acknowledge anything
implying a possible claim to suzerainty on the part of the emperor.

Eanred, the son of Eardwulf, enjoyed a reign of a length unprecedented in the Northumbrian annals, having worn the crown
from 808 to 840.   But its annals are almost a blank, though we get
indications that the kingdom was in a state of woeful decay.   The
Galloway Picts—as has been already mentioned—appear to have
freed themselves from the Northumbrian overlordship somewhere
during the troublous reign of Eardwulf—the last mention of an
English bishop of Whiterne falls in 803.   The bishopric of Hexham disappeared also in 821, the see being apparently amalgamated
with Lindisfarne, while the splendid cathedral of Wilfred is said to
have fallen into ruins.   Had it been sacked in some unrecorded
civil broil or in an invasion of northern enemies ?   For Angus Mac
Fergus, King of the Picts from beyond Forth, is said, though by
writers of late date and dubious veracity, to have been ravaging

Bernicia in 820.[1] That Northumbria was in no condition to contest the supremacy of England with Ecgbert, or even to defend
itself, is sufficiently shown by the tame fashion in which Eanred
did homage to the King of Wessex at Dore in 829. A few years
later the ravages of the Danes recommenced, and the northern
kingdom began to receive its full share of their attention. But all
this period is as shadowy as the times before Ida ; we have lost the
help of the old Northumbrian Chronicle, and have nothing to take
its place. From Ecgbert onwards Wessex becomes the centre of
history, and all that happened far from that small centre of light is
barely visible. The names of the last Northumbrian kings are best
preserved by their prolific coinage of small copper *stycas*. It is
interesting to note that the archbishops of York were also coining
freely, like their brothers of Canterbury, and generally without any
acknowledgment of the reigning king. Of one of these prelates, Wigmund (837-54), there exists, as has been mentioned above, a large gold
solidus,[2] with the inscription Mvnvs Divinvm, and a well-executed
portrait bust. We should be glad to know under what circumstances such a fine piece—unparalleled in the Old-English series—
was struck. But no information is forthcoming.

Meanwhile, in the fifth year after Ecgbert had achieved his
supremacy over all England, the northern storm began to beat
once more upon her coasts. In 834, wrongly called 832 by the
Anglo-Saxon Chronicle, " the heathen men ravaged Sheppey ".
From this year onward their incursions came almost without
a break, and affected all the kingdoms of England alike.
The war with them becomes the one all-absorbing topic in
the history of the time. Wherefore it is necessary to obtain some
conception of who they were, whence they came, and what was the
character of their plundering bands.

[1] See Skene, *Ancient Celtic Kings of Scotland.*
[2] British Museum, *Anglo-Saxon Coins,* i. 193.

CHAPTER XX

THE VIKINGS AND THEIR ORIGIN

THE phenomena of the Scandinavian invasion of Britain in the ninth century bear a resemblance, which appears more striking the more it is studied, to those of the Saxon invasion of Britain in the fifth. The stages are similar—first isolated ravages, then the establishment of a solid base, followed by deliberate conquest, lastly the formation by the victorious settlers of new states extending over a great part of the island. The operating force is no less similar—it does not consist of a whole nation migrating to new sites under its ancestral king, but of bands of adventurers headed by numerous petty chiefs, who only yielded an uncertain and temporary obedience to the generals-in-chief whom they from time to time elected. It is only occasionally that the English in the fifth century, or the Northmen in the ninth, appear to be conducting a rational strategic operation under the guidance of a single mind. There was normally a certain fitfulness and want of logical sequence in their movements, which bore witness to the conflicting desires of many leaders. When settlement began, in each case, it took the form of the establishment of several small states, not of one solid monarchy. The aims of Saxon and of Scandinavian were clearly the same—at first merely to get good plunder by unexpected descents on some rich centre of population, a city or (in the later century) a great monastery: then somewhat later to win land for settlement, finally to set up a small principality on the conquered land.

The methods and the aims of the two bodies of invaders were similar, because the composition of their hosts and their social organisation were much the same. In each case the nucleus of the migration consisted of warlike adventurers of royal or noble blood, accompanied each by his war-band of oath-bound followers, the *comitatus* of personal dependants, or of broken men from other tribes, who had sworn to adhere to the fortunes of a chief whom they had chosen for themselves. The Scandinavian coasts swarmed in the ninth century, as the North Sea coasts had in the sixth, with petty chiefs—younger sons of royal houses, dynasts who had been expelled from their own districts, or leaders of less noble origin but of tried reputation in war, whose fame had sufficed to win them a following. An expedition might be conducted by a single chief and his small squadron—as small as the three keels of Hengist, or those "three ships from Haerethaland" which made the first raid on Wessex in the days of King Beorhtric. More frequently the raid was effected by an alliance of several pirate admirals, with a force of twenty, fifty or a hundred ships. Later on great confederacies were formed, and an invasion might be conducted by an alliance of "two kings and five earls" like that of the "Great Army" with which Aethelred and Alfred fought at Reading and Ashdown in 871. In such case the vessels might be numbered by the hundred, and the host might reach 10,000 shields.

Probably the "imperium" of Aella or Ceawlin among the Saxons was much the same thing as the war-lordship of the Dane Guthrum. If we had as many details about the fifth and sixth centuries as we have about the ninth and tenth, the parallel might probably be pushed to further detail. But the Anglo-Saxon Chronicle gives us hard detailed fact, where Gildas prefers to indulge in vague rhetoric and lamentations destitute of names and dates. If the Celt had been as prosaic as the Saxon, we should know precisely what was the number of Aella's ships, the date of the fall of London or Lincoln would not be hidden from us, and we might trace the itinerary of Ambrosius Aurelianus even as we can trace that of Alfred.

The condition of Sweden, Denmark and Norway about the year 800 must have been singularly like that of the lands round the North Sea in 500. The pirates of the later age, indeed, were actually occupying some of the territory that had been owned by their predecessors. For the Danes had moved south and west, had spread over much of the land that had been deserted by the Angles, and had conquered and absorbed the Eutiones or Jutes of the Cimbric Peninsula. Their race, which three hundred years before had dwelt mainly in Scania and the other lands beyond the Sound —with Zealand perhaps added—had now possession of all the islands about the two Belts, and of the mainland as far as the Eider. It was on that river that they marched with—and often fought with—the Saxons. Beyond the Danes eastward lay the Goths (Geats, Gautar) in their two provinces of East and West Gauthiod, on each side of the long lake Wetter. North of the Goths again were the Swedes, in Swithiod, around the lake Maelar; their holy place was Upsala, and their boundary probably extended little farther than the Dal River, the modern Swedish Norrland being still the home of wild Lapps and Finns. The inland to the west of Swithiod was a vast forest, separating the Swedes in the most effective fashion from the Norwegians. Along the fiords of the rugged and much indented coast of Norway, where the salt water creeps for scores of miles into the heart of the mountains, dwelt many communities, all practically independent of each other, and not even normally subject, like the Swedes and Danes, to a single king. For monarchy in Norway was a plant of a later growth. The part of the land most thickly peopled was the shore looking south, round the "Vik," where the Skager Rack meets with the long fiord at whose head the future capital of the united land, the mediæval Opslo, the modern Christiania, was one day to rise. The wilder inlets of the Western coast had each their separate community ruled by Jarls great and small, up as far as the Trondjem Fiord, and for some way beyond. But the northern coast of modern Norway was still unpeopled by any Scandinavian inhabitants.

Dane and Goth, Swede and Norwegian, were all close akin in blood, language and manners. All were as yet untouched by Christianity, and only affected slightly and indirectly by the common culture of Europe. Yet it would be wrong to look upon the Northmen as savages, though their deeds were often savage enough. They had a primitive civilisation of their own, descending in legitimate line from that of the Bronze Age people, who had been in the Scandinavian lands long ere the Romans came to Britain. Their metal-craft was notable, as it had been in the Bronze Age: but its art was now affected at second hand by debased Roman models, copied and recopied through the various tribes which lay between the Rhine and the Baltic. It is interesting to trace on the bracteate medallions, set as gold pendants, which formed one of the most typical developments of northern art, traces of the figures or busts of Constantine and his house, gradually degenerating into rude representations of Scandinavian gods. The ultimate result bore as little resemblance to the original as did the first century coins of the Britons to the Philippic staters from which they traced their remote ancestry.

The Scandinavians were also great boat-builders. Tacitus, seven hundred years before the time at which we have arrived, had noted that the "island of the Suiones" (for so he called the Scandinavian peninsula) was rich in arms and ships.[1] Yet they had seldom or never left their own waters to join in the piratical assaults which the Saxons and other nearer Teutonic nations had made upon the expiring Roman Empire. No more than a single raid indeed is on record—that made by a king whom the Frankish chroniclers called by the uncouth name of Chocolaicus: he was apparently the Hygelac who occurs in the song of Beowulf, as the near kinsman of that hero. While ravaging at the mouth of the Meuse he was surprised and slain, in 515, by Theudebert, the son of the Austrasian king Theuderich. After this expedition we have—strangely enough—no notice of a Danish expedition into the western lands till that which sacked Lindisfarne in 793.

The vessels of the Scandinavians were not well suited for long voyages in the open sea, which may account for their long abstention from excursions far afield. They were long open boats, high at the stern and bows, worked mainly by oars, though they possessed a single mast, which could be hoisted and made to bear a broad square sail when the wind was favourable. But normally, as it would seem, they were worked with a single bank of oars, from twelve to thirty a side. They had no rudders, but were steered with a single large paddle strapped on the starboard side, like a Shetland "sixern" or a whale-boat. Originally, as it appears, the type was much smaller than it afterwards became; the length did not exceed seventy-five feet, and fifteen oars a side may have been the average provision; but the great sea-kings of later times built much larger vessels, which would carry 150 men or more. Such boats were well suited for working inside the fiords,

[1] *Germania*, § 44.

or in the narrow waters of the Belts and the Sound, but they were
eminently dangerous in stormy weather, if caught in the storms of
the North Sea, or—still worse—in the dreadful rollers that surge
through the Pentland Firth, or beat upon the Atlantic coasts of
Britain and Ireland. Countless unrecorded disasters must have
occurred to Viking fleets, after the fashion of that dreadful shipwreck in 876 when the shattered hulls of 120 galleys were piled up,
one over another, under the cliffs of Swanage. At first the
exploration of the Western waters by the earliest pirate squadrons must have been done cautiously, in spells of fine weather,
carefully waited for. They fled home before the gales of the
autumnal equinox, and did not crawl forth coast-wise again till
spring was fully set in.

The difficulty of deep-sea navigation in such vessels might be
sufficient to explain the long immunity of the Christian kingdoms of
the West from Viking raids, if we did not remember that—despite
all hindrances—those raids began at last. They began, too, at a
time when Christendom seemed far stronger than had been the
case for many generations. It was not while the Merovingian race
was decaying, and the frontiers of the Frankish kingdoms were
giving way before the Slav and the Saracen, that the Vikings appeared, nor while Teutonic England was no more than a fringe of
petty states along the coast of the German Ocean. The Northmen
began their ravages while Charles the Great was still in his prime,
and was going forth, conquering and to conquer, to South and
East and North, and while Offa of Mercia was ruling over something like a petty empire of united England. The home conditions of Scandinavia do not seem to have been changing of late:
it would be difficult to deduce from them why a maritime expansion should have begun among them just before the year 800.
There had been far better opportunities a century, or two centuries,
earlier, for the pirate to exercise his trade with profit. But down
to the end of the eighth century no signs of Scandinavian activity
in the Western seas are to be found. Nothing, indeed, can be
more marked than the total want of any trace of communication
between England and the lands beyond the North Sea in the days
of the Heptarchy. There are more signs of touch between them
in the Bronze Age than in the sixth or seventh centuries of our
era. Some of the early English kings had war-fleets—Edwin, it

will be remembered, conquered Man, and Ecgfrith ravaged parts
of Ireland. And there was much mercantile intercourse between
England and the Franks, and some even with the Frisians. But
neither in war nor in peace do we hear of any dealings with the
Cimbric or the Scandinavian peninsulas. The few notes about the
old seats of the invaders of England in Bede seem to be gathered
from old national tradition, not from modern knowledge. So do
the ethnographic details of the song of Beowulf. Meanwhile the
independent heathen tribes of old Saxony appear to have acted as an
effective buffer between the Franks and the Danes. There is nothing in the seventh or earlier eighth century to parallel the notices
of touch with the Northern nations that are to be found in Venantius Fortunatus, and other writers of the earlier Merovingian times.

Strange as the fact may seem, it would appear that the origin
of the Viking raids must be sought in the hostile advance of Christendom, represented by Charles the Great, towards the North,
rather than in any original intention of the Scandinavians to attack the South. As long as they were left alone, they confined
themselves to the practice of intestine wars in their own narrow
seas. But with the first invasions of Saxony by the Frankish
troops, invasions begun with a deliberate intent to conquer and
convert the whole Saxon race, a new period commenced. Charles the
Great had an iron resolution and an untiring hand: Einhard
calculates that his "Saxon war" lasted thirty-three years—from
772 to 804. Though these dates merely mark the beginning of
the first invasion and the end of the last revolt—many of the intervening years having been times of comparative peace, when the
Saxon race lay prostrate under the Frankish sword—yet the whole
period was in truth one long struggle. Again and again the
Saxons submitted, gave hostages, revolted, and were once more
tamed with fire and sword. The emperor refused to be beaten,
and finally achieved his purpose: the enemies' spirit was broken,
they received baptism and became obedient, if discontented, subjects of the empire.

One feature of this interminable war brought Charles and his
Franks into direct collision with the Scandinavians. Repeatedly
Widukind and other Saxon chiefs, when driven out of their own
dominions, crossed the Eider and sought a momentary refuge with
their old foes beyond the boundary stream. By sheltering the

exiles and lending them help, Siegfred King of the Danes found himself involved in disputes with the conqueror. Apparently he feared the consequences, and sent propitiatory embassies to Charles, who then lay in his winter quarters in Saxony (782). His successor Godfred was less timid or more powerful—he took up war with the Franks, and it was probably his subjects who were responsible for some sporadic descents on the Frisian coast, and other outlying tracts of Charles's empire, which took place at much about the same time that the sack of Lindisfarne occurred. To the Danes, no doubt, all Christendom seemed as one enemy, and they were not concerned to discover whether an attack on Northumbria would have any effect on the King of the Franks. But it may have been a Norwegian and not a Danish fleet which harried the sanctuary of St. Cuthbert. The advance of the armies of Charles the Great towards the North seems to have alarmed and stirred up all the Scandinavians, and not merely those whose frontier was immediately threatened.

Meanwhile from the year 800 onward there was almost permanent hostile contact between Frank and Dane: we hear of ravages in Frisia, of Danish armies massed in Schleswig, who drew the great entrenchment called the " Dane's Dyke " [1] across the neck of the Cimbric peninsula, and of land attacks upon the Abotrites, and other newly won subjects of Charles on the Baltic. In 808 the emperor himself was in Holstein with a great army, but ultimately turned back without carrying out the invasion of Denmark, which he had been projecting. Two years later the Danes are found ravaging the Frisian lands with a fleet of 200 ships—this is the first mention of a Scandinavian armament which reached such a considerable strength. In 812 King Godfred himself was in the field, but he was murdered hard by the Elbe by a domestic enemy, in the midst of his campaign. His nephew and successor, Heming, withdrew his army homeward at once, just in time to escape Charles, who had started out to seek the invaders, and was already on the Weser at the head of a great host. Heming sought peace with the emperor, and we hear for some time of no more Danish troubles on the Eider or the Saxon shore. At the moment of Charles's death in 814 the successors of Godfred were occupied in bitter

---

[1] Not the later Dannewerk, which was constructed some time later by the famous Queen Thyra.

civil wars, and some of them sought the alliance of the Franks to strengthen them against their kinsmen. A certain King Harald propitiated Lewis the Pious, the son of Charles, by allowing Christian missionaries to visit the lands of which he was in possession, and even, when driven out of his realm in 826, visited Ingelheim and allowed himself to be baptised. It was not till 833-37 that we again hear of Danish invasions becoming a serious menace to the empire. It must be noted that there is a corresponding gap in the history of Scandinavian raids on England in all these years. From the first group of raids in 793-94 down to the later years of Ecgbert, we have no record of any troubles caused by the pirates. Evidently the civil wars of the Cimbric peninsula gave a respite to the greater part of Western Christendom.

In one region alone do we find a long-drawn record of raids and ravages, continuing from the first moment of the Vikings' appearance. This was Ireland, which seems to have been enduring for a whole generation a most miserable fate. The earliest record of the coming of the Northmen in this quarter falls in the year 795—two summers after the sack of Lindisfarne. A fleet which is stated to have numbered over 100 ships came first to South Wales,[1] where it made a landing in Glamorganshire : but, being attacked and repulsed by King Maredudd, the " pagans " transferred their attention to the Irish coast. Here they found an easy prey, in a sacred island whose character was much the same as that of Lindisfarne, and whose attractions for the spoiler were the same. This was the isle of Rechru, off Dublin Bay, which now bears the Scandinavian name of Lambay, On it was a rich monastery founded by St. Columba, and full no doubt of treasures of gold, jewels and metal work, since it was a famous and popular sanctuary. It was plundered " with horrid ravage and harrying," [2] and seems to have served as a convenient base for further raids around St. George's Channel. For now, as always, an island was the best possible camp and stronghold that Vikings could find, since they were dealing with folks who had no war-navy to send against them. The English seem to have lost for many generations their old efficiency at sea : we hear nothing of a fighting fleet between the days of Ecgfrid of Northumbria and those of the great Alfred. The Irish had never owned war-vessels at all ; both

---

[1] Annales Cambriae, *sub anno* 795, and Gwent Chronicle.
[2] Wars of the Gaedhil and Gaill, *sub anno* 795.

their trade and the strange reckless explorations of their hermits and missionaries had been conducted in boats of the flimsiest sort. Sometimes they crossed broad waters in mere coracles of hide, which the first storm must infallibly have destroyed.

It would seem that the Vikings settled down to harry Ireland, while they left the English and the Franks practically unmolested for thirty years, because they found the conditions specially favourable. There was no great monarchy to cope with, such as that of Charles the Great : there was not even a confederacy with an energetic suzerain at its head, such as England showed in the times of Offa, Coenwulf, or Ecgbert. The English states were comparatively large, set beside those of the sister island, where "every *dun* (fortified mound) had its king". Dynasts claiming the kingly title were numbered by the dozen in Ireland, and though the tradition of a High-King (Ard Righ) existed, it had of late practically dropped into effeteness. The title was borne at this period by the O'Neils, who reigned in two branches, the one at Derry and the other in Meath. But they enjoyed no real power either over the strong kings of Munster, nor even over many smaller princes who dwelt nearer to their own borders. Indeed the normal condition of the whole land was civil war, and old feuds rendered it specially difficult to bring about any common action against an invader. As long as he confined himself to petty attacks on a few spots, each king rather rejoiced than lamented over the misfortunes of his hostile neighbours. It was not for many years, till the Vikings began to threaten the independence of the whole island, that combination, as the only alternative to extermination, was forced upon the Irish princes.

After the first attack on Rechru in 795 we find in steady succession a ravaging of the Isle of Man in 798, a preliminary raid on Iona in 802, and a complete desolation of that holy place in 806. This last was a blow that echoed round the West as a terrible sign of future woes. Iona was to the Scots and Irish far more than Lindisfarne had ever been to the Northumbrians. Despite of the waning power and energy of the Western Church, it was still the greatest of sanctuaries. Now the "heathen men" slew its community of sixty-eight coenobites, burnt its churches, and carried off its treasures, the gifts of ten generations of kings. The island community was afterwards refounded: but pious hands exhumed the bones of Columba, and carried them to Kells, in the Irish inland, where a new church was reared over them. It was a wise act, for Iona was desolated for a third time only a few years after (823-24).

In the year after the sack of Iona the Vikings appeared for the first time on the West coast of Ireland, to destroy the monastery of Innishmurray, off the coast of Sligo, and afterwards to land and harry some part of the neighbouring mainland. This was the first of a series of raids upon the inland, which was not to cease for three generations. In 812-13-14 the invaders are heard of everywhere in Ulster, Connaught and Munster, sometimes repulsed, but more often successfully plundering some great shrine, after having routed the bands of the local king. But the worst series of their incursions began in 820, precisely at the time when the Danes were at peace with the Emperor Lewis, and making no show whatever of hostility either in Frankland or in England. The explanation of this fact has been sought in the hypothesis that the original invaders of Ireland may have been Danes, who had arrived in the West by following the route through the Dover Straits and the Channel, and whose vigour in attack fell off when the civil wars in their homelands began in 814, while the later visitors may have been Norwegians, coming by the longer and more dangerous passage from Norway to Orkney, and then round the Hebrides to Ulster. The activity of these northern raiders would not be affected by the Danish civil wars, with which they had little concern. And thus the fact that Ireland was being thoroughly harried from 820 to 837, while the Franks and the English were unmolested, might be accounted for, the first adventurers being Danes, the later-comers Norwegians.

That the route to Ireland round Cape Wrath was actually in use by 825, seems to be demonstrated by a complaint made by an Irish chronicler in that year to the effect that all the settlements of monks in the islands of the Northern Sea had already been destroyed by pirates coming from the North. And these settlements had certainly extended to the Orkneys, and probably to Iceland.[1] It is impossible to doubt that this destruction must have been the work of Norwegians. The Irish chroniclers soon learnt to make a distinction between the Dubh-Gaill or " Black Strangers," by which name they designated the Danes, and the Finn-Gaill, or " White

---

[1] See Keary's *Vikings in Western Christendom*, pp. 171, 186-87.

Strangers," their title for the Norsemen. Unfortunately they do
not tell us to which category the early invaders between 795 and
814 belonged.

The raids of the Vikings, now probably all Norsemen, continued
with increasing fury from 820 to 831, and extended almost to the
heart of the Isle of Erin. After the last-named year they took a
new shape, under a certain Thorgils (or Turgesius as the Irish
chroniclers call him) who seems to have aimed at territorial conquest, and the setting up of a Scandinavian kingdom in Ireland.
The notes concerning him extend over many years: he sacked
Armagh thrice, ravaged all Ulster, Meath and Connaught, and as
one curious annal relates, set up his wife Ota, who seems to have
been a sort of prophetess, to utter oracles from the desecrated high-
altar of the famous abbey of Clonmacnoise.[1] In the latter part of
his time he was reckoned as actual king of all Northern Ireland.
Meanwhile his projects received every possible help from the insane
civil wars of the Irish: Felim King of Munster was ravaging the
lands of his northern neighbours from the one side, while Thorgils
was attacking them from the other. Things went from bad to
worse till in 845 Malachy, King of Meath, the head of the
southern branch of the O'Neills, slew the Norse king. We are
told that he seized him by treachery at a conference, and caused
him to be drowned in Loch Owel.[2] The half-compacted Viking
state at once went to pieces, and in a few years we find the invaders of Ireland owning nothing more than a comparatively small
territory, a number of scattered patches of land round certain
great ports which they had made their own, such as Dublin,
Waterford, Wexford, and Limerick. But from these bases they
continued to devastate the inland in sporadic raids with as much
energy as of old, and no corner was safe from them. Civilisation
and literature died down, as one after another the old seats of
Irish learning and piety were destroyed. Some of the natives
even abandoned Christianity, and took to allying themselves with
the spoilers—a detested class who were known as the Gaill Gaedhil or "Irish Strangers". The local kings maintained themselves
in the bogs and woods in precarious independence: but they had
at least learnt to some small degree the necessity for combina-

[1] *Wars of the Gaedhil and Gaill, sub anno* 843.
[2] See *Ulster Annals* and *Wars of the G. and G., sub anno* 844.

tion, and at a day still long distant were to unite under Brian Boroimhe to win the last great battle at Clontarf (1014), which made it certain that Ireland, save some few coast cities, was to remain a Celtic and not to become a Scandinavian land. Even at Clontarf, so great was the infatuation of the Irish, a king of Leinster, with a considerable body of auxiliaries, was fighting in the Danish ranks.

But the fortunes of Ireland must not be pursued too far. The thirty years of respite which England enjoyed during the reign of Coenwulf and the earlier years of Ecgbert came to an end in 834. To that same summer, we must note, belong equally the first considerable descent that the Vikings had made on Frankish territory since the death of Charles the Great—a plundering of Dorstadt and Utrecht, the two great towns by the Rhine-mouth, and their first landing in England—on the Isle of Sheppey—since the original raids in 793-94. In all probability it was the same fleet which was responsible for both these attacks, since the localities lie exactly opposite each other on the two sides of the North Sea.

The raiders in this case were almost certainly Danes from Denmark—the Irish Vikings were busily employed at the moment in following Thorgils, who had arrived two years before, and is recorded in this year to have been ravaging all around the coasts of Ireland. On the other hand the Danish civil wars had ended in the expulsion of Harald, the king who had allowed himself to be baptised, and had favoured the work of Christian missionaries, and the triumph of his kinsman Horik, a bitter enemy alike of the Frankish empire and of the Christian religion—the chroniclers called him *Fel Christianitatis*, the gall of Christendom [830]. At the same time the deplorable strife between Lewis the Pious and his sons had begun. In the very year when the Danes appeared to carry out the first sack of Dorstadt, Lewis was waging civil war in Italy against his eldest son Lothair. The pagans were once more united, the Christians, for the first time since the early days of Charles the Great, were divided. It was this juxtaposition of facts which accounts for the ever-increasing disasters of the next generation.

The doings of the invaders in England and in the empire must be kept in close connection. For the next thirty years the same pirate fleets were operating indifferently on each side of the North

Sea. If stoutly met and repulsed on one shore, they tried their luck on the other. And when we come on an unexpected gap of two or three summers in their ravagings in England, it is generally explained by the fact that we find them particularly active during that time in Eastern or Western Frankland. On the whole the Continental side of their activity was more prominent in this period ; plunder was richer, and the kings, we may add, were individually weaker in Neustria or on the Rhine than in England. Ecgbert was far superior as a fighting man to any of his Carlovingian contemporaries, and even his pious son Aethelwulf compares favourably with Charles the Bald or Charles the Fat. The English expeditions of the Vikings from 834 to 865 were pressed far less vigorously than their Continental expeditions ; it was only after the last-named year that the lands on this side of the North Sea became the more important front of the Viking attack, and drew off for a time the main body of their forces. It was the years from 865 to 878 which were the period of most desperate peril for England, when the " Great Army," a confederacy of all the chief pirate bands, was hard at work on this island, demolishing kingdom after kingdom, and only finally failing because it was met and turned back by Alfred of Wessex, the greatest man of his time. In the years after 878 we find Alfred enjoying a long space of comparative peace, won by the terror which he had inspired in the campaign of Ethandune, while the Franks once more became the chief victims of the Danish sword, and suffered the worst of their humiliations, the sack of Aix-la-Chapelle, their ancient capital (881), and the ignominious retreat of Charles the Fat, with the whole force of the empire at his back, from before the besiegers of Paris (886). Alfred's last Danish campaigns (892-96) were the direct result of the rally of the Franks under the gallant Arnulf, the successor of Charles the Fat, and his victory over the " Great Army " at Louvain (891). The host of Hasting, which so persistently attacked England for the five years that followed, was vainly seeking the "point of least resistance " in Christendom, when it had come to the conclusion that this point did not lie in the realm of Arnulf. Hence it was a turning-point not merely of English but of European history when that host, utterly fought out and humbled in spirit went to pieces in 896, when " the army dispersed, some to East Anglia, some to Northumbria, while those who were moneyless gat them ships and fared over sea southwards to the Seine. Thanks be to God, the Army had not utterly broken down the English nation."[1] Nay, rather, it was the English nation which had broken down the Army, for never again was such a confederacy seen, and the later ravages of the Vikings in the tenth century, though often serious enough, did not seem to threaten the complete destruction of Christendom, a thing that had seemed perfectly possible at more than one disastrous moment in the ninth century. The exploits of Sweyn and Cnut, a hundred years later, belong to a different series of events, and—as we shall presently see—are not to be counted as a mere continuation, or recrudescence, of the original raids of the earlier pirate hosts.

The absolute domination over land and sea which the Vikings seemed to possess for a good part of the ninth century appears at first sight sufficiently surprising. They can never have been very numerous, compared to the strength of the enemies of whom they made such havoc. The Scandinavian North was not very thickly peopled—more than half of what now forms the kingdoms of Norway and Sweden was not peopled at all. Unity also was lacking in the direction of their hosts. Norway had no king to lead its national force, but only many jarls, jealous of each other and divided by family feuds. Denmark had kings, but it is very rarely that we find one of them leading an expedition in the ninth century, though Siegfred, Godfred and Horik are so found on one or two occasions. But much more frequently the leaders were expelled princes, or members of the royal house who stood near enough to the throne to find life dangerous at home. Quite as frequently they were mere adventurers, who had won their way to command not by virtue of birth but by military prowess. The " king," who is so often found at the head of a Viking fleet, had usually no kingdom at home ; he was like the chief of whom Abbo sang—

Solo rex verbo, sociis tamen imperitabat.

A certain number of them won kingdoms abroad, like those princes who reigned at York or Dublin, or, later on, at Rouen. But usually they were kings of a host, not of a tribe or a region, and their kingship would disappear when their host melted away from

[1] A. S. Chronicle, *sub anno* 897 [for 896].

them, after a series of defeats, or a display of some personal foible of which the public opinion of their following did not approve, such as avarice, over-caution, or a hankering after the Christian faith.

Such leaders were obliged to pay attention to the desires of their host, which often dictated rather than obeyed a plan of campaign. Often, too, the expedition had not even a single general, but was managed in common by some three or four adventurers whose bands had united for the time being, and might split up after a stormy council of war. Hence came illogical and spasmodic action, which is often difficult to understand.

Having neither numbers nor unity of guidance to their credit, how did the Viking hosts contrive to bear down all opposition for several generations? The answer is, in the main, that they enjoyed two all-important advantages—the complete command of the sea, and the ascendency that trained war-bands could assert over hastily-raised regional levies, individual superiority in military efficiency.

Their command of the sea was absolute: during the first period of their raids they met with no opposition whatever on the water. No English war-fleet had been heard of since the days of Ecgfrith: Charles the Great had shown some intention of caring for naval affairs, but his unhappy descendants did not make any signs of copying his example: it was to be centuries before any of the realms that obeyed the Frankish house could boast of a fleet of its own. The Irish were even less given to maritime ambitions than the English or the Franks. Hence, until the great Alfred arose, a Viking fleet wandered at its own sweet will through the broad and the narrow seas. The same expedition might threaten Hamburg in May, Ghent in June, Winchester in July, and Leinster in August. When the local defence proved too strong, it could always move along to another point, where the landsfolk were less prepared or more feebly led. Moreover there was the certainty that no common action would be taken against it: the Frank and the Englishman had not learnt to co-operate, still less the Englishman and the Irishman. If a raiding squadron was heard of at Dorstadt or Utrecht, the King of East Anglia might think of strengthening his own coast defences, but would certainly not dream of giving help to the Frisian neighbour across the North Seas. Still less would the misfortunes of a King of Leinster affect the ruler of South Wales or of Wessex. Even within the Frankish empire it was hard to stir up Burgundy to help Neustria, or Bavaria to succour Saxony. And so, within the bounds of England, it is some time before we find any attempt of one kingdom to aid another— the first was the occasion when Aethelred of Wessex came to help Burhred of Mercia at Nottingham in 868, thirty years after the great series of Viking raids had started in 834. Free power to move in any direction, and consequent ubiquity, compensated for the want of numbers in the Viking hosts.

Another result of the non-existence of hostile fleets was that the Northmen could establish practically impregnable bases off the hostile coast, so long as they could find islands separated by a channel a few hundred yards broad from the mainland. Not merely outlying isles like Man, but watergirt localities like Walcheren, Thanet, Sheppey, or the isle of Noirmoutier at the Loiremouth, were perfectly safe against the armies of Christendom, which could only rage impotently from the opposite shore, for want of means to cross in face of a hostile naval force.

But no less important than the command of the sea was the superiority of the individual Viking in battle to the average member of the host that came out against him. The war-bands of the invader were the pick of the North, all volunteers, all trained warriors. In a Frankish or an English host the only troops that could safely be opposed to them, man to man, were the personal following of the kings and ealdormen of England—or the dukes and counts of the Continent. And these were but a small fraction of the hasty levy that assembled, when news came that the Danes were ashore at Bremen or Boulogne, at Sandwich or Weymouth The majority of the *hereban* of a Frankish county or the *fyrd* of an English shire was composed of farmers fresh from the plough, not of trained fighting men. Enormous superiority of numbers could alone compensate for the difference in military efficiency. If that superiority existed, the raider quietly retired to his ships, or to his fortified island base. If it did not, he fell upon the landsfolk and made a dreadful slaughter of them. How could it be expected that the ceorl, who came out to war with spear and target alone, should contend on equal terms with the Northman equipped with steel cap and mail shirt, and well trained to form the shieldwall for defence and the war-wedge for attack? Working against the hastily arrayed masses of the landsfolk, the Viking host was like a good military machine beating upon an ill-compacted earth-work.

Of later developments of northern tactics—how the invaders learnt to stockade themselves in good positions even on the main-land, how they got horses and became as lightly moving on shore as on sea—we must deal later in the proper places. These were characteristics of the second period of invasions, which do not appear in the first. And later also must we treat of the devices of the English and the Franks for self-defence—the rearing of the *burhs* and the development of the thegnhood in England—the castle-building and the creation of the feudal cavalry on the Con-tinent. Such shifts were only taught by bitter experience, and in 834 that experience was only beginning.

CHAPTER XXI

FROM ECGBERT TO ALFRED

834-871

ECGBERT had been for five years overlord of all England when the immunity from Viking raids, which his realm had so long enjoyed, came to an end. In 834 "the Heathen men ravaged Sheppey": the laconic statement of the Anglo-Saxon Chronicle gives us no details, but apparently this was a hasty and transient descent, followed by a swift departure. Undoubtedly it was the work of some detachment, small or great, of a powerful Viking fleet which in that same summer burnt Dorstadt, the great trading port at the mouth of the Rhine, and spoiled the lands around it. Perhaps it was before turning homeward in the autumn that the invaders made an experimental raid into the estuary of the Thames.

In 836-37 the Danes returned in force to the regions of the Rhine mouth and the Lower Scheldt, and sacked Antwerp and other towns. This was the main scene of their activity, but (as in 834) a section of the fleet found leisure for a dash at England. This time it was at Charmouth, in Dorsetshire, that the crews of thirty-five ships came to land, and started plunder. The king came out in person against them, probably at the head of his personal following and the shire-levy of Dorset alone. Though "there was a great slaughter made," yet "the Danes maintained possession of the battle-spot ".[1] Considering their very moderate force, this boded evil for Wessex: if thirty-five ships' crews could hold their own against the king even for a day, what was to be expected when fleets

[1] There is no reason to suppose that the two bishops and two ealdormen whose deaths are mentioned directly after this battle in the A. S. Chronicle fell in it, as say some of the later historians, Henry of Huntingdon and Roger of Wendover.

of several hundred galleys should appear ?   And already the Danish squadrons which had been ravaging Frisia and Flanders had reached that strength.

Yet there was an interval of two years before the next raid, and when it came it was of a new kind.   In 838 " a great hostile fleet came to the land of the West Welsh (the lately subdued Cornish-men) and made alliance with them, and together they waged war upon Ecgbert King of the West Saxons ".[1]   A league between the Vikings and any Christian people was a new thing, save in Ireland where already such unholy combinations had been seen.   Wherefore some historians have supposed, on grounds slight enough, that this fleet may have been composed of Irish Vikings—though the hypothesis seems not specially probable, since the Northmen were very busy this year beyond St. George's Channel, and actually took Dublin for the first time—it was then the obscure village of Ath-Cliath, but was soon to be a great Danish city under its later name.

Whatever was the origin of the fleet that came to Cornwall and leagued itself with the West Welsh, it had bad luck.   As soon as he heard of the league, Ecgbert marched westward with all the levies of Wessex, and smote the allies with a great slaughter at Hengestesdune—Hingston Down, near Plymouth.   The Danes fled to their ships, the Cornishmen renewed their oaths of allegiance, which they never seem to have broken again.   Perhaps they had found their allies uncomfortable comrades.

This was the last exploit of Ecgbert, who was now an old man—if he had reigned as a sub-king in Kent about 790, he must now have been nearly seventy years of age.   In the next summer he died, after he had ruled Wessex for thirty-seven years and seven months, and had presided over all England as " Bretwalda " for ten years.   Clearly he was a man of mark, but we know so little about him—far less than we know about Offa or Oswy—that it is dangerous to endeavour to make of him a definite historical figure.   To speculate whether he was one of those who bend their surroundings to their purpose, or merely one who used adroitly the opportunities which fate offered him, would be futile.   At any rate he was the father of a long line of able descendants, who may well have owed their vigour and their enduring courage to the blood that they drew from him.

[1] The A. S. Chronicle is here three years out, putting these events in 835.

Ecgbert's death was followed by a rearrangement of his king-doms. His eldest son Aethelwulf, who had been reigning hitherto as sub-king in Kent, moved on to rule over Wessex, as suzerain over the whole of the realms which had obeyed his father. But Kent, and with it Essex, Sussex and Surrey, was handed on to Ecgbert's younger son Aethelstan, who had hitherto been sub-king in East Anglia. The evidence of coins seems to make it probable that Aethelstan gave up his former holding to an Aethelweard, whom no chronicle mentions.[1] But since he owned a name common in the royal house of Wessex—it was borne afterwards by three princes,[2] one of whom was the well-known chronicler—we may guess that he was the son or other close kinsman of Aethelstan, and that the hegemony of Aethelwulf was duly recognised in East Anglia. In Mercia Beorhtwulf[3] had just succeeded Wiglaf, while in Northum-bria the long-lived but obscure Eanred had still one year to live.

We know much more of Aethelwulf than of his father, but apparently he was far less worth knowing. He was a man who would never have won the suzerainty over England for himself, but he was just strong enough to maintain it, when it had been left him by his strong-handed parent. Though not destitute of fighting power, and full of a laudable sense of his duty to his kingdom, he had the faults of a conscientious man. He was pious even to excess, he was an over-indulgent father, and he lacked apparently that capacity for righteous resentment which forms a necessary part of the mental equipment of a great king, if not of a good Christian. His character, no less than his career, bears a singular resemblance to that of the unlucky Emperor Lewis, his elder contemporary across the Channel. Like him Aethelwulf was a worthy man who fell upon evil days, and owed part of his troubles to his own deficiencies. Both suffered not only from the plague of the Viking invasions, but from unruly sons and disloyal subjects, whom a stronger hand might have tamed by the use of proper severity in the first instance. It is a curious coincidence that the later misfortunes of each were due in

---

[1] See Sir Henry Howorth's article in the *Numismatic Chronicle* for 1908.

[2] One was the youngest son of King Alfred, the second, the chronicler, was great-grandson of Alfred's elder brother Aethelred, ealdorman of West Wessex about 977-97. The third was the chronicler's grandson, and lived in the time of Cnut.

[3] He is said, but on bad authority, to have been Wiglaf's brother. Nothing is certain concerning his birth.

a large measure to an unwise second marriage, made in late middle age. Not less similar was their exaggerated meekness and long-suffering, due to a deep religious sense of their own unworthiness, which placed them at a grave disadvantage when they were dealing with kinsmen, or still more with churchmen, who were troubled with no such scruples. For Aethelwulf, like Lewis, felt himself helpless before a prelate who attacked him on his weak side, and he was cursed with such a one in Ealhstan, the fighting bishop of Sherborne. This able but turbulent priest, if he was the first of his rank in England to lead an army against the Danes, was also the first to lead a rebellion against his lawful sovereign. Fortunately for Aethelwulf the type was yet rare on this side of the Channel : a better-remembered bishop of the virtuous type was Swithun of Winchester, who is said to have been Aethelwulf's instructor in his youth and his minister in middle age.[1] We have sadly inadequate information about this saint, who must have been a man of mark if we may judge from the popularity which his name enjoyed for many a century after. But his biographies are of late date, and consist of little more than a string of miracles.

The accession of Aethelwulf was almost coincident with a sudden redoubling of the vigour of the Danish attacks on England. Very probably the invaders had realised that with the death of Ecgbert a strong barrier to their assaults had been removed. It does not seem that they were at this juncture thrown back on England by any rally on the part of the Franks. For Aethelwulf's early years are coincident with the civil wars of the sons of Lewis the Pious, and during those commotions the Danes were working their wicked will almost unopposed along the northern shore of Frankland.

Nevertheless in the first year after Aethelwulf's succession (840), we find not an isolated raid reported, but a deliberate coasting of the Danes along Wessex. First they are heard of as landing near Southampton, and there defeating Wulfheard ealdorman of Hampshire. Then a second descent follows on the Isle of Portland : Aethelhelm the ealdorman of Dorset came down to meet the invaders, "and for a good time he put the enemy to flight : but finally the Danes had possession of the field and slew the ealdor-

[1] Our only details are from Florence of Worcester i. 58. One could have wished for earlier authority.

man ". There can be small doubt that the two victories were won
by the same squadron, which probably made great havoc, and
returned well laden with plunder, though we are not told of any
great town or minster being destroyed. In the next year (841)
matters grew much more serious for England, though it was not
Wessex this time which bore the brunt of the invasion. A fleet,
no doubt after coasting down the Frisian shore, appeared in the
Wash. The crews came ashore in the Lincolnshire marshland,
started ravaging, and were attacked by Herebert, ealdorman of
Lindsey. But they slew him and many more, and then harried
all his land. After this the squadron turned south, and plundered in succession the shores of East Anglia and of Kent. To
show the widespread activity of the Vikings in this year—the year
when the Franks were tearing each other to pieces at the battle of
Fontenay—it must be added that a fleet under one Oscar sacked
Rouen and devastated all the lands about the Seine-mouth, much
about the same time that Mercia was being attacked.

In 842 we have the doings of the Danes on both sides of the
sea combined : a great fleet attacked in succession London—still a
Mercian town— ; Quentovic,[1] the great port of Picardy, and then Rochester. The second place ransomed itself, perhaps the two English
cities may have done the same, for though there was "slaughter"
at both, yet both were surviving and worth sacking a few years
later. The following summer saw the Danes once more on the
Wessex coast ; they landed for a second time at Charmouth in
Dorsetshire and once more beat a king on its beach, for Aethelwulf,
like his father in 836, came down hastily upon them, and was
repulsed ; as on the first occasion, "the Danish men maintained
possession of the battle-spot ".[2] Yet the struggle may have been
bitter enough to deter the victors from a return to Wessex for
some years. There is a blank in the Chronicle for four years after this
fight. But we find from the Frankish annals that for the first time
in the following winter the Danes had the hardihood not to go home
to their own land but to keep their Yule in Christendom. Noir-

---

[1] Not Canterbury (Cantwarabyrig) as some manuscripts of the A. S. Chronicle
write, but certainly Cwantawic in Picardy, as the attack on that place is specially
mentioned by the Frankish chronicler Prudentius of Troyes.

[2] Some historians have supposed that the two battles of Charmouth are the
result of an erroneous duplicate entry in the Chronicle. See note to Plummer's
edition, ii. p. 76. The date of Aethelwulf's fight is three years wrong.

moutier at the Loire-mouth was the place which they chose as
their quarters. Truly this was a disquieting symptom for their
enemies: hitherto winter, at least, had brought a cessation from
their ravages. In the next year (844) their main fleet made an
astounding exploration of the coast of the Spanish peninsula, as far
as Lisbon and Cadiz; but they took small profit thereby, for
Ramiro King of Asturias routed them, and took seventy ships, and
others were destroyed by the Moors, after their crews had made an
attack on Seville. Yet there were Vikings enough abroad that
summer to molest not only Spain, but Ireland and Northumbria.
England's share in the annals of 844 is a note that Redwulf King
of Northumbria was slain therein by the Danes. He was a prince
of the most ephemeral sort: he had just succeeded in expelling
Aethelred II., son of the long-lived Eanred, when the heathen
came down and destroyed him, after he had reigned only a few
months.[1] His rival returned to York to take up his crown once
more, for a second reign of four years (844-48).

For two years after Redwulf's death we have no mention whatever of Viking raids in England—a fact to be accounted for by
redoubled notices of their activity abroad. In 845 they attacked
Hamburg with a force of 600 ships, a royal fleet sent out by
Horik King of Denmark, not a mere gathering of the bands of adventurers. The thriving port at the Elbe-mouth was completely
destroyed—though it soon rose again from its ashes. Meanwhile a
second squadron, which represented the lesser leaders as opposed
to the king, pushed up the Seine, past the ruins of Rouen, and
affronted the walls of Paris; they forced their way inside its gates,
but were expelled before they had quite ruined the city—by a
miracle of St. Germanus, as the Franks said—by a supernatural
fog followed by a panic according to their own legend. This was
the farthest point inland which any Viking raid had yet reached—
but worse was to follow. The Paris expedition was led by a prince
named Ragnar, apparently the Ragnar Lodbrog who appears as a
semi-mythical personage in some of the Northern Sagas. There
seems, however, to have been a real chief of the name, the ancestor

---

[1] Of all the obscure Northumbrian kings, Redwulf is the obscurest. We have
a few rare coins belonging to him, but otherwise he is only vouched for by
" Matthew of Westminster ". The Chronicle, Simeon of Durham, and Florence of
Worcester have all got a bad gap in their Northern history from 827 to 867.

of a numerous progeny of sea-kings, with whom we shall have to deal during the next three generations, for they were busy in England for many a year. His three sons Ingwar (Inhwaer Ivar), Hubba and Halfdene, were all destined to make themselves "kings" in England, though their kingship meant the command of a host rather than the possession of a definite territory. The name of Ragnar is connected with a legend, assuming several variant shapes, which purports to account for the invasion of England by his sons.[1] The best known of them is that which represents the hero as having been shipwrecked on the coast of Northumbria, and thrown into a pit full of serpents by the usurper Aella (*circ.* 862-67). Another makes him murdered by a jealous courtier of Edmund of East Anglia. All are worthless, and belong to the tribe of "aetiological myths," which purport to account for observed effects by constructing imaginary causes. No such high purpose as revenge for a murdered father was required to set a ninth-century Dane upon a course of raiding and massacre.

But the coming of the sons of Ragnar to England was still twenty years away in the early days of Acthelwulf, and the chiefs with whom the King of Wessex had to deal at the commencement of his reign are for the most part anonymous. The unhappy time when the English were to know each of their main enemies by headmark and name had not yet arrived. We do not know, therefore, who were the leaders who in 846 essayed a landing in Somersetshire, and were there badly beaten at the mouth of the Parret by the warlike bishop Eahlstan of Sherborne and the ealdormen Eanwulf and Osric.[2] The locality of the fight suggests that the invaders may possibly have been Irish Vikings from Dublin or Wexford. After this battle, and perhaps in consequence of it, we have another gap in the Viking raids on England : no disembarkations are recorded between 846 and 850. On the Continent meanwhile the Danes were very active, especially in Aquitaine. Bordeaux was beset in 847 and taken in 848 ; while the Irish annals are full of fighting, and record three separate battles, in which the invaders were defeated by the native kings—an unusual phenomenon in Erin during the unhappy ninth century.

But in 851 England was for the first time assailed by the main

---

[1] For notes on Ragnar, see Keary's *Viking Age*, pp. 255-58.
[2] Osric was ealdorman of Dorset, Eanwulf of Somersetshire.

army of the Vikings, and no longer molested by mere raiding
squadrons. It seems that the fleet which had been operating of
late on the Garonne combined with another force, which had been
ravaging in Flanders and Northern France, and that their leaders
resolved to make something more than a mere raid upon England.
The sequence of the fighting which followed is most difficult to
follow, but if the Chronicle is to be trusted the campaign was somewhat as follows. The first appearance of the enemy was off the
coast of Devonshire ; it is probable that this was a mere detachment, or even a demonstrating force deliberately sent to draw off
the attention of King Aethelwulf from the main point of attack.
At any rate the landing force was decisively defeated by Ceorl
ealdorman of Devonshire at "Wicganbeorg," apparently Wig-
borough near South Petherton.[1] This place is so far inland that
we cannot tell whether the raiders had landed at the estuary of
the Axe or that of the Parret. Next we get a notice of a descent
at the other end of the south coast. A squadron ran into Sandwich and there was attacked by Aethelstan, sub-king of Kent [2]
and Alchere, his ealdorman. They "fought on ship-board"—
though this surely cannot mean that they had prepared a naval
force to resist the invaders,—and captured nine Danish vessels,
putting the rest to flight. But all this was preliminary skirmishing. Later in the same summer the main fleet of the Vikings,
with a strength of 350 ships ran into the Thames-mouth, apparently
under the command of one Roric. It touched on the southern shore,
and put ashore a great landing force, which marched on Canterbury. The metropolitan city was taken—assuredly not without
heavy fighting—sacked and burnt. The Danes then coasted up the
estuary to London. King Beorhtwulf of Mercia came down to defend
his chief port with all the levies of the Midlands. But he was
defeated, and London was stormed and plundered. We are not
told that King Aethelwulf had made any effort to succour his
vassal : was he distracted at the moment by some other threatened

---

[1] Not Wembury nor Weekaborough near Torbay, neither of these places
having names that can legitimately be derived from Wicganburg. See Stevenson's
Asser, pp. 175-76.

[2] Is this Aethelwulf's *brother*, once king of East Anglia (see above, p. 419) or
his *son* of the same name, who also seems to have been sub-king in Kent, presumably in succession to his uncle ? The second Aethelstan's date seems to lie about
850, and he probably died before his father *circ.* 851-53.

attack on his own realm? But a very short time after, when the Danes, spreading out from London, had begun to ravage Surrey, we find Aethelwulf and his son Aethelbald in arms against them with the full levy of Wessex. They encountered the raiders at Aclea[1] (apparently Oakley near Basingstoke) with satisfactory results, for "they inflicted the greatest slaughter upon the heathen host that ever we have heard tell of up to the present day, and got the victory". The fame of the success is recorded in Continental as well as in English chronicles; and it seems that the Viking landing force was absolutely destroyed.

This being so, it is almost inconceivable that a confused note occurring in the Chronicle and inserted in the middle of the campaign, can be correct, when it says that "the heathen men for the first time remained over winter, in Thanet".[2] If we had found it placed before the account of the battle of Aclea we might have accepted it—not without surprise. But written where it stands, it makes nonsense, and we can only suppose it to be a false duplication of the later entry under the year 855 which again states that "in this year the heathen men *for the first time* remained over winter, in Sheppey". Asser, it may be mentioned, puts the supposed wintering of 851 in Sheppey also, not in Thanet: while one of the best MSS. of the Chronicle omits the wintering-place altogether. It seems best to neglect the whole story: is it likely that the ships' crews would have stayed in Thanet after the landing army had been exterminated?[3]

The wholesome effect of the battle of Aclea seems to be marked by the absence of any record of Danish invasions in England during the year 852; while Aethelwulf's improved prestige and

---

[1] Usually this Aclea is identified with Ockley, in Surrey, near Horsham. But this place, in the Weald, though on the old Roman Stone Street, seems, for strategical reasons, less likely than Church Oakley, Hants, near the great road from London and Silchester to Winchester, in a good position for an army covering Wessex from an attack from the North-east. Moreover this village is named Aclei in Doomsday book, while the Surrey Ockley is called Hoclie. See a paper "The Site of the Battle of Aclea," by Mr. C. Cooksey in *Proceedings of the Hampshire Field Club*, 1904. Ockley, as he observes, is a most unaccountable place in which to find the Danish main army, Oakley an easy one. See also Stevenson's *Asser*, p. 178. A ring bearing King Aethelwulf's name was dug up in 1781 at Laverstoke, five miles from Oakley.

[2] We have now got over the chronological errors of the A.S.C., 851 is correct.

[3] For all this see Plummer's notes to the Chronicle, ii. 77, *sub anno* 851.

power to assert his supremacy over the neighbouring kingdoms is vouched for in 853 by an entry of an unexpected sort. "This year Burhred, King of the Mercians (Beorhtwulf had died in 852), begged of King Aethelwulf that he would assist him to make the North-Welsh obedient to him. He then did so, and went with an army across Mercia among the North-Welsh, and made them all obedient to him." The homage of Burhred was rewarded by his receiving the hand of Aethelswith, the daughter of Aethelwulf, who was wedded to him after Easter, at Chippenham. How Burhred, the last of the old series of Mercian kings, came to ascend the throne we do not know: he does not seem to have been the natural heir of his predecessor Beorhtwulf. For the latter had two sons old enough to sign charters, and one of them Beorhtferth is said to have slain Saint Wistan, the grandson of King Wiglaf.[1] What domestic convulsions, and disputes about the succession, may be hidden under this string of names it is impossible to say. We only know that both Wiglaf and Beorhtwulf left male issue, but that in each case the natural heir was excluded in favour of another candidate for the crown. Whether the succession was settled by the influence of the King of Wessex, by domestic strife, or by some peaceable decision of the Mercian Witan, cannot be ascertained.

In the same year that Aethelwulf's successful campaign in North Wales took place, we read that he sent his youngest son Alfred, then aged only four years (he had been born in 849), on a visit to Pope Leo IV. at Rome. The pontiff took him as his adoptive son, honoured him with the name and insignia of a Roman consul, and performed over him some ceremony which the writer of the Anglo-Saxon Chronicle, and Asser copying him, regarded as a royal coronation. The whole of the story is very strange: that so young a child should be sent on a long and dangerous journey apart from his parents is surprising in the first instance. Aethelwulf, however, sent many embassies to Rome, and we may suppose that he took advantage of one to introduce his youngest and best-loved son [2] to the Pope. A letter

---

[1] But this occurs only in Florence of Worcester. Saint Wistan, however, seems to be a real person: he was a popular saint in Mercia, his day being June 1st.

[2] Asser, at any rate, says that Aethelwulf " illum plus caeteris filiis diligebat," § 11.

of Leo chances to be preserved, in which he states that what he
had done was to take Alfred as his " spiritalis filius " and to
invest him with the belt and robes of a consul.[1] There was evidently no real question of a coronation—Alfred was the fifth son
only of his father and the lady Osburh, so that there could be no
prospect of his succeeding his father, even in a sub-kingdom.
Though English rulers had sometimes caused their elder sons to
be crowned as their colleagues during their own lifetime, and
Ecgbert had apparently got his second son chosen king in East
Anglia, such an idea would be wholly inappropriate when a child
of four years was in question. Probably, long years after, when
Alfred's brothers were dead and the crown of Wessex had actually
fallen to him, the dimly remembered ceremony at Rome was taken
as an anticipation or foreshadowing of his promotion to the kingly
status.

It was in the same summer that saw the child Alfred's first
visit to Rome that the Viking raids on England began again.
The enemy landed in Thanet, whereupon Ealchere and Huda, the
caldormen of Kent and Surrey—the sub-king Aethelstan was now
dead—made an attempt to force their way into the island, presumably by fording the Wensum at low tide, but possibly by boat.
They failed; "for some time they had the better, and many there
were slain and drowned on both sides, but both the ealdormen were
killed". The usual statement that "the heathen men maintained
possession of the battle-place " is not made, but we can hardly
doubt that this was so. Yet since no more ravages of the enemy
are recorded either in this year or the next, it is probable that the
invaders had been given their fill of fighting, and went off to easier
plunder on the Continent.

Yet they were back again on the Kentish soil eighteen months
later, when there occurred, in the winter of 854-55, that most
ominous symptom, a wintering of the host in England. The Yule
feast of the invaders was held in Sheppey, not in Thanet, where
they had last been heard of. There is no mention of any attempt
being made by the Kentish men to drive them forth, by passing
the narrow channel which divided the isle from the mainland.
Nor do we hear of any help being brought by their lord, Aethel-

[1] Epistolae Aevi Karolini (Pertz), iii. p. 602.

wulf, though, owing to the death of Aethelstan, he was now directly ruling Kent, and not administering it through a *subregulus*. Instead, we find two acts of the king recorded in 855 ; the first was his famous donation to the Church. " The same year Aethelwulf gave by charter the tenth part of his land throughout his realm for the glory of God, and his own eternal salvation,"[1] or, as Asser puts it, "he freed a tenth part of his realm from all royal service anc tribute, in everlasting alms to the cross of Christ, and offered it to the Triune God for the redemption of his own soul and those of his ancestors ". Whole libraries of books have been written in explanation and comment upon these words. All manner of designs have been ascribed to the king, from the institution of tithe and the creation of glebe lands for every parish (Selden's view) down to a mere "beneficial hidation" of certain lands intended for Church purposes, *i.e.*, a permission to reckon them for matters of taxation at less than their real extent in hides (a suggestion of Professor Maitland's[2]). It seems clear, however, that what Aethelwulf did affected only one-tenth of his own private royal estates—the tithe on the whole realm was not his to bestow. Apparently he "booked" one-tenth of his private lands for pious uses, by making them over to certain of his subjects, lay or clerical, with the understanding that they were to be applied to religious purposes. Two charters, apparently relating to this great gift, have been preserved. By one Aethelwulf grants certain lands to a thegn named Ealdhere, "pro decimatione agrorum, quam Deo donante caeteris ministris meis facere decrevi," with power to transfer them ; it is endorsed with a statement that the grantee has made them over to a monastery.[3] By the other the king grants, in 855, land to another thegn named Dunn, "pro expiatione piaculorum meorum et absolutione criminum meorum," with similar power to transfer, and the addition that the land is given free, "ab omni servitute regali, intus et foris, magnis et modicis, notis et ignotis".[4] From the statement that this is an expiatory gift, we must conclude that the thegn, as in the other case, was to transfer it to religious uses.[5]

---

[1] A. S. Chronicle, *sub anno* 855, and Asser, § 11. For the curious phrase *in sempiterno graphio*, see Stevenson's *Asser*, p. 191.

[2] *Domesday and Beyond*, p. 496.   [3] Birch, *Cartularium Saxonicum*, ii. 8-6.

[4] *Ibid.*, ii. 61.

[5] For all this see the invaluable note in Stevenson's *Asser*, pp. 187-90.

To diminish the royal revenue by giving away at one sweep a tenth of the royal estates seems sufficiently lacking in worldly wisdom, at a moment when the Viking invasions were in full vigour, and the "wintering" in England had just begun. But the other recorded act of Aethelwulf in 855 was at least equally unwise : we learn, to our surprise, that he chose this year for a long pilgrimage to Rome, which had been already in his mind for some time. He took with him his youngest son Alfred, who thus performed the long journey to Italy twice in three years ; it might have been guessed that Aethelwulf took the boy back to exhibit him to his spiritual father Leo, but for the fact that the old Pope was now dead, and Benedict III. was reigning in his stead. The travellers were received with much kindness by Charles the Bald, the King of the West Franks, who gave them honourable escort all through his dominions—a thing by no means unnecessary when the Vikings were abroad : the valleys of the Seine and Loire were both being devastated this year by a fleet under one Sihtric. At Rome Aethelwulf made magnificent offerings, bestowing, as is duly recorded in the *Liber Pontificalis*, to the church of St. Peter, a crown weighing four pounds of pure gold, two gold vases, a gold-mounted sword, two golden images, a silver-gilt candelabrum, and much more. He also made a great donation in gold to the priests and nobles of Rome, and in silver to the common folk. After a lengthy stay in Rome he began his journey home, but tarried long enough at the court of Charles the Bald to pick up there a second wife, and she a child of only thirteen. Aethelwulf had but recently lost his wife Osburh,[1] and was the father of a large family, nearly all of whom were older than his little bride ; his conduct, considering that he passed for a wise as well as a pious prince, is indefensible. Presumably there was some design of cementing a close

---

[1] That Osburh had been alive till very recently is indicated by the story told by Asser, about her offering an illuminated book of poems to whichever of her sons should first be able to learn it by heart: Alfred, though the youngest, was the winner. But he can hardly have been less than six at the time, and since he was born in 849, the story must belong to the year 855, the same on which Alfred was taken on his second journey to Rome. If, therefore, Osburh was alive just before her husband started, she must have died in his absence, and he must have been a widower of less than a year's standing when he married Judith. That Osburh was the heroine of the book-story, and not Alfred's step-mother Judith, is quite clear. Nor is there the least foundation for the hypothesis that Aethelwulf divorced her (see Stevenson, *Asser*, pp. 221-22).

political alliance with the Franks at the bottom of the marriage, rather than the senile admiration of an old man for a pretty child. For the king cannot have been much over fifty in 856, and may even have been a year under that age.

Aethelwulf's second wedding was celebrated at Verberie on October 1st, 856, and he was apparently back in England by the end of the year, after an absence of at least eighteen months. His home-coming was not happy, though we are told by the Anglo-Saxon Chronicle that his subjects rejoiced to set eyes on him again ; too many English kings had gone to Rome, like Ceadwalla and Ine, only to leave their bones there. But the time of Aethel-wulf's tarrying abroad had been most unhappily chosen. While he was away the Danes had been more troublesome than ever ; a strong hand had been especially necessary for their curbing, and had not been forthcoming, owing to the absence of the master of England. The Vikings, as we have already seen, were now fitted with a permanent base in Sheppey, but we are surprised to find them also operating for the first time in the very heart of England during the year of Aethelwulf's absence. A charter of Burhred issued in 855 dates itself by the statement that when it was written " the heathen men were in the land of the Wrokensaetas," [1] *i.e.* the Mercians around the Wrekin, in the modern Shropshire. Clearly, therefore, raids had begun to cut much deeper into England than before, since the Wrekin is as remote from the sea as any other part of England that can be designated. Presumably this region must have been reached either by ascending the Severn valley from the Bristol Channel, or by cutting across from the estuary of the Dee. In either case the penetration was something much more dangerous than anything that had been seen before. That the Anglo-Saxon Chronicle does not mention it can only be due to its excessive specialisation on the affairs of Wessex : but there is nothing startling in the fact, when we remember that during the last ten years the Vikings had often won their way much deeper into the interior of the lands of the Franks. It is, of course, prob-able that this raid up or down the Severn was only one of several unrecorded incursions of the year 855.

Aethelwulf's long absence at this critical time almost lost him

---

[1] See Rev. C. S. Taylor's " The Danes in Gloucestershire," in *Transactions of the Gloucestershire Archaeological Society*, vol. xvii. pp. 10, 11.

his throne. His eldest surviving son Aethelbald, who had probably
been acting as regent, conspired with Eanwulf, ealdorman of Somersetshire, and Ealhstan, the warlike bishop of Sherborne, in order to
prevent his father from resuming the crown on his return. Some
said, writes Asser, that the ealdorman and bishop over-persuaded
the prince, others that Aethelbald himself was an evil-disposed
youth and needed no persuading. At any rate, he and his party
made an attempt to drive out Aethelwulf when he appeared : but
the old king had plenty of supporters, and might probably have
crushed his son had he chosen. He chose, however, "such was his
ineffable clemency," to come to terms with him, and those terms of
unnecessary mildness. To avoid the chance of civil war while the
Danes were in the land, Aethelwulf offered to make over Wessex to
his rebellious son, and to reign himself in Kent, Sussex and Essex
alone, though he of course retained his nominal suzerainty over all
his dominions.

He survived this unhappy home-coming for two years, and died
late in 858. We know nothing of the end of his reign save the trivial
fact that, contrary to the custom of Wessex, he gave his young wife
Judith the full honours of a queen, and made her sit beside him
crowned on state occasions.[1] His will, preserved in Asser, was of
the sort that might have been expected from such a thriftless and
pious prince. He charged his private estates with an obligation to
clothe and feed one poor man for every ten hides for ever : this
was justifiable enough—though it is difficult to see how he could
bind his descendants, since he was but a life tenant of the lands.
But he also imposed a heavy tribute on them—300 gold mancuses a year to be sent to Rome, of which one-third was to maintain the lights in St. Peter's, one-third those in St. Paul's (the
great basilica outside the walls), and the other third to be a personal
gift to the pope. The royal estates were parted between his four
surviving sons and his daughter, the Queen of Mercia, subject to
these liabilities.

Aethelwulf left the states in which he was actually reigning at
the day of his death—Kent, Essex and Sussex—to his second son,

[1] See Asser, § 13, and, in dependence thereon, to explain the custom of refusing
the royal title to the king's wife in Wessex, the story of Beorhtric and the wicked
Queen Eadburh. Judith had been crowned at her wedding by her father's orders,
perhaps because he knew of this custom.

Aethelbert, but Aethelbald, the undutiful elder son, obtained a general suzerainty over all by his father's death. It is impossible to ascertain whether he held himself to have succeeded also to the Bretwaldaship, the superiority over all South Britain, which Ecgbert had won and which Aethelwulf seems in some measure to have preserved—as witness his dealings with the Mercians and the Welsh in 853. There is a certain indication that this claim was vanishing, in the fact that in East Anglia we find, a few years before, a king succeeding to Aethelweard who does not seem to be (like that prince and his predecessor Aethelstan) a descendant of Ecgbert of Wessex. This is Beorhtric, who must have reigned but a very short time— his existence is only established by a few coins of extreme rarity. The name is a Mercian one, and he may possibly be identical with the Beorhtric, son of King Beorhtwulf,[1] who was excluded from the throne by Burhred in 852, at his father's death. This short-lived king had a successor of enigmatic origin, Edmund, who was crowned on Christmas Day, 856, being then only fifteen years of age.[2]   Evidently, then, it was not his own sword that won him the crown, and presumably he represented some line which had a claim on the East Anglian throne. He was afterwards to be the best known of English martyr-saints, and several lives of him exist, but the only one which is of any value, that written by Abbo and dedicated to St. Dunstan about 980, merely tells us that he was " ex antiquorum Saxonum nobili prosapia " and "atavis regibus editus ". As he is said to have been raised to the throne by the unanimous choice of his " comprovinciales," it is clear that he was of East Anglian birth, and that the " prosapia antiquorum Saxonum " does not mean the line of the Old Saxons of the Continent, as some authors, mediaeval and modern, have translated it. If the traditional name of his father, Eahlmund, could be taken for certain, we should suspect him to have been of some branch of the Wessex line, probably a grandson of Aethelstan and a great grandson of Ecgbert, for Eahlmund is a name belonging to that house, and had been borne by Ecgbert's father, the " subregulus " in Kent. Thus Abbo might have meant merely that Edmund was of the old West Saxon line, which had got settled in East Anglia in 829, while his predecessor Beorhtric was

---

[1] Only known otherwise by his signing some of Beorhtwulf's charters as " filius regis ".   He was the brother of the Beorhtferth who murdered St. Wistan.
[2] *Annals of St. Neots, sub anno 856.*

not. In this case his election would probably represent a reaction in favour of the Wessex connection among the East Angles, and may have been made with the approval of Aethelwulf. But such a reading of the scanty facts forthcoming is only hypothetical.

Be this as it may, Aethelwulf's pre-eminence, whatever it was, passed in 858 to his son Aethelbald, who had now been ruling Wessex for over two years. This prince, already discredited by his unfilial conduct in 856, completed his spiritual ruin in the eyes of his contemporaries by making an incestuous marriage with his father's young widow, Queen Judith, who was even now only fifteen years of age. We know no other fact about his short reign, which only lasted for two years and a half, since he died somewhere in the latter part of 860, and was buried at Sherborne. No Danish inroads are recorded in his day: this does not prove that none took place, but there is such an ample list of such ravagings in the Frankish realms and in Ireland during 859-60 that it is easy to account for England being spared for the moment. It is to this time also that belongs the second of the great Viking raids down the coast of Spain — it was pushed far along the coast of the Mohammedan realms, and only ended at the mouth of the Rhone.

On Aethelbald's death his kingdom fell to his brother, Aethelbert, hitherto sub-king of Kent and Essex, while his widow Judith returned to France, where her father placed her in a nunnery. She eloped therefrom, a few years later, with Baldwin, afterwards Count of Flanders, whom she subsequently married. Their descendants in the eighth generation were to sit one day on the English throne, through the marriage of William the Conqueror with Matilda of Flanders.

Aethelbert was destined to reign not much longer than his elder brother, since he died in 866 after having worn the crown for six years only. But these six years, unlike Aethelbald's time, are marked by serious Danish invasions. The attack upon England was beginning to grow hotter, while, at least after 864, that on the Frankish lands seems to have begun to slacken for a space. Aethelbert did not continue his father's plan of allowing Kent and Essex to be worked as a sub-kingdom under Wessex: he held all three himself, and gave no endowment to his younger brothers, Aethelred and Alfred, who sign his charters as *fratres regis* merely, not as *subreguli*. Apparently the new king contrasted very favourably with his predecessor; we are told by Asser that he governed all his realms "with love and honour," and was adored by his subjects, and Asser is probably repeating the testimony of his patron Alfred.

His reign commenced with a fierce Danish inroad; in 860 a great fleet under one Weland, which had been bribed to depart from France by Charles the Bald, ran into Southampton Water. The crews came ashore in force, and marched on Winchester, the ancient capital of Wessex, which is only thirteen miles from the head of the estuary. Like other English towns it was not fortified, and the attack was so sudden that it fell into the raiders' hands. But before they had time to get off with the plunder, Osric, ealdorman of Hampshire, and Aethelwulf, ealdorman of Berkshire, came down upon them with the fyrd of their shires and inflicted on them a bloody defeat As happened all too seldom in these wars "the English had possession of the battle-spot". St. Swithun just survived to see his cathedral plundered and his see-town burnt, and died in the next summer (861).

We then find a rest for five years, during which the heathen were busy in France: it was probably some severe checks suffered by them across the Channel in 864 and 865 which threw them back once more on England. But in the latter year the greatest of all the invasions began—one which was to be followed by no retirement or evacuation of the land, but was to continue without a break till 872, and was to leave half England in Danish hands. In 865 a great force came ashore in Thanet: the men of Kent— either after some unsuccessful fighting, or perhaps without any fighting at all—tried to come to terms with them, and to bribe them to depart with a great sum of gold, "but during the truce and the promising of the money, the army stole away by night, and ravaged all Kent to the eastward". They then wintered in Thanet, and apparently were still there when King Aethelbert died in the next spring—taken away from the wrath to come, which his brothers had to face (866).

The fourth of Aethelwulf's short-lived sons now succeeded to all the lands that his brother had held. This prince, Aethelred by name, seems to have been well worthy of his position; he was pious like his father, but a hard fighter like his grandfather. To aid him he had his brother Alfred, now a lad of seventeen, who was to make his first campaign two years later. Aethelred never gave him a sub-kingdom, but made him his "secundarius" or junior colleague, after he had won his spurs.   But it was not Wessex that was to bear the first brunt of the invasion: in 866 an enormous swarm of allied Viking bands came over to England: it was the main body of the heathen "Great Army," under many chiefs, of whom Ingwar and Hubba the sons of Ragnar Lodbrog were the best-known names.   They did not use the base already in the hands of their comrades in Thanet, but descended on East Anglia, where, after plundering far and wide, they permitted King Edmund to buy peace from them: but it must have been an uncomfortable arrangement for him at the best, since the Army lay about in his realm all the winter, "and there they were a-horsed"; that is they provided themselves with horses by sweeping the countryside, both in order to give themselves the power of swift movement, and also in order to be able to carry plunder the better.   This was quite as ominous a stage in their proceedings as the wintering on English soil which had happened in 855, eleven years before.   It marks the moment when they were beginning to cut themselves loose from their ships and their base-camps by the shore, and to think of long raids by land as equally safe and sure.

The next year brought the most dreadful disaster for the English which had yet been recorded—not the mere slaying of a king in battle, nor the mere sack of a great capital city, nor the mere ravaging of a wide region—all this had been seen before—but all these disasters culminating in the dashing to pieces of one of the greater English kingdoms, which was never to recover from the shock.   The doomed realm was Northumbria, once the suzerain state of all England, but long a byword for its insane and never-ending civil strife.   It was surprised in the midst of its usual tumults by the Viking invasion.   After the death of that exceptional prince Eanred, who contrived by some strange luck to hold the crown for thirty-two years (808-40) and then to die in his bed, the old wars of succession had recommenced.   Eanred's son, Aethelred II. had been chased from his throne after four years of reign by the obscure Redwulf (844).   When that prince had fallen, only a few months later, while repelling a Danish raid. Aethelred came back for a few years, but was defeated and slain in 848 by a new pretender, one Osbeorht.   Osbeorht, in his turn, after thirteen years of reign, had to face a rebellion under one

Aella, who was "a tyrant, and not of the blood royal," according to Asser, and "ungecyndne cyning"—a king both unkind and of unkingly race according to the Anglo-Saxon Chronicle. Civil war lasting for five years had followed, Osbeorht having apparently maintained a hold on part of Bernicia, while Aella held York and the larger share of the realm. They were still fighting when the Danes appeared, passing northward, as it seems, by the great Roman road that brought them to Barton Ferry on the Humber, which they crossed unresisted.

Later English tradition constructed a romantic story about the introduction of the invaders into Northumbria—they were said to have been called in by an ealdorman named Beorn "Butsecarl" (the ship man) whose wife had been violated by the king, and who sought revenge by bringing down the strangers upon his oppressor. Oddly enough one version of the tale makes Osbeorht the ravisher, the other Aella:[1] both forms may be rejected as mere decorative myths, of the same sort as those of the Rape of Lucrece by Sextus Tarquinius, or that of Florinda by Roderic the Visigoth. Folk-tales always seek to explain great national disasters by the vengeance of heaven, or of man, on some private sin of the sovereign or his kin.

It is certain enough, however, that the Danes intervened in the war, and made themselves masters of York, even as they had taken Canterbury, London and Winchester a few years before. Yet York was fortified, which the other cities had not been, though Asser tells us that its walls were neither strong nor well built.[2] The disaster was sufficient to force the rival kings of Northumbria to patch up a peace, and to agree to attack the invaders with their united forces. With small delay they marched upon York, and beset it on March 21st, 867. The Danes shut themselves up within the city, but the Northumbrians broke in, and engaged in a bitter street fight. It went badly for them; after a long contest both of the kings were slain, and their army was well-nigh cut to pieces. Only a remnant escaped. This was practically the end of

---

[1] The tale as told by Geoffrey Gaimar makes Osbeorht the criminal: the version in a MS. belonging to C.C.C., Cambridge, printed in *Monumenta Historica Brittanica*, pp. 795-96 gives Aella as the offender. It also calls the injured nobleman Arnulf instead of Beorn.

[2] Murum frangere instituerunt, quod et fecerunt. Non enim tunc adhuc illa civitas firmos et stabilitos muros illis temporibus habebat (Asser, § 27).

the Northumbrian kingdom: the Danes seem to have remained in permanent possession of York, though it was not till some years later that they settled down, and divided up the whole kingdom of Deira among themselves (876). In the remoter parts of the land three ephemeral pretenders, Ecgbert I. (867-73), Ricsig (873-76) and Ecgbert II. (876-78) assumed the kingly title in succession, but they were at the mercy of the Danes, to whom they did homage, and paid tribute for permission to exist. Their power did not extend south of the Tyne,[1] and was brought to an end when their masters resolved to assume the kingly power themselves. Neither of the Ecgberts nor Ricsig contribute any coins to the long Northumbrian series.

In the spring that followed the fall of York the victorious army, still under Ingwar and Hubba, marched southward up the valley of the Trent, intending to invade Mercia (868). They had reached Nottingham when they were met not only by Burhred the king of the land, but by Aethelred of Wessex and his brother Alfred. No doubt Burhred had renewed on this occasion the homage that he had once given to Aethelwulf, and the West Saxon king was acting once more in the character of Bretwalda. The results of the campaign were not satisfactory to either party: the Danes, finding themselves overmatched, shut themselves up in Nottingham. The English kings besieged it for a long time, but failed to take it: finally—when provisions were giving out, or winter was drawing near—negotiations began. The Danes undertook to leave Mercia in the next spring, and to remain quiet in Nottingham meanwhile, on condition (we can hardly doubt) that they were paid a handsome sum in compensation. So Burhred and his Witan "permitted them to winter there without contention".[2]

The bargain seems to have been kept, for early in 869 "the Army went back again to York, and sat there one year". No doubt they were occupied in harrying the poor remains of Northumbria, though it is also probable that they were beginning to strike root in Deira, which had now been their own for two years.

[1] These princes are only found in Simeon of Durham, see *M. H. B.*, pp. 680-81. The Chronicle says that those Northumbrians who survived bought peace from the Danes.
[2] Ethelweard, ii. 4.

But in 870 the restless fit seized them once more, "they rode across Mercia into East Anglia, and took up quarters for the winter at Thetford". Their passage through Mercia was accompanied by all manner of devastation; it seems to have been in this year that they burnt the monasteries of the Fen-country, Peterborough, Croyland, Bardney and Ely. Edmund of East Anglia came out against them, and gave them battle at Hoxne, but his army was exterminated and he himself slain.[1] According to the tenth century life of the king he did not fall in the fight, but was taken prisoner, and murdered in cold blood—he was tied to a tree and shot to death with arrows—because he refused to promise tribute and homage to Ingwar and to reign as his vassal (November 20th, 870). It is quite possible that the tale is true,[2] and some such incident seems to be required, to account for the fact that, within thirty years after his death, Edmund was being worshipped as a saint, even by the sons of the Danes who slew him.[3] Had he merely perished in the battle, it is hard to see why his memory should have been honoured more than that of any other of the English kings who died in harness doing their duty. His body was translated shortly after his death to the royal manor of Bedricsworth, which changed its name in his honour to Saint Edmund's Burgh, and his body (miraculously incorrupt, according to the legends) became the chief treasure of one of the greatest of English abbeys.

East Anglia was reduced under the power of the Danes, and we can hardly doubt that Essex shared its fate in this winter, since everything north of Thames and east of London seems to be in their hands for the future. In the next spring (871) the army moved on to attack Wessex, leaving Burhred of Mercia alone for a time. Evidently he was considered an enemy who might be dealt with at leisure, while Aethelred of Wessex was a foe worth fighting. If he and his host were broken, there would be no great

[1] So, giving no details, say the Chronicle, Asser and Simeon of Durham.

[2] Abbo says that its details were related to him by St. Dunstan, who had them from a very old man whom he knew in his youth, who had been the armour-bearer of St. Edmund. There is nothing to prevent their story from being true.

[3] The earliest coins struck in honour of St. Edmund date back to the time of Guthrum-Aethelstan, the Danish King of East Anglia from 878 to 890. He may easily have been present at Edmund's murder, and have been impressed by his steadfastness and Christian courage.

difficulty in making an end of all the English. It is clearly for territorial dominion, and not for new plunder, that the Danes are now
contending. The " Great Army " was led in this year, not by Ingwar and Hubba, but by other chiefs—King Halfdene, the third son
of Ragnar, another king called Baegsceg, and five " jarls," Sidroc
the old and Sidroc the young, Osbeorn, Fraena and Harald. It came
by land across East Mercia, from its winter camp at Thetford,
crossed the Thames in its middle course, and seized Reading, then
no more than a royal manor on the slip of ground between the
Thames and the Kennet. The Danes drew a ditch and palisade
across from one stream to the other, and so secured for themselves a
well-protected camp, to serve as their base of operations. How far
they could depend on the Thames as a channel of communication
with the sea we cannot be sure. But we know that they were reinforced during their stay at Reading by " a summer-army from over
seas," and it seems quite possible that the light Danish vessels found
their way up the river.

If the Danes wanted fighting in Wessex, they got it to their
hearts' content. Eight battles in quick succession were fought, for
the landsfolk were attacking the invaders in force even before their
camp was finished. On the third day only after their arrival at
Reading, the fyrd of Berkshire, under Aethelwulf, its ealdorman
(the same man who had beaten the Danes at Winchester in 860),
fell on a raiding party at Englefield Green, in Windsor Forest,
routed it, and slew the jarl who was in command. Three days later
the royal army of Wessex came up, under the king and his brother
Alfred. There followed a general action outside the ramparts of the
camp : the Danes were driven back, and constrained to take refuge
within it. There followed a desperate attempt to storm the stronghold, which proved unfortunate : after the English had wearied
themselves out in numerous assaults, the enemy sallied forth, " bursting out from all the gates like wolves," and drove off the attacking
force. The ealdorman Aethelwulf, was slain, and many other
worthy thegns, and the army of Wessex seems to have drawn back
for some distance.

At any rate the Danes were now able to emerge from their palisades, and to take the offensive again, and were only opposed when
they had got many miles from Reading, and had reached the eastern
end of the Berkshire Downs. Somewhere on these hills, we cannot

say exactly where,[1] for all the range bore the name of Aescesdun (Ashdown), the invaders again found King Aethelred and his brother in front of them. We are told that the Danes lay high up the hillside in two divisions, the one headed by the Kings Halfdene and Baegsceg, the other by all the jarls: in front of their line was a single stunted thorn-tree, which was shown to Asser twenty years later as the spot round which the battle had been fiercest. The English were drawn up below in the valley, also in two divisions, the one headed by the king, the other by his brother. It is now that we get our first concrete personal notice of the doings of Alfred. We are told that he saw the Danes upon the move, and noted that, if they were to be deprived of the advantage of the offensive, it was time for the English to move also: it would never do to accept a defensive action on a down-slope. But Aethelred was hearing mass in the rear, and, like the pious prince that he was, refused to give an order, or to leave his prayers, till the celebration was finished. Whereupon Alfred took upon himself to order the army to advance, though his brother was still absent, and went forward to meet the advancing Danes. The struggle was fierce, but Alfred, " charging uphill like a wild boar, began to gain ground ". His brother came up not long after, and was soon in the heart of the battle. The fortune of the day never wavered ; the shield wall of the Danes was broken, and they dispersed into a horde of fugitives, seeking each for himself the nearest way to the fortified camp at Reading. King Baegsceg was slain, and all the five jarls, with many thousands of their men, for the pursuit was kept up all night and into the next day—a fact which shows that the battle-spot must have been very far west of Reading.

This was, with the possible exception of Aethelwulf's victory at Aclea, the greatest success that any Christian army had yet won over the Vikings. But the final results of the campaign were to be most disappointing. Halfdene, the surviving Danish leader, shut himself up with the wrecks of his army in the camp of Reading. Yet only fourteen days after we hear that he was again in the field,

---

[1] Aescesdun does not mean the " down of the ash," as Asser says (*mons fraxini*) but the down of Aesc—some ancient chief. That the whole range and not any par ticular part of it bore this name is conclusively proved by Mr. Stevenson in his notes to Asser, 235-38. It cannot be restricted to the ground about Compton Beau- champ, or Ashbury.

and fought successfully with Aethelred at Basing, a dozen miles
south of Reading. Presumably he must have been heavily reinforced : perhaps the Chronicle and Asser are wrong when they say
that a " great summer army from beyond seas," joined themselves
to the original invaders after, and not before, the battle of Basing.[1]
At any rate, the war was still lingering on, upon the borders of
Berks and Wilts, two months later, and the last fight of the campaign was at Marden, near Bedwyn,[2] more than twenty miles west
of Reading. This was a terrible defeat : " there King Aethelred
and Alfred his brother fought against the Army, and they were in
two bodies, and they put both to flight, and during a great part
of the day were victorious : and there was a great slaughter on
either hand, but the Danes had possession of the place of carnage,
and the bishop Heahmund of Sherborne, was slain and many good
men ". Worst of all, the worthy king died a few days later, at
Eastertide, perhaps of wounds got in the battle. He was buried
in haste at Wimborne, and his brother Alfred was immediately
saluted king in his stead. He left at least two sons,[3] but they were
mere children, and in this crisis a grown man and a tried warrior was
required to maintain the cause of Wessex against the heathen.
The election of Alfred was the obvious, indeed the only possible,
course for the Witan to take. How well he justified their choice
we have now to relate.

[1] A. S. Chronicle, *sub anno* 871, Asser, § 40.

[2] Almost certainly the Meratun of the Chronicle is not Merton in Surrey, nor
Merton in Oxfordshire, but Marden near Hungerford and Bedwyr.

[3] One was Aethelwald, the rebel of 901, from him or another son of Aethelred
descended Aethelweard, the chronicler.

CHAPTER XXII

THE REIGN OF ALFRED. THE EARLIER DANISH WARS (871-78)

GREAT historical figures—Caesar, Hadrian, Severus, Constantine—have occasionally crossed the scene, while we have been dealing with the history of Britain. But each of them appears for a moment only, and the main activity of no one of them was concerned with this island. Now at last we come to the story of a great man who was English born and English bred, whose whole life's work was devoted to English ends, and of whose character and aims, no less than of his mere battles and treaties, we have a competent knowledge—though there is still much withheld from us that we would gladly have learnt. The more prominent kings of the earlier Anglo-Saxon period, Ceawlin or Aethelbert, Edwin or Offa, or Ecgbert, are very little more than names to us. We recognise that they must have been men of mark, but we have concerning them but a few short annals, backed sometimes by a handful of anecdotes of greater or less authenticity. Indeed before we come to Alfred there is only one Englishman of whom we have a real intimate knowledge, because he left behind a mass of writings which enable us to understand and to admire his personality—and he was a monk, who saw history passing by him, but did not help to make it.   If the Venerable Bede had never lived, we should know far less about the seventh and eighth centuries, but it cannot be said that the actual course of events in this island would have been in the least affected. Alfred made history : indeed he was one of those rare spirits who not merely bestride their whole generation, and dominate it, but who actually turn back the flowing tide of circumstance, and avert what seem to be inevitable conclusions.   Though his work was done on English soil, he is a figure of more than insular importance, as the first successful champion of Christian Europe against the all-pervading, all-conquering Viking swarm.   Down to the moment of his appearance there seemed to be no reasonable probability that Christendom would end by beating off the heathen of the North.   When he died there was already a fair hope of it.   In a way Alfred is a landmark in the Dark Ages, as notable and as suggestive as Charlemagne himself; they built in different fashions and on a different scale; the one created an empire, the other only a national kingdom.   But Charlemagne's creation, though its effects were to last for a thousand years, was from the first something of an illusion, and became in the end a hindrance and a snare.   The idea of the Empire did more harm than good, in that it effectually prevented either a real kingdom of Germany or a real kingdom of Italy from coming into existence in the Middle Ages.   Alfred's work was all devoted to a practical and an attainable end; what he accomplished was never undone, for neither the conquest of Cnut nor the conquest of William of Normandy cancelled it.   There was never any reasonable probability, after the year 900, that England would fail to achieve national unity, or break up into a group of states—some English, some Danish.

But it is not merely the political achievements of Alfred that make him the most interesting figure in the Dark Ages: his personality is as attractive as it is commanding.   Charlemagne's crimes and vices are as notorious as his great achievements and his intellectual powers.   To set against Alfred's virtues there is no countervailing balance of faults or failings.   Yet he is very far from being the typical "good king" of the Dark Ages.   There was nothing of Aethelwulf, or of Louis the Pious, or of Edward the Confessor in him.   All these were "sore saints for the crown," princes in whose characters meekness ran into weakness, generosity into thriftlessness, piety into superstition.   They neglected their kingdoms, while they were busy on saving their own souls—a typical result of the religious ideal of their time.   Looking up and down the ages there is no one but St. Louis of France who can be compared to Alfred, and St. Louis—though a blameless man and a wise and conscientious king—was misled by his enthusiasm into wasting the strength of his realm, and ultimately his own life, on wholly unnecessary and unprofitable enterprises.   It is true that he was less fortunate than Alfred, in that his crusading had to be done abroad, while Alfred's lay ready to his hand at home, and involved the salvation, not the abandonment, of his native kingdom. But the West Saxon king was a more many-sided personage, and thereby more interesting to the modern observer. This great fighter and administrator was not merely the victorious general of a dozen campaigns, the founder of a navy, the rebuilder of the internal organisation of Church and State, but also a scholar and author ; one who loved alike the old national poetry of his own race and the literature of Rome. He undoubtedly set going that invaluable compilation which we call the "Anglo-Saxon Chronicle," the first great historical work written in one of the modern languages. He collected the ancient heroic songs of the English— though the compilation, to our unspeakable loss, perished in a later age. But he also translated himself, or caused to be translated by others, Latin books as different in their interest as Orosius' Universal History, Bede's *Ecclesiastical History of the English Nation*, Boethius's *Consolation of Philosophy*, and the *Pastoral Care* of Gregory the Great. And all this literary work was to forward a scheme which seems simply grandiose, when we remember that it was framed in the troublous ninth century—that "all the sons of freemen who have the means to be able to undertake it, should be set to learning English letters, and afterwards such of them as were fit for a more advanced education, and were to be prepared for higher office, should be instructed in Latin letters also ".[1] Truly this Alfred was no mere national hero, no ordinary "patron of arts and letters," but a man of great ideas, a figure of transcendent energy, unique and marvellous among kings. His own people admired and loved him—he was remembered as the *rex veridicus*, as "England's darling," but most certainly they did not fully comprehend the greatness of the man who ruled them for thirty eventful years. His life, such is the perverseness of fortune, has been left to us written not by a real historian of the type of Bede, who would have made it no less lucid in manner than edifying in matter, but by the Welsh bishop Asser, the most inconsequent and incoherent of biographers, who was constitutionally incapable of telling a story in logical sequence, or distinguishing events of primary from those of secondary importance. His one

[1] The words occur in the epistle of the king to Bishop Werfrith of Worcester, annexed to the copy of Gregory's *Pastoral Care* which Alfred was forwarding to him, and to his other bishops, as a first earnest of his great scheme.

redeeming vice was his garrulity, which has preserved for us many
illustrative anecdotes which a more serious historian would probably have omitted.

Alfred was in his twenty-third year when he succeeded to the
crown and the wars of his brother Aethelred in 871. He had been
born at the royal manor of Wantage in 849, the youngest of the
five children of King Aethelwulf and his first wife Osburh.[1] We
have already had occasion to mention his two visits to Rome as a
child in 853 and 856, and the honours which were conferred upon
him by Pope Leo IV. It must apparently be to the time immediately preceding the second visit that Asser's pretty story of his
winning the book of Saxon poetry from his mother, as a prize for
learning it by heart, must belong. It was not an incredible feat for
a sharp boy of six years old, and it is to be noted that he is expressly
said to have *recited* the poem to Osburh, and not to have *read* it,
according to the perverted version of the story that is often set forth.
Asser specially informs us that he did not learn to read for himself
till he had passed his twelfth year, and that it was not till a long
time after, *viz.*, in 887, when he had attained his thirty-eighth
year, that he began " legere simul et interpretari ". By this curious
phrase it is apparently meant that he then began to read off Latin
into English extempore. For it can hardly mean that the faculty
of reading came to him without his having previously learnt his
letters, which would be absurd. But since we are told that down to
this time he had been wont to have books recited to him, because
" *per se ipsum aliquid adhuc de libris intelligere non posset,*" [2]
we must take it that he could not make much of either Latin or
English manuscripts. Yet he had from youth onward been wont
to carry about with him in his breast a little book in which were
written certain psalms and " hours " that he had *read* as a boy
(*quas in juventute legerat*).[3] Clearly no one would carry about a
prayer-book unless he could make something of its contents.[4] Writing was a very different matter : Asser tells us that his master
repeatedly asked him to copy out texts of Scripture for him into
his pocket-book (" encheiridion ").

Alfred's mother died apparently in 856, his father in 858, when

---

[1] She was the daughter of a thegn named Oslac, who was Aethelwulf's high-
butler (*pincerna*) and was a Jute from the Isle of Wight by descent (Asser, § 2).

[2] Asser, § 77.   [3] *Ibid.*, § 88.   [4] *Ibid.*, § 86.

he was only nine years of age, so that his training devolved on his brothers; their ministers must have been the "nutritores" who, according to Asser, somewhat neglected the education of the boy. But at least they brought him up well according to their lights: as a youth he was night and day most constantly set on hearing and learning all that he could of Saxon poetry. He became a mighty hunter, "for in that art his skill and fortune was incomparable, as it was in all other of God's good gifts". He was, of course, like every prince of the house of Ecgbert, trained to arms; his first recorded campaign was in 868, when in his nineteenth year he marched, with his brother, against the Danes who were holding Nottingham. "But, alas! what he most longed for, training in the liberal arts, was not forthcoming according to his desire, for in that day good scholars were non-existent in the realm of Wessex."[1] Long after, he would say that the greatest hindrance of his life had been that, when he had the right age and leisure for learning, he could get no masters; but that when, in after days, he was able to collect scholars and authors, he was so beset with wars, administrative cares, and bodily infirmities, that he was not able to read as he wished. Despite of this he has left the bulk of translations behind him to which allusion has already been made, beside the collection of English songs and the "encheiridion" which have been lost.[2]

Concerning the bodily infirmity from which Alfred all through his life was a sufferer, Asser gives a long and most confusing story, or rather two separate and irreconcilable stories. He tells us that even from infancy the prince had a "genus infestissimi doloris," though in other respects his body was comely and well built. Then that, when a lad, some time before his marriage, he prayed at the Cornish shrine of St. Gueriir, to which chance took him during a hunting expedition, that this painful ailment might be changed for any other—provided that it did not make him a useless cripple, as leprosy or blindness might do. The prayer was heard, and his first ailment disappeared, but another took its place, under which he laboured for some years. But when he was married, at the age of nineteen, at the end of a long series of bridal feasts and ceremonies, he was seized by what was apparently a third disease, which afflicted

[1] Asser, § 23.
[2] Though the latter survived till the days of William of Malmesbury, who had read it.

him for the whole of the rest of his life. The physicians could not
give a name to it, nor could any remedy ever be found. Some said
that it was put upon him by witchcraft ; others that the devil was
being allowed to persecute him (as in the case of righteous Job) ;
others that it was a recurrence of the disease which had afflicted him
in infancy ; [1] others, again, that it was some unusual form of fever.
We are told that it afflicted Alfred for long periods at a time, and
that when it was absent he was never sure for a single day that it
might not return. It was painful, yet did not much affect either
his bodily or his mental activity. Indeed during the thirty-two
years that he lived after his marriage it is clear that he surpassed all
men in his labours, and never tired or slackened. What the afflic-
tion can have been it is idle from Asser's vague narrative to guess—
possibly some form of intermittent neuritis. Epilepsy, which some
have suggested, seems incredible : it was a known disease, and moreover one which could not have failed to prostrate the king completely at untoward moments—of which we have no trace in the
narrative of his life.[2]

The marriage feast which formed such an unhappy landmark in
Alfred's physical health took place in his twentieth year. His bride
was Ealhswith, daughter of a Mercian ealdorman named Aethelred
Mucel [3] and his wife Eadburh, a member of the old Mercian royal
house. The date of his wedding, 868, which is the same as that of
his march, in company with his brother, to assist King Burhred in
the siege of Nottingham, suggest that the alliance between Mercia
and Wessex was being knit together by a new marriage tie in this
critical moment. We know practically nothing of Ealhswith, save
that she bore Alfred six children, three sons and three daughters, of
whom the two eldest (the Aetheling Edward and his sister Aethelflaed) showed characters of exceptional power and virtue. She survived her husband by five years, yet is never mentioned once in the

[1] Which Asser, § 73, calls the *ficus*, which may perhaps, from the Anglo-Saxon
Leechdooms, be identified with hæmorrhoids. See notes on Stevenson's *Asser*,
p. 296.

[2] Yet a man may be a great general, though suffering from epilepsy. The
Archduke Charles was disabled by a fit of it during two critical days of his Eckmühl
campaign, with disastrous results.

[3] Called by Asser, § 29, Comes Gainorum—probably a corrupt reading, for we
know of no district of Mercia inhabited by a tribe called Gaini. The identification
with Gainsborough is impossible.

course of all his biography, for good or evil. Her name does not occur even in the rather full description of the education of Alfred's children given us by Asser. It is hardly possible to avoid the deduction that she must have been a common-place personage, who was fitted to give little help to her husband's great schemes. If she had been a woman of mark, like her daughter Aethelflaed, she could hardly have failed to win at least some mention from the chroniclers. There is perhaps some reticence hidden under Asser's statement, given under his note of Ealhswith's marriage, that he had often seen at court her mother Eadburh, who was a matron of great worth and much venerated. He does not add the almost obligatory sequel that her daughter resembled her, which we should have expected to find. She is set down in her husband's will for a maintenance from Wantage, Ethandun and other royal estates, and this is absolutely all that we know of her.

Aethelred, it will be remembered, died, perhaps of his wounds, a few days after his defeat at Basing—the sad end to the campaign that had opened so handsomely at Ashdown. The Witan without hesitation chose Alfred to succeed him, and he had barely leisure to bury his brother at Wimborne Minster when he had to hasten back to the field. Before he had been one month a king he had fought his first battle as general-in-chief—and lost it. The Danes, pressing their advantage, had evidently advanced southward and westward, for it was at Wilton, in the heart of Wiltshire, that Alfred met them.[1] We are told that his army was small, but that for a long day he defended his position against the attacks of the enemy, till at last the Danes drew back. Whereupon the men of Wessex pursued rashly, broke their line, and were scattered by an unexpected rally of the Vikings. Let no one blame them, plead the Chronicle and Asser; they were but a handful, the fighting men of the kingdom having been worn down to a miserable remnant by eight pitched battles waged in one year, besides skirmishes. "God alone knows how many Danes had perished in that campaign." But the more they were slain off, the more they seemed to increase in numbers, from new reinforcements.

Immediately after the battle of Wilton, as it seems, Alfred was driven to sully the glory of his new crown by buying peace from

---

[1] Ethelweard, contradicting all the other chroniclers, says that Alfred was not at the Battle of Wilton, being occupied in burying his brother.

the enemy, after the same fashion that was only too well known
already to other Frankish and English kings. The "Army" consented to retire from Wessex on receiving a subsidy; it had suffered very heavily, and was willing to turn for a moment to other
realms where the resistance was less fierce. It could return when
it pleased, for oaths counted but little. Alfred knew this, and was
aware that he was probably buying but a short respite. But time
was at the moment invaluable to him, in order that he might win
a breathing space to reorganise the exhausted kingdom.

As a matter of fact the respite lasted for nearly four years
(872-75), during which Wessex was apparently unmolested. How
Alfred employed the time we are not told, save in regard to one
point: he started a national navy—the modest beginning of the
mighty force that he was to develop in his later years. It must
have been a small affair at first, for both Asser and the Chronicle
think it an achievement worth note that the king's galleys in 875
were able to attack a squadron of seven Viking ships, to take one,
and chase the rest out to sea.[1] But that there should be a royal fleet
of any sort at all, in existence, was a mighty step in advance: no
other Christian king had yet found the right way of dealing with
the Vikings. Nothing is more probable than that Alfred at the
same time began the reorganisation of the land force of the realm.
At least he must have made efforts to replace with new fighting
men the thegnhood that had fallen at Reading and Ashdown, at
Basing and Wilton.

Meanwhile the storm, averted for a moment from Wessex, beat
all the more fiercely upon Northern and Central England. The
years 872-75 were those in which the final ruin of Mercia took
place. The army which had quitted Wessex betook itself to
London, which was still counted, as in Offa's days, as a Mercian
town. There it sat all the winter of 871-72, living apparently on
the country, till King Burhred bought peace and bribed it to
depart. It was apparently during this wintering of the Danes in
London that their king Halfdene struck there some remarkable
coins—the first specimens of Viking mintage; they bear his name,
and sometimes that of the city; one shows a copy of an ancient
Roman device, two emperors crowned by a victory. Oddly enough

---

[1] Asser, §48, A. S. C. *sub anno* 875. The former says *six* ships only were
fought, the latter seven.

both Alfred and Ceolwulf, the last King of Mercia, employed this same archaic type.[1]

Burhred's subsidy moved the Danes from London, but not (as he had hoped) from Mercia. We read that, despite of the treaty, the army only removed itself as far as Lindsey, where it made its camp at Torksey, and abode there many months (873) till it had extracted a second subsidy from the Mercians—or perhaps from the men of Lindsey only. For its next move was into the heart of Mercia proper: it shifted itself in 874 into the valley of the Trent, and encamped at Repton, not far from its old camp at Nottingham. King Burhred, in utter despair, abandoned his people—whether after a battle or without fighting is not quite certain. But he, at any rate, fled out of England altogether, retired to Rome, and died there as a monk not long after. When he was gone the Danes made a pact with one Ceolwulf, whom the chronicles call "an unwise king's-thegn," [2] on the ignominious terms that they would make him King of Mercia during their good pleasure. He was to be their vassal for the present, but if they bade him resign his lands to them at any time, he must depart. To this miserable treaty he solemnly pledged himself, taking an oath and giving hostages. That he was recognised for some time is shown by his coins, on which he duly calls himself King of Mercia. How long the arrangement lasted is not quite certain, but he was gone—either dead or deposed—by the year 880. Such was the end of the once-mighty empire of Offa.

After this the "Great Army" broke up into two halves. One under King Halfdene returned to Northumbria (875). Here York and much of Deira was already in Danish hands, but Bernicia, now ruled by the obscure Ricsig, still had left something that was worth plundering. Halfdene pitched his camp by the Tyne, and wasted the land cruelly from sea to sea. This was the time at which the monastic community abandoned Lindisfarne in despair, and started on nine years of unhappy wandering, bearing with them their palladium, the relics of Saint Cuthbert.[3] But it was not on the Bernicians alone that Halfdene spent his wrath: he invaded also the land of the Picts, making a great slaughter of

[1] See *British Museum Anglo-Saxon Coins*, i. p. 203.
[2] Or "cuidam insipienti ministro " as Asser calls him, § 46.
[3] Simeon of Durham, *sub anno* 875.

them, and the Strathclyde Welsh also felt his sword. Having, as it seems, trampled out all open resistance in the North, the army returned to York in 876, and there settled down, not for a winter encampment, but for permanent habitation. "In this year," says the Anglo-Saxon Chronicle, "Halfdene portioned out the lands of Northumbria, and they thenceforth continued ploughing and tilling them." It is to be wished that we had more details concerning the settlement. Apparently every Dane who desired it obtained his endowment of land; but the Northumbrian peasantry had not been exterminated—though the thegnhood, clergy, and upper classes had been driven forth or destroyed. Deira became a region with a Danish population of freeholders great and small; the former were called *holds*, and appear sometimes both in the Chronicles and in laws as persons of the status of a very important thegn.[1] But under these *holds* and freemen were English servile dependants, whom in the tenth century the Danes called *liesings*, or freedmen.[2] Since their *weregeld* was the same as that of a Saxon ceorl, it is almost certain that their blood and origin were the same also. The settlement did not extend to Bernicia, where the wrecks of the old English population lived on, tributary to the Danes at York, but not annexed to their realm. There was a last king of English blood called Ecgbert II. from 876 till 879: after his death we hear only of high-reeves at Bamborough, who were destined to survive till the suzerainty of Wessex came to the North. Meanwhile their position must have been precarious and miserable.

Half of the "Great Army" had not followed Halfdene to the Tyne in 875, but had remained in the Midlands. They were under three kings, Guthrum, Oskytel and Amund, who made their winter camp for the Yule of 875-76 at Cambridge, not dispersing nor setting themselves to division of the land. Presumably they must have been living on the systematic plunder of East Anglia and Essex, and no doubt they were also bleeding their dependant Ceolwulf of Mercia whenever they lacked more. But after a year's delay they took in hand once again the invasion of Wessex—presumably they thought that King Alfred's blackmail of 871 had

---

[1] An ordinary thegn's weregeld, according to the " North People's Law " was 2000 *thrymsas*, an earl's 8,000, a hold's 4,000. He was therefore valued at much above the normal thegn.

[2] Some *liesings* may have been non-English. The class existed in Scandinavia.

already bought him an ample respite. His realm was now the only part of England that was still fairly intact and worth plundering. It seems likely also that the host at Cambridge had lately been recruited by all the minor swarms of Vikings, for the Continental annals of 874 and 875 are singularly silent regarding the raids of the heathen, though there had been much trouble both on the Loire and in Frisia in the summer and autumn of 873. In that year the main contingent of the Northmen in France had waged a long campaign with Charles the Bald about Angers, and had finally returned to the sea, after a treaty of the usual sort. Apparently they had mainly gone off, to join either Halfdene in Northumbria or the three kings who were devastating Central England. It is very notable to find that the Irish annals also speak of the years following 870 as a time of comparative peace from the normal pest of invasion. " Now for a while were the men of Ireland free from the plunderings of the strangers."

In 875-76, therefore, it would seem as if the entire Viking swarm, usually dispersed over the whole of the Western realms, had gathered together for the destruction of Wessex. King Alfred was about to fight not only for himself but in behalf of the whole of Christendom ; he had everybody's adversaries thrown upon his hands at once, when the new invasion came. When the blow fell it was delivered with surprising vigour. The army left Cambridge by a sudden night march, and reached Wessex before its departure from its base was known. Then crossing Berkshire and Hampshire with undiminished speed, it seized Wareham, and stockaded itself in the angle between the rivers Frome and Trent, " in a position extremely strong by nature, and only approachable on dry land on its west front," while it was open on the water side to ships coming up from Poole Harbour. The reason for the choice of this spot was that the Cambridge Danes had made an agreement for joint operations with the " Western Army," i.e., their kinsmen who had been wont to work by sea on the Irish and Welsh coasts.[1] These latter brought their fleet round to Wareham and joined them. Alfred's few vessels were evidently unable to show themselves in

---

[1] Ethelweard's Chronicle is, for once, of use here. It is he who tells us that "exercitus qui in Grantanbricge fuerat conjecit statum cum occidentali exercitu, quod ante non usi sunt, juxta oppidum quod Werham nuncupatur " [iv., § 3]. The "occidentalis exercitus" can mean nothing but Danes of the Irish Sea.

face of such a force. The junction being completed, the host at
Wareham had two advantages ; it possessed the power of throwing
detachments ashore whenever it pleased in Wessex, and could
readily be supplied with provisions by sea.

Nevertheless the campaign did not go so badly as might have
been expected from this ill beginning. Alfred collected the whole
force of Wessex in front of Wareham, in such strength that the
enemy did not dare to give him battle, and stayed within their
entrenchments on the defensive, though they seem to have succeeded in carrying out some raids in Dorsetshire, perhaps by landing expeditions in his rear.[1] Apparently there was a deadlock
between the main armies, which must have lasted for a long time,
perhaps until winter was near. But finally the Danes offered to
depart on receiving a subsidy of the usual sort. To this Alfred
consented, and a treaty was concluded ; the Danes gave him some
hostages, and swore to keep their word on a holy relic of their
own, a great gold ring or bracelet, such as is mentioned as sacred
by many Northern historians.[2] But when Alfred's suspicion was
lulled, and his outposts less carefully guarded, all that part of the
army which had horses burst out of Wareham by night, pierced
the English lines, and hurried along the coast to Exeter, which
they seized and fortified. Alfred, as we are told, rode after this
detachment with such mounted men as he possessed, but they had
the start of him, and were not overtaken till they had reached
Exeter, behind whose entrenchments they "could not be come at".

Presumably part of the Saxon host was left to blockade the
rest of the Danes in Wareham, for otherwise Wessex would have
been at their mercy. But after the New Year the Vikings evacuated their base-camp, and went on shipboard, intending to join
and succour their friends at Exeter. Here Providence intervened
on Alfred's side : a Channel storm swept down on the fleet as it
was passing under the cliffs of Swanage, and almost annihilated it.
A hundred and twenty ships were wrecked and their crews drowned.
Hence no help came to Exeter, which was besieged for many

---

[1] At any rate "depopulata est ab iis pars major provinciae illius" (Ethelweard,
ibid.).

[2] The Chronicle and Ethelweard tell us that they had never before consented
to swear oaths to any king on this sacred ring (*armilla, beage*). For references to
similar rings, see notes to Plummer's A. S. C., ii. pp. 90, 91.

months by Alfred. At last the garrison offered to depart, giving as many and a; great hostages as the king might choose; this time there was no question of the wonted blackmail. In August they moved off, and kept their word so far that they left Wessex; but it was only to enter into the neighbouring Mercia, where they established their camp at Gloucester.[1]

The Danish leaders then, as we learn, called upon their miserable vassal Ceolwulf to fulfil the pact which they had made with him in 874. They bade him give up great part of his kingdom, which they proceeded to apportion among themselves, and then told him that he was at liberty to keep the rest. There seems no reason to doubt that the annexed portion was the region which afterwards formed the Mercian Danelaw—the lands east of Watling Street, including all Lindsey, nearly all the land of the Middle Angles, and part of the old original Mercian settlement, viz., the region that afterwards formed the counties of Derby and Nottingham. To Ceolwulf, apparently, they left the land of the Hwiccas and Magesaetas on each side of the Severn, with the Western part of old Mercia (Staffordshire, Shropshire, Warwickshire, Cheshire). Such at least was the boundary between English and Danish Mercia a few years later. This settlement did not result in the creation of a single kingdom such as that which Halfdene had established at York. We find instead many "earls" (jarls), each seated in a central town and with an "army" dependent on him.[2] The five most important were those of Stamford, Lincoln, Derby, Nottingham and Leicester, afterwards known as the "Five Burghs". There were also earls and "armies" at Northampton, Bedford, Cambridge and Huntingdon. The whole formed a very loose confederacy. It is impossible to say whether all these petty states were established at once in 877: we have no details about them till thirty years after. But it is certain that the Danish settle-

[1] The chronology of the campaign of 876-77 is difficult to follow. In the Chronicle the capture of Exeter is put under 876, but repeated again as the first entry of 877, followed by the note of the evacuation of Wareham and the wreck of the fleet. Probably we must conclude that the seizure of Exeter fell in November or December, 876, and the naval disaster early in 877. Ethelweard seems to put both events in the later year, but is apparently working from the Chronicle and misunderstanding it.

[2] For proof that the 'Five Burghs' had jarls, and were not always ruled by a 'patriciate of Lawmen' (as many suppose), see chapter xxiv.

ment of East Mercia formally began in this year. It seems to have been thickest, if we may judge from the proportion of Danish to surviving English place-names, in Lincolnshire, Leicestershire and Nottinghamshire. Farther south the traces of Danish settlement are more slight and scattered.[1] But of this more hereafter. The social organisation must have been much the same as in the kingdom of York, with a basis of servile English dependants under the yoke of a land-owning class of Danish freeholders

The settlement of such a widespread area must have greatly depleted the ranks of the "Great Army": yet a very large body still clung together in Gloucestershire under King Guthrum, preferring the life of plunder and battle to a quiet establishment on the land. They now apparently leagued themselves once more with the pirates of the Irish Sea, for a renewed attack on Wessex, despite of the treaty to which they had so recently pledged their oath. The leader of the host was Guthrum: we hear nothing in this year of the two other kings, Amund and Oskytel, who had taken part in the invasion of 786. Presumably they were among those who had gone off to settle in Mercia. The auxiliary squadron of pirates, however, was commanded by a leader with a well-known name, Hubba, the brother of Halfdene and Ingwar, who has already come under our notice in Northumbria and East Anglia. His horde had been wintering in South Wales, where it had wrought much devastation, so that it was close at hand to co-operate with Guthrum's force at Gloucester. It cannot be doubted that their plans had been carefully thought out, in order that Wessex might be distracted by a double attack.

The special peculiarity of this treacherous invasion was that it was made at midwinter, soon after Twelfth Night, in the second week of January, 878, an unheard of time for the commencement of a war. The King of Wessex, whatever his suspicions of Guthrum's faith, cannot possibly have suspected that he would strike at this moment. It was the strangeness of the season and the suddenness of the blow that made the attack for the time successful. The Army, as the Chronicle puts it, "stole away" into Chippenham, in the heart of Wiltshire, there stockaded itself, and then commenced to devastate all the surrounding country. "In the

---

[1] The shires of the 'Five Burghs' in Domesday Book are assessed on a six-carucate system, the rest of the Danelaw on the normal five-hide unit.

same winter "[1]—presumably a few days or weeks later—Hubba's fleet came ashore in Devonshire and began to ravage it.

The utter unexpectedness of the invasion made it for a time irresistible: there was complete panic in Wessex. Large districts offered tribute and homage to Guthrum: many men of note fled over-seas to the Franks without thinking of resistance. It seemed as if the defence of the realm had completely broken down, despite of all King Alfred's care, and the blood and treasure that had been spent in the two preceding years. But the worst of the panic only lasted for a few weeks: the elements of resistance soon began to draw together. We hear that Aethelnoth, ealdorman of Somerset, soon collected a small force in the forest tract of his shire [2]—Selwood presumably. Odda, ealdorman of Devon, gathered many thegns and their following at a fortress named Cynuit,[3] to oppose the bands of Hubba. The king himself with his military household and some other nobles took refuge in the famous isle of Athelney, where he built himself a stockade in the marshes of the Parret, from which he made frequent sallies against the raiding bands that came out from the great camp at Chippenham.

It is to this lowest period of his fortunes that the famous tale of the king, the cowherd's wife, and the burnt cakes belongs. It is found first in a very bad and late authority, the Annals of St. Neot's, which was compiled after the Norman Conquest, though not later than the first quarter of the twelfth century.[4] That Alfred was so friendless that "he long lay hid with a certain cowherd of his own" who did not know him by sight, is in itself most unlikely. On Twelfth Night, when the Danish invasion began, he must have had his court about him, and there is no conceivable reason why he should have fled alone—indeed his *comitatus* would surely have refused to quit him, and we know from Asser that they were with him in Athelney during the worst weeks of disaster.

---

[1] So the Chronicle. Asser and Ethelweard use the vaguer term " in the same year ".

[2] Ethelweard, iv. § 3.

[3] Asser, § 54. Where Cynuit lay is unfortunately not to be ascertained. Mr. Stevenson [notes to Asser, p. 262] seems to prove that it is *not* Kenwith, near Bideford, as is generally supposed. Indeed the name Kenwith appears to be an archæologist's invention, the spot now known by that denomination having been called Henniborough down to the eighteenth century.

[4] For a discussion of its age and value, see Stevenson's *Asser*, pp. 97-110.

But it is useless to spend time in "breaking a butterfly"; the quaint tale is only worth mentioning because it has achieved such a world-wide popularity. But there is a much more tangible and equally interesting connection between Alfred and the marshy refuge of his adversity: in 1693 there was dug up, a little to the north of the farm that still bears the name of Athelney, the gold and enamelled jewel bearing the inscription AELFRED MEC HEHT GEWYRCAN, which the king must certainly have dropped during his stay there. It now is the most valued possession of all the antiquities owned by the University of Oxford, which vainly believed for so many centuries that it might count Alfred as its founder.[1]

The period of the complete domination of the Danes in Wessex seems to lie within the months of January, February and March, 878. The tide had begun to turn before Easter, which fell on March 23rd in that year. The first great success of the English was due not to the king himself but to the nobles of Devonshire. Ealdorman Odda and many thegns had established themselves in Cynuit, a place, says Asser, not properly walled, but only fortified after our fashion (*i.e.*, with stockade and ditch), but extraordinarily strong by natural position, and only accessible from its eastern front.[2] Hubba came up against them with his host—the crews of about thirty ships—looked at the fort, and preferred to try starvation rather than an open assault. He had heard that the Saxons were short of provisions, and there was no good water supply. "But matters went not as he expected. For the Christians, before they had begun to suffer any serious inconvenience from want of supplies, got an inspiration from on high that it would be far better to take the chance of death or victory. They made an unexpected sally upon the heathen at dawn, had the advantage over them from the first, and slew the king and the larger part of his host, only a remnant escaping to their ships."[3] The Chronicle says that 840 Danes were slain, Asser raises the number to 1,200.[4] At any rate this band was practically annihilated as a fighting force.

[1] It is, oddly enough, very hard to determine what purpose this jewel was intended to serve. It has been called a locket, the ornament of a helm, or the butt of an "aestel" or book-pointer. Professor Earle's little monograph, *Alfred's Jewel*, still leaves the point uncertain.

[2] Asser, § 54.   [3] *Ibid.*

[4] Most versions of the A. S. Chronicle add that it was on this occasion that the great Danish war-banner called the Raven was captured. The Annals of St.

This victory fell before Easter, and must have freed the West.
But it was not till more than a month later that Alfred challenged
the main body of the Danes to battle. He had sent the summons
all round Wessex, and had ascertained that the levies of Wilts and
Hants could join him. Why we hear of no aid from Surrey or
Sussex, Berkshire or Kent, it is hard to say. Were these the regions
which are said to have submitted to Guthrum, or were they enduring some separate trouble of their own, from another Danish force,
of which no record has chanced to survive ? At any rate forty days
after Easter Alfred sallied out from Athelney at the head of his
military retinue. He rode as far as Ecgbert's stone (near Penselwood), on the east side of Selwood, and there met, by agreement,
all the *fyrd* of Somerset, Wiltshire and Hampshire,[1] " who were
filled, as was natural, with immense joy on seeing their king once
more, as it were alive again after all his tribulation ".[2] They
pitched their camp there for one night, and on the next day passed
on to Iglea (Iley, near Warminster), where they abode the second
night. On the third day they advanced to Ethandun (Eddington),[3]
and then joined battle with the main army of the Danes, which
had moved out of its encampment at Chippenham, ready to risk a
general engagement, when the raising of the king's banner had been
reported to them.

Concerning the great struggle that followed we have no details,
save that the English fought " *densa testudine*," in one thick
shield-wall, not in two divisions as at Ashdown. The victory was
well disputed, and the fighting lasted for many hours, but at last
the heathen broke, in no feigned flight, as at Wilton, but in com-

Neot's give a wild tale concerning it : " they say that the three sisters of Ingwar and
Hubba, the daughters of Lodbrog, wove that flag and finished it in one day. In
every battle when it was displayed, if the Danes were destined to win, there appeared in the middle of the banner as it were a living flying raven. But if defeat
was to come, the flag would hang down straight, and would not float out at all. And
this was often tested " (A. S. N., 10).

[1] Only Gaimar, 3170, adds the Dorsetshire *fyrd* to the list of troops that served
in this campaign. But I have little doubt that he is right.

[2] Asser, § 49.

[3] For a dissertation on the location of Ecgbert's Stone, Iglea and Ethandun,
see Stevenson's *Asser*, pp. 270-77, the last authoritative exposition of the subject.
Ethandun has been sought in many places by different historians, from Somersetshire
to Berks, but Camden's old identification with Eddington still stands.

plete rout.   Alfred smote the fugitives with a great slaughter,
pressed them hotly as far as the stockades of their base-camp at
Chippenham, and drove them within its gates, capturing all the
cattle and stores that were left without, and killing every man who
was too slow to gain the shelter.   He then encamped and palisaded
himself just outside the Danish stronghold, blocking its exits.
Guthrum and his men were too broken in spirit to venture on a
sally : they held out for fourteen days, and on the fifteenth, having
exhausted nearly all their food, asked for terms of surrender, and
offered to give as many hostages as Alfred should choose, and to ask
for none in return while the negotiations were proceeding.   It might
possibly have been worth while to refuse to treat, and to make an
example of the broken host.   But the Viking, when fighting without
hope of quarter, was a dangerous enemy, and Alfred was merciful to
a fault.   He exacted a number of hostages, and put terms of a new
sort on the enemy ; not only did he require that the army should
depart from Wessex, but he stipulated that Guthrum and his chief
men should be baptised, and swear to accept Christianity from his
hands.   There were some sad precedents of broken baptismal vows
already on record, on the Continent, but Alfred resolved to take
the risk.   Indeed his surest security was not any oaths given, but
the fact that the Danes had received a thorough defeat, and were
broken in spirit as they had never been before.

Three weeks later Guthrum and twenty-nine other leaders
came to Aller, near Athelney, and were there baptised.   The king
was given the new name of Aethelstan, and had Alfred himself
as one godfather and Ealdorman Aethelnoth for the other.   The
"chrysom loosing," or taking off of the baptismal bands, was celebrated eight days after by a great feast at the neighbouring royal
manor of Wedmore.   This fact has led many historians to call the
pact concluded at Chippenham in the preceding month "the Treaty
of Wedmore".   The Vikings were entertained magnificently for
twelve days longer, and then allowed to return to their camp at
Chippenham.   From thence they removed to Cirencester,[1] just outside the border of Wessex : Alfred and his subjects must have
remembered how closely the situation now resembled that of the

---

[1] Apparently in the autumn of 878 (see Plummer's *No'es to A. S. Chronicle*, ii
95).   The Chronicle seems to put the transference in the next spring.

autumn of 877, when the army that had sworn oaths of peace at Exeter retired for a few months to Gloucester, before making its treacherous attack on Wessex at mid-winter.

But this time there was no such double-dealing on hand. The Danes had received a lesson which they never forgot, and Guthrum was intending to carry out his pledge. He withdrew his host after some delay eastward, and took possession of East Anglia and Essex, where he and they settled down (880) and established a kingdom similar to that which Halfdene had set up in Northumbria four years before. It is uncertain whether this had formed part of the terms of peace concluded at Chippenham, as is often asserted. The Chronicle, Asser, Ethelweard, and the other better authorities give no hint of it, though the arrangement is sufficiently likely in itself. This settlement was made in spite of a strong temptation to break the treaty and turn once more against Alfred. For a great Viking host from the Continent entered the Thames-mouth in 879, and fortified itself at Fulham. Guthrum might easily have united with it, and have attacked Wessex again. But he did not : the two hosts, as we are told, got into communication,[1] but the only result was that the newly arrived horde departed again after a time, and recrossed the Channel, after which it settled at Ghent and harried all Flanders. Possibly some of Guthrum's men, who neither wished to settle down nor to adopt Christianity, went off with the fleet. But the king himself and the bulk of his host remained in East Anglia, and apparently kept the peace honestly. They never threw off the Christianity which they had adopted, and it is most curious to find not only coins struck by Guthrum under his new name of Aethelstan, but others of his minting on which the name of St. Edmund appears in the place of honour.[2] For the East-Anglian Danes became fervent worshippers of the English martyr-king whom their fathers had slain. Guthrum reigned over them for eleven years (879-90), apparently always keeping, save for one short interval, on good terms with Alfred. In 886 they con-

[1] So Asser, § 58. Eodem anno magnus paganorum exercitus de ultramarinis partibus navigans in Tamesin, adunatus est superiori exercitui (to Guthrum's host) sed tamen hiemavit in loco qui dicitur Fullonham, juxta fluvium Tamesin.

[2] See British Museum, *Anglo-Saxon Coins*, i., xxix., Guthrum's moneyers strike these pieces.

tracted the well-known agreement called " Alfred and Guthrum's
Frith," of which more hereafter.   It not only defined accurately
the boundaries between their realms, but provided for an elaborate
system of *weregelds* and compensations between Englishman and
Dane.

CHAPTER XXIII

THE REIGN OF ALFRED—LATER YEARS (879-900)—THE KING AS STATESMAN AND SCHOLAR—THE LAST DANISH WAR

THE victory of Ethandun and the Pact of Chippenham form the central turning-point in the history of the struggle between the kingly house of Wessex and the Vikings, though half a century more was to elapse before that struggle came to an end, with the final submission of all the Danes settled in England to the heirs of King Alfred. This, however, was the last occasion on which the invaders succeeded in making a solid lodgment in Wessex: in the next great struggle in 892-96 the fighting was mostly in regions which Alfred had not owned in 876-78, and which had fallen under his domination since that date. For from Guthrum's defeat onward the borders of Wessex continued to grow, and Alfred at the time of his death had become suzerain over the larger part of the regions that had done his ancestor Ecgbert homage seventy years before. He had already commenced that reconquest of Central and Northern England which his descendants were to complete.

The immediate result of Ethandun was to throw the main stress of the Viking raids on to the Frankish realms for some thirteen years. In the time 878-91 fall the very worst humiliations suffered by the Carlovingian monarchy. It was in 881 that the Danes burnt Aachen, and desecrated the tomb of Charlemagne ; in 882 that the miserable treaty of Elsloo was made by Charles the Fat ; and in 885 that this unworthy inheritor of the imperial crown refused to fight for the relief of Paris, though all the armies of the Franks were ranged beneath his banner, and preferred to pay a "Danegelt" and abscond. It was not till 891 that the first notable check was given to the Vikings by the Emperor Arnulf's great victory on the Dyle, which delivered Inner Germany, though it did not save France. Meanwhile Alfred was enjoying a well-won immunity from attack, interrupted only by one short episode in 885-86, when there befell an isolated piratical descent on Rochester and a short war with the East-Anglian Danes, which must almost certainly be connected with that descent, and was probably caused by it. It was not till 892 that the "Great Army" from the Continent, after its defeat by Arnulf, transferred itself to England once more, and gave Alfred three years of hard fighting, in which the strength of the realm that he had reorganised during the long years of peace was demonstrated by a series of glorious successes.

The years 879-92, therefore, form an almost peaceful interval between the two periods of fighting, in 871-78 and 892-97, when Alfred's work as a general was more important than his work as an administrator. In the meantime he was not absolutely undisturbed, for there were always pirates on the seas, but he had sufficient leisure to work out some at least of the great schemes that he had pondered over in his much-troubled earlier life. We realise his well-deserved good fortune when we find frequent years [1] in the Anglo-Saxon Chronicle containing nothing but notes of embassies exchanged with Rome, or of events on the Continent with which the English were not directly concerned. This was indeed a case of "happy is the nation which has no history": for history in the Chronicle tends to be a record of military operations, and shrinks to a very narrow stream when wars are not afoot.

Before dealing with Alfred's civil and domestic activities, it may be well to explain the political importance of these central years of his reign. His position after the Pact of Chippenham and the departure of Guthrum's host was no more than that of King of Wessex, Sussex, and Kent. He did not even hold all that his father Aethelwulf had owned and governed, since Essex was relinquished to the Danes. London was also still in their power, though it seems to have been more or less in ruins ; but London since Offa's time had been reckoned a Mercian possession rather than the greatest town of Essex. The really important political question which concerned the future of the West Saxon realm at this moment was the fate of Mercia—not of those eastern parts of it which now formed a group of Danish burghs under many jarls, but of the western half, which the unhappy Ceolwulf II. had once governed. It seems pretty certain

---

[1] Such as 881, 883, 884, and the six years ' 887-92 ' [i.e., really 886-91].

that this phantom monarch had disappeared not long after the partition of Mercia in 877.   No successor was chosen to succeed him by the local Witan, and in the early eighties we find only ealdormen in his place.   Of these the chief[1] was a certain Aethelred, whose administrative sphere had probably been in the land of the Hwiccas before the break up of the Mercian kingdom.   He is found signing charters as "dux," *i.e.*, ealdorman, some years before Burhred's abdication and flight to Rome.   After the disappearance or death of Ceolwulf II. he seems to have achieved a certain pre-eminence over the other surviving magnates, and is even called on rare occasions *subregulus* : the Chronicle and charters occasionally style him also "Lord of Mercia" (Myrcna hlaford), so that his position was evidently something greater than that of an ordinary ealdorman,[2] After the departure of the Danes from Cirencester in 879, when he must have been left more or less his own master, he no doubt allied himself to Alfred.   The fact that he did not then take the title of king suggests that he accepted a position of inferiority towards the ruler of Wessex, as his predecessors, Wiglaf and Beorhtwulf, had done sixty years before.   But we cannot be sure that he definitely became his subject before 886, when "all the English submitted to Alfred except those who were under the bondage of the Danes".[3] The connection between the two was made firm by the marriage of Aethelflaed, Alfred's eldest daughter, to the ealdorman, probably at this same time,[4] and by the gift to him, certainly in 886, of London, then just recovered from the Danes.   It was apparently given him as a separate holding, not as a part of Mercia.   From that year on-

---

[1] But not the only one.   Mercian charters in Alfred's later years are often signed by three or even four ealdormen.

[2] Ethelweard, by a slip, no doubt, twice calls him *rex* in iv. § 3, but in other places *dux*.   Celtic sources sometimes make the same error (see Plummer's notes to A. S. C., ii. 118-19).   He is *subregulus* in a single charter (Birch, 561), *hlaford* in several (K. C. D., 313, 327, 339), and in the Chronicle, *sub anno* 911.

[3] A. S. C., *sub anno* 886.

[4] They are sometimes said to have been married in 880, but Aethelflaed is definitely said by Asser to have been kept at her father's court till she was marriageable (adveniente matrimonii tempore copulata est Merciorum comiti), which means thirteen to fifteen, not ten, and she cannot have been born before 870 (since her father only married in 869), and may have been a year younger yet.   The Worcester Charter, which seems to make her wedded in 880, is apparently wrongly dated, the indiction year corresponding to 887 (Birch, C. S., 547).   There are plenty of charters by the two signing together after 886.

ward Aethelred, though retaining a certain independent status (he sometimes granted charters without naming Alfred in them), was undoubtedly to be reckoned the subject rather than the ally of Wessex, so that the boundaries of that realm might be considered to extend as far as the Dee on one side and the Chilterns on the other. Aethelred, it may be remarked, seems to have waged many wars with the Welsh as well as the Danes: the *Annales Cambriae* tell us that in 877 Rodri, King of Gwynedd, was slain by the Saxons, and in 880 that Rodri's death was avenged by a victory at Conway. In the last case at least Aethelred must have been the enemy. Asser records that some years after this (but before 892 [1]) the South Welsh kings, Howell, Brochmail and Fernmail, were compelled by the " tyrannous force " of Aethelred and the Mercians to submit to King Alfred and take him for lord.[2] The North Welsh at this same time are said to have been allied with the Northumbrian Danes, " from whom they got no good, but rather harm," so that they, too, a little later than their southern brethren, did homage to Alfred and repudiated the unnatural alliance with the Vikings.

The submission of the Welsh kings was probably made after the events of 885-86, and the formal union of Mercia to Wessex. But we must return for a moment to that time. The trouble in it began with the landing of a Danish host at Rochester, the only incursion (as we have already pointed out) that happened between 878 and 892. This host was a fraction of the " Great Army " which lay that year at Amiens, and had been wasting all the lands of the Somme. It sat down before Rochester, which was now fortified and well defended; but before it had made any impression on the place Alfred came up with the whole *fyrd* of Wessex, beat the invaders, and compelled them to escape to sea, leaving behind them their horses, and their camp full of plunder and captives. It seems clear that Guthrum's Danes in East Anglia must have given some help or encouragement to this host, for we read that " the army which dwelt in East Anglia wantonly broke the peace ".[3] After the relief

---

[1] Before 892, because Hemeid, another Welsh king who submitted to Alfred at the same time, died in that year.

[2] Asser, § 80.

[3] Exercitus qui in Orientalibus Anglis habitavit pacem quam cum Aelfredo rege pepigerat opprobriose fregit (Asser, § 72).

of Rochester Alfred sent out a fleet from Kent against their coast "*praedandi causa*". One cannot conceive that the righteous king would have taken such a step without provocation. This fleet met sixteen Danish galleys at the mouth of the Stour, captured them and slew their crews. But the whole naval force of East Anglia then turned out, fought a second battle in the same estuary with the English fleet, and defeated it. This was not to be the end of the matter. Alfred in the next year (886) *post incendia urbium stragesque populorum*,[1] after considerable fighting, therefore, seized London, which had hitherto remained in the hands of the Danes; he "honourably restored the city and made it habitable," after which he handed it over to be kept by Aethelred, ealdorman of Mercia.[2] Ethelweard distinctly says that London had to be besieged before it was taken, and is probably right, though neither Asser nor the Chronicle mention a siege. Presumably from the language used by the two last-named authors the city was in a dilapidated condition, and needed rebuilding as well as repeopling with a new body of English inhabitants. Apparently Alfred planted there military settlers, the *burhware* of whom we hear a few years later. It would seem that the *cnihten-gild* of London, which appears in early charters, was the association of these original men of war, who were at first rather a garrison than mere colonists.[3] The border of the Danelaw was still so close that no one averse to hard blows would have dared to take up a grant of land or houses in the newly restored city.

Soon after the fortification of London, Guthrum and his people seem to have come to terms with Alfred, and to have made peace on the lines which he dictated. The document known as *Alfred and Guthrum's Frith* must belong to this year (886) as it precisely defines the boundary between Dane and Englishman according to the new condition of affairs. The frontier lies "up the Lea to its source, then straight across to the Ouse at Bedford, then along

---

[1] Asser, § 83.

[2] That London was not reckoned as a recovered part of Mercia, but as a new conquest bestowed on Aethelred personally, is (I think) shown by the fact that Edward the Elder resumed possession of it, and of Oxford, in 910 on Aethelred's death, while he allowed the Mercian state to exist a few years longer, while his sister Aethelflaed lived.

[3] *Cniht* = the military follower of a thane (see the statutes of the Cambridge Thegns' Gild and the Exeter Gild).

the Ouse to Watling Street ".   This line left London, with Middlesex, most of Hertfordshire and part of Bedfordshire (if we may use
names of a later date) to Alfred, and this, no doubt, was the amount
of territory that he had just won.   Beyond the spot near Stony
Stratford, where the Ouse is crossed by Watling Street, the definition of borders is not continued, obviously because Guthrum's
power did not extend over the rest of Danish Mercia, where
Northampton, Leicester and Derby were held by jarls who did
not owe him allegiance.   The *Frith* then proceeds to make rules
as well for peaceful intercourse between Englishman and Dane as
for the weregelds and other compensations due when individuals had
met and slain each other.   The two nations are valued at similar
rates, with obvious fairness and seeking for equality, save that the
Dane seems to get some preference, in the fact that his freemen are all
valued as if they were thegns of moderate value, and not reckoned
at the mere assessment of the English ceorls.   These later are
equated with the Danish *liesing* or freedman, who was a servile
dependant, presumably of English blood.

Having disposed of the political history of Alfred's central years,
we may turn to the far more interesting subject of his domestic
reforms during these fifteen years of comparative peace.   To the
reorganisation of the fighting force of Wessex, military and naval,
we have already had occasion to allude.   The fleet, whose origins
date back to before the campaign of Ethandun,[1] was largely increased in the time that followed.   We have mentions of small
successes by sea in 882, besides the considerable expedition already
alluded to in 886, when the coast of East Anglia was scoured.
It does not, however, seem to have been till the very end of Alfred's
reign that he worked out his new ideas in naval architecture, and
built the ships that were "nigh twice as long as those of others,
some with sixty oars and some with more, and they were both
swifter and steadier and also higher than others, shaped neither
like the Frisian nor the Danish vessels, but so as seemed to him
that they would be most efficient ".[2]   These improved galleys did
not make their *début* till 897.   But meanwhile the king had
already a fleet, and used it effectively.

Alfred's military reforms are more difficult to disentangle from

[1] See p. 449.   [2] A. S. Chronicle, *sub anno* 897.

those of his son, but a certain amount can be made out concerning them.   One was the systematic fortification of important towns: we note that after 878 the Danes are no longer able to seize every place near which they land, as they had been wont to do during the earlier campaigns.   Rochester is found prepared, and stands a siege in 885, so do Exeter and another unnamed Devonian fortress in 893, and Chichester is found well able to defend itself in 894. How carefully London was restored, presumably by the patching up of its Roman walls, when Alfred recovered it, we have already seen.   The only case where in these later wars we hear of an English stronghold being captured was that the Danes took Appledore in Kent, in 892, and this was " prisco opere castrum," [1] an ancient earthwork of early Saxon days, as opposed to one of the new *burhs*.

It would seem that the system by which Alfred's *burhs* were maintained was not unlike that which Henry the Fowler employed in Germany a generation later—probably the latter borrowed the idea from England.   To each stronghold, whether an old city like Winchester or Rochester, newly fortified, or a modern fortress created for strategical reasons, there was allotted a district consisting of a certain number of hides of land around it.   All the thegns dwelling on these hides were responsible for its defence: apparently they were bound to keep up a house within it, and either to reside there in person or to place a competent fighting man therein as a substitute.   These were the " burhware " or garrison-settlers of whom we hear repeatedly in Alfred's later wars. In 893 we are told in the Chronicle that the field army was distinct from " those men whose duty was to defend the burhs," and again that when a Danish force appeared on the Lower Severn the Western ealdormen were assisted by " the king's thegns who were then at home in the burhs ".   A regular system had evidently been established.

Now there exists a precious relic of the old English military organisation called the " Burghal Hidage " giving a list of all the lands dependent on the burhs of Wessex, with an appendix of three lines, apparently added at a later date, which includes Essex, Worcester and Warwick.   It has generally been attributed to the

[1] Ethelweard, iv. 3.

early years of Edward the Elder, Alfred's son, but there seems good reason for thinking that it may date back to his father.[1] The main document does not give statistics for any of the regions which were definitely Mercian, and were from 880 to 910 under the rule of Ealdorman Aethelred : Gloucester, Hereford, Worcester, Warwick, do not appear in it—though the last two are mentioned in the appendix.   This surely means that the burghal system was not yet fully organized in Mercia : for though Worcester was made a burh by Aethelred some time before Alfred's [2] death, Warwick only became one under Aethelflaed so late as 914.   Oxford, which does appear in the list (along with Buckingham), must probably have been given to Aethelred by Alfred, like London, as a personal possession, not as part of Mercia.   For when the ealdorman died in 910 Alfred's son Edward is recorded to have resumed these two places, though he allowed Mercia as an entity to continue for some years longer, under the rule of his sister Aethelflaed, the widow of Aethelred. Being mutilated at its beginning, which lies in the south-east, the Burghal Hidage does not deal with Kent or London.   It starts with the Sussex towns, works west to Devon, and then returns to Oxford, Berks, Buckingham and Surrey, Southwark being the last burh mentioned, before the total amount of hides is cast up as an addition sum.   There is no mention of Hertford, or of the other numerous fortresses constructed by Edward from 913 onward, while the fact that the vague heading " Essex, 3000 hides " appears in the appendix would seem to render it probable that this short addendum was made just when Alfred's son was building his burhs at Maldon, Witham, etc., at the same time as Hertford. On the other hand every place in Wessex mentioned in the Anglo-Saxon Chronicle as a fortress between 890 and 900 is duly recorded,[3] not only large towns like Exeter and Chichester, but the insignificant Wimborne and Twyneham (Christ Church).[4]

Taking into consideration these indications, and the notorious fact that Alfred was an originator and reformer, while Edward was

[1] For a long consideration of the Hidage, attributing it to the years 911-19, see Chadwick's *Anglo-Saxon Institutions*, 205-17.

[2] This foundation is vouched for by the Charter Kemble C.D., 1075.

[3] With the exception of Appledore which (as we have already seen, p. 468) was not a " burh " with proper " burhware ".

[4] Mentioned in 900, just after Alfred's death.

but an inheritor, it seems natural to ascribe the whole burghal
system to the father rather than to the son.   Indeed the repeated
mentions of *burhware* and their garrison duty during the wars of
892-96 almost compel us to believe that the new arrangements
were in full working order by the first-named year.

There were evidently many improvements made in the field
army, as well as in fortification, during Alfred's central years.   One
was the division of the *fyrd*, or national levy, into two halves,
of which only one was called out for service at once, the other
relieving it at stated intervals.   This arrangement is mentioned
during the campaign of 893 ; it was the only one by which a large
force could be permanently kept in the field.   Something of the
same sort was put into practice for the king's personal military
retinue, in times of comparative peace, when it was only necessary
to have the nucleus of a force in hand.   All the fighting men of
the royal household (*bellatores et ministri nobiles* [1]) were bound
to follow the king's court for a month, and then went home to
their estates for two months, coming back to relieve each other in
turn.   All of course were called out together in the case of serious
war.

It seems probable that Alfred was also the originator of that
extension of the thegnhood, as a professional military class, which
is found working in the tenth century after his death.   We are, as
in the case of the *burhs*, not able to separate his work from that
of his heirs with absolute certainty.   But when we reflect on his
original genius, and remember that he had to face the worst crisis
of the Danish wars, when fighting men had to be procured at all
costs and in every possible way, we are inclined to credit him with
the invention of this expedient for multiplying them, even though
the first clear record of it dates from much later times.   It took the
shape of enlisting into the ranks of the nobility-of-service, liable to
permanent military duty, of all the more prosperous and energetic
of the middle class both in the countryside and in the towns.   The
ceorl who " throve so that he had fully five hides of land, and a
helm and mail shirt, and a sword ornamented with gold," as also
" church and kitchen, belfry, *burh-geat*, with *setl* [2] and special service

[1] Asser, § 100.
[2] For the *burh-geat* and *setl*, see Stevenson in *Eng. Hist. Review*, for 1891, pp.
489-95.

in the king's hall" was entitled to be *gesithcund*,[1] or as another law phrased it, "of thegn-right worthy". A second draft of the first-mentioned document even allows the ceorl who has the complete military equipment, but not fully the five hides of land, to slip into the privileged class. Moreover "the merchant who has fared three times over the high seas at his own expense" is granted the same boon—as a premium for wealth and energy, for he clearly must be a man of substance, no less than the ceorl who has obtained the five hides. It appears from other laws that the attaining to be "of thegn-right worthy" did not ennoble the blood of the promoted ceorl, though it made his weregeld equal to that of a thegn, and gave him the personal rights of the class. But it is only when his son and his son's son have continued to prosper, and to keep the necessary possessions, that their descendants will all remain of *gesithcund* rank.[2]

In return for their personal promotion in the social scale, the ceorl and merchant had of course to assume the duties of a thegn, and to follow the king to war whenever he raised his banner, no longer getting off with the more incidental military service required from all freemen as members of the *fyrd*. Often the service must have been the garrison duty in a burh, for the wealthy ceorl with five hides must have been precisely the sort of person whom the king wished to connect with the nearest fortress to his place of residence, and to fix there by his "burh-geat" and obligatory residential home within it. In London the merchant-thegn must have been a well-known figure, perhaps he may have been found in smaller numbers in *burhs* like Southampton, Hastings, Portchester, Exeter, Southwark or Rochester. However recruited, the professional fighting class in England was obviously growing both more numerous and more efficient in Alfred's day, even if these later rules were not perfected by him. It is probable, on the other hand, that the relative importance of the ceorls in English society must have been diminished in the end, when all the wealthier and more energetic members of their order were gradually promoted

---

[1] All this comes from the document called "Of Ranks of the People" (Be Leod gethincthum). See Liebermann's edition of the Anglo-Saxon Laws, i. 456-57. The editor dates this document as an ancient original, worked up by a reviser in or after 1027. " *Sie verrathen, neben älteren Kernen, Spüren von Abfassung nach* 1027."

[2] Also from the "Ranks of the People," § 11, in the continuation called "North-People's Law".

into the thegnhood. This was probably an important factor among the numerous causes which seem to have led to the depreciation of the status of the poorer freeman, during the last two centuries of the existence of the Anglo-Saxon monarchy.

Nothing concerning these reforms can be deduced from Alfred's Collection of Laws, which is, in truth, rather a disappointing document to the student of constitutional history. It is not a complete and all-embracing code, cancelling earlier legislation, but rather a revision of the laws of the ancient kings, especially of those of Ine, with a view to the changed state of society in the ninth century. It begins, however, with a curious preface, in which is inserted a great part of the Mosaic Law from Exodus xx.-xxviii., some fifty clauses of the severest retaliatory ordinances, followed by the note that Our Lord, though He came into the world not to destroy but to fulfil the law, inculcated mercy and mild-heartedness, and laid down the golden rule that we should not do unto other men that which we would not have them do unto us. Wherefore Christian kings and synods have rightly reduced the harshness of the old Mosaic ordinances, and for the most part replaced death and mutilation by money penalties. There remains, however, one crime which cannot properly be compounded—treason against a man's lawful lord: Jesus Himself could not remit the penalty of Judas.[1] This is a notable point: earlier English kings had no such conception of treason as the unpardonable sin, and indeed the statement of the weregeld payable for a slain king is found repeatedly in Anglo-Saxon legislation. Alfred then proceeds to state that his Dooms are a selection from those of the kings who were before him, such as Aethelbert, Ine and Offa. He has selected those which pleased him, and those which displeased him he has cancelled, using the counsel of his Witan, and sets other decisions in their stead. But—and this is most curious—he adds that he has not made many changes, because "he knew not how it might like them that came after him".[2] Hence Alfred's laws are of a more archaic type than we might have expected, repeating old dooms in the old form, where we might have expected something more different from the laconic and often puzzling language of Ine and Aethelbert. Once more we are plunged into the midst of minute and tedious recapitulation of the penalties for cutting and

---

[1] Alfred, Laws, Preface, 49, § 7.   [2] *Ibid.*, Preface, 49, § 9.

wounding, trespass, brawling, cattle stealing, etc., etc. We could
wish that he had shown less regard for the counsel of his Witan
and the susceptibilities of future generations, and had issued a
new and original *Code Napoleon* of his own.

This we feel all the more strongly because we know that Alfred
had a great juristic reputation in his own day. Asser has a most
curious paragraph concerning this. " His subjects, both noble and
simple, used to have the most violent dissensions in the courts of
his ealdormen and reeves, and hardly any man would accept the
doom passed upon him by reeve or ealdorman as good law. And
under the stress of these violent and obstinate wranglings, they
would pledge themselves each one to undergo judgment by the
king, and both sides would hasten to fulfil the agreement. And this
although the man who was conscious that he had not true justice
on his side was most unwilling to come, of his own accord, to the
judgment of such a judge, and appeared unwillingly, compelled to
plead by the force of law and his own pledge. For he knew that
nothing of his malice would escape notice, since the king was a most
efficient investigator in dealing with lawsuits, as he was in every
other branch of business. And he would make sagacious inquiries concerning almost all the litigation that took place in his realm outside
his presence, to see whether decisions were just or unjust. And if
he detected any unjust dealing of the judges, he would interrogate
them in a mild fashion, as was his disposition, either personally
interviewing them, or sending some trusted minister, concerning the
reasons why they had given such bad decisions, whether by ignor-
ance, or from some other fault, from love or fear of the one side, or
hatred of the other, or even for greed of bribes." Whereupon some
got dismissed from their offices, but the majority set themselves to
study law in an honest fashion, " so that it was a strange sight to
see the ealdormen, who were almost all illiterate from infancy, and
the reeves and other officials, learning how to read, preferring this
unaccustomed and laborious discipline to losing the exercise of their
power ".[1]

All this paragraph is very curious and interesting, because it
does not agree with our fundamental conception of Anglo-Saxon
law. In the courts of the reeve or the ealdorman, that is to say, in
the burgh or the shire, the " suitors were the judges," and the king's

[1] Asser, § 106.

official was theoretically only the mouthpiece of the assembly, declaring the " doom " which they decided was applicable to the case
before them. The only way in which regular appeals to the king
could be made was that, if one of the lower courts failed to do justice within a proper limit of time, the litigant could appeal to the
shire moot, and if this also failed the king might be asked to force
the shire moot to act. Asser speaks as if the reeves and ealdormen
were real judges, giving decisions on their own responsibility, and
as if the appeal to the king was normal. We must perhaps conclude that, whatever their theoretical position, the royal officials
often forced their own views on the suitors of the court, who might
naturally be subservient to persons of such importance, so that
the "doom" was practically the ealdorman's and not the suitors'.
And the appeals to Alfred must be regarded as extrajudicial appli-
cations, under a private voluntary pledge-agreement, or as a sort of
foreshadowing of the Chancery cases of the later Middle Ages, not
as mere moving the king to force the local courts to act. There
was nothing to prevent him from acting as an arbitrator if privately
consulted by two litigants. Asser, being a Welshman, and un-
skilled in the technicalities of English law, has probably miscon-
ceived the legal meaning of the business which he frequently saw
laid before the king. But his testimony cannot be disputed as to
the fact that Alfred was perpetually revising law suits, or again concerning the way in which he compelled his officials, small and great,
to study the law which they had to administer. Since they had to
learn reading in order to master it, they were clearly referred by the
king to written codes, such as Ine's, Offa's, or his own.[1]

From Asser we get also certain meagre information as to King
Alfred's Budget, not (alas!) details as to its amount, or its heads—
how much came from royal demesne estates, how much from legal
fines, how much from taxation—but a notice as to the way in which
he spent his revenues. He instructed his ministers to divide the
total of his annual revenues into two equal halves. The first half
was devoted to purely secular purposes ; and this he subdivided into
three parts. The first of these thirds was spent on his military
retinue and noble officials, who abode at his court in due turn of
office. The second third was spent on his artificers, of whom he

[1] For all this see the admirable note on pp. 342-43 of Stevenson's edition of
Asser.

kept an enormous number, sought out from many nations, men instructed in every sort of art that exists in the earth. The last third
was spent on the strangers who came to him from every race, far
and near, some asking money and some not, in accordance with their
relative personal importance—such people no doubt as the Scandinavian sea-captains, Ohthere and Wulfstan, who gave him so
much curious geographical information.

So much for the secular expenses. The second half of Alfred's
revenue was devoted to purposes which he regarded as directly or
indirectly connected with religion. He divided it into four parts
of equal amount : the first was spent entirely on the poor, on St.
Gregory's principle, "neither little to whom much should be given,
nor much to whom little, nor nothing to the man who should have
something, nor something to the man who should have nothing ".
The second fourth served as the endowment of the two religious
houses which Alfred founded, a monastery at Athelney, his old
camp of refuge in 878, and a nunnery at Shaftesbury. The third
quarter was spent on his great school, of which more hereafter,
where boys of all conditions were reared in English and Latin learning. The last fourth was a kind of special emergencies fund, which
Alfred employed to make gifts to any church or monastery which
was in great temporary need, not only in Wessex or Mercia, but
sometimes in Wales, Cornwall, France, Brittany, Northumbria, or
even Ireland. There were a special series of gifts to Rome, carried
by various ealdormen and abbots, which are mentioned in 883,
887, 888, 890, and probably were sent in other years also ; they
are called the " Alms of the West Saxons and of King Alfred," but
whether they were occasional donations, or represented Offa's old
grant, or some other national subsidy, it is not possible to decide.
But sometimes we are told, as in 889, that there was no regular
embassy in a particular year, though the king sent to Rome two
letters by the hands of couriers. The most astonishing notice of
the king's liberality is the statement in several manuscripts of the
Chronicle, under the year 883, that two English envoys, in pursuance
of a vow made by Alfred " when they sat down before the host that
was in London," [1] carried alms to Rome, and also to India, to St.
Thomas and St. Bartholomew. This seems a very far journey, con-

[1] Probably in 872, long years before ; possibly in 879, when the Danes were at
Fulham, near London.

sidering the state of the East and the difficulties of the road, and the fact has been generally doubted.[1] Indeed the words might be construed to mean that gifts for the Indian shrines were sent to Rome, to be forwarded from thence if possible. But it is certain that Alfred did correspond with Elias, patriarch of Jerusalem, who sent him letters begging for charity to ransom captive bishops and monks of Cappadocia, and no doubt received a favourable answer.[2]

Of all Alfred's expenses those which interest us most are the sums given to foreign scholars, and to the schools. It may be said without exaggeration that he revived learning in England when it was almost absolutely extinct. The generation of Alcuin, when men of culture were still bred in the island, had long been dead when Alfred came to the throne. The picture which he himself gives, in his letter to the bishops to whom he sent the gift of new copies of Gregory's *Pastoral Care*, is most distressing. He says that in old days the English clergy had been as eager to teach as to learn, and men came from abroad to England for wisdom and instruction. " But so clean fallen away was learning now in the Angle race, that there were very few on this side Humber who would know how to render their service-book into English, or to read off an epistle out of Latin into English, and I ween there would not be many on the other side of Humber. So few of them were there that I cannot think of so much as a single one South of Thames when I took to the realm." Alfred then calls to mind his memory of the days of his youth, when Wessex had not yet felt the ravages of the heathen to any great extent—the churches had been well furnished with libraries and the clergy were numerous, but they profited little by the books, because they could not well understand the Latin in which all were written. " We have lost both the wealth and the wisdom, because we were not willing to bend our minds to the pursuit of learning."

The moment that he had the power and the leisure, Alfred set to work to collect about him the few scholars who were yet to be found in England. All the four who are first mentioned were Mercians, a fact which bears out the king's just-quoted statement

[1] See note to Stevenson's *Asser*, pp. 288-89. The only corroboration comes from William of Malmesbury, who says that jewels brought back by the English envoys from India were still at Sherborne (*Gesta Regum, c.* 122).

[2] See Asser, § 9, and Stevenson's note thereon.

that Wessex had become absolutely illiterate.   These four were Plegmund, afterwards Archbishop of Canterbury (890-914); Werfrith,
Bishop of Worcester (873-915), with Aethelstan and Werwulf,
who both became the king's chaplains.   While they were still the
only men of learning that he could find, he kept them about his
court, and would always contrive to have one of them at his side,
for at every spare moment of night or day he wished to have books
read to him, Latin or English, and it was not till 887 (as Asser
tells us) that he was able to read freely for himself.   To these four
Mercian scholars were afterwards added several foreigners, Asser
himself, a South Welshman, to whom we owe most of our details
of Alfred's life, though he was a sadly inadequate biographer,
John the Old Saxon, and Grimbald the Frank, a monk of St.
Bertin.   All these, after serving the king for some time, received
great preferment—Asser was made in 892 Bishop of Sherborne;
John, abbot of the king's foundation at Athelney ; Grimbald, abbot
of the new minster at Winchester.   From this little band of men of
letters Alfred gradually developed once more a body of learned
clergy, though the task of reclaiming the English to letters proved
no easy one.   We are told, in particular, that he found it almost
impossible to find men with a vocation, to set in the monasteries
which were to be the sanctuaries of learning.   Parents would make
over young boys to him, but few grown men would submit themselves to the rigour of the monastic rule : those who took orders preferred to become secular priests.   To fill up the new community
of Athelney Alfred had to import foreign monks of many races,
including some stray Franks, of whom Asser tells us a dreadful
tale—how they not only schemed to murder their abbot, John the
Old Saxon, but to fix a charge of shameful sin upon his memory.

But, hard as the task was, Alfred succeeded in carrying it
through.   "God Almighty be thanked! We have now teachers
in office," he could write.   But he was not contented with having
a learned clergy : it was his object to build up a learned laity also.
We have already seen how his admonitions sent middle-aged and
illiterate ealdormen and reeves to con over the alphabet.   But the
more promising method was to catch the young.   Hence came the
institution of his great school, to which he allured the children of
almost the whole of his thegnhood and many of less noble birth
also.   "In which school books of both tongues, Latin and English,

were assiduously read, and they had time to learn writing also, and became studious and ingenious in the liberal arts, before they had the strength to turn themselves to other avocations, such as hunting, and the other accomplishments in which noble youths should be conversant." [1] Aethelweard, Alfred's younger son, was brought up in this school, and became a good scholar. His elder brother Edward and Alfred's second daughter Aelfthryth were also great readers of books, as Asser informs us, and never fell into the idle and unprofitable ways that are a snare to princes.

Alfred's exertions gave England for many years an educated governing class, in which laymen as well as clergy were included. How long the impulse lasted may be judged from the fact that three full generations after his death there were lay magnates capable of writing freely in Latin. His kinsman Aethelweard, the descendant in the fourth degree of his brother Aethelred, *patricius, consul, et quaestor*, as he oddly styles himself (presumably meaning that he was an aetheling and an ealdorman, and had been a king's reeve), was able to compile a chronicle, which he dedicated to his distant cousin Matilda, the great-granddaughter of Alfred, [2] somewhere about the year 975. Its Latin is pompous and rhetorical, adorned with affected Greek words and inappropriate classical tags, [3] but it is astonishing to find in the tenth century a high secular official of royal descent who can write a Latin book of any sort, still more so one who does it for pure love of historical research and love of family antiquities. The phenomenon is unparalleled in the lands of Continental Christendom.

How Alfred worked with his scholar-chaplains on the translation of the Latin books which he turned into English is sufficiently shown by their internal evidence, which fully bears out the statement of Asser that he did it largely "*sensum ex sensu ponens*" not by literal rendering of word for word. The king himself, in his preface to the *Pastoral Care*, says also that "he turned into English the book that is called *Pastoralis*, sometimes word for word, sometimes sense for sense, just as he learned it of Plegmund

---

[1] Asser, § 75.

[2] Through Eadgyth, her mother, daughter of Edward the Elder, who married the emperor Otho I.

[3] He thinks it fine to call Edgar "anax," and Eadwig the Fair "pancalus" A slain prince " sub Acheronteas peregrinam tentat regionem undas," etc.

and Asser, Grimbald and John; and after he had learned it so that he could understand it and render it with fullest meaning, then he Englished it". This implied a very free treatment of the text: in the translation of Orosius's General History, in particular, the king inserted whole paragraphs of his own, including a complete reconstruction of the geographical chapters concerning Germany, the Baltic lands, and the North, and a narrative of the voyages of two explorers who had come to his court and told him of their voyages, Ohthere, the Norseman, who had rounded the North Cape and discovered the White Sea and "Biarmaland," and Wulfstan, the Dane, who had travelled in Prussia and Esthonia, at the east end of the Baltic. The translation of Boethius's *Consolation of Philosophy* is equally free, if not so much interpolated. Alfred turns into definitely Christian language much that the ancient senator of Theodoric had put in vaguer phrases, for Boethius wrote as one inspired by the theism of the Greek philosophers rather than by doctrinal Christianity. Alfred paraphrased the words of Boethius into terms that suited a day when religious thought must be necessarily and formally Christian. In this he was apparently following earlier Latin commentators on the *Consolation*, who had made similar, if less notable and widespread, dealings with the text.

We know a good deal of Alfred's intercourse with his scholars, but unfortunately very little of his dealings with his artificers (*operatores*), to whose sustentation, according to Asser, he devoted no less than a sixth of his revenue.[1] They were very numerous, and worked in all manner of crafts—no doubt smiths, builders, illuminators, carvers and jewellers are included. Of the gold work that he inspired we have the one surviving specimen in the famous Athelney jewel, to which allusion has already been made. Some of these productions must have been very large and valuable— the *aestels* (book-markers?) which he sent to each bishop of England along with his translation of the *Pastoral Care* were worth fifty *mancuses* each, and the mancus of the ninth century was a gold piece valued at thirty pennies, and weighing about 65 grains. Apparently work in gold and silver was sometimes applied to domestic or church decoration, for Asser makes allusion to "*aedificiis aureis*

---

[1] Asser, § 101.

et argenteis incomparabiliter, illo edocente, fabricatis.[1] But architecture, as we are told, was specially dear to him: not merely the military art applied to *burhs* and town walls, but the civil branch appealed to him. "He constructed in wonderful style royal halls and chambers of stone and wood. Ancient kingly residences of stone were moved by his orders from their former positions, and sumptuously rebuilt in more suitable places."[2] His fortress of Athelney and the monastery within it were finished "*pulcherrima operatione*". It is curious to find that among his retainers, along with his jewellers and architects, we find his huntsmen and hawkers mentioned, to whom he gave much instruction, being skilled above all other men of his time in field sports. Nor did his ingenuity disdain such small inventions as the candle-clocks to which Asser devotes a whole paragraph—waxen tapers of a fixed length and weight, protected by lanterns of horn, of which six would exactly measure out a day of twenty-four hours. Truly this was a many-sided man.

After fifteen years of comparative peace from 878 to 892, Alfred was, as we have already said, subjected to one more great Danish invasion—the indirect result of the checks which the "Great Army" had suffered from the Emperor Arnulf in 891 and in minor operations which followed his great victory on the Dyle.[3] Alfred had probably some notice of their setting forth, which must have been a lengthy business, for they collected no less than two hundred and fifty vessels at Boulogne, and shipped on board not only their material but their horses. Indeed one authority tells us that they built galleys in the harbour of Boulogne, which must have taken months.[4] This force, as we are told, was the same army which had been lying in Flanders and Brabant, and had fought the Germans. The names of its leaders are not given. But at the same time a smaller fleet of eighty vessels came into English

---

[1] But perhaps the *aedificia* were merely shrines.   [2] Asser, § 91.

[3] There seems to be almost certainty that the A. S. Chronicle is a year out in its dates here, and that the original landing was in the autumn of 892, and not in that of 893. Indeed Ethelweard says that the "Great Army" had been defeated by Arnulf *one year* before, and the battle of the Dyle was certainly in 891, and the Annals of St. Neot's start the Danes from Boulogne in 892.

[4] "Barbari Bononiam petunt, ibique construunt classem," says Ethelweard, who in this campaign is an authority not to be despised, and gives many facts omitted by the A. S. Chronicle.

waters, commanded by Hasting, or Haesten, the most famous of
all the Viking leaders of this age, whose name had been the
terror of the Western Franks for thirty years, and whose ravages
had extended even to the Mediterranean. He came not from
Flanders but from the Somme, where he had been conducting
separate operations of his own. Presumably the two hosts had
agreed to concert their operations, since there would be a great
advantage in distracting Alfred by a double attack ; but it is possible that the other chiefs had refused to put themselves under the
command of Hasting, who had a bad reputation for greed and
selfishness.

The " Great Army " came ashore late in the autumn in a rather
unexpected place, the mouth of the harbour of Lymne on the
borders of Kent and Sussex, which lies on no good water-way, and
is not near any considerable town. But in those days it had a
long tidal creek running inland for four miles, though this has now
silted up completely. Inland from it lay only the vast forest of
the Andredsweald, some 120 miles long. It was probably owing to
the remoteness of this landing-place from Canterbury and London
that hardly any opposition was offered : the only fighting that
took place was the storm of an old earthwork " prisco opere castrum " at Appledore, which " a few ceorls " tried to defend. The
Danes dragged their ships up to this point, and made it their base-
camp, stockading themselves in haste. A very short time afterwards the other fleet, under Hasting, appeared in the Thames
estuary, and landed at Middeltune on the Swale (the modern
Milton), a much more obvious goal for an invading army : here
they too built themselves a " winter camp ". From both strongholds
plundering bands went out at once, but it is notable that no attempt was made to begin serious operations against any of the
English fortified places in Kent, such as Rochester or Canterbury.
No doubt these were well guarded by their " burhware ". But we
have no mention of any English field-army being at hand, as might
have been expected even in this late season of the year. Possibly,
however, the fyrd was already in arms, though no notice of its
presence occurs.

Alfred's main dread seems to have been that this invasion
might be supported by the Danes already settled in England, the
Northumbrian and East Anglian hosts. Accordingly we are told

that he endeavoured to overawe them, and succeeded so far that
they gave him hostages, and promised to keep the peace. A word
is perhaps needed in this place to explain the position of these
settlers. The Eastern army had apparently given no trouble since
Alfred and Guthrum's "frith" of 886. They were now under the
rule of a king called Eohric (Eric), apparently an elected successor
of Guthrum, who had died in 890, and had been buried as a
Christian at Hadleigh ; whether he was kin to Guthrum is uncertain.
The Northumbrian Danes we have not mentioned since Halfdene
established himself as king at York and "divided up the land" in
877. Since then their history had been most obscure. Halfdene had
reigned only one year when he was expelled by his subjects "because
of his tyranny".[1] After a long interregnum the Northern host raised
up as king one Guthred or Cnut, the son of Harthacnut, who was a
Christian, and is said to have been sold as a slave in his youth.
Owing to his religion he treated his English subjects with great
consideration, and lived on the best of terms with the Bishops
Wulfred of York and Eardwulf of Lindisfarne, who had been
wandering unhappily in the wilds for some years. Eardwulf is
said to have helped largely in making him king. He reigned from
883 till 894, apparently dying just at the moment when the invasion of Hasting and the "Great Army" was giving Alfred
trouble.[2] We are told by Simeon of Durham, that he had been on
good terms with the King of Wessex, a statement that squares in
sufficiently well with the fact that hostages were sent in by the
Northumbrian in the beginning of 893.[3] An extremely rare
Anglo-Danish penny, which bears Cnut-Guthred's name on one
side and Alfred's on the other, would seem to bear witness to a
close connection between them, if not to the Northumbrian's actual
submission to Alfred as suzerain.[4] But early in 894 Guthred was

[1] According to the Irish chroniclers he then came over to their island, and was
killed in battle in Strangford Lough. See Steenstrup, *Normannerne*, ii. 91.
[2] So Simeon of Durham, who should be the best authority for Northern affairs,
but Ethelweard makes him die in 896.
[3] That the Guthred of Simeon of Durham and Ethelweard, and the Cnut, whose
name appears on a numerous series of Northumbrian coins, were one and the same
was first suggested by Mr. Haigh, and has been practically demonstrated by Steenstrup, *Normannerne*, ii. 73 *et sqq.*
[4] See British Museum *Catalogue of Saxon Coins*, i. 201. The only possible
way of refusing credence to the idea of Cnut's doing homage to Alfred is to say that

succeeded by another Dane, one Siefred (or Sievert or Sigferth),[1] who was unfriendly to Wessex, and (as we shall see) threw himself into the wars of 893-96 with energy on the side of the Vikings.

The campaign of 893 seems to have begun early in the year, and to have continued throughout its course. When the earliest possible moment for operations began, Alfred mobilised both his thegnhood and the *fyrd*, making the arrangement that one-half of the latter should always be in the field, while the other half came out to relieve it at intervals. The king placed himself in Kent, encamping between the two winter camps of the Vikings, " as near as he could for the wood-fastnesses and the water-fastnesses," so that he might be able to reach either of them, in case they should seek any open country. But they would not issue from their strongholds to seek a decisive battle : " the army did not come out of their station with their whole force oftener than twice, once when they first came to land, before the *fyrd* was assembled, and a second time when they finally resolved to evacuate their position ". This did not prevent them from sending out small raiding bands, who crept out through the woods of the Weald and looked for unguarded points. Alfred sent out similar detachments against the plunderers, and there was much petty skirmishing, but no decisive engagement. Meanwhile he opened negotiations with Hasting and the smaller force at Milton on the Swale, who apparently found themselves cooped in, and were anxious to get away from a dangerous situation. Hasting offered to depart, took oaths, and gave hostages : he even handed over his two sons to be baptised. The king became the godfather of the one, Ealdorman Aethelred of the other.[2] But on being permitted to depart he only transferred himself across the Thames Estuary to Bemfleet in Essex, and built another camp there on ground that was safe to him, for the East Anglian Danes (no doubt by previous agreement) received him in friendly guise, and adhered to his cause, breaking their oaths with Alfred. He then began to ravage the

this coin was struck by an ignorant Danish moneyer, who put together two types at random.

[1] Probably Cnut-Guthred and Siefred reigned together for a short time in 893-94, for there are some rare pennies bearing both their names. See British Museum, *Saxon Coins*, i. 221. Siefred broke the peace before Guthred's death.

[2] The sequence of all this is given in very confused order by the A. S. Chronicle. See Mr. Plummer's *Notes*, ii. 107-8.

neighbouring English lands (the regions around London no doubt) and sent word to the "Great Army" at Appledore, bidding them despatch their ships round the North Foreland to join him, while their main force should break out across the Lower Thames, and come round on land to Essex. These schemes seemed possible, because a new distraction had been prepared to draw off King Alfred from his central position in Kent. The Danes of Northumbria, or part of them headed by Siefred, had come into the plot, and had agreed to attack West Wessex by sea. A smaller squadron of forty ships sailing down the Irish Sea was to fall upon the north coast of Devon; the main fleet, strengthened up to 100 vessels by aid from the East Anglian Danes, was to go along the Channel under Siefred's command against the south coast.

The timing of the campaign did not succeed : indeed all such complicated schemes were at the mercy of wind and weather. But the "Great Army," leaving only a small division in charge of their ships, came out in force through the Andredsweald, and, keeping to the woods so as to conceal their march, descended upon West Surrey, East Berkshire, and North-East Hampshire, where they took much booty. But they had gained only a few days' start when they were attacked by the English main army, which no doubt passed from Kent across Surrey, when the news of the departure of the enemy from Appledore came to hand. This army was commanded for the moment by the Aetheling Edward, Alfred's eldest son, his father being absent from headquarters, apparently in Wessex. The Vikings were intercepted at Farnham, where a pitched battle took place : they were routed with great loss, their king was wounded, and only a disordered remnant escaped across the Thames. These were chased into Thorney, a marshy island on the Hertfordshire Colne, where they stockaded themselves. The Aetheling and his force beleaguered them in this last refuge for some time, till both besiegers and besieged were short of provisions. Then the fyrd went home, both because its food had run out, and because Alfred himself was reported to be at hand with the relieving body of levies whose service was just beginning—a sufficiently unmilitary proceeding which we are surprised to find occurring when such good soldiers as Alfred and Edward were in the field. But the king's corps never arrived at Thorney, for on his way thither he got the news that the fleets of the Northumbrian Danes had descended on Devonshire

and were beleaguering the one Exeter, and the other an unnamed
town on the north coast, perhaps Pilton by Barnstaple, which is
the *burh* of North Devon in the *Burghal Hidage* list. The king
resolved to march to the relief of Exeter with his main host, only
detaching his son with a fraction of his troops—probably Surrey
and Kentish levies—to observe the Danes in Thorney. These last,
we are surprised to hear, had not taken the opportunity of escaping
to Essex, because their wounded king could not safely be moved.
Hence they were still in their old stockade when the Aetheling
appeared once more in front of them: he was soon joined by
Ealdorman Aethelred, who came up to his aid from London with a
Mercian force. Between them they succeeded in constraining the
wrecks of the "Great Army" to come to terms: the Vikings gave
hostages, and promised to quit Alfred's realm. But when they had
been let go they only retired into East Anglia, and joined their
compatriots there, who were in arms against the English.

Meanwhile Alfred had reached Exeter: on his near approach
the Northumbrian expeditionary force hastily retired to their ships,
and fled out into the Channel. But they continued to hang about
the south coast, where we find them still lingering in the spring of
the next year.

Hasting now appears as taking up the main stress of the campaign. His own force at Bemfleet had been joined by the ships of
the "Great Army" from Appledore, and the proportion of their
crews who had not gone off on the disastrous raid through the
Andredsweald. Probably many of the East Anglian Danes of
King Eric were with him also. Leaving his camp and the ships in
charge of a garrison, he had gone out to ravage Alfred's borders.[1]
He was in Aethelred's territory, but whether in the direction of
Hertford and Buckingham, or even farther afield we cannot say, as
the Chronicle merely tells us that his sin was great, in that he was
devastating lands in the possession of the ealdorman who had become his son's godfather only a few months before. During his
absence the English force lately victorious at Thorney, presumably
with Edward and Aethelred in command, strengthened by the

[1] The A. S. C. annal only says that he was ravaging in Aethelred's ealdormanry. Had he possibly gone out on an attempt to relieve the host beleaguered in
Thorney by a blow at Mercia, and not got back in time when this manœuvre
failed? Ethelweard mixes up this raid with the subsequent move to Buttington.

London *buhrware* and other succours, marched on Bemfleet. The
garrison came out to meet them, but they routed it, and captured
the camp, with the ships lying beached beside it, and an enormous
bulk of plunder, besides the wives and children both of Hasting's
own force and of the men of the "Great Army". Among the
prisoners were Hasting's own wife and his two young sons. The
ships were either broken in pieces or carried off to London and
Rochester. The captives were sent to Alfred, who was apparently
still in the West Country. At some subsequent period the magnanimous king sent them back in safety to Hasting, probably at
the moment when the viking finally left England.

The long campaign of 893 was not yet at an end. Hasting
returned from his raid to find his fleet destroyed and his companions
scattered, but he did not give up the game. He established himself
at Shoebury, not far from the ruined camp at Bemfleet, and there
rallied the fugitives. His next move was to strike West once more,
with the assistance of considerable reinforcements drawn from the
East Anglian Danes, and (what is more surprising) from the Northumbrians also. The course of the raid was along the north side
of Thames and then across Gloucestershire to the Severn. Possibly
Hasting was wishing to get into communication with one or both
of the Northumbrian fleets which had been driven off from Devonshire by the king. Or, again, he may have been tempted to attack
Mercia because it was not yet so fully provided with *burhs* as
Wessex: we shall presently see that nearly twenty years later important frontier places like Warwick, Tamworth, Stafford, and
Chester still required fortification. At any rate Hasting pressed
right across Mercia to the Severn before he was brought to bay.
But he was presently beset by a very large force: not only was
Aethelred out against him with the local levies of the land, but
two ealdormen, Aethelhelm of Wiltshire and Aethelnoth of Somerset, brought up the fyrd of Central Wessex, and some of the kings
of the Welsh joined in on the other side—probably those princes of
Gwent and Demetia whom Asser records as having done homage to
Alfred a few years before.[1] These converging forces caught Hasting
between them, and he was compelled, after a fight, to stockade him-

---

[1] They are called "people of the North Welsh" by the Chronicle, but North
Wales means everything beyond Bristol Channel, as opposed to West Wales, *i.e.*,
Cornwall.

self and assume the defensive at Buttington, apparently Buttington
in Tidenham, on the estuary of the Severn, not the village west of
Shrewsbury of the same name.[1] Here he remained shut up for
many weeks, perhaps awaiting the expected arrival of the Northumbrian fleet of Siefred from Devon. But we are told that King
Alfred " was in the West, against the fleet," all this time, perhaps
with a naval as well as a military force. After having eaten all their
store of food and many of their horses, the Danes made a sally
against the force who were blocking the eastern side of their camp,
and cut their way through, but with enormous loss. " That part
which got away only escaped by flight." Hasting then fled back
into friendly Danish territory, presumably East Mercia, and finally
returned to Shoebury.

But all this was not the last act but only the last act but one of
the extraordinary campaign of 893. Late in autumn, apparently,
Hasting, having recruited his ranks with many adventurers from
East Anglia and Northumbria, made one last raid. " Going at one
stretch day and night" apparently across the territory of his allies,
north of Watling Street, he suddenly appeared once more on the
extreme northern border of Mercia, and seized the " waste chester," the old Roman Deva on the Dee, where he repaired the
broken walls and fortified himself. This time he had escaped the
notice of his enemy ; the Mercian *fyrd* was not gathered in time
and never overtook him. But they came up at last, and found
him unwilling to fight in the open : " whereupon they beset the
place two days, and took all the cattle of the Danes and slew all the
men whom they overtook outside, and burned all the corn, and
with their horses ate up all the neighbourhood ". Then, after a
time, it would appear that they went home, autumn being spent,
for it is recorded that this was just about a full twelvemonth since
the " Great Army " first came from Boulogne, and this, as we know,
had happened late in 892.

The campaign had been a very successful one for Alfred : his
defensive system of fortification in the South had proved successful,
his *fyrd* had proved able to win battles in the open, and even once
—at Bemfleet—to storm a camp. He had destroyed hundreds of

---

[1] See Rev. C. S. Taylor in *Proceedings of the Gloucestershire Archæological
Society* for 1894. There is to be said in favour of the other Buttington the fact that
A. S. C. says that Hasting went " up be Saeferne " as if he had gone up-stream.

ships and thousands of men. Mercia had suffered severely, it is true, but south of Thames the "Great Army" had accomplished nothing more than short and sporadic raids, and had never touched the heart of Wessex. Yet there was still much to be done : Hasting was stockaded in Mercian territory—though only in its remotest angle,—and the Northumbrian fleet had not yet left the Channel, though where it wintered we do not know—possibly in Cornwall, or even in the lands of the Franks.

The events of the following year (894) were much less crowded and less important. Apparently in, or before, early spring the Danes at Chester evacuated their camp, being completely destitute of povisions, and entered North Wales, where they plundered for some time, and then marched north-eastward to enter the friendly district of Northumbria. From thence they turned into East Anglia, and finally returning to their old haunts in Essex, fortified a new camp in the Island of Mersey, a little farther north than Bemfleet and Shoebury. About the same time—perhaps midsummer—the fleet which had been so long in the Channel at last turned eastward to join the friendly force in Essex. On its way it made a descent in West Sussex, but the *burhware* of Chichester turned out against the landing-party, attacked it with great energy and slew several hundreds of raiders. The ships, however, reached Mersey and were united to their compatriots. Then, late in the autumn, the united land and sea force pushed once more up the estuary of the Thames, and established themselves on the Lea. They built a new camp some twenty miles up that river, and dragged their ships up to its shelter. The Chronicle tells us nothing meanwhile of what Alfred and his helpers were doing ; assuredly the *fyrd* must have been out in arms, but we hear nothing of its doings, or of why it did not give battle to the Danes during their advance to the Lea. Some explanatory fact of paramount importance has evidently slipped away unnoticed.

The Chronicle once more becomes lively and intelligible in 895. The campaign began by an attack on the Danish camp upon the Lea, carried out by the *burhware* of London and other local forces. It was repulsed, and four king's thegns of note were slain. But in summer Alfred himself came up with a great army, and encamped opposite the Danes, while all the corn in the neighbouring regions was hastily reaped, to prevent them from finding food. The enemy remained quiescent behind their stockades, and thus Alfred was enabled to devise a plan for their discomfiture.   Having pitched on a suitable spot some miles below their camp, he blocked the Lea—presumably with stakes and booms—and built a fort on each side of the obstruction.[1]   Before the works were quite finished the Danes discovered their meaning, and, despairing of ever getting their vessels out of the trap, resolved to abandon them, and to strike once more at Mercia by land.   It is noteworthy that during all this later fighting they seem to have left Wessex alone, as too strongly guarded, while throwing all their force upon the territories of Ealdorman Aethelred.   On this occasion they turned north-westward, and passing, as we gather, through friendly Danish territory, the lands of the Bedford and Northampton jarls, reached the Upper Severn at Quatbridge, near Bridgnorth, where they stockaded themselves as usual.   The men of London meanwhile took possession of the abandoned fleet, destroyed such of the vessels as were not worth keeping, and brought the rest in triumph down the Lea to their own harbour.   This was the second large Viking fleet which Alfred had captured entire.

For the rest of 895 there was another "stale-mate," such as had been seen so often during these last campaigns.   The Danes were too strong in their entrenchments to be dealt with by storm : on the other hand, the *fyrd* lay about them in such strength that they dared not come out and offer battle.   At the most they could feed themselves in a precarious way by small raids.   They endured this semi-starvation till winter, when presumably the Mercian army went home, and kept their Yule at Quatbridge.   But in the next spring there was no more heart left in them, and when the time for campaigning began, and the royal hosts, no doubt, began to muster against them, they gave up the game.   "The army broke up : some went to Northumbria, some to East Anglia, and those that were without resources got them ships there, and went southward over seas to the Seine."   And, surely enough, in the Frankish annals of the year 896 we find the Viking ravages recommencing on the south coast of the Channel after a gap of four summers.

"Thanks be to God, the army had not utterly broken down the English nation," writes the chronicler at this moment.   Instead it

---

[1] Only Henry of Huntingdon says that he drained the Lea into three channels.

had been itself broken up, and while its more unquiet spirits left England and returned to the Continent, the rest scattered themselves among the English Danes and were absorbed by them. There must have been some sort of a treaty concluded between Alfred and his enemies—perhaps Hasting had his wife and sons restored to him at this time, but this wily chief is not named during the campaign of 895-96, and we do not know for certain that he took part either in the fighting on the Lea or in the last raid to Quatbridge. Hostilities with the settled Danes continued for at least some time after the "Great Army" had disappeared : it was to guard against marauding East Anglian and Northumbrian galleys in the Channel that Alfred built the improved war-galleys already mentioned,[1] which justified their existence by destroying more than twenty pirate vessels during their first year of service.[2] But after this the notes of war die away, and it would seem that some sort of "frith" must have been reconstructed between Alfred and his neighbours.[3]

It seems, in short, that for the last four years of his life (897-900) Alfred was at peace. The work of defence was done, Wessex was saved, and with it the future of the English nation. Within a few years of his death his hard-fighting son Edward was to take the offensive, and to repay on the settlers of the Danelaw all the evils that his ancestors had suffered during the terrible years of the later ninth century. It may well be supposed that Alfred's declining years were peaceful—the Chronicle gives us no notes in them save the *obits* of an ealdorman and a bishop of London. The internal evidence of some of his literary works is said by scholars to point to their having been the product of the very last years of his life.[4] It would be pleasant to believe that he was able to secure in

---

[1] See p. 467.

[2] There is, at the end of the annal for 897, a long description of a petty fight between nine of Alfred's ships and six Danes, in a haven of the Isle of Wight, which looks like the narrative of an eye-witness.

[3] Where are we to insert an extraordinary statement in Ethelweard, iv. § 3, that Aethelnoth, the well-known ealdorman of Somerset, led an army against York, and apparently devastated all the land between the Welland and the woods of Kesteven ? He seems to put it in 895. But his dates are in much confusion, and the text of this sentence is hopelessly corrupt—indeed the meaning may not be that which I suppose : in any case some words must be changed to make sense. It would be tempting to think that this was a raid in 895 or 896 to bring pressure on the English Danes.

[4] See Professor Earle's notes on the metrical version of Boethius's *Consolation*.

the evening of his days some of that leisure for which he had so often sighed in vain.

He died, aged only fifty-three, on October 26th, 900,[1] and was buried at Winchester ; his bones lay for two centuries in the New Minster, which he had founded for his scholar-chaplain, Grimbald, close under the shadow of the cathedral. In 1110 the monks of this community migrated, and built the great Abbey of Hyde, on the north side of the city. They took Alfred's tomb, which is said to have been a magnificent sarcophagus of porphyry,[2] with them and rebuilt it before their new high altar. At the dissolution of the monasteries, under Henry VIII., Hyde Abbey was unroofed and became a quarry for builders. Alfred's bones are said by some to have been taken and placed with those of the other Saxon kings in the great chests which are still visible in Winchester Cathedral.[3] But when in the reign of George III. the magistrates of Hampshire cleared away the ruins of Hyde, to build a county jail, and the vaults were cleared and levelled, a great coffin, which many supposed to be Alfred's was broken, and with its contents cast away. It did not, however, correspond to the porphyry sarcophagus spoken of by early authors. But it matters little whether sixteenth or eighteenth century vandals violated the tomb of England's noblest king. His living memory is his best monument.

Alfred had five children who survived infancy. His eldest issue was Aethelflaed, the spouse of Ealdorman Aethelred : then came the Aetheling Edward, his successor. Of his two younger daughters, Aethelgifu became Abbess of Shaftesbury, a foundation of her father's ; Aelfthryth, a learned lady, married Baldwin II., Count of Flanders, son of her father's stepmother, Judith. His youngest child was Aethelweard, of whose progress in learning Asser speaks with enthusiasm,[4] a prince who survived till 922, and left issue.[5]

---

[1] For doubts on this date see Mr. Stevenson in *English Historical Review*, 1898, p. 71, etc. The A. S. Chronicle is certainly wrong in putting this date in 901, but this seems a mere clerical error. The balance on the whole seems in favour of 900, as see Plummer's *A. S. Chronicle*, ii. 112.

[2] "Mausoleum constat ipsius factum de marmóre pretiosissimo," says the Annals of St. Neot's, which, if valueless for the ninth century, are good evidence for what was visible in 1100.

[3] The inscription on one states that Alfred's bones are within.

[4] See Asser, § 75.

[5] His sons, Aelfwine and Aethelwine, both fell at the battle of Brunanburh in 937, according to William of Malmesbury, who is probably accurate in this bit of genealogy.

BOOK V

THE KINGS OF ALL ENGLAND

CHAPTER XXIV

THE RECONQUEST OF THE DANELAW (900-940)

ON the death of Alfred, his elder son Edward was duly chosen king by the Witan.[1] Although his father had reigned for nearly thirty years, and he himself had commanded armies and won victories, and even signed charters as "rex" for some years back, his election was not absolutely undisputed. The Anglo-Saxon law of kingly succession left many problems, as has already been pointed out. When Alfred had received the crown in 871, his nephews, the sons of his elder brother Aethelred I., had been set aside as minors, incapable of taking up the burden of the Danish war. One of them, Aethelwald, who must by now have been a middle-aged man, many years older than the Aetheling Edward, made a bold bid for the crown. At the head of his personal following he seized the *burhs* of Wimborne and Twyneham (Christ Church), and obstructed all the approaches. When Edward marched against him with a hastily collected force, he swore to his adherents that "one of two things, either there he would live, or there he would lie dead". But notwithstanding his boast, his heart failed him ; he stole away by night and sought the Danes in Northumbria. There seems to have been anarchy at York at the time—Siefred, the last king, was dead or expelled—and the Northumbrians took the extraordinary step of hailing Aethelwald as their sovereign. Presumably they thought that his name would serve them well, and break up the union of Wessex : while he was content to use the sword of the heathen to win his

---

[1] The choice is very clearly put by Ethelweard's "A primatibus electus".

father's crown. For two years he was nominally king,[1] and we find
him ravaging his own paternal acres with the Danes at his back.
He never won any support in Wessex, however; apparently public
opinion had been outraged not only by his want of patriotism, but
by the fact that he had carried off a nun to be his wife. His election of course meant open war between Danes and Englishmen, for
the East Anglian King Eric and the Midland "armies" joined in, as
was natural, with their Northumbrian brethren.

The chronology of King Edward's reign is very difficult to
determine, as the Anglo-Saxon Chronicle—our main source—is demonstrably incorrect by two, or three, or even five years at several
times.[2] The dates given for its events are therefore in many
cases doubtful. Apparently, however, the war between Edward and
the Danes who followed his cousin extended only over the two
years 901-2. In the first of these Aethelwald came down to Essex
with a Northumbrian fleet, and was joined by the East Anglian
Danes, who owned him as suzerain, as if he had been Alfred's
legitimate successor. In the following year he headed them in a
great raid upon English Mercia. "They ravaged all over the land
of Mercia till they came to Cricklade, and then they crossed
Thames, and took in Braden (the Forest along the edge of Wiltshire), all that they could lay hands on." Edward's way of dealing
with such a problem as a Danish raid differed fundamentally from
that which his father had been wont to use. The adversary was now
of a different sort: he had not to deal with the "Great Army,"
which was a wandering fraternity with no territorial base and no
fields or flocks of its own. The settled Danes of England had
houses and wives, cornfields and cattle; therefore the best way
to stop their raiding was not to commence a long stern-chase after
their lightly moving host, but to strike at their homes. While
Aethelwald was ravaging Hwiccia and Wiltshire, Edward gathered
up the fyrd of Kent and East Wessex, and struck at the Danish
settlements about Bedford, Cambridge and Huntingdon, "he overran all their land between the Ouse and the Dykes,[3] and as far North

---

[1] We have apparently a memorial of his kingship in a rare Anglo-Danish penny,
with the inscription ALVALDVS (British Museum, *Anglo-Saxon Coins*, i. p. 230).

[2] See Mr. Plummer's note on the chronology of Edward's reign in his *Notes to
the A. S. C.*, ii. 116-17.

[3] The Dykes on the present borders of Cambridge and Suffolk, which mark the
old border of Mercia and East Anglia, and perhaps that of the Iceni and Catuvellauni in earlier days.

as the Fens ". This naturally brought back the enemy, who came up in great force and mighty wrath just as Edward was turning home again. His forces had apparently been spread in several columns, to do the more damage, but " it was proclaimed throughout the whole army that they should return together ". Unfortunately the Kentish division was late (though sent for seven times, as the Chronicle tells us), and was overtaken by the Danes while isolated. There followed a furious battle, most destructive to the leaders on both sides, at a spot called the Holme, which cannot be identified. On the side of the Danes there fell their two kings, Aethelwald and Eric, with three other chiefs of name ; the English lost Sige-helm and Sigewulf, the two ealdormen of East and West Kent, an abbot named Kenwulf, and many important thegns. " Of the Danish men there were the more slain, but they had possession of the place of carnage."[1] It was no small gain to be rid of the traitor Aethelwald, even at a great sacrifice. The Northumbrians do not seem to have elected any king in his place, and relapsed into anarchy, which made them less dangerous for the next few years. The East Anglians chose in Eric's place one Guthrum, a nephew of the original Guthrum whom Alfred had baptised.

In the next year (903) a treaty was made between Edward and the Danes at Yttingaford (Linslade ?), and brought the war to an end in its third summer. No doubt the removal of Aethelwald and Eric made it easy. While some versions of the Chronicle say that it was made " even as King Edward ordained," others speak as if Edward was forced (apparently unwillingly) to make peace by the stress of circumstances. Soon after he and Guthrum II. made a " frith," reproducing the old agreements of 886 between Alfred and Guthrum I. with certain modifications and much detailed cal-culation of weregelds.[2]

---

[1] The battle-spot of " the Holme " is unknown, but must be somewhere in the direction of Bedfordshire or Cambridgeshire. The date given in most MSS. of the Chronicle as 905 is three years out : for the battle where Sigewulf falls in 902, in Ethel-weard's narrative (iv. 5) and the " Mercian " version of the Chronicle, is clearly the same as that which the other versions put in 905 (see Plummer's *A. S. C.*, ii. 123). Simeon of Durham also brings us to 902, by mentioning the death of Brihtsig, a supporter of Aethelwald.

[2] The peace of Yttingaford is put under 906 by most versions of the A. S. C., but that is only because they have wrongly got the battle of the Holme and the death of Aethelwald in 905, three years too late. The place is shown by a charter (Kemble C. D. 1257) to be somewhere near Leighton Buzzard, on Watling Street. Lieber-mann (*Gesetze*, etc., I. 128) puts this treaty later : but 903 seems correct.

Edward would then seem to have enjoyed a space of peaceful rule for over six years (903-10). We have few notes concerning its events, and these are for the most part mere *obits* of notable personages or records of natural phenomena. But an entry in the Mercian version of the Chronicle under 907 deserves mention: in this year Aethelred of Mercia and his spouse, Aethelflaed, repaired and repeopled Chester, which was no longer to be left, as in Alfred's day, as a point of vantage for the Vikings. The strategical position of the old Roman city was, of course, most important: not only did it cut off any communication between the North Welsh and the Northumbrian Danes, but it gave a point of observation on the dealings of these same Northumbrians with their Irish brethren across St. George's Channel.

There appears to have been a close and persistent intercourse between York and Dublin in the first half of the tenth century. In the annals of the family descending from the two great Viking brothers, Ingwar and Halfdene, the conquerors of Northumberland in 866-76, connections with both shores of the Irish Sea continue for three generations. Some members of the house appear as kings of Limerick, Man, or the Hebrides, others, generally of the Dublin branch, intermittently reigned at York in rapid and irregular succession, among other kings who were not of their house. The names Anlaf, Guthfrith, Regnald, Sihtric were borne by so many uncles and nephews that it is very difficult to keep their individualities apart. The turbulent Northumbrians were not particular about the title or origin of the kings: they had already accepted the Wessex prince Aethelwald, when political reasons seemed to make it a profitable move. The occupation of Chester was important, in regard to this connection, because it gave the King of England a harbour looking out on the sea over which the communication between Dublin and York took place, for Edward was, it must be remembered, the possessor of the navy which Alfred had created, and in 910 had over 100 vessels at sea. It is to be noted that Aethelflaed, Edward's sister and Aethelred's wife, is mentioned by the chroniclers [1] for the first time when co-operating with her husband in the restoration of Chester; she had been married to him for twenty years, but only now begins to appear in formal

---

[1] But the Charter Kemble, 1075, shows that they fortified Worcester together before Alfred's death.

history as his fellow-worker. Charters of an earlier date, however, show that for many years she had been practically the co-regent of her spouse the ealdorman of Mercia. Her importance came not only from the fact that she was a princess of royal blood, but from her energy and masculine spirit, which enabled her to take Aethelred's place, not only in peace but in war, after his death. She was evidently as capable as her brother Edward—more so perhaps when we consider the disabilities of a woman in those troubled times. The Welsh and Irish annals usually call her "queen," and the power which she and her husband exercised was indeed more than that of mere governors. As long as one of them survived, Mercia was still practically a vassal kingdom allied to Wessex, rather than a mere province of it.

The war between King Edward and the Danes broke out again in 910. Apparently it began by an unprovoked raid into the Severn Valley: "The barbarians broke the peace both with the king and with Aethelred who then ruled in Mercia," says one Chronicle.[1] "They despised whatever peace King Edward and the Witan offered them," says another,[2] "and overran the land of Mercia. And the king had gathered some hundred ships, and was then in Kent, and the ships were going south-east along the coast toward him. So the 'Army' [the Danes] thought that the most part of his force was on the ships, and that they should be able to go unfought wheresoever they chose." A concentration of the English in the direction of Kent and Essex would leave the West Midlands ill guarded. "So they devastated the territory of Mercia far and wide, till they came right inland to the Avon,[3] which is the boundary between the Mercians and the West English, and then they crossed the Severn into the Western lands [Herefordshire, etc.] and there took no small prey." Returning from thence they had recrossed the Severn at Quatbridge,[4] in Shropshire, when they found a mixed army of Mercians and Wessex men barring their

---

[1] Ethelweard, iv. 4.   [2] The main Wessex version of the A. S. C.

[3] The Somersetshire Avon, not the Warwickshire one, which does not "bound Wessex and Mercia". All this is from Ethelweard, iv. 4.

[4] This place, the Cwatbridge of the A. S. C., where the Danes had been in 896, is clearly the passage named here by Ethelweard, as Cantbridge, with one letter miswritten. It is unlikely that the obscure bridge by Cam in Gloucestershire is meant. For the battle takes place in Staffordshire immediately afterwards, not in Gloucestershire.

way, under Edward himself. There followed a pitched battle between Tottenhall and Wodnesfeld (Wednesfield, near Wolverhampton) in Staffordshire,[1] which was as disastrous to the Danes as Ashdown and Ethandun. No less than three of their "kings" are said to have been slain, Halfdene, Ingwar and Eowils,[2] beside two Earls Ohthere and Scurfa and six or seven "holds"—the greater landed proprietors of the Danelaw. Presumably Halfdene and Ingwar were kings of the Northumbrians for the time being; they seem to have been the sons of that Halfdene who had established the Danish kingdom at York,[3] and had been expelled so soon after by his subjects.

It would appear that the great ealdorman Aethelred died in this same year (910)[4] some time after the battle of Tottenhall, a fact which accounts for the appearance of his widow and not himself as the builder, during its autumn, of the second of the " burhs " with which her name is to be so regularly connected during the next seven years. This fort was Bromesberrow (Bremesburg), near Ledbury in Herefordshire,[5] a spot which was no doubt suggested by the ravages of the Danes in that region during the past summer.

---

[1] There is immense confusion in the A. S. C. here. The normal Wessex version makes two campaigns out of one, and has two pitched battles, one at " Teotanhele " in August, 910, of which no detail is given, save that the English were victorious; the other at a place unnamed in 911, in which the two Danish kings and thousands of their followers are slain. The Mercian version has one battle only at Totanheal in 910, and is undoubtedly right. For Ethelweard, who is here an independent authority, and gives the details cited above, which are not in the A. S. C., has only one battle, and puts the death of *three* Danish kings at it: he alone mentions Ingwar, the third slain king. But he calls the fight Wodnesfeld not Tottenhall. As the two places are within four miles of each other this does not much matter. Simeon of Durham has only one fight, at Tottenhall in 910. The Annals of St. Neot's have also one battle only, with two kings slain, at ' Wodnesfeld,' in 910. I cannot doubt that the two battles are identical, and that 910 is the real date.

[2] Mr. Plummer ingeniously suggests (note to A. S. C., 911) that " Eowils cyng," called in one text Eowilisc cyng, is really " Eowil Wilisc cyng," a Welsh Howel and no Dane. Eowils is not a possible Scandinavian name.

[3] See pages 451 and 482.

[4] The Wessex version of the A. S. C. makes Aethelred die in 912, but is (as usual) several years out. Ethelweard is right here in giving 910, Simeon of Durham coincides by mentioning Edward's resumption of Oxford and London under 910. So does one Mercian version of the A. S. C. It is possible, however, that Aethelred died early in 911.

[5] See Rev. C. S. Taylor's *Danes in Gloucestershire*, p. 23, for an account of the great fort on Conigree Hill, above Bromesberrow.

The fact that they had regularly made Mercia and not Wessex their main objective for attack, in every campaign since 893, had no doubt been caused by the lack of systematic fortification in this quarter such as that which Alfred had introduced in Wessex. Aethelflaed began to remedy this deficiency on a liberal scale the moment that she became mistress of the Mercian lands.

Aethelred must have been many years older than his spouse; they had no male issue, but only one daughter named Aelfwyn, who seems to have been young and unmarried, the child of Aethelred's old age. If they had had sons, the sub-kingdom of Mercia would probably have survived for many a year. On his brother-in-law's death, King Edward took under his own hand London and Oxford, with the districts depending on them—no doubt the later counties of Middlesex, Hertford, Buckingham and Oxford, which he regarded as Wessex land, London having been actually given to Aethelred by Alfred in 886, while the territory of the Chiltern-saetas was originally West Saxon in population and history, and had not become finally Mercian till the eighth century. But the rest of Aethelred's wide dominion, from Chester to Cotswold, was left under the control of his widow, who ruled them with quasi-regal power till her death eight years later. It is clear from the enthusiastic way in which she co-operated in all her brother's subsequent campaigns, that Aethelflaed did not consider the annexation of London and Oxford to the crown as in any way an unbrotherly act. In the year after her husband's death we find her proceeding with her system of building *burhs* to protect the line of the Severn from the Danes. Her foundations of 911 were Bridgnorth and Scargate (Shrewsbury?)[1] both situated in the region which the enemy had devastated in 910.

In this same year (911)[2] King Edward appears to have made a solid advance against the Danes of East Anglia. Not only did he build two *burhs* on the north and south sides of Hertford, which was in his own old territory, but he also moved forward into Essex, and while his main army kept guard, and defied the enemy to attack it, constructed a fortress at Witham. Whereupon "a good part of the people who had before been under the dominion

[1] See Rev. C. S. Taylor's *Danes in Gloucestershire*, pp. 23-24.
[2] Wrongly put under 913 in the Wessex version of A. S. C.

of the Danes submitted to him "—evidently the inhabitants of Southern Essex.

It seems that after this the Danes must have asked and obtained terms, since when they next appear in arms we are particularly told that they were "transgressing the *frith*". The first move was made by the jarls of Northampton and Leicester who, soon after Easter (apparently of 912)[1] broke the peace by a raid upon "Hocneratun"[2] and its neighbourhood, where they made much slaughter, followed immediately by another on Lygton (Leighton Buzzard), where they were repulsed by the landsfolk, who had hastily assembled in arms. This seems to have checked their ambitions. Meanwhile Aethelflaed was still busy *burh*-building : this year she fortified Tamworth, the old residence of Offa and so many other kings, in the early summer, and Stafford before Lammas—both good centres of defence against the Danes of Northampton and Leicester, who had just taken up arms against her brother.

In 913 King Edward had the stress of the fighting ; he had not only to deal with the Danes of East Anglia and their neighbours of East Mercia, but with a great Viking fleet. Summoned in, no doubt, by the appeal of their insular kinsmen, a numerous squadron, starting from Brittany, appeared in the Bristol Channel. Their leaders were two jarls named Ohthere and Hroald (Harald ?).[3]

---

[1] Though the Wessex version of the A. S. C. gives the date 917, having no news of King Edward since the time of his fortification of Hertford, in the year which it calls 913, but which is really 911. There are no entries of the king's doings in 914-15-16; and then we get the outbreak of the Northampton and Leicester Danes ascribed to 917. There was really no such pause in King Edward's activity, and the doings ascribed to him in 917-18-19 are really those of 912-13-14. Florence of Worcester and Ethelweard are much more nearly right, but the former is one year out, by counting too late. That Ethelweard correctly gets the Danish raid on the Bristol Channel into 913 is proved by the fact that he casually mentions that Christmas Day in the next year fell on Sunday, which was the fact in 914.

[2] Hook Norton, Oxfordshire, according to Mr. Plummer (*A. S. C.*, ii. 396).

[3] In fixing this Viking raid to the year 913 I am following Ethelweard, who (see last note but one above) puts it in the year before that on which Christmas Day fell on a Sunday (*i.e.* 914), and *Annales Cambriae* which have under 913 the note, "Otter venit in Britanniam". The Wessex A. S. C. (wild as usual !) puts it in 918. Simeon of Durham muddles this invasion with the Danish raid into Herefordshire before the battle of Tottenhall, and gets it into 910, which is almost as bad. The Mercian version of A. S. C. omits it altogether !

Having coasted round Land's End, they first came ashore in South
Wales, where they ravaged Gwent and captured Cimeliauc, Bishop
of Llandaff, whom King Edward afterwards ransomed for forty
pounds of silver. The "army" then pushed up through Irchenfield (South Herefordshire), as if to attack Mercia from the rear.
But they were opposed by the *burhware* of Hereford, Gloucester
and other neighbouring towns, who defeated them in battle, and
slew Hroald and the brother of Ohthere. The Danes then fortified
themselves in a "park," where they were besieged by the Mercians
till they delivered hostages, and swore to quit King Edward's realm.
We are told that Edward was out at this time with the Wessex
fyrd, on the south side of the Bristol Channel, watching the fleet,
which twice threw landing forces on shore, once at Porlock and
once at Watchet. On each occasion the Danes who came to land
were utterly cut to pieces, save some few who swam out to their
ships. The invaders then "sat down" on the desolate isle of
Bradanrelice (Flat Holme) until many died of hunger, for all
their efforts to forage were defeated. They then drew off, first to
Demetia (Western South Wales) and then to Ireland, where Ohthere
is heard of a year later as helping a King Regnald to lay waste
Dublin.[1] The interest of this inroad is that it was the last Viking
raid from over the High Seas of which we are to hear for some
sixty years. When Danish ships appear in the reigns between
Aethelstan and Aethelred II. it is always the Irish Danes who are in
question. The hordes which had so long infested Frankland were
beginning to find their ravages restricted, and either to draw together into the solid settlement in Normandy, which they finally
occupied about this very time, or to retire to Ireland, the Hebrides,
Iceland, and other quarters, where actual colonisation had begun.

Ohthere's fleet disappeared at harvest-time. When it was gone
King Edward transferred himself to the East, and sat four weeks
at Bedford,[2] where he forced the local jarl Thurketil to submit to
him, with all his "holds" and the townsmen, and some also of the

[1] Only mentioned among English sources by Simeon of Durham, and dated by
him two years wrong—*i.e.* 912, since he wrongly starts Ohthere in 910.

[2] Not Buckingham, as four Wessex versions of the A. S. C. have it, by a stupid
slip of the pen. The mention of the four weeks' stay of Edward and the submission
of Thurketil proves that Bedford is meant, as does also the context and the next annal,
that of "919" (*i.e.* 915) where there is clearly duplication. Buckingham, of course,
was always English, and appears as one of Alfred's *burhs* in the Burghal Hidage.

Danes who were dependent on the neighbouring jarl of Northampton. Thurketil, in the next year but one, went over seas into Frankland, together with the men who would follow him, "with the peace and aid of King Edward". Probably he joined Rolf in Normandy, and aided in the settling up of his new duchy, which had started in 911 after the treaty of Clair-Sur-Epte.

In the year when this lively campaign was going on near the Lower Severn, Aethelflaed of Mercia was, as it seems, leaving the defence of the South and West to her brother, while she concentrated her attention on the North and East; early in the summer she strengthened her border against the Northumbrians, by building a *burh* at Eddisbury in Delamere Forest, looking out towards the Mersey; in the autumn she fortified Warwick, as a continuation of the line formed by Stafford and Tamworth against the jarls of Leicester and Northampton. It was no doubt all-important to keep the two hostile forces apart, and to secure that invaders landing by the Severn mouth should have no undefended passage into the Danish Midlands.

In 914, if our dating be correct, King Edward was mainly occupied with the settlement of the newly conquered Bedford, where he built a second supplementary *burh*. Aethelflaed, on the other hand, was busy far to the north; she built " Cyric-byrig " (Cherbury on the Welsh frontier, facing Powys), and " Weardbyrig," (apparently Warburton on the Mersey),[1] close to Eddisbury, which she had fortified in the previous year. And, finally, in the early months of the winter, she set up a *burh* at "Rumcofa," apparently Runcorn, at the very mouth of the Mersey. These two forts were intended to guard the mouth of that river (as the mouth of Dee was already guarded by Chester) against descents from the sea, similar to that which had been in the previous year so successfully repelled at the estuary of the Severn.

Having made sure of Bedford, King Edward in the next year (915) turned eastward again toward Essex, and strengthened the frontier which he had established on the Blackwater in 911 by

[1] Not Warborough on Thames, which some have suggested; that would have been in Edward's own dominions. There is a very rare penny of Aethelstan, struck at the mint " Weardbyrig ". It seems odd that we should have a mint at work in such an out-of-the-way place as Warburton, only newly built. But we cannot concede that Aethelflaed could have worked on the Middle Thames.

building a *burh* at Maldon, only five miles from his earlier strong-hold at Witham.   There now remained in the hands of the Danes only Colchester and the northern third of the old kingdom of the East Saxons.   For the first time since 910 we hear of no similar advance on the part of his martial sister the Lady of Mercia.   She was this year distracted by a new trouble.   We are told of a South Welsh war which broke out in June.   On St. Cyricius' Day (June 16), as the Mercian version of the Chronicle informs us, Abbot Ecgbriht was "guilelessly slain," assuredly by the Welsh. For the annal proceeds to note that within three days Aethelflaed had sent out her forces against them.   The Mercians stormed Brecon, the capital of the principality of Brecheiniog, "and made prisoners there of the Welsh king's wife and some four and thirty other persons".   Apparently this was not Elen the spouse of Howell Dda, high-king of South Wales, but a princess of Brecheiniog, whose husband had probably been the person guilty of the raid in which Abbot Ecgbriht had been slain.

The next year, however (916), was to see fighting of a very different degree of importance, a complicated double campaign against the Danes of East Mercia, by Edward and Aethelflaed in combination.   The summer was so full of stirring events that it provides one of the longest entries in the whole Anglo-Saxon Chronicle.[1]   Early in the spring, before Easter, Edward seized and fortified Towcester, which must have lain in the principality of Thurferth, jarl of Northampton.   It will be remembered that already in 913 some of the "holds" depending on that city had done homage to the king.   This advance was probably intended to secure their prince's allegiance.   Some weeks later, during May, Edward commanded a second *burh* to be built at "Wiggin-gamere," apparently upon the frontier farther east, possibly Way-mere in Hertfordshire,[2] but more probably somewhere in the direction of Essex.   This was a challenge to the whole of the Midland and East Anglian Danes, and it was promptly accepted.   In July

---

[1] Entered wrongly, as usual, in the year 921—five years out, like most other events of this period—in the main Wessex version of the Chronicle.

[2] Certainly not Wigmore on the Welsh border, as many historians have stated. Edward and Aethelflaed never trespassed by *burh*-building on each other's territory. Waymere, suggested by Steenstrup and Sir James Ramsay, seems to me too much to the rear.

"between Midsummer and Lammas" the hosts of Northampton
and Leicester, with assistance from their neighbours farther north,
made a descent upon the new fort at Towcester. "They fought
against the burh the whole day, and they thought that they should
have been able to take it by storm, but the folk who were within
defended it till reinforcements came up, and then the Danes departed
from the burh and went away." They took their revenge, however,
by pushing a raid into the Chiltern country, where they wrought
much damage between Aylesbury and Burne-Wood "coming upon
men unprepared".

This was only one of three simultaneous campaigns which went
on during the month of July, 916. Aethelflaed was playing her
part by drawing off the attention of the Danes of the North-Midlands. "Before Lammas the Lady of the Mercians, God helping
her, got possession of the town that is called Derby, and there were
slain within the gates four of her thegns, which was to her a cause
of sorrow." The fact that these chiefs fell inside the place shows
that Derby must actually have been taken by storm.[1]

At about the same time—between Midsummer and Lammas
day—there was equally hard fighting on the other wing of the
English advance, along the line of the Ouse. The East Anglians,
joined with the "army" of Huntingdon, went out with a new
design; they would build offensive *burhs*, like their foe, and
establish ἐπιτειχίσματα, as the Greeks would have called them, on
Edward's soil. Moving forward to Tempsford, where the Ouse and
the Ivel join, "they abode and built there, thinking that from
thence they could by war and hostility get more of the land
again". Having established this great base-camp, they went forward against Bedford, but suffered a severe check in front of it
from the garrison. This turned them in another direction: a force,
composed of East Anglian and Mercian Danes combined, went off
against the newly-built fort at "Wiggingamere". But the garrison
defended it well, so that the army left the *burh* and went their
way. They were indeed required to defend their own stronghold
at Tempsford, for an English force, drawn out of all the nearer
burhs, had marched against the base-camp of the enemy. There
followed a great battle, as deadly to the Danes as Tottenhall had

[1] Wrongly under 917 in the Mercian version of the Chronicle. We are fixed to
916 by this being the year before Aethelflaed's death in 917.

been six years before. Tempsford was stormed, and in its defence
there fell Guthrum II. the King of East Anglia, two jarls, Toglos
and Manna,[1] and "all who would defend themselves"; the rest
were made prisoners. Pressing this decisive advantage to the
uttermost, Edward then sent his army against Colchester; harvest
was now on, but reinforcements had nevertheless been got up from
Kent and Surrey, to strengthen the local forces of the *burhs* of
Essex, Hertfordshire and Bedfordshire. The result was splendid:
the great town of Colchester was taken by storm, and all its defenders slain or taken "save the men who fled away over the wall".

The Eastern Danes seem now to have despaired of their own
strength, and called in to their aid a fleet of their landless countrymen—pirates, or *aescmen* (ship folk), as the Chronicle calls them.
The combined force, leaving the destroyed city of Colchester alone,
marched against Maldon, the nearest English garrison. But fortune was ever unkind : "they beset the *burh* and fought against
it, but aid came to the *burhware* from without, and the 'army'
had to go away. Then the garrison and the reinforcements together followed hotly after them, caught them up, put them to
flight, and slew many hundreds, as well of the pirates as of the
others."

This battle outside Maldon was the last blow required to finish
the business. The resistance of the Danes collapsed : when King
Edward came up with the whole of the *fyrd* of Wessex and established himself at Passenham on the Ouse, the surrenders began.
First Thurferth, the jarl of Northampton, with his chief men "and
all the army which owed obedience to Northampton as far as the
Welland" came in and did homage "seeking King Edward's peace
and protection". Half the English army then went home, but the
king with the other half went on to Huntingdon, where "all who
were left of the inhabitants submitted". A *burh* was built and
garrisoned here, and then Edward marched to Colchester, whose
ruined walls he rebuilt. While he lay there he received the submission of the "army" of Cambridge, and (what was more important) that of the whole of East Anglia. "All the army swore
union with him, and that they would all that he would, and would
observe peace toward all to whom the king granted his peace, both
by sea and land." The long annals of the year end with the state-

---

[1] Probably jarls of Huntingdon. They were father and son.

ment that King Edward built a *burh* at "Cledemuth"—assuredly
not a fort at the mouth of the South-Welsh Cleddau, as some
have supposed, but probably in the direction of East Anglia. Not
to mention that the Demetian river would have fallen rather into
Aethelflaed's sphere of operations, we may add that no instance of
Edward building isolated and outlying *burhs*, in territory where he
had no grip, occurs elsewhere in his long record of campaigning.

At the end of 916 there remained in arms against King Edward
none of the Midland Danes save those of Leicester, Stamford, Lincoln and Nottingham, all of whom must have been not only discouraged by the fate of their friends, but much worn down by long
fighting, since they had borne their share in the last campaigns.
Their subjection was not long delayed, and followed in the next
spring (917), which was the date of the last joint advance made by
Edward and his untiring sister against their common enemy. It
was practically unresisted, and resembled (as has been aptly said) a
royal progress rather than a strategical operation. Very early in
the year the important city of Leicester and the "army" dependent on it came into Aethelflaed's hands by surrender. The Danes
promised obedience and homage. It is more surprising to read in
the next paragraph of the Chronicle that the Northumbrians followed suit : "the people of York also made covenant with her,
some having given a pledge and others having bound themselves
by oath, that they would be at her orders ". It looked as if the
end of the independent Danish states of England was near, but
there was yet many a battle to be fought, and many a rebellion
to be crushed, before they were finally tamed. Meanwhile King
Edward, after the surrender of Leicester, had passed on to Stamford, its next neighbour. There, too, the "army" surrendered without
fighting, and permitted the king to build a *burh* just outside their
gates, on the south side of the Welland, and to place a garrison
there.

It was while he lay at Stamford, superintending the new fortifications, that the king received the news of the death of his sister
the Lady of Mercia, who died at Tamworth on June 12th, 917, in
the year that saw the happy completion of the task that she had
taken in hand after her husband's death. All Mercia was now
once more under English supremacy, and not only Mercia but
Northumbria. Aethelflaed must have been about forty-seven or

forty-eight at the time of her death—the house of Alfred, as we shall note during several generations, were vigorous but not long-lived.   She is undoubtedly the most interesting figure among Anglo-Saxon princesses—yet we know but little about her personality. Asser does not chance to have left any anecdote concerning her, and we have on record her acts not her character.   Clearly, how-ever, she must have been a woman of quite abnormal capacity.   It was not the wont of the Old English to entrust power to female rulers ; the obscure case of Seaxburh in the seventh century is the only parallel.   And Aethelflaed was not a mere regent ad-ministering a sub-kingdom in peaceful times, but a resourceful sovereign facing endless wars and working out a victorious policy to its end.   If she had been Mercian born we could better have understood the loyalty with which her subjects served her—but she was an alien, who yet continued to bear rule when her husband was dead—like Catherine II. of Russia.   We are nowhere told that she was considered to be acting as the guardian or representative of her daughter Aelfwyn, Aethelred's only child ; she is treated as ruling in her own right.   What was the legal basis of her position (if such conceptions may be spoken of in the tenth century) we do not know.   Did the Mercian Witan hail her as lady-regnant, or did her brother suggest or confirm her election ?   It is impossible to say : the only thing that is clear being that before her husband's death she was in some measure his colleague and co-regent, as their charters show.   Apparently an exceptional personality secured her an exceptional position.[1]

On hearing of his sister's death King Edward went to Tam-worth, and saw to her burial at Gloucester by the side of her husband Aethelred.   He then received the personal homage of all the Mercian magnates, and not only of them but of other less im-mediate subjects, who had commended themselves to Aethelflaed— Howell Dda King of Dyfed, and Cledauc and Juthwal, Welsh princes of less note and smaller dominions.   Indeed " all the Welsh race sought him to lord," and his suzerainty was no doubt acknow-ledged in Gwynedd and Powys, no less than in Dyfed.   It would seem that Edward was at first undecided as to whether the Mercian sub-kingdom should not be permitted to continue, and to devolve

[1] For notes on Aethelflaed's position, see Rev. C. S. Taylor's *King Alfred and His Family in Mercia.*

on his niece Aelfwyn, who must now have been at least fourteen years old,[1] and was certainly therefore marriageable.   In the meantime the actual governance devolved on the Mercian ealdormen, of whom there seems to have been three or four at this moment: presumably one of them had charge of the young princess.   In the next year, however (918, if our calculations are right), Edward resolved to make the provisional arrangement permanent, and to treat the Mercian lands as a mere fraction of his kingdom of England.   He carried his niece off into Wessex, where she was placed in a nunnery with or without her own consent.   She was alive thirty years after, as is proved by a charter of Eadred[2] conferring lands on the "*religiosa femina*" Aelfwyn.   This seems a hard act on the part of King Edward, and has provoked much angry comment by historians of all ages—from Henry of Huntingdon downward.   There was probably good political justification for it: we could wish that there were better authority than a late Welsh chronicle for the statement that Edward discovered a plot to marry her to Regnald the new Danish king at York,[3] which would have involved the ruin of all his plans, by the creation of an over-great sub-kingdom, composed of Mercia and Deira conjoined.   At all events Mercian independence was now an anachronism, and Edward was undoubtedly acting for the best interests of the nation.[4]

From Aelfwyn's deposition in 918 we must turn back a year, to glance at her uncle's proceedings in the autumn that followed her mother's death.   Stamford having been regularly fortified, he moved on to Nottingham, which submitted, like all the other Danish towns, without another blow.   Edward "commanded it to be repaired, and to be occupied as well by English as by Danes ".   After this "all the people settled in Mercia" made their submission, *i.e.* the Danes of Lincoln and the other smaller settlements

---

[1] Her name occurs in a charter of 904, a three-life lease confirmed by her parents, in which the Bishop of Worcester grants them lands; she is inserted as the third and youngest life (Kemble, *C. D.*, 339).

[2] Birch, C. S., 869.

[3] See Lappenburg's *England under the Anglo-Saxon Kings*, ii. 116-26.   But Caradoc of Llancarvan is worthless as an authority.

[4] We need pay no attention to the theory that Aethelred and Aethelflaed had another child, Aethelstan, who became a monk at Glastonbury.   His supposed existence has been caused by errors of identification.   But see Taylor's *House of Alfred in Mercia*, 22-25.

in Lindsey and Kesteven came in to do their homage, and so completed the submission of the Midlands. This was a part of England more thickly peopled by the invaders than any other district, so that its tame surrender is all the more remarkable.

The next year showed no relaxation in Edward's energy. His sphere of operations in 918 was on the Mersey, where the line of advance had stood still since Aethelflaed had built the *burhs* of Warburton and Runcorn in 914. This time the frontier was advanced beyond the boundary river; while Edward himself lay at Thelwall (quite close to Warburton), and fortified it in his usual style, a division of his army went north to Manchester, repaired it (were Roman walls still visible?) and garrisoned it. The reason for this attention to the lands by the Irish Sea was undoubtedly because there had just been a change of king at York. An adventurer from Ireland, Regnald, grandson of the celebrated Ingwar, had been very busy in the western waters for the last few years. He had ravaged the Isle of Man in 914. A little later we hear of him in Bernicia, where he set upon Ealdred of Bamborough, the high-reeve who possessed some precarious sort of sovereignty between Tyne and Forth. Ealdred called in Constantine, King of the Scots, to his aid, but they were defeated with great slaughter by the Vikings, and Regnald ravaged Scotland as far as Dunblane. It was after this northern raid, which ended in a check in 918, that the pirate king descended upon York, where he " broke " the city, and expelled the prince—whoever it was—that had done homage to Aethelflaed in 917. Edward, therefore, did well to strengthen his north-western frontier, which was equally exposed to the Northumbrian and the Irish Vikings.[1]

But Regnald, as it appears, did not intend to give trouble, or to stir up the Midland Danes to revolt. In the succeeding year (919), when King Edward advanced once more, this time to strengthen his inland frontier by building a *burh* at Bakewell in Derbyshire, he received offers of homage from all the lords of the northern lands. Not only Regnald but Ealdred of Bamborough submitted, "and with them all who dwell in Northumbria both English and Danes," but also the king of the Strathclyde Welsh, Donald, and—what is more surprising—Constantine the Scot

---

[1] All these details are from Simeon of Durham, i. 72-3, who seems trustworthy where Northern affairs are concerned.

himself. This submission has sometimes been questioned by patriotic North Britons, who remember that all the claims of another
and a greater Edward in the thirteenth century started from the
passage in the Anglo-Saxon Chronicle which is here in question, as
their first base. But further reflection on the circumstances of 919
serves to make the fact less improbable than it might appear at
the first glance.

All the lands north of Forth and Clyde had been suffering
dreadful misery from the Vikings for three-quarters of a century.
The heathens had destroyed Alclyde in 870; they had sacked at
one time or another most of the strongholds of the Pict and the
Scot. And they had established (just as in Ireland and in England)
a "Danelaw" of conquered land. On the North it embraced the
Orkneys, Caithness and Sutherland ; on the West it took in all the
Hebrides, and much on the mainland facing them. Nearly all,
indeed, of the original Scot kingdom, in Argyle and the Isles, was
now part of a Norse jarldom of the "Sudereyar," the "Sodor" of
later contraction, that has puzzled many a beginner who reads of
the Bishops of "Sodor and Man". It is true that the Pictish and
Scottish kingdoms had coalesced in 843, probably as much under
Viking pressure as did English Wessex and Mercia. Owing to the
curious Pictish custom of succession through female kin in preference to male, the Scottish king, Kenneth son of Alpin, had
obtained the crown of the greater realm. The fact that on his
death and that of his brother Donald, it did not revert to a
relative on the side of their Pictish mother, but was passed on to
Kenneth's son, Constantine II., marks the end of the old system. It
was probably felt to be impossible to split the two kingdoms once
more (they had now been united from 843 to 863) when the Danes
were all over the land. It will be remembered that the descent of
the "Great Army" on Britain falls just at this conjuncture, and
that Halfdene ravaged all the lands beyond Forth in 875.[1] Constantine II. himself was slain by the Danes in 881. His nephew of the
same name, Constantine III., was reigning through most of the
time of Edward the Elder, and for many years after, since he ruled
the Picts and Scots from 904 to 944. He had suffered many things
from the Vikings, and especially from that Regnald who now held

York. What can be more rational than to trust the Chronicle, when it states that he took the opportunity of connecting himself with the newly-risen power of Edward, which had just shown its capacity for humbling the common enemy? The loose form of commendation, "taking King Edward for father and lord," must not be pressed into a feudal sense, or made to cover the ideas which a lawyer of the thirteenth century would attach to it. But to believe that Constantine made himself the ally of Edward, and owned himself as his inferior, seems entirely probable. It is hard to see how the compiler of the Anglo-Saxon Chronicle can have had any political object for inventing his statement : the idea of claiming imperial rights by falsifying past history is not one that can be rationally ascribed to him.

King Edward had still four years to live, after the eventful summer in which he received the homage of the kings of the North, but no annals from them have been preserved. Presumably, as we have already noted in the reign of Alfred, the absence of "history" in the chronicler's sense bears witness to a space of peace and prosperity. Like his father, Edward enjoyed a few years of well-won quiet before his death : " hic finis ; hic nomen, nec non pertinacia cessit ejusdem ".[1] He died in 924, "at Farndon in Mercia," probably Farndon on the Trent, and not the more southernly village of the same name in Northamptonshire.

As drawn for us by the dry annalists of the Chronicle, he seems little more than a formidable engine of war, a sort of infallible military machine which gets through its task with admirable accuracy, if not always with great speed. Fortunately we know a little more about him : he had been well educated by his father, "used books frequently," and took delight in the old Saxon sagas, though he had not the broad literary interests of Alfred. He was the father of an enormous family, fourteen children in all, by three wives. It would appear that he must have had some share of his father's taste for art, for his coins form a perfectly abnormal section in Anglo-Saxon numismatic history, so much so that their character can only be explained by the supposition that he took a personal interest in their types. At the beginning of his reign they copy the simpler types of his father, but presently the series develops an

---

[1] Ethelweard, iv. 5.

interesting and variegated array of new devices—a church tower with elaborate arcading, another quite different sort of church, represented from a side view, symmetrical sprigs of roses, a flying dove bearing an olive branch,[1] the hand of Providence descending from clouds, a large open flower like a marigold, several varieties of freely drawn curves and arabesques, form the reverses of his numerous pennies. When his bust appears on the obverse, it is frequently engraved with great skill and beauty : there is one of his portraits which may be called the best head on the English coinage from Offa down to Edward I.[2]

There is some reason to believe that we may ascribe to Edward's last four years of peace the rearrangement of the territorial distribution of the Midlands, or at least its commencement. When we contemplate the modern map of the shires between Humber and Thames, we recognise at once that we have to do with divisions much later and much more artificial than those of Wessex. The first thing that strikes the eye is the uniform naming of the shires after their chief towns—of the seeming exceptions Rutland dates from after the Norman Conquest, and Shropshire is only a variant that has prevailed over " Scrobbesbyrigscire "[3] because of the unwieldiness of Shrewsburyshire to a modern English mouth. Looking at the East-Midland shires, we note at once that they represent the Danish units of organisation which Edward found and conquered. To the towns of Bedford, Northampton, Cambridge, Huntingdon, Derby, Nottingham and Leicester we find appended an " army " and " people owing obedience to the town," in the case of most of them a "jarl" also is mentioned. It is hardly possible to doubt that the modern shire simply corresponds to the holding of the Danish " army " which Edward subdued. The casual mention of the Chronicle that the lands " owing obedience to Northampton " reached as far as the Welland, exactly describes the modern frontier of its shire. As to the remaining lands of East Mercia, Nottingham undoubtedly bore the same relation to the district around it, which now bears its name, as did Bedford or Derby to

---

[1] Probably Noah's dove, typifying peace after the Deluge, i.e. after the subsidence of the Danish flood.

[2] For all these coins, see plates vii. and viii. of the second volume of the British Museum *Catalogue of Anglo-Saxon Coins*. The fine portrait is vii., No. 8, a copy in general design from the head of some late Roman emperor.

[3] As in A. S. C., *sub anno* 1006.

their regions. While Lincolnshire must surely, on the analogy
of the rest, be composed of the tributary lands of the "armies"
of the two great Danish strongholds of Lincoln and Stamford.
But why these two were ever united for any administrative purpose,
when either of the two regions was ample to build up a shire, we
cannot say. Under these new divisions, created by the Danes and
taken over by Edward, as convenient units for his purpose, the old
Mercian boundaries lay completely submerged. The ancient line
between Gyrwas and Middle Angles, or South Mercians and
Middle Angles, has no relation whatever to the tenth-century limits
between the tributary lands of one or another Danish "Army".

The origin of the West-Midland shires, those formed from the
Mercian sub-kingdom of Aethelred and Aethelflaed, is much more
difficult to discover. The Chronicle does not mention the name of
one of them before the reign of Aethelred the Redeless.[1] And
when later authorities do casually name them, in narratives dealing
with the times of Edward or his immediate successors,[2] we cannot
be sure that they are not committing unconscious anachronisms,
using later territorial names for mere convenience' sake. These
counties, from Cheshire to Oxfordshire, were as far from reproducing the boundaries of the older Mercian ealdormanries as were
those of the Danish Midlands. Hwiccia is not exactly represented
by Gloucestershire and Worcestershire, for it had included the
lands along Avon which formed the southern half of the later shire
of Warwick, while it did *not* include the Forest of Dean, which had
belonged to the ealdormanry of the Magesaetas, though it was
thrown into the later shire of Gloucester. So, too, Shropshire is
a unit composed for about two-thirds of its area of old-Mercian
land, but its southern third had been Magesaetan soil. On the
whole, the best hypothesis for accounting for the shape of the
counties in the basin of the Severn is to believe that they were put
together by grouping in blocks of a convenient size the lands
"attributed" to the *burhs* which Aethelflaed created. If we
suppose that like her father in Wessex, and her brother in the
South-East Midlands, she attached a certain hidage to each of her
fortresses—an almost inevitable hypothesis—we can understand

---

[1] Cheshire is the first named, in 980.

[2] *E.g.*, when the Abingdon Chronicle mentions the *comprovinciales Oxeneford-
ensis pagi* as involved in litigation with the abbey in Aethelstan's time.

that for convenience these sections were dealt with in certain unions, which gradually become permanent. Thus Gloucestershire would be formed of the lands attached to Gloucester and Winchcombe,[1] Herefordshire of those belonging to Hereford and Bromesberrow, Cheshire of those which appertained to Chester, Eddisbury, Runcorn, Warburton, Thelwall; Shropshire of those belonging to Shrewsbury ("Scargate?"), Bridgnorth and Chirbury;[2] Warwick of those around Warwick and Tamworth. In the cases of Oxford, Worcester and Stafford there is no sign of more than one ancient burghal centre in the shire. If we had a Mercian "hidage" corresponding to that which exists for Wessex,[3] we should probably find the explanation easy to work out. But of all the *burhs* of the lands held by Aethelflaed only Warwick and Worcester are mentioned[4] (and those in a sort of appendix) in the Wessex "burghal hidage" on which so much has already been written. On the whole, the final shaping out of all this region into shires must have taken some time, and probably was not complete till the time of Aethelred II.

One thing is clear. Whenever the new West-Mercian shires took formal shape, they were never furnished like the old Wessex shires with an ealdorman apiece. In the regions which had been under Aethelred and Aethelflaed there were never in the times after 917 more than three ealdormen, though there were finally seven shires. But in the Eastern regions, which had been Danish, there were apparently a considerable number of "earls"—the name now begins to appear as designating in Danish lands the person who would have been an ealdorman on English soil. We have so few charters from the end of King Edward's reign that we cannot draw any deductions as to the number of Danish magnates whom he continued in territorial office. But in his son Aethel-

---

[1] For there was a "Winchcombeshire" which Eadric Streona (among other high-handed deeds) arbitrarily annexed to Gloucestershire; provincias provinciis pro libito adjungebat, nam vicecomitatum de Wincelcumb, quae per se tunc erat, vice-comitatui Glocestiæ adjur it (Heming, *Cartulary*, 280).

[2] Some of these districts would be very small, *e.g.*, those of the smaller Cheshire *burhs* But so were those of the districts attributed to some of Alfred's Wessex *burhs*, *e.g.*, Pilton 160 hides, Lidford 140 hides, and Lyng 100 hides.

[3] See for all this Mr. C. S. Taylor's *The Mercian Shires*, though he puts their origin a little later than I should prefer.

[4] Oxford occurs, of course, but was not really Mercian; and though held by Aethelred (886-910) was taken from his widow in the latter year.

33

stan's day there were certainly as many as thirteen earls with
Danish names about the year 930-31 ; they were holding office not
only in the East Midlands but in Northumbria and East Anglia
also. But if we put aside two for East Anglia, and three for Northumbria, there remains eight for the eight units of the Mercian
Danelaw. Probably the jarls who submitted to Edward, and
never gave trouble afterwards, were allowed to continue in their old
position till death. Thurferth *dux* who continues to sign charters
down to 932 is almost certainly the Thurferth Jarl of Northampton
who submitted in 916. And very probably some of the other
Danish signatories of Aethelstan's early charters—Fraena and
Grim, Styrcar and Gunnar, Hawerd, Scule and Halfdene, Ingwar,
Hadder, Guthrum and Urm, and Regnwald—represent the old
jarls of the "armies" of the "five boroughs" and their neighbours.[1]
But in the next generation the number of earls on Danish soil is
cut down to a much smaller number. The same was the case
equally in Wessex : it is clear that when Edward the Elder came
to the throne there was an ealdorman for every southern shire, but
that by the end of his eldest son's reign there were only three
or at the most four, ealdormen south of Thames, a system of grouping several shires into one ealdordom having been begun by Edward
and completed by Aethelstan. The object of this change was
probably military and not political, a unit such as the three shires
of Somerset, Dorset and Devon, or Hants, Wilts and Berkshire
being more conveniently handled by one ealdorman than three,
and its levies not being too widely scattered to be easily gathered
in haste under one leader. On the other hand, so long as the
Danelaw was newly subdued, the king would find it in his interest
to leave it much subdivided, lest the control over several towns and
several "armies" should be too tempting to an earl of Danish
blood.

Edward the Elder, as we have already said, had children by
three wives, Ecgwyn, Aelflaed and Eadgifu. He was succeeded by
his only son by Ecgwyn, Aethelstan, who in 924 was already
thirty years of age. It is alleged by certain late authors, especially

---

[1] As Mr. Chadwick has shown in his dissertation on this point (Anglo-Saxon
Institutions, 184-85) Scule and Regnwald are Northumbrian, and possibly one or two
more. But there remain a great number of Danish *duces* to be distributed into
Mercian lands.

William of Malmesbury, that there was something irregular about his birth—that his mother was of low estate, and never properly wedded to Edward. But this hardly squares in with the anecdotes related by William himself, to the effect that Aethelstan as a child was the special favourite of his grandfather Alfred, who, when he was no more than six years old, invested him with a scarlet cloak and a golden sword, much as he himself had been decorated by Pope Leo half a century before. It is also said that he was fostered with great honour by his aunt Aethelflaed, the lady of Mercia, and her husband, who trained him in the duties of a ruler of men. William adds that his father nominated him in his will as his successor—a thing which was not in the power of an Old English king—though he might have presented him to the Witan as a colleague during his lifetime.[1] But all this story is rendered more than doubtful by the plain fact that in many charters of Edward, from the year 908 onward, Aethelstan signs as *filius regis* directly after the bishops, and before his next brother Aelfweard, the elder son of Aelflaed, the king's second spouse.[2] Unless he had been regarded as the nearest of kin and natural heir, his signature would not have been placed in this position. It was probably, therefore, not a thing of crucial importance to Aethelstan that Aelfweard chanced to die only twelve days after his father, though it would have been, if there had been doubt as to his own eligibility for the throne.[3]

The Anglo-Saxon Chronicle throughout the reign of Edward the Elder is full and interesting in its notices of events, though in all its versions they are dated with distressing inaccuracy. But when we arrive at the reign of Aethelstan the pen seems to fall

---

[1] As in the cases quoted on p. 369.

[2] *E.g.*, in Kemble, C. D., Nos. 1090-91-94-96 and 342.

[3] William of Malmesbury, besides all his stories about Aethelstan's doubtful birth, has another set of legends about opposition offered to his succession, not (as we should have expected) in the name of his next surviving brother the Aetheling Edwin, but by a certain Alfred, who must be some representative of Aethelwald the Pretender of 900 and the house of Aethelred I. His plot failing, he was sent to Rome, where, making a false oath before the Pope that he had never been guilty of intended treason, he was seized by a fit of epilepsy and died within three days. For all this stuff, some of which William acknowledges that he got out of " *Cantilenis per successiones temporum detritis,*" see W. M., i. 136-56. There are two (forged) charters supporting the story about the pretender Alfred, Kemble, C. D., 354 and 1112.

into the hands of a new and very inferior scribe, whose entries are short, vague, and occasionally quite cryptic in their meaning. His only redeeming grace is that under the year 937 he has inserted, instead of a mere mention of the battle of Brunanburh, the long and triumphant song concerning that victory which is the best known, and one of the most striking, fragments of Anglo-Saxon poetry. We may pardon him much for preserving this bold ballad, but the chronicle of Aethelstan's reign (as of that of his brother Edmund) remains distressingly incomplete. Nor does Ethelweard (who had some useful independent facts to supply in King Edward's time) help us the least here : he has only nine lines on the sixteen years 924-940. The Chronicle which Simeon of Durham has transmitted is hardly more profitable—it devotes twenty-five lines only to the reign. Henry of Huntingdon puts us off with an execrable Latin translation of the "Song of Brunan-burh," and little else. Florence of Worcester mainly translates one of the versions of the Chronicle, but gives a few notes of his own, one or two of which are demonstrably wrong. Finally William of Malmesbury comes centuries too late, to smirch the fame of the king with disgraceful stories drawn from folklore or ballads. The result is exasperating : we know that we are dealing with the reign of a great and victorious king—yet we can state little in detail concerning his doings. What there is to know must be put on record.

Edward the Elder died, as it seems, in November, 924, and Aethelstan was crowned at Kingston-on-Thames before the end of the year. His first political act whose memory has been preserved was that, on January 30th following, he met at Tamworth and accepted as his vassal Sihtric, whom the Northumbrians had recently saluted as king on the death of his brother Regnald. This is Sihtric Caoch,[1] so called to distinguish him from many kinsmen of the same name. To bind the alliance Aethelstan gave the Dane the hand of his sister of the full blood, the only daughter of Ecgwyn, though Sihtric was one-eyed and advanced in years; he had at least one grown-up son. The marriage, however, was not destined to have any serious political results. The King of York

---

[1] According to the *Annals of Ulster*, Regnald had died as far back as 921. Sihtric had been expelled from Dublin, and was on the look-out for a new crown. Caoch = blind, *i.e.*, one-eyed.

died in the next spring (926), whereupon Aethelstan moved up
into Northumberland with an army, drove out Guthfrith the
eldest son of Sihtric, and formally annexed his realm to the crown
of England. This was a bold act, but premature. The Northumbrian Danes were not yet ripe for complete annexation, as
their constant rebellions were to show, and it would have been
wiser to leave them for a few years more under vassal-kings,
selected for their loyalty or want of ambition.

But Aethelstan, at least, knew how to keep them in subjection,
and for the rest of his reign Danish Northumbria was governed as
a regular portion of the English realm, though under Danish legal
customs and by Danish earls. For the king made no attempt to
rule them by alien English ealdormen, or to enforce Wessex law
upon them. He opened, however, at York a royal mint, which
struck for him a large issue of pennies precisely resembling his
southern issues, and quite different in appearance from the Anglo-
Danish coins struck there both before and after his reign.

After the driving out of the young Guthfrith, Aethelstan
advanced to the farther edge of Northumbria, and held a great
council at Eamot or Dacor (Dacre near Ullswater) on the Cum-
brian border (July 12th, 926). There he received the homage of
Ealdred, son of Ealdwulf, the English high-reeve of Bamborough,
of Eugenius King of Strathclyde, of Constantine III. King of the
Picts and Scots, and of several princes of Wales, of whom Howell
Dda of Dyfed is the best known.[1] After this Aethelstan could
with good justification take the style of " Rex totius Britanniae "
which appears so frequently on his coinage, and the even more
sounding titles of " basileus," " rex monarchus " and " dispensator
regni totius Albionis" which are set forth, with others, in his
charters. He had indeed achieved a position which as much surpassed that of his father Edward as Edward's, in its turn, had
surpassed that of their ancestor Ecgbert, the first King of Wessex,
who had claimed supremacy over North and South alike. For he

[1] If we could trust Florence of Worcester and William of Malmesbury (which we
cannot), we should believe that there had been serious fighting before these princes
did homage. Florence says that Ealdred resisted and took refuge with Constantine
of Scotland before both submitted. William that Aethelstan "proelio vicit et
fugavit" both Howell and Constantine. William has the still more startling statement that he beat both the Scot and the Demetian out of their kingdoms, and then,
in pity, restored them. This is wholly incredible.

was reigning directly, and in his own right, over every one of the old English kingdoms, as well as enjoying a suzerainty over all the Celtic kings of Britain, from Scotland to Cornwall.[1] He was, in fact, the first true King of all England, and at the same time the "Emperor" of Britain.

But he had to fight hard for his empire. The position which he had attained made him the common foe of all the minor kings. A few years before his father Edward had appeared to Scots and Strathclyde Welsh as a deliverer from the Viking danger. Now Aethelstan seemed to have become the danger himself, since he had lightly suppressed the Danish kingdom of York and had pushed up his own frontier to the Forth. King Constantine, in particular, found himself checked in a plan for absorbing Strathclyde, with much more, into his own kingdom. He had succeeded in placing his nephew Eugenius on this old Welsh throne, and no doubt intended to keep it under his power. Moreover since the time of the break-up of the kingdom of Northumbria, the house of Kenneth had been encroaching on the old Bernician district of Lothian, and some-times raiding as far as the Tyne, whether as enemies of the line of the high-reeves of Bamborough, or as their allies against the Danish kings of York. All this would have to come to an end, when the new "basileus" of Britain became the neighbour of Scotland, and the guardian of the northern boundaries of North-umbria.

Six years, distinguished in the Chronicles by nothing more im-portant than the *obits* of some bishops, are recorded between Aethelstan's great council at Eamot and the outbreak of the wars which made the middle period of his reign glorious. In 933, however, we suddenly find him attacking his vassal Constantine with great vigour. The Scot, as we are told, had "broken his

---

[1] I frankly cannot believe one of William of Malmesbury's statements about Aethelstan's dealings with the Britons, *viz.*, that he was the first to shut the Dam-nonians beyond the Tamar, and to expel them from Exeter, of which they had hitherto shared the possession with the English. This story is contrary to all that we know of Devonshire: Exeter had been English since Ine's time (see p. 328). Is it credible that more than two centuries later the Damnonians were still its half owners ? Devonshire has long been appearing as a regular Wessex shire with an ealdorman, and a *Fyrd*. It had fought splendidly against the Danes, while we have no mention of any trouble from the Britons since 832. Alfred possessed estates in Cornwall, and used to hunt there, as Asser tells (see p. 446). Cf. *Crawford Charters*, p. 102.

frith "; he had allied himself with the Viking prince Anlaf, one of the sons of the late Sihtric of York, and given him his daughter in marriage. This king " Anlaf Quaran "—Anlaf of the Sandal— was leader of an Irish pirate fleet, and had designs on his father's old realm in Northumbria. He must carefully be distinguished from his cousin Anlaf Guthfrithson, King of Dublin, with whom he often co-operated. On hearing that Constantine had leagued himself with the Vikings, Aethelstan came north with a great force, both naval and military. His land army devastated the Pictish regions as far as " Dunfoder," i.e. the fort of Dunnottar on its headland near Aberdeen. The fleet went farther, and wasted the shores of the Moray Firth as far as the Northmen's settlement in Caithness : presumably the Orkney earls were allies of Anlaf; but perhaps any "heathen" settlement was fair game for an English fleet —as any English coast-region was for a Viking squadron (933). This chastisement did not tame Constantine, though apparently he submitted for the moment.[1] He nursed his wrath, allied himself more closely with the heathen, and became the chief organiser of a great alliance against Aethelstan which was to be crushed at Brunanburh, three years later.

This same year 933 is marked by the Anglo-Saxon Chronicle with the bald statement that " Edwin the Aetheling was drowned at sea ". Round this simple record, apparently treated as an accident, a number of legends have clustered. Edwin the son of Aelflaed, was Athelstan's eldest surviving half-brother, and his natural heir, since he had no children. The first authority giving a lurid explanation for Edwin's end is the chronicle preserved by Simeon of Durham, which definitely states that Edwin was drowned by order of the king. William of Malmesbury fills up the outline by a long tale to the effect that the Aetheling, for having been implicated in the supposed plot of Alfred nine years before, was turned adrift on the Channel in an oarless boat, with one companion, by his brother's order. He perished, but his follower came ashore in Picardy with his body, which was buried at St. Bertin. Fortunately for the reputation of Aethelstan, the chronicle of that abbey, drawn up only thirty years later, mentions Edwin's death by shipwreck

[1] At least Florence of Worcester says that he asked for peace and gave his son as a hostage, which seems likely enough.

as a pure accident, and speaks of the gratitude of the king to the monks who buried his brother's corpse.[1]

It was four years after Aethelstan's invasion of Northern Scotland that the league against him, headed by King Constantine, "the grey-haired warrior, the old deceiver," came to a head. It was a motley alliance of ancient enemies, united by the common fear of the English domination. The Picts and Scots marched in company with the Strathclyde Welsh, against whom they had fought for so many generations. The Vikings, equally hateful of old to Pict and to Briton, had come over in great force. Not only was Anlaf Quaran there, in company with his father-in-law, but also his cousin Anlaf Guthfrithson of Dublin. All the pirate fleets of the North and West had joined them. The mustering place of such a host can only have been on the coast of the Irish Sea, somewhere between Mersey and Clyde, and nearer to the northern than the southern of these two limits, for it is incredible that a Scottish host could have penetrated very far into Northumbria before fighting came to a head.[2] But the topography of the campaign cannot be made out with any certainty, owing to the tiresome chance that no single chronicle of those who tell of it has given any precise local indications. Aethelstan and his eldest surviving brother Edmund had brought up the full levy of Wessex and Mercia, but possibly rebellion may have broken out among their newly subdued subjects of the North, since no Anglo-Danes are mentioned in their host. They met the allies at Brunanburh (or, as various authorities write it, Brunanwerc, Brunefeld, Brunandun), otherwise called Weondun or Wendune. A dozen sites at least have been suggested for the battle, of which Birrens or Burnswark, the old Roman fortress of Blatum Bulgium on the north-eastern side of Solway Firth, seems on the whole the most likely. For precisely on the north shore of Solway would be

---

[1] See the quotation from Folcwin's Chronicle of St. Bertin in Plummer's *Notes to the A. S. C.*, ii. pp. 137-38.

[2] Florence of Worcester's statement that Anlaf of Dublin took his fleet into the Humber mouth seems simply incredible. To get there he would have had either to sail up the Channel, challenging the large naval force, of which Aethelstan, like his father Edward, was possessed, or else to round Cape Wrath. And the Humber would have been a very bad junction-point for meeting the Scots. Apparently Florence was misled by reading of some great gifts made by Aethelstan to the monks of Beverley, which were really given on his way to the Scottish campaign of 933, four years before.

the natural point of junction for a ship-force from Ireland and a
land-force of Scots, Picts and Strathclyde Welsh.[1] It is very
possible that the allies took advantage of the ruined Roman
entrenchments when they pitched their camp.

Here was fought a very long and stern engagement: even two
generations later it was still remembered as "the great battle".[2]
It went on from dawn to night—as the "Song of Brunanburh"
tells us—a length of continuous fighting which suggests that, in
its later stages at least, the English may have been battering at an
entrenched camp rather than waging war in the open. But this is
not a certain inference; many of the details of the "Song of
Brunanburh" seem to refer to a regular clash between two embattled hosts—the "northern men" are "shot over their shields,"
there is "hard hand-play," "clashing of bills," "conflict of banners". The victory, at any rate, was complete, and there was a
long and bloody pursuit. Anlaf of Dublin escaped to his ships
with a small band "the bloody relic of the darts," and pushed off
for Dublin. The fight then had been not far from the water.
Constantine fled apart to his northern realm by land. Five kings
are said to have been slain, and seven Viking earls. One of the
former was Constantine's son and heir; Eugenius of Strathclyde
may have been another, as he seems to disappear from history at
this moment. As to the other three " kings " the title was so cheap
among the Vikings that it is useless to make further inquiry. An
Irish chronicle gives their obscure names.

At any rate the slaughter was exemplary, and Aethelstan's triumph surpassed all the glories of his ancestors. "Carnage greater
had not been in this island ever yet, of men slain by the edge of
the sword, as the books of old writers tell us, since the Angles and
Saxons came to land here from the East, and sought Britain over
the broad seas." There was no more trouble during Aethelstan's
life from Scot or Dane, and his empire seemed too firmly compacted ever to be shaken. Yet, as we shall see, this was mainly
the result of his personal ascendency, and when he was gone the

---

[1] Here I agree with Dr. Hodgkin, *Political History of England*, i. 264. The
other alternative site which has something to be said for it is Bromborough in
Wirrall, by the mouth of the Mersey. But this is too far from the base of the Scots.

[2] "Usque ad praesens 'magnum' praenominatur 'bellum,'" says Ethelweard,
writing about 970-80.

Danelaw showed that it still retained particularist ambitions, and was not yet ready to settle down as a loyal province of the new kingdom of All-England.

Aethelstan enjoyed the fruits of his triumph for three years (937-39), during which the Anglo-Saxon Chronicle gives no details whatever as to his administration. All that this silence tells us is that no enemy dared to raise a hand against him so long as he lived. We know that he exercised a great influence not only over Britain, but over the whole of Christendom : an Irish annalist calls him " the main beam of the honour of the Western world ". His power indeed was well known on the Continent, where he sometimes seems to have lent naval help against the Northmen to his neighbours. But he was most renowned as the brother-in-law of most of the crowned heads of Europe. His numerous sisters had been sought in marriage by all the greater sovereigns. One Eadgifu became the wife of Charles the Simple of France, and the mother of Louis IV., the last capable Carolingian king. This prince, driven out when a boy after his father's murder, was brought up at Aethelstan's court and returned from thence in 936 to rule the West-Frankish realm : hence came his nickname of Louis d'Outremer. Another sister, Eadgyth, married Otto the Great, son of Henry the Fowler, the restorer of the Western Empire : a third named (like her elder sister) Eadgifu wedded Louis II. King of Provence,[1] a fourth, Eadhild, became the wife of Hugh the Great Count of Paris,[2] whose power overshadowed that of the legitimate Carolingian king. A fifth, Aelfgifu, married "a prince under the Alps," possibly one of the kings of the obscure realm of "Lesser Burgundy".

An infinite amount of lost diplomatic history must lie beneath the story of these marriages, but not a detail of it has been preserved save the curious story in Ethelweard,[3] to the effect that when Henry the Fowler asked for a sister of Aethelstan as bride for his son Otto, the liberal English monarch sent him both

---

[1] A blind prince, who had been mutilated by his rival for the imperial crown, Hugh King of Italy, but retained his own kingdom, and was father by Eadgifu II. of Charles Constantine, the last Carolingian ruler of Provence. As he died in 923 he must have wedded his English wife in her father Edward's lifetime.

[2] She was not, however, the ancestress of all the Capetian kings of France, who came from Hugh by another wife.

[3] Preface, section D.

Eadgyth and Aelfgifu, requesting him to select which he pleased. Otto chose the elder sister, and the younger was passed on to the sub-Alpine prince.

Aethelstan's court seems to have been a general refuge for dispossessed princes. He sheltered not only his nephew Louis d'Outremer, but Alan Count of Brittany, and the heirs of Herlouin Count of Ponthieu. If we may trust Northern traditions there were also exiled Scandinavian princes sometimes about him. He is said to have had friendly dealings with Harald Harfagr, the first king who made Norway into a single state, and this is possible because the Vikings were enemies of both. Many of Aethelstan's enemies were Harald's expelled rebels.[1]

Of Aethelstan's not unimportant legislative work we must speak in its proper place. Here we are dealing only with his political career—or rather with that shadowy reconstruction of it which the meagre entries of the Anglo-Saxon Chronicle make possible. He died at Gloucester on October 27th, 939, and was buried not with his kin at Winchester or Wimborne, but at the Abbey of Malmesbury to which he had been a great benefactor. As he left no issue, the crown passed to his eldest surviving half-brother, Edmund I., a mere lad of nineteen years.

---

[1] But the long story of the friendly practical jokes which they played on each other in the *Saga of Harald Harfagr*, is an invention, though it is quite possible that Aethelstan did foster Harald's son Hakon.

CHAPTER XXV

FROM EDMUND TO EDWARD THE MARTYR, 939-978

THERE appears to have been no trouble or dispute as to the succession on the death of Aethelstan. The obvious successor was his eldest surviving half-brother Edmund, the son of Edward the Elder by his third wife, Eadgifu, the daughter of that Sigehelm, ealdorman of Kent, who had fallen in 902 at the battle of the Holme. Edmund, though he had borne a creditable part at the victory of Brunanburh in 937, was still only nineteen, so that he must have been no more than sixteen when he took the field with his brother in that eventful campaign. There were other descendants of Aethelwulf of more mature age surviving,[1] but by this time the crown had stayed so long in the line of Alfred that no one seems to have taken any count of the more distant kinsmen of Aethelstan.

We have often had to notice in the days of the Heptarchy that the death of a great conquering king was generally followed by a tentative insurrection on the part of the subject-allies who had been wont to give him homage and tribute. This old phenomenon was repeated when Edmund succeeded Aethelstan : he was but a boy, and the experiment of rebellion was well worth trying ; possibly he might prove incapable,—though after his exploits at Brunanburh it was impossible to hope that he might fail in courage or energy. In the spring after the death of Aethelstan (940) the Northumbrian Danes took arms, and proclaimed as their king that

[1] The sons of Ethelweard, the brother of Edward the Elder, had both fallen at Brunanburh. But the father of Ethelweard, the chronicler, who descended from Aethelred I., must have been alive and a grown man at this time, since his son was born about 940—as must be deduced from the fact that he begins to sign Edgar's charters as *minister* in 963. It seems probable that there was at least one other line of royal aethelings in existence at the time.

Anlaf Guthfrithson, King of Dublin, who had already given so much trouble. Since Brunanburh he had apparently been occupied in Ireland, raiding the lands of Meath and Leinster. The crisis was threatening, for the Northumbrians burst into North Mercia with the intention of involving the Danes of the "Five Boroughs" in their movement.[1] They were successful; the first note as to Anlaf's invasion is that he beset Northampton, which lies very far to the south, and could hardly have been attacked unless the towns more to the north had submitted to the rebel. But this place remained loyal and beat off the invaders. Thereupon they swerved westward, and fell upon Tamworth, on the border of English Mercia. Here they were more successful: Aethelflaed's *burh* was stormed and much plunder taken. But King Edmund and the fyrd were now at hand: Anlaf had to fall back, and threw himself within the walls of Leicester,[2] which must therefore have made treasonable submission to him at the moment of his appearance in Mercia. Edmund laid siege to the place, and would have captured the Northumbrian king if he had not fled over the wall at night. We are perplexed to hear that Wulfstan, Archbishop of York, was the companion of Anlaf in his flight, for this prelate, as his name shows, was English born. But no more fighting took place, and we learn, much to our surprise, that Edmund consented to a pacification, by which the five Danish boroughs of the North Midlands were left to Guthfrithson. It is difficult, on the facts known, to understand how King Edmund consented even for a moment to such a cession, but the fact is vouched for by Simeon of Durham, and incidentally corroborated by the Anglo-Saxon Chronicle mentioning in 942 the *recovery* of these towns by the King. Obviously he must have lost them first, if he recovered them later.

The treaty between Edmund and Anlaf is said to have been

[1] There is terrible confusion about this time between the doings of Anlaf Quaran and Anlaf Guthfrithson, but I follow Simeon of Durham in taking the invader of Mercia in 940 to be Anlaf Guthfrithson, for he carefully distinguishes him from his successor Anlaf *filius Sihtrici, i.e.,* Quaran. [S. D. *sub anno,* 941.] The title, "Anlaf of Ireland," applied to him by the A. S. C., suits best with the fact that Guthfrithson was King of Dublin.

[2] Not Chester, as some have taken it. But there is always a difficulty at this time between Legracester or Lehercester (Leicester) and Leigecester or Legecester (Chester). See the Mint signature in Brit. Mus., *Anglo-Saxon Coins,* ii.

drawn up by the two archbishops, Oda of Canterbury and Wulfstan of York, concerning whom we may note the curious anomaly that Wulfstan was English by birth, but had joined in the rebellion of the Dane Anlaf, while Oda was Danish by birth, yet was the loyal supporter of Edmund. He was the son of one of the Viking companions of Ingwar, but had come under the patronage of Aethelhelm, ealdorman of Wilts, with whom he went on a pilgrimage to Rome as a boy. He entered orders, and had been made Bishop of Ramsbury by Aethelstan in 927; in 941 he had just been promoted to the primacy of All England. He was the first Dane to rise to high position in the Church.

The prosperity of Anlaf Guthfrithson was destined to last but a short space. Less than a year after he had been recognised as king by Edmund he attacked Bernicia, where the English high-reeves of Bamborough were still ruling as vassals of Edmund. After sacking Tyningham in Lothian and burning the church of St. Balthere he "perished" (942), perhaps slain in action, for we are told that "for this reason" the men of York sacked (not for the first time) the shrine of Lindisfarne, and committed great massacres. They chose as the successor of Anlaf Guthfrithson his cousin Anlaf Quaran, the son of Sihtric.

On hearing of the death of Anlaf Guthfrithson, King Edmund resolved to attack his successor, and coming up in the spring of 942 with a great army reconquered the Five Boroughs. The Anglo-Saxon Chronicle tells us in a short song of triumph how Leicester, Lincoln, Nottingham, Stamford and Derby were "redeemed" by "the bulwark of warriors, the offspring of Edward, Edmund the King". Apparently Anlaf Quaran thought himself too weak to continue the struggle. Early in 943 he sued for peace, and consented to be baptised, and to do homage for the Kingdom of York, which he was permitted to retain.

Anlaf was expelled from York almost immediately after, by his cousin Regnald, brother of the late King Guthfrith. He seems, however, to have maintained his hold on some part at least of his realm—perhaps its western or northern corner. Regnald hastened to submit himself to King Edmund, and received baptism and did homage, just like his predecessor [943 late months].

Apparently civil war between the two cousins continued, and

probably encouraged by it, Edmund resolved to make an end of both. The Chronicle tells us that in 944 he came up with a great host to York, and utterly expelled from Northumbria both kings, Anlaf Sihtricson and Regnald Guthfrithson.[1] It is quite possible that Regnald was reigning at York, and Anlaf II. on the west coast opposite Ireland, when the conquering army of the English fell upon them.[2]

This reading of the position seems to be made very probable by the entry of the Anglo-Saxon Chronicle for the next year, 945. Here we are told that Edmund ravaged all " Cumberland " (a new name for us), and then let it out to Malcolm, King of the Scots, " on condition that he should be his fellow-worker as well by sea as by land ". Now Cumberland can hardly mean the whole or part of the land of the Strathclyde Welsh, who were at this time ruled by the kinsmen of Malcolm, and do not appear as enemies either of him or of Edmund. I take it that by this name we are to understand the obscure Viking settlement on the Solway Firth, whose existence we have to presuppose in order to account for the predominant Scandinavian nomenclature of all the countryside of the modern Cumberland and Westmoreland—a land of " garths " and " thwaites " of " fells " and " becks ". This region had not been part of the original settlement of the Danes, which Halfdene had established around York. Indeed, it seems rather to have been a land of refuge after the disasters of 866, for the expelled English clergy of Northumbria. It was there that Bishop Eardwulf of Lindisfarne, carrying the relics of St. Cuthbert, had found shelter first with

---

[1] For chronology here, see Mr. Beaven, *E. Historical Review*, June, 1918. A. S. Chronicle, A and G, give the baptism of Anlaf to 641 and his death to 642. The version of D, on the other hand, puts the invasion of Mercia, the siege of Leicester, the baptism of Anlaf and Regnald all under 943. Simeon of Durham makes Aethelstan die in 939, and puts the rebellion of York, the sack of Tamworth, the siege of Leicester and the baptism of Anlaf all in that same year, 939. He kills Anlaf after the sack of Tyningham in 941, and makes his cousin, the son of Sihtric, succeed him in the same year. Florence of Worcester puts the rebellion of York in 941, the reduction of the Five Boroughs by Edmund in 942, the baptism of Anlaf I. and Regnald in 943.

[2] Ethelweard, who has hardly anything else to say about Edmund's reign, gives the curious statement that the two " desertores," Anlaf and Regnald, were expelled from York by Archbishop Wulfstan and the ealdorman of Mercia (*dux Myrciorum*), who subdued York for King Edmund. I know not what to make of this statement, which Ethelweard most unaccountably puts under the year 948—a quite impossible date.

Eadred, Abbot of Carlisle, and then at the mouth of the Derwent (*circ.* 870-80). Eadred was still Abbot of Carlisle and a person of importance when, in 883, he induced the Danes of York to take Guthred-Cnut as their king.[1]   But, some time after this, Cumberland was certainly overrun by Vikings, who settled there in great numbers, and imposed their own names on many of its villages and natural features.   Moreover, as these names show, the new settlers were of Norse rather than Danish extraction.   The period of this conquest and immigration must surely be between 890 and 920,[2] and the settlers must have been Norsemen of the same blood as those who established the Viking States in Ireland, the Orkneys and the Hebrides.   Probably they were often under the suzerainty of the kings of the House of Ingwar, who ruled at Dublin, though they may just as often have been reckoned among the vassals of the Danish King of York.[3]   If we suppose that in 945 Edmund fell upon this state—where Anlaf Sihtricson may well have been reigning—and did his best to destroy it, the story seems to work out well.[4] Feeling unable to retain it for himself, and unwilling to assign it to a Scandinavian jarl, he may well have handed it over to the Scots to tame.   For the house of Kenneth and Constantine was already dominant in Strathclyde, and was only too ready to push its power farther south.   Other readings of the problem are possible, but this seems to fit the political situation best.   Certainly it is far more probable than the usual interpretation that Edmund fell upon the Strathclyde Welsh, who were already ruled by princes of the Scottish house, and handed over their lands to Malcolm.

This is the last act of Edmund recorded in the Anglo-Saxon Chronicle, which remains during his reign as bare and bald as in that of Aethelstan.   But we know that he must have had other spheres of activity.   For example, an entry in the *Annales Cambriae* under 943, is to the effect that Idwal, King of Gwynedd, and his brother

---

[1] See Simeon of Durham, *Historia Regum*, pp. 114-5.   See also p. 482 above.

[2] The only historical note to aid us is that Florence says that Carlisle was restored by William II. in 1093, just 200 years after its sack by the Danes.

[3] If we could believe the Egil Saga, we might point out that two earls with Norse names, Hring and Adils, ruled here at the time of the battle of Brunanburh.

[4] We may note, however, that the *Annales Cambriae* and the *Brut-y-Tywysogion* say that Strathclyde was devastated by the Saxons at this time.

Elised [1] were "slain by the Saxons," must imply a rebellion in North Wales and a retaliatory incursion by the over-lord. We know too that Edmund was deeply interested in the misfortune of his nephew, Louis d'Outremer, King of France, and tried to bring pressure on the over-great vassal, Hugh Count of Paris (his own brother-in-law), who had put his master in durance vile. But nothing came of his intercession in this quarter.

By the English of the next generation Edmund was perhaps best remembered as the original patron and friend of the famous Dunstan, to whom, as the Chronicle (notwithstanding its lack of entries in this period) finds space to note, he gave in 943 the abbacy of Glastonbury, the first step in the chain of preferment which was to lead him to the archiepiscopal chair of Canterbury. But of the saint more hereafter : in Edmund's day he was not a figure of any great importance.

Edmund was destined to reign not quite six years. His death was unworthy of so gallant a king, but was brought on by his own hot temper and imprudence. " It is well known how his days ended, that Leofa stabbed him at Pucklechuch," observes the Chronicle. The tale, as told by later historians, runs as follows : The king was feasting on St. Augustine's Day (May 26, 946) at his royal vill of Pucklechuch when a notable outlaw, one Leofa, insolently slipped in among the guests, and set himself down at one of the tables. The royal major-domo (*dapifer*, *discthegn*) detected him, and endeavoured to turn him out : the ruffian (*pessimus cleptor !*) drew his dagger upon the thegn, whereupon the king, forgetful of his dignity and of common prudence, sprang from his seat to help his servant. Leofa in the scuffle dealt him a mortal wound, and was immediately cut to pieces by the horror-stricken guests.[2] So perished in a miserable brawl this promising young king, before he had finished his twenty-fifth year. He was buried at Glastonbury, the abbey of his favourite Dunstan, who had been favoured with a premonitory warning of his death.

Edmund had been twice married, despite his youth at the time of his decease. By his first wife, Aelfgifu, a lady of great virtue,

---

[1] But the *Brut-y-Tywysogion* makes Elised Idwal's son.

[2] So Florence of Worcester *sub anno* 946 for the outline ; William of Malmesbury adds picturesque details. The general outline of the story is probably quite correct.

who was reverenced as a saint in the next generation, he had two sons, Eadwig and Eadgar.[1] He had only married his second wife, Aethelflaed of Domerham, daughter of Aelfgar, ealdorman of Wilts, shortly before his murder, and had no issue by her.

The king's eldest son being only six or seven years of age, the Witan proceeded, after the usual custom of the English, to elect as his successor his only surviving brother, Eadred, then a young man of about twenty-two years of age : he seems to have been the last-born of all the large family of Edward the Elder. He was crowned at Kingston-on-Thames (as his first charter carefully states[2]) as successor to his brother, " who had ruled the realms of the Anglo-Saxons and Northumbrians, the Pagans [Danes] and the Britons for seven years," after having been chosen by the magnates and blessed by the bishops, to be king and ruler of the fourfold realm. Eadred is said by the first historian who gives any details about him[3] to have been a worthy heir of Alfred and Edward so far as brains and energy went, but to have been weakly in body, little better indeed than an invalid, for his digestion was so weak that he could not eat flesh like other men. Yet his acts seem as vigorous as those of his brother, and he had strength and perseverance enough to carry to a successful end the long strife of the kingly power with the rebellious Danes of York.

In the spring after his election (947) Eadred went up in person to Northumbria, where he met Archbishop Wulfstan and all the Northern Witan at Taddenesscylf (Tanshelf, near Pontefract), and there received their oaths of allegiance as sole and immediate King of Northumbria. He intended to rule it by ealdormen, as Aethelstan had done, and not to concede any under-king to the Danes. But before the year was out the Danes " belied their pledge and their oaths," rose in rebellion, and chose as their king Eric Blood-Axe, an exiled prince of Norway, who was wandering in the northern waters with a pirate fleet. This Eric, with the ominous

---

[1] She has wrongly been called his mistress by some historians, because she signs some of his charters as " *concubina regis* ". But this is a literal translation of her perfectly honourable Saxon title, and Ethelweard calls her *regina*.

[2] Kemble, C. D., No. 411.

[3] Osbeorn's eleventh-century life of Dunstan says that Eadred was seen " *constanti languore periclitari* ". But it is the much earlier biographer, who signs himself " B.," and wrote in 1000, who gives the curious and unappetising details about the king's dinner.

nickname, was an elder son of Harald Harfagr, the unifier of Norway. He had ruled for some time in his native land, but had been driven out by his younger brother Hakon [1] the Good. Having still a strong following he had taken to the sea, and maintained himself for a space as a Viking, plundering in Scotland and the Northern Isles. The *Heimskringla* tells us that " he was a great and fortunate man of war, but bad-minded, gruff, unfriendly and silent ". He had slain his brothers Biorn, Olaf and Sigrod, with many other men of mark, before he was expelled from his kingdom, and had the reputation of a tyrant. Nevertheless, the aid of his strong arm and his large fleet was too tempting to be refused, when the Northumbrians were plotting rebellion, and he was installed as king at York, apparently in the end of 947.

This brought down King Eadred upon the oath-breakers. In the next spring he came up to the North and ravaged the whole valley of the Ouse, pushing his invasion as far as Ripon, where the great minster that St. Wilfred had built was burnt—not, as we should guess, with the king's approval, for he was a pious man and a great friend of monks. He failed, however, to take York, and when he was on his homeward march the Danes sallied out from the strongly fortified city and cut up his rearguard at Chesterford (Castleford, near Ferrybridge). " Then was the king so wrath that he would have marched his forces in again, and destroyed the whole land." But on hearing of his halt, and of his determination to resume the campaign, the Northumbrians were stricken with fear. They expelled their king, Eric—after he had reigned a single year —did homage to Eadred, and paid him a great sum as compensation for their outbreak. Their land was once more broken up into ealdormanries (948).

But the tendency to particularism among the Yorkshire Danes was still deeply rooted. In the very next year (949) an old pretender to their throne once more came on the scene—this was Anlaf Quaran, whom Edmund had driven out in 944. Since then he had been in Ireland, and had apparently made himself King of Dublin for a space. The Yorkshiremen, having failed to establish their

[1] This Hakon is said by the *Heimskringla* to have been foster-son of Aethelstan, and to have been reared in England. But the dates are all wrong, as Aethelstan is made to be still reigning when Eric came to York, and Yatmund (*i.e.*, Edmund) is said to be the English king who expelled Eric, instead of his brother Eadred.

independence with the aid of the pirate-horde of Eric Blood-Axe
had now reverted to their old alliance with the Irish Vikings.   It
would seem that their choice was justified by the greater resisting
force displayed by Anlaf, who maintained himself as king at York
for more than two years (from the end of 949 to the spring of 952).
Possibly he was admitted to homage and confirmed in the position
of *subregulus* by Eadred, though the English chroniclers give no
hint of this.   The *Heimskringla* says that, after the expulsion
of Eric Blood-Axe, the King of England (whom it wrongly calls
Edmund) placed York under a king Olaf (which is the same name
as Anlaf), to defend it, and that this prince fought fiercely against
Eric.[1]   If we could accept this story, the reign of Anlaf Quaran
from 949 to 952 becomes explicable.   It seems unlikely that
Eadred, who was a man of great vigour, would have allowed a
rebel king to exist at York unsubdued (and apparently unattacked)
for such a long time.   But confronted by the inveterate particularism of the Danes of Northumbria, he may not impossibly have
tried the old experiment of giving them a sub-king, bound by
stringent oaths of homage.   And the experiment may have been
considered moderately successful if Anlaf kept out Eric, for Quaran,
at least, was a baptised Christian, and knew the weight of the
sword of Wessex, while the Norseman was a heathen adventurer of
the most bloody and untamed sort.

But Anlaf proved unable to hold what he had won against the
more formidable adventurer.   In 952 " the Northumbrians expelled
King Anlaf and received again Eric, the son of Harald ".   The
hypothesis that the former had been reigning as Eadred's liegeman
seems to be somewhat helped by another entry in the Anglo-Saxon
Chronicle under this same year, 952, *viz.*, that Eadred—apparently before Eric's reappearance—arrested Wulfstan, Archbishop
of York, and cast him into prison at " Judanbyrig," because he had
been often accused of treason.   If we read this to mean that
Wulfstan was detected intriguing for the return of Eric and the
expulsion of Anlaf, who was reckoned Eadred's vassal, matters
become a little more clear.   But if Anlaf was a rebel and York
independent, how did Eadred succeed in laying hands on the archbishop ?   And what need was there that he should be "accused,"

---

[1] But the Norse history is certainly wrong in stating that Eric, after much
fighting, fell in battle against Anlaf.

if he were openly supporting an unrecognised pretender to the Northumbrian throne : his guilt would not need the evidence of any accuser. Judanbyrig, where Wulfstan was confined, was certainly not Jedburgh, as many modern historians have asserted : a prison in the remotest part of disloyal Northumbria would not have held him long. Apparently we are to look for it at the Essex town of Ythanceaster.[1]

Eric Blood-Axe maintained himself at York for the whole of 953 ; but in the spring of 954 he was driven out once more by his fickle subjects. We are told by Simeon of Durham that they acted from sheer dread of King Eadred, who had sworn that the whole province should be laid waste, in punishment for its repeated treasons. But the men of York appeased him with great gifts, and accepted as their earl Oswulf of Bamborough, their English neighbour from Bernicia. Eric was soon after slain by Magnus, the son of Anlaf Quaran. This was the end of the Danish kingdom of York ; its submission was not followed by another revolt ; we have reached the last entry in the troubled annals of the Danish kingdom of Northumbria. The men of York were at last tamed ; probably they had seen little reason to congratulate themselves on their last independent sovereign, who (if Norse sources can be trusted), was a tyrant of the worst sort. Eadred's perseverance had finished the work of subjection to which Edward, Aethelstan, and Edmund had set their hands before him without satisfactory results.

There is little more to record of the reign of this resolute king. We have a note that in 952 he made a great slaughter of the townsmen of Thetford because they had slain an abbot named Eadhelm. But whether this means that there had been serious trouble in East Anglia, or not, we have no means of judging. Another recorded deed of Eadred's later years is that in 954, after the expulsion of Eric Blood-Axe, he released Archbishop Wulfstan from prison, but did not restore him to his see of York, giving him instead the Mercian bishopstool of Dorchester-on-Thames. The *Annales*

---

[1] There are some coins struck at "Geothabyrig" by Aethelred II. Sir John Evans, in the *Numismatic Chronicle* for 1895, suggests that this is identical with Judanbyrig, and that it is represented by the modern Idbury (Oxon.). But Ythanceaster seems equally possible philologically, and more likely historically as it was an old town, representing the Roman fortress of Othona. See Plummer's *Notes to A. S. C.*, ii. 140.

Cambriae give us a hint that Eadred was forced to the same
intervention in Wales which so many of his predecessors had tried.
Howel Dda, the celebrated legislator, having died in 950, there
followed the usual anarchy that attended the passing away of a
powerful king.   In the midst of Welsh civil wars we get the statement that Cadugan, son of Owen and grandson of Howel, was
"slain by the Saxons".   But where and why we are not told.   Had
he been raiding in the land of the Magesaetas?   Or had Eadred
sent troops into Wales to support one of the factions?   We note,
however, that there is no further mention of the English in the
annals of the wars of the descendants of Howel and their rivals the
Kings of Gwynedd.

The only other fact concerning Eadred's later years, which
stands recorded, is that he did his best to induce Dunstan to accept
the bishopric of Crediton, but could not prevail with him, owing to
the obstinate diffidence in his own power to rule and administer
such a charge which the young abbot displayed.   This made no
change, however, in their friendly relations ; it is said that Dunstan
was the king's closest friend and most trusted councillor.   Eadred
used Glastonbury, we are told, as a sort of " safe deposit " ; whenever
he was on the move he handed over to Dunstan his private papers
and his " bocland " charters,[1] the choicest of his furniture, and his
plate and valuables, including the ancestral treasures of the royal
house—a course that must have seemed somewhat offensive to the
lay custodians of the " hoard ".   When Eadred was seized with his
last fatal illness he bade his friend bring him all his property, that
he might dispose of it before he died.   Dunstan, as his biographer
tells, was on his way to Frome, where the king lay sick, with a long
train of laden waggons, when a voice from heaven sounded in his
ear : " At this moment King Eadred has died in peace," whereupon
the abbot's horse suddenly fell down under him dead, " not being
able to endure the presence of the supernatural ".   The sorrowing
abbot arrived in time to find his patron's corpse almost deserted by
his courtiers, who had gone off to pay homage to his nephew, and
was suffered to take it up, to celebrate the funeral rites, and to lay
it by the tombs of Edward the Elder and Alfred in the Minster at
Winchester.

[1] Quamplures rurales cartulas et veteres praecedentium regum thesauros, necnon
diversas suae adeptionis gazas (Anonoymi, *Vita Dunstani*, § 19).

Dunstan's name begins to appear so frequently in the history of the succeeding reigns that it may be well to give some account of one who exercised so much influence over many kings, and left behind him a name more notable than that of any other early Archbishop of Canterbury save Thomas Becket. His character and personality, as drawn for us by his biographers, of whom the first wrote less than twenty years after his death,[1] and was well acquainted with him, were curious and not at all English in type. If we did not know that he had been born of a good Wessex family, and had many kinsmen highly placed in Church and State, we should have suspected him of having been a Celt, for his whole temperament bore a greater resemblance to that of the Irish saints, those men of dreams and visions and self-torturing asceticism, than to that of the more sober English churchmen who attain the same honours from their countrymen. His whole life, as recorded by all his biographers—the earliest no less than those in whose time he had become a focus of wild legends—is full of supernatural sights and warnings. His whole career, we are told, was originally settled by the fact that, when a mere child, he chanced to fall asleep in the church of Glastonbury, and saw an old man in shining apparel, who told him that he should one day rebuild and amplify the buildings. This led him to get his parents' leave to settle there as a scholar, for the ancient sanctuary seems to have been at that time as much a school as an abbey. He was afterwards at the king's court, where many young boys of noble rank were being reared in English and Latin letters, according to the scheme which Alfred had devised thirty years before. Dunstan surpassed all his contemporaries in every kind of learning, and showed such an interest in out-of-the-way studies, combined with ecstatic piety, that his young companions grew jealous, accused him of prospering in knowledge by the use of occult arts, and obtained from King Aethelstan that he should be expelled from the court. This done, they beat him soundly, and threw him into a muddy pond. His own cousins are said to have been among his most prominent accusers and enemies.

[1] This is the priest who signs himself only B., and calls himself humbly *vilis Saxonum indigena*. Bishop Stubbs in his preface to the *Memorials of St. Dunstan* decides against his identification with the well-known scholar Byrhtferth of Ramsey, a pupil of Dunstan. The book was written in, or just about, the year 1000, while Dunstan died in 988. The second life, by Adelard, is only a little later: the other two by Osbeorn and Eadmer are of Norman date and much less valuable.

Disappointed at this sorry reward for zealous study, Dunstan thought for a moment of turning aside into secular life, all the more readily because he had fallen in love with a certain maiden, who showed no objection to his attentions. But his uncle, Bishop Aelfheah of Winchester, combated his desire strongly, and bade him follow the way of his early dream and become a monk. The young man was so torn between the earthly and the spiritual desires that he fell ill, and when (as he imagined) at the point of death yielded to his uncle and took the vows. Everything that Dunstan did, he did with energy,.and we afterwards find him wrestling with the flesh with wild ascetic frenzy. He built himself a cell only five feet high by two and a half broad, in which he could neither stand nor lie, and shut himself there for long periods. We are not surprised to hear that, after much prayer and fasting, he was visited by devils in the shape of bears, dogs and foxes, who tried to distract his attention from prayer by fawning upon him and whispering wicked suggestions in his ear. He was also troubled with spiritual disturbances of the " poltergeist " character ; large stones dropped from the air, or were hurled at him with inconceivable force when nobody was by. One of them, when examined, turned out to be a rock of a description not to be found in any part of Somerset, and was set aside as a relic.[1]

The fame of Dunstan's sanctity spread abroad, and brought him under the favourable notice of King Edmund, who (somewhere towards the end of his reign) made him Abbot of Glastonbury, when he had only reached his twenty-second year—a wonderful piece of promotion. We hear that he had many enemies about the court, who continually tried to prejudice the king against him ; but he was blessed with an even greater number of admirers, not only clerks and thegns but ladies of high rank and wealth. When he was not busy with his spiritual exercises or distracted by visions, he was evidently a delightful and many-sided companion. He was a mighty singer and harper—a curious legend, found in his earliest biographies, tells how his harp once played of its own accord, while he was otherwise engaged. He was a skilled smith and jeweller ; ornaments and utensils made by him were preserved as relics long centuries after. His hand was also skilled in draughtsmanship, and at least one manuscript containing pictures that he drew has been

[1] See the Life by " B.," Rolls Series, p. 29.

preserved.[1] In all kinds of designing his taste was good, and he even condescended to instruct ladies in church embroidery. But he was no mere artist and amateur, but also a sound and conscientious adviser in matters of state : it was for this reason more than the others that King Eadred made him his familiar friend and counsellor, and would have promoted him to a bishopric long before he had reached the age of thirty. Evidently his dreams and visions were a chapter of his life which was kept apart from his practical activity, and did not in the least impair it. Yet they pervaded every year of his life, and he held that he had received premonitions of every important political event of his time : before Edmund's murder he had seen the devil, in the shape of a black man, dancing in glee ; the death of Eadred, as we have already heard, was announced to him by a voice from heaven ; his first acceptance of episcopal preferment was directly caused by a vision of St. Peter, who chastised him for refusing to take up " the office of an apostle ".

It is easy to see how the visionary side of Dunstan's character must have made him an object of suspicion and contempt to many of the lay courtiers, magnates and officials of the kings who successively did him honour. They might, not merely from jealousy but on reasonable grounds, dread the influence in politics of one whom they must have regarded as either a madman or a romancer, and have made every effort to undermine his influence. That he fought through all his troubles, and received the homage of the whole nation as a saint, is the best evidence that there was in him some spiritual power which could not be denied. Madmen and hypocrites may win influence for a moment, but cannot retain it, and so far as we can trace Dunstan's political activity was directed to sane and reasonable ends.

The death of his devoted friend and patron, King Eadred, brought much trouble, not only to the young abbot of Glastonbury, but to all England. The natural heir to the throne was the elder of the two sons of Edmund, who during his uncle's reign had grown up to the age of fifteen. There was no grown man of the royal house who stood anywhere close in kinship to Eadred, though remote descendants of Aethelred I. still survived. Hence it was

---

[1] The Glastonbury book in the Bodleian Library, with a figure of Dunstan himself kneeling.

not unnatural that the Witan made the experiment of electing the
boy Eadwig, though there was no previous example in the history
of the Kings of Wessex of a sovereign of such tender years.[1]   But
Edmund's son was evidently a lad of a prepossessing sort.   Ethelweard, in his pedantic style, tells us that for his personal beauty he
was named " Pankalus," the All-fair, and that he was worthy of
love.   And Ethelweard must have known him well, since he was his
relative and contemporary.   Of what caused all the troubles that
followed Eadwig's coronation at Kingston in 956 we have hardly
sufficient evidence to enable us to come to any safe conclusion, for
the Anglo-Saxon Chronicle runs almost dry during this reign,
favouring us with only two or three entries of a deliberately cautious
and cryptic wording.   The early biographer of Dunstan gives us
a definite and comprehensible story, but it is obviously an *ex
parte* statement written to justify Eadwig's enemies.   It seems,
however, safe to conclude that there were two parties at court, each
of which hoped to secure control over and manage the young king.
The magnates being divided, much depended on the personal influence of those members of the royal house who were about Eadwig's
person : we seem to detect that on one side was his grandmother,
Eadgifu (his mother, St. Aelfgifu, was dead) ; on the other, a young
widow of princely blood named Aethelgifu—perhaps a descendant
of Aethelred I. and a kinswoman of Ethelweard.   The latter got
complete possession of the young king, who announced that he was
about to marry her daughter—a mere child, no older than himself.
The allegation of the other party, which comprised not only the
queen-dowager but Archbishop Oda, Dunstan and Aethelstan,
Earl of East Anglia, the most powerful of the former advisers of
Eadred, was that Aethelgifu had obtained her control over Eadwig
by the most shameful means—tempting the lust of a precociously
vicious boy.   What truth there was in the statement we cannot
say : the royal house of Wessex had not been wont to produce
decadents, and its standard of morals had been high : Eadwig was
not more than fifteen when he was elected, nor than sixteen when
he was crowned a few months later ; his mother had been a saint,
his father had successfully taken up the rule of a kingdom at

---

[1] Though, as we have seen (p. 316), a King of Northumbria had been elected
and crowned when only eight years old.   Edmund, hitherto the youngest king of
Ecgbert's house, had been eighteen when chosen.

eighteen, and is never accused of evil-living. The insinuation that
he had become besotted on a woman of twice his own age, and
resolved to cover their connection by the disgraceful expedient of
marrying her daughter, seems as improbable as it is disgusting.
On the other hand, we cannot deny that boys ripened young in the
tenth century; occasional Neros crop up even in well-conducted
families: there were cases in earlier English history of young
kings [1] who are said to have started on a career of outrageous vice
as early as Eadwig. And something seems to be required to explain
the widespread outburst of wrath against the unhappy boy which
occurred in the next year. It is not sufficient to allege the jealousy
of his grandmother for the woman who had supplanted her as first
lady in the realm, or the conspiracy of a clerical party against a
king who refused to submit to its control; for the latter hypothesis
there is indeed practically no evidence.

The meagre outlines of Eadwig's ruin are told us as follows.
The first friction took place at his coronation banquet in 956, when
the young king, instead of sitting out the long ceremony, left early,
and betook himself to the " bower " of Aethelgifu and her daughter,
an unwise act, for they were not yet married, and his conduct was
liable to misinterpretation.[2] Archbishop Oda suggested, amid
general approval, that the newly-anointed monarch should be
begged to return to his loyal magnates and finish the evening with
them. But none of the bishops or ealdormen seemed inclined to
carry the errand, for it was pretty well known where the king would
be found, and how he would take the interruption. At last Abbot
Dunstan and Bishop Kinesige of Lichfield consented to go: they
found Eadwig alone with the ladies, in very private and familiar
conversation, with the crown of England lying promiscuously in a
corner. There was a stormy scene, in which Dunstan " *increpitavit
mulierum ineptias*," placed the crown on the king's head, and
pulled his unwilling sovereign back to the banquet.

This was a matter that was never likely to be forgiven, either by
the king or by his mother-in-law elect. Eadwig went on as he had
begun; he married Aethelgifu's daughter—her name was Aelfgifu
like that of his own mother—and placed himself entirely in the

[1] See especially the case of Osred of Northumbria, p. 325.
[2] And is given its most scandalous interpretation, with details, in the earliest
life of Dunstan, § 21.

hands of her and her friends.   Her name appears high in his charters of 957 with the odd and unwonted title of "the king's wife's
mother" affixed.[1]   Aethelgifu's enemies were punished ; the queen-
dowager was stripped of her estates,[2] as were many of her friends,
and Dunstan was expelled from Glastonbury and thrust into exile.
He retired to the abbey of Blandinium in Flanders, and abode
there for a year.   What followed we can only guess from Eadwig's
charters, which show that in 956-57 he was giving away lands and
grants right and left, in a most thriftless style, evidently to buy
support from subjects of doubtful loyalty.[3]   That he was not anti-
clerical in his policy seems to be shown by the fact that many of
these grants are to monasteries.   But his rule was not a success:
this modern Rehoboam, as he is styled, and his new advisers pleased
no one.   In the autumn of 957 a general revolt broke out in the
North, and both the Mercians and the Northumbrians elected
Eadgar, Edmund's younger son, a lad of fourteen, as their king.[4]   It
does not appear that there was any fighting, for even in Wessex
there was little vigorous loyalty to the unfortunate Eadwig.   He
only retained the ancient heritage of Ecgbert by submitting to his
enemies: Archbishop Oda declared his marriage uncanonical, on
account of nearness of kin,[5] and Aethelgifu and her daughter
were driven from court (958).   A horrible story is told by one of
Dunstan's later biographers to the effect that Aethelgifu[6] was
mutilated and murdered by her enemies near Gloucester ; but it is
not found till a century and a half after the reign of Eadwig, and
was possibly invented by moralists anxious to provide a proper
chastisement for all the enemies of the saint.

After ruling for one year over Wessex only, Eadwig died before
he had attained the age of twenty.   The only recorded event of his
restricted reign is that, on the death of Archbishop Oda in 958, he
appointed Aelfsige of Winchester as his successor : this prelate, if

[1] Kemble, *Corpus Dipl.*, 1201.   [2] See the early *Life of Dunstan*, § 24.
[3] See Plummer's *Notes to the A. S. Chronicle*, ii. 150.
[4] According to the life of St. Oswald popular opinion was mainly stirred up by
the fact that the king openly lived with two women at once, *i.e.*, his wife and his
mother-in-law (*H. Y.*, i. 402-3).
[5] In what this consisted we cannot say; possibly there was some relationship
by fosterage or sponsorship; but it is more likely that Aethelgifu was more nearly
related to the royal house than the chroniclers deign to tell us.
[6] Not her daughter, as some have it, but "adultera," *i.e.*, the elder lady.   The
younger was Eadwig's wedded wife.

we may trust late authority, was probably one of Eadwig's few
consistent supporters, as he is said to have insulted Oda's tomb
and memory : the story adds that by a just visitation of heaven he
never lived to exercise the office of primate, as he died of cold in
the Alps, while making his way to Rome to receive his pallium.
Eadwig expired on October 1st, 958, after a reign of four
years. Dunstan, as one of his later biographers assures us, had a
vision in which he saw the wretched lad's soul carried to Hell by
black demons ; but he prayed so hard and long that it was inti-
mated to him that the punishment of his late master had been
commuted to a long spell of Purgatory.[1] We should be grateful
for a few less visions and a little more political information concerning this dark and unhappy reign.

Eadgar had already reigned for two years as king of all
England north of Thames when his brother died. Since he was
only fourteen years of age at his election, it is clear that he must
have been under tutelage : the faction which set him up and ruled
in his name was apparently composed of the English ealdormen
and Danish earls of the North and the Midlands, and certainly was
supported by the queen-dowager Eadgifu. It is not fair to ascribe
the insurrection to the clerical party : Oda adhered to Eadwig
when the scission of the realm took place : Dunstan was in exile.
If the movement had any acknowledged head, it was apparently
Aethelstan, the ealdorman of East Anglia, who had been Eadgar's
foster-father, and stood to profit most by the exaltation of his
ward. We are told that under Edmund and Eadred he had been
known as the " Half-king," on account of the influence that he possessed. All the mentions that we have of him are to his credit :
but as he was on the winning side, and moreover was a close friend
of Dunstan, this is but what might have been expected. That he
was no mere ambitious self-seeker, anxious to exercise the powers
of a regent, seems to be shown by the fact that in 958 [2] he resigned
his ealdormanry, and retired into a monastery within a year after
Eadgar had been made king. His province, and some part at least
of his political power, passed to his sons, Aethelsige, Aethelweald
and Aethelwine, of whom the first two can be proved by charters

---

[1] Osbeorn's *Life of Dunstan*, R.S., 104-5.

[2] Not 956, as is sometimes wrongly asserted. See Searle's *Anglo-Saxon
Genealogies*, table 27 of the Nobles.

to have been already ealdormen before their father retired to his monastery.[1] The third, Aethelwine, succeeded ultimately (962) to the paternal ealdormanry of East Anglia : he is always mentioned by the chroniclers with great respect—Aethelwine *Dei Amicus* is his style—and was apparently the most prominent of Eadgar's ministers during the greater part of his reign. It seems likely that this influential family-group may have been the main controlling power during Eadgar's minority, but they probably worked in friendly alliance with the magnates of the North, of whom Oswulf of Bamborough, Earl of Bernicia (953-65), was apparently the chief. Undoubtedly Ealdorman Ordmaer must have been another of the party, since Eadgar was married very young to his daughter, Aethelflaed the Fair, who was the mother of his eldest son and heir, Edward the Martyr.[2] When the young king issued his code of laws we find that he committed the enforcement of it to Aethelwine, and two other ealdormen, Oslac of Northumbria and Aelfhere of Mercia : the last-named, however, was—as subsequent events showed—not a firm friend of the other two, and opposed them after Eadgar's death.

We gather that Eadgar remained faithful during his whole reign to the group of magnates who had placed him on the throne in boyhood. He was also closely allied to their clerical friends, Dunstan and Abbot Aethelwold of Abingdon. For the house of Aethelstan, the " Half-king," were staunch friends of Dunstan. Their first act after Eadgar's coronation as King of Mercia was to bring him back from his exile in Flanders. He was made in quick succession Bishop of Worcester (957) and of London (959), and after Eadwig's death promoted to the primatial seat of Canterbury (960), whereon he sat for twenty-eight years. His chief supporters and friends were Aethelwold, who had been his pupil at Glastonbury and was made Bishop of Winchester in 963, and St. Oswald, Bishop of Worcester (961-71), and Archbishop of York from 971

---

[1] Aethelweald signs charters as *Dux* (ealdorman) from 956 onward, Aethelsige from 950 onward to 958 : Aethelwine succeeded to East Anglia on his brother's death in 962, and held it till about 990, exercising great power under Edward II. and Aethelred II., as well as under Eadgar.

[2] Ordmaer's daughter must have married Eadgar not later than 961, as their eldest child was born in 962, when the king was only nineteen. This lady was nicknamed Eneda "the Duck". She died young. Ordmaer's ealdormanry is not known, but was probably in Wessex.

to 992. Quite a disproportionate amount of the facts that have come down to us from the reign of Eadgar are concerned with the clerical reformation carried out by these prelates, with the approval of the king, and of Aethelwine *Dei Amicus* and his other ministers. Of this more hereafter.

Of the secular annals of England during Eadgar's sole reign (959-75) there is much less to tell than might have been expected. By all accounts it was a Golden Age : the king, loyally supported by the great magnates, lay and spiritual, enjoyed a reign of sixteen years of unbroken prosperity. The realm was undisturbed by invasions from abroad, and only troubled by trifling tumults from within on two occasions. Of these all that we know is that in 966 Westmoreland was harried by Thored Gunnar's son, one of the Anglo-Danish rulers of the North. Apparently the Scandinavian settlement in Cumbria must have given trouble—perhaps stirred up to revolt by the Irish Danes—and received prompt chastisement.[1] Two years later (968) we have the more inexplicable note that King Eadgar ordered Thanet to be ravaged, presumably as a punishment for some local insubordination, which is surprising in this ancient and usually loyal corner of the realm.[2] If there was any fighting of a more serious sort during this reign, it was when in 965 an English army entered North Wales and ravaged the kingdom of Gwynedd, which was then ruled by the three sons of King Idwal. As these princes were always engaging in civil war, it is probable that the suzerain was intervening in behalf of one of them. The invading army is said by the Welsh chronicles to have been headed by "Alvryt" or "Alfre," who seems to be Aelfhere, the ealdorman of West Mercia. We hear of no trouble in South Wales in Eadgar's time. Normally, indeed, the surrounding kingdoms seem to have been in a condition of quiet vassalage from Scotland down to the Bristol Channel.

---

[1] This is the first mention of the name Westmoreland in English history. That Thored was not a rebel but the executioner of a royal mandate seems proved by the facts that his father, Gunnar, was already an earl under Aethelstan, and that he himself was for many years Earl of York, and became the father-in-law of Eadgar's son, Aethelred II. See Plummer's *Notes to the A. S. C.*, ii. 159.

[2] Concerning this enigmatic entry, we have no help, save from Henry of Huntingdon, Book V., who says that " *Rex jussit praedari insulam Tenet, quia jura regalia spreverant, non ut hostis insaniens, sed ut rex malo mala puniens* ". But his authority is too late to be of any real service to us.

The most notable mention of Eadgar's undisputed imperial position in Britain occurs in curious context. We are surprised to find that in 973, when he had already been reigning as sole king for fourteen years, he resolved to have himself crowned, his Mercian election in 957 and his succession to Wessex in 959 having, as it seems, not been accompanied by this ceremony,—an inexplicable omission on the part of the ealdormen and bishops who were then guiding the career of the young lad. We may, however, safely omit the only explanation that has ever been given for it—the silly tale found in some of Dunstan's eleventh-century biographers,[1] to the effect that he seduced a nun, and as penance vowed not to be crowned for seven years. For, his coronation being in 973, his vow would have to start in 966, when he had already been sole king for seven years, and had reached the age of twenty-three. It is the reason why he was not crowned in 957 or 959 that has to be sought—and sought in vain. There is no doubt, however, that he was anointed and crowned with great state at Bath on May 11th, 973, by the two archbishops, Dunstan and Oswald. The compiler of the contemporary section of the Anglo-Saxon Chronicle breaks out into a long poem to celebrate the event, and the life of St. Oswald gives an elaborate account of its details, which seem to have been used as a model for all later coronations. When the festivities were over, Eadgar went to sea with a very great fleet— probably collected at Bristol—sailed round Wales, and came to Chester, where he was met by vassal kings, six or eight in number,[2] who plighted their troth to him, and swore that they would be his fellow-workers by sea and land. These kings were apparently Jago (Jacob) and Howel of North Wales, sons of Idwal; Magnus and Siferth of Man and the Isles, Kenneth of Scotland, his son Malcolm, Dunwallon (Dufnal) of Strathclyde, and " Juchil "[3] of South Wales. Later tradition, both English and Welsh, relates that Eadgar caused his vassals to row him in state upon the Dee, while he steered this extraordinary crew of kings.[4] They went, it is said,

[1] Osbeorn, R.S., p. iii, and Eadmer, *ibid.*, 209.

[2] Six in the Chronicle, but Florence of Worcester and other later writers say *eight* were present.

[3] Juchil is quite unidentifiable, evidently a blundered name.

[4] The Assembly is mentioned not only by the Anglo-Saxon Chronicle, but by the *Brut-y-Tywysogion*, and the *Annales Cambriae*, which is interesting as showing the impression made by Eadgar on the Welsh.

from his palace to the suburban church of St. John the Baptist, where
they offered up prayers together, and then back from St. John's to
Chester, a great fleet following in their wake.   Eadgar, so the story
runs, remarked on his return that any one of his successors who
should ever again preside over such a pageant (*pompam talium
honorum*) might call himself with truth King of All England.

That Eadgar should have been esteemed and loyally served both
by his vassals in Britain and by his own wilder subjects in Northumbria, is explained to a certain extent by the fact that, according
to the Anglo-Saxon Chronicle, he was a great lover of all that came
from abroad.   "One fault he had, all too much," grumbles the
chronicler in verse, "that he loved too much foreign vices, and
brought heathen customs into this land, and enticed hither out-
landish men and harmful folk.   But God grant him that his good
deeds may be more availing than his misdeeds, for his soul's protection on its long journey."   There must be some exaggeration here :
the king beloved by Dunstan can hardly, at least, have brought
heathen customs into the land.   Presumably Eadgar favoured Danes
too much to please a Southern Englishman.   He certainly placed
very many of them in high offices, spiritual no less than secular.
Hence, no doubt, came the fact that (save for the obscure affair in
Westmoreland mentioned above) they gave him no trouble.   As to
the accusation that he "loved foreign vices," we cannot be sure what
is meant : perhaps nothing more than a love for Scandinavian customs is implied.   There are, however, some ugly accusations against
Eadgar's personal character in some of the later chroniclers—just as
there are against that of his brother Eadwig.   Had he picked up
the Norse tendency to practical polygamy, like that of Harald
Harfagr ?   Yet we can hardly believe that he would appear in such
a favourable light in contemporary literature if he had been a
specially evil liver.   The story which has been often told against
him, in modern as well as mediæval writers, that he privily slew
Ealdorman Aethelweald, the first husband of Queen Aelfthryth—
the spouse of his later years—is sufficiently disproved by two facts.
The first is that Aethelweald's brother, Aethelwine *Dei Amicus*,
remained his most trusted minister till the end of his reign ; the
second, that there was an interval of two years at least between the
ealdorman's death and the king's marriage to his widow.   The
whole story, as told by Gaimar and William of Malmesbury, is a

variant of the tale of David and Uriah. But Aelfthryth, by all accounts, was an evil woman, and dark legends naturally gathered around her name.

Before passing on to Eadgar's premature decease, and all the woes that came therefrom, it is necessary to give some account of his ecclesiastical policy, which, in the Anglo-Saxon Chronicle, as in other contemporary records, is described at all too great length, while his secular policy is so sadly neglected. Ever since the chaos of the Danish invasion in the ninth century, the monastic life had been out of gear in England : it will be remembered that Alfred had only been able to fill his new foundations with boys and aliens.[1] Matters had certainly got no better since his day, and we find that in 950 there was hardly a monastery in England that lived by rule. Both those that had escaped the ravages of the Danes, and those which had been founded or rebuilt since those ravages ceased, were apparently liable to that same sort of criticism which Bede had passed upon the religious houses of Northumbria two centuries before. The best of them, like Glastonbury or Athelney, seem to have been as much schools as regular communities : the worst were places where idle clerks lived the lives of laymen, with small profit or edification to themselves or the community at large. In a great majority, as it appears, the places of the original monks had been gradually filled by secular canons, some of whom were actually married, while others ought to have been. They did not live in common, nor observe the Benedictine rule on which the original monastic life of England had been modelled. When, under Edward the Elder and Aethelstan, the realm had become safe from the Viking enemy, and religious men had leisure—so to speak—to take stock of its spiritual condition, they naturally felt that the state of things visible was eminently unsatisfactory. If monasteries existed, they ought to be monastic ; and at this time there was a strong movement of reform visible on the continent, of which the rumour had reached England. The revived Benedictinism of Fleury and other Frankish houses of the better sort provoked the envy and admiration of the more spiritually-minded of the insular clergy. The first persons who are said to have made an effort to improve the condition of the English monasteries were Aelfheah the Bald, Bishop of Winchester (934-51), the uncle of Dunstan, and the

[1] See p. 477.

Danish Archbishop, Oda (942-58). But Dunstan himself was the chief supporter of the movement: as Abbot of Glastonbury, he reformed his own convent, not without much opposition from members who preferred the old laxity. The second house which is said to have been thoroughly set in order was Abingdon, whose abbot, Aethelwold, had been Dunstan's pupil at Glastonbury. He took the trouble to send some of the brethren to Fleury, in order that they might pick up every detail of the revived Benedictinism, and so instruct the community in full. It is said that at Eadgar's accession Glastonbury and Abingdon were the only houses in England that deserved to be called monasteries in the proper sense of the word.

When Dunstan became archbishop in 960, and Aethelwold Bishop of Winchester in 963, they were able to put their ideas as to monastic reform into practice. The king gave them his active support, as did his great minister Aethelwine, whose name of *Dei Amicus* was bestowed on him first by admiring reformers. With this aid the archbishop and his friend were able to carry out drastic reforms all over the southern primacy. Dunstan himself seems to have been far the milder and more tactful of the two, working by persuasion rather than by force, preaching far and wide, gathering willing novices, who were stirred up by his enthusiastic sermons, and promoting to abbacies men whom he had inspired with his own zeal. Aethelwold was a more drastic personage, who called in the secular arm whenever he was met by opposition. Having got papal bulls to back him, and secured the king's approval, he made a clean sweep from the Winchester monasteries of all the canons who would not take the full monastic vows, and send away their wives. We have a lively picture of how he stood triumphant at the " Old Minster," with the king's thegn, Wulfstan of Dalham, at his side, offering the choice of the monastic habit or instant expulsion to the cowering clerks, who craved in vain for delays. Almost the whole body was driven out, and their places were taken by a detachment of monks from Abingdon. The same purge was accomplished at the New Minster and the great royal nunnery of Winchester. Aethelwold afterwards travelled all over England, acting as a sort of inquisitor or vicar-general to purify monasteries. He also restored many old houses that had perished in the Danish wars, such as Ely, Peterborough and Thorney

Dunstan was evidently doubtful as to the wisdom of such violent compulsion : it is curious to note that he did not even expel the secular canons of his own cathedral church of Canterbury, who survived some time after his day.   St. Oswald, Bishop of Worcester, and afterwards Archbishop of York, seems to have been equally moderate : he was a great patron of monks and restorer of monasteries, but we have no tales of violence associated with his work at Worcester, while, when he went north to York, he seems to have found the public opinion of the Anglo-Danish clergy so much opposed to him that he accomplished comparatively little.   But all over the South the reform was carried out during Eadgar's reign, not without much wrath on the part of the canons and their kinsmen.   For the expelled seculars seem to have been in many cases men of the noble class, with powerful connections, who much resented their fate. Aelfhere, ealdorman of Mercia, was especially their patron, and (as we shall see) gave them vigorous help when King Eadgar was once dead.

It must not be supposed that Dunstan's only aim was the revival of strict monasticism.   His aims were far broader : not only was he an advocate of higher and stricter living for the secular clergy also, but he did his best to preach moral reformation among the laity ; his code of Ecclesiastical Canons is very severe, not only against concubinage, and marriage within the prohibited degrees, but also against drunkenness, brawling, and other normal vices of the laity.   In pursuit of his ideals he was unswerving ; a powerful thegn who had made a marriage against canonical law was excommunicated by Dunstan ; he went to Rome and obtained a dispensation from the Pope ; but the primate refused to pay any attention to it, saying that the authority of Christ was the one thing to be obeyed.[1]   In a good cause he would resist even the Pope.

Eadgar, to the deep sorrow of all his subjects, died, aged only thirty-two, on July 8th, 975.   He was the last king of his line who preserved the ancient traditions of the house of Ecgbert, and ruled his realm successfully, in close union with the magnates spiritual and temporal.   Some historians have thrown doubts alike on his ability and his morality, and have written of him as if he had been exalted by his contemporaries only as the friend of Dunstan and

[1] This comes from Adelard's life, § 12, written less than thirty years after Dunstan's decease.

the tool of a clerical party. This is an unreasonable view, and has no solid evidence to support it. The fact that in the midst of troubled times this " Rex Pacificus " enjoyed seventeen years of unbroken prosperity, and that his death was at once followed by rapid decay in the body politic, is sufficient evidence in his favour, and needs not to back it the eulogistic verses of the Anglo-Saxon Chronicle.

Dying so young, Eadgar left no grown-up heir: nor had he any brother who could take over charge of the realm during the minority of his children, as Eadred had done in the case of Edmund's offspring. By his first wife, Aethelflaed the Fair, Ordmaer's daughter, he left one son Edward, then thirteen years of age ; by Queen Aelfthryth, who survived him, he had two children, Edmund, who died in 970, and Aethelred, who was only seven years old at his father's decease. There was no reason why Edward should not be saluted at once as king, though it was clear that for some years he must be in the hands of tutors and guardians. But we learn, to our surprise, from the life of St. Oswald, the nearest contemporary authority to give any details, that his stepmother made a serious attempt to induce the Witan to give her son the crown, or perhaps rather a share of the kingdom, and that she got support from a party probably composed of her own powerful kinsmen. But the idea of a wanton partition of England was overruled, and Dunstan, Oswald and Aethelwold are all said to have championed the cause of Edward, who was duly elected and crowned at Kingston-on-Thames.

The new reign commenced and continued among strife. Before Edward's first year was out we hear of dissensions among the magnates, who had dwelt peacefully together for so many years in Eadgar's time. What were the sides it is hard to make out, nor is it easy to determine the causes for which they fought, though probably the control of the king's person was the real aim of each. One point over which there was much wrangling was the old controversy between the monks and the secular canons. Aelfhere, the great ealdorman of Mercia, as we are told, expelled the monks from many of the newly-reformed houses, and restored the canons. It is said that he found opportunity to distribute a part of their lands among their friends and supporters, and that his action was (perhaps in consequence of this) not unpopular ; he worked " *cum con-*

silio populi et vociferatione vulgi". On the other hand Aethelwine of East Anglia and Brihtnoth of Essex took arms to defend the
monasteries, which remained unharmed throughout their provinces.
In the midst of all this Oslac "the great earl," who had long ruled
York and Deira, was banished by the Witan. The terms of regret
in which the departure of "the hoary-haired hero, wise and word-
skilled" is deplored by the Anglo-Saxon Chronicle, suggest that he
was a friend of Dunstan and of Aethelwine. But who were his
enemies, and why he was "driven out over the gannet's bath, the
whale's domain," we are not informed. A comet is said to have
foretold future evil during the autumn of 975, and a sore famine
to have made 976 a most unhappy year. But civil strife is of worse
omen than comets, and more destructive than famines, and this
seems always to have prevailed during the boy Edward's reign.

The Chronicle gives us no information about this time save that
it mentions two great Witans, held the one at Kirtlington in 977
and the other at Calne in 978. Both, if we may trust later historians, witnessed much disputation between the friends and the
enemies of the monastic reformation. But it is probable that the
questions of the guardianship of the king and the guidance of his
policy were equally fertile sources of debate. At Calne an extraordinary incident occurred. "All the chief Witan of the English
nation fell from an upper chamber, except the good Archbishop
Dunstan, who remained supported on a beam, and there were some
grievously maimed, and some did not escape with life." This chance,
a testimony to the badness of Anglo-Saxon building, becomes a
miracle in Dunstan's biographies, and it is his enemies who are
precipitated through the floor, while he remains aloft supported by
the only joist which did not break.

In 978, on March 14th, King Edward was cruelly murdered, apparently by the contrivance of his step-mother Aelfthryth. According to the earliest version of the story which survives[1]—that in
St. Oswald's life—the young king paid a visit to the royal vill of
Corfe, where his little brother and the queen-dowager were residing.
As he sat on his horse at the gate, the retainers of Aelfthryth
thronged around him, and her butler brought him out a horn of

[1] Gaimar and William of Malmesbury add many and romantic details, some
inconsistent with the plain story in the early eleventh-century life of St. Oswald
quoted here.

wine to drink his welcome. While he was thus distracted, one thegn suddenly grasped his right hand, pretending to kiss it, while another stabbed him from behind on the left, inflicting a mortal wound. Edward fell dead from his horse: his body was taken up and buried with maimed rites at Wareham. But a year later Ealdorman Aelfhere of Mercia took it up, found it incorrupt, and gave it honourable sepulture at Shaftesbury. "There has never been among the English a worse deed done than this, since first they sought Britain," moans the Anglo-Saxon Chronicler, who finds some poor satisfaction for the impunity of the assassins in the fact that if men slew him God has made him a saint in heaven: "his murderers would blot out his memory, but the Avenger on High has spread his fame in heaven and earth. Those who would not bow to his living body now humbly bend on their knees before his dead bones."

CHAPTER XXVI

AETHELRED THE REDELESS AND EDMUND IRONSIDE, 978-1016

NOTHING can give a more unfavourable impression of the
condition of England in 978 than the fact that the murder
of Edward the Martyr went unavenged. The kingdom had been
rent by faction, yet no party seems now to have taken as its war-
cry the punishment of the slayers of the innocent lad. There
were saints in the land—Dunstan, Oswald and Aethelwold—yet we
do not hear that any one of them demanded the punishment
of the murderers or denounced the atrocity, though on late authority [1] we are assured that Dunstan bitterly regretted it, and pro-
phesied that the sword should not depart from the house of the
boy Aethelred, in whose interest the crime had been wrought, and
that his kingdom should be transferred to a stranger—a prediction
which was amply fulfilled. But we should have expected that, if
there had been any right feeling left in the land, the queen-dowager
would not have been allowed to profit by the crime of her retainers,
and to place her son on the throne unopposed. There were still
aethelings in existence who came from the royal line of Ecgbert
and Aethelwulf, and who might have been raised up against the
child of the murderess. Indeed the chronicler Ethelweard, one of
them, was at this moment an ealdorman in Wessex.[2] It must be
to him and Aelfhere of Mercia [3] that the compiler of the Anglo-
Saxon Chronicle makes bitter allusion when it says that "Edward's
earthly kin would not avenge him, but left the vengeance to his
Heavenly Father". Presumably, the majority of the magnates felt

---

[1] Osbeorn's *Life of Dunstan*, R.S., 115. The prophecy is an echo of 2 Samuel
xii. 10.

[2] He commences to sign charters as *dux* in 977, the year before Edward's
murder.

[3] Who was *regis Edgari propinquus*, we know not by what descent.

that Aethelred, who was but ten years old, could hardly be made responsible for his brother's death, that the memory of Eadgar had great claims on the gratitude of his people, and that anything was better than a war of succession.   But this does not explain why they should have left the queen-dowager in possession of her son's person, to rear him to manhood, still less why her retainer, the thegn Aelfric, who is said to have been one of the actual murderers of Edward, should have been permitted to obtain an ealdormanry, no doubt by Aelfthryth's favour, only a few years after his crime.[1]   One thing is certain, that all the magnates acquiesced in the consequences of the crime at Corfe, though many of them may have deplored it.   Aethelred was elected king without opposition, and crowned by Dunstan and Oswald, the two archbishops, at Kingston on April 14th, 978, only a month after his brother's assassination.

For the next few years the realm must practically have been under the governance of Queen Aelfthryth and of the faction of magnates who adhered to her.   But there seems to have been no revolution in the *personnel* of the governors of England, such as might have been expected.   The greater ealdormen of Eadgar and Edward's time continued to hold their provinces till their deaths—that of Aethelwine *Dei Amicus* did not befall till 992, Aelfhere of Mercia lived till 985, Brihtnoth of Essex till 991; Ethelweard the chronicler-ealdorman survived till well into the next century.   It cannot be said, therefore, that the youth of King Aethelred was spent under the guidance of newly promoted or inexperienced counsellors.   Dunstan, Oswald and Aethelwold also survived, all three, for some part of the new reign.   The drastic bishop of Winchester lived to 984, the saintly northern primate till 992. Dunstan, the greatest of the three, saw ten years of Aethelred's reign, and ere he died witnessed the commencement of the working out of his own prophecy—if ever he made it.   He seems to have retired from public affairs soon after 980, and to have spent his

---

[1] This Aelfric gets terribly confused with his contemporary Aelfric Cyld, ealdorman of Mercia, in whose company he signs some charters. He seems to have been ealdorman of Hants and Berks, 983-1003. He is the traitor who wrecked the campaigns of 992 and 1003, but surely not the ealdorman Aelfric who fell at Ashington in 1016, nearly forty years after Edward's murder. (But see Searle's *Anglo-Saxon Genealogies, Nobles*, No. 25.)

last years mainly in the exercise of his spiritual duties as archbishop. We are told that his zeal and activity remained with
him to the end, and that his last sermons were his best. Ere we
come to his death in 988 we shall have one more mention of him to
make, in which the young king, the last of his many masters, cuts
a sorry figure.

In his earlier years, then, Aethelred II. did not win his name of
the Redeless, the man destitute of counsel, through the absence of
counsellors to whom he might apply. It was given him rather because of his talent for choosing the worse rather than the better
advice. But his full capacity for mismanagement did not display
itself till the older generation of magnates had died out, when
he was free to listen to the evil inspirations of his chosen friend
and *alter ego*, the miserable double-dealing Eadric Streona, the
worst man to be found in the records of English history down to
the moment of the Norman Conquest. Aethelred himself was not
exactly a coward or a weakling: he had his moments of energy
and action, but they were always ill-timed and misdirected. The
more we study his career the more does he seem like a man stricken
with judicial blindness, inevitably forced to take the wrong turning
and make the wrong decision, whenever an alternative was placed
before him. The curse of a brother's blood seemed to lie upon
him, and to bring ill-luck to his every action. He has sometimes
been compared to John Lackland : but there is this difference between them that, while both were equally vicious and selfish, John
often guided his plans with much ingenuity and worldly wisdom,
and only failed because he made no allowance for the moral factors
in human life and policy, while Aethelred seemed as destitute of
practical wisdom as of conscience. John had many petty triumphs
of cunning; his remote ancestor had none. Otherwise they were
not unlike : both were cruel and debauched, treacherous, contrivers
of murder, oath breakers Both were given to strange outbursts
of energy and passion, and equally strange lapses into sloth and
apathy. Both died broken men, oppressed by adversaries who
were trampling down their realm. And the death of each was welcomed by his subjects as the removal of a long nightmare.

Aethelred's long reign of thirty-eight years falls into three
parts, whose annals reproduce in the most accurate way the three
stages of the history of England in the ninth century. For, like

that century, his period begins with the sporadic Viking descents which are mere coast-raids for plunder, and accomplish nothing serious (978-91).   Then we have a second stage, when once more a "Great Army" throws itself upon England, and begins to press inland and do widespread mischief (991-1012).   Lastly there comes the third stage, when the invaders, elated by their earlier successes, take in hand the conquest of the whole realm (1013-16).   And having an Aethelred to face them, and not an Alfred, they succeed in their purpose.

The record is an exasperating one to follow, for in 978 there was no reason whatever why England should not have beaten off the enemy with ease.   She was now a united realm—not a group of loosely federated States as in 834.   She had a large fleet, which under Eadgar had been counted by the hundred ships, and could still assemble in great force—whereas in 834 she had been altogether destitute of a navy.   And she had the tradition of victory ; Alfred, Edward the Elder, and Aethelstan had made such havoc of the Vikings that the English had learnt to face them with confidence, and to beat them at their own game.   But all this was of no avail when the Redeless King guided the helm of the state.   The rage of the nation at being beaten neither by superior numbers nor superior courage, but simply because of the mismanagement of its own resources, is well expressed for us by the entries in the Anglo-Saxon Chronicle, whose main version fell into competent hands again about the year 990, and continues to be very racy reading throughout the second half of Aethelred's reign. The compiler, who was evidently working at his entries from year to year, was a man with a considerable power of irony, who is normally writing in a white heat of indignation at the unnecessary disasters that he has to record, he tells us how "anything that may be counselled never stands for a month," how "when the enemy is eastward, then are our forces kept westward, and when they are southward, then are our forces northward," how "when the leader groweth feeble, then is the army sore hindered".   And, like many a more modern patriot, he goes off wildly on the cry of treason, whenever a worse disaster than usual has occurred.   His vivid descriptions enable us to follow contemporary history in a way that has been impossible since Asser laid down his pen in Alfred's reign.   And bitter is our regret that a similar annalist was not writing in the glorious days of Aethelstan, a time far more worthy of such a narrator.

Aethelred had been but two years on the throne, and was still but twelve years of age, when the first note of distress is struck. In 980 there were Viking descents on Southampton, Thanet and Chester, a phenomenon that had not been seen since Ohthere's fleet in 913 got such poor welcome in the Bristol Channel : they do not seem to have been very dangerous, though some havoc was done owing to the want of preparations for defence. These first evil portents were followed by similar ones in 981-82, when a small fleet, apparently from Ireland, fell upon Padstow, and ravaged some part of the coast of Devon, as well as the opposite coast of South Wales. After this came a gap of six years, during which no further attacks are recorded—a phenomenon that recalls the similar cessation of raids during the first invasions, between the first sack of Lindisfarne and the serious attacks that only began in 834. The years however were not altogether quiet. We hear of quarrels in the Witan, and of the exile in 985 of Aelfric Cyld, the son and successor of the great Ealdorman Aelfhere of Mercia. Clearly a royal minority was demoralising to the magnates, who fought out their quarrels unhindered by any restraining power.

In this space the young king Aethelred came to man's estate. The first note of his personal activity is characteristic : in 986, being now eighteen, he quarrelled with Aelfstan, bishop of Rochester, but instead of taking any legal proceedings against him, wasted his see-lands at the head of a band of his household men, and laid siege to his city. Thereupon Dunstan begged him to desist from such strange proceedings, but Aethelred refused till the primate paid him a hundred pounds of silver, on which he raised the siege and went away. It was the deed of a captain of mercenaries or a Viking chief rather than of a king, but all his later acts were of a similar pattern.

Two years later Dunstan died (988), and in the same year the Viking raids recommenced with a new descent on the north coast of Devon and Somerset, and the sack of the little town of Watchet ; this was another move on the part of the Irish Danes, who are recorded by the Welsh annals to have been busy this year all along the coasts of Demetia, where St. David's was sacked. Their leader was Guthfrith, son of Harald, King of the Western Isles. The

power of such a petty prince was not dangerous ; but a more re-
doubtable invader was at hand. This was Olaf Tryggveson, an
exiled scion of the house of Harald Harfagr, who had been an
adventurer in the Baltic since his youth, and had gradually built
up for himself a considerable squadron of pirate ships. For he
could not approach his native Norway, which the sons of Eric Blood-
Axe had conquered many years before, and long held. After
many exploits in the East, he and his fleet drifted over to the
British Isles, where they were a terror alike to English, Scots,
Welsh and Irish for about four years (991-92-93-94). It is unfortunate that the *Saga* which bears his name is too late to help us
in disentangling his doings from those of other marauders in the
British seas about this date. But such details as it gives us do
not fit in at all well with the notices in the Anglo-Saxon Chronicle
—indeed the only point in which they agree is that Olaf finally
became a Christian, made his peace with King Aethelred, and departed from England in friendly guise, never to return.[1]

It appears certain, however, that it was against Olaf's fleet
that the English fought, in 991, the most important battle that had
taken place since Brunanburh—a battle celebrated by a song as
vigorous and more lengthy than that which told of Aethelstan's
victory—though this was a defeat of the most disastrous kind.
The Chronicle only tells us that "this year Ipswich was ravaged,
and after that, very shortly, was Brihtnoth the ealdorman slain at
Maldon". The song helps us out with many details; evidently
after sacking Ipswich the pirates coasted down the shore of Essex
and landed near Maldon, at the mouth of the Blackwater. They
were faced not by the full levy of Eastern England, but by that of
Essex alone, under its ealdorman, who must have been advanced
in years, as he had held office ever since the time of Eadwig.
Brihtnoth gave the enemy "hard hand-play," but was mortally
wounded, and fell with all his chosen thegns around him. His
body was barbarously mutilated by the victors. We should have
heard, if an Alfred or an Edward the Elder had been on the
throne, of a second battle a few days later, when the king with all
the *fyrd* of England should have come upon the scene. Instead of
this we learn that the disgraceful expedient tried so often in the
ninth century was repeated. By the advice of Archbishop Sigeric,

[1] See pp. 396-400, of the *Saga*, translated in Laing's *Heimskringla*.

as the Chronicle informs us, the king and the Witan resolved to buy peace from the invaders. " It was decreed that tribute should be given to the Danish men, on account of the great terror which they caused by the sea coast, and this first tribute was 10,000 pounds." [1]

Next year, however, something more worthy than mere bribery was devised against the enemy. " The king and the Witan decreed that all the ships which were worth anything should be gathered together at London, in order that they might try if they could anywhere entrap the Army from without," *i.e.*, if they could close in upon the Vikings from the sea side, and so surround them with superior forces and exterminate them. Apparently, then, Olaf's fleet was still hanging about the eastern coast. The command of the great armament assembled was taken not by the king himself but by two admirals, ealdorman Aelfric (the reputed murderer of Edward the Martyr) and Thored a Northumbrian earl, with whom were associated two bishops, Aelfstan of London and Aescwig of Dorchester. The Anglo-Saxon Chronicle informs us that Aelfric (for whom it has no words too hard) wrecked the scheme by sending treacherous news of it to the enemy. Nay worse, on the night before battle was expected, he withdrew himself from the fleet and fled. The Vikings therefore escaped from the encircling movement, all save one ship which was taken and its crew slain. But shortly after the squadrons of London and East Anglia fell in with the enemy and fought a hard battle in which they apparently had the worse, as we are told that the Vikings captured the admiral's galley on which Aelfric had been. [2] But there clearly was no very decisive victory : the enemy seems to have moved up northward, as if to get out of the way of the English fleet. In the next year (993) they are found sacking Bamborough, after which they moved down the coast and entered the Humber, landing right and left to plunder Yorkshire and Lindsey. The lands-

---

[1] The text of the Treaty chances to have been preserved. See Liebermann's *Gesetze der Angelsachsen*, i., 220-23. It names 22,000 pounds, instead of the 10,000 of the Chronicle. It also gives the names of two colleagues of Olaf, the Jarls Guthmund and Jostein.

[2] So, at least, I interpret, as does Dr. Hodgkin, the confused wording of the A. S. C. Others make the English take the ship from the Danes, which seems incredible; if Aelfric had joined the enemy we should surely have been told, and he would not have retained his ealdormanry till 1003.

folk came out against them in force under three leaders—Fraena, Frithgist and Godwine, who were apparently magnates of the Mercian Danelaw. But they were badly beaten and " the leaders first of all began the flight," as the Chronicle observes with suppressed bitterness. The only other note which we have concerning this year is that King Aethelred caused Aelfgar, son of Ealdorman Aelfric, to be seized and blinded. If this was in revenge for his father's cowardice and treachery in the preceding summer, as some historians assert, it is strange that Aelfric himself is found still holding his ealdordom for ten years more.[1]

In 994 [2] Olaf Tryggveson found a comrade in his piracy of a rank and status much the same as his own. This was Sweyn (Swegen), son of Harald " Bluetooth," King of Denmark. He had fallen out with his father, and had been compelled to take to the Viking life. Nor did he succeed at once in recovering his position when his father fell in battle with him, for, after he had reigned for a short time in Denmark, the Swedes intervened, and drove him forth again. He was now wandering at large with a great fleet, and ready for any mischief. Sweyn was an apostate, and a cruel foe to all Christians. He had, along with his father Harald, been compelled to submit to baptism by the Emperor Otto I. many years before. But while his parent had taken kindly to the enforced change in his faith, and had done much to further the spread of Christianity in Denmark, Sweyn had reverted to paganism at the earliest opportunity, and had made himself the leader of a party of reaction. He was a church-burner and a slayer of priests. Olaf and the Dane united their squadrons, and at the head of ninety-four ships took in hand no smaller an enterprise than an attack on London. They ran up the estuary of the Thames, landed near the city and " continued fighting stoutly against it ". Among other devices we are told that they tried to set it on fire. But the Londoners, always hard fighters since Alfred set his new military

---

[1] He witnesses Aethelred's charters in 997-98, as *dux Wentanensium provinciarum*, Kemble, C. D., 698, 703, and is certainly the commander who in 1003 is accused by the A. S. C. of " falling again to his old tricks " and showing cowardice. But I can hardly believe that he is the Aelfric killed at Assandun in 1016. This would make him hold his office over thirty years, and be too old for battle.

[2] Or possibly in 993, for there are indications of an early visit of Sweyn (see Plummer's *Notes to A. S. C.*, ii. 177).

colony in the restored city, made a splendid resistance, and "after sustaining more harm and evil than they had ever supposed that any citizens could do unto them," the Dane and the Norwegian raised the siege. It is characteristic to find that there is no mention of King Aethelred appearing with an army of succour. Apparently London saved itself, without external aid.

Olaf and Sweyn fell back down the Thames, plundering both in Essex and in Kent as they retired. They then seem to have settled down on the south coast, where their men "got themselves horses"—even as the "great army" had done in 866—and rode at large over Sussex and Hampshire. Instead of raising all England for a battle, the miserable Aethelred resolved to repeat the experiment of 991, and to offer tribute on condition that the enemy should depart. The two kings accepted the terms; they gave hostages for the fulfilment of the treaty, and were granted the town of Southampton for their winter quarters, while 16,000 pounds of silver was being collected to pay them off. Olaf Tryggveson trusted himself in the hands of the English, visited Aethelred at Andover, and was there confirmed, after which he solemnly swore that he would never come to England again in warlike guise, a pledge which (as we are astounded to hear) he loyally fulfilled. Olaf was a chivalrous prince, if we may trust the picture of him given in his interesting *Saga*, and he was a genuine convert to Christianity; during one of his raids, as the *Saga* tells us, he had been much impressed by the teaching of a certain hermit in Scilly, and had been baptised by him. Yet we may, perhaps, suspect that the most efficient reason for his keeping his oath was that just at this moment he received invitations from his native Norway, to come over and deliver the land from the lecherous tyrant, Earl Hakon, who was then ruling there. In 995 he sailed thither: the earl was slain by his own revolted subjects, and Olaf became king. He reigned for five years, doing many valiant deeds, and extirpating paganism in his realm by the strong arm when persuasion failed. The old faith of Odin had many martyrs while he ruled; if half the tales of his *Saga* are true, his methods of conversion would have pleased Charlemagne or Torquemada.[1]

[1] *Cf.* the horrible story of the torture of Raud the Strong, *Heimskringla*, i. 448-9.

Sweyn the Dane would have nothing to do with Christianity, and his share of the 16,000 pounds of silver would not have contented him long, but, as it chanced, external circumstances drew him also out of England. His old enemy, Eric of Sweden, who had driven him out of Denmark, died in 995, and the time was propitious for a snatch at the paternal crown. He went home with his armament, and after some fighting recovered his realm. Thus it came to pass that England seems to have been completely free from Viking ravages in 995-96.

When the raids commenced again in 997, it does not seem that Sweyn was concerned in them, and their locality suggests that a fleet based on Danish Ireland may have been the invading force. The theatre of war was all about the Bristol Channel, and the enemy landed and wrought devastation in South Wales as well as in Devon and Cornwall. They then rounded Land's End, and raided about the mouth of the Tamar, going as far as Lydford and Tavistock. Not one word is said about any opposition being offered by the ealdormen of West Wessex, Ordwulf, the king's uncle, who was responsible for its defence—still less by the king himself. Hence we are not surprised to see the sphere of the operations of the Vikings spreading eastward in the next year (998), when we are told that their fleet ran into Poole harbour, settled down at the mouth of the Frome, and sent out raiding expeditions "as far as they would into Dorset". From thence, still pushing up-channel, the Danes landed on the Isle of Wight, and harried the neighbouring shore of Hampshire and Sussex for provisions. Here they were in the ealdordom of Aelfric, the cowardly admiral of 992, so that it is not astonishing to hear that "forces were often gathered against them, but as soon as they should have joined battle, there was ever, from some cause, flight begun, so that in the end the enemy ever had the better of it". Of a general levy against the invaders, or the preparation of a fleet there is not a word as yet. Such measures, were, however, taken at last in the following year, when, ever pushing eastward, the invaders came into the Medway, and defeated the *Fyrd* of West Kent by Rochester. "Then the king and Witan decreed that they should be attacked both with a land-force and a ship-force. But when the ships were ready, then those who had the

36

decision[1] delayed from day to day, and distressed the poor folks
on board ; and ever as things should have been forwarder they
were set more backward, and ever they let the enemy's force increase, and ever they drew back from the sea, and ever they (the
Vikings) went after them, so that in the end neither sea-force nor
land-force effected anything, save distress of the people and waste
of money, and the encouragement of the enemy." What precisely
was the series of operations here hinted at we cannot say, but
clearly there was no general engagement when the great levy by
land and sea had been called out. The Vikings avoided action
when outnumbered, and Aethelred had not the wit or the courage
to force it on them.

In the following year (that thousandth year from the birth
of Christ whose number many men thought mystical and ominous[2])
the main body of the Danes suddenly departed from England,
and went adventuring in the duchy of Normandy, or "Richard's
land" as the Chronicle calls it, from the name of its then ruler,
Richard the Good. Why they went we are not directly told, but
we must probably connect the fact with a note to be found two
years later in the Chronicle, to the effect that King Aethelred had
taken into his service Earl Pallig, the husband of Gunhild, sister
of Sweyn of Denmark, with some ships' crews of his followers, and
had " well gifted him with houses and with gold and silver". We
can hardly doubt that Pallig was one of the chief leaders of the
fleet that had made itself so troublous in 997-98-99, and that he
was now bribed to play the part of sheep-dog instead of wolf.[3]
Very probably other chiefs were taken into the king's service at
the same time, for so can we best explain the existence of many
recently arrived Danes dwelling in Southern England two years
later.

In the absence of the main Viking fleet, and probably with

[1] " Deman," the doomsmen, a very queer word to find here, it being properly
applied to local judges; cf. p. 374, above.

[2] Though the expectation that the world was to come to an end in 1000, often
insisted on by modern historians, does not seem to have been so widespread as was
supposed.

[3] Pallig is spoken of in 1001 as having been hired and entertained by the king
some little time back, and as revolting in that year. The service presumably began
in 999. He was probably a member of the house of Palna-Toki the famous Jomsborg Viking. See Stevenson, *Notes to the Crawford Charters*, p. 144.

the assistance of Pallig and other mercenaries, King Aethelred took in hand in the year 1000 an enterprise of the most surprising kind. For once he is found assuming the offensive and operating with great—if perhaps misdirected—vigour. At the head of a land army, composed presumably of the levies of Northumbria, he "went into Cumberland, and ravaged it well nigh all". No doubt the Irish-Scandinavian colonists about the Solway Firth had been aiding and abetting the raids of their kinsmen during the last few years, and deserved chastisement as rebels. At the same time Aethelred had brought a fleet round to the west coast: it had been intended to co-operate with the land force, but failed to do so, probably being turned aside by storm; but it fell upon the Isle of Man[1] and devastated it. This was part of the dominions of Regnald, King of the Isles (989-1004), whose father Guthfrith had given trouble in the year 988, and who had probably taken a prominent part himself in the later raids: a long-deferred punishment was thus inflicted on him and his subjects.[2]

The tale of this unwonted display of energy by the English forms but a small interlude in the story of their disasters. In the next year (1001) we begin to hear again of Viking raids. A squadron assailed the Hampshire coast, and its landing force pushed inland and had a sharp battle with the *Fyrd* in which two high-reeves (here apparently sheriffs are meant) fell. Next a descent was made at Exmouth, apparently by the main fleet of the enemy, recently returned from Normandy.[3] While the Vikings lay here they were joined by Earl Pallig, who treacherously fled from King Aethelred's court, despite of all the endowment that had been lavished on him. With his aid, and perhaps under his leadership, the invaders ravaged the borders of Wilts and Dorset, and beat the fyrd at Penselwood: again, as earlier in the year, we hear that two high-reeves, presumably those of Wilts and Dorset, were slain in the fight. Thence

---

[1] Not on Anglesey, as in many translations of the A. S. C. "Mon" serves for both, but here means Man.

[2] That the invasion of Cumberland was not an invasion of Strathclyde, now ruled by Scottish sub-kings, as some Scottish historians, mediaeval and modern, have asserted, seems clear. Henry of Huntingdon has got matters right when he says that Aethelred made this raid because there was a "maxima mansio Dacorum" in Cumberland (Book v., *sub anno* 1000).

[3] We have only Florence of Worcester's authority for this return. But it seems correct.

they marched east, apparently unopposed, reached Southampton
Water, and burned Bishop's Waltham. "This was in every wise
a heavy time, because they never ceased from their evil doings."

Knowing the king's character, we are not surprised to learn
that his next move was to bribe the invading swarm to depart,
by a third paying of tribute, even heavier than those of 991
and 995. This time the Danes extorted as much as 24,000
pounds, half as much again as the sum that had been given to Olaf
and Sweyn six years before. Yet this was no royal army, but
a miscellaneous assembly of pirates. Apparently they left the
land after getting their tribute, and the chronicler then turns aside
to tell of domestic strife, how Leofsige, ealdorman of Essex, murdered the high-reeve Aefic, and how the king forfeited his ealdormanry and drove him out of the realm. Whether this was an isolated
act of lawlessness, or an incident of some unrecorded court intrigue
no man can say, for lack of further details.

Two other notices only survive from the year 1002, but both
were pregnant with much importance in the future. The first is
that King Aethelred, now aged thirty-three, having lost his wife
Aelfflaed [1] the mother of his twelve eldest children, sought and obtained the hand of Emma, the daughter of Richard, Duke of
Normandy. The marriage probably was intended to cement an
alliance between two powers now equally plagued with Viking
raids, for the pirates of this day were as ready to attack their
settled relatives in Normandy or Northumbria as to fall on ordinary
Franks or Englishmen. Emma received a large endowment from
her husband, in which was included the city of Exeter, which she
put under the rule of a countryman of her own, one Hugh, who
was made king's-reeve there. This was the first recorded coming of Norman adventurers to England—the phenomenon which
was to be such a predominant feature in the reign of Emma's and
Aethelred's son Edward the Confessor.

The last incident recorded in the Chronicle under the year 1002
is one of a very different sort, the celebrated but enigmatical
"Massacre of St. Brice" (Nov. 12th, 1002). We are assured

---

[1] Who is said by Ailred of Rievaulx to have been daughter of that Northumbrian
Danish Earl Thored, son of Gunnar, of whom we have heard before. But Florence
of Worcester makes her daughter of an otherwise unknown *Comes Agilbertus* in his
genealogy, and calls her Aelfgifu.

by the Chronicle that Aethelred was told that there was a conspiracy against him, that the Danes settled in England were plotting "to bereave him treacherously of his life, and after all his Witan," whereupon he ordered them to be slain, and the order was carried out. It is clear that the phrase "all the Danes that were in England" does not mean the inhabitants of the Mercian Danelaw and the North. They had given no trouble of late, and had suffered from, and fought against, the Vikings just as their English fellow-subjects had done. Earls with Danish names held many provinces both before and after the massacre, and the king himself had taken as his first wife the daughter of an Anglo-Dane. Moreover, they represented well-nigh half the population of England. Apparently the men whose treason (real or supposed) was delated to Aethelred were of another class. Probably they were the adventurers and broken men (like Earl Pallig in 1001) whom he had taken into his service as mercenaries. Very possibly he may have enlisted quite a number of them after the recent treaty and tribute, made and paid in the last spring. Quite possibly they may have been concerned in some plan to renew trouble in conjunction with the pirate fleets that were always hovering in the offing. How far the slaughter extended we do not know; Henry of Huntingdon, who wrote early in the twelfth century, tells us that he had heard, when a boy, old men who said that Aethelred sent secret letters to each city, in accordance with which the English on a fixed day fell on the unsuspecting Danes and slew them. But such authority is useless; in ninety years the memory of a tale can assume very exaggerated and distorted shapes. William of Malmesbury, whose authority is still less than that of Henry, says that Earl Pallig's wife and child were among the slain in the massacre; they had been captured and held as hostages when he absconded a year before. This is possible, but it seems unlikely that he or his friends should not have reclaimed them at the time of the treaty made in the spring before St. Brice's Day.[1]

Whatever may have been the scope and the effect of Aethelred's order, we cannot doubt, after reading the Anglo-Saxon Chronicle,

[1] The only local tradition about the massacre is an Oxford one, introduced into a forged charter of 1104, in which we are told that the Danes in that city fortified themselves in St. Frideswide's church-tower, and that it was burnt over their heads. The fact is quite probable, but the authority is poor.

that a considerable slaughter took place. The act is entirely in keeping with all that we know of the king's character and methods. Of course it had no such result as he hoped; the massacre only gave the Danes a good excuse for renewing their assaults on England. In the spring of 1003 they reappeared in greater force than they had ever shown before, and under the command of Sweyn their king. If, as is said by William of Malmesbury, his own sister Gunhild, the wife of Pallig, had been one of the victims of St. Brice's Day, he had every reason to seek revenge. Sweyn came this time not as an exiled adventurer (as he had been in 994) but as a reigning king, with the whole force of Denmark at his back. Not only had he long mastered his paternal kingdom, but in the year 1000 he had defeated and slain his old friend Olaf Tryggveson at the great sea-fight of Swold, the most famous of all the northern naval battles. Since then he had been suzerain over the greater part of Norway. England had never before had to face such a formidable enemy, who brought against her the full force of more than one kingdom. The presence of an Alfred was needed, and instead the defence was in the hands of a sovereign who did not even take the field in person, but handed over the conduct of the war to a subordinate of tried incompetence. The Danish army first appeared at the mouth of the Exe: it then captured Exeter with ease, through the treason or culpable negligence of the Norman Hugh, whom Queen Emma had set there as governor. From thence, after acquiring an enormous booty, the enemy went up into Wiltshire. There they were found by a large force from East Wessex, but it was under the charge of Ealdorman Aelfric, the disgraceful admiral of 992. "When he should have led on the *fyrd* he had recourse to his old devices: as soon as the armies came in sight, he feigned himself ill, and began retching and vomiting, and said that he was grievously sick, and thus betrayed the people whom he should have led. . . . When Sweyn saw that the English were not single-hearted and were beginning to disperse, he led his army against Wilton, and spoiled the town and burned it. And then he went to Salisbury, and after east to the sea, to meet his ' sea-horses' (*i.e.*, his fleet)." Satisfied with this harrying of all Wessex from Devon to Hants, he then brought the campaign to an end, and apparently went home for the winter.

The Danish version of the wars of Sweyn and Aethelred, as

given in the Heimskringla, tells us that the King of Denmark from the first aimed at nothing less than the complete conquest of England. He had sworn over the " bragging cup," we are told, either to slay or expel Aethelred. But this story, besides being recorded far too late to give us any confidence in its veracity, does not square with the actual course that events took in 1003-14. For some time the idea of political conquest does not seem to have entered into the king's head ; he merely ravaged England on a larger scale than his predecessors, and more than once accepted a tribute and took his departure for a season. It was only after learning by long experience of the worthlessness of Aethelred, and the ever-growing discontent of his subjects, that he rose to the idea of making himself King of England.

This is clearly shown by the events of 1004. Sweyn this year delivered his attack on East Anglia, which seems to have been free from the Viking attacks since the time of the battle of Maldon. He burned and plundered its chief towns, Norwich and Thetford, after several sharp contests with the fyrd, which was led by a hard-fighting ealdorman of Danish blood, one Ulfkytel, whose prowess was such that his name has been preserved in the Heimskringla, almost alone among the generals of Aethelred.[1] "The enemy themselves said that they never had met a worse hand-play among the English nation than Ulfkytel had brought to them." Nevertheless he was defeated, and Sweyn won his way back in safety to his fleet. Probably he wintered in this region, but in the next spring the host went back to Denmark, "and staid a little space ere it came again". Perhaps a destructive famine, which raged over all England in 1005, was the cause of his departure. Aethelred's court, during this year, appears to have been the scene of much strife and turmoil : "then was Wulfgeat deprived of all his possessions and Wulfheah and Ufegeat were blinded, and ealdorman Aelfhelm was slain". Wulfgeat is said to have been long the favourite and adviser of the king, but a charter of 1015 tells us that "inimicis regis se in insidiis socium applicavit"—though we know not who these foes may have been. Aelfhelm was apparently Earl of Deira, and the two blinded thegns are said (on the late

---

[1] He is called Ulfkytel Snelling, and is said (probably in error) to have been slain by Jarl Thorkil the Tall.

authority of Florence of Worcester) to have been his sons. In this same late source we are told that the whole intrigue was the work of the king's new favourite Eadric Streona—a name that grows only too familiar in the annals of the next few years. But all possible crimes were fathered on to this unscrupulous person by tradition, and it is possible that Florence of Worcester had no better authority for this statement.

About the same time as these tragedies occurred the first trouble on the Northern border of which we have heard for some time. Malcolm, King of Scots, attacked Northumbria, and penetrated as far as Durham. But he was defeated in front of it by Uhtred, son of Waltheof, who as a reward was made Earl of all Northumbria.

The absence of the Danes from England only continued for one year; they returned in the summer of 1006 and landed at Sandwich, where they seem to have made their base-camp. From thence plundering expeditions went out into Kent and Sussex, but the main army seems to have been "contained" by the assembly of a very great force in front of them. "The king had commanded all the people of Wessex and Mercia to be called out, and they lay out over against the Army throughout harvest-time. But this availed no more than on previous occasions, for the army made sallies in whatsoever direction it would." After Martinmas the fyrd dispersed homeward, thinking that the winter would keep the Danes quiet. But the reverse was the case: when the landsfolk were gone from in front of them, the Danes executed a sudden and daring strategic move. They went on board ship, landed again in Southampton Water, and about Yule executed a raid of the most sweeping kind through Hampshire and Berkshire, moving by Reading and Wallingford to a point on the Berkshire Downs, known as Cwichelmshlew (Cuckamsley or "Scutchamfly" Barrow) "and this they did as a piece of bravado, for it was an old saying that if they should ever reach this hill, they would never reach the sea again". The fyrd of Hampshire and Wiltshire tried to intercept them on their return march, but were badly beaten at East Kennet near Marlborough, and the Danes marched back to their ships past Winchester. "Then might the Winchester-men see the army, daring and fearless, as it went by their gates towards the sea, fetching treasure and food for over fifty miles from the

water." Aethelred meanwhile was far away in Shropshire, whither
he had gone to abide for mid-winter : he never was where he should
have been.   All that he did was to summon his Witan and to conclude that "hateful though it might be, they must pay tribute
once more to the army".   So the maw of the spoiler was stopped
once more with a great gift—no less than 36,000 pounds of silver,
which was duly made over in the spring of 1007, and bought
nearly two years' respite for England from the sated plunderers.
It was at the moment of this humiliating peace that Aethelred
gave to his favourite, Eadric Streona, the great ealdormanry of
Western Mercia, which was at this time about equivalent in size to
the old bishopric of Lichfield, and stretched from Chester to Tamworth and Shrewsbury.

As in 992, the payment of an exorbitant tribute was followed
by a serious attempt to reorganise the national defence, which went
wrong not from the badness of the scheme but from the incapa-
city of those set to administer it.   The plan devised in 1008 was
more ambitious than anything which Alfred or Edward the Elder
had contemplated.   The text of the ordinance, as set out in the
Chronicle, is difficult to follow, but apparently every three hundreds, throughout the realm, in inland shires as well as coast shires,
was to provide a ship, and every ten hides a small boat, while every
eight hides was to furnish a helm and coat of mail.   The former
obligation is extraordinary, and furnishes an early precedent for
Charles I.'s well-known demand for ship-money, 600 years after.
As to the clause dealing with armour, it seems to mean that
large landowners were to provide a fully-equipped man for every
eight hides that they possessed, while small landowners were to club
together, in contributory groups, so arranged that the sum total
of each group's land made up just eight hides.   Probably the
armed men were told off to the ships : at any rate this is suggested
by the contemporary will of Archbishop Aelfric, who bequeaths
"his best ship with sixty helms and sixty coats of mail to the king,
and a ship each to the men of Kent and Wiltshire," obviously to
help them with their contribution to the national navy.   Wiltshire being an inland county, it is clear that the obligation was,
as the Chronicle implies, made incumbent on all regions whatever
their posiiton.[1]

[1] See note to Plummer's A. S. Chronicle, ii. 185-86.

In 1009 this vast fleet was actually prepared, and collected at Sandwich, to meet the expected coming of the Danes "so many ships as were never before seen, as books tell us, among the English nation in any king's days". But the result was not merely disappointing but disgraceful. The fleet got involved in petty civil war. Brihtric, the brother of the king's favourite Eadric Streona, accused of treason one Wulfnoth Cyld, apparently a powerful thegn of Sussex, but better known as the father of the famous Earl Godwine.[1] Wulfnoth justified the accusation, whether it was originally false or true, by tempting away twenty ships-crews, with whom he took to piracy in the Channel. Brihtric, his accuser, was given a squadron of eighty vessels, and told to destroy the rebel. He was caught in a storm, some of his ships were wrecked, and others forced to run ashore. While they lay helpless, Wulfnoth came down upon them and burned them. This was the sole campaign of the new fleet : the crews were dismissed after Lammas (Aug. 1st), both because their stores were used up, and because it was considered that the time was over in which the threatened Danish invasion might reasonably be expected. But all calculations of King Aethelred were habitually incorrect. The enemy appeared in great strength before August was out, and found no fleet to ward him off. This time the Danes were led by a Jarl named Thorkil the Tall, one of the celebrated Jomsborg Vikings and were shortly afterwards reinforced by another squadron under two other jarls named Heming and Eglaf, of whom the former was the brother of Thorkil. But Sweyn himself did not appear this year, though the invasion seems to have been made with his aid and approval. The Vikings put Canterbury to ransom, and then ravaged far and wide in East Wessex. The *fyrd* was called out against them, but (as the Chronicle tells us) when Aethelred had intercepted the raiders by getting between them and their ships, a decisive battle was prevented by the cowardice or treachery of his favourite Eadric Streona "as it ever is still". The Danes then made an ineffectual attempt on London after midwinter, and finally retired into Kent, where they lay till Lent repairing their ships, no man hindering them.

---

[1] That Godwine was the son of this Wulfnoth Cyld is stated by version F of the A. S. Chronicle, and seems to be correct. But that Wulfnoth was a nephew of Eadric Streona seems to be a mistake of later historians; for a refutation of the idea, see Freeman's *Norman Conquest*, i. 701.

When the campaigning season of 1010 began, Thorkil's host struck at the one part of England which seems to have been hitherto free from their ravages during the whole of Aethelred's reign—the inland of East Mercia. They first shipped themselves round to Ipswich, which they destroyed, and then after a victory over Ealdorman Ulfkytel at Ringmere in Norfolk, spread their bands all over the lands of Cambridge, Bedford, Buckingham, Oxford and Northampton, "ever burning as they went," till at the end of autumn they returned to their base camp in Kent, where their ships lay. It is exasperating to read in the Chronicle that "at the proper time they were neither offered tribute nor fought against : but when they had done the most evil there was peace and truce made with them ". For King Aethelred, after his usual fashion, entered into negotiation with Thorkil and his company when the spring of 1011 came round, and promised them once more a great " gafol " on condition that they should bring their plundering to an end. But nevertheless, despite the suspension of hostilities, as we are told, the Danes would go about in parties plundering the miserable peasantry at their will. The tribute-collection apparently was slow, and in September the invaders, weary of waiting, took a most outrageous step. They suddenly beset the city of Canterbury, and captured it, through the treachery of Aelfmar Abbot of St. Augustine's, as we are told. This man they let go free, but they carried off to their ships as hostages Aelfheah the archbishop, Godwine Bishop of Rochester, Aelfweard the king's high-reeve, an abbess named Leofruna, and an infinite number of monks and nuns. Where, meanwhile, was King Aethelred ? It seems hardly credible, yet must be accepted as true, that he was directing a campaign against the South Welsh, for the Celtic chronicles record under this year a great invasion of Dyfed, and devastation reaching as far as St. David's by the army of the Saxons under their leaders " Edrich " (undoubtedly Eadric Streona) and " Ubrich " (apparently Uhtred, ealdorman of Northumbria). Possibly the king was trying to force the Welsh to contribute to the great sum of ransom-money which he was collecting for the Danes, but it is hardly likely that his methods were effective.

Be this as it may, the king and Ealdorman Eadric came to London in April, 1012, and (ignoring the atrocities committed by the Danes at Canterbury six months before) began to pay them off.

The money made over is said to have amounted to the huge sum of 48,000 pounds of silver, even a greater sum than the last *gafol* of 1007. The matter did not go off without a horrible tragedy. The Vikings appear to have demanded some extra ransom for the unfortunate Archbishop Aelfheah, which he (very rightly) refused to give them: for he had been captured by treachery, and the sum demanded would have ruined the tenants of his see-lands. A mob of drunken pirates dragged him out of his prison at Greenwich on Palm Sunday, 1012, and after a mock trial before their "hustings" or general assembly, shamefully pelted him to death with the bones and horns of the oxen which had been slaughtered for their feast. He had been mishandled in this bestial fashion for some time, when a Dane, kinder than his fellows (he is said to have been a Christian convert),[1] put an end to his agony by a blow from an axe. This brutal murder is said to have been done without the consent, or even the knowledge, of Jarl Thorkil, who gave over the archbishop's mangled body to the Londoners next morning. It was buried with much reverence in St. Paul's, and Aelfheah—justly reckoned a martyr, for he died to save his flock from ruin—became one of the most venerated of English saints. King Aethelred seems to have remained undisturbed by the primate's death, and completed the payment of his tribute without making any objection. Nay more, he took into his pay Jarl Thorkil and forty-five ships' crews, when the rest of the "army" had departed, covenanting that he should have their service in return for regular pay and rations.

Such an end to the war had not been intended by Sweyn of Denmark, who came over in person to England next summer with the whole force of his Danish and Norwegian subjects, so all Aethelred's money had been spent for naught. The Danish fleet, after first showing itself in Kent, sailed round to the mouth of the Humber, from whence Sweyn ascended the Trent, and put his army ashore at Gainsborough. He had no sooner shown himself than it became apparent that Aethelred had at last broken down the long patience of his much-enduring subjects. The Anglo-Danes, in whose territory Sweyn was now lying, offered to take

---

[1] Florence of Worcester says that this man was named Thrym. A *minister* of that name signs Cnut's Charters, probably the same man. See *Crawford Charters*, p. 149.

him as king : first Earl Uhtred and the Northumbrians, then the
men of Lindsey, then those of the other Danish shires of the
North Midlands[1] submitted to him and gave him hostages.
Having accepted their homage, and left his son Cnut and his
ships on the Trent, Sweyn advanced as far as Watling Street as
if in friendly territory, but commenced wholesale ravaging as soon
as that ancient boundary was passed. The behaviour of the people
soon showed that the submission of the North had not been the
result of a Danish conspiracy against English supremacy, but of
the general discontent of the realm against the redeless king. For
first Oxford and then Winchester, old English strongholds, yielded
readily to the invader, and made over hostages to him. Sweyn
then marched on London, but here he met, at last, with strenuous
resistance. Ever since the refoundation of the ancient city by
Alfred, its "burhware" had been true to their traditions. Moreover Aethelred himself was within their walls, and with him his
new general, Jarl Thorkil, who kept his recently sworn oath, and
did not desert to the Danish king, as might have been expected.
The Danes attacked London in vain : we are told, in enigmatical
words, that "much of Sweyn's people was drowned in the Thames,
because they kept not to any bridge". At any rate the invaders
turned aside to complete the subjugation of Wessex before dealing
with the stubborn city. The army marched *via* Wallingford,
meeting submission on every side, as far as Bath, where Aethelmar,
ealdorman of West Wessex, came in, and did homage with all
the thegnhood of his shires. After this "all people held Sweyn
for full king" and the Londoners themselves sent to offer their
submission. Nor were they to be blamed, for Aethelred and Jarl
Thorkil retired with their ships to Greenwich, and lay there,
evidently meditating flight, while they plundered the country-side
for food and money just as if they had been pirates. Aethelred
first sent off his wife Emma and then his younger sons, Edward
and Alfred, to be taken care of by his brother-in-law Richard of
Normandy. He himself followed at mid-winter, sailing out of
Thames and then down to the Isle of Wight, from whence he ran
across to Rouen.

[1] The Chronicle uses for these shires the phrases " the five burhs," *i.e.* Lincoln,
Stamford, Derby, Nottingham, Leicester, and " all the army north of Watling
Street," an archaic phrase, which would include Northampton, Cambridge, etc.

There was probably a full and complete recognition of Sweyn as king by all England after Aethelred's departure, over and above the local homage done to him at Bath and elsewhere, but we have no record of it. For all intents and purposes, whether elected by a formal Witan or no, he was acknowledged by the whole realm. But his reign was to be reckoned by days rather than by months. He had gone northward to rejoin his fleet and his son Cnut, when he died suddenly at Gainsborough on Trent upon February 3rd, 1014. The English had their own version of the cause of his death, which probably resulted from an apoplectic fit. On his way north he had imposed a great contribution on the Abbey of St. Edmund's Bury, a shrine revered as much by Danes as by Englishmen, and had promised to burn it if the money was not forthcoming. On the day when the time for payment expired, he was giving orders, we are told, for a force to march against Bury, when he cried out: " Help, comrades! Here is Saint Edmund who comes to slay me ! " Whereupon he rolled from his horse, as if struck by the spear of an invisible adversary, and expired in great torment."[1] Whatever the manner of his death, he certainly reigned for no more than six weeks after Athelred's flight to Normandy.

The removal of Sweyn was certainly for the benefit of England : he was a mere pirate king, treacherous, cruel and greedy, who had started as a parricide, and had all the apostate's hatred for Christianity, though he is said to have conformed to it once more in his latest days.[2] He was the last of the old generation of pagan sea robbers, and was more barbarous than most of his own followers. His son Cnut was to prove himself a very different sort of king, though in his first youth he showed some of the violence and bloodthirstiness that his father had taught him.

Sweyn's death, however, caused vast confusion, not only in England but all over Scandinavia. For his unwilling subjects in Norway at once revolted, and proclaimed as king Olaf Haraldson (a cousin of their last king Olaf Tryggveson), afterwards better known as Olaf the Saint : he was destined to be a thorn in the side of Sweyn's

[1] All this legend in detail may be found in Florence of Worcester, who is obviously copying from some local Bury legend.

[2] The *Encomium Emmae*, i. 5, makes him, just before his death, exhort his son Cnut *de Christianitatis studio* !

heir for many a year. At the same time the Danes who were at home in Denmark elected Harald, the younger son of the late king. But the army which lay at Gainsborough chose Cnut, who was present with them, and was his father's favourite. He was at this moment a very young man of no more than nineteen.

The homage of the army, however, did not carry with it the homage of all England. When Sweyn's death was reported, the English turned once more to the old king, despite of all his misdoings. "The whole Witan, clerks and laymen, took counsel to send after Aethelred, and they declared that no lord would be dearer to them than their natural lord, if he would but rule them better than he had done hitherto." The exile sent over his younger son Edward [1] with lavish promises "he would be to them a loving lord, and amend all those things that they had abhorred, and all things should be forgiven which had been said or done against him". During Lent he returned from Normandy with his fleet, and met with complete submission in the South.[2] But the Anglo-Danes of the North Midlands, dominated by the presence of Cnut and his army at Gainsborough, denied their homage. Wherefore Aethelred marched against them with the full *fyrd* of Wessex and Mercia, and began to burn and plunder as soon as he reached Lindsey. Cnut, we are surprised to hear, absconded with his fleet, and "abandoned the poor folk who were deceived by him". He went out to sea, and only touched at Sandwich on his way home to Denmark. His descent there was in order to land the unfortunate hostages whom his father had taken from Wessex and the Midlands: they were put ashore with their noses, ears and hands chopped off—a very horrible deed which boded ill for Cnut's after-life. But this is the worst act that was ever recorded of him, and one whose reputation he lived down. Aethelred soon after

---

[1] So the A. S. Chronicle, but Edward was, in 1014, only ten years of age. I suspect that Edmund is meant.

[2] There is a long narrative in the *Saga* of St. Olaf in the *Heimskringla* concerning a campaign which Olaf is said to have made to assist Aethelred against the Danes, in company with Jarl Thorkil. But it will not in any way fit into the history of the A. S. Chronicle. Olaf is made to capture Canterbury and to break through London Bridge, both of which are being held against Aethelred by Danes, apparently just after Sweyn's death. But we are clearly among errors and fictions, for the battle of Ringmere (see p. 571) is put after Aethelred's return to London, and Ulfketyl is made to fight for the Danes!

lost what small share of popularity he may have regained at his
return, by levying a tax of 20,000 pounds from the exhausted land
to pay his friend Jarl Thorkil's crews.

While Cnut was absent in Denmark, settling matters with his
brother Harald, who consented to refit his fleet and lend him
succours if only he would quit his realm, England had about a year
of respite from battle—not, however, from murder and sudden
death, for the annals of 1015 start with a double assassination
which recalled Aethelred's worst days. He had assembled the
Witan at Oxford, nominally to debate on the reorganisation of
his wasted realm, really, as it seems, for revenge. For his favourite
Eadric Streona—once more all-powerful,—allured into his own house
and there murdered Sigeferth and Morkere, the sons of Arngrim,
two great Anglo-Danish thegns from North Mercia, who had probably been prominent among those who submitted to Sweyn in
1013. The king then confiscated all their possessions, and im-
prisoned Sigeferth's widow Ealdgyth at Malmesbury. A new figure
now comes upon the scene—Edmund the Aetheling, Aethelred's
eldest surviving son,[1] who was, not without good reason, a con-
temner of his father and a hater of his father's grasping favourite.
He was now twenty-two years of age, and must surely have seen
something of war during the last few years, though the Chronicle
says nothing of his earlier doings.

Edmund, as we read, but a short time after the murder of the
two thegns, went to Malmesbury, carried off the widowed Ealdgyth, and married her in open disobedience to his father. He then
betook himself to the land of the Five Boroughs, took possession of
all Sigeferth's and Morkere's estates, and received the willing homage of their dependants. It looked as if civil war between Aethelred and his son was about to break out, but this disaster was
prevented by a greater one. Cnut appeared once more at Sandwich, with a great fleet fitted out and manned by the help of his
brother Harald, just as autumn came on. He coasted along Kent
and Wessex, ravaging as he went, and landed at Wareham.
Aethelred thereupon took to his bed, and lay sick for a long time
at Cosham, near Portsmouth. He handed over the defence of the
realm to Eadric Streona, who raised great levies: but the Aethel-

---

[1] He had only just become his father's natural heir, his eldest brother Aethelstan having died this spring. His second brother Ecgbert had died in 1007.

ing Edmund also came south with a force of Anglo-Danes. The
two armies met, and went together against Cnut, but when they
were in presence Eadric, as we are told, hindered Edmund from
giving battle on favourable terms, and tried to betray him to the
enemy. Foiled in this, he absconded and joined the invader, bringing over with him the crews of forty ships—apparently Aethelred's
Anglo-Danish fleet under Jarl Thorkil. For it seems that this
mercenary chief, who had hitherto adhered to the old king, and
had followed him to Normandy in 1014, now joined Eadric in his
treachery, and went over to the side of Cnut.[1] Edmund was forced
to retire northward, and all Wessex once more submitted to a
Danish master: a year of the governance of the restored Aethelred
had been sufficient to reduce even the ancient heritage of Ecgbert
to despair. The king himself, still sick, retired to London: so
ended the year 1015.

In the next month a curious political situation was seen. The
old English shires, both Wessex and Eadric Streona's West-
Mercian ealdormanry, were subject 'to the Dane, and partly—at
least in arms in his behalf. Edmund, on the other hand, was
maintaining the cause of England at the head of the Anglo-Danes
of North Mercia and Northumbria alone. Very early in the year
Cnut, accompanied by the traitor Eadric, advanced from Wessex
into Central Mercia, and began to ravage from Warwick eastward.
Edmund called out the levies of the Danelaw against them, but
found his force unsteady: "nothing would content them save that
the king should be with them (an unwise wish!) and that they
should have the help of the ' burhware' of London". When these
came not, Edmund's force melted away. A little too late Aethelred did appear, and an army was once more assembled: " But when
they had all got together, it availed nothing more than it oft had
before : the king was told that they who should aid him would
betray him, and he went off from the host and retired to London ".

The Aetheling Edmund retired in despair to York, where
Uhtred, now Earl, as it seems, both of Deira and Bernicia, remained
faithful to him. But when they had rallied the Northumbrian
forces they took them not straight against Cnut, but to punish
Eadric Streona by ravaging his ealdormanry. While they laid

[1] For possible reasons for this defection see Stevenson's note to *Crawford
Charters*, p. 141.

waste Shropshire, Cheshire, and Staffordshire, the young Danish
king was devastating the Mercian Danelaw in a similar fashion,
from Bedford as far as Lincoln and Nottingham. At last the news
reached Earl Uhtred that the enemy had reached the Humber, and
was marching on York. He thereupon left the Aetheling to his
own resources, and hastened back to defend his own land. But he
found Cnut so strong, and discouragement so general, that he was
forced to yield. He gave hostages and made his submission, though
most unwillingly, as we are told. But this surrender availed Uhtred
little : he was murdered a few days later by an old enemy named
Thurbrand, as every one supposed with the connivance of the
Danish king.[1] Cnut then placed his brother-in-law Eric, a jarl
lately expelled from Norway by Olaf Haraldson, as governor of
both the Northumbrian earldoms, and turned southward to deal
with Aethelred and his son. It seems, however, that Bernicia still
held out against him, under Uhtred's brother Eadwulf Cudel.

The Aetheling Edmund, after his desertion by Earl Uhtred,
had returned with the wreck of his following to London. Almost
immediately after his arrival Aethelred did England the only good
service that was in his power, by dying on April 23rd, 1016, of
the lingering sickness that had been afflicting him for the last nine
months. If he had only expired, or been deposed, a few years
earlier—anywhere before Sweyn's invasion of 1013—the crown of
England might have been saved for his house. But now it was
too late, though his son Edmund did all that was humanly possible
to rescue the land from the spoiler. But the strength of the realm
was wasted, and demoralisation had gone too far.

The summer campaign of 1016, however, was a glorious effort
to stave off ruin, and by it Edmund won most deservedly the
name of "Ironside" [*ferreum latus*] by which he is best remembered. He was hailed as king on his father's death by the
citizens of London and the few magnates who still remained faithful: but his kingdom must have been for the moment little larger
than the circuit of London's walls, since Wessex, Northumbria
and all Eadric's Mercian shires were subject to Cnut, with much
more of the Midlands also. Having placed London in as good
a posture of defence as was possible, Edmund started for a raid

---

[1] Simeon of Durham, i. 281. He is always trustworthy for local northern
affairs.

into Wessex, hoping that the landsfolk would rise in his behalf now that his wretched father was removed.[1] Cnut meanwhile arrived before London, and sat down to beleaguer it (May 6th-8th), cutting a canal round Southwark so as to get ships on to the Upper Thames, and constructing lines of circumvallation about the whole circuit of the city. The citizens withstood him manfully, and he was soon distracted from the siege. For Edmund had not been deceived in his expectations, and had been joined by many Wessex thegns the moment that he showed himself in the old heritage of Ecgbert. He was soon at the head of a considerable army, with which he cut up a Danish detachment at Penselwood, near Gillingham, on the borders of Dorset and Somerset. A few days later he fought with another host at Sherston, near Malmesbury, where we are told that not only Danes under Jarl Thorkil, but Mercians under Eadric Streona, and Wessex forces under two other Englishmen, Aelmaer 'Darling,' and Algar, son of Meaw, were ranged against him.[2] The battle was indecisive, but the enemy fell back towards London, so that Edmund had the real advantage. He followed with an ever-growing army, and, making a rapid march, broke through Cnut's lines, drove the Danes back towards their ships and entered the town in triumph. Two days later he took the field, and defeated his enemy at a pitched battle at Brentford, though with much loss, for many who pursued too far in the hope of plunder were thrust into Thames by a rally of the Danes. Cnut seems to have retired into his fortified camp at Greenwich, from whence he still menaced London. But Edmund, having raised more levies by a hasty visit to Wessex, now appeared a second time, in such force that his rival, who had once more attacked London during his short absence, at last unwillingly evacuated the estuary of the Thames. The great fleet dropped down its reaches, and transferred itself to the mouth of the Orwell, in Suffolk, where Cnut lay for some time plundering the land for provisions. All Southern

[1] According to the *Encomium Emmae*, London surrendered for a moment to Cnut, after Aethelred's death, and before Edmund's return. But its dates are wrong, since it puts the battle of Sherston before the death of the old king.

[2] Florence of Worcester's tale about Eadric's stratagem at Sherston, of crying aloud that Edmund was dead, and showing the head of a dead man, is a mere folk tale. Henry of Huntingdon tells it of Ashington.

England now adhered to Edmund, who seemed to have saved his crown.

But there was still more fighting to be done. When the English king appeared opposite to him in the Eastern regions, Cnut took to the sea again, and relanded in Kent, in the estuary of the Medway. His rival followed, crossed the Thames and brought the Danes to action at Ótford. They were routed and fled into Sheppey, where they were safe owing to the intervening water of the Swale ; for England had no longer a fleet to pursue them. At this moment Eadric Streona deserted Cnut, came to King Edmund at Aylesford and sought pardon and peace. It was granted him, "than which nothing could be more ill-advised," as the chronicler remarks. It would have been better to have cut off the head of this odious traitor at once. But Edmund was magnanimous, and Eadric promised to bring, and actually brought, to his aid a great force from his West Mercian shires during the next stage of the campaign.

After his defeat in Kent, Cnut once more took his fleet out to sea, and crossing the mouth of the Thames came ashore once more in Essex, and began ravaging far and wide. The indefatigable Edmund followed once more, by the long land route that was imposed upon him, and came upon the Danes on the low downs south of the estuary of the Crouch at Ashington (Assandun) near Rochford. Here was fought the fifth and last of the great pitched battles of the campaign of 1016. It was the most strenuously contested of all, but it ended in disaster, brought about according to the Anglo-Saxon Chronicle by the deliberate treachery of Eadric Streona, who "began the flight with the Magesaetas (the Herefordshire and Shropshire *fyrd*), and so betrayed his royal lord and the whole people of England ". If later chroniclers can be trusted, we may believe that the treachery had been previously concerted with Cnut. The slaughter was such as had been seen in no previous battle : there fell Ulfketyl, the brave ealdorman of East Anglia, Godwine, ealdorman of Lindsey, another ealdorman named Aelfric,[1] Aethelweard the son of Aethelwine *Dei Amicus*, Eadnoth, bishop of Dorchester, "and all the nobility of the English race ".

Edmund fled westward with the wrecks of his army into Glou-

---

[1] Not apparently the traitor of 991 and 1003, who has not been heard of since the last date, and was apparently disgraced. See Stubbs' edition of the *Lives of Dunstan*, R.S., p. 396.

cestershire, resolved apparently to keep up the struggle. Thither Cnut followed him, and an unexpected end came to the war, for " by the advice of Eadric and other counsellors" a peace and a partition of England were concluded. Apparently the Danes were tired out,[1] and willing to take a part for the whole—to accept a great tribute and a cession of lands instead of persisting in the attempt to take the whole realm. In an interview on the Eyot of Alney, near Deerhurst,[2] the two kings met, exchanged hostages and drew up a pact confirmed by pledges and oaths. Cnut was to have Northumbria and Danish Mercia, Edmund Wessex, London, Essex, East Anglia, and English Mercia, and he kept his crown.[3] These were better terms, after all, than those that Alfred made with Guthrum in 878. But Alfred surrendered only a vague supremacy over Northern England, which he had never really enjoyed : Edmund was forced to give away provinces which had been under his father's complete domination.

Yet had Edmund lived he might perhaps have vindicated himself like his great ancestor, and have died once more an imperial king. Death intervened to prevent the partition of England, for on November 30th, only a few weeks after the treaty of Deerhurst, Edmund expired at Oxford, worn out apparently by the fatigues of the tremendous campaign that he had just gone through. Later tradition held that he was insidiously murdered by Eadric Streona, but no good authority adds this to the already sufficient burden of sins to be laid on the national scapegoat. We part from Edmund with bitter regret—his last campaign vied with the best exploits of Alfred and Edward the Elder, and he seemed capable of building up a lost cause and reforming a ruined realm.

[1] This fact is stated with special clearness in the *Encomium Emmae*, ii. § 9.

[2] Apparently not the isle of Olney near Gloucester, but some meadow surrounded by backwater of the Severn, now vanished. See Rev. C. S. Taylor's *Danes in Gloucestershire*, p. 28.

[3] The Chronicle only says that Cnut had Northumbria and Mercia (or, according to Version D, " the North Parts ") while Edmund had Wessex. Florence of Worcester (in the revised text, not that given in M. B. H.) states the arrangement named above, save that he does not mention English Mercia. But this certainly stayed with Edmund, for (1) Eadric, its earl, remains Edmund's vassal, and (2) the king dies at Oxford, which must have been in his share. It is incredible that London, after its long and gallant defences, should have been surrendered. Henry of Huntingdon, who gives it to Cnut, is almost certainly wrong. See Plummer's *Notes to A. S. C.*, ii. 199.

CHAPTER XXVII

CNUT AND HIS SONS (1016-1042 A.D.)

THE sudden death of Edmund Ironside did not lead, as might have been expected, to an immediate renewal of the war that had been ended by the pact at Deerhurst. There was one possible heir whom the Witan of Wessex might have nominated as the dead king's successor ; but he was young and untried—though no younger than Edmund I. had been when he took up Aethelstan's succession. The Witan, however, refused to make the experiment, thinking anything better than a resumption of the struggle with Cnut. A word as to the dynastic situation is required to make it clear. Of the numerous family of Aethelred the Redeless by his first wife, Aelfflaed, all the sons save two had predeceased their father, unmarried or without issue.[1] They must have been a weakly race, as they all five died before attaining the age of twenty. Edmund Ironside had survived to the age of twenty-two, had been able to fight one glorious campaign, to marry and to beget sons. But his two children Edmund and Edward (apparently twins) were infants in the cradle when their father died.[2] There was no possibility of making them pretenders to the crown in such a troubled time. There remained of Aethelred's first family only the Aetheling Eadwig, one of the youngest children of Aelfflaed, and he was probably not more than eighteen. Aethelred's second family consisted of two sons and a daughter—

---

[1] Of these five princes Aethelstan, the eldest, was born about 986 and died apparently in 1015. Edward died before 1004 and Ecgbert before 1005, both as boys. Eadred and Eadgar, both younger than Edmund Ironside, seem to have been dead before 1015, i.e. neither can have reached the age of twenty.

[2] As Edmund married in 1015, after midsummer, and is said to have left two sons when he died in November, 1016, they must have been twins, unless the second was a posthumous child, which is nowhere asserted. Indeed his *sons* are spoken of clearly at his death, not his *son*.

of the former Alfred was born, as it seems, in 1003 and Edward (afterwards to be known as the Confessor) in 1004. Of taking them as representatives of the line of Wessex there could be no question while their elder half-brother Eadwig was alive. On that prince rested the hopes of any resolute patriots who dreamed of continuing the struggle against Cnut. But such persons, though they seem to have existed, were too few and too weak in influence to resist the majority who only thought of " peace at any price ". The Wessex Witan made its choice in favour of accepting the Dane, and avoiding further wars.

" The whole land chose Cnut as king," says the author of the *Encomium Emmae,* " and of its own accord submitted itself to the man against whom it had previously made such a strenuous resistance." Florence of Worcester tells the tale at considerable length.[1] By a prearranged plan Cnut met the Witan of Wessex at London, and challenged them to say whether at the conference of Deerhurst their late master had made any reservation of the right of succession to his brothers or his sons. To which they replied that all men knew that Edmund had never intended that any part of his realm should pass to his brothers, and that he had wished Cnut to be the protector and guardian of his infant sons, till they should reach the age when they might reign. " Wherein, as God is witness, they gave false evidence, and lied foully, thinking that Cnut would be propitiated by their lies, and that they would get no small reward from him." He then proposed himself to them as king, and they swore that they were willing to elect him, and to obey him humbly, and would pay a tribute for his army. And so they did, and contemned the sons of Aethelred, and declared them outlawed.[2] It seems that the Aetheling Eadwig first fled over seas, and then returned to raise rebellion, but " he was betrayed by those whom he thought his best friends," and we are told that Cnut had him hunted down and slain. The infant

---

[1] Henry of Huntingdon has another version, followed by Scandinavian writers and accepted by Professor Freeman, that Cnut and Edmund at Deerhurst had taken each other as brothers, and agreed to share their rights, so that the Dane could claim to be Edmund's heir. This is surely most unlikely, when Edmund had sons. Florence's story, on the other hand, seems quite credible.

[2] All this story, which seems probable enough, is told at length by Florence of Worcester.

sons of Ironside were sent out of the kingdom, nominally to be fostered by Olaf King of Sweden, really, as it is said, with a hint to that prince that they need never be seen again. But the Swede resented the proposal, and passed the boys on to Stephen King of Hungary, who brought them up in all honour, and married one of them to his own daughter, and the other to a kinswoman of the Emperor Henry II. The children of the younger brother, Edward, were Edgar Aetheling and St. Margaret, afterwards Queen of Scotland, both figures of high importance in the history of the later years of the eleventh century. But more than a generation was to pass before a descendant of Edmund Ironside was to set foot again in England.

At the same time that Cnut sent away the two sons of Edmund and slew the Aetheling Eadwig, we hear that he also suppressed a mysterious person whom the Chronicle calls "Eadwig the King of the Ceorls". Was this some other member of the old royal house, who tried to raise the lower classes in insurrection when the Witan had voted for submission? Or may we possibly conceive that both the Chronicle and later writers copying it have made one prince into two, and that Eadwig the son of Aethelred made a stand at the head of the ceorls, and was called their king? This last alternative is distinctively favoured by the entry of the facts in Simeon of Durham, who says that Cnut "*exlegavit clitonem Edvium, regis Edmundi germanum, qui rex appelabatur rusticorum*". But Simeon is too far from the events that he records to make his testimony decisive against that of the Chronicle, even though the latter was certainly not always kept up to date in Cnut's time, and was occasionally "written up" with such inaccuracy that events of importance might be misplaced by as much as four years.[1] The "King of the Churls" must remain an unsolved mystery.

It is possible, however, that another slaughter recorded under the year 1017 may have been connected with the suppression of the unfortunate Aetheling Eadwig. "At this time," says the Chronicle, " was Eadric the ealdorman slain in London, very justly,

---

[1] *E.g.* the visit of Cnut to Rome, which is placed under 1031, though it most certainly took place in 1027, as is shown by several undoubted Continental authorities, and by the fact that Cnut's presence in Rome synchronised with the crowning of the Emperor Conrad II. (see below, p. 595).

and also Norman, son of Ealdorman Leofwine, and Aethelweard, son of Aethelmaer the Great, and Brihtric, son of Aelfheah, in Devonshire." The execution of these magnates suggests that Cnut had discovered, or suspected, some plot against him on their part. Any treason on the part of Eadric Streona was not only possible but probable. According to the author of the *Encomium Emmae*, Cnut called the wily ealdorman to him and said: "Can you, the man who betrayed your late master, become my faithful servant? I will repay your service with the reward that you have deserved, but never try treachery again." Whereupon he called in to him Eric, Earl of Northumbria, and said : "We must pay this man what we owe him ; that is to say, he must be killed, lest he deceive us again ".[1] So Eric beheaded him, and his body was cast unburied outside the walls of London as a warning to traitors. As to the others who suffered at the same time, we are told that Cnut retained Norman's father Leofwine as ealdorman of the Hwiccas for many years, while Aethelweard's brother Aethelnoth was promoted to the Archbishopric of Canterbury in 1020. It does not look, therefore, as if he had been making a clean sweep of English magnates in a suspicious mood, since he treated so handsomely the nearest relatives of the men executed in 1017. Florence tells us that these three nobles were "*sine culpa interfecti*". On the other hand, Emma's encomiast says that they had all been unfaithful to Edmund, and were executed, like Eadric, because the king doubted their loyalty. "But those who had been faithful subjects to Edmund he much loved."

Cnut certainly made no attempt to rule England by Danes alone, but from the first gave the highest offices to Englishmen. He kept Leofwine as ealdorman of the Hwiccas till his death somewhere after 1023, and made his son Leofric ealdorman of Mercia (Eadric Streona's old dominion) in 1026. Another favourite of his was Godwine, son of that Wulfnoth Cyld of Sussex who had raised insurrection against Aethelred in 1009.[2] This man he made Ealdorman of all Wessex in 1020, and it seems that he had been entrusted with part of it as early as 1018, when he began to sign charters as *dux*. The Chronicle informs us that at the beginning of 1017 Cnut had divided all England into four parts, of

[1] *Encomium Emmae*, ii. § 16.   Florence, *sub anno* 1017.   [2] See p. 570.

which Eric ruled Northumbria, Thorkil (Aethelred's old mercenary) had East Anglia, Eadric Streona Mercia for a short space, while the king kept Wessex for himself and set no one else over it. But this arrangement, if it ever existed, was very short-lived, for we find several more subdivisions in existence very soon after. In especial, Leofwine's Hwiccian ealdormanry seems to have been in existence even in 1017, Eadwulf Cudel held Bernicia about 1016-19, apparently while Eric was still ruling in the rest of Northumbria; Wessex had been transferred from the king to Godwine as early as 1020. The ealdormanry of the Magesaetas was in exist- ence again (independent of that of West Mercia), perhaps as early as 1020, under Earl Eglaf; certainly in Cnut's later years under Earl Ranig. There was also an earldom, perhaps two, in the Eastern Midlands during the later part of Cnut's time, which em- braced the Mercian Danelaw. It is not quite certain whether this government, sometimes called that of the " Middle Angles," was the same as that of East Mercia or not. But at any rate it is clear that Cnut's quadri-partite division of the realm in 1017 must have been a most ephemeral arrangement. So far was he from making a permanent reduction in the number of ealdormen (or earls as they now begin to be called in English as well as in Danish regions) that he seems to have had quite as many of them in authority during the greater part of his reign as had been seen in the later days of Aethelred the Redeless.

But in 1017 Cnut's plans must have been as enigmatic to his subjects as his personal character. It remained to be seen whether he would prove a great administrator or a mere hard-handed tyrant. There was as much reason to fear the one as to hope for the other. Some of his early doings might have justified the most gloomy anticipations—the mutilation of the hostages at Sandwich, the making away with Earl Uhtred at the very moment of his sub- mission, the executions at London in 1017, foreshadowed a reign of blood and terror. And pitiless taxation seemed to be promised by the extortion which Cnut practised in the first winter of his sole sovereignty over England: he raised no less a sum than 72,000 pounds of silver from the realm, besides a special contribution of 10,500 more from the city of London, whose inhabitants had been such consistent and formidable enemies to him and to his father. On the other hand, Cnut, if cruel, was clever; he had shown already

that he was skilled in diplomacy, and that he was not too obstinate
to consent to compromises.   England was now all his own : but if
he wished to rule a wealthy and contented rather than an im-
poverished and rebellious realm, it was clearly to his own interest
to give peace and good governance to his new subjects.   Only the
more brainless among conquerors treat the lands that they have
subdued as a mere prey.   Cnut began from the first year of his
reign to display signs of politic consideration, and to show that he
wished to reign as an English king, not as a mere crowned pirate.

The first of his acts on record which indicates his intention to
place himself in the position of Aethelred's lawful successor was a
very strange one.   He was apparently only twenty-one years of
age, but he offered his hand in marriage to Aethelred's widow
Emma of Normandy, though she was apparently at least ten years
his senior, and had three children by her first husband.   She is said
to have been a lady of great beauty,[1] but as Cnut had certainly
never set eyes upon her, this can hardly have been the reason for
which he made his suit to her.   We are told that he attached
great importance to building up a firm alliance with Emma's
brother Richard, who might, if left hostile, make the Norman
duchy a base for operations against England, when in a few years
his sister's children should have grown up to man's estate, and be
able to claim their father's throne.   The match is said to have
been pleasing to the Danish army, because they were glad to see
the king ally himself to a distinguished Scandinavian stock, and to
the English because they thought the reappearance of the queen-
dowager as a queen-regnant to be a sign of Cnut's intention to
restore the old *régime*, and to settle down in the seat of his predecessor.   But Emma's conduct appears to be simply odious—she
deliberately sacrificed the rights of her elder children to her ambition.   Her encomiast tells us that the only condition which she
placed on her assent was that Cnut should guarantee that any son
whom she might have by him should be declared his lawful successor.   For she had heard that he had already two children by an
English lady named Aelfgifu, daughter of that Ealdorman Aelfhelm of Mercia whom Aethelred had murdered in 1006.   These
boys were not born in wedlock—or at least not in Christian wed-

---

[1] *Encomium Emmae*, ii. § 16.

lock—but Emma was well aware how lightly legitimacy was regarded by the Danes, and she was determined that if she had to
sacrifice her elder children, her proposed husband should do the
same. Cnut made no objection, and their marriage was duly
celebrated in July, 1017; it apparently preceded by five months
the slaughter of Eadric Streona, a person whom the queen had as
little reason to love as the king. In the next year Emma bore to
Cnut a male child, Harthacnut, who was destined to reign as his
mother had designed, but not without much trouble and delay
caused by the existence of his illegitimate half-brothers. Emma's
elder children, Alfred and Edward, were brought up with care
and affection by their uncle Richard II. of Normandy, and apparently never met their unnatural mother again for some twenty
years.

The year 1018 saw two events which afforded much better promise for the time that was to come than any of Cnut's acts in 1017.
Having collected the enormous "Danegeld," already spoken of, he
used it to pay off the greater part of his Scandinavian army,
which had been lying as an incubus on the land ever since his
accession. He now, as it seems, regarded himself as securely seated
on his throne, and intended to rule as an English king, not as the
master of a foreign host. He only retained of his fleet forty ships
and their crews, as a sort of standing navy: this was precisely the
same mercenary force that Aethelred had maintained during his
later years, and probably amounted to about 3,200 men. The
remainder of the host was paid off and sent home. Probably some
of it was wanted in Denmark, where Cnut had to guard the crown
that had come to him on the death of his brother Harald in the
end of 1016. It is notable that he did not visit his other realm in
person till 1019, being apparently far more interested in the affairs
of England. Indeed for the whole of the rest of his reign he spent
much the larger part of his time on this side of the sea, and only
visited Scandinavia in times of stress, when his presence there was
necessary. The dismissal of the "Great Army" was a most important landmark in Cnut's policy. It showed that he had no
intention of ruining England for the benefit of his countrymen,
and it freed his English subjects from the fear that he might be
intending to divide up the realm among his confederates. For no
general distribution of land to the Danes took place, though im-

portant chiefs like the Earls Eric, Thorkil and Eglaf,[1] and certain
other Danish followers of the king, such as Osgod Clapa[2] and
Tofig, received ample endowment. But forfeited estates must
have fallen into Cnut's hands in plenty after the death of Eadric
Streona and those who suffered with him, so that there would be
no need to provide for these Danes by new confiscations from un-
offending Englishmen. The crews of the forty ships, the *thingmen*
or *housecarls* who formed the king's standing bodyguard, seem to
have received the handsome pay of eight marks each per annum,
with their maintenance, but no landed property.[3] This fact shows
the most striking contrast between the policy of Cnut and that of
William of Normandy, the next conqueror of England. Cnut kept
his fellow-countrymen, who had followed him to victory, in the
condition of stipendiaries. William parcelled out among his some
three-fourths of the land of the realm that they had won for him.
But it must be remembered that the Norman was more in the condition of the managing partner of a great joint-stock enterprise,
than in that of a king leading a national armament. The host
that won the battle of Hastings had been collected from every
land of Western Europe, and not more than half the adventurers
were William's natural born subjects. He was forced to satisfy
them by giving them land when they demanded it, and so earned
the undying hatred of the evicted English thegns. Cnut had
neither the need nor the wish to act in this fashion, and, since he
left the native landholders undisturbed, was easily able to win their
loyalty.

The second important event recorded by the Chronicle under
the year 1018 is that the king held a great general assembly at
Oxford, at which "both Danes and English agreed to live under
King Eadgar's laws". This meeting, no doubt, was summoned to
hear Cnut's solemn promise to administer the realm according to
ancient constitutional usage, for the laws of Eadgar must have
represented at this time the same ideal of peace, legality, and

----

[1] Apparently this earl is the same as the pirate chief mentioned in 1010, he was
Thorkil's kinsman.

[2] For whom see pages 607, 610 and 615.

[3] This rate is given us by the Peterborough version of the A. S. C., under the
year 1039, when we learn that Harold Harefoot gave his crews eight marks a man,
" in like manner as had been done in the days of King Cnut ".

efficient administration which in a later age, after the Norman Conquest, was associated with the oft-quoted, but practically non-existent " Laws of Edward the Confessor ". Cnut himself in later years was rather a prolific legislator, but nothing could have been more politic at the commencement of his reign than this simple republication of the ancient law of the realm. It evidently had an excellent effect.

From this time onward the reign of Cnut assumes a new character. The Chronicle tells us no more of murders, executions, exceptional taxation or outbursts of cruelty. A few magnates were expelled from the realm from time to time, but it is notable that they were Danes, not Englishmen.[1] One single crime, the murder of his cousin Jarl Ulf in a fit of passion, is ascribed to Cnut's middle age—but this took place out of England, and is only recorded (with a folk-tale added to explain it) by Scandinavian historians. To his subjects on this side of the seas the king appeared for the remainder of his life in nothing but an amiable aspect. The change was extraordinary, but not inexplicable. He was still a very young man—only twenty-two at the most—he was eminently adaptable, and his ambition was to rule by policy rather than by the strong hand, and to be respected as well as feared. There can be little doubt that, unlike his father Sweyn, he honestly preferred the status of a civilised Christian monarch to that of mere pirate king. He felt that he had risen in the scale when he acted as became the successor of Eadgar and Alfred, rather than as the heir of Harald Bluetooth and his other barbarous ancestors. He preferred the comparatively rich and cultured England to his native Danish moors—which indeed he hardly had seen since first he set out on his adventures by his father's side in 1013. His confidence in, and preference for, English courtiers and ministers was probably genuine and not feigned; by the end of his reign they had practically superseded his Danish countrymen in all the more important posts which the latter had filled in his earlier years.[2] It is notable that Cnut not only placed English bishops in

---

[1] Jarl Thorkil is said to have been " driven out " in 1021 and Jarl Eric in 1023, but they were both given great promotion in the king's Scandinavian lands, and must not be reckoned as disgraced.

[2] The only prominent exceptions that suggest themselves are Osgod Clapa, who was " Staller," or marshal in Cnut's latest years, and survived to hold the same office under Edward the Confessor, and Ranig Earl of the Magesaetas.

some of the Scandinavian sees—this would have been but natural, since qualified Danes were rare—but employed English commanders and troops in his Baltic wars. His whole policy and mental attitude contrasts in this respect with that of William the Conqueror, no less than did his dealings with land, mentioned above. The Norman, unlike Cnut, was too old to be adaptable; he never learnt the English tongue or understood English ideas. He despised his new subjects, and extruded them from every post in Church and State. The underlying difference between them was that Cnut considered that he had bettered himself when he became an Englishman; William would have held that he had lowered himself if he had abandoned Norman manners and methods. No small portion of the difference between the effects of the Danish and the Norman conquests resulted from these simple facts. The alien king who respected his English subjects and their civilisation altered little; he who regarded them as his inferiors not only swept away the old governing class, but introduced new ideas that were gradually to transform the realm.

Nothing displays Cnut's consistent plan for conciliating public opinion better than his dealings with Church affairs. He always posed as a most religious and conscientious king; in his legislation, offences against ecclesiastical law are dealt with no less fully and drastically than offences against secular law. His letter to his subjects drafted after his visit to Rome in 1027 is a sermon as much as a statement of administrative principles. To work on Sunday or to marry a nun provokes his wrath as much as breaking the peace, or theft. He was ostentatious in his addiction to Church ceremonial, and ready to profess his own sinfulness and fallibility to an almost suspicious extent. Most of all did he love to propitiate English religious feeling by honouring the national saints. In 1023 he celebrated with special pomp the translation of the body of St. Aelfheah—the victim of his vassal Thorkil's drunken sailors[1]—from London to Canterbury. He showed a special veneration for St. Edmund of East Anglia—whose wrath was said to have destroyed his father—and honoured his abbey with rich gifts. When he visited the relics of St. Cuthbert he walked five miles with bare feet along the highway to the saint's new shrine at Dur-

[1] See p. 572.

ham.[1] He built a memorial church at Assandun, the place of his great victory in 1016, where prayer was made for the souls of all, both English and Danes, who fell on that bloody field. Apparently he made some ceremony of contrition at Edmund Ironside's tomb, for in the twelfth century a rich pall, embroidered with peacocks, Cnut's gift, was still covering the sepulchre, and a charter was shown in which he confirmed the rights of the Abbey of Glastonbury "for the pardon of my offences, and the forgiveness of the sins of my brother Edmund ".[2] Apparently contrition, or its outward appearance, was an emotion which came easily to Cnut; a contemporary observer watched him while visiting a foreign church (St. Omer) with which he had no special connection ; he notes that the royal eyes were shedding copious tears, and that the penitent smote his breast continually, and heaved heart-breaking sighs.[3] Certainly Cnut had a good store of crimes to his account, for which penitence was profitable ; let us hope, therefore, that his pangs of conscience were genuine, even if somewhat exuberantly displayed. In English folk-lore he was certainly remembered as a godly man, as witness the well-known tale of his rebuke to the flattering courtiers who bade him command the incoming tide to respect his throne: "Vain and frivolous is the power of kings, nor is any one worthy of the name of King save Him to whose nod, sky, land and sea are obedient by eternal law". So, as the legend continues, he never would wear his crown again, and dedicated it over the high-altar of Winchester Cathedral, where it hung for many a century.[4] Thus, no doubt, would Cnut himself have wished to be remembered ; but whether the memory truly represents the man is another matter.

It would be a very inadequate conception of this strange personage that we should obtain, if we only looked upon him as one who wished to play the part of a model king, and achieved his end indifferent well. Cnut was not merely the reorganiser of England, he was the builder up of a great, if ephemeral, northern

---

[1] So at least says Simeon of Durham, who is always a good authority on northern affairs (*Hist. Eccl. Dunelm*, iii. § 9).

[2] William of Malmesbury, *Gesta Regum*, ii. 184. But charters were lightly forged in the twelfth century.

[3] *Encomium Emmae*, ii. § 20.

[4] The story is first found in Henry of Huntingdon, vi., *sub anno* 1036. authors embroidered it with more or less taste.

empire, of which England was the centre. When he first could
call his position secure in 1017, he did but own the realm that he
had himself won on this side of the sea, and the Danish kingdom
which had fallen to him by his brother Harald's death in the preceding year. But there descended to him from his father a claim
of a certain sort to supremacy over Norway and all its dependencies. For Sweyn, after he had slain Olaf Tryggveson at the
battle of Swold in 1000, had set up earls to rule Norway under
him, and had died its suzerain. In the confusion that followed
his decease the Northern kingdom had broken loose again, and was
now in the hands of that Olaf Haraldson who has already been
mentioned.[1] This prince, like his cousin and predecessor, Olaf
Tryggveson, was at once a great man of war, and a zealous Christian; he was also a lover of peace and order, who tried to put
down family feuds and Viking cruises. If his courage and skill
won him much admiration, his hard dealing with pirates and man-
slayers, and his inquisitorial pursuit of those who still made offerings to the heathen gods, got him many enemies. His throne was
not a very stable seat, and many Norwegian exiles fled to England
or Denmark to stir up Cnut against him. According to the
Heimskringla, the King of England offered Olaf peace, on condition that he should do him homage and become his man, but
received the uncompromising answer that Olaf "would defend
Norway with battle-axe and sword as long as life was in him, and
would pay tribute to no man for his kingdom".[2] This was apparently in 1022, when Cnut was about to pay his second visit to
his Danish realm, and it was expected that an invasion of Norway
would promptly follow his arrival in Eastern waters. But things
went otherwise at this time: Cnut learnt that Olaf was closely
allied with his brother-in-law Onund, King of Sweden, who dreaded
any further extension of Danish power in the North, and so resolved
to defer his attack on Norway to a more favourable season. He
returned to England in 1023, to be present at the translation of
St. Aelfheah, and it was not till 1025 that he again went eastward, taking with him a great fleet, which included many vessels
manned by English thegns and seamen, as well as the forty ships
of housecarls who formed his personal following. Apparently he

---

[1] See p. 574.   [2] Laing's *Heimskringla*, ii. 194-95.

was encouraged to bring matters to the decision of the sword by
the continual arrival of discontented Norsemen of high estate at
his court, who kept informing him that Olaf's subjects were ready
for rebellion, and would make little resistance. In this they were
wrong, for the threat of a Danish invasion caused many waverers
to rally to the cause of the national king, while Onund the Swede
came down in force to aid his ally. The enemies of Cnut were so
bold that they advanced beyond their own frontier, and fought
with his great fleet at the mouth of the Helge River, within the
borders of the Danish province of Scania. The battle was indecisive : the Anglo-Saxon Chronicle tells us that "there fell many
men, as well Danish as English, on King Cnut's side, and the
Swedes had possession of the field of slaughter ".[1] The version of
the *Heimskringla*—whatever it may be worth—is that King
Olaf had prepared a sort of water-trap for his foe—that he had
dammed up the stream of the Helge, and then suddenly let it go,
by cutting the dam. Cnut's ships, lying in its mouth, were driven
out to sea, and many of them grievously damaged by floating logs
and trees. The Swedes and Norsemen then fell upon them, and
made great havoc, but withdrew when the Danes rallied and were
reinforced by outlying ships, which had not been caught in the
water-shoot. But Cnut was in no condition to renew the struggle,
and gave up for the time his attempt to conquer Norway.[2] He

[1] It is apparently in error that the Chronicle makes the Swedes have possession
of the field. They certainly withdrew, after a partial success.

[2] There is considerable doubt as to whether there were not two battles at the
Helge River, one in 1025 and the other in 1027. The A. S. Chronicle only knows
of one, and places it in 1025, but says that Cnut's opponents were " Ulf and Eglaf "
instead of Onund and Olaf. There were two well-known earls of these names, but
they were Cnut's own men—Ulf the son of Thorgils Sprakaleg,who had married his
sister Estrith, and Eglaf, who had commanded the marauding Danish fleet of 1009,
and had afterwards acted as one of Cnut's trusted officers—apparently he had held
an earldom, probably that of the Magesaetas, about the year 1020. For their history
see Stevenson on the Crawford Charters, pp. 144-45. We have no knowledge that
they had broken into rebellion, though the *Heimskringla* makes Cnut incensed
with Ulf for supporting his wife Emma's plan of declaring their son Harthacnut
King of Denmark without his royal permission (see Laing's *Heimskringla*, ii. p. 246).
Afterwards Ulf was certainly vicegerent for Cnut in Denmark. It seems very unlikely
that he should have been in arms against his lord in 1025, and leagued with the
Swedes. The *Heimskringla* knows of only one battle, that where Onund and Olaf
inflicted a check on Cnut by the stratagem of the broken dam. Apparently, however,
it fixes the engagement to the year 1027, as the narrative of only one winter's events

returned to Roeskilde in Zeeland, and is said to have there committed the one notable crime of his later life, the murder of his
cousin Jarl Ulf, the son of Thorgils Sprakaleg, who had married
his sister Estrith, and had been acting as his regent in Denmark.
Danish legend said that they had hard words over a game at chess,
and that Ulf had taunted the king with his failure in the late battle,
whereupon Cnut bade one of his housecarls slay him, under circumstances of peculiar atrocity, for the earl had gone into a church,
and was stabbed as he knelt by the altar. When the king's wrath
was passed he made great show of contrition, and gave rich gifts
to the church which he had desecrated (Sept., 1025 ?). He then
returned to England.

It may possibly have been penitence for this deed, among other
causes, which led Cnut to make a pilgrimage to Rome in the winter
of the following year (1026-27). He was present there on Easter Day
(March 26th) in the latter year, and assisted at the coronation of
Conrad II., the first of the Franconian line of emperors, by Pope
John XIX. He seems to have transacted a quantity of profitable
political business during his stay in Rome. He betrothed his only
daughter Gunhild, a child of eight or nine, to Conrad's eldest son,
Henry, afterwards emperor, and obtained from the newly-crowned
monarch not only some privileges for English travellers and pilgrims, but a slight rectification of the frontier on the Eider in
favour of Denmark. At the same time he got a grant of relief of
tolls and taxes for English pilgrims from Rudolf III. of Burgundy,
who had also been present at the coronation, and from the Pope a
promise that archbishops visiting Rome to receive their pallium
should be less heavily mulcted, and that the " Saxon School" in
Rome should be let off taxation. Most of these advantages gained
are detailed in a long letter which Cnut addressed to his English
subjects from Rome: it is a curious document in which, after

divides it from Olaf's expulsion from Norway in 1028. Cnut was certainly in Rome
on March 25, 1027, yet he might possibly have been back in Denmark by June. In
his letter to his people written from Rome, apparently in April, he speaks of his intention to go straight back to Denmark to deal with " certain people and nations
who would, if they could, deprive him of life and crown ". But he hopes to be in
England before summer is out. Yet the *Heimskringla* makes him come with a
great armament directly from England before the battle of the Helge. On the whole
I am inclined to take the view given in the text—that there was only one battle, that
it took place in 1025, and that the A. S. Chronicle errs about the names " Ulf and
Eglaf ".

giving an account of his successes, he promises " to reform his life in
every respect, to rule the realms and people that he owns justly and
piously, to give equal justice, and, with God's aid, to amend anything that he may have done contrary to the right through the
indifference or negligence of youth ". He threatens all officials
abusing their power with his wrath, and bids his subjects not only to
observe with all care his secular laws, but to be very diligent to pay
their tithes, and Church-scot, and to send St. Peter's pence to
Rome.[1] How long it took Cnut to return from Rome to his own
dominions we cannot be sure; it is not certain, indeed, whether he
came straight to England, or first visited the Baltic, according to
the intention expressed in his letter. But in the year 1028, that
which followed his return, he delivered his second and successful
attack on Norway. "This year King Cnut went from England
with fifty ships of English thegns to Norway, and drove King
Olaf out of the land, and took entire possession of it," says the
Chronicle. This statement agrees perfectly with the late Norse
narrative in the *Heimskringla*, which tells how Cnut, avoiding
the Skager Rack and the Vik, and the neighbourhood of Sweden,
where Olaf was waiting for him, made his attack on the West side
of Norway, where he knew that his rival was most unpopular.
The chiefs, for the most part, fell away from King Olaf, moved not
merely by their dislike for his strong hand but by Cnut's insidious
liberality. " He enriched all men who were inclined to enter into
friendly accord with him, both with land and money, and gave
them greater power than they had before." All malcontents were
promised revenge for their old wrongs, and jarldoms and official
posts were dangled before the eyes of the ambitious. The greater
part of Olaf's host melted away from him, and he was forced to
retire overland into Sweden, from whence he finally sought refuge
for two years in Russia. Cnut was saluted as King of Norway in
a great *thing*, held at Trondjem, and for the rest of his life maintained his suzerainty there with small difficulty. He made Jarl
Hakon, son of that Jarl Eric who had once ruled Northumberland
for him,[2] his viceroy, and after Hakon had been lost at sea, two

---

[1] The letter is quoted textually by Florence of Worcester, but wrongly under the
year 1031, an error into which he has been led by the A. S. Chronicle.

[2] Hakon's grandfather of the same name was the jarl who had ruled before
Olaf Tryggveson, and his son Eric had held Norway for Sweyn before he held
Northumberland for Cnut.

years later, replaced him by his own eldest natural son by Aelfgifu of Northampton, a lad of fourteen named Sweyn. This arrangement he did not regard as a violation of his oath to Queen Emma that their children should reign over the realms that he had possessed at the time of their marriage, for Norway was a new conquest. It was probably in compensation to her that he proclaimed their son Harthacnut King of Denmark, and placed him in authority there, though he was but ten years old. In the short interval between Earl Hakon's death and Sweyn's arrival in Norway, the exiled king Olaf Haraldson made a desperate attempt to recover his crown : he returned from Russia with his personal following, and set up his standard in Norway : but the majority of the Norse freeholders remembered him in no friendly fashion : they mustered in Cnut's name, and overwhelmed Olaf by numbers at the battle of Stiklestad (Aug. 31st, 1030). Yet it was not long after his death that the Norwegians began to regret him : Sweyn and his mother Aelfgifu proved even harder rulers than their old king had been, and national feeling grew more and more averse to the Danish yoke. Olaf was ere long declared a saint and a martyr, and though Cnut was acknowledged as suzerain in Norway as long as he lived, yet the moment that he was dead the Norsemen expelled Sweyn and his mother, and crowned Magnus the son of " Olaf the Holy ". This rising, however, was still six years in the future in 1030, and from that year till 1035 not only Norway, but its dependencies, Iceland and the Earldom of Orkney, formed part of Cnut's empire. So did, as it appears, the Viking-State in the Hebrides and Man, and almost certainly also the Scandinavian settlements in Ireland.

The same was the fate of Scotland, whose connection with Cnut requires a word of special notice. During the chaos that prevailed from 1013 to 1016, while Sweyn and Cnut were waging war against Aethelred the Redeless and his son, the King of the Scots had such an opportunity for aggression against his southern neighbours as had never been granted to any of his predecessors for many a year. Malcolm II., it will be remembered, had attacked Bernicia even before these last times of trouble, but had been turned back in 1006 by Uhtred, the son of Waltheof, who had been made earl of all Northumbria by King Aethelred in reward for his prowess.[1] When

---

[1] See p. 568.

this Uhtred was assassinated, by Cnut's contrivance or consent, in 1016, and Eric of Norway was made earl in his place by the Dane, it appears that the Bernicians tried to hold out for themselves under Eadwulf, nicknamed Cudel, the brother of their murdered ruler. But Malcolm the Scot came down upon them early in 1018, aided by Eugenius the Bald, King of Strathclyde, and fought a great battle with them at Carham on the Tweed,[1] in which " all the people who dwell from Tees to Tweed were well-nigh exterminated, and all their leaders slain ". Eadwulf himself however escaped, and being "*ignavus valde et timidus*," patched up a peace with the victor, by ceding all Lothian to him, so that the Tweed instead of the Forth became the northern boundary alike of the Bernician earldom and of the English realm. This cession cannot surely have been made without the consent of Cnut, who in this year had become the effective king of all England.[2] Yet it is not till after his return from his visit to Rome in 1027 that the Chronicle records a visit of Cnut to the North, ending in a setting to rights of affairs on this border.[3] "As soon as he came home "—presumably, therefore, in the early summer of 1027—" he went into Scotland, and the King of the Scots, Malcolm, submitted to him, and became his man (but that he held only a little while), and two other kings, Maelbeth and Jehmarc."[4] It is certain that the homage of Malcolm was secured by the confirmation to him of his recent conquests in Lothian, which remained ever after an integral part of the northern realm. This fact, passed over so lightly by all the contemporary chroniclers, was to have the most far-reaching effects within a few generations. For it was round this nucleus of English-speaking Bernicians that the later Scottish kingdom crystallised into a Teutonic instead of a Celtic state. Before sixty years had passed Edinburgh had become one of the chief residences of the descendants of Malcolm II., and Lothian

---

[1] All this comes from Simeon of Durham's Chronicle of the Church of Durham, iii. § 5.

[2] Simeon in his *De Obesessione Dunelmi*, § 6, speaks as if the cession was made by Eadwulf only, on his own responsibility. But this, possible in 1017, seems impossible in 1018.

[3] Having wrongly got the visit to Rome into the year 1031, the A. S. Chronicle makes the homage of the Scot king fall in that year also. But 1027 being a certain date for the Pilgrimage, it must be that of Malcolm's submission also.

[4] The former is probably *not* the famous Macbeth. The second name, evidently miswritten, may be that of a Scandinavian king in the Isles.

the centre of their realm.   When a century had gone by the royal
house was English-speaking and half-English in blood,[1] and already beginning to forget the time when their ancestors were mere
Gaelic-speaking sovereigns of the lands beyond Forth.   Nor was it
merely the kings who were changed—the Welsh of Strathclyde and
the Picts of Fife and Fortrenn were gradually assimilated by the
English of Lothian, and became indistinguishable from them, till by
the year 1300 the only part of Scotland that remained purely Celtic
was the Highlands.

But great as was to be the importance of the cession of Lothian
in the future, all that could be seen in Cnut's time was that the uneasy homage of the King of the Scots had been won by the sacrifice
of a devastated province.   Lothian remained part of Cnut's empire,
but had ceased to be part of his immediate domain.   For the rest of
his life Malcolm II. seems to have remained a quiet vassal ; he died
one year before his suzerain (1034).   But the moment that Cnut
was gone the Scots, under Malcolm's grandson Duncan, threw off the
English supremacy, and invaded Northumberland—though little to
their profit.   The overlordship of even the greatest king never
survived him, and had to be won back again by his successor if he
were sufficiently able and powerful.

There is singularly little on record concerning the last five years
of Cnut.   The Chronicle fills them up with mere records of natural
phenomena (" wildfire " such as was " never before remembered," etc.)
and the *obits* of certain bishops.   Florence of Worcester helps us to
the fact that it was in 1032 that Cnut completed the great restoration
of the Abbey of St. Edmunds Bury, to which allusion has been
already made,[2] and that at the same time he displaced canons there
in order to make room for monks.   But if we may trust continental
sources—there is no corroboration from English writers—the last
few years of the reign were disturbed by a threat of war with Robert
of Normandy.   The duke is said to have made up his mind to
champion the cause of his two exiled cousins, Alfred and Edward,
(who had been dwelling at Rouen ever since their flight from Lon-

---

[1] It will be remembered that Malcolm's grandson Duncan I. wedded a daughter
of Earl Siward, while his great grandson, Malcolm III., married St. Margaret, sister
of Eadgar Aetheling ; their son, David I., married Matilda, daughter of Earl Waltheof,
and David's son Henry married Ada, daughter of William de Warenne, Earl of Surrey.

[2] See p. 591.

don in 1015), and to have collected a fleet for the invasion of
England.   According to the Norman tale he sailed, with the
Aetheling Alfred in his company, but was driven by storms against
the rocks of the Channel Islands, where so many of his vessels
perished that he abandoned the enterprise, and soon after went on
a pilgrimage to Jerusalem, never to return.[1]   It is impossible to
estimate the importance of this breach between Cnut and Robert,
or to fix its exact date, for want of trustworthy evidence.   Evidently, from the silence of the Anglo-Saxon Chronicle, the matter
was not taken very seriously on this side of the Channel.

Cnut died at Shaftesbury on November 12, 1035, apparently in
the thirty-eighth year of his age, and certainly in the eighteenth
year of his reign as King of All England.   He was bitterly regretted
by his English subjects, to whom he had honestly fulfilled the
pledge that he had made at Oxford in 1018—that he would give
them good and strong governance under the laws of their ancestors.
Certainly he left behind him not the dilapidated realm that he had
taken over from Edmund Ironside, but a flourishing and well-
administered state.   The rapidity with which the traces of the
disasters of Aethelred's reign were removed is surprising.   Probably
no small part in the recovery was due to the fact that Cnut had
given his English subjects the opportunity of peaceful trade with
the whole of his broad dominions.   Not only the North Sea but the
Baltic was opened to them, while in his later years he was keeping
good peace in both by his complete naval supremacy.   And the
Scandinavian, and even the remoter Wendish, lands were well worth
trading with, since they eagerly sought what England could produce—things that had hitherto been luxuries only to be got by
piracy, fine woollen stuffs, jewellery, metal work, embroidery—as
well as the continental goods from the South, brocade and silk,
gold and ivory, wine and oil, spices and glass,[2] which came to Lon-

[1] For a discussion of this story see Freeman's *Norman Conquest*, i. pp. 471-76.
The details in William of Jumièges are sometimes unlikely and frequently incredible.   But there probably was some sort of friction between Cnut and Robert
about 1031-33.

[2] All these commodities are named by the merchant in Aelfric's *Dialogues*, an
early eleventh century work, as the " precious things not produced in this country,"
which he goes over seas to procure : " and I wish to sell them dearer here than I
buy them there, that I may get me profits to maintain myself, and my wife, and my
sons ".

don as a half-way house. No doubt the bulk of this trade was conducted by Danes or Anglo-Danes : but it is not merely the carrier
who is enriched by commerce ; the merchant, the middle-man and the
producer all make their profit, when trade develops and grows
prosperous. The immense quantity of Cnut's silver pennies that
survive bear witness to active trade—they are as common as those
of Aethelred, though his reign was only half as long, and while
Aethelred's money was largely coined for purposes of tribute only,
Cnut's must have been struck for purely commercial reasons, since
he never paid tribute to any man, though (unless the *Heims-*
kringla wrongs him) he was as adept as Philip of Macedon in
using bribes to aid the work of his sword. Probably the towns
recovered more quickly than the country-side from the results of
the earlier ravagings of Cnut and his father, before they came to
be English kings. But there is every sign that by the time that
his reign ended the whole land was in a very flourishing and satisfactory condition.

Owing to Cnut's settled policy of ruling England by means of
Englishmen, the fate of the dominions at his death was settled, not
in the interests of the imperial Scandinavian monarchy which he
had striven to create, but by local and particularist ambitions.
He had apparently intended that England and Denmark should
remain united under his one legitimate son Harthacnut, the son
of Emma, while Norway—ruled since 1030 by his natural son
Sweyn—remained a subject kingdom. Harthacnut was already
established as sub-king in Denmark long before his father's death,
but England was also destined for him, and an oath had been required from Archbishop Aethelnoth of Canterbury that he would
crown none save the son of Cnut and Emma.[1] Probably other
magnates had made similar pledges. But when the Witan met at
Oxford, immediately after the king's death, it became evident that
the arrangement was not to stand. Earl Leofric, the son of
Leofwine, and now ruler of Mercia, together with nearly all the
thegns north of Thames, and the *lithsmen* in London, *i.e.*, the
thing-manna-lith, the crews of Cnut's standing fleet, chose
Harold as King over All England. This Harold—nicknamed Harefoot for his fleetness—was the brother of Sweyn of Norway, the

[1] I see no reason to doubt the long story to this effect in the *Encomium Emmae*,
iii. 1.

other son of Aelfgifu of Northampton, the mistress of Cnut's early
years. He was now a young man of nineteen or twenty, active,
energetic and evidently ambitious. His father had acknowledged
him, but apparently had intended to give him no share in his heritage. But the facts that he was half-English by blood, that he had
been reared in England, and was there when his father died, and
that he was at least two years older than Harthacnut, gave him
many advantages.[1] Perhaps the fact that his grandfather Aelfhelm
(the victim of Aethelred and Eadric Streona, murdered in 1006) had
been for many years Earl of Deira, may have given him some help
among the Northern thegns, of whom some may have been his
kinsmen. At any rate the whole of Northern and Central England
favoured his candidature, rejecting Harthacnut, the son of the
stranger Emma, as too young to take up the responsibilities of
royalty. This meant the disruption of Cnut's empire, and certain
war with Denmark, but there was also opposition within England
itself. The Queen-Dowager Emma maintained the cause of her son
Harthacnut, and was at first supported by Godwine, the great Earl
of Wessex, who was already by this time the most important figure
among the English magnates. Cnut had trusted him to the uttermost, and had not been deceived in him. He had been taken into the
circle of the Danish royal house by his marriage with Gytha, the
daughter of Cnut's first cousin, Thorgils Sprakaleg, and the sister of
Jarl Ulf. Several of his children received Scandinavian names—
notably the eldest, Harold, who must have been given it in memory
of his ancestor, King Harald Bluetooth of Denmark, Sweyn's father.
Godwine had long been ruling all Wessex—an earldom larger and
more important than any other—as the king's vicegerent: its territories had been enough to support three ealdormen in the time of
Aethelstan. Whether from loyalty to Cnut's memory, or because
he thought that he would be more powerful under the boy Harthacnut than under his elder half-brother, Godwine at first persisted
in supporting the claim of the son of Emma to the crown of all

---

[1] The silly story mentioned by the A. S. Chronicle, and backed (of course) by
the *Encomium Emmae*, to the effect that there was doubt as to the parentage of
Sweyn and Harold, may be rejected with contempt. Cnut had acknowledged his
sons, and actually placed Sweyn as sub-king in Norway, under the tutelage of his
mother Aelfgifu. The tale that she foisted two changelings on him was put about
by Emma's friends, and may be compared with the "warming-pan" story about the
birth of the Elder Pretender.

England. When he was overruled by the Northern earls, he persisted in his protests till a compromise was reached, by which Harold was to be king north of Thames and Harthacnut in Godwine's earldom of Wessex alone. The queen-dowager settled down at Winchester with a guard of her late husband's housecarls, to await the arrival of her son from Denmark, and Godwine administered Wessex in his name. But this arrangement was wrecked by the non-appearance of Harthacnut, and in his absence the party of Harold grew stronger, and he began to make overtures to the southern magnates to come over to his party. The reason of the delay of Harthacnut was that he had become involved in troubles of his own in Denmark. Early in 1036 the Norwegians drove out Sweyn, the son of Cnut, and his mother Aelfgifu, and proclaimed Magnus, son of St. Olaf, as king. The fugitives took refuge with Harthacnut, who granted them his protection, and so took up war with Norway. Sweyn died of disease during the winter of 1036-37, but this did not free his brother from the prospect of war; probably he was set on reasserting his father's claim to suzereignty over Norway in his own behalf. In the next spring (1037) the armies of the two Scandinavian realms met on the Gotha river, their boundary, but no decisive battle took place, for the jarls and chiefs on both sides came to an agreement not to encourage the enmity of the two kings, "who were both young and childish," but to make peace. This was done, Harthacnut being forced to surrender his claim of supremacy over Norway. Meanwhile the summer had slipped away.[1]

While the King of Denmark was thus distracted, he lost his chance of retaining Wessex. The year 1036 had been eventful in England. The compromise made at Oxford was bound to fall through unless Harthacnut appeared, and the fate of Wessex was trembling in the balance when a third party intervened. Alfred, the younger son of Emma and Aethelred, presented himself on the South coast with a body of 600 mercenaries raised in Normandy and the Boulonnais, evidently with a view of making a snatch at the paternal crown while the sons of Cnut were at variance. He is said to have given out that he only wished to visit his mother Emma at Winchester—a plea about as credible as that of Edward

---

[1] All this comes from the *Heimskringla*, but seems trustworthy, despite of the lateness of the authority.

IV. when (returning from exile before Barnet) he said that he only intended to visit London in order to claim his Duchy of York. Emma was devoted to the cause of her younger son Harthacnut, and had always shown complete indifference to the fate of the children of her first marriage. And a friendly visitor need hardly bring 600 foreign soldiers in his train. There was no enthusiasm shown on Alfred's appearance; indeed his first attempt to land in Kent was repelled by force. When, however, he had got ashore he was dealt with very treacherously; Earl Godwine, who was still the leader of Harthacnut's faction, met him at Guildford in friendly guise, feasted him and billeted his men in small parties about the town. But at midnight a descent was made upon Guildford by a body of King Harold's supporters, who seized the aetheling and his followers in their beds, without a blow having been struck. It was universally believed, and apparently with truth, that Godwine was guilty of complicity in the plot, since he had no wish to see a new pretender appear, to complicate the political situation. But he apparently took no part in the atrocities that followed : Harold put out Alfred's eyes, and shut him up in the monastery of Ely, where he shortly afterwards expired. Of his men some were slain, others tortured and mutilated, and the rest sold as slaves. " Never was a bloodier deed done in this land since first the Danes came hither," says one of the versions of the Anglo-Saxon Chronicle. Both of the dominant political factions seem to have been implicated in it, Godwine having betrayed the aetheling, if Harold was responsible for the horrid cruelty displayed to the prisoners. The stain on the great earl's character was indelible, and during the rest of his long life the charge of being guilty of Alfred's "martyrdom" was repeatedly brought up against him.[1]

[1] I have followed here the main narrative of the *Encomium Emmae*, which gives the most rational account of the matter, and does not contradict the A. S. C. in any important particulars. But it seems unlikely that the Encomiast is right in saying that Alfred was lured to England by letters forged by Harold in his mother's name. The aetheling must surely have known that Emma was committed to the support of her younger son, for whose claim she had been striving all her life. The treachery of Godwine is implied by the *Encomium* and definitely stated by the Abingdon version of the A. S. C. Professor Freeman's vindication of his innocence in *Norman Conquest*, i. 489, etc., is unconvincing. The number of Alfred's followers is given at 600 by Florence of Worcester, who calls them

Early in the next year, while Harthacnut was facing the Norsemen on the Gotha river, his supporters in England abandoned his
cause, "because he stayed too long in Denmark," and Harold was
taken as king over all England.   Queen Emma had to fly over the
seas in wintry weather, and took refuge at Bruges with her kinsman Baldwin, Count of Flanders.   Godwine's peace with Harold
was easily made—he had already won the young king's grace by
his complicity in the horrid business at Guildford.   For about three
years (spring of 1037 to March 17, 1040) Harold enjoyed a supremacy that was never disputed, though all through the time he was
being threatened by an invasion from Denmark.   The impression
conveyed by the chroniclers as to his character and policy is unfavourable.   We are told that he was cruel (his treatment of
Alfred sufficiently justifies this charge), careless, and irreligious.
But every one of the writers was influenced by partisanship, at first
or second hand, for the house of Emma and Aethelred, and it is
likely enough that Harold gets scant justice from them.   Emma's
encomiast tells us that when Archbishop Aethelnoth refused to
crown him, because of his pledge to the dead Cnut, he "not only
spurned bishops' blessings but seemed alienated from all religion
whatever.   For when other men went to church and heard mass,
like good Christians, he would go a hunting in the forest with his
dogs, or occupy himself in other trifling pursuits, so as to avoid
ceremonies that he detested."   The charge is not a very serious one
after all!   And since no other definite accusations are made
against Harold by his bitter enemies, we may conclude that the
murder of Alfred was his only crime of serious importance.   A few
details may be collected about his reign.   Both the Welsh and
the Scots thought it safe, when Cnut was dead, to trouble the
borders of England.   Duncan, the grandson and successor of Malcolm II., invaded Northumbria in Harold's last year, and besieged
Durham, but was routed with great slaughter by a sally of the
inhabitants, who built up a ghastly trophy of severed Scottish
heads in their hour of triumph.[1]   The luck of the Welsh was better
in 1039, when Gruffyd, King of Gwynedd, then newly come to the
throne, defeated an English army at Rhyd-y-Groes on the Severn,

Normans; the Encomiast says that he " *elegit commilitones* " in Normandy, and
strengthened them with " *Bononiensium paucos* " before sailing.
[1] Simeon of Durham, *Hist. Dunelm. Eccl.*, iii. 9.

and slew Edwin the brother of Earl Leofric of Mercia, and other thegns.[1] This warlike prince was to be for twenty years the bane alike of his neighbours the kings of South Wales, and of the Mercian and Magesaetan marchmen. No such fighting man had reigned for many a year among the Britons. But it does not appear that Gruffyd's victory had any more important effect than Duncan's defeat on the general history of England.

On March 17, 1040, King Harold died at Oxford, just at the moment when his brother Harthacnut's coming—so often rumoured and delayed—was actually about to take place. Though married [2] the young king left no issue, so that his cause perished along with himself, and there was no obvious successor whom his partisans could set up against the claimant from Denmark. He was buried at Westminster, in the monastery which was the humble predecessor of the great foundation of Edward the Confessor. But he was not destined to lie long in his tomb.

Harthacnut, after losing his chance of retaining Wessex in 1037, had delayed for two full years before he set out to attack his brother. Since he was at peace with Norway and Sweden, it is to be presumed that he had been vexed with domestic troubles in Denmark. But he had collected a great fleet in the autumn of 1039, and had coasted down to Flanders, where he landed to confer with his mother Emma, who still lay at Bruges under the protection of Count Baldwin. It is said that his coming might have been yet more tardy but for her constant appeals. Harthacnut stayed for the winter at Flanders, deferring his attack till the campaigning season should come round. Hence he had not yet started when the unexpected news of his brother's death was brought to him in March. We are surprised to find that he did not land at Sandwich till June 18, 1040. Evidently the intervening months had been spent in negotiations with the Witan, many of whose members must have had good reason to dread his arrival—some because they had been concerned in the original election of Harold in 1036, others, like Godwine, because they had been comprised in the murder of Harthacnut's brother Alfred. For the king was to be accom-

[1] Apparently Crossford, six miles West of Shrewsbury, which name translates Rhyd-y-Groes.

[2] His wife's name is not known, and her existence is only proved by a legacy to her, in the will of Bishop Aelfric of Elmham.

panied not only by his mother, but by his half-brother Edward, the last surviving son of Aethelred. He had sent for him to Normandy, at Emma's request, and promised him a fraternal welcome in England.[1]

Matters, however, were settled by June, Harthacnut giving some sort of a promise of amnesty. He landed at Sandwich among many ceremonious rejoicings, and was crowned king. His first royal act was to order the body of his brother Harold to be exhumed, and cast on the marshy foreshore of the Thames. It floated about, till it was secretly recovered and buried by certain Danes in their cemetery—either St. Clement's, Strand, or St. Olaf's, Southwark. Harthacnut's later acts give no better impression of him than this disgusting exhibition of spite. His reign began with the levy of enormous tribute—he had sixty-two ships of *thingmen* in pay—where Cnut had been wont to keep forty and Harold only sixteen. To give them eight marks each required a very heavy "gafol," and the tax was to be permanent. There was resistance against the impost in Worcester, where two of the king's housecarls, charged with its collection, were murdered in a riot. Harthacnut took the matter hardly, sent a whole army against the shire, under Godwine and Leofric, and harried it from end to end. Of the other deeds of his short reign—which lasted less than two years—we know that he consented to the treacherous slaying of Eadwulf, Earl of Northumbria, who was killed when visiting him under safe conduct by his enemy Siward, to whom the king then gave his earldom. "And so he became a belier of his *wed* " (pledge), observes the Anglo-Saxon chronicler. He also dabbled in simony, selling the vacant bishopric of Durham to one Eadred for a great price.[2]

It was a relief to every one when this unworthy son of the great Cnut died suddenly, before he had completed his second regnal year and twenty-fifth summer. He was present at the marriage feast of a Danish magnate, Tofig the Proud, who was wedding the daughter of Osgod Clapa his *staller* or marshal. As he " stood at his drink " —perhaps as he was proposing the health of the married pair— " he fell to the earth in a horrid convulsion ; and then they who were nigh lifted him, but he after spake not one word, but died on

[1] This appears in the last chapter of the *Encomium Emmae* : apparently Edward was made in some degree his brother's designated heir.
[2] Simeon of Durham, *Hist. Eccl. Dunelm.*, iii. § 9.

the sixth day before the Ides of June" [June 8th, 1042]. And so ended the short period of the reign of the Danish House in England, to the satisfaction of the whole nation, for Cnut's sons had done their best to make all men forget the blessings that they had received from their father.

CHAPTER XXVIII

EDWARD THE CONFESSOR, AND HAROLD GODWINESON. CONCLUSION (1042-1066)

AT the moment of Harthacnut's sudden death his half-brother Edward, the last surviving son of Aethelred the Redeless, was actually present in England.[1] He had been entertained at Harthacnut's court with all honour during the greater part of the short reign which had now ended : indeed, according to one absolutely contemporary authority he had been treated, either formally or practically, as *regni socius*.[2] On his brother's decease he was, therefore, the most obvious claimant to the crown whom the Witan had to take into consideration. Against him there might have been raised up two other claims ; the one was that of his own nephew Edward the Exile, the son of Edmund Ironside, who had been dwelling in Hungary ever since he was sent out of England as an infant in 1017 ; he was now a young man of twenty-six, but absolutely unknown on this side of the high seas. The other possible pretenders were the sons of Cnut's sister Estrith, by her husband Jarl Ulf, the man who had been so cruelly slain by his brother-in-law in 1025 ; their names were Sweyn, Osbeorn and Beorn. If England had been treated during the last twenty years as an appanage of Denmark, and had been governed by Danes in Danish interests, one of these young men might well have obtained the crown. But this, as we have seen, had never been the case ; Cnut had ruled England mainly by English officials, and his sons

---

[1] This, though denied by Freeman (*N. C.*, ii. 3-16) on late authority, seems certain (see Plummer's *Notes to A. S. C.*, ii. 221).

[2] " Hic fides habetur regni sociis, hic inviolabile viget foedus fraterni amoris," says one version of the last paragraph of the *Encomium Emmae*, while the other says that " Hic fratribus concorditer regnantibus, mors media intercidit, et Hardechnutonem abstulit ".

had followed his example. There were in 1042 a fair number of
Danish magnates in the Witan, such as the Earls Siward of Northumbria, Thorer of the Middle Angles, and Ranig of the Magesaetas,
and the great *ministri*, Osgod Clapa and Tofig the Proud, who
have already been mentioned. But they were in a minority, and
dominated by the native element in the council. It seems, however, that the claim of Sweyn Estrithson was at least raised. We
have his own word to that effect—for what it may be worth. He
told the chronicler, Adam of Bremen, with his own mouth, that he
chanced to be in England in the autumn of 1042, having run over
from Denmark to announce to Harthacnut that Magnus of Norway had renewed the war which had been stopped in 1037.[1] He
found his cousin just dead, and Edward already elected ; yet he
nevertheless put himself forward as a claimant.[2] But he soon consented to withdraw, having designs that were more easy to carry
out on Denmark itself. He said that Edward promised him the
heritage of England after his own death—the same tale that
William of Normandy afterwards put about—but this seems hardly
likely. It was, however, perhaps part of the " pact with which he
was mitigated," according to his own story, that his brother Beorn
was made shortly afterwards Earl of Danish Mercia—of the land
of the Five Burghs, and somewhat more. Sweyn, at any rate,
retired to Denmark, where he claimed the throne and fought for
several years with varying fortune against Magnus of Norway, who
repeatedly drove him out into Sweden. His brother Beorn ruled
his earldom till he was murdered in 1049, and never seems to have
given any trouble to King Edward.

It is notable that Godwine made no attempt to help Sweyn
Estrithson's claims, though he might well have dreaded the accession of the brother of the Aetheling Alfred, whom he had
betrayed, in 1036, into the murderous hands of Harold Harefoot.
But he did not set himself to oppose the general voice of the
English nation by backing the cause of a stranger. Indeed it is
expressly said that he and Bishop Lyfing of Crediton were mainly
responsible for Edward's quiet recognition, and spared neither pains
nor money in buying off opposition.[3] The earl had, no doubt,

[1] See p. 603.
[2] " Quod sceptrum sibi Anglorum reposceret " (see Adam, iv. 74).
[3] Florence of Worcester, *sub anno* 1042.

been able by this time to form an estimate of the character of the new king, and thought that he should be able to assert a domination over him.

Edward was at this time thirty-seven years old—no king of England since Ecgbert had come to the throne at such a mature age. But maturity with him did not imply strength, and twenty-six years of exile had taught him patience and resignation, but had drained the fount of energy in him. Apparently he had spent his time in Normandy among priests rather than among fighting men ; certainly he showed no family likeness to the capable and turbulent cousins with whom he had been living. Yet the Normans, clerks and laymen alike, were far dearer to him than any Englishman. He was himself half-Norman by blood and wholly Norman by education. How could he love the former subjects of his father, who had served Cnut with content while he himself lay in exile, and who had slain his brother Alfred when he tried to claim his rights ? It was but natural that the kinsmen who had harboured him with great kindness all the days of his youth should be better liked by him. Hence came the eagerness with which, so far as was in his power, he promoted Norman clerks to English bishoprics, and gave land and office to Norman laymen. But he was too weak to carry out any consistent policy of this kind. Like Charles II.— a king whom he resembled in no single other trait of character—he was very anxious "not to go on his travels again". He knew that the Witan which had made him might unmake him, if he showed too great disregard for their wishes. Hence he aspired to no more than to getting a certain share of his desires fulfilled, by playing off one party of the English magnates against another.

But it would be wrong to represent Edward as a Machiavellian manipulator of politics. He clearly had neither the will nor the brains to make himself a despot, and he was—according to his lights—a very conscientious man. Above all things he was religious, in the strictest eleventh-century sense of the word. His fasts and prayers, his rigorous observation of all ceremonial, his lavish almsgiving, his liberality to all ecclesiastical personages and institutions, were the admiration of his age. Not the least of his merits, in the eyes of admiring clerks, was that vow of chastity, which caused him to leave his kingdom without an heir, to be fought for by strangers. He was austere in his living, equable in temper, save on rare occasions where he burst out into fits of passion—but never used strong language—and thrifty in all things save his charities. He would seem to have been a bad judge of character, for many, or most, of his favourites were men unworthy of honour—the bloodthirsty and treacherous Earl Tostig, the cowardly Ralph "the Timid," whom he made Earl of the Magesae-tas, the Norman bishop Ulf, "who did nothing bishop-like, so that it is a shame to tell of," and the other Norman, Robert of Jumièges, the domineering primate, who had such an ascendency over his master "that if he said a black crow was white, the king would rather trust his mouth than his own eyes". But some of his other clerical *protegés* have a better record.

Edward was in personal appearance a very kingly figure—he had a handsome ruddy face, his hair and beard in old age were long remembered for their beautiful snow-white hue; his hands were small and graceful, his stature well proportioned; his aspect was benevolent and majestic. But the spirit within him was that of a monk rather than a king, and a strong will was wanting. All through his reign he was the tool of men of sterner mould. The reasons for which he received, after death, the rather undeserved honour of canonisation were twofold. The English looked back to him as the last king under whom they had been ruled according to their own ancient customs, and spoke of the "good laws of St. Edward" as if he had been a great legislator—which was far from being the case. The Normans, on the other hand, affected to regard him as the donor of the English crown to their great duke, and as the righteous patron of all things Norman. Hence he was popular with both races,—more especially with the clergy who remembered his piety and his lavish endowment of the Church.

Edward was not crowned till some nine months or more after his election; the ceremony was perhaps delayed till the claims of Sweyn Estrithson had been got rid of, and all the magnates conciliated by the grant of their desires. After the hallowing had been duly accomplished at Winchester, on the first day of Easter, 1043, we get our first note from the Chronicle of a royal act of the Lord's anointed. It does not appear to be one very characteristic of a saint. "Fourteen days before St. Andrew's Mass (Nov. 16th) the king was advised to ride from Gloucester, and in his company the Earls Leofric [of Mercia], Godwine [of Wessex], and Siward [of

Northumbria] with their followers, to Winchester, unawares upon
the lady Emma. And they bereaved her of all the treasures that
she possessed, which were incalculable, because before that she had
been very hard with the king her son, insomuch that she had done
less for him than he would, both before he was king and also
after." Edward's conduct was entirely comprehensible, if hardly
filial. His mother had neglected him all her life, and had reserved
all her affection for the children of her second marriage. Apparently
she had got possession of much land and great part of the royal
hoard, by the liberality of Cnut and Harthacnut, and showed no
desire to share them with her son. She was now deprived of all
save a moderate competence, but permitted to live free and undisturbed for the rest of her life at Winchester ; from this time forth
she ceased to have any further influence on the politics of the realm.

For the next seven years matters seem to have gone fairly well
in England. The king was in the hands of the three great Earls,
Godwine, Leofric and Siward, who managed for a time to keep the
peace with each other, and to share the power between them, though
we can hardly doubt that the jealousies which afterwards led to
civil war were already working. That Godwine had the pre-
eminence over his colleagues is sufficiently shown by several events
recorded in the Chronicle. In 1044 Eadsige, Archbishop of Canterbury, asked for a coadjutor, because of his great age and infirmities. Siward, Abbot of Abingdon, was appointed to the place
" by the king's wish and Godwine the earl's," the matter being
kept from the Witan "so that it was known to few men ere it was
done ". In the next year Godwine induced the king to marry his
daughter Ealdgyth ; it was well known that Edward had taken a
vow of chastity, and that the union was but nominal. The lady
was fair but pious and staid :—

Sicut spina rosam, genuit Godwinus Edivam,

and the royal pair seem to have lived on friendly terms. Whether
Godwine's new position as the king's father-in-law did him more
good than harm is doubtful. It must certainly have provoked much
wrath and jealousy among the other greater earls. In this same
time Godwine extended his power outside Wessex, by persuading
the king to give earldoms to his two elder sons ; Sweyn the eldest
was given the land of the Hwiccas, and several adjacent shires, in

1043. Harold, the second son, received East Anglia in 1045. By what transference of land from deceased or deposed earls this arrangement was made we cannot be sure. But there was a considerable shifting of boundaries in King Edward's early years. It was perhaps to balance the promotion of the two sons of Godwine that Beorn, the brother of Sweyn Estrithson, received his large earldom in Danish Mercia, while Ralph the son of the king's sister Goda (Godgifu), by Drogo, Count of Mantes, was made earl of the Magesaetas, probably in succession to the Dane Ranig, who had been holding it in the time of Cnut and his sons.[1] But the net result of the rearrangement was decidedly in favour of Godwine's family rather than of the other party.

The foreign politics of England in the years 1043-49 seem mainly to have been concerned with the vicissitudes of the struggle in Scandinavia between Magnus of Norway and Sweyn Estrithson. The Norse king was a very powerful and ambitious prince, and on more than one occasion, when he had for a time driven Sweyn out of Denmark, expressed his intention of attacking England. Indeed, when he was at the height of his power, he is said to have sent a formal challenge to King Edward, bidding him prepare to fight or submit.[2] It was apparently to resist this threatened Viking raid, that we hear in several successive summers of an English fleet being collected at Sandwich (1044-5-6), though it is only in the last year that we are told in definite words by the Chronicle that the gathering was to resist Magnus. Fortunately for England Sweyn Estrithson, though often driven out of Denmark, always came back to distract his rival from broader schemes of conquest. Twice Sweyn sent to ask aid from King Edward, and Godwine is said to have been inclined to grant it, but the majority of the Witan overruled him—a sign that his power, however great at this time, had its limits. Probably the Witan was right—Sweyn unaided sufficed to keep Magnus in check, till the Norwegian king

[1] It is pretty certain that Florence of Worcester is wrong when (*sub anno* 1051) he says that Sweyn's earldom included Herefordshire. It was really partly Hwiccian, and composed of Gloucestershire, Oxon, Berks and Somerset (see Freeman's *Norman Conquest*, ii. App. c.).

[2] This is found only in the late *Heimskringla*, in the last chapter of the Saga of Magnus, but the contemporary entries in the A. S. C. show in 1046 that an invasion was expected from Norway, and that the fleet collected at Sandwich was to resist him: "but Sweyn's contention with him hindered his coming hither".

died in 1049. The northern realm then fell to his uncle, Harald
Hardrada, who though a great fighting man never succeeded in
beating down Sweyn to extremity, as his nephew had repeatedly
done.

It seems probable that we should connect with the threatened
invasions of Magnus the expulsion from England of several important personages of Scandinavian blood—it is likely that they
were suspected of being in secret correspondence with the Norseman. In 1045 we are told that Heming and Thorkil, kinsmen of
Cnut, were "driven out" along with their mother Gunhilda. In
1046 Osgod Clapa the "staller" was exiled. He retired to Flanders and for some time vexed the east coast of England by small
piratical descents. But evidently the main danger from the East
was considered to be at an end in 1049, when King Edward, as we
are told, disbanded the greater part of the small force of "lithsmen," professional mercenary sailors, which he had inherited from
Harthacnut. He paid off nine ships' crews out of fourteen, and
apparently disposed of the remaining five not long after. The
cessation of the tax required to pay them was a relief to the
country, but the policy of cutting down the standing navy was
as unwise in the eleventh as in the twentieth century.

Already, before this date, the first signs of the civil war which
was to be the landmark of Edward's central years were to be des-
cried. The troubles commenced by a misdeed of one of Godwine's
sons—it may truly be said of him that the earl's enemies were of
his own house, for though his second son Harold was a tower of
strength to him, a wise counsellor and a good general, his eldest
son Sweyn, and his third, Tostig, were lawless young ruffians, who
seem to have inherited wild Viking blood from their Danish mother
the daughter of Thorgils Sprakaleg. Returning from a campaign
against the South Welsh in 1046, Sweyn passed through Leominster, where he was captivated by the beauty of Eadgifu, abbess of
the nunnery there. He carried her off by force and made her his
mistress.[1] This was the kind of crime which provoked the usually
meek King Edward to wild wrath, and public opinion was so deeply
stirred that Godwine did not dare to defend his son, who was very
properly deprived of his earldom and banished. He retired for a

[1] According to Florence of Worcester he wanted to marry her; but the A. S.
Chronicle says that " he kept her as long as he listed, and then let her fare home".

time to Denmark, and served under his relative and namesake
Sweyn Estrithson against the Norwegians. But in 1049 he came
back to Flanders, and from thence began making piratical descents
on the English coast, with a little squadron of seven or eight ships.
Having thus made his existence known, he had the impudence to
propose to the king, who was then lying at Sandwich with his fleet,
that he should be recalled from exile and restored to his earldom.
This proposal, we are told, was seriously taken into consideration,
but it was resisted not only by Earl Beorn, but by Sweyn's own
brother Harold. They had each received a shire or so from the
outlaw's forfeited earldom, and refused to give them up. Sweyn,
however, was allowed the king's peace, in order that he might
visit England and plead his cause in person. He took the most
shameful advantage of this permission : he induced Beorn to meet
him, as if for a reconciliation, but when the unsuspecting earl had
consented to ride with him to see the king, he had him seized by
his retainers and carried on board a ship. Beorn was murdered on
the high seas, and his body cast on shore at Dartmouth. This
foul crime—a bad case of "murder under tryst"—provoked a
great outburst of wrath, "the king and all the army proclaimed
Sweyn *nithing*," the worst word of contempt and ignominy in the
Old-English vocabulary, and all his own ship's-crew save two deserted him as he fled to Flanders. Earl Harold, to mark his
horror at his brother's crime, solemnly bore Beorn's body from
Dartmouth to Winchester and buried it beside the tomb of his
uncle Cnut.[1]

After this it is most astonishing to hear that in the next year
negotiations for Sweyn's "inlawing" were once more taken in hand,
the intermediary between the exile and the Witan being Bishop
Ealdred of Worcester, who was passing through Flanders on his
way to a council in Italy. As the earl's piratical inroads do not
seem to have been a very serious menace to the realm, we can only
account for his pardon by supposing that his father Godwine was
unscrupulous and foolish enough to put paternal fondness before

---

[1] The exact details of Sweyn's return to England and his murder of Beorn are
related differently in the various versions of the A. S. C.   In one we are told that the
king resolved to pardon Sweyn at once, in another that he utterly refused, and there
are many other discrepancies.   See the interesting note in Plummer's A. S. C.,
ii. pp. 229-30.

moral right and political expediency, and to force the king to re-call him. The act was as unwise as it was immoral, for Sweyn's well-deserved unpopularity weakened his father's position to a marked extent. It seems that he was given back some, but not all, of the counties of his former earldom.

In the autumn of 1050, the year of Sweyn's pardon, there was a trial of strength between Godwine and his enemies, whose result showed that the Great Earl's power was waning. On the death of Eadsige the aged Archbishop of Canterbury [1] (October 29) God-wine had proposed to replace him by a relative of his own,[2] a monk named Aelfric, and the chapter of Canterbury (no doubt on a hint from the earl) met hastily and elected Aelfric without the king's con-sent. But Edward had made up his mind to bestow the primacy on the chief of his Norman favourites, Robert of Jumièges, whom he had already promoted to the bishopric of London. At the Mid-Lent meeting of the Witan in March, 1051, Godwine's wishes were overruled, after much wrangling, and Robert was chosen archbishop. He at once journeyed to Rome for his pall, and made such haste that he was back in England before the autumn.

He had not yet returned, however, when open strife broke out between Godwine and the party that was backing the king from jealousy of his father-in-law. During the summer of 1051 Eustace, Count of Boulogne, the second husband of Edward's sister Goda, landed at Dover on a visit to his kinsman. He brought a con-siderable armed retinue with him, and proceeded to quarter it on the townsmen; the king's guests had from time immemorial a right to be lodged when on their way to visit his presence. The French men-at-arms were insolent and exacting, and one of them fell into a brawl with the householder on whom he was billeted, in which the burgess was wounded and the Frenchman killed. Count Eustace thereupon armed and mounted his retinue, and attacked the men of Dover: there was a considerable fight in the street, with many casualties on both sides. At least seven of the count's men were slain, and he was driven out of the town by

[1] Eadsige's coadjutor Siward (see p. 613) had predeceased the old archbishop, or he would no doubt have taken his place, with Godwine's help, since he was the earl's nominee.

[2] The relationship cannot be traced.

main force.[1] Eustace rode straight to his brother-in-law, who
then lay at Gloucester, and demanded the condign punishment of
the strong-handed Kentishmen. Edward, without making any inquiry, sent orders to Godwine, bidding him burn and ravage Dover
—just as his brother Harthacnut had ravaged Worcester under
similar circumstances ten years before. The Great Earl refused:
not only did he think the Dover men guiltless, but he saw a fine
opportunity of posing as the protector of Englishmen against lawless foreigners. He replied to the king's message by bringing a
counter-charge of robbery and oppression against certain Norman
followers of Earl Ralph of Hereford, who, having been established
on the Welsh border by their master, had built there a castle
(called Richard's Castle from Richard le Scrob, the chief of these
foreigners) and from thence had been blackmailing the neighbouring land.

Such a reply meant civil war, and Godwine gave orders to
raise the *fyrd* of Wessex, and called in his sons Harold and Sweyn
to his aid. Their forces were gathered at Beverstone in Langtree
hundred, on the border of Gloucestershire and Wiltshire, observing
the king, who still lay in Gloucester city. Edward showed no
signs of wavering, but called in the Mercians and Northumbrians
to his aid. Siward, Leofric, and Ralph of Hereford all came up,
and the feeling was so strong against the overweening Earl of
Wessex, for taking arms against his master, that " all were united
in opinion to seek out Godwine's forces if the king so willed ".
But when the armies were facing each other " then thought some
that it would be great folly to join battle, for all that was most
noble in England was present in one army or the other, and they
weened that it should expose the land to our foes, and cause great
distruction among ourselves ". So it was settled that hostages
should be exchanged, and that all the Witan should meet in London at Michaelmas for a peaceful settlement. This compromise
proved ruinous to Godwine: his followers felt many qualms at
finding themselves arrayed in arms against their lawful king. When
the Witan met, and the earl brought up the Wessex *fyrd* to Southwark to back his claims, it was noted that they were half-hearted,
and that many began to slink home after a few days. On the

[1] So the best version of the A. S. C. The Peterborough version says that
nineteen were slain on one side, and twenty on the other.

other hand the levies of Siward and Leofric were numerous and
resolute. The strength of his adversaries seemed so great, that
Godwine refused to come to the meeting of the Witan, unless he
was given the king's personal safe-conduct and more hostages.
Edward and his advisers replied by a counter-demand that the
earl and his sons should surrender the homage-rights which they
owned from various thegns scattered outside their own ealdormanries
—for owing to the practice of voluntary commendation they had
many dependants in other earls' lands.[1] To this Godwine and
Harold consented, hoping thereby to get the safe-conduct. But
on the following day Bishop Stigand of Winchester appeared at
Southwark to tell the earl (with all regret, for he was one of his
partisans) that he must come to the Witan with twelve followers
only, or be held contumacious. He and his sons would be outlawed, unless he submitted and came to meet the king, without
guarantees, within five days. The Wessex *fyrd* had dwindled so
rapidly that Godwine dared not push matters to the arbitrament
of the sword. Nor would he trust himself among his enemies. He
resolved to fly, dismissed his levy, save his personal retainers, and
rode off by night with his wife, and most of his family, to Bosham,
where he took ship for Flanders. But his sons Harold and Leofwine
made off by another route, and shipped themselves from Bristol to
Ireland.[2]

It seemed that the Great Earl's power was finally broken. The
moment that his flight was known the king, in a full meeting of the
Witan, declared him, with all his sons, outlawed. Their earldoms
were distributed among the victorious party; West Wessex and
part of Hwiccia (Gloucestershire at least) were given to a certain
Odda; Harold's East Anglian dominions to Aelfgar, the son of
Leofric of Mercia; an Earl Sigrod, whose name appears in charters
of this year, may also have been given his endowment out of the
spoils—we cannot say where. Spearhafoc, bishop-elect of London,
was ousted from his see, in order that it might be given to the
king's Norman chaplain William. But the most extraordinary act

---

[1] For this interpretation of the rather obscure note of the A. S. C. about the
thegns see Plummer, ii. 237.

[2] All Godwine's doings in 1051 are described with varying details by different
versions of the A. S. C. The Peterborough version (Mr. Plummer's " D ") is mainly
followed here.

on Edward's part was that he sent his blameless wife Ealdgyth, Godwine's daughter, into a nunnery—an odious deed.

In the end of the year the Chronicle informs us that Edward received a visit from his cousin William the Bastard, Duke of Normandy. "The king received him and as many of his companions as pleased him, and then let him go away again." This visit had all-important issues depending on it, for it was on this occasion, according to William's story, that his cousin promised to make him heir to the crown of England. It is needless to point out that Edward had no power to do any such thing—he might have commended him to the Witan, no doubt, but such a commendation would have provoked only wrath and indignation, and was certainly never made. It is odd to find the saintly sovereign, according to the tales told by his relatives, behaving like those modern *oncles à hériter*, who are always promising to leave their property to different relatives. Sweyn Estrithson, William of Normandy, and later Harold Godwineson were each positive that he had left them the succession of the crown! Very probably he did hold out hopes to all three in turn. William in especial, a young man of twenty-five, of boundless energy and capacity, was no doubt in complete possession of his cousin's good graces during his short stay at court. His Norman blood, his considerable powers of diplomacy, and his formal piety were all in his favour. Edward may have promised him anything that he asked.

Earl Godwine's absence from England was to endure but a short space. He had made no real trial of his strength in 1051, but had rather placed himself in an impossible position by unskilful diplomacy, and retired to recover himself. He was aware that Wessex was loyal to him, and that he had many supporters even outside it. He had but to present himself, and his partisans would join him. Accordingly in the spring of 1052 he appeared with a small fleet off Dungeness, while his son Harold, with nine vessels hired in Ireland, ran into the Bristol Channel and defeated a Somersetshire levy which tried to resist his landing at Porlock. The king had set forty ships under the Earls Odda and Ralph to watch for him in the Dover Straits, but they had been storm-bound at Sandwich, and then retired to London, leaving the sea clear. Thus Godwine and his sons were able to unite at Portland, from whence they sailed along the coasts of Hampshire, Sussex and Kent, levying contributions, and calling in the coast-folk to their aid. "They collected all the *busscarls* (professional sailors) whom they met with," says one version of the Chronicle. "Everywhere hostages were given them and provisions, whenever they desired," says another. By the time that they entered the mouth of the Thames they had a great fleet, and though fifty ships had been collected against them the king's men dared not offer battle. Though the invaders had done considerable harm, by ravaging every place that did not instantly submit, public opinion was evidently not estranged from them. The Londoners in especial showed much favour to Godwine, and allowed him to pass his vessels under their bridge without molestation. Presently a great land force from Kent, Surrey and Sussex came to his aid. The king had also an army behind him, "but it was loathful to almost all of them to fight against men of their own race," and it was felt that Godwine had been hardly treated in the preceding year. The Archbishop Robert, and Edward's other foreign favourites tried to screw him up to fighting-point, but could not succeed. He gave leave for negotiations with the rebels, and Stigand, bishop of Winchester, as an old friend of Godwine and his sons, was sent out to meet them. Seeing their cause lost, Archbishop Robert and Bishop Ulf, with many other French and Normans, fled, and, after cutting their way through a hostile London mob, took ship and went over seas.

After this Godwine could demand all that he pleased. He showed great moderation ; he and his son Harold got back their earldoms, but his eldest-born Sweyn, the original cause of troubles, never came back to England. He died on a pilgrimage to Jerusalem, whither his own conscience or his father's orders had driven him. Queen Ealdgyth was restored to her place and honours, the king apparently taking her back with the same equanimity that he had dismissed her. Not only Leofric and Siward kept their old earldoms undisturbed, but even Ralph of Hereford, though he was a foreigner and justly unpopular. William, bishop of London, was allowed to come back to his see after a short absence, but Archbishop Robert and Bishop Ulf, with certain other Normans, were outlawed. Their preferments were filled up, somewhat uncanonically, Stigand taking over the archiepiscopal chair despite of Robert's vehement protests from abroad. Pope Leo IX. refused to acknowledge Stigand. But when both Leo and William were dead, the intruder bought his pall from Benedict X. in 1058—this turned out an unfortunate investment for him. Benedict, after reigning for less than a year, was expelled by Nicholas II., and declared an anti-pope ; wherefore ecclesiastical purists (Normans especially) continued to hold that the position of the last English primate had never been legally set right. Several scrupulous bishops went and got themselves consecrated overseas, to avoid his hands. This mattered very little to Stigand, who was a person of no delicacy of feeling,[1] so long as the house of Godwine was in power : but it was to be his ruin in 1070.

Earl Godwine survived his return to power but a few months : perhaps the fatigues and emotions of the last two years had been too much for an old man—if he was thirty when he first got an ealdormanry from Cnut in 1018, he must, when he died in 1053, have reached the age of sixty-five. We are told that his death was sudden—while sitting at the king's banquet he was seized by a paralytic or apoplectic fit, sank down speechless, and died within three days (April 15th, 1053). No attention need be paid to the story—borrowed in part from a well-known folk-tale—with which post-Conquest writers [2] befouled the memory of his last days. It was said that the conversation at the royal table had strayed on to an infelicitous topic—the murder of the king's brother Alfred in the days of Harold Harefoot. " If I had any guilty knowledge of his death," the earl is made to say, " may God choke me with the morsel of bread that I hold in my hand." He swallows it, gasps, and falls down dead. The ordeal by the morsel of bread (*corsnaed*) sometimes practised by the Old-English, was evidently in the mind of the inventor of the legend.

Godwine's character was unduly blackened by Anglo-Norman chroniclers, but it is hopeless to attempt to make a national hero out of him. He was evidently grasping and unscrupulous, though he often showed a surprising moderation, and seems to have wished well to England as well as to himself and his house. His death had no cataclysmic effect on English politics, because he left behind

---

[1] He continued to hold Winchester as a plurality along with Canterbury, which was rightly considered scandalous, down to his deposition by William the Conqueror.

[2] William of Malmesbury, *Gesta Regum*, 197, and Wendover, *Flores Historiarum*, i. 492.

him an heir who equalled him in capacity, and surpassed him in popularity. Harold Godwineson, now about thirty-one years of age, was already an administrator and soldier of proved capacity; he was ambitious, no doubt, but just, merciful, courteous, and untiring in work. For the next thirteen years he was practically prime minister to his brother-in-law the king, yet contrived for the greater part of the time to exercise his power without coming into friction with the elder earls Leofric and Siward, who had been his father's enemies. It is characteristic of his moderation that, on taking over his father's earldom of Wessex, he surrendered East Anglia to Leofric's son Aelfgar, instead of passing it on to one of his own numerous younger brothers.

The first events of importance recorded under the time of Harold's pre-eminence belong to the year 1054, when we hear of an invasion of Scotland beyond Forth, where no English army had penetrated since the time of Aethelstan. In this land there was now reigning Macbeth, a king more celebrated in legend than in serious history. He had slain in 1040 that Duncan I., the grandson of Malcolm II., who had made the unsuccessful attack on Durham during Harold Harefoot's reign.[1] Macbeth son of Finlay had been *Mormaer*, or Earl, of Moray; he had wedded Gruoch, granddaughter and heiress of Kenneth IV., the king who had been slain by Malcolm II., and perhaps put in a claim to the crown in virtue of this marriage, though he is said to have had royal blood in his own veins. The legendary details about Duncan's death are clearly wrong: he was a young man who had been reigning only six years, and he was not slain by treachery in Macbeth's own castle, but perished (whether in battle or by assassination) at Bothnagowan, "the smith's bothy," near Elgin. He left two infant sons, Malcolm and Donald Bane, who were carried off by their fosterers to the court of Earl Siward of Northumbria, who was their grandfather,[2] for Duncan had married his daughter. Macbeth appears, contrary to all our preconceived ideas, to have been a successful and popular king. He reigned undisturbed for thirteen years, and apparently found leisure for a pilgrimage to Italy in 1050, for the chroniclers[3]

[1] See p. 605.

[2] See Freeman's *Norman Conquest*, ii. 35. She was only his *Consanguinea* according to several chroniclers.

[3] Marianus Scotus, Florence of Worcester, and Simeon of Durham copying Florence.

tell us that "he scattered silver broadcast in Rome". In 1054
however Siward invaded Scotland, evidently in the cause of his
grandson Malcolm, who was now grown to man's estate and accompanied him. Presumably Macbeth had been refusing the homage to the King of England which Malcolm II. and others of his
predecessors had paid, since we are told that Siward acted under
Edward's orders, and had some of the royal housecarls with him.[1]
The King of the Scots was defeated in a great battle at Dunsinnan
Hill near Perth "on the Day of the Seven Sleepers," where Osbeorn,
Siward's elder son, perished " with all his wounds in front," as his
father proudly noted, and many good thegns with him. Malcolm
obtained by this victory some part of the Scottish kingdom—apparently Strathclyde and other southern regions. But Macbeth
did not fall at Dunsinnan as legend tells, but prolonged the war
for three years more beyond the Mounth, till Malcolm slew him in
battle at Lumphanan in Aberdeenshire in 1057. Thus Scotland
came under the power of a king with English blood in his
veins, reared in England and speaking English, like his subjects
in Lothian. The fact was to have no small influence in the development of Scottish history—all the more because Malcolm
wedded some years later an English princess, that Margaret, granddaughter of Edmund Ironside, who so well won the name of a
saint from her husband's admiring subjects.

Earl Siward died in the year following his victory over Macbeth
(1055), "and was buried in the minster at Galmanho (in York)
which he had himself built to the glory of God and all his saints".
His death, however, if legend can be trusted,[2] was more like that
of one of his Viking ancestors than that of a pious Christian.
When he felt that his last moments were at hand, he groaned
"Shame on me, that after missing death in so many battles, I must
now die the death of a cow". And he bade his men clothe him in
his shirt of mail, and gird him with his sword, and place his shield
on his arm and his helmet on his head, that he might face man's
last enemy like a warrior. And so arrayed he gave up the ghost.
His only surviving son Waltheof was a mere child, and was held

---

[1] The cause was probably *not*, as some have urged, that Macbeth had given
shelter to some of Edward's expelled French favourites. See Plummer's *A. S. C.
Notes*, ii. 243.

[2] This tale, like that of his observation on his son's death, comes from the late
authority of Henry of Huntingdon, vi. p. 760.

too young to succeed to the Northumbrian earldom, which was
bestowed on Godwine's third son, Tostig—a bad choice, perhaps
that of the king rather than of Harold, for Edward delighted in
the young man, and loved him as he loved none other of his house,
though he was selfish, arrogant and cruel.[1]

It was perhaps for opposing Tostig's preferment that Aelfgar
the son of Leofric, ealdorman of East Anglia, was outlawed in
this year "almost without guilt," according to one version of the
Chronicle, "quite guiltlessly" according to another. His father
did not share in his disgrace, and retained his earldom undisturbed.
Aelfgar did his best to justify the action of those who had exiled
him ; he fled to Ireland, hired eighteen ships of Vikings, and came
back to ravage the west coast of England. Presently he joined
himself to Gruffyd ap Llewellyn, King of North Wales, and set himself to harry Herefordshire in his company. The allies inflicted a
dreadful defeat on Earl Ralph, because (as the chronicler tells us)
the earl must needs try to make his thegns fight on horseback in the
continental fashion, which they neither understood nor liked. They
were routed disgracefully, with a loss of 400 or 500 men, and the
victors burst into the city of Hereford, burnt the minster, and slew
many of the cathedral clergy as well as of the citizens. Harold
then came up with a great body of the *fyrd*, and reoccupied
Hereford, which he proceeded to fortify. But instead of invading
Wales he offered Aelfgar pardon and peace : the exile abandoned
Gruffyd, and was restored to his earldom—perhaps at his father's
intercession.

The Welsh war, however, remained, even when Aelfgar had
submitted, and the following year (1056) was marked by a second
disaster. Eight days before midsummer Gruffyd inflicted another
great defeat on the Herefordshire *fyrd*. This time it was led by
a fighting bishop, one Leofgar, who had once been Harold's chaplain. The Anglo-Saxon Chronicle relates, with some show of
righteous indignation, not only that "he forsook his ghostly weapons, his chrism and his rood, and took to the spear and the sword,"
but that "he wore his moustaches after he was ordained ".[2] As a

---

[1] The *Vita Aedwardi*, however, says that the king was moved by Queen Ealdgyth
and by Harold.

[2] A passage often mistranslated (see Plummer's *Notes to the Anglo-Saxon
Chronicle*, ii. p. 246).

commander he was probably unskilful, and certainly unfortunate; he was left dead on the field along with Aelfnoth the sheriff and many other thegns. Reinforcements hurried up to repair the disaster. But Gruffyd apparently evaded them; "it is difficult to describe the distress, and all the marchings, and the camping, and the toil and the destruction of men and horses, which the army of the English endured," no doubt in a profitless campaign among the hills, where the enemy refused battle. At last the earls, Harold and Leofric, came to the front, and matters took a turn for the better: Gruffyd was forced to do homage, "to take oath to be a faithful and loyal under-king" to the monarch of England; apparently he also suffered some slight diminution of territory on the line of the Dee [1] (1056).

In the year following this peace Earl Leofric died, to the grief of all men, "for he was very wise for God, and also for the world, which was a blessing to this nation". He was buried at Coventry, in the priory founded by himself and his wife Godgifu—the Lady Godiva of the well-known local legend. His son, Aelfgar succeeded to all his lands from the Wash to the Dee, nine broad shires, but was not permitted to keep along with them his former earldom of East Anglia, of which the larger part seems to have been passed on to Harold's brother Gyrth, the fourth of Godwine's numerous band of sons, while Essex, Bedford and Hertford were cut off, and made into a separate earldom for the fifth son, Leofwine, with the addition of Kent and Surrey, which Harold gave him from his own great Wessex holding. Thus the house of Godwine dominated all England save Mercia.

Another event of even greater note—though of negative rather than positive importance—which befell in the year 1057, was the sudden appearance and disappearance of a claimant for the succession to the crown. The Aetheling Edward the Exile, the son of Edmund Ironside, had been dwelling all his life in Hungary. He was now a man of forty, and by his wife Agatha, a kinswoman of the Emperor Henry III., had three children Eadgar, Margaret, and Christina. Why he had not presented himself in England before it is impossible to conceive. The Confessor may, no doubt,

---

[1] According to the *Annales Cambriae* and the *Brut y Tywysogion*, Gruffyd was helped in this campaign of 1056 by Magnus, son of Harald King of Norway. There is no mention of this in the English sources or in the *Heimskringla*.

have had little love for his father's first family, and may have
shared in the common dislike of mankind for the sight of an heir-
expectant waiting for his heritage.   Ten years had passed since
Edward's accession before he took notice of his nephew : but in
1054 he invited him to return to England.   It must be remembered that this was a year after Godwine's death, when Harold
was already predominant at court, so that the summons must have
been sent at his suggestion, or at least with his consent.   Wars
between his host, the King of Hungary, and the emperor—whose
dominions he had to cross—made Edward the Exile two years late
in reaching England.   But in the spring of 1057 he appeared, only
to die a few days after his arrival, and before he had even seen his
uncle the king.   There is no hint that there was anything suspicious about his death ; if there had been, Norman tradition
would certainly have fastened a charge of murder upon Harold.[1]
The succession question was thus left as open as before, for Eadgar
the only son of Edward the Exile was a child of about three or four
years of age.   If the king, his great uncle, had survived for fifteen
years longer, Eadgar might very probably have worn the English
crown.   But the Confessor, as it chanced, had only nine winters
more to live, and Eadgar was still a mere boy, too young to stand
up for his rights, when the crisis came in 1066.

From 1057 till 1065 matters in England were practically at a
standstill, though twice events of stirring interest seemed likely to
set the whole realm aflame.   In 1058 Earl Aelfgar quarrelled with
Harold ; strife broke out between them, and the Mercian was outlawed by the Witan—who appear as the humble supporters of the
son of Godwine.   Aelfgar called into his aid his old ally the king of
North Wales—he seems at this moment to have given him his
daughter Ealdgyth in marriage—as well as a Viking fleet which
chanced at this moment [2] to be in the Irish Sea.   It seemed as if there
was to be a pitched battle for the control of England and the

---

[1] The remark in the Worcester version (D) of the A. S. C., "We wist not for
what cause it was done that he might not his kinsman King Edward behold," seems
to be a repining at Providence, not a statement that he was forcibly withheld from
an audience by interested persons, though it might have the latter meaning read
into it.   But the silence of later chronicles acquits Harold.

[2] *Ex improviso*, says Florence of Worcester, who is the sole authority to give
any details about this puzzling business.   The Chronicle merely says that Aelfgar
was outlawed, allied himself with Gruffyd, and then was inlawed again.

king. But nothing of the kind happened : Harold, as in 1055,
showed himself marvellously ready to accept a compromise and to
avoid civil war, when mere self-interest would have dictated the
pressing of his advantage to the uttermost and the crushing of his
rival. Within a few months Aelfgar was "inlawed," and had recovered his earldom and his position in the state. He held them undisturbed till his death in 1062, and we have no trace of any further
quarrels between him and Harold. His eldest son Edwin succeeded peaceably to the whole heritage of Leofric, no attempt being
made by Harold to turn Aelfgar's decease to account for the ag-
grandisement of his own house.

The other notable feature of Harold's time of predominance
was a Welsh war, ending (unlike the earlier ones) in his complete
triumph. In 1063 Gruffyd had once more given trouble by making
raids into the borders of Mercia. Harold took the field against
him unexpectedly at mid-winter, hoping to surprise him in his
residence of Rhuddlan on the Clwyd. He captured the town and
the king's treasures, as also his ships—this is the first and the last
time at which we hear of a Welsh naval armament. But Gruffyd
himself escaped into the mountains. He was not left undisturbed
in his fastnesses : when the spring of 1064 came round, Harold
collected a fleet at Bristol and sailed round into Cardigan Bay, to
attack Wales from the outside, while his brother Tostig led a land
army from the inland. Gruffyd was defeated in several skirmishes,[1]
and chased from hill to hill, till most of his followers deserted him
and surrendered. The king kept up the war a little longer, but in
August his own people, angered at his obstinacy, slew him and
sent his head to Harold.[2] This ghastly trophy the earl forwarded
to King Edward—it was a strange gift for a saint—along with
the gilded beak and ornaments of his royal galley. North Wales
was placed in the hands of two chiefs, Bleddyn and Rhiwallon, the
sons of Cynvyn, who made complete and satisfactory submission
to Harold and his master. South Wales went to a prince named

[1] According to the late authority of Giraldus Cambrensis (*Descriptio Cambriae*,
p. 217) Harold set up pillars on each battle spot, with the inscription *Hic fuit
victor Haroldus.*

[2] The *Brut y Tywysogion* waxes sorrowful on this : "Gruffyd, the head and
shield and defender of the Britons, fell through the treachery of his own people;
the man who had been hitherto invincible was now left in the glens of desolation,
after having taken immense spoils and after innumerable victories".

Caradoc, the son of a Gruffyd ap Rhydderch whom his namesake
of Gwynedd had slain nine years before. He was an unruly person
who gave trouble to Harold in the succeeding summer. But the
blow inflicted by the death of the warlike king of the north,
sufficed to keep Wales from giving any serious trouble for many
years : though Caradoc made a raid upon Portskewet in 1065, it
had no sequel of any importance. It seems that Harold's victory
was followed by considerable annexations beyond Offa's Dyke, the
first appreciable addition to England on its western side that had
occurred for three centuries. In South Wales the frontier was
advanced from the Wye to the Usk ; in Mid-Wales Ewyas, and
other parts of the defunct principality of Ercyng became English,
along with other regions beyond the Dyke that now form parts of
the shires of Hereford, Radnor and Shropshire. It is probable that
there was also a slight advance of the border opposite Chester, in
the modern county of Flint.[1]

It must have been somewhere soon after the termination of the
Welsh war in 1063, and very probably in that next year 1064 for
which the Chronicle supplies no entries, that a chance befell Earl
Harold which was to have the most disastrous effects not only for him
but for all England.[2] He had, for reasons to us unknown, taken
ship at Bosham in Sussex—which seems to have been a sort of
family port for him and his house—and was sailing the Channel when
he was driven southward by a sudden storm. His ship was stranded
on the coast of Ponthieu, where Guy, the local count, seized him and
held him to ransom, after the detestable custom of those times.
But Guy was a vassal of William Duke of Normandy, who saw his
own advantage in the affair, and compelled the count to surrender
his captive. Harold was taken to Rouen, and placed in the hands
of the duke, who gave him an honourable reception, but soon let
him understand that his liberation and return to England could only
be secured on certain conditions. These, as it appears, were no less
than that he should do personal homage to William, should " become his man," and as a corollary should swear to support to the
best of his ability the scheme, which the duke had apparently formed
as early as 1052, of getting himself acknowledged as the successor of
King Edward on the English throne. It is quite possible that the

---

[1] For speculation on all this see Freeman's *Norman Conquest*, ii. p. 473.

[2] As to the date of Harold's voyage see Freeman's Appendix in *N. C.*, vol. ii.

Confessor had held out some hopes to his cousin when the latter visited London, during the days of the exile of the house of Godwine: he loved his Norman kinsmen best of all men. But it is quite certain that the return of Edward the Exile and his children to England in 1057 had placed one hopeless bar in William's way, and that the growth of Harold's power, as he remained, year after year, supreme in the councils of the kingdom, interposed another. It is hardly to be conceived that the earl had not begun to speculate on his own chances of obtaining the crown. Though the English were loyal to the house of Alfred, yet that house, if Edward were to die soon, would be represented by a young boy, and the memory of the disasters that had always supervened on the crowning of a minor in the tenth century must have been very vivid. The stories of the evil days of the boy-kings, Eadwig, Edward the Martyr and Aethelred the Redeless, were not likely to be forgotten. And the intrusion of the Danish monarchs for a whole generation had broken the charm of the undisputed hereditary claim of the old house of Wessex to rule England. Harold himself, it must be remembered, had the Danish blood-royal in his veins. His mother Gytha was the great-niece of Sweyn, and the cousin of Cnut. Through her he was also the first cousin of Sweyn Estrithson, the present King of Denmark, who held himself to have claims on England as Cnut's nearest heir. There was a comparatively recent example, too, before the eyes of all Western Europe, of the substitution of a new royal house for an ancient legitimate line, which must have caused all great magnates to ponder. When Hugh Capet, the strongest of the earls of France, seized the crown of Charlemagne and excluded the last male heir of the Carlovingian house, he accomplished a usurpation which had a more than local significance. Hugh's grandson was now reigning peaceably at Paris, and the old royal line had never reasserted itself. What had happened to the house of Charles Martel might happen to the house of Ecgbert. The one was not more decadent than the other. Harold would have been more than human if he had not been considering, for the last ten years, the possibility that the succession question might turn in his own favour.

But when a prisoner in the hands of the capable and ambitious William of Normandy, his own personal safety became the one important point. William's enemies had a way of disappearing, either into endless captivity or into the grave. The conscience of even a scrupulous man might tell him that promises made under duresse are not binding, and Harold must have reflected on the fact—more obvious to him than to his captor—that the English crown went by the choice of the Witan, and was not to be had for the mere claiming. At any rate it is clear that the great earl stooped to the ignominious necessity of accepting the terms openly or secretly laid before him. In the presence of a great assembly of the barons of Normandy, held at Bonneville as it seems, he made the oath required of him, and pledged himself to serve the duke's purpose. The legend which relates that, by a trick, Harold was made unwittingly to swear on no ordinary relic, but on all the bones of the saints of Normandy gathered into two great coffers, may pass for what it is worth. William, no doubt, took care that the pledge was given publicly and under impressive surroundings. To modern observers, these decorative adjuncts have no bearing on the question whether Harold's subsequent breach of his promise was blameworthy or justifiable. But there is no doubt that to the eleventh-century mind they seemed of much importance. The oath-breaker, however much constrained to his oath by threats, had become the enemy of God and the Saints.

Having once manœuvred Harold into this false position, Duke William affected to treat him with confidence and distinction. He took him in his company for a short campaign against the Bretons, in which the earl, according to the Bayeux tapestry, saved certain of the Normans from destruction at the fords of the river Coesnon. He gave him a gift of arms—perhaps according to the continental idea it answered to something like the ceremony of knighting him. He is said also to have promised to give him the hand of his daughter Adela—a mere child at the time, so that the marriage had to be deferred. And finally he let him depart, after he had made over his youngest brother Wulfnoth as a hostage.[1]

[1] The authority for placing Harold's visit to Normandy in 1064 is mainly William of Poitiers, who makes the events befall *after* William's conquest of Maine, which occurred in 1063-64. Henry of Huntingdon is probably wrong in putting his version of the tale in 1063, before Harold's Welsh campaigns against Gruffyd. The Norman writers are certainly wrong in asserting that Harold went to Normandy by order of King Edward, who sent him to make arrangements for William's quiet succession! William of Poitiers, 107-8, and Orderic Vitalis, p. 492 A). The Anglo-Saxon Chronicle and Florence of Worcester entirely omit the visit. But there is no doubt that it took place. The version in the Bayeux tapestry seems singularly clear and

Harold, if our dates are correct, must have had special reasons in the end of 1064 for wishing to get back promptly to England. There was great trouble impending in the North Country. It will be remembered that Tostig, Godwine's third son, had been given the earldom of Northumbria on the death of Siward in 1055, though there were heirs still surviving to both the houses which had previously held that great charge. Siward himself, and that Eadwulf whom Siward had slain in the days of Harthacnut, had both left male issue. The intrusion of an earl from Wessex seems to have been taken in evil part by the Northumbrians, but they might have endured it if Tostig had been a wise and conciliatory ruler. This was far from being the case : he was a tyrannous and bloodthirsty young man, a great raiser of tolls and taxes, yet one who neglected to be on the spot when his presence was most needed, for one of the accusations made against him is that he was a habitual absentee. He dwelt much at the court, where he was a far greater favourite with King Edward than his brother Harold, and sometimes went much farther afield. We are told that he was on a pilgrimage to Rome when Malcolm King of Scots made an incursion and did much harm to Northumberland, in 1061.[1] But the cause of the trouble in 1064 was a sin of commission, not one of omission ; "in his own chamber in York, he slew by treachery Gamel, son of Orm, and Ulf, son of Dolfin, who had come to him under sworn safe-conduct". He is also said to have procured the murder of Cospatric, son of Arkell, at the king's court.[2] Of these magnates two were kin to Earl Eadwulf, the third a nephew of Siward, so that there was evidently method in their murder. Open insurrection against Tostig broke out in the following year (1065), led by three thegns, Gamelbeorn, Gluniarain,[3] and Dun-

coherent, and I have utilised it above for several details. William of Malmesbury says that Harold was out for a pleasure sail "ut animum oblectaret" (Gesta Regum, ii. 228) when his vessel was driven off the English coast by a storm. This seems the most probable explanation of his adventure. The story of the betrothal to Adela (Henry of Huntingdon, book vi.) presupposes either that Harold's first wife, the mother of his five children, was dead, or that they were not born in legitimate wedlock.

[1] Simeon of Durham, sub anno 1061.

[2] Florence of Worcester, and Simeon of Durham copying him, have the strange statement that Cospatric was made away with at court by the contrivance of Queen Ealdgyth. to please her brother Tostig. This seems inconsistent with all that we know about her character.

[3] This curious name is Dano-Irish, and had been borne by two Danish kings of Dublin.

stan, of whom the two former were evidently Anglo-Danes, the third an Englishman. They raised the whole earldom against their master, and, accompanied by 200 thegns more, seized York, slew Tostig's housecarls and officials, and sacked his palace. They then held a tumultuous assembly, which purported to be a general *moot* of Northumbria, and declared the earl outlawed. In place of him they elected not some member of the old local houses, but Morkere, the son of Earl Aelfgar, obviously in order to enlist in their cause Edwin his brother, the Earl of Mercia.

The subsequent course of this rebellion is very surprising. The Northumbrians went southward into Mercia, where they were joined by Earl Edwin, who brought with him many Welsh allies. When they had got outside his earldom they began devastating the land cruelly, and so advanced as far as Northampton and Oxford. We should have expected to find Harold marching against them with all the forces of the South and East, in the king's name. But he did nothing of the kind: apparently he was convinced that his brother had been greatly to blame, and that the rebellion was justified. We are told that he made himself the mediator between the Northern Men and the king, who was ready to back Tostig's cause. All the demands of the insurgents were conceded : Morkere was confirmed as Earl of Northumbria ; Tostig was bidden to depart from the realm ; no penalty was exacted, as it surely should have been, for the wanton devastations in the Midlands. Presumably Harold refused, unlike his father in Sweyn's case, to back a bad cause, and preferred to sacrifice a relative rather than to start civil war. In so doing he showed himself more patriotic than careful of his own interests. For though he did his best to conciliate the two sons of Aelfgar, and apparently not long after asked and obtained the hand of their widowed sister Ealdgyth, yet they were estranged from him by old family grudges, and never were his faithful allies. By their possession of the two great northern earldoms, their power almost balanced his own. If Harold had been nothing more than a long-sighted schemer in his own interest, he would have taken advantage of their open rebellion against the king to crush them, and would have placed Northumbria at least in the hands of some respectable member of his own house, who might be trusted not to repeat the misdeeds of Tostig. Harold's action was, indeed, so strikingly disinterested and patriotic that malevolent explanations were found for it. Tostig is said to have declared that his brother had been the real instigator of the northern rebellion, because he was jealous of his own influence with the king, and wished to get rid of him out of the realm. This seems absolutely incredible.

It is certain, however, that the earl's exile cut King Edward to the heart : he is said to have fallen into a state of morbid melancholy on discovering that his own wishes had no weight whatever in the settlement of the affairs of the realm, and we are assured that his grief actually hastened his death. He was now in his sixty-third year, an age to which no other king of the short-lived house of Alfred had attained, and seemed both to himself and to his subjects a very old man. In the following winter (1065-66) his state of health grew so alarming that he hurried on the dedication festival of the Abbey of Westminster, on whose rebuilding and re-endowment he had busied himself for many years, in order that he might see it hallowed ere he died. But on the day of the ceremony, December 28th, 1065, he was too ill to be present, and the queen had to take his place. Eight days later he died, on January 5th, 1066. A number of legends cluster about his death-bed. ` We are told in the *Vita Aedwardi*, a work of fair authority, and written no long time after his death, that he troubled the hearts of all who stood about him by uttering dire prophecies about the approaching ruin of the realm, which was doomed by God to destruction, because of the wickedness of its rulers, clerical and lay. He had seen in a vision, so he said, two saintly monks, long since dead, whom he had known in his youth, who told him that for a year and a day after his own death England would be given over to the power of the enemy, and wasted by fire and sword, in devilish fashion. He had replied to his monitors that he would warn his people to repent, and that they should be saved, even as the Ninevites were saved by the preaching of Jonah. To which answer was given that the English would not repent, nor would the mercy of God be granted them. Other obscure words he spoke as to the end of these evils, which later generations twisted into a prophecy of the restoration of the old royal house through the marriage of Henry I. and Matilda the grand-daughter of Edward the Exile. But Archbishop Stigand is said to have whispered to Earl Harold that the dying king, " worn out by age and infirmity, was babbling he knew not what ". All this sounds like the imaginings of the next generation, which held Edward a saint, and thought that he must have had some divine intimation of the impending woes of England.

We get on to firmer ground when the *Vita Aedwardi* tells us that, after uttering his vaticinations, the king turned to more practical things—that he commended his wife and his household, especially his foreign retainers, to the care of Earl Harold, whom he thus tacitly or openly acknowledged as his own inevitable successor. This is corroborated by the Anglo-Saxon Chronicle, which says, in verse, that "the wise king committed his realm to that highly born one, Harold's self, the noble earl, who in all time had faithfully obeyed his rightful lord by word and deed, and naught neglected which needful was to his sovereign prince ". There can be little doubt that Edward had accepted the situation which had grown up around him, that he saw that neither the child Eadgar nor William of Normandy could possibly be his successor, and that, perhaps with much reluctance, he acquiesced in Harold's exaltation.

No bequest of the dying king could place the crown on the great earl's head. That was the right of the Witan; but Edward's illness had lasted long enough to allow of every preparation being made for the crisis that would follow his decease. Edward was buried in the newly consecrated Westminster on the day that followed his death, at dawn, and Harold was elected and enthroned at the celebration of high-mass on the same morning (January 6th).[1] The throne cannot have been vacant for more than twenty-four hours. The fact that no opposition whatever is recorded sufficiently proves that all the necessary arrangements had been made with diligent care beforehand. The coronation and anointing was performed by Archbishop Ealdred of York, although Stigand was certainly present in London : this seems to prove that Harold and his friends regarded the position of the southern primate as so doubtful and irregular, that they would not allow him to perform the ceremony, though he was their firm partisan, lest it should be declared that his un-canonical status had vitiated the whole function.

It would be hard to call Harold a usurper. At least he was no more deserving of the name than Cnut, whose title was fully acknowledged by all men. Indeed the Danish monarch's election

---

[1] See Hermann's *Miracula Sancti Edmundi*. "Edwardus finit hominem vigilia epiphaniorum. . . . Quo regali tumulato more, ante diei missam, Theophaniorum die, statim cum introitu missae inthronizatur in solio regni Haroldus."

to the crown was the best precedent that the new king could quote. Duly chosen by a full Witan, he had a claim which it was hard to dispute.   Yet he knew from the first that his right would be challenged : though the Earls of Mercia and Northumbria had been conciliated, and no voice had been raised in favour of the boy Eadgar, it was certain that William of Normandy would assert his pretensions. Possibly Harold made some attempt to soothe him,[1] but he must have known from his personal acquaintance with the duke that the probability of a compromise was small. William's strength lay in his fighting power, not in the legal merits of his claim, and his self-confidence could only be checked by a defeat following a trial of armed strength.   Nor was William the only possible enemy —both Sweyn Estrithson of Denmark, who alleged claims of his own to the English throne [2] and Harald Hardrada of Norway, who is said to have threatened an onslaught on England in King Edward's day, might think the time propitious for a snatch at the crown. All through his nine months reign Harold Godwineson must have lived under constant fear of invasion: "little quiet did he enjoy the while that he wielded the kingdom," as the Anglo-Saxon Chronicle observes.

Harold had been crowned on January 6th, a date so early in the year that he had several months before him during which he could make his preparations, before any enemy could cross the seas. We are told that his activity and practical wisdom won golden opinions. "He set to work to remove unjust laws, and to devise good ones, to make himself the patron of churches and monasteries: he was attentive and respectful to all ecclesiastical persons; he showed himself dutiful, courteous and kindly to all good men, but a terror to ill-doers. He bade his earls, governors and sheriffs arrest all who troubled the kingdom, and set himself energetically to provide for the defence of the country by land and sea." [3] Apparently he travelled much about the realm, for he was certainly at York, courting the favour of the Northumbrian thegns, when his troubles actually began in May. It was at the end of April that the famous star appeared—known since the eighteenth century as the recurrent "Halley's Comet"—which seemed to all men ominous of

---

[1] See Freeman's *Norman Conquest*, iii. p. 262, etc.
[2] See p. 610.   [3] Florence of Worcester, *sub anno* 1066.

coming disaster, and which is represented so quaintly, with an angular and awestruck crowd below, in the Bayeux Tapestry.

While Harold was conciliating and organising the thegnhood, preparing for the mobilisation of a fleet, and coining great sums of money,[1] William of Normandy was making equally great preparations on the other side of the Channel. After one great outburst of wrath on the news of the coronation of January 6th, the duke had announced his intention of invading England with every man and ship that he could raise. He broached the scheme to a parliament of his barons at Lillebonne, but at first without success: the assembly thought the plan too ambitious, and England too strong. But by personal pleadings with his more influential vassals, William began to secure the support that he required. Many great lords, who had refused to pledge the fortunes of the duchy for the expedition, were ready to take shares in it as a private adventure, when they had received definite promises of English lands and gold, in proportion to the contingents which they might bring to the host. In the end, every Norman baron of note seems to have come into the bargain. But the forces of all Normandy were insufficient for the enterprise, as William was well aware, and he had resolved to interest all his neighbours small and great. Not only feudal princes like Eustace of Boulogne and Alan of Brittany were tempted into the enterprise, but individual barons and knights from every Western region. We find in the host multitudes from Anjou, Brittany, Poitou, and Flanders, and stray adventurers from lands so far off as Apulia and Aragon. It took months for William's invitations to make their way round Europe, and for the contingents to assemble; but the delay was necessary, since all the shipping of Normandy would not have sufficed to transport them, and hundreds of new vessels had to be built. The mustering place for the fleet was St. Valery-en-Caux, one of the Eastern ports of the duchy. Not the least important of William's preparations was to open negotiations with Pope Alexander II., from whom he wished to obtain a bull formally approving his expedition. It was procured with no great difficulty, not so much because King Harold had shown himself a perjurer, as because

---

[1] The number of his coins, considering the shortness of his reign, is remarkable; he only reigned nine months, yet his pennies are as numerous as those of Harold I. or Harthacnut, who reigned several years.

the Roman Court was highly offended at Stigand's long-protracted
intrusion into the See of Canterbury, which had only been possible
owing to the tacit support that the uncanonical archbishop had received from Harold, during the years when the great earl directed
all the counsels of King Edward.

The troubles of 1066 began in May, just as the portentous
comet was beginning to wane. They commenced not with a Norman invasion—for William was not yet ready—but with a raid by
a domestic enemy. The exiled Earl Tostig had taken refuge in
Flanders, whose count, Baldwin, was the brother of his wife Judith.
During the spring he had collected personal adherents of his own,
and enlisted a considerable body of adventurers, Flemings and broken
Northern pirates, so that he had finally enough men to man sixty
ships. He had apparently opened negotiations both with William
of Normandy and with the kings of Scandinavia, offering his help
to any enemy of his brother Harold.[1] But we know not in whose
cause it was, save his own, that he presented himself off the coast of
Kent in May. There he began to impress all the seamen that
he could catch, and to exact contributions: he then moved towards
the Isle of Wight. But presently learning that his brother was
coming against him, " with a sea force and a land force such as no
king in the land had before gathered," he fled northward, and came
ashore in the Humber—a bad choice, for his name was hated in
Northumbria. There Edwin the earl fell upon, defeated and
drove him away: all his crews, save enough to man twelve ships,
then deserted. It was with this shrunken armament alone that
Tostig reached Scotland, where he was harboured by King Malcolm
for a time. Off the Scottish coast there soon appeared Harald
Hardrada, King of Norway, with a great fleet of 300 galleys. Possibly the Norseman had come out on his own initiative to fish in the
troubled waters of English politics, but it is more probable that
Tostig had summoned him to the adventure earlier in the spring.[2]
The earl hastened to do homage to Hardrada, and to become his
man. They then coasted along Northumbria and, after ravaging
Cleveland and capturing Scarborough, ran into the mouth of the

---

[1] See Plummer's *Notes to the A. S. C.*, ii. p. 254.
[2] The *Heimskringla* says that Tostig had already visited Norway to ask Harald's
aid; Florence of Worcester and Simeon of Durham say that he met Tostig "ut
prius condixerant," without any mention of such a visit by the earl.

Humber. Edwin and Morkere, the brother-earls, had raised their
men, and stood to defend York with a considerable army, at Fulford, two miles south of the great city (September 20, 1066). But
they suffered a crushing defeat, their army was scattered, and the
citizens of York began to treat for surrender, and gave 150 hostages
to the Norse king. It looked for the moment as if England was
once more to have a Scandinavian master, and this Harald, the
brother of St. Olaf, would have made no unworthy successor to
Sweyn and Cnut, for he was a mighty man of war, who had fought
all over the East, from the Bosphorus to Novgorod. He had commanded the Varangian Guards at Byzantium, and had won the
hand of the sister of the Russian king. He had waged long wars
with Sweyn Estrithson, and had often subdued great parts of his
dominions, but he had lately made peace with the Dane, and now
had his hands free for the invasion of England. Harald was in
character very unlike his brother St. Olaf, being greedy to take and
slow to give, and a master of shifts and devices. But his courage
and strength (he is said to have been nearly seven feet high) were as
great as his cunning, and hitherto he had been reckoned the most
fortunate of kings. In attacking England, however, he had taken
in hand too heavy a task—he had his namesake the son of Godwine
to face, not an Aethelred the Redeless.

Only five days after the battle of Fulford the King of England
appeared at the gates of York, with all his housecarls and a strong
levy from the South. The son of Godwine had long been waiting
off the Isle of Wight, with a great fleet, for the expected arrival of
the Norman duke. But July and August had passed, and still the
invader came not—at first his host was not fully gathered, later
contrary gales prevailed, and the northern winds, which were propitious to Hardrada, were a hindrance to William. On September
8th, as we are told, the provisions of Harold's fleet were utterly exhausted, the men were starving and beginning to desert, and he was
forced to send the whole squadron round to London to refit—a
most unhappy chance. But he himself with his army was still
guarding Kent and Sussex : the " land force was kept everywhere by
the sea, though it was in the end of no benefit ". Only a week after
the departure of the fleet came the unexpected news of the Norwegian invasion of Yorkshire, and Harold was constrained to commit the guard of the South Coast to the uncertain aid of the winds,

and to hurry northward with the flower of his army. He was five days late for the battle of Fulford, but on September 25th he was at the gates of York, which the citizens gladly threw open to him. On the same day he brought the Norwegian king to action, at Stamford Bridge on the Derwent, seven miles east of York. The invader was taken unawares—Harold's rapid march had surprised him while he was waiting for the appearance of hostages from all Northumbria, who were to be handed over to him at that spot on this very day. There followed a long and bloody battle, the greatest victory that the Englishmen ever won over the Scandinavians, for the forces on either side were greater than those which fought at Ashdown or Ethandun, at Tottenhall, or even Brunanburh. But its details are utterly unknown to us—it is sad that we cannot trust for a moment the noble narrative of the *Heimskringla*, the grandest battle tale among all the *Sagas*. So many of its statements are utterly incorrect that we cannot accept the rest.[1] Harold may have offered his brother Tostig pardon and an earldom, and have promised Tostig's ally no more than the famous " seven feet of English ground—or more since he is taller than other men ". The Norsemen may have fought on all day in their shield-ring, and have broken at evening when their king had fallen pierced by an arrow. But we have no contemporary authority to bear out the vivid narrative of the Northern historian, and the one fact given by the Anglo-Saxon Chronicle, *viz.*, that the battle ended with the desperate defence of a bridge against the pursuing English, does not appear at all in the *Heimskringla*. But there fell Harald Hardrada, and Earl Tostig and nine-tenths of the Northern host, and the survivors, under the king's son Olaf, were glad to depart after obtaining a truce ; they could man only twenty-four ships out of the 300 that they had brought into the Humber.

Just three days after the battle of Stamford Bridge, on September 28th, 1066, William of Normandy came ashore on the long

---

[1] The whole story is one tissue of mistakes. Morkere is made Harold Godwineson's brother, and is said to have been slain at the battle of Fulford. Tostig is said to be Harold's elder instead of younger brother, and to have been exiled only after the death of Edward the Confessor. But it is most hopeless of all to find the English army composed entirely of mounted knights and bowmen, just the arms in which it was deficient, and to find it described as directing countless cavalry charges against the defensive Norse shield-wall. In fact the tale looks like that of Hastings transferred to Yorkshire with the parts inverted by some incredible error.

beach of Pevensey with all his host. The winds had betrayed Harold Godwineson, and had shifted round to the south only a few days after he marched for York. This was a rare chance in English history; for our island kingdom has been often saved and rarely harmed by the rough airs that beat about it. Harold's "fleet in being" had not yet refitted itself, or come out from London; his army was far away in the North, and the Norman had an undisturbed voyage and a quiet landing. How many men William the Bastard brought with him it is impossible to say; the chroniclers are lavish with figures like 50,000 or 60,000 which we can not accept for a moment. Wace, a twelfth-century authority, tells us that he had heard from his father, a contemporary, that the ships were precisely 694 in number,[1] reckoning small and great together. Many must have been horse transports, others were filled with stores. An army of 12,000 or 14,000 men is probably as much as we can allow,[2] of which 3,000 or 4,000 may have been cavalry. After completing his landing, William moved fourteen miles along the coast to the town of Hastings, where he erected a fortified camp, and drew his ships ashore. He then commenced to send out plundering bands right and left, but made no attempt to march on London, though for many days he had no enemy in front of him, and met with no resistance, save from the townsfolk of Romney, who beat off some of his raiders. Evidently he had resolved to fight near the coast, and not to separate himself from his fleet till he had gained a victory.

Harold probably received the news of the Norman landing not earlier than October 2nd. Without a moment's delay he marched south again from York with the housecarls and the thegnhood— but the fact that he apparently reached London on October 6th or 7th seems to hint that only those of his host who were provided with horses can have kept up with him. The Earls Edwin and Morkere were following with their northern levies, which had suffered severely at Fulford, and must have needed reorganisation and reinforcement. They never caught the king up, and were absent from the battle

---

[1] In another passage he says that the total provided by the duke and his co-adventurers was to have been 752, so that 694 allows for a shortage on their contracts.

[2] For an ingenious set of calculations, see General James's article in the *Royal Engineers' Journal* for 1907.

which followed, probably from slackness rather than treachery. But Harold was ill-repaid for the self-denying consideration which he had shown for the house of Leofric in 1065, and got no profit from his matrimonial alliance with it. The slowness of the earls seems all the more inexcusable, considering the way in which Harold had flown to their aid against the Norsemen of Hardrada.

The king appears to have remained three or four days in London, no doubt to allow the dismounted part of his host to come up, and to draw in reinforcements from East Anglia and the Midlands. On October 11th he marched out again to face the Normans, though (as the Anglo-Saxon Chronicle reminds us) his army was still incomplete. The northern earls, and the levies of the extreme west were alike missing. A rapid march of two days brought the army to the outskirts of the Andredsweald, looking out on the coast-plain which the Normans had now been ravaging for more than a fortnight. It is said that his brother Gyrth pleaded with Harold to take the defensive, to clear the neighbourhood of provisions by devastating the country-side, and to await the arrival of all his outlying forces. But Harold seems to have thought that it was his duty as king to protect his subjects, rather than to harry their farms, and resolved to put his fate to the arbitrament of the sword without delay.

The position which he chose is that where the road from London to Hastings emerges from the forest, on the ground named Senlac, where the village of Battle now stands. The road passes along a sort of high-lying isthmus or saddleback, and then crosses a hill some 260 feet high, down one of whose side-slopes it descends into lower ground. This hill formed the battle-ground; it has a front of about 1,000 or 1,100 yards, sloping southward with a gradient of about one in fifteen, but at the right and left rear, where the hill is joined by the isthmus bearing the road, the slope is much steeper—one in eight on the right rear, one in four—almost precipitous—on the left rear. The existence of the flank-protection caused by these declivities made the position very strong, and the direct rear, save on the narrow ridge where the road comes in, was steepest of all. If modern indications can be trusted, the ground in front of the hill was very marshy on its western side.[1]   Behind

---

[1] I cannot sufficiently praise Mr. Baring's map and accurate contour-description of the ground in the Appendix to his *Domesday Tables*. I verified it carefully on January 8th, 1910, before writing the above paragraph.

the whole was the forest, so close that when the English army
moved on to its fighting ground, it seemed to the Normans to
spring directly out of the wood.[1] If we may trust the most detailed, though not the earliest, narrative of the battle, Harold had
fortified the front of his position with a hastily dug ditch, and an
abattis of intertwined brushwood, of which plenty lay close to
hand in the brakes at his rear.[2] But the earlier writers speak only
of the shield-wall of the English, and the dense masses crowning the
hill, many ranks deep.   It is possible that Wace has overrated the
amount of fortification executed by Harold's men, who must have
reached the ground late and wearied ; and conceivably it amounted
to no more than a flank protection on those parts of the side slopes
where the ground was least steep and most accessible, and to the
damming up of the marshy brook to the right.[3] On the other
hand Harold knew all about Norman tactics, having served a campaign under William's leadership, and may well have utilised the
old Danish device of entrenching his chosen ground ; he must have
been perfectly well aware of the danger from the rush of the duke's
mailed horsemen, to whom he had not a mounted man to oppose.
However much or little he had fortified himself, we know that his
army was strong enough to cover the whole ridge, so that it
must have numbered some 12,000 or 13,000 men—much the same
as William's force.   But in quality it was less homogeneous ; only
the two or three thousand housecarls who stood round the royal
standards in the centre were professional soldiers ; in the rest of
the line the thegns and wealthier ceorls, with mail-shirt and helm,

---

[1] " Ex improviso diffudit silva cohortes,
    Et nemoris latebris agmina prosiliunt "
                              —(Guy of Amiens, lines 363-64).

[2] There has been an immense controversy on the so-called " Palisades " of
Hastings: against the silence of William of Poictiers, Guy of Amiens, Baldric,
Henry of Huntingdon, and others, we have to set the elaborate description of
Wace, who wrote perhaps ninety years after the battle.   His lines 7815-20 run :—

        " Fait orent devant els escuz
        De fenestres [*fresnettes* or *sevestres ?*] et d'altres fuz;
        Devant els les orent levez
        Comme cleies joinz et serrez
        Fait en orent devant cloture,
        Ni laisserent nule jointure "

M. Bémont suggests *sevestres*, Mr. Young of All Souls *fresnettes* for the impossible
fene tres.

[3] See again Mr. Baring's notes in the book just quoted.   I think, however, that
he might allow for a little more fortification.

must have been lost among the ill-armed masses of the *fyrd*, who came to the fight with no defensive weapons but the shield, and were ill-equipped, with javelins and instruments of husbandry turned to warlike uses.

When Duke William was informed that the king had come out to meet him, and had taken up his position, he accepted battle with joy. He marched out the eight miles from Hastings, halted his army on the ridge of Telham, which faces the English line and slightly dominates it at a distance of somewhat over a mile, and there deployed his force in three lines, while descending into the intervening valley. The host was arrayed in geographical order, as it were ; the Western allies and mercenaries from Brittany, Anjou, Maine and Poitou formed the left, the Normans themselves the centre—which was the strongest division—the French and Flemish auxiliaries the right. In each corps a front line was formed with the archers and other men armed with missile weapons—there were even a few crossbowmen present, an arm only just invented.[1] Behind them were deployed the heavy-armed foot with spear, shield, helm, and mail shirt, who must have formed the main body of the army. Last rode in the rear the most formidable striking force, the squadrons of mailed knights to whom the English had nothing to oppose. Apparently the duke had arrayed his host so as to make it equal to the entire front of the enemy, and to attack the hill along its whole slope. But there is no mention of an attempt to outflank Harold, an operation which would have been made difficult by the steep declivities and the neighbouring woods.

On reaching the lower slopes of the English position the archers began to let fly their shafts, and not without effect, for as long as the shooting was at long range there was little reply, since Harold had but few bowmen in his ranks, and the abattis, whatever its length or height, would not give complete protection to the English.[2] But when the advance reached closer quarters it was met with a furious hail of missiles of all sorts—darts, lances, casting axes, and

[1] The order comes out clearly from William of Poictiers and Guy of Amiens : first archers, then *galeati*, or *pedites quirites* as Guy calls them, then the horse. It is Guy who mentions the crossbowmen (line 338) :—

> " Praemisit pedites committere bella sagittis
> Atque *balistantes* inserit in medio ".

[2] Baldric, 1,407, " Spicula torquentur, multi stantes moriuntur ".

stone-clubs, such as William of Poictiers describes and the Bayeux Tapestry portrays—rude weapons more appropriate to the neolithic age.[1] The archers, having reached a point from which they could get no farther forward, gave way to the heavy-armed foot, who pushed up to the front of the English shield wall, and got to hand-strokes with the adversary. The fight was long and furious, but the assailants made no headway, "they could not penetrate the thick wood of English spears". It was time for the cavalry to deliver its blow, on an enemy who, if not shaken, was at least already heavily engaged.

It was apparently at this moment that there occurred the often recorded exploit of the minstrel Taillefer, who rode far ahead of the other horsemen, cheering them on, and playing like a juggler with his sword, which he repeatedly tossed up into the air, and caught again. He rode down an Englishman who ran out to meet him, cut down another, dashed into the mass, and was cut to pieces. Behind him came the whole knighthood of Normandy, and their Eastern and Western allies, pricking up the slope; the infantry opened up to let them pass, or perhaps had already recoiled. The impetus with which the horsemen dashed against the English shield-wall and abattis was tremendous, but though the line may have swayed back at points, and the stakes may have been torn down, no breach was made. After a long exchange of blows the Bretons and Angevins on the left wing were beaten off, and fell back down the hill in disorder, many (as William of Poictiers tells us) being unhorsed and overthrown as they recoiled into the bed of the little brook which they had easily avoided in ascending the slope. All along the hillside the onset wavered, and the knights drew back. The duke had to ride along the line and rally it, baring his head to show that a rumour that he had already fallen was false. But the rout of the Bretons was to his advantage rather than to his hurt: a great body of the English shire-levies came pouring down the slope in pursuit, breaking their shield-wall, and rushing forward in wild disorder. William turned the horsemen of his still intact central division against them, and, caught in the rough valley below their position, the half-armed peasantry were ridden down in a moment: thousands fell, and few were able to regain the position and re-form alongside of those who had not joined in their mad pursuit.

[1] *Lignis imposita saxa*, W. P., 201 D.   They are clearly shown on the Tapestry.

But Harold's main body still stood steady, and only the first act of the battle was over. A second series of cavalry attacks were now directed by William against the English mass, which proved as impregnable as ever, despite of its severe losses. Hard fighting raged for several hours along the whole front, and many fell on both sides. It was at this time apparently, that Harold's two brothers, Earls Gyrth and Leofwine were both slain—the latter, if we may trust one good contemporary authority,[1] by William's own hand. The duke had two horses slain under him, and was repeatedly in imminent danger. At several points breaches were made in the English line, but they were repaired, and nothing decisive had occurred when William, taking his inspiration from the earlier incident which had occurred on his left, tried the device of a feigned flight. By his orders a large part of the army, apparently the French on his right, gave way and retired hastily to the valley. This time the English host thought that the battle was indeed over, and great masses of them came down in pursuit, to their own destruction, for the retreating squadrons turned upon them, and troops drawn from the intact Norman centre took them in flank. The whole horde is said to have been practically destroyed.[2]

There was still left on the hill top a compact body of combatants, including the most efficient part of the English army, for Harold had succeeded in keeping the whole of his housecarls steady around their standards, on the central summit of the position, where the ruins of Battle Abbey now stand. The Normans, inspired by the hope of victory, renewed the attack upon this sturdy remnant, but at first with little effect. The shield-wall still held, and the great axes still cut down man and horse when the charges were pressed home. The duke then tried the last of his devices ; he brought his archers to the front again, and in the intervals between the attacks bade them shoot with a high trajectory, so that their arrows should fall into the heart of the mass, and not be intercepted by the shields of the front line. This plan proved most effective, for the centre-ranks of the English were thinned by the hail against which it was impossible to guard, and presently King Harold himself was mortally

[1] Guy of Amiens.

[2] There is some confusion between the two flights, the feigned and the real, in the authorities, *e.g.*, Guy of Amiens makes the first flight of the Bretons a device, and the second a real rout.

wounded by a shaft in the eye. He lent on his shield in agony by his standards, but the resistance still went on, though it was slackening, and at last several rifts were cut by the charging horsemen in the shield-wall. Through one of them a band of knights penetrated, who slew and shamefully mutilated the dying king, and cut down his banners. The housecarls refused to fly and died to a man, in their ranks, as honour and old custom dictated when their lord had fallen. But the rest of the English host—it can have been no great remnant—fled north-westward and plunged into safety among the brakes of the Andredsweald. They were still capable of turning on the pursuers, and the chroniclers tell how at the ravine behind the north-west slope of the position [1] a body of Normans was suddenly charged and cast down the bank with considerable loss by a rally of some desperate band. William brought up reinforcements, but found, when he reached the spot, that the enemy had disappeared in the dark and gained the woods. The day was all his own, and the slaughter had surpassed anything that had been seen on earlier fields. Of all the English magnates who are known to have been on the field only one, Esegar the "staller" (master of the horse) is known to have survived; he had been carried wounded from the field early in the fight. The house of Godwine had been broken—beside the king there had fallen both his brothers, Gyrth and Leofwine, and his uncle Aelfwig—who had taken the field though old and in orders—he was abbot of the royal monastery at Winchester. Of all the numerous kin of Godwine there survived only the young children of Harold and Tostig,[2] and Wulfnoth, the hostage at Rouen,[3] who was destined to spend all his life behind prison bars. No one was left to maintain the cause of the new line, while the old was represented only by the child Eadgar Aetheling. The victory of Hastings was to mean not only defeat but conquest for England.

Many a moral has been drawn from this great fight. The first obvious modern application of it is that even a formidable fleet did not guarantee England from the possibility of a raid by an enemy who was prepared to take the risk of destruction. The second is

---

[1] Its position is proved, I think, by Mr. Baring in pp. 229-30, of his Hastings Appendix to *Domesday Tables*, repeatedly quoted above.

[2] Tostig's sons, who had been sent to Norway, survived there, and started a noble house which lived on into the later middle ages—see the genealogy in the *Heimskringla*, iii. 98-100.

[3] See p. 631.

that neither desperate courage, nor numbers that must have been at least equal to those of the invader, could save from defeat an army which was composed in too great a proportion of untrained troops, and which was behind the times in its organisation. A thousand horsemen or a couple of thousand bowmen might have saved Harold from destruction. But the English stood by the customs of their ancestors, and, a few years before, Earl Ralph's attempt to make the thegnhood learn cavalry tactics[1] had been met by sullen resistance, and had no effect.

Historians, mediaeval and modern, have repeatedly set themselves to prove that the battle of Hastings was a blessing in disguise to England; it is always tempting to try to justify the decrees of Providence, and it is easy to dilate on the disadvantages of insularity, and the profit that came to the English realm from its being bound up for five generations with the Duchy of Normandy. Much that is doubtfully true has been written to prove that the organisation of Church and State was improved, that civilisation was advanced, that art and architecture received a new impulse from the advent of William the Bastard. But the most recent research tends to make us less eager to subscribe to this acceptance of the accomplished fact.

Many of the old commonplaces concerned with the Norman Conquest must go. We have long learnt to discard the old screed of eighteenth century historians to the effect that "William the Conqueror introduced the feudal system into England"—for England was already feudal in one sense when he arrived—its earldoms of late were growing marvellously like continental countships, and the "commendation" of the small man to the great had become normal, though not universal, long before Senlac field. On the other hand certain aspects of continental feudalism were hateful to the Conqueror, and he did his best to keep them out of his new realm. But there are other contradictions to long-established views which we have only begun to accept quite recently. It was supposed that the Normans had a well-developed system of castle-building long ere 1066, and that they introduced it, full blown, on to English soil. Modern research has shown that no pre-conquest castles of the developed type existed in the Duchy, and that the English stone castles are none of them so early as had been supposed

[1] See p. 625.

—castle-building was, indeed, evolved on English soil, not imported in a complete and advanced stage.[1]

Nor was there in architecture at large a sudden advance from barbarism to the solid and majestic style that we now call "Norman" immediately after, and solely in consequence of, the Conquest. The study of the surviving remnants of Old-English building, only recently taken seriously in hand, shows that England had a "Romanesque" architecture of her own, which was developing with regularity, in the tenth and eleventh centuries. It was, no doubt, behind that of the continent, but it was already on the move, and was sufficiently in touch with the contemporary art beyond seas to make us sure that evolution would have continued in the same direction which was actually pursued. For architecture does not necessarily depend on political conditions, and a style which commends itself to the taste of an age passes from land to land despite of boundaries and wars. The sons of the architects who built the Anglo-Saxon churches of Bradford-on-Avon or Earl's Barton in the days of Edward the Confessor,[2] would have been rearing something much more advanced by the year 1100, whether there had been a Norman conquest or no. If only we had the Abbey of Westminster as the Confessor left it at his death, we should be able to judge far better of what would have been the fate of Anglo-Saxon architecture, had the battle of Hastings taken another course. It was evidently a magnificent edifice, likely to be the parent of much progress. And if it be objected that Edward was a lover of foreigners, and built under their influence, this is only a proof of what we have just said above—that Art overleaps boundaries, and can travel irrespective of political conquests. The 'Norman' style was really Burgundian. The Romanesque architecture of Scandinavia or Scotland did not come into being through the advent of an invader.

Let any one who believes that the Norman Conquest led in every sphere of civilisation to a rapid and satisfactory development, compare the neat silver pennies of the later issues of Edward the Confessor and the short reign of Harold Godwineson, with the

[1] See Mr. H. Round's "The Castles of the Conquest," in *Archæologia*, 58, part i. (1902), for a summing up of this conclusion.

[2] For reasons for ascribing Bradford to Edward's age rather than to an earlier generation, see Rivoira's *Origini della Architettura Lombarda*, chapter iii. ; this great book inspires all the paragraph above.

shapeless ill-struck issues of Henry I., Stephen, and the early years of Henry II. A relapse into barbarism might rather be deduced from the comparison.

For good or ill the Norman Conquest was accomplished—but the more that we study it, the less easy is it to acquiesce in the easy and comforting conclusion that all was for the best—that the survival of an English England must necessarily have been a disaster. We are told that the insular Church and State were alike decadent, and the failings of Archbishop Stigand are held up for disapproval, along with the misdeeds of Earl Tostig. But Stigand is a less hateful figure than Odo of Bayeux or Ralf Flambard, on whose characters, as typical Norman prelates, any one might dilate who wished to set forth the opposite theory. And the Earls of the latter days of the English kingdom on the average compare favourably with those of the early Norman reigns. Even Tostig might pass as an honest man and a considerate ruler compared with Robert of Bellesme or Geoffrey de Mandeville. It is absurd, re-membering the existence of such men, to speak as if the Conquest had brought immunity from the feudal danger to this realm. Nor is it fair to say that the English state was hopelessly out of gear : Under an Aethelred II. or an Edward the Confessor, the crown might seem helpless, but so it was in the reign of Stephen. And when an Eadgar or a Cnut was on the throne England appeared as a well-ruled realm and a great imperial power. Surely Harold Godwineson, the wise, the just, the merciful, but also the strong handed, was the kind of ruler under whom the days of Cnut might have come again.[1] Hastings blinds us too much to the glories of Stamford Bridge, a victory that vied with or excelled Ethandun and Brunanburh. During his nine months' reign Harold had shown himself a most resourceful, active and capable ruler, and it seems hard to find him guilty of inadequacy because of the tactics of one fight. It might even be said that the chance arrow from on high which slew him turned a still possible victory into a defeat, while if William the Bastard had fallen, lopped down by the axe that slew his horse in an earlier phase of the fight, Hastings might have served historians to point another moral. For the eleventh century produced no such

[1] I cannot comprehend the spirit which induces J. R. Green in his *Conquest of England* to belittle Harold (pp. 582-85) : the evidence for his character is all the other way, save for the carpings of malignant Norman chroniclers.

other general among England's enemies, and William's death would have wrecked his army.

The optimist may hold that the future development of this realm under continental influences was so infinitely superior to what that development would have been under purely national influences, as to compensate England in the end for all that she suffered in and after 1066. But the breaking up of the old governing class, the general confiscation of estates, the trampling of the nation beneath the feet of an alien aristocracy, were a heavy price to pay for that problematical gain. Episodes like William's ravaging of Northumbria in 1069, whose after-effects endured for whole centuries, and surpassed anything that the Dane ever wrought, cause us to doubt the theory that paints the Norman as the spreader of civilisation. Were the tyranny of Rufus, the grinding oppression of Henry I., the anarchy of Stephen, necessary stages in the evolution of a nation? Can the introduction of Wager of Battle be considered a happy juristic reform? May it not be said that William the Bastard turned England from her true line of development towards the sea—she was a great naval power when he found her—and involved her in that unholy game of gambling for French provinces which was not to end till the Hundred Years War was over, after four centuries of wasted effort? It was a bitter day when the Norman grip tightened upon her—nor was it in error that the Northern poet Thorkil Skallason sang :—

> Cold heart and bloody hand
> Now rule the English land.

ROMAN GOVERNORS OF BRITAIN

Down to its Division into Two Provinces under Severus

	A.D.			A.D.
Aulus Plautius	43-47	M. Appius Bradua	circ.	126-129
P. Ostorius Scapula	47-52	L. Mummius Sisenna	circ.	129-133
Aulus Didius Gallus	52-57	Cn. Minucius Seveus	circ.	133-138
D. Veranius Nepos	57-59	Q. Lollius Urbicus		138-144
C. Suetonius Paulinus	59-61	Cn. Papirius Aelianus	circ.	144-150
P. Petronius Turpilianus	61-63	Cn. Julius Verus	circ.	155-160
M. Trebellius Maximus	63-69	M. Statius Italicus		160-161
M. Vettius Bolanus	69-71	S. Calpurnius Agricola		161-165
Q. Petillius Cerealis	71-74	C. Julius	circ.	166-170
S. Julius Frontinus	74-78	L. Ulpius Marcellus	circ.	170-175
Cn. Julius Agricola	78-85	Q. Antistius Adventus	circ.	175-180
Sallustius Lucullus	85- ?	L. Ulpius Marcellus again	circ.	183-184
Metilius Nepos	circ. 95-98	P. Helvius Pertinax	circ.	185-187
T. Avidius Quietus	circ. 98-101	D. Clodius Albinus		192-197
L. Neratius Marcellus	circ. 101-103	Virius Lupus		198-200
P. Pomponius Mammiliaus	circ. 103-109	Pollenius Auspex	circ.	200-205
Q. Roscius Falco	circ. 118-122	L. Alfenius Senecio	circ.	205-209
A. Plaetorius Nepos	122-126			

CHRONOLOGICAL TABLE OF KINGS

I

KINGS OF KENT

Aethelbert I., 560-616.
Eadbald, 616-640.
Earconbert, 640-664.
Ecgbert I., 664-673.
Lothere, 673-685 [with Eadric, 684].
Eadric, 685-686.
Anarchy, 686-690.
Wihtraed, 694-725.
Eadbert, I., 725-748.
Aethelbert II., 748-762.
Kent was divided among several kings, vassal to Mercia, 762-796.
Eadbert II., " Praen," 796-798.
[Coenwulf of Mercia], 798.
Cuthred, 798-805.
Baldred, 805-823.
Ecgbert, of Wessex, 825.
Aethelwulf, of Wessex, 825-839.

Aethelstan, brother of Aethelwulf, 839-850 ?.
Aethelwulf (again), 856-858.
Aethelbert (son of Aethelwulf), 858-860.

II

KINGS OF EAST ANGLIA

Raedwald, 593-617.
Eorpwald, 617-628.
Sigebert, 631-634.
Egrice, 634-635.
Anna, 635-654.
Aethelhere, 654-655.
Aethelwald, 655-664.
Ealdwulf, 664-713.
Aelfwald, 713-749.
Beorna, 749 ——?.
Aethelbert, ——793.
[Kings of Mercia], 793 to 823.
Eadwald, 823-829 ?.
Aethelstan I., son of Ecgbert, 829-839 ?.

Aethelweard, 839-852 ?.
Beorhtric, 852-856 ?.
St. Edmund, 856-870.

———

Danish Kings

Guthrum I., 878-890.
Eohric, 890-902.
Guthrum II., 902-916 ?.

III

KINGS OF MERCIA

Creoda, died, 593 ?.
Pybba, 593-606 ?.
Cearl, 606-626 ?.
Penda, 626-655.
Peada, 655-656.
[Oswy of Bernicia], 656-659.
Wulfhere, 659-675.
Aethelred, 675-704.
Coenred, 704-709.

Ceolred, 709-716.
Aethelbald, 716-757.
Beornred, 757.
Offa, 757-796.
Ecgferth, 796.
Coenwulf, 796-821.
Ceolwulf I., 821-823.
Beornwulf, 823-825.
Ludican, 825-827.
Wiglaf, 827-829.
[Ecgbert of Wessex], 829-830.
Wiglaf restored, 830-839.
Beorhtwulf, 839-852.
Burhred, 852-874.
Ceolwulf II., 874.

IV

NORTHUMBRIA

Kings of Bernicia

Ida, 547-559.
His elder sons, in uncertain order, 559-586.
Aethelric, 586-593.
Aethelfrith, 593-617.
Edwin of Deira, 617-633.
Eanfrith, 633-634.
Oswald, 634-642.
Oswy, 642-655.

Kings of Deira

Aella, 560-588.
Aethelric of Bernicia, 588-593.
Aethelfrith of Bernicia, 593-617.
Edwin, 617-633.
Osric, 633-634.
Oswald of Bernicia, 634-642.
Oswin, 644-651.
Aethelwald, 651-655.

Kings of all Northumbria

Oswy, 655-671.
Ecgfrith, 671-685.
Aldfrid, 685-705.
Eardwulf I., 705.
Osred I., 705-716.
Coenred, 716-718.

Osric, 718-729.
Ceolwulf, 729-737.
Eadbert, 737-758.
Oswulf, 758-759.
Aethelwald Moll, 759-765.
Alchred, 765-774.
Aethelred I., 774-779.
Aelfwald I., 779-788.
Osred II., 788-790.
Aethelred I. (restored), 790-796.
Osbald, 796.
Eardwulf II., 796-806.
Aelfwald II., 806-808.
Eardwulf II. (restored), 808-810.
Eanred, 810-840.
Aethelred II., 840-844.
Redwulf, 844.
Aethelred II. (restored), 844-848.
Osbeorht, 848-867.
Aella, 861-867.

V

KINGS OF WESSEX

Ceawlin, 560-592.
Ceolric, 591-597.
Ceolwulf, 597-611.
Cynegils, 611-643.
Coenwalch, 643-645.
Anarchy, 645-648.
Coenwalch restored, 648-672.
Queen Seaxburh, 672-674 ?.
Aescwine, 674-676 ?.
Centwine, 676-685 ?.
Ceadwalla, 685-688.
Ine, 688-726.
Aethelheard, 726-740.
Cuthred, 740-756.
Sigebert, 756-757.
Cynewulf, 757-786.
Beorhtric, 786-802.
Ecgbert, 802-839.

VI

THE HOUSE OF ECGBERT, KINGS OF ALL ENGLAND

Ecgbert, 802-839.

Aethelwulf, 839-858.
Aethelbald, 858-860.
Aethelbert, 860-866.
Aethelred I., 866-871.
Alfred, 871-900.
Edward the Elder, 900-924
Aethelstan, 924-939.
Edmund I., 939-946.
Eadred, 946-955.
Eadwig, 955-959.
Eadgar, 959-975.
Edward II., the Martyr, 975-978.
Aethelred II., 978-1016.
Edmund II., Ironside, 1016.

Danes

Cnut, 1016-1035.
Harold I., Harefoot, 1035-1040.
Harthacnut, 1040-1042.

Edward III., the Confessor, 1042-1066.

Harold II., Godwineson, 1066.

VII

DANISH KINGS OF YORK

Halfdene, 876-877.
Guthred-Cnut, 883-894.
Siefred (Sievert), 893-896.
?   ?   ?
Aethelwald, of Wessex, 900-902.
?   ?   ?
Regnald, 918-921 ?
Sihtric Caoch, 921-926.
Guthfrith Sihtricson, 926.
[Aethelstan, 926-939.]
Anlaf I., Guthfrithson, 940-942.
Anlaf II., Quaran, 942-944.
[Edmund and Eadred, 944-947.]
Eric Blood Axe, 947-948.
Anlaf Quaran (restored), 949-952.
Eric Blood Axe (restored), 952-954.

TABLE I

KINGS OF NORTHUMBRIA

N.B.—The names in capitals are those of Kings

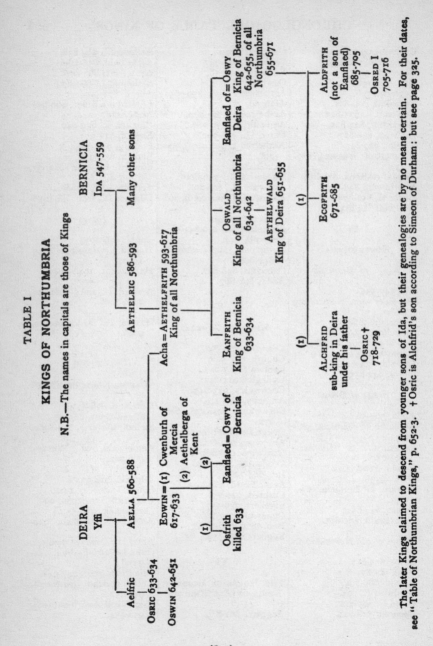

The later Kings claimed to descend from younger sons of Ida, but their genealogies are by no means certain. For their dates, see "Table of Northumbrian Kings," p. 652-3. † Osric is Alchfrid's son according to Simeon of Durham: but see page 335.

TABLE II

KINGS OF MERCIA

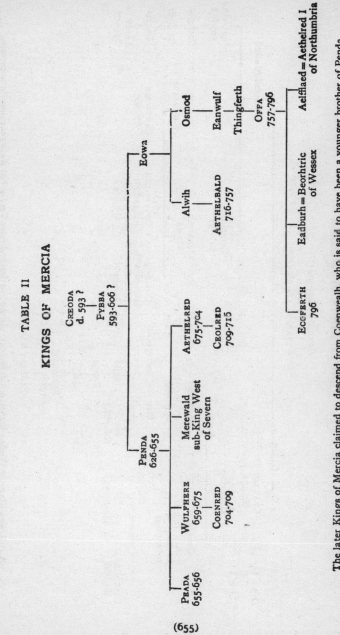

CREODA
d. 593 ?

FYBBA
593-606 ?

PENDA
626-655

Eowa

PEADA
655-656

WULFHERE
659-675

Merewald
sub-King West
of Severn

AETHELRED
675-704

Alwith

Osmod

COENRED
704-709

CEOLRED
709-715

AETHELBALD
716-757

Eanwulf

Thingferth

OFFA
757-796

ECGFERTH
796

Eadburh = Beorhtric
of Wessex

Aelfflaed = Aethelred I
of Northumbria

The later Kings of Mercia claimed to descend from Coenwealh, who is said to have been a younger brother of Penda and Eowa. The genealogy is not clear.

TABLE III

EARLY KINGS OF WESSEX

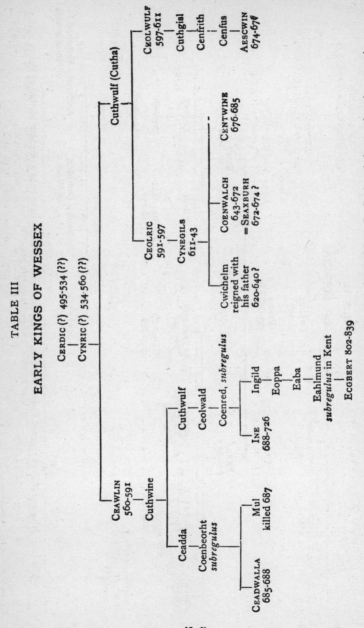

N.B.—The Kings of Wessex between 726 and 802 claimed to descend from Cerdic, but their genealogy is uncertain.

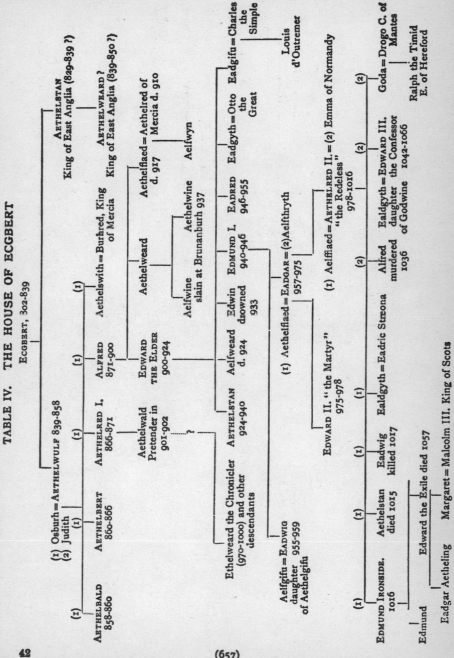

TABLE IV. THE HOUSE OF ECGBERT

ECGBERT, 302-839

42

INDEX

Dorchester-on-Thames, bishopric of, 227, 279, 282.
Dore, Northumbrians do homage to Ecgbert at, 395.
Dover, Eustace of Boulogne's misdeeds at, 617.
Druids, Celtic priesthood, Caesar's description of, 25, 27-31, 59, 74.
Dubnovellanus, British king, 53; flies to Rome, 55.
Duncan, King of Scots, 599; defeated at Durham, 605; slain by Macbeth, 623.
Dunstan, St., Abbot of Glastonbury, 529; his early life and character, 535-537; his
    quarrel with King Eadwig, 539-540; promoted by Eadgar, 542; his monastic
    reforms, 546; upholds Edward the Martyr, 549; crowns Aethelred II., 553;
    his relations with Aethelred, 556; dies, 556.
Dunwich, bishopric of, founded, 275.
Durham, besieged by Scots, 605.
Dyrham, Ceawlin defeats the Britons at, 246.

EADBALD, King of Kent, his conversion to Christianity, 271-272.
Eadbert, King of Northumbria, his war with Aethelred of Mercia, 331-332; conquers
    Strathclyde, 333; abdicates, 334.
Eadbert, "Praen," King of Kent, his usurpation, 384; crushed by Coenwulf, 385.
Eadgar, son of Edmund I., chosen King of Mercia, 540; King of All England, 541;
    recalls Dunstan, 542; his prosperous reign, 543-544; his imperial position,
    544; character of, 545; his ecclesiastical policy, 546; dies, 548.
Eadgar, Aetheling, grandson of Edmund Ironside, 584, 627.
Eadgifu, daughter of Edward I., marries Charles the Simple, 522.
Eadmund. See Edmund.
Eadred, King of England, succeeds Edmund, 530; his Northumbrian wars, 531-533;
    his friendship with Dunstan, 534, 537; dies, 534.
Eadric, King of Kent, his war with Ceadwalla, 311-312; his laws, 354.
Eadric Streona, favourite of Aethelred II., 568: made ealdorman of Mercia, 569; his
    evil deeds, 570-571; murders two thegns, 576; deserts to Cnut, 577, 579; be-
    trays Cnut and follows Edmund II., 580; betrays Edmund, 580; executed by
    Cnut, 584-585.
Eadsige, Archbishop of Canterbury, 613, 617.
Eadwig, King, son of Edmund I., 538; his quarrel with Dunstan, 539; revolt against,
    540; dies, 540.
Eadwig, son of Aethelred II., opposes Cnut and is slain, 583.
Eahlstan, Bishop of Sherborne, defeats the Danes, 420, 423; intrigues against Aethel-
    wulf, 431.
Eahlswith, wife of King Alfred, 447.
Ealdgyth, wife of Edward the Confessor, 613, 620, 621, 634.
Ealdgyth, wife of Harold II., 627, 633.
Ealdorman, position of, in the early English states, 370-371, 373.
Ealdred, of Bamborough, does homage to Edward the Elder, 508.
Eamot (or Dacor), synod at, 517.
Eanflaed, daughter of Edwin of Northumbria, 274; influences Oswy against the
    Celtic Church, 289.
Eanfrid, King of Bernicia, slain by Cadwallon, 278; his Pictish marriage, 307.
Eanred, King of Northumbria, 348, 399; does homage to Ecgbert, 435.
Eardwulf, King of Northumbria, his escape from Aethelred's assassins, 347; becomes
    king, 397; exiled, 397; restored by help of Charles the Great, 398.
Eardwulf, Bishop of Lindisfarne, 482.
Eardwulf, Cudel, Earl of Bernicia, defeated by the Scots, 598; murdered by Siward,
    607.
Earl, title of, 454, 514.
East Anglia, kingdom of, founded, 228; subject to Kent, 265; powerful under Raed-
    wald, 270-272; harried by Penda, 282; annexed by Offa, 337; recovers its
    independence, 393-394; vassal to Ecgbert, 396; conquered by the Danes,
    438; reconquered by Edward the Elder, 504.
Easter, debates on the "Paschal Controversy," 267-268; 290.
East Saxons, kingdom of, founded, 222; subject to Kent, 265; conversion of the, 265,
    283; subject to Ecgbert, 393.

43

ROMAN BRITAIN

ENGLAND & WALES

ABOUT THE YEAR 910 A.D.